"GRITTY . . . WITH ALL THE BLOOD AND GORE, THE COURAGE AND TERROR OF MASSES OF MEN KILLING THEIR ENEMIES."

—*Washington Post Book World*

"MESMERIZING . . . DRAMATIC . . . THE STORY OF FEARLESS MEN like 'Chesty' Puller, who located a Japanese machine gun in the the night by striking a match and then jumping out of the path of fire . . . And Lt. Kenneth Frazier, who, unable to escape the cockpit of his burning plane, rolled the plane over and fell out . . . A vivid portrayal of the horrors of war, with no punches pulled . . . a fitting memorial to the men who placed their nation's pride and prestige above their own lives."

—*Grand Rapids Press*

"The author writes in the tradition of Bruce Catton. . . . Each battle is described from the bottom up. An invasion isn't arrows on a map but men stumbling through waves up to their necks, bullets splashing closer and closer."

—*West Coast Review of Books*

RICHARD WHEELER is author of *Iwo, Siege of Vicksburg, Sherman's March, We Knew Stonewall Jackson, Voices of the Civil War,* and *Voices of 1776.* He fought with the Marines in the Pacific and was a member of the company that raised the flag on Mt. Suribachi—the incident that more than any other dramatized the valor of The U.S. Marines in World War II.

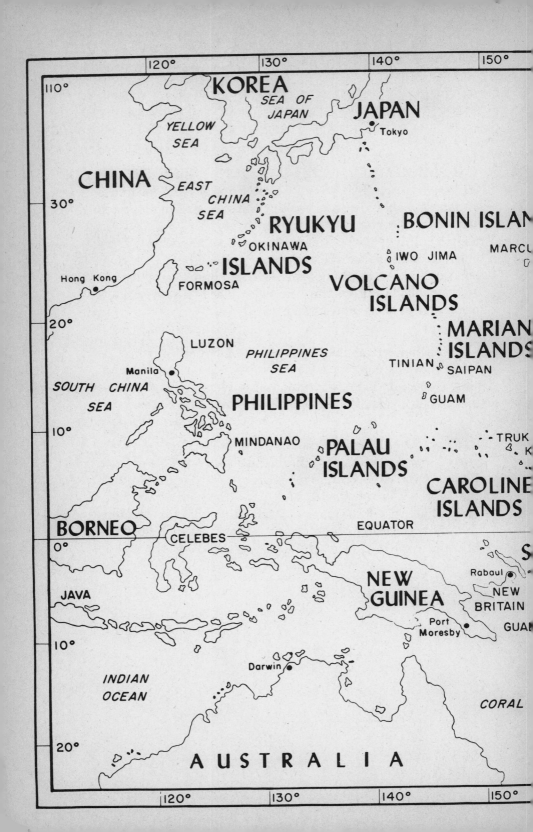

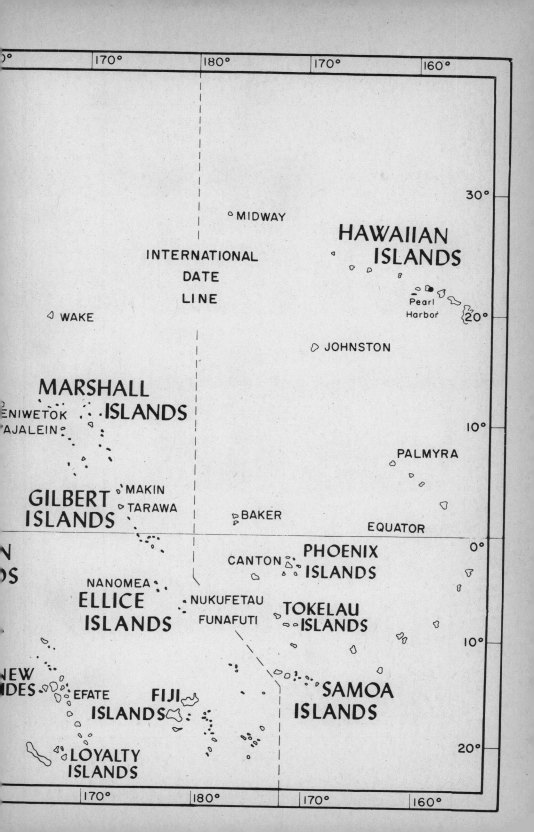

RICHARD WHEELER

A SPECIAL
VALOR

The U.S. Marines
and the Pacific War

A MERIDIAN BOOK

NEW AMERICAN LIBRARY

NEW YORK AND SCARBOROUGH, ONTARIO

This is an authorized reprint of a hardcover edition published by Harper & Row, Publishers, Inc., and published simultaneously in Canada by Fitzhenry and Whiteside Limited, Toronto.

 MERIDIAN TRADEMARK REG. U.S. PAT. OFF. AND FOREIGN COUNTRIES
REGISTERED TRADEMARK—MARCA REGISTRADA
HECHO EN WESTFORD, MASS., U.S.A.

SIGNET, SIGNET CLASSIC, MENTOR, PLUME, MERIDIAN AND NAL BOOKS are published *in the United States* by New American Library, 1633 Broadway, New York, New York 10019, *in Canada* by The New American Library of Canada Limited, 81 Mack Avenue, Scarborough, Ontario M1L 1M8

Library of Congress Cataloging in Publication Data
Wheeler, Richard.
  A special valor.

  Bibliography: p.
  Includes index.
  1. World War, 1939-1945—Campaigns—Pacific Ocean.
2. United States.   Marine Corps—History—World War, 1939-1945   I. Title.
[D767.9.W47   1985]   940.54′26   84-25578
ISBN 0-452-00737-2 (pbk.)

First Meridian Printing, March, 1985

1 2 3 4 5 6 7 8 9

To my mother,
Margaret Wenrich Wheeler,
who spent the war years making shirts for Marines

Other Books by Richard Wheeler

IWO
SIEGE OF VICKSBURG
SHERMAN'S MARCH
WE KNEW STONEWALL JACKSON
VOICES OF THE CIVIL WAR
VOICES OF 1776

Contents

Preface

When I enlisted in the Marines at the outbreak of World War II, I was an aspiring author hoping to encounter a story worthy of a book. My luck was sensational. Fate not only plunged me into the classic Battle of Iwo Jima but made me a member of the company that raised the flag on Mount Suribachi. It took me years to develop as a writer, but a series of books on American military history that I wrote between 1965 and 1980 included two on Iwo Jima, *The Bloody Battle for Suribachi* and *Iwo.* With the publication of the latter, I thought I was through with projects based on my Marine connections, but then my publisher suggested I use them to assemble a much bigger story, that of the Corps' entire role in the Pacific war. This was the start of *A Special Valor.*

Much of the material in the book was obtained directly from veterans of the fighting. Many were interviewed, while others sent me cassettes or written memoirs. These obliging men also made available such things as letters they had written home, battlefield reports, unit rosters, casualty lists, and newspaper clippings they had saved for thirty-five years. Particularly helpful was a stack of on-the-spot articles written by Marine Corps combat correspondent William K. Terry. Another correspondent, Elvis Lane, provided some excellent unpublished material from a notebook he kept on Okinawa. Periodicals of special usefulness were *Leatherneck, Marine Corps Gazette,* and Lowell V. Bulger's *Raider Patch.* My research included a trip to the Marine Corps Historical Center in Washington, D.C., where I was aided by Brigadier General Edwin H. Simmons, Henry I. Shaw, Jr., and Benis M. Frank. Frank's Oral History Collection produced a bonanza of facts, fresh insights, and anecdotes.

I owe a particular debt to Lawrence M. Hebach, who gave me liberal access to his remarkable World War II library. Former Master Gunnery Sergeant Mark R. Moyer, USMC, also provided some essential books. Most of the maps used in *A Special Valor* were either borrowed from or adapted from publications of the Marine Corps Historical Branch, and the majority of the photographs came from the Defense Audiovisual Agency at Anacostia, also in Washington. Major Yoshitaka Horie, a Japanese supply officer instrumental in arming Iwo Jima with such items as the mortar ammunition that knocked me out of the fight, helped with the Japanese side of the story. My long-time friend and assistant, Kathleen Bross, conducted a number of the interviews and handled much of the correspondence involved. Most of the veterans who contributed to the project are mentioned in the text. Those not named are: Jack Bishirjian, James C. Buchanan, I. J. Fuertsch, Herman Kogan, Jerry Loper, Leonard J. Mooney, Leonard R. O'Leary, Rolla E. Perry, Gordon L. Pouliot, John Radmore, Ray Roberts, Clifford Sharon, Robert D. Sinclair, Eric W. Turner, Jr., and Thomas H. Young.

A SPECIAL
VALOR

Prologue: The Corps Finds a Mission

Even before the First World War, there were American military experts, including certain Marine Corps officers, who foresaw the possibility of a conflict between the United States and Japan. The Empire's expanding power in the Western Pacific was beginning to threaten America's political and economic interests. During World War I, the two nations were among those allied against Germany, but the Treaty of Versailles compounded America's Pacific apprehensions. In the distribution of the spoils, Japan was given mandate over the Central Pacific islands formerly controlled by Germany, which augmented the Empire's influence and strength.

Many American military experts were now convinced that war with Japan was inevitable, and at least one man made a fair prediction as to how the war would be fought. Marine Corps Major Earl H. "Pete" Ellis, who had been decorated for heroism in France, said that Japan would strike first, and that it would be necessary for the United States Navy to counterattack across the Pacific toward the Empire, utilizing not only American bases such as Hawaii and Guam but also some of the enemy's islands. Japan, Ellis reasoned, would have these islands fortified, and they would have to be taken by amphibious assault. The major was troubled by the fact that the United States had no amphibious specialists.

This type of operation, which required troops to emerge from the sea, unshielded in the face of heavy fire from concealed and bulwarked weapons of all kinds, was the toughest known. Some military authorities, in fact, felt that it was impossible to take islands which could be fortified so that every yard of their shorelines could be showered with fire from within. Wrote Ellis: "It is not enough that the troops be skilled infantrymen and artillerymen of high morale; they must be skilled water men and jungle men who *know it can be done*—Marines with Marine training."

In order to get a personal look at Japan's Pacific outposts, Pete Ellis disguised himself as a commercial traveler and undertook a secret mission to the Marshalls and the Palaus, where the motives of all foreigners were suspect. A brilliant strategist, Ellis was also a man with a burning thirst. On the island of Koror in the Palaus he took up residence with a native woman, drank heavily, and prowled around Japan's installations. He was carefully shadowed by plain-clothed policemen. On May

1

12, 1923, according to another of Koror's native women who knew him, Ellis went "crazy drunk" and was dead within a few hours. The Japanese authorities simply reported that the American had fallen ill and died—which might have been true. But it is also possible he was poisoned, the victim of a classic cloak-and-dagger counterstroke.

Back in the States, the Commandant of the Marine Corps, Major General John A. Lejeune, had already asked his superiors in the Navy for authorization to make the Marines into the amphibious specialists the nation appeared to need. During these years, the Corps, in spite of its splendid record in World War I, was uncertain of its future. Its successes in France, in fact, were a part of the trouble. The Marines had served as ground forces in the same manner as the Army; and the Army, understandably, was chagrined that the Marines, although relatively few, had been given so much publicity. It was this wartime publicity, augmented by continued good relations with the American public, that was sustaining the Marines. But military budgets were being tightened, and Corps leaders feared a ground swell of Congressional support for the Army-oriented officials who were asking, with some justification, "Why maintain two different branches of the service with the same function?" To ensure its survival, the Corps had to win itself a new and significant role in the nation's defense structure.

One of the strongest advocates of special amphibious training for the Marines was Major Holland M. Smith, another veteran of the fighting in France. Smith bore the nickname "Howlin' Mad," probably as much because the words fitted his initials as because of his temperament, although he could be emphatic enough when fighting the Army or Navy over Marine Corps rights. The major envisioned a day when the Marines, supported by naval gunfire and aerial bombing and strafing, would be able to make successful landings on islands the Japanese considered to be impregnable. Smith wanted the Marines committed to what he termed "a novel principle of war, the principle of doing the impossible well."

Once the Navy's approval and aid had been won, Smith and his colleagues began shaping the necessary tactics, made studies of the logistics involved, and found beaches suitable for practice operations. Nothing was left unexamined. Things that were known about Japanese amphibious techniques were analyzed and tested, and, if found practicable, were adopted. The Navy's gunfire vessels developed softening-up and support procedures, while Navy and Marine fliers experimented with maneuvers concerned with close air cover.

A dozen years of work, replete with both triumphs and failures, led to the establishment in 1933 of the Fleet Marine Force, which was later defined by the Navy Department as "a balanced force of land, air, and service elements of the U.S. Marine Corps which is integral with the U.S. Pacific and/or Atlantic Fleet. It has the status of a full-type command and is organized, trained, and equipped for the seizure or defense of advance naval bases and for the conduct of limited amphibious or land operations essential to the prosecution of a naval campaign." Holland Smith considered this "the most important advance in the history of the Corps." In 1934 the Marines put together a landing operations manual that became a standard not only for the Corps but, seven years later, also for the Army, which at the same time called upon the Corps to help train several of its divisions in amphibious techniques.

As the prewar days grew short, there was still one serious problem to solve. The Navy had no small boats capable of doing an efficient job of beaching either troops or heavy equipment such as tanks and trucks. Barely in time, some excellent landing craft were developed in cooperation with Andrew J. Higgins, a New Orleans boat manufacturer; and an equally useful amphibian tractor was designed by Donald Roebling, Jr., grandson of the man who designed the Brooklyn Bridge.

All of this does not mean that, by the eve of World War II, the Marines had brought their amphibious efforts to perfection; but they considered themselves to be at least reasonably ready—assuming that their manpower would burgeon through wartime enlistments—to tackle even the toughest of Japan's fortified islands.

Pete Ellis would have found a world of pleasure in drinking to that!

1   *War Comes to Wake Island*

===== Less than five hours after the conclusion of the surprise air attack that devastated the American fleet at Pearl Harbor, the Japanese paid their first visit to tiny Wake Island, 2,000 miles to the west, which they planned to invade. The date was December 8, not December 7, 1941, for Wake lies west of the international date line. The strike was made by thirty-six twin-engine planes from Roi in the Marshalls, about 700 miles to the south. The craft came roaring down out of the cover of a rain squall, machine guns rattling and bombs plummeting, the blasts shaking the island and raising clouds of debris. The runs were completed in ten minutes, and as the raiders began climbing back to cruising altitude for the trip home, according to a Japanese participant, "the pilots were grinning widely, and everyone waggled his wings to signify *banzai.*"

Severe punishment had been inflicted, especially upon the island's air facilities, manned by Marines, and of modest proportions to begin with. Out of eight Grumman Wildcat fighters parked on the strip, seven had become twisted junk, with some in flames; the other had perforations in its reserve fuel tank. The island's four remaining planes, also Wildcats, were whole only because they were away on patrol. Of the fifty-five Marine aviation personnel on the ground, twenty-three had been killed or fatally hurt, and eleven others had taken lesser wounds. The strip and its environs were strewn with bloody figures, some of them dismembered. The living were moaning and calling for aid. A huge gasoline tank and a number of fifty-gallon drums were blazing wildly, their black smoke trailing toward the sky. Tents and buildings about the airfield had been leveled, and precious communications and maintenance equipment was damaged and in disarray.

The island's nonaviation Marines, 388 men of the 1st Defense Battalion, led by Major James P. S. Devereux, escaped unharmed, although their camp had been hit hard. Most of these men had not been in camp but in the gun emplacements scattered about the island. Of Wake's sixty-nine Navy men, two were dead. An Army Air Corps communications team, six men, had come through safely. Also on the island were seventy employees of Pan American Airways and 1,146 civilian construction workers. The civilian camp and a set of seaplane facilities, including a shoreside hotel, had received their share of bombs and bullets, and several buildings were shattered and afire. The *Philippine*

4

Clipper, a four-engine flying boat lying in Wake's lagoon, had taken numerous bullets but was still operable. At least ten civilians had been killed, and a number of others had been wounded.

War had come to Wake with a staggering suddenness, although some such move by Japan had been expected. As tensions between the two nations had mounted, the United States had been well aware of the island's strategic importance. It was an outpost facing the line formed by Japan's mid-Pacific mandates, which she had been fortifying. The United States, in turn, had been fortifying Wake, but it was the old story of "too little too late." The island had been provided with about 500 servicemen, a dozen planes, six 5-inch guns, twelve 3-inch antiaircraft guns, some .50-caliber and .30-caliber machine guns, and hand weapons of a number not even sufficient to go around. The crews of the all-important bigger guns were short of men, and there were machine guns with no crews at all. Various maintenance items and other materials were in scanty supply.

"God knows why Wake did not have more men and defenses," lamented James Devereux in later years. "I can't understand why our leadership was caught napping." Devereux, a short man of slight build, was thirty-eight at the time of the crisis and had been in the service for eighteen years. He had signed up, he once joked, because he liked the red stripe on the trousers of the Marine dress uniform. His overseas duties had included tours at Pearl Harbor, in Nicaragua, the Philippines, and China. He led without bluster, was competent and thoroughgoing, and had the respect of his men and his superiors. "He's the kind of guy," said a fellow officer, "who would put all the mechanized aircraft detectors into operation, and then station a man with a spyglass in a tall tree."

In this case, there was no radar, and no alarm system. There wasn't even a tall tree. To make things worse, enemy planes could not be heard approaching because of the persistent pounding of the surf. The expedient adopted for spotting both planes and ships was an observation post atop a water tank, which put the horizon at a distance of ten miles.

Wake, an atoll shaped roughly like a V with the point in the southeast, is actually three islands. Wake proper makes up the base and the lower portions of the V, while Wilkes is the western extremity, and Peale, across the lagoon, is the northern. The atoll's composite land mass is only about four square miles, but it has a twenty-mile coastline. Its lagoon bristles with coral heads, and its shores hold thick patches of scrub brush. Hardly noticed by man until the arrival of the Air Age, Wake was for centuries a place known mostly to land crabs, a strange

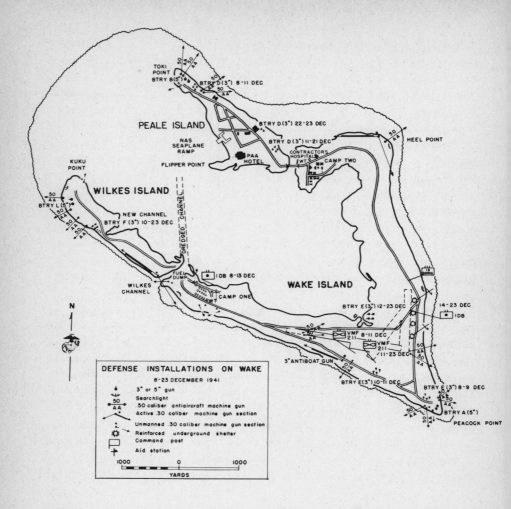

DEFENSE INSTALLATIONS ON WAKE
8-23 DECEMBER 1941

3" or 5" gun
Searchlight
.50 caliber antiaircraft machine gun
Active .30 caliber machine gun section
Unmanned .30 caliber machine gun section
Reinforced underground shelter
Command post
Aid station

1000   0   1000
YARDS

breed of rat, and a variety of birds, one a flightless rail. The United States annexed the island in 1899, and in 1935 Pan Am established a station there, a refueling stop for its trans-Pacific clippers. It was not until January 1941, eleven months before the outbreak of the war, that the government began turning Wake into a naval air station. The job was assigned to a civilian construction crew under Nathan D. "Dan" Teters, previously a college football star and a World War I Army sergeant, a big man with just the right combination of toughness and amiability to make him an excellent field superintendent.

There were no women on Wake when the Japanese made their strike. Mrs. Teters, a tall, personable blonde who was popular with civilians and servicemen alike, was there until mid-November. The men, as she explained later, regarded her as a kind of barometer. "They figured that as long as I was allowed to stay on the island things couldn't be so bad." When the Navy brass at Pearl Harbor ordered her to leave and she was walking to the plane, she saw groups of men watching her with a sober expression. "I think they realized then that they were in for it."

The strike demonstrated just to what extent the men were "in for it." Many of the survivors, stunned by the experience, could hardly credit the damage to life and property that surrounded them. But others moved quickly to care for the wounded, who were placed in trucks and the island's single ambulance and taken to the civilian camp (known as Camp Two) in the northern part of Wake proper, where there was a one-story hospital. Since preparations for further trouble with the enemy had to be started at once, there was no time to bury the dead. They were gathered and deposited, as decently as possible, in a large freezer room in a civilian storehouse. No tomb was ever darker or colder. Nor, perhaps, was there ever a more dramatic illustration of the uncertainty of human life. The victims had gone from peace to war and from life to death within a matter of moments, and their corpses had been removed from the earth's warm light to a place of cold darkness a short time later.

In overall charge at Wake was a tall, slender Navy man, Commander Winfield S. "Spiv" Cunningham, who had entered the Naval Academy in 1916, and, a year later, became memorably aware that he was part of a long-standing tradition when he marched in the funeral procession for Admiral George Dewey, whose career had begun under Farragut at New Orleans in 1862. Cunningham went on to serve for years at sea in various parts of the world, and also became a naval flier. When he reached Wake, only ten days before the enemy attack, observers noted with some surprise that his personal effects included a set of golf clubs. He was not really expecting to play golf on the atoll, had brought his clubs simply because he did not know what else to do with them.

The raid, as Cunningham would recall in his memoirs, left him awesomely conscious of the depth of his responsibilities. "I drafted a report . . . for coding and transmission to Pearl Harbor, and tried to shake the confusion out of my mind." He decided that this was no time to wonder how the Japanese, who were thought to have inferior planes and weak eyes, had managed to strike with such deadliness. "Wake's future had to be considered."

The preparations for the enemy's return, undertaken at top speed, included restoring disrupted telephone lines, sandbagging and camouflaging gun positions, constructing air-raid shelters, clearing debris from the airstrip, repairing and servicing the remaining Wildcats, and digging revetments in which the precious planes could be housed. Dan Teters and about 200 of his civilian workers, some operating bulldozers or other pieces of heavy equipment, plunged in beside the military, and their help was indispensable. Most of the Pan American employees were evacuated in the *Philippine Clipper.* Of the remaining civilians on the island, hundreds gathered their belongings, headed into the brush, and concealed themselves in dugouts and foxholes. They had not bargained for this precipitation into peril, and were not only alarmed but also angry with the United States government.

With the coming of evening a cold drizzle enveloped the island, but the preparations continued swiftly. "We worked into the darkness," says Spiv Cunningham, "and through the first night of the war." The weather was clear again by dawn. Marine PFC Verne L. Wallace at last found time to sit down and take a letter from his pocket that he had not yet opened, one from his girl in Pennsylvania. At the time it was written, the attention of most Americans was focused on the turbulence in Europe, into which it seemed the nation would be drawn. The girl said: "As long as you have to be away, darling, I'm so very, very happy you are in the Pacific, where you won't be in danger if war comes."

There was no shortage of rations on Wake, and the bleary-eyed men enjoyed a good breakfast, including plenty of hot coffee. According to James Devereux, the coffee was especially appreciated. "There are times in war when coffee is almost plasma for the spirit." By the time they finished their second cup, some of the men had forgotten their weariness and began to make jokes about their situation. The work was resumed with a will.

It was about 11:30 A.M. when the Japanese airmen came over the horizon to make their second raid, the formation of twenty-seven bombers conspicuous against a clear blue background. Watching from a position high in the sky south of Wake was a combat air patrol, two of the island's Wildcats piloted by Second Lieutenant David D. Kliewer and Technical Sergeant William J. Hamilton. It was two against twenty-seven, but the Marines did not hesitate, nosing their small planes into screaming dives. They cut one of the bombers from the pack, the din intensified by the throbbing of their guns and the return fire from the enemy's top turret. The bursts from the turret were ineffective, but those of the Wildcats struck home, and the bomber erupted into flames and went careening toward the sea, no one parachuting clear. The Americans had to break contact with the formation then, for black puffs of flak from the Marine antiaircraft guns on the island were beginning to appear around it. As the bombers made their runs, the ack-ack sought them hotly, and another kill was scored. The plane exploded and fell to the sea in pieces. Again, no chutes appeared against the blue. Four additional bombers were seen to be trailing smoke as the raid ended and the formation started for home. Unknown to the Marines, ten more had been damaged.

The known score might have caused more rejoicing on the atoll, except that the destruction wrought by the enemy was again heavy. The Pan American installations on Peale were now almost completely wrecked, as were the beginnings of the naval air station, in the same area. Destroyed along with one of the government buildings was a million dollars' worth of equipment and supplies. The civilian camp, too, was again a target, and nearly all of its buildings had now been shattered, burned, or at least damaged. Fifty-five men in the camp were killed or wounded by bomb bursts or machine-gun bullets. The dead, according to Cunningham, "were lying in clusters." Bombs struck the hospital, and three patients died, while others were wounded. One of those for whom it was the second wound was Master Technical Sergeant Andrew J. Paszkiewicz, a twenty-year Marine. On the first day a leg had been mutilated. Today his wound was minor, serving chiefly to stir him to a torrent of colorful profanity aimed not only at the enemy but also at the luck that made him twice a victim. Flames sprang up in the hospital, and the medical personnel rushed to evacuate the wards, which they did successfully, although the building burned to the ground.

On Wake itself, a gasoline truck trying to escape destruction by zig-zagging its away across the airfield to the cover of the brush, its tires squealing, moved directly under a falling bomb, and the vehicle dissolved into a mass of flame and flying metal, three Marines a part of the dissolution. Another Marine died when a bomb landed on the rim of his foxhole, and five civilians working with a Marine gun crew were wounded. No one knows how much harm was done to the atoll's original inhabitants. Along one of the beaches, terns and frigate birds, stunned by bomb blasts, were seen lurching and staggering about as though drunk.

The work of salvage and repair and the other preparations for the next attack were begun almost before the bombers vanished over the horizon. Three large earth-covered magazines near the east coast of Wake proper were emptied of their ammunition, two for conversion to hospitals and the other to be used as a shelter for the Army Air Corps' radio, now the last undamaged set on the island and precious for communicating with the outside world. "We worked all afternoon and night installing our transmitting equipment in the magazine," relates Staff Sergeant Clifford Hotchkiss, the radio crew's technician. "This was an ideal site for our operations. The antenna was installed adjacent to the entrance, and was of the vertical mast type, approximately twenty-five feet in height. This could be disassembled or erected in five minutes' time."

The radio "igloo" also became Commander Cunningham's headquarters, the island's nerve center. James Devereux had his headquarters in a dugout near the battered Marine camp (Camp One) at the western end of Wake proper. The major's chief concern at this time was a set of antiaircraft guns near the point of Wake's V that he feared had been photographed by the enemy and was marked for special attention. The battery was moved to a spot about 500 yards distant, a heavy job that required the aid of about a hundred civilian construction workers and took all night to complete.

Four Wildcats, ignoring the odds, met the twenty-six Japanese bombers that approached Wake at 10:45 on the morning of December 10. During a short, hot action that was cheered on the ground, Captain Henry T. "Hank" Elrod sent two of the enemy craft into the sea. But this time the island's ack-ack caused damage to only one bomber during the runs. As Devereux anticipated, a concentration of bombs was placed on the spot from which the battery had been removed. The enemy's chief accomplishment during this raid was to hit a shed on Wilkes, the least developed island, that held 125 tons of dynamite. The explosion, by far the most spectacular that any of the Americans had ever seen, rocked all three of the islands and showered them with sand, crushed coral, and other debris. Wilkes was stripped of most of its brush, and its gun positions were considerably damaged, their ready ammunition exploding like firecrackers. Miraculously, personnel losses on Wilkes were limited to one Marine killed, four Marines hurt, and one civilian sent into shock. The raid's toll was also low on the other islands.

As the bombers departed and the Americans realized that this time they had escaped lightly, their morale escalated. They might be weary and shaken, but it was clear their digging and their other work had begun to pay off. They were learning how to take care of themselves under some of the worst conditions warfare can bring. "We felt good, almost cocky," says Cunningham. "Surely help would come from Pearl Harbor any day now, and meanwhile we could wait it out."

But another kind of threat was imminent. Plowing a steady course from the Marshalls toward Wake was a naval task force, Destroyer

Squadron 6 under Rear Admiral Sadamichi Kajioka, composed of the admiral's flagship (the new light cruiser *Yubari*), two old light cruisers, six destroyers, two destroyer transports, two regular transports, and two submarines. There was no aircraft carrier; the operation had not seemed to warrant one. The landing force on the transports numbered only 450 men. As explained later by an unnamed officer on Kajioka's staff: "It was the beginning of the war. We could not mass as many men as we considered necessary, and it was planned in an emergency to use the crews of the destroyers to help storm the beach." This would raise the landing force to nearly 2,000 men.

The fact that the Japanese even considered making the assault with 450 men—especially when they believed the island held 1,000 Marines (there were actually only about 400 still on their feet)—tells something of their philosophy of warfare. They placed much more emphasis on individual ability and bravery than upon numbers and material power. This was the outgrowth of the Bushido code, developed centuries earlier by Japan's *samurai* caste in connection with the Shinto religion. The code stressed aggressiveness, courage, honor, loyalty, self-sacrifice, stoicism during suffering and pain, and a contempt for death. Commonly, you either won a battle or you died—if not at the enemy's hands, at your own. It was a terrible disgrace to become a prisoner of war; suicide was infinitely preferable. The Emperor was venerated, and it was a privilege to die for him; Shinto taught that he was of divine origin. Heroic ancestors were also held in reverence, and were the objects of emulation.

The beleaguered Americans on Wake Island would have been surprised to know how the Japanese regarded the war they had launched with their strike on Pearl Harbor. It was considered an assertion of their rights. Their nation, they felt, had been denied its legitimate role of leadership in the Eastern world. For many years the Western powers had been dominating the region and exploiting it economically, while treating its people like inferiors. Japan's leaders dreamed of creating a rich and powerful empire, one of benefit to all people of their color, and one safe not only from Western exploitation but from Russian communism. To many of the Japanese the war was a holy crusade. This feeling was reinforced by Shinto, which affirmed Japan's divinity and was construed as prophesying her domination of the world. It was the age-old story of a dominated people yearning not only to be free but to be dominant themselves.

The Japanese task force, with no lights showing, made its landfall at about 2:00 A.M. on December 11, and drew up five or six miles off

Wake's southern coast. Shortly before three o'clock the vessels began moving in slowly, their aim to shell the Marine gun positions to rubble before the assault force was landed. The atoll's dark mass looked lifeless, and Admiral Kajioka assumed he had caught the Americans wrapped in oblivious sleep. But Major Devereux's headquarters had already been alerted by a phone call from a lookout. The man was not sure what he was seeing, and reported the ships as "just something moving out there." Devereux hurried to the beach with his night glasses. At first he could make out nothing, but soon he announced, "Well, there they are."

Commander Cunningham was notified, and his first thought was that the gunnery contest with the warships was going to be an unequal one. "What could six old 5-inch guns do against the batteries of longer-range weapons they were sure to have?"

While the Marines, preserving blackout conditions, were readying the guns and otherwise going into general quarters, some of the civilians who were huddled in foxholes in the brush got the idea the ships were an American rescue force, and several groups came to the beach carrying their luggage. Appalled when they learned the truth, these men made a hasty return to their cover. By this point in the campaign, however, a good many more civilians had joined Dan Teters in helping with the defense.

Not only were Devereux's six guns old, but some of their fire-control equipment had been damaged during the air raids. On the plus side, the weapons were well emplaced. Each extremity of the V held a two-gun battery. Their camouflage made them difficult to spot. If the warships came close enough, the guns might do some damage. It was decided that the enemy's first fire should not be returned, that he be led to believe that all of the island's shore batteries had been silenced from the air. This might lure him in. Major Devereux returned to his command-post dugout and phoned the gun crews, telling them that none was to fire a single round until he gave the order.

In the first faint light of dawn the flagship *Yubari*, leading the somber formation, reached a position about 8,000 yards south of Peacock Point, the atoll's apex. Here the vessels swung west on a course parallel with the southern surf line, and at 5:30 their guns began flashing and booming, the missiles shrieking to a violent union with the shore. With the sand and coral trembling and rising in spouts about them, the Americans pressed deeper into their holes. When the warships reached the western end of Wilkes, several remained in that area, slipping closer to shore, while the *Yubari* and two others doubled back, this time making their parallel run at about 6,000 yards. The shelling accomplished little beyond the destruction of a set of diesel tanks, the contents of which flamed high and added an amber cast to the early daylight.

Both divisions of the force now had guns trained on them. In the east, at Peacock Point, was Battery A, commanded by First Lieutenant Clarence A. Barninger, and in the west, at the end of Wilkes, was Second Lieutenant John A. McAlister's Battery L. Even the third set of guns, Battery B under First Lieutenant Woodrow M. Kessler, across the lagoon at the north tip of Peale, was ready for action against any ship that showed itself beyond the west end of Wilkes.

The crews of Batteries A and L were eager to fire, and the phone in Major Devereux's dugout rang repeatedly as the commanders begged permission. The corporal at the phone kept responding, "Hold your fire till the major gives the word." Soon the nearer vessels were only about 5,000 yards offshore, but the order to hold remained in effect. The gun crews grew angry, and one man growled, "What does that dumb little bastard want us to do? Let 'em run over us without spitting back?" At about six o'clock the *Yubari*, moving eastward, passed Peacock Point and made another reversal of her course, a destroyer near her. Within ten minutes the flagship was only 4,500 yards from Battery A. Major Devereux quietly ordered, "Commence firing."

In Lieutenant Barninger's words: "At the opening salvo, the cruiser turned and raced away from the battery on a zigzag course, picking up speed rapidly. She concentrated her fire on the battery position, which had been disclosed by the initial firing. None of the salvos came into the position. The first salvo from our guns which hit her was fired at a range of 5,500 to 6,000 yards. Both shells entered her port side about amidships just above the waterline. The ship immediately belched smoke and steam through the side, and her speed diminished. At 7,000 yards two more hit her in about the same place. Her whole side was now engulfed in smoke and steam and she turned to starboard to try to hide in the smoke. At this time the destroyer which had accompanied the cruiser came in at high speed, tried to sweep between us to lay smoke, but a shell struck the forecastle of the destroyer. The destroyer immediately turned and fled. We continued to fire on the cruiser. The only hit I am certain of after this time was a hit on her forward turret. A shell hit the face of the turret, and this turret did not fire again."

Battery L, at the west end of Wilkes, was handicapped by broken range-finding equipment, but, after Lieutenant McAlister had judged the range to the nearest vessel, the destroyer *Hayate*, the guns opened fire. The first two salvos were too high. The third made a direct hit, causing a terrific explosion. Debris, smoke, steam, and sea water were spewed in all directions. The vessel broke in half and sank within a few minutes, and the Japanese who had survived the blast, some badly hurt, were left struggling in the water. The Marines at the guns, at first amazed, shortly broke into wild cheers, but were curbed by an old China hand, Platoon Sergeant Henry A. Bedell, a small, wizened man with a booming voice, who ordered, "Knock it off, you bastards, and get back on the guns. What do you think this is, a ball game?"

Battery L scored three more hits, but none as dramatic as the first. Meanwhile, across the lagoon on Peale, Battery B was sending long-range fire at three destroyers that had appeared beyond the tip of Wilkes. The vessels returned the fire, hitting all around the battery and shaking up its crew. As the men recovered and continued the fight, one of the guns was disabled by its own recoil. The remaining gun scored a hit that started a deck fire. By this time—less than an hour after the opening shot—all of the ships in the task force were zigzagging seaward, in full retreat, some of them laying down smokescreens. The men of the sunken *Hayate* who were floundering in the water were left to drown.

At Peacock Point, Lieutenant Barninger of Battery A was still watching the wounded flagship *Yubari*. "After we ceased firing, the whole fleet having fled and there being no other targets to engage, the cruiser lay broadside to the sea, still pouring steam and smoke from her side. She had a definite port list. After some time she got slowly under way, going a short distance, stopping, and continuing again. She was engulfed in smoke when she crept over the horizon."

Although the Japanese were now out of range of the island's guns, they still had its four serviceable fighter planes to contend with. Marine Major Paul A. Putnam, Wake's air commander, was himself piloting one of the Wildcats. The other pilots were Captains Hank Elrod, Herbert C. Freuler, and Frank C. Tharin. In the face of heavy flak from the task force, the little squadron made repeated attacks with .50-caliber machine-gun fire and 100-pound bombs dropped from improvised racks. Returning to the island for additional bombs, the Wildcats flew a total of ten sorties, with two replacement pilots, Sergeant Hamilton and Second Lieutenant John F. Kinney, taking a hand. In all, the squadron dropped twenty bombs and expended 20,000 rounds of machine-gun bullets. A destroyer was blown to pieces—thought to be Hank Elrod's work—and four other vessels were damaged. The crew of one was left fighting a billowing gasoline fire. All of the aircraft suffered flak hits, and Hank Elrod was forced to make a crash landing on the beach. Although his Wildcat was a total loss, he climbed from the wreckage unhurt. Among the Marines who came rushing to the scene was Major Devereux, and Elrod told him, "I'm sorry as hell about the plane." Captain Freuler made a perfect landing on the strip, but just barely; his engine was hopelessly battered. This left Wake with only two serviceable air-craft.

But the battle had been won. Admiral Kajioka, according to one of his officers, decided "to retire to Kwajalein and make another attempt when conditions were more favorable." Two vessels had been sunk and seven damaged, some of them seriously. The force had suffered perhaps 700 casualties, most of them deaths. On Wake, four Marines had been wounded. Assessing the battle later, a high-ranking Japanese naval officer stated: "Considering the power accumulated for the invasion of Wake Island, and the meager forces of the defenders, it was one of the most humiliating defeats our navy had ever suffered." American naval historian Samuel Eliot Morison was to write that December 11, 1941, "should always be a proud day in the history of the Corps. Never again, in this Pacific War, did coast defense guns beat off an amphibious land-ing."

As the action ended, Commander Cunningham went to Devereux's command-post dugout to congratulate the major and his men. Then a group repaired to the nearby Marine Officers' Club, which was still in usable condition. The refrigerator was not working, so the beer was warm, but nobody cared. "It was like a fraternity picnic," says Cunning-ham. "War whoops of joy split the air. Warm beer was sprayed on late arrivals without regard to rank." But the celebration was necessarily brief; everyone had work to do. Cunningham went to his headquarters and, just before 9:00 A.M., performed the proudest task of his naval career: he reported the victory to Pearl Harbor.

An hour later Wake's two surviving Wildcats, piloted by Second Lieu-tenants John Kinney and Carl R. Davidson, were in the air attacking thirty Japanese bombers nearing the island. The pair shot down two of the planes and sent one swinging homeward in a crippled condition. The antiaircraft gunners on Wake shot down one and drew black smoke from three others. As usual, the Japanese wasted no time making their runs and departing. This time they inflicted no casualties and did only minor damage.

That afternoon at about four o'clock, Lieutenant Kliewer was patroll-ing the ocean in one of the Wildcats when he spotted a Japanese sub-marine, fully surfaced, and he made a strafing and bombing attack. The bombs missed but fell close, and when the craft submerged she left an oil slick. Kliewer believed he had made a kill, although this never became official.

All in all, it was a remarkable day for Wake's defenders. Morale was further improved by a commendation from Pearl Harbor assuring the men they had performed their duties "in accordance with the highest traditions of the Naval Service." Moreover, they were promised reinforcements. The only gloomy aspect of the day was a rather gruesome burial service. A civilian dragline operator scooped out a long ditch, and the rigid corpses from the freezer room were placed in it, side by side. After a firing squad had loosed three volleys into the air, a bulldozer covered the ditch. Wake had no military chaplain, but, as the men of the burial party stood with bowed heads, a civilian lay preacher said a short prayer. Among the saddest men in the party was a construction worker whose son, also a workman, was among the interred. Spiv Cunningham issued orders that thereafter all of the dead be buried where they fell, or in the nearest practical space.

2 | *Submission and an End to Pride*

In the United States, the story of the victory was broken with animated radio reports and banner newspaper headlines such as MARINES KEEP WAKE. Commentators and editorial writers compared the island's defenders to the little band of Texans who had fought so heroically at the Alamo in 1836. The story was grabbed to the bosom of a people grievously shaken by the news of Pearl Harbor, and it helped rekindle both their spirits and their pride. The Marine Corps also benefited. Never before had it got this much attention. Enlistments were stimulated and the foundation was laid for the Corps' legendary role in the Pacific war.

Reported along with the authentic news about Wake was an untruth. When Commander Cunningham sent his victory message to Pearl Harbor it was in code, and in keeping with a practice of the time, initiated to confuse the enemy's code experts, it was padded, front and rear, with unrelated material. It started out: SEND US STOP NOW IS THE TIME FOR ALL GOOD MEN TO COME TO THE AID OF THEIR PARTY STOP CUNNINGHAM MORE JAPS. . . . Someone at Pearl turned this line of nonsense into a tale of defiant courage. When the men on Wake were asked if they needed anything, the story went, they responded with, "Yes, send us more Japs!" Repeated with enthusiasm all over America, the fabrication became a kind of rallying cry, but it was resented when it reached Wake. The tired defenders had seen far too many of the enemy already, and no one was making flippant remarks about the situation. As Cunningham explains: "We were doing our best, and we were proud of it, but our best seldom included that disregard for sanity that marks so many romantic visions of the thin red line of heroes."

What Wake's defenders needed was not more of the enemy but their own promised reinforcements. At Pearl, Admiral Husband E. Kimmel, commander in chief of the Pacific Fleet, had formulated a workable plan for a relief expedition. It was based on the use of three fast carrier forces made up of vessels that had not been at Pearl during the Japanese attack and had thus escaped harm. One force was to carry troops, planes, equipment, and supplies to Wake; another was to make a diversionary strike in the Marshalls; and the third was to patrol the waters east of Wake, its orders to cover Pearl and be available to provide emergency aid for the relief force. But as a result of the handicaps, uncertainties, and doubts created by the attack on Pearl, the plan was developing slowly. In the Marshalls, at the same time, the Japanese were busy restoring and enlarging their Wake Island task force, determined to make their second assault at the earliest possible moment. Meanwhile, the strikes from the air were continued.

The Americans on Wake entered a period during which time seemed to stand still. According to James Devereux: "The days blurred together in a dreary sameness of bombing and endless work and always that aching need for sleep." Not everyone on the island was as busy as the major and his working parties. There were men who, between raids, idled about, napped in their shelters, and suffered from boredom. The raids, which were always brief and inflicted few casualties, became more of a nuisance than a horror. There were other problems. Numerous men were stricken with diarrhea; some became so weak they had to be carried to the hospital. The island's rat population, crazed by the bomb bursts, swarmed into foxholes and other shelters, sometimes biting. The hundreds of birds killed during the raids were a sanitation threat; they had to be gathered and buried.

There was the usual "griping and bitching" among the Marines. One would snap, "I've never seen such a fouled-up detail!" Another would ask, "Why don't we just let the Japs have this damned island? What good is it anyway?" Still another would say, "Knock it off, you guys. It's your own fault you're here. You're both 'brave volunteers.' "

The Marine antiaircraft gunners continued to score hits, now and then knocking a plane into the sea. But no Japanese bodies washed up on the beach. The defenders looked in vain, as one Marine officer put it, for the sight of "a nice fresh corpse." Men in combat are always heartened by tangible proof of the slaughter they achieve. The higher the body count, the greater their own chances of surviving.

Top-priority targets of the Japanese airmen were the Marine gun positions. In a report from Peacock Point on one of the strikes, Lieutenant Barninger said: "The Point was pretty badly torn up. Battery communications were left in such a condition that all wires had to be relaid. . . . Bomb hits in the center of the battery position shook many of the men in their foxholes, but none was injured."

If this period of the defense had its particular heroes, they were the island's aviation personnel—not only the Marine pilots but also the maintenance crew, composed of Marines, Navy men, and civilian volunteers. The squadron, down to one serviceable Wildcat on December 14, was built up to four by the morning of the seventeenth. According to the squadron commander, Major Putnam, the maintenance men "did a truly remarkable and almost magical job. With almost no tools and a complete lack of normal equipment, they performed all types of repair and replacement work. They changed engines and propellers from one airplane to another, and even completely built up new engines and propellers from scrap parts salvaged from wrecks. They replaced minor parts and assemblies, and repaired damage to fuselages and wings and landing gear." A Navy man with the crew, Aviation Machinist's Mate First Class James F. Hesson, earned the Navy Cross, second only to the Medal of Honor. The pilots continued to take the Wildcats up to patrol and to make their valiant attempts to intercept. If results against the impossible odds were minimal, the planes at least survived the torrential return fire. But by December 19, as a result of mechanical breakdowns, the squadron was again reduced to two planes, with one suffering engine trouble.

It was now eight days since the Japanese naval assault had been repelled and the defenders had been promised reinforcements. The mood remained generally hopeful, but men were asking, "Why the hell doesn't somebody come out and help us fight?"

On December 20, a day of overcast and rain, the island finally received a friendly visitor, a Navy patrol bomber, a PBY, that had flown the Midway route from Pearl. According to one observer, the big flying boat settled on the surface of the lagoon "as lightly as a gull." The neatly uniformed crewmen stepped ashore near a few haggard and disheveled Marines, and a young ensign asked, "Where is the Wake Island Hotel?" One of the astonished Marines replied, "There it is, sir," and pointed to a pile of rubble.

The visitors brought sealed orders for Spiv Cunningham, and they contained great news: The relief expedition—Task Force 14 under Rear Admiral Frank J. Fletcher—was on the way! Cunningham was to prepare to receive a fresh fighter-plane squadron, a detachment of ground troops, and an assortment of equipment and supplies. The word sped around the island, and morale soared.

Early the next morning, as the PBY's crewmen gathered on the shore of the lagoon to make their flight home, they were joined by Major Walter L. J. Bayler, a communications specialist whose job on the island was finished and who was needed elsewhere. He was carrying a flock of messages the defenders had given him for transmission to their families. As he stepped from the dock to the plane, the major turned and looked back. The American flag was snapping on its pole, and the men who had come to see him off were grinning broadly. There was a distinct optimism in the air. "As I waved a last good-bye and took my seat in the plane, my smile was as cheerful as theirs." Bayler was to become famous as "the last man off Wake Island."

The PBY left Wake at about 7:00 A.M. Less than two hours later the island was attacked by nearly fifty Japanese planes, both bombers and fighters. The armada did little physical damage but put a blight on the spirit of the morning. The Americans saw that it was composed of naval aircraft, which meant that a carrier was somewhere in the vicinity. This portended the approach of another landing force. The situation was developing into a race between this force and Admiral Fletcher's relief expedition. Unfortunately, Fletcher wasn't racing but was proceeding slowly, anxious about the mission and getting no reassurance from his communications with the high command at Pearl. That this command was in a state of change did not help matters. Admiral Kimmel had been relieved by Vice Admiral William S. Pye, but Pye was really only a stand-in until Admiral Chester W. Nimitz arrived from Washington.

On Wake that day, the carrier-plane strike was followed by one of the usual visits of the land-based bombers. Peale got special attention. In the director pit of its antiaircraft battery was a legendary Marine, Platoon Sergeant Johnalson E. Wright. Probably the fattest man in the Corps, "Big" Wright was said to weigh 320 pounds. His bulk was maintained, at least in part, by copious beer drinking. For years, Wright had carried a silver dollar he swore was a good-luck piece, and some of the men of his crew had begun to believe in the charm, for so far all had been lucky. But today, in the very act of squeezing his coin, Wright was killed by a bomb, and several others were wounded. When word spread around Wake that Big Wright was dead, some of the defenders felt that perhaps everyone's luck was running out.

The bomb that got Wright also damaged the antiaircraft battery's fire-control equipment. This battery was further diminished by Major Devereux, who transferred one of its guns, along with some of its equipment, to the antiaircraft battery on Wake proper in order to bring the unit up to its full four-gun strength. The third antiaircraft battery, that on Wilkes, was by this time reduced to two guns. Although no longer spectacular in their degree of destruction, the enemy's raids were nonetheless whittling down the island's defenses.

The next day, December 22, was a bad one for Wake's airmen. The last two operational Wildcats, piloted by Captain Freuler and Lieutenant Davidson, were aloft when the island was approached by another formation of carrier planes, this time thirty-three dive bombers and six Zero fighters. Showing the same remarkable courage that had stamped the squadron's performance from the start, the two men plunged to the attack. Freuler got two of the Zeroes, the second exploding so near him that his Wildcat was scorched, riddled by debris, and almost knocked out of control. A third Zero came in from behind, and the captain felt bullets stabbing into his shoulder and back. Unable to maneuver out of the way, he put the Wildcat into a steep dive, barely managing to pull up before reaching the sea. The Zero did not follow, and Freuler coaxed his crippled craft back to the island, making a crash landing on the airstrip. The plane was demolished. When the captain was lifted out he was covered with blood from his bullet wounds, but he had escaped serious injury in the crash. As for Lieutenant Davidson, when the raid ended he was missing. His friends watched the sky for much of the afternoon, but he never returned. The squadron was now out of planes, and only twenty of its original fifty-nine men were still on their feet. Major Putnam went to Major Devereux and said, "We're reporting as infantry."

By ten o'clock that night, the American relief force was about 500 miles from Wake. The Japanese assault force was closing in. It was the same force as before, its damages repaired, its sunken destroyers replaced, and its size increased by four vessels. This time it was supported not only by a strong carrier force but also by a screening force made up of cruisers and destroyers. Admiral Kajioka was again in command of the assault, given a rare chance to save face, and this time he had 1,500 amphibious troops. If this number proved insufficient, his destroyers were to ram their prows up on shore and disgorge the hundreds that composed their crews. The assault was to be made by surprise in the dark, not given away by a preliminary bombardment.

The night was moonless, rainy, and blustery. On one of Kajioka's vessels was a young journalist, Kayoshi Ibushi, who later wrote a dramatic account of the expedition. "The storm came down upon the ship, and the terrific wind whistled over the mast. The angry waves tossed the ships around as if they were toys. Suddenly a blinking light was seen on a destroyer up ahead. It was the signal 'Island is sighted.' Our course was changed, and our speed gradually reduced. The island appeared faintly in the darkness. The admiral ordered, 'Break off and land the naval landing party.' The honorable first order of 'Charge' was given, and the daring officers and men, with white sashes, bravely went down to the surface of the sea. The hardships encountered in lowering the landing barges were too severe even to imagine. Now we, the naval landing force, on the barges which we had boarded, must charge into enemy territory. . . ."

The barges, along with two transports that were to double as landing craft, began their long run toward the preferred landing beaches, the southern shores of Wake proper and Wilkes. By this time the atoll was ringed by warships, and their composite power was enormous. All but the landing craft, however, stood at a respectful distance. As a senior Japanese officer said afterward, "Due to the previous experience with the American shore batteries, we did not want to come within range." The lookouts on shore, their work made harder by a high, thunderous surf and the extreme darkness of the night, spotted the northern vessels first; some of their unshielded lights showed as fuzzy yellow specks in the black mist.

When the word reached Devereux's headquarters, which had been transferred from the western end of Wake proper to one of the magazines near the island's east coast, the major ordered the Marines of all three islands to be extremely alert, but discounted the idea of an attack from the north. He had established his main defenses along the southern shoreline, since this seemed the most likely place for the enemy to land. The defenses, however, were pathetically short of men. More than half of Devereux's command was tied to the surviving 3-inch and 5-inch gun positions, some on each of the islands. The 5-inch guns had to be kept ready to counter shellfire from the ships, and the 3-inch guns would be needed at daylight to fight the carrier planes that would surely arrive to support the Japanese assault troops. To cover the 4.5 miles of southern shoreline—now being approached by approximately 1,000 of the enemy, backed by 500 reserves and the destroyer crews —Devereux had about 200 men who were not tied to gun positions: a mixture of Marines, Navy personnel, and civilian volunteers. The major's "mobile reserve force" was made up of one truck carrying eight Marines armed with four machine guns.

It was 2:35 A.M. when Gunner Clarence B. McKinstry, at one of the gun positions on Wilkes, heard the throb of a motor in the darkness offshore, and the position's crew opened up with .50-caliber machine-gun tracers. The pink streaks illuminated the first of the craft to land. Sergeant Henry Bedell, the little man with the big voice, and PFC William F. Buehler ran to the beach and began to lob hand grenades among the Japanese as they scrambled out of the surf. A few fragments scored, but Sergeant Bedell was quickly shot down, his big voice stilled forever, while Buehler took a wound and retreated. Another craft landed, and the Japanese officers shouted for the men to form a skirmish line.

On Wake proper, the Marines had set up a 3-inch gun just in from the beach about 2,000 yards west of Peacock Point, and now they aimed the weapon at the dark hulk of an approaching transport. At least one

Japanese rifleman on board would never forget the next few moments. The transport rode up on the reef "with a loud crunching sound. The enemy opened fire all at once. One shell exploded on the ship's bridge, and several men fell where they stood." The rest began to clamber down ladders and ropes into the surf. "The water was so deep we could hardly walk. Rifles in hand, we struggled desperately forward." The men flopped on their stomachs on the beach, and the fire from the 3-inch gun, joined by that of machine guns and rifles, kept them pinned there. "The enemy's tracer bullets which came flying through the dark looked like a show of fireworks." The transport on the reef now burst into flames, and the beach took on a flickering red cast.

An observer on Admiral Kajioka's flagship, which was several miles from the atoll, decided that "the scene was too beautiful to be a battlefield." The Japanese rifleman, now on the beach, had no such illusions. "An inch at a time we crept toward the enemy." At a distance of twenty yards from the Marine line the invaders rose and charged. "One large figure appeared before us to blaze away with a machine gun from his hip as they do in American gangster films." A Japanese lunged at this man with his bayonet thrust forward, and they both went down.

All of the landing craft managed to place most of their occupants on shore, and soon the thin lines of Americans on Wilkes and Wake were fighting about 1,000 Japanese. The night was filled not only with gunfire, grenade bursts, and pyrotechnics, but also with shouts, curses, and shrieks of pain in two tongues. There was much confusion, and on both sides it was often hard to tell friend from foe. Visibility was worsened by squalls of rain. The Japanese made inroads, but in places were held back. They suffered disproportionate losses. Many who ran forward screaming *"Banzai!"* became still shadows on the damp ground, their blood draining invisibly. Then American communications began breaking down. Some of the phones failed mechanically; the invaders cut the lines of others. As commander of the defense, Major Devereux found himself operating in the dark, both literally and figuratively.

Spiv Cunningham, in his radio igloo, informed Pearl Harbor of the landing. Then, while casting about for a course of action, he remembered that there was supposed to be an American submarine patrolling near Wake. A ray of hope! He tried to contact the craft, but was answered instead from Pearl: no friendly vessels were in Wake's vicinity, and there would be none for the next twenty-four hours.

Actually, Admiral Fletcher's relief expedition was being called off. The decision was not popular with the task-force men; they were needed by fellow Americans in terrible trouble. According to a Marine lieutenant with the force: "Reactions varied from astonishment to shame and anger. There were even some staff officers who counseled Admiral Fletcher to disregard orders and make a dash at Wake." The operation, backed by the other two task forces, would have had a good chance of succeeding. The saga of Wake Island might have been turned into a spectacular victory at a time when America was desperately in need of one. But the confidence of the nation's leadership had been badly shaken by the disaster on December 7, and the courage to make bold decisions was temporarily lacking. The general attitude at Pearl during the Wake crisis was negative and defeatist, though some officers retained enough spirit to assert that the day on which Admiral Fletcher turned back would go down as the blackest in the Navy's history. Matters were not helped when Japan's radio propagandist, Tokyo Rose, was heard to taunt, "Where, oh where, is the United States Navy?"

In a message he radioed to Pearl an hour before daybreak, Spiv Cunningham confirmed the enemy's presence on Wake, but added that the issue was in doubt. This seemed to be the right thing to say, even though the breakdown in communications had left Cunningham with little knowledge of what was happening. Actually, the statement was at least momentarily true. The defenders were exploiting their one advantage, a familiarity with the terrain, and in some points the invasion had been stalled. On Wilkes, in fact, Captain Wesley M. Platt was reorganizing the defenders for a counterattack.

The knots of Americans on Wake proper, while suffering losses themselves, continued to stop some of the Japanese and to make others pay a high price for their gains. One group of defenders was made up of Major Putnam's airmen and a number of civilian volunteers, including big John P. Sorenson, who was killed in the act of running at the enemy hurling rocks. Putnam, crouching close to the ground, blasted two charging Japanese with his .45 pistol. As the pair fell, the helmet on the head of one clanged against Putnam's. During another skirmish, the major was shot through the neck. Feeling no pain, he was unaware he was wounded, though he wondered why he kept nodding off at such a critical time. Hank Elrod, a demon as a pilot, was just as pugnacious on the ground. "Kill the sons of bitches!" he shouted as he stood up and fired his Thompson submachine gun, laying several charging Japanese at his feet. Elrod himself was soon shot dead, unaware that his work as a pilot and foot soldier had earned the Medal of Honor.

About the same time that Elrod died, just before daybreak, Lieutenant Kinichi Uchida, the Japanese company commander leading the attack at this spot, suddenly vanished from the ranks. According to a

Japanese participant: "To the continuous calls of 'Unit Commander, sir, Unit Commander, sir,' there was now no answer. Lieutenant Uchida, who had landed with and stood at the head of his troops, and who had laughed during the attack on the enemy, was no more." Uchida had been shot through the head.

This fight was taking place just east of the center of Wake proper, near the airstrip's parking area. At the strip's eastern extremity was a small group of Americans under Corporal Winford J. McAnally. They had already beaten off several attacks. In the earliest light, one of McAnally's Marines shouted, "What the hell is that?" as two oddly equipped Japanese approached through the brush. They were wearing goggles and had heavy tanks strapped to their backs. "Men from Mars!" McAnally cracked as he opened fire with a .50-caliber machine gun. The two Japanese were the first flamethrower operators to be seen in the Pacific war, and they were also the first to die.

Although the Americans everywhere were glad when daylight came and the enemy was visible, the sight of the encircling vessels, gray slabs under low-hanging clouds, was a new discouragement. The fleet represented a power they had no chance of besting without outside help. If by some miracle they managed to defeat the first invaders, a fresh force would be landed. Besides, the Japanese had enough gunfire vessels in the fleet to stand at a safe distance and bombard the atoll into submission. Even now, a few shells were whining in and were shaking the ground with their bursts. The Japanese on Wake proper and Wilkes had ensured their immunity to this fire by marking their positions with flags bearing the Rising Sun. Although a destroyer that grew careless and came within range of the 5-inch guns on Peale was hit several times, the blow meant nothing. As if determined to rob the Americans of every vestige of hope, the first carrier planes now swept in to bomb and strafe them. These were some of the same craft that had devastated Pearl Harbor, "gallant Eagles of the Navy," as the Japanese styled them.

James Devereux, at his command-post igloo near the east coast of Wake proper, remained unable to learn what was happening to the majority of the defenders scattered over the 4.5 miles stretching westward. Devereux had ordered his executive officer, Major George H. Potter, Jr., to set up a last-ditch defense line a hundred yards south of his igloo. At first numbering about forty men, mostly clerks and communications people, the line was bolstered by thirty gun-position personnel Devereux called down from Peale, where no Japanese had landed. Potter's force was under attack, and was barely holding. At the same time, the few shreds of information Devereux got from the west seemed to indicate that most of the rest of the Americans had been overwhelmed. A terrified civilian came running from the west announcing that he had seen Marines being bayoneted. "They're killing 'em all!" he cried. "They're killing 'em all!" Devereux had no way of knowing that many of the defenders were still fighting, and fighting well. Near the western end of Wake itself, Second Lieutenant Arthur R. Poindexter, commanding about seventy Marines, Navy men, and civilians, had set up a perimeter defense that was so strong the enemy had stopped attacking it.

On Wilkes, Captain Platt's counterattack was succeeding remarkably. Nearly 100 of the enemy would be dead by the time it ended, with Platt losing only sixteen of his seventy men: nine Marines and two civilians killed, and four Marines and one civilian wounded. Ironically, Devereux thought that Platt and his men were being wiped out. Observers looking across the lagoon from Peale saw the flags the Japanese had planted to mark their positions and reported them as flags of victory.

Ever since the enemy had landed, Devereux had been in telephone contact with Commander Cunningham, in his command post to the north. Now, at 7:00 A.M., the two men discussed something galling that had to be faced: the possibility of surrendering. They had not only the lives of the servicemen to consider but also those of more than 1,000 civilians. Moreover, they were worried about the hospital igloo that was in the no-man's-land between Potter's line and the enemy. "Is any help coming?" Devereux asked. Cunningham told him there was not. Devereux pondered for a few moments in silence, explaining later: "I tried to think of something—anything—we might do to keep going, but there wasn't anything. . . . We could keep spending lives, but we could not buy anything with them." It was Cunningham, as the atoll's top commander, who made the decision to surrender, and it was the correct one, even though the defenders were not yet defeated. They could have carried on—perhaps for as long as a day or two—but the outcome would have been the same, with their casualties going much higher. Devereux told the commander, "I'll pass the word."

At this point, no one on the island was closer to the developing situation than the six Army communications men in Cunningham's igloo. "I burnt out the power transformer in our transmitter," recalls Sergeant Clifford Hotchkiss, "and we prepared as best we could for our surrender. We were scared to death, as we knew not what was in store for us."

The Japanese were already moving against the underground hospital between the lines. One of the Americans inside was Ted Abraham, Jr., a civilian serving as medical secretary to the Navy doctor, Lieutenant Gustav M. Kahn. Abraham relates: "We had extended a white sheet on a long stick out the entrance of the hospital so that it was visible from ground level. A squad of Japanese soldiers entered our unit by coming down a cement ramp." Those Americans not bedridden were standing inside the igloo in a group, and Abraham was clutching his typewriter case to his breast. Inside the case was not only his trusty "portable" but also his medical notes and a personal diary of the entire siege carefully kept in shorthand, an item he prized. "The Japanese seemed very nervous. The leader thrust his rifle inside and fired immediately, killing the fellow standing directly in front of me. I dropped my typewriter like a hot potato!" The case was not retrieved, but Abraham would later reconstruct his diary from memory.

The Americans in the igloo were ordered outside, and most were able to climb the ramp without help. Those who were dressed were made to strip to their underwear, and all of the men—the able-bodied, the wounded, and the sick—were seated on the ground in four rows. Their hands were lashed behind their backs with telephone wire picked up from the atoll's surface, and an extra strand was run from each man's hands up around his throat like a noose, and this was drawn tight enough so that it was impossible for him to struggle to free himself without choking. As if this were not enough, the group was covered by several machine guns.

Major Devereux now approached the hospital in the custody of a Japanese enlisted man he had met after leaving Potter's line under a white flag. There was an officer with the men who had captured the hospital, and Devereux asked him, "Do you speak English?" The officer answered, "Yes, a ritter." Devereux announced, "Well, we are surrendering." The officer broke into a smile, offered Devereux a cigarette, and told him he had attended the 1939 San Francisco World's Fair. At this time Spiv Cunningham, who had shaved and put on his formal blue uniform, arrived in a truck to make the official surrender. Devereux left with a party of Japanese for a walking tour of Wake and Wilkes to inform whatever American survivors he could find that the atoll had been given up.

The major was amazed at the number of defenders he found not only alive but still fighting. In front of their positions were many enemy dead. At one time Devereux and his party came up behind a unit of Japanese who were retreating before an American advance. Most of the Marines the major contacted could hardly believe what was happening. When they caught sight of the party approaching under its white flag, some thought that Devereux was the captor and the Japanese the captives. At one spot a sergeant said, "This must be a hoax. Marines never surrender." It was when the major boated across the channel to Wilkes that he got his own biggest surprise. Captain Platt was in complete control. The only live invaders in evidence were two wounded prisoners. (Another wounded man was lying among the dead, pretending to be one of them.) When the Marines released the two prisoners, one ran to a nearby corpse, fell down beside it, and cried in Japanese, "My brother! My brother!"

The invasion as a whole cost Admiral Kajioka's forces nearly 300 casualties, a high percentage of which were fatalities. On the American side, about thirty were killed; the number of wounded was considerable but undetermined. The breakdown for the entire siege was about 1,150 casualties for the Japanese, and, officially, 171 for the Americans. The Marines lost forty-nine killed and thirty-two wounded; the Navy, three killed and five wounded; and Dan Teters's civilians, seventy killed and twelve wounded.

It took most of the day for the victors to round up the Americans on the three islands, all of whom were marched to Wake. One squad of Japanese, searching the brush for civilians, came upon a small dugout in which one lay drunk. Prodded into an awareness of what was happening, the man refused to come out without his shoes, which he had

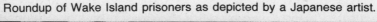

Roundup of Wake Island prisoners as depicted by a Japanese artist.

mislaid. The Japanese stood outside with great patience until the man found his shoes, fumbled into them, and came lurching from the entrance. Less patience was shown the Marines. The officers got reasonable treatment, but the enlisted men, able-bodied and wounded alike, were trussed in the same manner as the earliest captives and jammed into two of the underground magazines for some hours. Many sickened as the air became foul, and a few nearly choked to death as a result of their neck wire. At last the men were taken to the airport, where the civilians had been gathered.

Late in the afternoon Admiral Kajioka, resplendent in a white uniform garnished with medals and a dress sword, came ashore to take possession of the atoll for the Japanese Empire. The admiral brought with him a proclamation stating that the peace-loving Japanese people had been forced to take up arms "against the challenge of President Roosevelt." Those prisoners who showed no hostility would not be harmed, "but whoever violates our spirit, or whoever is not obedient, shall be severely punished by our martial law."

The majority of the Americans spent their first two days of captivity at the airport with no shelter, no food, and little water. Then they were moved into some of the damaged but usable barracks in the civilian camp, and their treatment became somewhat better. But this was the Christmas season, which made their isolation from their nation and their families all the more distressing.

The Americans soon learned they could make no blanket assessment of their captors. Some obviously took a savage pleasure in giving them discomfort and pain, but others were inclined to be amicable. A young enlisted man told Spiv Cunningham that his parents lived in the Hawaiian Islands and he was worried about them. "You think they all right, please?" Given the assurance he wanted, the youth exclaimed, "Pretty soon war be over, and we all shake hands." An officer of apparent education and culture came to Cunningham and tried to convince him that the Japanese were a fair people seeking only justice. He argued that their launching of the war was morally defensible. Finally he asked, "Did you really send that message, 'Send more Japs'?" Cunningham said he had not. The Japanese responded with a smile, "Anyhow, it was damned good propaganda."

On January 12, 1942, twenty days after their capture, the Americans —minus about 100 civilians who were to be kept on Wake as a labor force—were loaded aboard a Japanese ship for transport to the Orient. This robbed the men of all hope of being rescued. Now they were certain to remain prisoners—with all of the isolation, hardship, and misery this portended—for the duration of the war.

Memorial painting by James Pearl.

At this time Major Devereux was suffering from what he called "the death of pride." Never mind that Wake's small garrison had conducted a defense that would doubtless go down as one of the most heroic in American military history. The siege had ended in defeat and in the humiliation of his Marines at the enemy's hands.

On the afternoon of the surrender, however, there had been at least one moment the major did not want to forget. He was sitting near the airport in a black mood, watching parties of his men being brought in under guard. A large group led by a veteran sergeant, Edwin F. Hassig, was approaching on a course that would carry it close by his position. All of the men were at least partly stripped, with many down to their undershorts. Some of those without shoes were limping, their feet bruised by the coral. Dirty and unshaven, shoulders bent and heads down, the men were infinitely weary from the long siege and depressed over the surrender. Suddenly Sergeant Hassig noted that he and the group were nearing their commanding officer, and he turned and shouted, "Snap outta this stuff! Goddammit, you're Marines!" To a man, they raised their heads and squared their shoulders, and when they passed Devereux they were marching in perfect cadence, showing all the pride of a unit on parade.

3 | *Into Hostile Jungles*

===== Major Devereux needn't have feared that he and his men were the only Marines to surrender to the Japanese during the early part of the war. They weren't even the first. Some 200 U.S. Embassy guards in North China laid down their arms immediately after the attack on Pearl Harbor, and about 150 garrison troops on Guam, the American island in the Marianas, surrendered to a greatly superior landing force on December 10. In the spring of 1942, after a series of desperate actions, about 1,400 Marines attached to the U.S. Army in the Philippines became a part of the capitulations on Bataan and Corregidor. There were 105 Marines among the unfortunate thousands of Americans and Filipinos who made the Bataan Death March.

For the first five months of the war, Japan's leaders maintained a remarkable impetus in the creation of the "Greater East Asia Co-Prosperity Sphere" they envisioned. Their armed forces were successful not only at Guam, Wake, and in the Philippines but fanned out over a vast area south of the home islands. The new empire—which absorbed rich possessions of the British, the French, and the Dutch—had an outer rim that extended westward from Hong Kong into Burma, ran southward through the Andaman Islands and Sumatra, made an easterly swing that took in Java, Bali, Timor, northern New Guinea, New Britain, and the Solomons, then arced northeastward to the Gilberts and on through the Marshalls to Wake. Only the Marshalls were not a part of the conquest; they were Japanese mandates.

The conquest received its first check as the result of a naval battle in the Coral Sea, northeast of Australia, on May 7 and 8. Commander of the Allied force was Admiral Fletcher of the Wake Island fiasco. Fletcher actually suffered a tactical defeat, since he took the heavier losses, including the carrier *Lexington* sunk; but the Japanese were bested strategically, for they were turned back from a move against Port Moresby, on the southern coast of New Guinea.

From June 3 to 6 occurred the great Battle of Midway, in the Central Pacific, with Fletcher, ably seconded by Rear Admiral Raymond A. Spruance, again in charge on the Allied side. Admiral Isoroku Yamamoto—commander of the Imperial Combined Fleet, architect of the Pearl Harbor strike, and Japan's most admired naval figure—lost four carriers sunk. The admiral had been cherishing a hope of finishing off America's Pacific Fleet, and Midway curbed him harshly. Because of Japan's limited industrial capacity, the four carriers could not be replaced. The intelligent Yamamoto had been against starting the war in the first place. He was one of those Japanese officers who had spent time in the States and had come to understand the American potential for creating a superior military machine.

For the sake of morale, the Empire's people were told that Midway was a decisive victory. A seed for the claim was that, in combination with the operation, a detached Japanese naval force had landed about 2,500 men in Alaska's Aleutian Islands. "As a result of the Battle of Midway," said the official report, "Japan has secured supreme power in the Pacific." In Tokyo, thousands of deluded citizens celebrated by parading in the streets. To keep the truth hidden, the battle's wounded were brought home secretly and were placed in isolation, one man explaining later that during his stay in the hospital he was allowed no communication with the outside. "It was really confinement in the guise of medical treatment, and I sometimes had the feeling of being a prisoner of war."

It now became possible for the Allied forces in the Pacific, the larger part of which were American, to assume the offensive. They had bases in southern New Guinea and Australia, and also scattered among the island groups stretching eastward from Australia to Samoa, and some of these bases lay strategically near Japan's southernmost line of conquest. Troops, however, were not abundant. An even graver problem was a shortage of equipment and supplies. Although the United States was already in full production as the "Arsenal of Democracy," the lion's share of the output was going to Europe, since President Franklin D. Roosevelt and England's Prime Minister, Winston S. Churchill, had given priority to the defeat of Germany and Italy. During this period of the war, the forces in the Pacific had to manage with what they could get.

As the United States set the stage for the first offensive action, the question arose as to which branch of the service should take the lead. The Army's General Douglas MacArthur, who had fled the doomed Philippines at Roosevelt's order, was mustering his forces in Australia and southern New Guinea, forces that included both American and Australian units. MacArthur had been placed in command of the Southwest Pacific Area, which covered Australia and the island route, now held by the enemy, leading northward to the Philippines. Admiral Chester Nimitz, operating from his headquarters in the Hawaiian Islands, commanded in the rest of the Pacific: south, central, and north. MacArthur felt strongly that the job of leading the attack should be his.

But the nod from Washington—after some spirited sessions between Chiefs of Staff General George C. Marshall and Admiral Ernest J. King —went to Nimitz, since the operation would depend largely on the use of the Navy's facilities. Of primary importance was the necessity of using amphibious troops, and this meant the Marines, who were a part of the Navy and whose leaders had been preparing for an island war with Japan for twenty years.

The trouble was that during the planning of the initial invasion there was a shortage of Marines in the Pacific. The assault force had to be built around two regiments of the 1st Marine Division, composed mostly of "boots," recent volunteers who were only half trained. Fortunately, the division had a nucleus of "old breed" Marines, tough regulars who had been training for years, some of whom had seen service as protectors of American interests in such places as China, Haiti, and Nicaragua. One of these veterans was the division's commander, Major General Alexander Archer Vandegrift. Of old Virginia stock, "Archie" had grown up listening to tales of the Civil War. One of his grandfathers had died in the fighting, while the other was twice wounded: at Antietam and in Pickett's Charge at Gettysburg. Among the boy's heroes were Robert E. Lee and Stonewall Jackson, and he himself developed something close to Jackson's winning combination of audacity and wariness. Vandegrift had been a Marine Corps officer for thirty-three years.

D-day was set for August 1, 1942, and the targets were Guadalcanal and Tulagi, neighboring islands in the southern Solomons, formerly British protectorates, now among the southernmost outposts of Japan's new empire. Guadalcanal was of special interest to the Allies because it held the beginnings of a Japanese airport. Tulagi had an excellent harbor. Victory in this operation would not only remove these outposts as a threat to American communications with Australia but would also give the Allies an advanced base for further assaults on Japanese-held territory.

The code name of the operation was "Watchtower," but its planners soon began calling it "Operation Shoestring." Top planner, under the Hawaii-based Nimitz, was Vice Admiral Robert L. Ghormley, who commanded the South Pacific Area from New Zealand. In actual charge of the expeditionary force was the ubiquitous Admiral Fletcher, but his main concern was its aircraft carriers, *Saratoga, Enterprise,* and *Wasp,* and their support vessels. Rear Admiral Richmond Kelly Turner, known for his unabating energy and strong language, commanded the amphibious forces—those vessels and troops to be directly involved in the landing. A modest amount of long-distance, land-based aerial aid

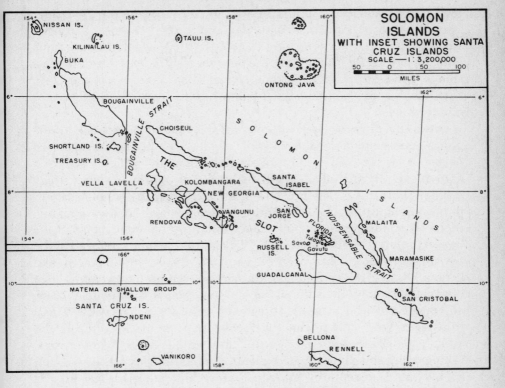

was to be provided by General MacArthur's fields in Australia and southern New Guinea, and by Army, Navy, and Marine planes stationed in the islands east of Australia. Admiral Fletcher was pessimistic about the whole plan, and was reluctant to risk his precious carriers in waters close to enemy bases that would surely send planes against them.

Archer Vandegrift, headquartered in New Zealand, had only a few weeks to assemble his troops from several parts of the Pacific, including the coast of California. It rained heavily while the transports were being combat-loaded at Wellington, which made a difficult job harder. Some of the supplies stored in cardboard containers were ruined. Marine workers in drenched dungarees groaned to see cartons of cigarettes and candy, or "pogey bait," turn soggy. The dock, according to one man, "was covered with drifts of mushy cornflakes and thousands of rolling C-ration cans."

With too many tasks to complete in his allotted time, Vandegrift asked his superiors for an extension of the deadline, and was granted a single week. D-day was rescheduled for August 7. The units the general assembled were the 1st and 5th Marines (or regiments) of his own 1st Division, the 2nd Marines of the 2nd Division, the 1st Raider Battalion, the 1st Parachute Battalion, and the 3rd Defense Battalion. The total number of men came to about 19,000, which seemed to be enough, at least for establishing the beachhead. This was one of the few things Vandegrift could feel fairly good about. He would say later: "Seldom has an operation been begun under more disadvantageous circumstances."

One of the general's special problems was that he had to seek intelligence concerning Guadalcanal and Tulagi, which he had never heard of before he received his orders to seize them, and which were little known even in Australia. An offbeat source of information was a Jack London short story, "The Red One," set on Guadalcanal. London seems to have been repelled by the entire Solomon chain: "If I were a king, the worst punishment I could inflict upon my enemies would be to banish them to the Solomons." Tiny Tulagi was the more civilized of the two target islands. It had been the capital of the British Solomons, and it held a street of shops, a hotel, a wireless station, and a number of bungalows built for the administrators. Guadalcanal, twenty miles south of Tulagi, was about eighty miles long and twenty-five wide. Those Australians who knew it called it "a bloody, stinking hole." From the air it looked like a green jewel of an island, with its towering mountains, rolling hills, and river-divided plains. But its jungles were wet, unfriendly, and unhealthful. They held crocodiles and giant lizards, and they teemed with insects, including ferocious white ants and poisonous spiders and scorpions. Their mosquitoes were virulently malarial. The island had a native population of ebony-skinned, bushy-headed Melanesians, most of whom hated the Japanese invaders.

The various elements of Fletcher's expeditionary force rendezvoused 400 miles south of the Fiji Islands—about 1,500 miles southeast of Guadalcanal—on July 26. The force comprised eighty-two vessels: three carriers, one battleship, fourteen cruisers (three of which were Australian), thirty-one destroyers, five minesweepers, five fueling vessels, four destroyer transports, and nineteen regular transports. Many of the American crews included Coast Guardsmen.

At a conference of the operation's commanders, Fletcher announced, "Gentlemen, in view of the risks of exposure to land-based air, I cannot keep the carriers in the area for more than forty-eight hours after the landing." The decision appalled Kelly Turner, for his amphibious fleet would be in grave danger without carrier cover, and it would take five days for him to put all of the Marines and their equipment and supplies on shore. Vandegrift, still wrestling with his own administrative problems, was furious at the new complication. To top things off, the invasion rehearsal in the Fiji Islands was, as the general put it, "a complete bust."

Unknown to Vandegrift and the other commanders, the operation had one great advantage: it was an absolute secret from the enemy. Even when on July 31 American bombers from bases in the New Hebrides Islands, southeast of the Solomons, began making daily strikes on Guadalcanal and Tulagi, Japan's war leaders suspected nothing. They did not dream that the Allies would take the offensive at this time. No taunts were broadcast by Tokyo Rose, for those who provided the grist for her propaganda were as ignorant of Allied plans as everyone else. The operation was to begin as a kind of reversed Pearl Harbor.

The Japanese hadn't had time for any masterful fortification of the target islands. There was even a shortage of troops. Allied intelligence personnel judged the total number to be around 7,000, but the estimate was far too high. Guadalcanal, in fact, had only 2,230 men, and about 1,700 of these were laborers. Little Tulagi and two nearby dots of land, Tanambogo and Gavutu, were somewhat more formidable. They held 1,500 men, about 900 of whom were prepared to fight.

Even as Turner and Vandegrift made their plans based on the figure of 7,000, they were pretty sure they'd be able to establish their beachhead, although they expected the job to involve some heavy fighting. Vandegrift was already looking beyond this first phase of the campaign. He was convinced that whatever the original number of enemy troops his Marines had to face, this number would soon grow. The waters of the Solomon Islands belonged to Japan, and it was going to be very difficult for the Allied forces to keep the Imperial Navy from bringing in reinforcements from the northwest. There was a handy passage—the Allies would soon be calling it The Slot—extending down through the Solomon chain from Rabaul, in the Bismarcks, where the Japanese had their largest South Pacific base. Rabaul was less than 600 miles from Guadalcanal. Vandegrift believed that Guadalcanal and Tulagi could be occupied, but he was far from certain they could be held. This concern was shared right up the ladder of command to Washington.

The voyage through the warm blue waters between the Fiji Islands and the southern Solomons took six days, with the landing force distributed on board the twenty-three transports and destroyer transports. Although the Marines were uncertain about what they were getting into, they were bolstered by their famed *esprit de corps*, the result of their tough training. They were, after all, "the best fighting men in the world." When not in attendance at briefings, they spent their time cleaning and oiling their firearms, sharpening their bayonets and knives, writing letters home, reading battered paperbacks, playing cards. They "shot the breeze" in small groups, their topics ranging from the pleasures of lovemaking to the brutal job ahead. When they began to boast of what they were going to do to the enemy, the talk often became bizarre. One man displayed a pair of pliers he said he intended to use to pull the gold teeth of the dead: "I'm going to make myself a gold necklace." Not to be outdone in ghoulishness, another youth declared that he planned to collect Jap ears and pickle them. One of the days at sea was a Sunday, and the services conducted by the chaplains were especially well attended. This was the moment of truth, and among the worshippers were Marines known for their colorful blasphemies and dissolute ways who were now singing hymns in zealous tones and bowing their heads in earnest prayer.

During the last two days of the voyage the weather was overcast, which provided a perfect screen for the approach, eliminating the danger of discovery by Japanese patrol planes. On the final day, August 6, Americans listening to radios heard Tokyo Rose ask derisively: "Where are the United States Marines? No one has seen them yet!" They were under the clouds in the waters south of Guadalcanal, drawing ever closer. That evening General Vandegrift wrote his wife: "Tomorrow morning at dawn we land in the first major offensive of this war. . . . Whatever happens you'll know that I did my best. Let us hope that best will be enough."

Dawn was still mostly darkness when a sharp-eyed Japanese lookout on Tulagi, twenty miles north of Guadalcanal, spotted the fleet coming around Cape Esperance, at Guadalcanal's northwestern tip. A Tulagi radio operator hastened to contact Rabaul: "Large force of ships, unknown number or types, entering the sound. What can they be?"

Not present were Admiral Fletcher's carriers and their support vessels; they were lurking in waters to the south. The invasion fleet was in two parts, with the smaller (code name "Yoke") heading across the sound, or Sealark Channel, toward Tulagi, and the larger ("Xray") bearing sharply eastward along Guadalcanal's northern coast. The waters of the sound were dark and almost still, and a faint breeze from Guadalcanal permeated the fleet with the stench of jungle swamps. Americans standing along the rails and peering at the island's hazy outline found the atmosphere creepy. Many of them jumped as the fleet's warships boomed into action against both Guadalcanal and Tulagi. The paths of the big shells were marked by red arcs, and the target areas twinkled and rumbled. Aboard the support ships themselves, all was noise and

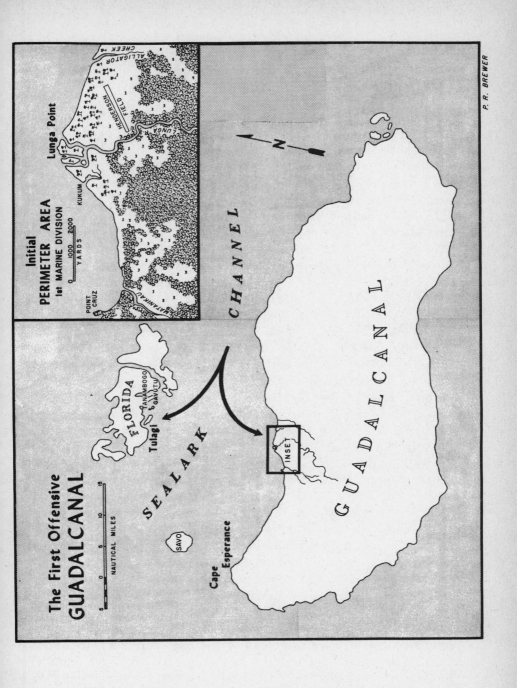

Initial
PERIMETER AREA
1st Marine Division

CREEK
ALLIGATOR

Lunga Point
HENDERSON FIELD
LUNGA
KUKUM
0   1000   2000
YARDS
POINT CRUZ
MATANIKAU

The First Offensive
GUADALCANAL

CHANNEL

FLORIDA
TANAMBOGO
GAVUTU
Tulagi

SEALARK

SAVO

Cape
Esperance

GUADALCANAL

INSET

0   5   10   15
NAUTICAL MILES

N

P. R. BREWER

vibration. Marine Corporal Jasper Lucas, serving with a gun crew on the heavy cruiser *Quincy*, was to say later, "Our teeth rattled in our heads." There was no return fire, for there were no functioning shore batteries.

The stunned Japanese believed at first that they were experiencing only a hit-and-run attack, but with the coming of full daylight they became soberly aware of what was happening. The transports lowered their landing craft to the water, and thousands of Marines in full combat gear swung over the rails and clambered down cargo nets to drop on board. The Japanese radioman on Tulagi informed Rabaul: "Enemy has commenced landing." The commanders at Rabaul made hurried preparations to dispatch a flight of bombers and fighters to the scene.

The Japanese effort was to be robbed of the element of surprise. Scattered through dozens of islands in the Bismarcks and Solomons were Australians and New Zealanders belonging to an arm of the Royal Australian Navy known as the Coastwatchers. Aided by parties of loyal natives, these intrepid men maintained radio stations hidden in Japanese territory. This remarkable intelligence network was to prove of inestimable value to the Allies through all of their work in the Solomons, for they would get advance notice of many of the enemy's movements.

The assault on Guadalcanal and Tulagi had the support not only of warships but also of dive bombers and fighters from Admiral Fletcher's carriers. The planes skimmed along above the beaches, motors roaring, bombs crashing, and machine guns strafing. The noises heartened the Marines about to head for shore in their blunt-nosed Higgins boats, their persons weighted down with helmets, packs, gas masks, canteens, firearms, hand grenades, bayonets, and knives. H-hour, the time of landing, was 8 o'clock on the Tulagi side of the channel, 9:10 on Guadalcanal.

Neither operation was opposed. But the boats heading for the southern coast of Tulagi crunched up on a coral reef, and the men had to jump out and wade in through the surf. On both islands, the Marines forming apprehensively along the beaches found nothing standing in their way but quiet jungle vegetation, some areas of which had been torn up by the preliminary bombardment. On Guadalcanal, most of the Japanese had withdrawn into the hills. Those on little Tulagi (roughly 1,000 yards wide and 4,000 yards long) were concentrated in its southern section, considerably to the east of the area where the Marines had landed. Tulagi lay in one of the southern bights of the large island of Florida, and a battalion of 2nd Division Marines, operating independently of the Tulagi landing, was in the process of seizing this unmanned island as a security measure and to eliminate the possibility of flight by the Tulagi garrison. The Japanese radioman sent a final message to Rabaul: "Enemy forces overwhelming. We will defend our posts to the death, praying for eternal victory."

It was the 1st Marine Raider Battalion that led the assault on Tulagi, about 1,000 lean, sinewy, superbly trained commando-type troops under one of the most respected officers in the Corps, Lieutenant Colonel Merritt A. Edson, a medium-sized man with cool blue eyes and thin, carrot-colored hair who was known as "Red Mike." Edson's executive officer was Lieutenant Colonel Samuel B. Griffith II, who was not only an expert on guerrilla warfare but also a writer, a China scholar, and a translator of the Chinese language. The Raiders had burlap tied around their helmets and camouflage paint on their faces, the paint looking especially weird on those men who had a cheek distended with a chew of tobacco. Armaments included rifles, pistols, machine guns, mortars, bayonets, knives. Hand grenades hung from pack straps where they curved under armpits, and the chests of some of the men were criss-crossed by bandoliers. A veteran sergeant said later: "We must have looked mean enough to scare the pants off a brass monkey."

The Raiders pushed into the jungle and up over a ridge to the island's northern shore. During the 1,000-yard trip, they met no resistance. Meanwhile, the 2nd Battalion, 5th Marines, 1st Division, was being boated to Tulagi in their support. The Raiders now formed a line across the island and began probing along the ridge toward the southeast. The underbrush was a tangle of vines and plants with giant leaves, and the men perspired as they worked their way through it. The going was slow. Three hours after their landing, the Raiders were still unopposed. "What the hell is this," cracked one man, "just another training exercise?"

It had been the same on the big island, Guadalcanal, where the 1st and 3rd Battalions, 5th Marines, 1st Division, had pushed into the jungle on the north coast just west of Lunga Point, about twenty-five miles from Cape Esperance. During the landing operation there had been a moment of excitement when an aerial observer reported seeing "many enemy troops" moving through a jungle clearing. A second look told the pilot that the figures were actually cows. The Marines moved inland about 600 yards and set up a hasty defense line. Coming ashore behind them were their reserves and their support elements, led by their artillery. And the fleet's cargo transports had edged closer to the beach and were unloading their vital supplies.

At about 11:15 A.M. the fleet received word through one of the Coast-watchers in the northern Solomons that twenty-seven twin-engine

Shore party personnel unloading supplies.

"Betty" bombers were on the way from Rabaul. The transports prepared to hoist anchor for evasive action, and Fletcher's carrier pilots were alerted. Along with the enemy bombers were eighteen Zeroes, and piloting one of these was Flight Petty Officer 1st Class Saburo Sakai, a leading Japanese ace. He had flown in China, the Philippines, and the Dutch East Indies, and he had fifty-six planes to his credit, including the Flying Fortress piloted by American hero Colin Kelly. This would be Sakai's first mission against carrier craft. He relates: "We flew southward along the line of the Solomons. Shortly before noon the pilots were able to make out the waters of Lunga Roads off Guadalcanal. We gradually distinguished the shapes of the enemy ships in the area. I had never seen so large a convoy before."

Sakai, who was proud of the sharpness of his eyesight, soon determined the number of ships to be about seventy. In addition, he saw myriad landing craft moving about in the waters near shore, their white wakes "having the appearance of brushstrokes of a giant but invisible artist." The beaches were already piled with supplies, and, as the bombers made their first run over the fleet, antiaircraft fire seemed to be coming from batteries on the island as well as from the ships. Sakai was amazed at what the Americans had accomplished in only a few hours. Nothing he had seen of Japanese invasions could match this. "I realized that any foe who could push ashore this rapidly was going to be a hard one to beat." Sakai was disgusted to note that the Japanese bombs merely raised geysers in the water about the ships. The bombers had been obliged to remain at a high altitude because of the antiaircraft fire and a pass by American carrier planes, which the Zeroes now began to engage.

It turned out to be a bad day for Saburo Sakai. Although he augmented his record, perhaps by as many as four kills, his own windshield was shattered by a .50-caliber machine gun, and two jagged slivers from the bullets slammed into his brain. "I felt as though I had been hit on the head with a club." His senses reeled and his plane fell toward the sea, but, revived by the cold air rushing through his smashed windshield, he was able to pull up in time. Sakai was in sad shape, his entire left side paralyzed, his right eye sightless, and his left eye very dim. He burst into tears, and the vision of his left eye improved, for part of the trouble there was caused by blood trickling down his forehead. After a period of aimless and erratic flying, while his senses fluctuated and he tried to settle upon a course of action, Sakai turned his Zero toward Rabaul, nearly 600 miles away. He had to contend not only with pain, critical disabilities, and a steadily fading consciousness, but also with a damaged plane, a failing gas supply, and a black squall that loomed in his path. But he made it, setting the Zero down on the same strip he had departed from, nearly nine hours earlier. The feat was one of the most remarkable in the history of aerial combat. As the little plane rolled to a stop, the blackness in Sakai's brain was nearly total, but he was aware that friends were climbing upon the wings. He felt the touch of eager hands, and heard someone cry, "Sakai! Sakai! Never say die!" The great ace would recover, except for the blindness in his right eye, and toward the end of the war he would fly again.

The Bettys that Sakai had helped to cover had scored one hit. A 250-pound bomb struck the destroyer *Mugford*, killing seventeen men and wounding another seventeen. A fire sprang up near a store of explosives, but the crew was able to put it out. A second strike from Rabaul came at about 3:00 P.M. The eleven unescorted dive bombers failed to score. The two attacks cost the Japanese a total of thirty bombers and fighters. Some were lost to antiaircraft fire and some to the carrier planes, while still others had to ditch on the way home for lack of gasoline. In all, a dozen American planes went down. Some of the pilots were rescued by destroyers.

The Marine Raiders on Tulagi, struggling southeastward through the jungle, had encountered their first resistance shortly before noon. The company on the left flank, working its way along the northern coast, entered one of the island's deserted villages. Everywhere were signs of damage inflicted by Fletcher's carrier planes. There wasn't a whole pane of glass to be seen. Marines who went into the houses discovered that the Japanese had left in a hurry. Private James G. Hall was surprised at the sight of "bathtubs half filled with water, layouts of Jap clothes, and half-eaten food on the tables." But the enemy had not gone far. Mortar shells began bursting in the streets, and the explosions were accompanied by the whine of snipers' bullets. Here the Americans took their first land casualties of the Pacific offensive. Several Marines were wounded, and a young Navy doctor was killed while trying to help them.

From that time, the Marine advance was resisted. According to one of the company commanders, Major Justice M. Chambers: "As we pushed them back upon themselves, it became progressively harder to work them out. Casualties began to get pretty heavy in both killed and wounded. We found that the Japanese had many dugouts both for machine guns and for riflemen."

The defenders made a few small-scale counterattacks. About fifteen Marines of C Company were moving abreast in a cleared area when one of the men shouted, "Christ, look what's coming!" It was a dozen of the enemy, several of whom were brandishing swords. All were shrieking, *"Banzai! Banzai!"* The Marines dropped prone and began firing. But it was Browning Automatic Riflemen belonging to units on the squad's flanks that did the best work. All twelve of the enemy were cut down before they reached the prone Marines. One fell in front of PFC Mario L. Sabatelli, "only about three feet away." The man's mouth was open and his sword was sticking in the ground beside him. For about half an hour after this experience, Sabatelli and his comrades found themselves joking and laughing almost hysterically. "I guess that was our reaction."

By late afternoon the Raiders had captured about two-thirds of the island. Red Mike Edson estimated that the remaining strongholds held 300 or 400 Japanese. Since it would not be possible to complete the conquest that day, Edson ordered his companies to consolidate for the night.

Simultaneously with the beginning of the action on Tulagi just before noon, Marines of the 1st Parachute Battalion, under Major Robert H.

Williams, had been crouched in about twenty landing craft headed for the islet of Gavutu, two miles east of Tulagi. Gavutu, only 500 yards long and 300 wide, had a 300-yard causeway running from its northwest shore to still smaller Tanambogo, the totality resembling a barbell. Each isle had a commanding hill, the one on Gavutu about 150 feet high, and the one on Tanambogo about 125 feet. The "barbell" was the site of a Japanese seaplane base that had been put out of commission by the invasion's preliminary bombardment. Most of the defenders had escaped harm by sitting out the sea and air attacks in caves and dugouts, and were ready for the Marines. This was the Corps' first contested landing, a microcosm of invasions to come.

The parachute battalion, deployed in three waves, with one company in each, approached Gavutu from the east. Among the men in the first wave was Private William Keller, formerly an Ohio farmhand. As his boat neared shore, Keller got the urge to pray. "I was on my knees, repeating the Twenty-third Psalm, when someone bumped me and said, 'Over the side, Keller.' I got ashore before I received any enemy fire, but then I saw dust kicked up on either side of me. My squad leader said, 'Keller, they are shooting at you.' I answered, 'Yes, but where the hell are they?' He told me the fire was coming from the island's hill, which was on our left. I took cover behind a coconut tree and tried to spot the enemy. In the meantime, Major Williams asked for volunteers to storm the hill. I was not in the group. The next thing I remember was a call coming down the hill that Major Williams was wounded, and to send a stretcher."

Another officer who was wounded early, though only lightly, was Captain Harry Torgerson. A sniper's bullet skimmed along his wrist, leaving a thin red line and carrying away the entire works of his wristwatch. After that, as the action progressed, each of Torgerson's habitual glances at his wrist to determine the time was met by the sight of an empty watch frame. He found this "the damnedest thing."

After several attacks the hill was occupied, but most of the Japanese were still alive, inside a network of caves. They continued to rake the beach with machine-gun and rifle fire, and ricochets whined everywhere. Bullets also came whistling across the causeway from Tanambogo, even though that island and its hill were under attack by American dive bombers and destroyers. Soon every tenth Marine on Gavutu was a casualty. In an effort to bolster morale, a Catholic priest moved about among the troops, shouting as he went, "God bless you, boys. Give 'em hell!"

By 2:30 in the afternoon the Marines occupied most parts of Gavutu, but the concealed enemy remained unconquered. Major Charles A. Miller, who had taken command when Williams was wounded, requested reinforcements to complete the capture of Gavutu and to assault Tanambogo. While awaiting this aid, Miller continued his attack. Some of the Marines resorted to an unusual expedient. Finding a number of fiber mattresses of enemy make, they set them afire and tossed them into caves. Thick yellow smoke came billowing out, and through it stumbled the coughing and tear-blinded occupants, who were shot down. A few other caves that yawned quietly were cautiously entered, and in one was a group of the enemy who had used knives to commit hara-kiri. This was the beginning of a commonplace practice of self-destruction among beleaguered Japanese defenders in the Pacific. To strengthen the will of those soldiers who might hesitate to kill themselves in defeat, officers spread the word that it would do no good for them to allow themselves to be taken alive, since the Marines would only torture them fiendishly, and then kill them. This was not hard for the Japanese to believe, for their own code, based on medieval concepts of total war, permitted the practice of torture.

It was late afternoon when the first American reinforcements, jammed together in their Higgins boats, arrived off Gavutu. The unit was Company B, 1st Battalion, 2nd Marines, under Captain Edward Crane. Major Miller directed Crane to seize Tanambogo. Darkness was closing in as the captain guided his small landing force to the island's northeastern shore. He had the support of destroyer fire that was at first heartening, but then became a terrible disadvantage. As the landing began, one shell fell short and burst among the boats, and another ignited one of the enemy's fuel dumps, the resulting glare illuminating the scene and making it easy for the Japanese to aim their machine guns and rifles. Crane's command was badly shot up, and the mission resulted in a confused withdrawal.

For the Marines on Gavutu, now in foxholes, the coming of night brought no respite from danger. From Tanambogo came machine-gun fire marked by tracers, and also mortar fire that crashed, flashed, and scattered debris. Some of the Japanese nearby fired machine guns from their caves; others stole out, climbed trees, and sniped with their rifles; and still others crept about and hurled hand grenades. The situation, according to one Marine, was hellish. "We couldn't talk; we couldn't whisper; we could scarcely even breathe." Private Bill Keller became furious with a member of his squad who lit up a cigarette. "That was the closest I ever came to shooting one of our own men." In spite of the night's many hazards, few Marines were killed or wounded.

4 | *Slaughter on the Ilu*

══════Across Sealark Channel on the big island, Guadalcanal, the Marines had spent the afternoon of D-day pushing inland without opposition. The only injuries were shin bruises caused by accidental encounters with fallen trees, finger cuts inflicted by knives that slipped while engaged with coconut shells, and red welts raised by insect bites. Most of the men were enervated by the struggle through the jungle, since the heat had grown as the day progressed. The disappearance of the sun in the west, however, was viewed with mixed emotions. The Marines were glad to be rid of its warmth, but were unhappy at losing its light. Most believed the jungle ahead to be filled with Japanese soldiers waiting till nightfall to attack. As the various units settled into defensive positions, the front began to ring with the fire of sentries shooting at shadows. The rest of the men had to hug the ground. According to Major Donald Dickson of the 1st Battalion, 5th Marines, "It was dangerous even to get up to go to the head."

On southern Tulagi, where Red Mike Edson's Raiders held an irregular east-west line facing the enemy's remaining strongholds, some on hillsides and some in a ravine, the threat of night action was real enough. Company commander Justice Chambers noted that "the Japanese were everywhere, and all night they were sniping, shouting at us, throwing grenades, whistling, and using all the tricks of the trade we had read about in the training pamphlets but, I suspect, none of us ever believed." It was here that the Marines experienced their first nighttime *banzai* charges. The sword-wielding leader of one of the groups was heard to shriek in perfect English, "Die, you dirty bastard Marines, die!" But, mostly, it was the Japanese who died, riddled with bullets. As a Tulagi Marine put it: "They launched several so-called suicide attacks, and they were successful—as far as the suicide part was concerned."

The American casualties who could not be properly attended during the night were evacuated to aid stations at dawn. Here and there in the front lines lay a dead Marine, the object of sober glances from his former buddies. The time given to grief was necessarily short. One man walked to where a comrade lay on his back, two crimson holes in his chest, stood looking down at him for a moment, said, "So long, fella," and promptly returned to his own position and his preparations for the day's fighting. Most of the Marines were tired-faced that morning; to one man his squadmates even seemed a little older.

The Raiders soon received reinforcements. Companies E and F of the 5th Marines, who had landed the previous day, came forward to help with the sweep to the southern end of the island. The attack was supported by both 60-millimeter and 81-millimeter mortar shells, which leaped from their tubes in a high and visible arc and landed with a roar, pulverizing the coconut log defenses and dismembering their crews. Caves encountered were blown with demolitions, the occupants sealed in, some still alive. By nightfall Tulagi was declared secured, though mopping up would be continued for some days. For his leadership in the assault, Red Mike Edson was awarded the Navy Cross.

On Guadalcanal, the Americans had spent the day expanding their beachhead and continuing with their unloading operations, again without opposition—except from the sky. About noon, a large formation of Betty bombers appeared in the north, over Florida Island. Armed with deadly aerial torpedoes, the planes swarmed in low to attack the shipping in the channel. They were met by a storm of antiaircraft fire, with both the warships and the transports participating, and the flak bursts threw a black canopy over the scene. The bombers began tumbling into the water, some exploding and bouncing their fragments upon nearby ships. One transport was the recipient of a gory assortment of arms, legs, and other human parts, which the crew swept overboard. A crippled bomber crashed into the transport *George F. Elliott*. News correspondent Richard Tregaskis was watching from Guadalcanal and saw "a huge flash of fire, as red as blood," burst along the transport's upper deck. Next, "a clump of sooty black smoke billowed out . . . and towered up into the sky." Abandoned by her crew, the *Elliott* continued burning for many hours. The only vessel hit by a torpedo was the destroyer *Jarvis*, which was able to limp from the area. She came to a dreadful end the following day. Alone in the sea, trying to make her way to Australia for repairs, she was discovered by a flight of enemy bombers and was sent to the bottom with all hands. As for the attack on Guadalcanal, it had cost the Japanese about twenty planes.

Some three or four hours after the raid, the advancing Marines reached the coveted enemy airport, which was to be named Henderson Field in memory of Major Lofton Henderson, a Marine air hero killed at Midway. This important piece of ground was as yet only a rough clearing with an unfinished strip. At the field's edges were dugouts about thirty feet long and ten feet wide that were covered with coconut logs and sandbags. In nearby areas were Japanese encampments consisting of rows of tents, grass shacks, and a few more substantial structures. As on Tulagi, it was obvious the enemy had left precipitously.

There was prepared food on the tables, and lockers held starched white uniforms, swords, and other gear, as well as personal keepsakes. The Marines were surprised and deeply angered to find that the keepsakes included American letters and snapshots taken from the captured defenders of Wake Island. The discoverers vowed revenge. Entering a quartermaster's building, the Marines found all kinds of supplies: a vast store of rice, dried fish, beer, *sake*, cigarettes, candy. Three small, brown-skinned Japanese laborers were captured, and an interpreter learned the reason for the hasty flight to the hills. There were only about 600 combat troops on the island. The invasion had startled and confused these men, and they had retired to await reinforcements.

There was plenty of action that day on the tiny Siamese-twin islands of Gavutu and Tanambogo. Additional American reserves, the 3rd Battalion, 2nd Marines, landed on Gavutu in the morning. The original invaders, after their harrowing night, were busy shooting the snipers out of the trees. It was "good hunting," according to Captain Harry Torgerson. The Japanese in caves, however, were "another matter." Torgerson made a name for himself during this phase of the struggle. He secured a supply of TNT blocks from an offshore Navy vessel, and had his men tear down a Japanese shack to obtain long boards. The TNT blocks, equipped with fuses, were lashed to the end of the boards, and the captain had some remarkable javelins. Covered by Marines firing into the caves to keep the enemy back, Torgerson and his helpers hurled the javelins through the entrances, each time falling flat as the rocks and earth flew and the air was rent by what Torgerson calls "a roar like a steam-boiler explosion." Eighteen caves were subdued, and there were no Marine casualties, although Torgerson got too close to one of the blasts and lost the seat of his pants.

Across the causeway from Gavutu, Tanambogo was still firmly in enemy hands. "Our planes," relates Bill Keller, "kept dropping bombs on it, but to no avail. The Japs would stay in their caves till a run was over, then come out screaming and put up the Rising Sun for us to see. One of the bombers targeted Gavutu by mistake. I was at the base of the hill at the time, and I was sure the bomb was coming right down my throat. It hit the hill above me, and debris flew everywhere. I got up and shook myself, and was relieved to find I was okay." The mistake cost the Marines three killed and nine wounded.

The decisive battle for Tanambogo began in the afternoon as the destroyer *Buchanan* opened up with her 5-inch guns. The crash of the first shell, coming after a period of relative quiet, startled the Marines on Gavutu. A man holding a Reising submachine gun jerked the trigger and shot a comrade in the stomach. Salvo after salvo rocked Tanambogo as Lieutenant Colonel Robert G. Hunt, commander of the 3rd Battalion, 2nd Marines, prepared his attack. One company would make the assault by boat, while another would charge across the causeway.

The Marines in the landing craft, accompanied by two light tanks, approached the beach under fire. One of the boats carrying a tank got hung up on a reef near shore. Says the vessel's commander, Boatswain's Mate 2nd Class B. W. Hensen: "Rather than lose time lowering the ramp, I told the tank commander to run right into the ramp and knock it down. The tank knocked the ramp down and started up the beach with a squad of Marines behind it. The commander had his head sticking out of the top of the tank, trying to fire its machine gun, and that's the last I saw of him." The commander, Lieutenant Robert J. Sweeney, was soon shot through the head. This tank, however, went on to do some effective work with its 37-millimeter gun.

The other tank got ashore with less trouble, but soon met with disaster. Lumbering inland, it got ahead of its infantry protection, and about fifty of the enemy swarmed around it. One thrust an iron bar into its tread. Trying to churn clear of the obstruction, the vehicle backed over a coconut stump and was stopped dead, unable to move in any direction. Now the enemy attacked it with Molotov cocktails, and the heat of the flames forced the crew to throw open the hatch. As they struggled to get out, the Marines were hit with hand grenades and more Molotovs. Only one tankman, his clothing afire, got to the ground alive, and he was seized, beaten, kicked, and stabbed. During these moments, several distant Marines were rapidly picking off the Japanese with rifle fire. Remarkably, the burned and battered tankman survived. Forty-two of the enemy were shot dead.

By this time the Marines making up the other half of the attack were charging across the causeway from Gavutu. They were raked with small-arms and mortar fire, and some fell. The rest clenched their teeth and kept going. As they reached Tanambogo, a number of the enemy, armed with swords and knives, rose shrieking from holes and ran at them. Some of the Marines fired point-blank, while others lunged with their bayonets, and the *banzai* was quickly shattered. The Marines spread out from the causeway, and were soon in contact with the company that had made the assault in boats. By late that night most of Tanambogo was in American hands, although neither that island nor Gavutu would be declared secured until the next day.

Capturing the small harbor islands of Tulagi, Gavutu, and Tanambogo cost the Americans 248 casualties: 108 dead and 140 wounded. An estimated 1,500 of the enemy were destroyed. About twenty survived as prisoners, and some seventy escaped by swimming from the small islands to Florida, where they vanished into the jungle. Perhaps as many as 600 of the dead were conscript laborers (the Marines called them "termites"), who'd had no choice but to help with the fighting, but most of whom had fought well. Those enemy dead not sealed in caves were buried, not as a concession to decency but as a measure required by sanitation; the climate was hot and the flies myriad.

It rained during the night of the Tanambogo conquest, August 8–9. Over on Guadalcanal, about 1:00 A.M., the soggy Marines heard the buzz of a plane coming from the murk above. To newsman Richard Tregaskis it sounded like one of the enemy's, and it was. "We stood in the drizzling rain, silently, and watched the Jap plane dropping flares in several sectors of the sky." This was the prelude to an attack on Admiral Turner's amphibious fleet—a night attack by warships that came as a complete surprise and resulted in one of the worst defeats ever inflicted on the United States Navy.

This early in the war the Navy had not yet acquired a real "battle awareness," was not yet fully attuned to the enemy's methods and capabilities, and was not sufficiently self-confident. It was a time when the prevailing mood of Allied forces everywhere in the world was one of apprehension rather than confidence. Adolf Hitler had expanded his European conquests deep into Russia, and the German and Italian forces in North Africa were threatening the Suez Canal. In the Pacific the Japanese still loomed tall as a result of their original victories.

The attack aimed at Kelly Turner's amphibious fleet was launched from Rabaul and was commanded by Vice Admiral Gunichi Mikawa, leader of the 8th Fleet, or "Outer Seas Force." The admiral was fifty-three, square-jawed and stern-eyed, although gentle and soft-spoken. Like many Japanese officers, he was of an intellectual bent but was also a man of action. A true *samurai*, Mikawa spurned directing the mission from Rabaul, which was his prerogative, in favor of leading it in person. He had eight vessels: five heavy cruisers, two light cruisers (including the *Yubari*, of Wake Island experience), and one destroyer. His aim was to make a hit-and-run attack, smashing Turner's shipping and opening the way for the Japanese reinforcement of Guadalcanal.

During the thirty-three-hour trip around the east coast of Bougainville and down through The Slot, Mikawa had been concerned about detection by Allied patrol planes. Although he was, in fact, spotted more than once, his intentions were not divined. It was reported to the American commanders that the fleet included seaplane tenders (which it did not), and this led them to believe that the enemy was planning another attack by air and that it would be made by daylight. The Japanese leader had his own apprehensions about an air attack, for he knew that Admiral Fletcher's carrier force was somewhere south of Guadalcanal. Very obligingly, Fletcher retired as Mikawa advanced. Fletcher's fears for the safety of his carriers got the better of his judgment, and he left the battle arena even earlier than he had announced he would at the Fiji Island conference.

The Japanese, through consummate skill on their part and drastic miscalculation on the part of the Allies, managed to descend upon the screening force (the warships) of Kelly Turner's amphibious fleet as a pack of wolves attack sheep. Commanded by a red-bearded Briton, Rear Admiral V. A. C. Crutchley of the Royal Navy, the vessels were hit while patrolling in the darkness around Savo Island, north of Guadalcanal's Cape Esperance. The one-sided battle, in which the Japanese used both guns and torpedoes, was over in less than an hour. To the Marines on shore, it was simply a series of explosions, rumblings, and illuminations, but to the Americans, Britons, and Australians afloat, many of whom were asleep in their bunks when the firing began, the Battle of Savo Island was a nightmare of destruction and death. Four cruisers, *Canberra, Astoria, Quincy,* and *Vincennes* were either sunk or left in a burning and terminal condition; the cruiser *Chicago* and the destroyers *Ralph Talbot* and *Patterson* were damaged. Deaths totaled 1,024 and the wounded numbered 709. The Japanese escaped with three vessels lightly damaged and with personnel losses of thirty-five killed and fifty-one wounded (although on the way home a cruiser fell prey to an American submarine, sinking with a loss of thirty-four dead and forty-eight wounded).

Two of the stricken Allied cruisers were still afloat and burning as the night faded. In the firelight and the gray light of dawn, the waters around Savo Island—on their way to fame as "Ironbottom Bay"—were revealed to be covered with vast patches of oil, thousands of pieces of wreckage and equipment, and hundreds of men, some huddled on rafts, some afloat in life jackets, and some clinging to fragments of flotsam. Numbers of dead bobbed around restlessly. Of those men who had gone under, some had been alive in the sinking ships, while others had survived the sinkings only to be jerked down, screaming in horror, by sharks. Many of the living bore wounds or burns, or both. All were exhausted. Destroyers and small boats nosed around carefully, pulling the men on board.

Even before the attack, when he learned with consternation that Fletcher was withdrawing his carrier force earlier than anyone expected, Kelly Turner had informed Marine General Archer Vandegrift that all of the amphibious shipping, warships and transports alike, must join in the retreat, even though the job of unloading the supplies and equipment was less than half finished. Now, on the afternoon of August 9, after some frantic last-minute ship-to-shore operations, the transports and the surviving warships weighed anchor and retired. Remaining on the transports were not only a multitude of items badly needed on the beach but also about 1,400 Marines. Those on shore who watched the last vessels disappear eastward along Guadalcanal's coast at sunset were chilled as they turned their gaze across the empty waters of Sealark Channel. Marines on a beachhead are always heartened by the sight of the Navy's silver silhouettes, which represent their sustenance and their link with home. Abandoned in waters controlled by the enemy, Vandegrift's Marines—about 11,000 on Guadalcanal and about 7,000 on the islands across the channel—were left with rations for thirty-seven days and with four units of fire: enough ammunition to last them through four days of sustained fighting. And no one knew when the Navy would return.

The outlook was dark. The Marines were now susceptible to air attacks, to bombardments from the sea, and to counterattacks by Japanese reinforcements ferried down The Slot from Rabaul. Vandegrift told his officers to explain the situation to the men, holding back nothing. "But," the general added, "also pound home that we anticipate no Bataan, no Wake Island. Since 1775 Marines have found themselves in tough spots. They survived, and we will survive—but only if every officer and man gives his all to the cause." The majority of the men who learned of the general's words were willing to fulfill their commitment as Marines, but not everyone believed this would do much good. One private was to say later, "I had it figured this way: Our necks were out, and it was just a question of how far down the Japs were going to chop." Unknown to this Marine, some of America's top war planners viewed the situation with the same kind of pessimism.

Vandegrift had three pressing tasks: to set up his lines, to make the airport usable, and to remove his tangled piles of supplies from their visible positions on the beach to orderly dumps concealed by the palms. The airport was the key to American survival. It must be made ready, and almost at once, to begin receiving fighters and bombers sent from carriers and land bases. With air support, which would at least inhibit enemy operations, Vandegrift figured he could hold out until the Navy was able to return with strength enough to win control of Solomon Islands waters.

Deciding to operate on the defensive, except for patrol actions, the general planned his perimeter in such a way as to encompass and protect the airport. The line was an irregular east-west oval more than ten miles in circumference, with its northern portion on the beaches of Lunga Point, where it extended from the mouth of the Ilu River in the east to a point well beyond the village of Kukum in the west. Its southerly half was made up of a series of jungle outposts running, in part, along the Lunga River. The perimeter occupied only a very small part of the island, with its area of more than 2,000 square miles. An attack could come from any direction, by sea or land. The Marine riflemen in the lines had the support of machine guns, mortars, and heavier weapons, including artillery and tanks. The airport, where antiaircraft guns were installed, became the project of engineers and pioneers working largely with captured tools and machines, among the latter two small gasoline-fueled trains with hopper cars, comical-looking to the Americans but fine for moving fill.

Air raids came daily, and lone-wolf patrol planes (given such nicknames as "Washing Machine Charlie" and "Louie the Louse") harassed

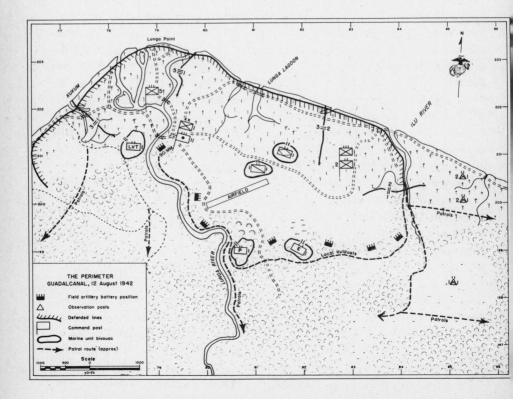

THE PERIMETER
GUADALCANAL, 12 August 1942

Field artillery battery position
Observation posts
Defended lines
Command post
Marine unit bivouac
Patrol route (approx)

Scale
1000 500 0 1000
yards

the perimeter at night. Destroyers made frequent visits and cruised the Lunga coast, gathering intelligence and laying down bombardments. The first substantial exchanges of gunfire on land occurred during American patrol activities west of the perimeter, at the Matanikau River, beyond which the majority of the island's Japanese were encamped, some in native villages.

From a man in Japanese naval uniform taken prisoner during a patrol the Americans learned that the enemy was short of food and was coming down with jungle ailments. The interpreter got the impression that at least some of the men might be willing to surrender. Lieutenant Colonel Frank B. Goettge, Vandegrift's intelligence officer and also an old friend, wangled permission from the general to take a Higgins boat and twenty-five men along the coast west of Lunga Point to the mouth of the Matanikau, and there go ashore and make a proposal of surrender. Shoving off late in the day on August 12, Goettge did not accomplish his landing until after dark. The patrol had scarcely reached the edge of the jungle before the shadows exploded with small-arms fire. The Marines hit the ground, with Goettge shot dead and with several others wounded. The ill-fated patrol was kept pinned down during the night, and its casualties mounted. Three men escaped, one by one during the early morning hours, by creeping back to the surf and plunging in. The last of these men swam away at daylight, and after a time he paused to tread water and look back. He saw sabers flashing in the sun as the patrol was finished off. The survivor spread his story, and from that time it was difficult for Marine officers to get their men to take any of the enemy alive.

On August 15, six days after Kelly Turner's battered amphibious force had sailed away, four American destroyer transports appeared off Lunga Point, having made a daring run with cargoes of aviation gasoline, bombs, belted antiaircraft ammunition, and tools and spare parts for aircraft repairs. Landed along with the supplies was Henderson Field's first operations officer, Major Charles H. Hayes, his staff, and 120 naval aircraft maintenance personnel under Ensign George W. Polk. The airport was already primitively operational, although it was still barren of planes.

That same day the island's Japanese, too, heard from their distant friends. Transport planes from Rabaul dropped baskets containing food, small-arms ammunition, and medicines, along with messages of encouragement. Some of the baskets fell inside American lines, and one of the messages was translated: "Help is on the way. *Banzai!*" This gave no encouragement to the Marines.

Apprehensions about the enemy, however, were presently rivaled by other concerns. Sanitation measures were breaking down and the men were filthy. Itchy and painful fungus infections were appearing, particularly on feet too long confined by socks and shoes soggy from the frequent rains and the wet grass and sand. An acute form of dysentery was hitting hundreds, some of whom had to head for the latrine trenches twenty or thirty times a day and became so weak they had to be helped by luckier comrades. Also appearing were the first few cases of malaria.

Had they known about it, Vandegrift's harried men would have found a degree of cheer in something that happened in the Gilbert Islands, some 1,200 miles northeast of Guadalcanal, on August 17. About 220 men of the 2nd Marine Raider Battalion, arriving by submarine from Pearl Harbor, made a hit-and-run attack on the Japanese atoll Makin. Tall, lean, and leather-faced Lieutenant Colonel Evans F. Carlson was in command, and his executive officer was Major James Roosevelt, one of the President's sons. The purposes of the mission were to overcome the defenders and destroy their installations, gather intelligence, test hit-and-run tactics, divert some of the enemy's attention from Guadalcanal, and boost the morale of the Americans at home. Costing thirty men dead and missing, and well over that number wounded, the bold venture achieved adequate success on the first four counts and extravagant success on the fifth. Carlson and his men were glorified in the stateside press, and home-front morale was indeed boosted. The raid's long-range military effect, however, was not a happy one. The Japanese were alerted to the necessity of building up their defenses in the Gilberts, and one of the Gilberts was Tarawa.

Fortunately for the American effort on Guadalcanal, its true import was not immediately grasped by the majority of Japan's war planners. In spite of their navy's setback in the Coral Sea, which frustrated the invasion of Port Moresby, they were still thinking more in terms of completing their conquest of New Guinea than of struggling to hold territory already taken. It was true, of course, that the Americans had to be evicted from Guadalcanal, but early intelligence seemed to indicate that the invasion force was relatively small and would prove no problem, especially since the Japanese soldier had a great edge in fighting ability. It had been written into the training manuals that Western troops were "haughty, effeminate, and cowardly" and had "no stomach for fighting in rain or mist or in the dark." It was well known that they sought their victories through material superiority and fought mostly for personal glory, that they lacked the all-important spiritual incentive that was a part of every Japanese.

Assigned the responsibility of retaking Guadalcanal, with his head-quarters at Rabaul, was the commander of Japan's 17th Army, balding and mustached Lieutenant General Haruyoshi Hyakutake. With his thin-rimmed glasses and sensitive features, the general looked more like a scholar than a soldier. He believed he could accomplish his mission with 6,000 men: a Special Naval Landing Force of 500, the 3,500-man Kawaguchi Detachment, and the 2,000-man Ichiki Detachment. So badly had the Japanese underestimated both the strength and re-solve of the Americans that the 6,000 troops were not even committed as a body but in dribbles.

After dark on August 18, the Marines at Lunga Point heard the wash of enemy vessels speeding eastward along the coast: six destroyers car-rying 915 men, nearly half the detachment commanded by the coura-geous but rash Colonel Kiyono Ichiki. The party and its supplies were put ashore at Taivu Point, about twenty miles east of Vandegrift's Ilu River flank. Ichiki radioed Rabaul: "We have succeeded in invasion." General Hyakutake had given the colonel the option of awaiting the arrival of the second half of his detachment, due within a week, before doing anything, but Ichiki decided to act quickly, and in his diary recorded a neat summation: "18 August, the landing; 20 August, the march by night and the battle; 21 August, enjoyment of the fruits of victory."

By the time of Ichiki's landing the Marines in the perimeter had gained some new and useful friends from close by. A party of male natives bearing gifts of fruit and led by a British Coastwatcher, Captain Martin Clemens, had come out of the jungle and offered to serve Van-degrift as scouts. The general was delighted to have them. Clemens, a former star athlete at Cambridge, was fair-complexioned and well formed. In his tropical shirt and shorts he looked to the Marines like a typical British movie hero, the kind, as one said, "who is always sitting at a small table on a hotel veranda in Cairo or Singapore or someplace like that." The captain had spent months eluding the island's Japanese and radioing reports of their activities to Allied listening posts. Upon his arrival in camp, Vandegrift was surprised to note that "he had appar-ently suffered no ill effects from his self-imposed jungle exile." Clemens had come out thirsty, however, and one witness swears that he drained a bottle of brandy at nearly a gulp, and then spent hours at a *sake* party, yet showed no signs of being affected except for growing somewhat louder in his speech.

While Colonel Ichiki was preparing to march upon the perimeter from the east, the Marines were still occupied in the west, at and beyond the Matanikau River. Three companies of the 5th Regiment assaulted the villages of Matanikau and Kokumbona, killing sixty-five of the enemy and losing four men killed and eleven wounded. When resistance petered out, the three companies returned to the perimeter. That same day, August 19, Vandegrift sent patrols probing eastward from the Ilu River, and the men under Captain Charles H. Brush, Jr., caught one of Ichiki's patrols in an ambush, killing thirty-one of its members, only three escaping into the jungle. Found in the pockets of the dead were diaries, dispatches, and other materials indicating that the men were part of a force new to the island, and that their commander was planning an attack. Among the papers were even sketches of the Ilu and the Marine lines.

On August 20, while Vandegrift was strengthening his eastern flank against the expected attack, thirty-one aircraft piloted by Marines— twelve Douglas SBD "Dauntless" dive bombers commanded by Major Richard C. Mangrum and nineteen Grumman Wildcats under Captain John L. Smith—circled in and landed on Henderson Field. The sight electrified the perimeter, and men cheered, laughed, and banged one another on the back. Vandegrift was infinitely relieved. "I was close to tears, and I was not alone." Thus was born the Cactus Air Force ("Cactus" was the code name for Guadalcanal). Also on that day additional supplies were landed by ship; three transports slipped in. And Commander Joseph P. Blundon, leader of the Seabee battalion slated to arrive some days later, came in on a PBY that touched down briefly in Lunga waters. While Blundon was reporting to Vandegrift, a flight of Japanese bombers appeared over the island, and the commander made his first acquaintance with a foxhole. "I just lay there and trembled with patriotism while the bombs fell around us."

Colonel Ichiki stuck to his schedule. That afternoon, leaving 125 men to guard his supplies, he began his twenty-mile march along the northern coast from Taivu Point to the mouth of the Ilu. Even though his patrol of the previous day had not returned, the colonel was still highly confident, and radioed Rabaul: "No enemy at all. Like marching through a no-man's-land." The Marines were waiting just beyond the Ilu (or the Tenaru, as they called it as the result of a mistake on their maps). The 2nd Battalion, 1st Regiment, under Lieutenant Colonel Edwin A. "Al" Pollock, held a line from the lapping surf southward through a grove of coconuts on the river's bank. Infested with crocodiles, the Ilu was shallow, sluggish, and green-hued, and it had a sandbar, a natural bridge, across its mouth; the river seeped, rather than ran, into the sea. Pollock's men had machine guns and mortars, and were supported also by artillery, with tanks in reserve.

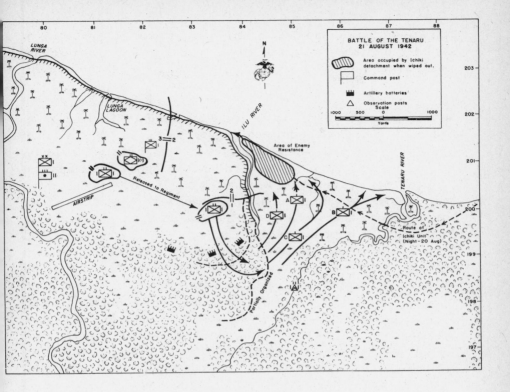

It was just after midnight when the Marines manning lonely outposts on the Japanese side of the Ilu began hearing metallic clankings, excited talking, and other noises that told of the enemy's approach. Sending up signal flares, the Marines tumbled back across the river to join the men who were now gripping bayoneted rifles or hand grenades, or were huddled around squat machine guns or jutting mortar tubes, men who were suddenly oblivious of the drone of the mosquitoes, ears attuned to more ominous sounds, eyes trying to pierce the darkness of the far bank.

When the Japanese began coming, it was evident at once they were using the beach route toward the sandbar. Seventeen-year-old Private Richard W. "Bill" Harding, among others, was surprised at their lack of caution. "We could hear them walking along the beach toward us, and jabbering. They didn't even have scouts out." Shortly Ichiki opened with his support weapons, and shells crashed brightly among the entrenched Marines, while machine-gun tracers crisscrossed above them. Then about 200 Japanese at fixed bayonet came charging across the sandbar, shrieking their battle slogans, working the bolts of their rifles, and firing from the hip as they ran. The noise and the pyrotechnics doubled and trebled as the Marines responded with the fire of rifles, machine guns, mortars, and 37-millimeter guns loaded with canister, which turned the weapons into giant shotguns.

"We cut them down by dozens," says Bill Harding. But some of the sprinting, screaming men reached the Marine lines. Corporal Dean Wilson's BAR jammed as three of the dark figures hurtled toward him. Dropping the firearm and seizing a machete, Wilson disemboweled the leading man and also chopped down his companions. More than one Japanese was stopped by a bayonet thrust. But now the survivors dropped to the ground and utilized the shadows to creep about among the Marines, looking for targets for their hand grenades and knives. A grenade flashed in front of machine gunner Albert A. Schmid, who had been firing doggedly and had accounted for many of the charging Japanese, and suddenly he could not see. His eyes seemed to be caked with dirt, and he reached up to brush it away. His fingers encountered a pulpy mass of flesh and blood. Al thought he was finished, but he would survive to regain a part of his sight and accept the Navy Cross.

Bill Harding had crept from his foxhole to check on a buddy, and, finding him okay, was making his way back on his stomach, tracers from across the river snapping above him, when he saw, some distance to the left, a dark figure sliding toward the same hole. In the temporary light of a flare the man was revealed to be a Japanese, and Bill's first thought was, "I'm going to have to fight for my own foxhole!" He was "scared as hell." Dragging his bayoneted rifle with him, Bill kept going, and so did the enemy. Bill did not fire, for fear of giving away his exposed position to other Japanese. A hot machine-gun bullet nicked his right hand. It made him start, and it stung fiercely, but he kept moving. As the two men neared the hole, the Japanese crawled around one side and Bill the other. At last they came face-to-face, and Bill struck out in a clumsy fashion with his bayonet. It pierced the other's arm, and he gave a sharp cry. Bill now dropped his weapon, threw himself on the enemy's back, and locked an elbow around his neck. The man kicked and struggled with the strength of the desperate, but Bill held on. "Finally he went limp. I kept up the pressure for another minute or two to make sure he was dead. By the time I let go my arm was numb."

As Bill lay there, sweating and panting, he spotted a second figure, and it was crawling toward him. "Oh God," he thought, "not another one!" Bill kept very still, and the Japanese, apparently thinking him dead, began crawling past him, only a foot or two away. Bill's rifle was lying on that side, and he had a hard grip on its barrel, close to the bayonet hilt. Using the bayonet as though it were unattached, he thrust with all his strength at the enemy's side and felt the steel slide home. The man screamed and flailed about, the bayonet stuck in his rib cage. Bill tried to pull it loose but could not. He rose to his knees for better leverage. At that moment a bullet slammed into one knee and a shell roared behind him, shattering a hip and a leg, and breaking a hand. With the impression that he was "all lit up like a Roman candle," Bill fell into the foxhole he had been trying so hard to reach, and passed out. Although his part in the war was over, he would make a good recovery.

Battalion commander Al Pollock reinforced the line where it had been punctured, and soon the Japanese were finished, only a few managing to retreat over the sandbar. When Colonel Ichiki, who had remained on the east bank with the bulk of his troops, learned that his first attack had been smashed, he tried a second time, again in the darkness, sending a reinforced company wading through the surf out- side the sandbar. The drenched men came ashore on the left flank of Pollock's line. Their attack faltered at a single strand of barbed wire strung along the beach. The Marines hit this line with everything they had, including artillery, and the result was another slaughter. It wound down at dawn with the Marine riflemen popping at the few survivors cringing on the beach or at the bobbing heads of those trying to swim away. Al Pollock strode around happily, repeating the old target-range order, "Line 'em up and squeeze 'em off." This was not callousness but exhilaration at the dispersion of a mortal threat to his command. As visibility sharpened, the Marines observed scores of enemy dead lying on the sandbar and along the beach, where the surf was tinged with red. One man shook his head and said, "Who ever told those dumb bastards they were soldiers?" This Marine would have been surprised to know that Ichiki's troops were considered to be some of Japan's best.

Until now the Americans had no idea of the total number of Japanese they were facing, but this information was opportunely provided by one of the native scouts under Martin Clemens, Sergeant Major Jacob Vouza. In his forties, Vouza had recently retired from Guadalcanal's police force after serving with distinction for twenty-five years. At pre- sent the sergeant major was in bad shape. Captured by the Japanese while scouting three or four miles east of the perimeter, he had refused to answer questions about the Americans and was tied to a tree, beaten with rifle butts, stabbed in the chest and throat with a sword, rendered unconscious, and assumed to be dead. After the enemy left, Vouza came to, chewed through his ropes, and began dragging himself toward the perimeter, arriving just before sunrise, as the fight on the beach was winding down. Martin Clemens was called and found Vouza to be "an awful mess," and now helpless. "We dragged him behind a jeep and he told me his story as best he could, in spite of the gaping wound in his throat." Vouza even gasped out a report on Japanese weapons and dispositions. Colonel Pollock arrived and asked the blood-caked man about the enemy's numbers. Vouza felt there were between 250 and 500. (Actually, Ichiki had about 400 men left after his two disastrous charges.) Pollock was reassured; the Marines could take action based on the sergeant major's information. Vouza was thought to be near death but would make an amazing recovery, soon returning to his duties.

Now aware he was facing a foe of no great threat to the perimeter, Vandegrift went on the offensive. While Pollock and his men kept Ichiki occupied by firing across the mouth of the Ilu, Lieutenant Colonel Lenard B. Cresswell's 1st Battalion, 1st Marines, crossed the river to the south, out of Ichiki's sight, then swung northward through the jungle and trapped the Japanese in the corner formed by the Ilu and the sea. The fighting should have ended with the entrapment, but no white flag appeared among Ichiki's men. Vandegrift would say in his report: "I have never heard or read of this kind of fighting. These people refuse to surrender. The wounded will wait until the men come up to examine them and blow themselves and the others to pieces with a hand grenade."

One of the Marines who learned of the enemy's ways at first hand that day was BAR man Andrew R. Poliny, who took part in the encircling maneuver. "As we came to a slight depression in the coconut-grove terrain, there lay two Japs who seemed to be playing dead. Our battalion commander was present, and he ordered the pair bayoneted. As a Marine approached to do the job, one of the Japs rolled over with a pistol in his hand and shot him in the face, just above the right eye. Seeing this, I opened up on both Japs with my BAR on full automatic, and that was the end of that." On another occasion, Poliny was on the scene when two Japanese carrying a wounded comrade approached the Marines as though wanting to surrender. As the three drew near, a sergeant who did not like the look of things suddenly shouted, "Cut 'em down! Cut 'em down!" The two Japanese dropped their burden and reached inside their shirts for grenades. Says Poliny: "They never got to use them."

The majority of Ichiki's men fought back desperately as the vise closed, killing or wounding a number of Marines. But in the end the battle became one of extermination. While the Japanese ran in all directions, some even jumping into the sea, they were hit not only by every land weapon the Marines had but were also strafed by some of the newly arrived Grumman Wildcats. The unfortunate men died by dozens and by scores. In this fighting without quarter, Vandegrift sent a platoon of tanks across the sandbar to help with the mopping up. The Japanese managed to disable two, but the treads of the others were soon red with churned flesh.

Two of the swimmers escaped to carry the story of the massacre to the 125-man detachment left at Taivu Point to guard the supplies. By sunset there were only a few live Japanese in the coconut grove on the beach near the Ilu. They were gathered around Ichiki, who had been wounded, and who now gave his last order: "Burn the colors." With an American tank clattering toward the group, Ichiki drew his sword and committed hara-kiri. It was August 21, the day on which the colonel had expected to enjoy the fruits of victory. Nearly 800 Japanese corpses were scattered through the coconuts, along the beach, in the surf, on the sandbar, and in the Ilu—food for crocodiles and grisly work for American burial parties.

Colonel Clifton B. Cates, commander of the 1st Marines, had come forward from his command post to watch the battle's finale. "Never at any time in France during World War I did I see such a congestion of enemy dead." It occurred to the colonel that these "sons of heaven" had been shot to the wrong address.

The Marines who had achieved the entrapment returned to their lines by way of the sandbar. Andy Poliny said later: "I will never forget the speech our battalion commander made that evening. He told us we were now real men and good Marines, and that we were going to kick the Japs' asses all the way back to Tokyo. After a hot meal of canned red beans and beef stew we crawled into our foxholes for a little rest. It's true that many of the men had no stomach for food that night even though they hadn't eaten all day. The adjustment to this kind of combat would take some time."

In his report from Rabaul to Imperial Headquarters in Tokyo, General Hyakutake said, "The attack of the Ichiki Detachment was not entirely successful." Why it was made in the first place was a mystery to the Marines. Ichiki had violated not only the military fundamentals but also the dictates of common sense. His actions were apparently based on an utter contempt for his foe and a boundless faith in his detachment's spiritual power, which, aided by Divine Providence, was supposed to conquer all. The colonel's concept of the situation was entirely unrealistic. Rear Admiral Raizo Tanaka, the wily old sea dog in charge of the naval side of the effort to reinforce Guadalcanal, was to say later that the Ichiki episode "made it abundantly clear that infantry-men armed with rifles and bayonets had no chance against an enemy equipped with modern heavy arms. This tragedy should have taught us the hopelessness of 'bamboo spear' tactics." Japan's military leaders were an odd combination of men who thought in feudal terms and men whose thinking was progressive. Unfortunately, the actions of even the intelligent moderns were governed to a great degree by the old codes, which were an integral part of Japan's ideology.

The Battle of the Tenaru, as it came to be called as a result of the mistake on the hastily prepared military maps, had an important psychological effect on the men of the perimeter. Like their comrades on the small islands across the channel, they now had a victory to their credit, and at the moderate cost of forty-three dead and fifty-six wounded. They had lost much of their apprehensiveness at facing the military machine that had swept through Southeast Asia and fanned across the Pacific with such remarkable speed, for they had destroyed a part of that machine with relative ease. "It was wondrous," says Vandegrift, "to see the infectious wave of confidence that swept over the Marines on Guadalcanal."

5 | Toward Edson's Ridge

===== Even though Japan's war planners maintained their schedule for the New Guinea campaign, they now began to take the Guadalcanal problem seriously. The great Admiral Yamamoto himself assembled the naval support for the next landing operation. When the remaining troops of the Ichiki Detachment and about 500 others, some 1,500 in all, headed for Guadalcanal, they were accompanied by three aircraft carriers, eight battleships, six cruisers, and twenty-two destroyers. Probably never in history had so small a landing force been so heavily covered. Of course, Yamamoto was thinking of drawing American naval forces into a decisive fight. Admiral Fletcher's carriers were in waters southeast of the Solomons at this time, having been watching over the sea route by which the Marines were being supplied. On August 24, with planes from *Enterprise* and *Saratoga*, Fletcher intercepted the Japanese advance. The Battle of the Eastern Solomons consisted entirely of aerial assaults, with Japanese damages including the loss of a light carrier and with the *Enterprise* absorbing three bombs. Since neither side was critically hurt, the battle was considered inconclusive, but the enemy's heavy warships turned back.

The Marine fighter planes on Guadalcanal had a share in this battle, going up to meet a large flight of enemy bombers and fighters coming in for a neutralizing strike on Henderson Field. At the cost of four planes and three pilots, the Marines broke up the raid, downing ten bombers and six fighters. Upon their return to the field the fliers climbed from their planes grinning and whooping. This was the first significant work done by the Cactus Air Force.

Although the Japanese carriers and their escorts turned back from their mission, the landing force, led by Admiral Tanaka and composed of five transports, one light cruiser, and five destroyers, was ordered to continue to Guadalcanal. The worried Tanaka sent his five destroyers ahead to bombard Henderson Field, a serious threat to his approach. The vessels cruised off the Lunga coast through much of the night of August 24–25, sending in salvos that shook up the Marines but did little damage. Then the destroyers raced northward to rejoin Tanaka for the purpose of escorting him in. During the morning the admiral was subjected to the raid he feared. The Marine fighters and dive bombers had the welcome company of a flight of Navy planes, dive bombers on loan to Henderson Field by courtesy of the *Enterprise*, now retiring for repairs. Also helping with the raid was a flight of Army bombers from a base in the New Hebrides. Tanaka's flagship, the light cruiser *Jintsu*, was badly damaged and the admiral himself was knocked senseless for a few moments. A destroyer and a transport were sunk, with the loss of many men. After the last of the aircraft left, Tanaka reorganized his fleet and probably would have tried to continue with his mission, but orders from Rabaul now turned him back to Shortland Island, just south of Bougainville. This had become the springboard for the runs down The Slot, which the Americans would soon dub the "Tokyo Express."

The Cactus Air Force had hit its stride. It already had its own Army planes; a part of the 67th Fighter Squadron had arrived from New Caledonia. From this time, Henderson Field would act the eager host, if irregularly, to all types of planes from every source that could spare them. Nobody cared what branch of the service the craft represented. Aware of the monumental importance of their task, the fliers worked in harmony; they lived together, fought together, and sometimes died together. The ground crews maintained a strenuous pace, handicapped by the enemy's raids and a paucity of equipment and supplies, trying to keep a sufficient number of planes armed and flying. The aviation people enjoyed none of the advantages usually associated with their branch of the service. They had no comfortable and convenient quarters in a zone of relative safety. They lived much like the men in the front lines, and they took more than their share of bombs and shells, for the airfield was the enemy's main target.

Japan's war planners now shifted their priorities: the conquest of New Guinea was placed second to the reinforcement and recapturing of Guadalcanal. To avoid the wrath of Henderson Field and of American carrier planes, the troop buildup was scheduled to be accomplished by stealth during a succession of nights. The first convoy to arrive in the area, however, erred in its timing. At dusk on August 28 it was caught by Henderson's pilots. Badly hurt, it was obliged to turn back. After this mistake, the system began to work; the buildup got under way. But the developing campaign suffered from a lack of harmony among its leaders, and confusion was rife. As always, there was a mixture of modern and feudal military concepts. Admiral Mikawa, hero of the Battle of Savo Island, warned: "Our operations must be conducted in accordance with careful and deliberate plans based on accurate information, and we must abandon the bad habit of underestimating the enemy and overestimating our own forces." Major General Kyotake Kawaguchi, when about to sail from Shortland to take command of the next attack on the American perimeter, spoke to his officers in spiritual terms: "Our

Major General
Kyotake Kawaguchi.

faith is our strength. Men who fight bravely, never doubting victory, will be the victors in the long run." He swore that the enemy would be smashed, and the officers responded by shouting, "On to Guadalcanal!" In a private talk with a news correspondent, Kawaguchi was not so confident, confessing that he believed the task of retaking Guadalcanal was going to be a tough one. Then, fearing he had said too much, the general reassumed the pose of the unbeatable *samurai*.

It was in the darkness of the last day of August that Kawaguchi arrived on the beach at Taivu Point, the same spot where Ichiki had landed. Some of the Ichiki survivors emerged from the jungle like ghosts, bodies thin and uniforms tattered. The newcomers were received with joy but were warned to obliterate all signs of their landing, since the enemy's planes patrolled the coast daily and were quick to attack the unwary.

Henderson Field got a boost on September 1 with the arrival, by transport, of the 6th Naval Construction Battalion (Commander Blundon's Seabees), sent to assume responsibility for the field's development and maintenance. Seabees were something new in American military circles. Organized about the time of Pearl Harbor, they were drawn chiefly from the nation's construction industries, and were expected to fight as well as to work. When the men of the 6th arrived on Guadalcanal the Marines eyed them curiously, for many were older than the average serviceman; some had gray hair. The younger Marines called out such things as "Hey, pop, what the hell are *you* doing here?" and got such responses as "We came to protect you kids!" It would not be long before the Marines and Seabees established a warm comradeship based on mutual respect. Blundon's men were much needed on Guadalcanal. The commander was aware that the campaign's fate depended to a great degree on their progress with the airport and on their learning to fill its shellholes and bomb craters almost as fast as the enemy made them. "We pitched our camp at the edge of the field to save time," he said later. "We dug our foxholes right up alongside the landing area."

General Vandegrift found some encouragement in the rapid development of his air arm. The field gained a new top commander on September 3, big, tough Brigadier General Roy S. Geiger, a World War I aviator and a friend of Vandegrift's for thirty-three years; they had been classmates at Marine Officers' School at Parris Island in 1909. Another plus for Vandegrift's cause was that supplies were filtering through, even though his needs were in competition with MacArthur's in New Guinea and those of the Allied forces preparing to invade North Africa. Rations were still low, but captured rice and other stores were helping. It was ironic that many of the island's Japanese were suffering from hunger while the Americans were eating Japanese food and calling it barely palatable.

Bright spots notwithstanding, there was no room for real optimism. The enemy had complete control of Guadalcanal's waters by night, and was managing to knock out some of the vessels making the supply runs during the day. Vandegrift knew of the enemy buildup on the island and realized that the next attack could come anywhere along the perimeter, and at any time. From afar came the bad news that the carrier *Saratoga*, while cruising in waters about 250 miles southeast of Guadalcanal, had been holed by a submarine and had retired for repairs.

A few of the American officers on Guadalcanal had radios capable of picking up short-wave broadcasts from the States, and each evening groups of men crowded around the sets to listen to the news. On hearing a commentator announce that, to judge by reports coming from Washington, Guadalcanal might end up a lost cause, a private exclaimed, "Well, I'll be a sad son of a bitch! Don't they know we got Marines on this island?" Not so easy to disregard was the radio's report that American war industries were being hurt by strikes and absenteeism. According to one observer (Lieutenant Edward L. Smith of the Navy's Medical Corps): "In shocked silence the men listened. Then in the gathering darkness they melted into the jungle to man their guns for the night watch. . . ."

By this time Vandegrift had begun pulling some of the troops over from the harbor islands, using them to strengthen the perimeter. One of the first things these Marines learned was that on Guadalcanal it was hard for a man to get enough rest. At night there were bombardments from the sea and harassment flights by "Washing Machine Charlie" and "Louie the Louse," and in the daytime there were air raids. Paratrooper Bill Keller soon devised a system for coping with the daytime strikes: "I would stand on top of a little hill and watch the Jap planes come in from Rabaul, would wait until I saw the bombs being released, and would then decide which side of the hill to retire to."

Vandegrift soon ordered Red Mike Edson to lead his 1st Raider Battalion, backed by the 1st Parachute Battalion, about 700 men in all, on a raid by boat eastward to Taivu Point, where it was known the Japanese had been landing. This turned out to be a good idea, but only because General Kawaguchi's force of about 4,000 well-armed men was no longer there. The general had started westward for an attack around the rear of the perimeter, planned for some days later. Only about 300 Japanese remained at Taivu Point with Kawaguchi's reserve supplies.

Covered by aerial bombing and strafing and by salvos of shells from destroyers, the landing was made on September 8 at the village of Tasimboko (the home village of Sergeant Major Jacob Vouza before the Japanese invasion of the island). Losing two dead and six wounded, the Marines killed twenty-seven of the enemy, some of them Ichiki survivors, uniforms in shreds and rags wrapped around their feet in place of shoes. No sadness was felt at the destruction of these unfortunates. "By this time," recalled one Raider, "most of us had the same feeling about the Japs. We just wanted to kill them." Vouza's village was burned, and large quantities of equipment and supplies were destroyed. Paratrooper Bill Keller was present: "We dragged artillery pieces into the ocean, chopped holes in the canned food, and slashed sacks of rice and then ran with them to spoil as much of the contents as possible." Both guns and food stores would have been appropriated by the Marines, but they were in a hurry. As it was, the men returned to their boats and to the perimeter with an assortment of the enemy's lighter weapons, and with such things as canned crabmeat, British-made cigarettes (seized by the Japanese during one of their own forays in the Pacific), beer, and *sake*. One squad brought back a prized souvenir: General Kawaguchi's dress uniform. A Japanese diarist who survived the day wrote: "It is maddening to be subjected to these insulting raids by the Americans."

General Kawaguchi now had 6,000 troops on the island, a composite of units known as the 35th Brigade. Not all of the men were with the general in the eastern zone. About 2,000 were west of the perimeter near the Matanikau River. This number should have been greater, but landings in that area had not gone as well as those in the east at Taivu Point. The last contingent to come down The Slot, 1,100 men of the 124th Infantry Regiment under Colonel Akinosuka Oka, were aboard forty-eight slow-moving barges. Delayed by stormy weather, the vessels were caught in the daylight by Henderson's pilots. Over half of Oka's command was bombed and strafed out of existence. Those men who made it ashore were not only exhausted but also in a state of shock.

The two elements of Kawaguchi's command were thirty miles apart, the perimeter between them. As he personally began leading the eastern force in a southwesterly direction around the perimeter, the general dropped off 1,000 men a mile or two east of the Ilu River. He was planning a three-pronged attack, with all elements acting simultaneously. The Ilu force was to hit the perimeter from the east and the Matanikau force from the west, while Kawaguchi himself, with 3,000 men, was to make the main attack, striking from the south against the perimeter's rear. The rallying cry was "Remember the Ichiki suicide!" And the purpose of the operation was not only to capture the airfield but also to annihilate the Marines and give rest to the souls of their victims.

Kawaguchi's march around the perimeter, begun on September 7, took several days. The troops were obliged to cut their way through dense, rain-soaked foliage, to climb over gnarled roots, to pick their way up and down hills, through swamps, and across stagnant streams. They perspired copiously and were bitten by insects; they acquired patterns of scratches and bruises; and they sagged with fatigue and were smitten with dysentery. They fumed and swore, and were mocked by parrots who picked up some of their phrases. Neither Henderson Field's air searches nor the perimeter's ground patrols discovered the expedition, although after Edson's raid the Americans knew that something big was in the wind. The only direct information the perimeter received came

Edson's Ridge.

from a group of natives who wandered in and claimed that the Japanese were making a tunnel through the jungle.

"Well, they're coming," said the American officers to one another. "But where will they hit?" A tactical study of their maps revealed the most likely spot, a rugged and relatively barren ridge rising from the jungle about a mile south of Henderson Field. Running north and south, the height offered an excellent avenue of approach. If the Japanese gained it, they would command the field. The ridge had not been occupied by the Marines. The entire south side of the perimeter, in fact, was thinly manned. Vandegrift had set up with his greatest strength along the coast and on his flanks.

It was Red Mike and his Raiders, again accompanied by the parachute battalion (now commanded by Captain Harry Torgerson, who had lost the seat of his pants while blowing caves on Gavutu), that were ordered into the breach. These Marines had seen heavy combat across the channel and had just returned from Tasimboko. Their reward for their good work, as is always the case with first-rate troops, was another tough

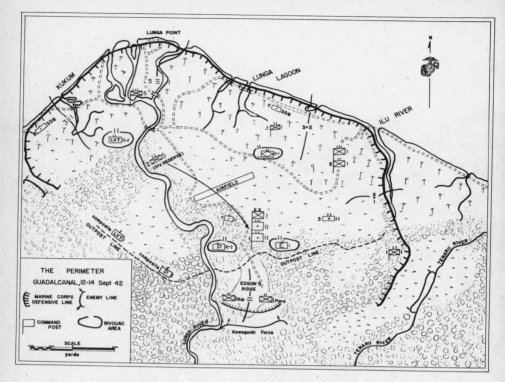

THE PERIMETER
GUADALCANAL, 12-14 Sept 42

MARINE CORPS
DEFENSIVE LINE   ENEMY LINE

COMMAND
POST   BIVOUAC
AREA

SCALE
yards

assignment. Both units, and especially the Paratroopers, were under-strength as a result of casualties. And nearly all 700 men were weary and shaken. As they plodded toward the ridge on September 10, they had no knowledge of the nature of their mission. Edson had chosen to tell them they were moving into a rest area. During the afternoon they took up a position along the southern face of the ridge and began digging in. The next morning the usual bombers from Rabaul approached the perimeter. Their target was nearly always the airfield, but this time they hit the ridge, their 500-pound bombs churning the ground and killing or wounding several men. After the planes droned away, a corporal stood up, surveyed the damage, and said, "Some goddam rest area!"

That afternoon Kelly Turner, who had been at New Caledonia consulting with South Pacific commander Robert Ghormley, flew in to Henderson Field to see Vandegrift. The admiral brought the bad news that the Japanese were assembling another huge fleet, with amphibious elements, which indicated they were planning strong backup measures for the operation presently under way on Guadalcanal. Moreover, Admiral Ghormley had concluded that his own South Pacific strength was

insufficient to sustain the Marines against increased pressure. Vandegrift was momentarily staggered, but then made up his mind that if he
could not hold the airfield he would take his men into the jungle and
resort to guerrilla warfare. Kelly Turner, not as pessimistic as Ghormley, promised to do everything he could to see that Vandegrift was
reinforced. The admiral left Guadalcanal by air on September 12.

General Kawaguchi and his three battalions, somewhat the worse for
wear, were now assembled at their jumping-off place, the northern
slopes of Mount Austen, about four miles southwest of Henderson Field.
At dusk the men took up their gear and began the march toward the
perimeter to launch the attack. Coming to a grassy plain, the battalions
drew up to make their final dispositions. The critical moment was near,
and faces were solemn in the pale light of a new moon. Almost to a man,
these troops were prepared to do their duty, and to die "gloriously for
the Emperor" if necessary; but, like all soldiers in spots like this since
the dawn of warfare, what they wanted most devoutly was to stay alive
and get back to their homes. A private who was engaged to be married
lamented to a friend that his enlistment in the Army had taken him
from Japan so unexpectedly that he had had no time to say good-bye
to his fiancée. Everywhere in the ranks, last-minute pacts were made;
those who survived the night were to write to the families of those who
did not. Their dispositions completed, the troops pressed into the deep
shadows of the last stretch of jungle.

After being drenched by an early evening rain, the 700 Americans
strung along the southern face of the ridge were trying to get some
desperately needed rest when, at nine o'clock, a Japanese patrol plane
droned overhead and dropped a green flare. Within half an hour a
bombardment was launched by a cruiser and three destroyers lying off
Lunga Point. The big shells sounded like approaching freight trains as
they cut through the darkness, but most failed to hit the ridge, although
the near misses made it tremble. When the guns fell silent, mortar shells
began to arc from the jungle, to be followed by machine-gun and rifle
fire. Then fragments of Kawaguchi's brigade began trotting forward,
the men slapping their rifle butts and chanting, "U.S. Marines be dead
tomorrow! U.S. Marines be dead tomorrow!" A part of the attack
reached the thin line and even broke through in one spot, but there was
no follow-up, and the Marines were able to re-form, although seven
men who had been cut off were never heard from again; not even their
bodies were found. At dawn the Japanese faded back into the jungle.
Red Mike Edson concluded that they had been merely probing, but
Kawaguchi had intended the attack to be decisive. He explained later:

"Because of the devilish jungle, the brigade was scattered all over and completely beyond control. In my whole life I have never felt so helpless." To worsen matters, neither of the general's flank attacks had developed, beyond the firing of a few artillery shells by the detachment in the east.

The Japanese leaders at Rabaul had lost radio contact with Kawaguchi, and that morning they were perplexed. The general should have been in possession of Henderson Field by earliest light and should have reestablished communications. Air transports had been readied to begin troop and supply runs to the island. The first planes were warming up, and their crews hoped to get there in time to witness the surrender ceremonies. To solve the mystery, four scout planes were sent in, and they returned with bullet damages, proof enough that the field was still in American hands. The explanation seemed to be that Kawaguchi had postponed his assault, and the transport crews were ordered to stand by until the next day.

The Marines used the hours of grace to good advantage. Red Mike drew his line into a better position farther back on the ridge, improving the fields of fire for his automatic weapons and giving the Japanese a longer route to travel over open terrain. Colonel Pedro del Valle's 11th Marines, the 1st Division's artillery regiment, prepared to give the new line close support. At Edson's request, Vandegrift moved his reserve battalion closer to the front. It might well be needed, for many of the Raiders and Paratroopers were now critically fatigued. All of these preparations were not accomplished without enemy interference. Vandegrift wrote home: "Another Sunday—and what a way to spend it! Planes roaring away overhead, Jap Zeroes darting in and out of the clouds and our boys chasing them. One of our pilots, Major [John L.] Smith has shot down 13 Jap crates to date."

By evening General Kawaguchi had two of his three battalions poised for action. The third would never make it to the front, much to the general's frustration. According to historical precedent, however, the 2,100 men he had were enough for the job at hand. Edson had 700, and sound military practice calls for troops attacking a fortified position to outnumber the enemy three-to-one. It was true that Edson had a reserve battalion, but, at least conditionally, so had Kawaguchi.

The attack that night was launched in the same way as the first one, with "Louie the Louse" dropping a green parachute flare at nine o'clock. This time the guns of seven destroyers began booming, but their fire was restricted to Henderson Field; the gunners were not sure who held the ridge. Even while Henderson rumbled and quaked, a Marine in Red Mike Edson's lines who was watching the jungle said, "Jesus, here they come!" Supported by the fire of machine guns and mortars, Kawaguchi's men began to swarm into the open, officers leading with raised *samurai* swords, symbols of Japanese military prowess for hundreds of years. Most of the troops were well armed, but here and there, remarkable for their incongruity, were small groups carrying bamboo spears. Under the flickering light of the patrol plane's follow-up flares, the panorama was unreal. To Captain Harry Torgerson, the Japanese "looked for all the world like children in Halloween costumes." But the war cries were real enough. The usual *"Banzai!"* rang out everywhere; and issued in English, their purpose to demoralize, were such phrases as "Gas attack!" and "Marine, you die!"

Edson's rifles and machine guns were rattling now, and their muzzle blasts stabbed through the shadows. From behind the lines came the first of Pedro del Valle's 105-millimeter howitzer shells, whooshing through the air in a shallow arc, clipping leaves from the trees. To Bill Keller the shells seemed low indeed: "I wasn't about to stand up, for fear of losing the top of my helmet." The enemy's ranks were torn by furious bursts. Edson's mortars did similar work on a smaller scale. The battlefield teemed with flashes and resounded with detonations. Kawaguchi's men still shouted, but now the war cries were mingled with screams of pain. The slopes were littered with bodies, some very still and others writhing in the midst of grass fires started by the shells.

Back in the fringes of the jungle, the enemy's light machine guns, or Nambus, began to locate the heavy machine guns in the Marine lines. Three of the busiest belonged to Captain William McKennon, commanding one of the parachute companies, and he went around checking on them. "We were beginning to lose men, but as fast as a machine-gun crew went down, their places were taken by others." The attack, according to the captain, "was almost constant, like a rain that subsides for a moment and then pours the harder." As the leading Japanese approached the line, the crack and flash of hand grenades joined the tumult. The Marines in the higher spots merely pulled the pins of their missiles and let them roll down the slopes, which some of the enemy were climbing on hands and knees. Bill Keller had a tight grip on his BAR. "I could hear three of them jabbering as they climbed toward me, and I opened fire. I must have got one of them, for someone down there carried on terribly." Bill was unable to do much more, for he was soon found by two hand grenades. Hit in the face and in the back, he passed out. When he came to, he was in the rear of the ridge in the care of two hospital corpsmen. Many another Marine was to be thankful for the skilled ministrations of the medical personnel that night.

Red Mike was everywhere, at the front and just behind it, shouting orders, praising those men who kept their nerve and ridiculing those who quailed: "The only thing the Japs have that you don't is guts!" Major Kenneth D. Bailey, who had been carrying hand grenades to the front, grabbed at dazed men stumbling rearward and used the old World War I taunt, "Get in there and fight. Do you want to live forever?" The line was bent back on both flanks, but then it settled into a tight horseshoe and held. And at eleven o'clock there was a letup in the horror as the Japanese drew off to the jungle to regroup. The Marines consolidated their horseshoe and awaited the next attack.

It came before midnight. Newsman Richard Tregaskis, who had been trying to sleep in a bivouac between the ridge and Henderson Field, now gave up. A "cascade of sound" emanated from the ridge, and " 'Louie the Louse' was flying about, and flares were dropping north, south, east, and west." The crackle of gunfire was heard also from the direction of the Ilu River. This was Kawaguchi's eastern attack getting under way against Lieutenant Colonel William McKelvy's battalion of the 1st Marines. Repeated thrusts here would gain the Japanese nothing but casualties. There were no sounds coming from the Oka zone in the west.

The second attack on Edson's lines was also major, but it was soon broken up. Other attacks followed, with the same result, although more than one group of the enemy closed with the Americans. Hand-grenade duels took a toll on both sides. During one of the close encounters a big Marine sidestepped a bayonet thrust and at the same time reached for the throat of his attacker, whom he quickly throttled. Mortar shells from the jungle shook the American position. One Raider was on his feet as a barrage began, and his comrades saw his body twist in a sheet of flame and heard him cry, "God have mercy on me!" He was dead almost before the words were out.

During all of the fighting Del Valle's artillery kept whooshing and crashing. The fire had been pulled in close to the lines, and some of the advancing Japanese became so demoralized while trying to avoid the bursts that they scrambled up the slopes and jumped into occupied foxholes. They were knifed to death and tossed out. Many of the shellfire victims lying in groups on the field were badly mangled. Entrails were scattered about, and here and there lay an arm or a leg or a head. Of those not dead but helplessly maimed, numbers were moaning or wailing or calling for aid. Marines who heard the shrill cry *"Oka-san!"* could not know it meant that a dying youth was calling for his mother.

At 2:30, during a lull in the fighting, a weary and disheveled Red Mike Edson stabilized his lines and then rang up Vandegrift at his headquarters not far behind the front and said, "We can hold." The Raiders and Paratroopers, at a cost of more than one-third of their number (upward of 250 in killed, wounded, and missing), had made one of the great stands of the war. At about four o'clock the 2nd Battalion, 5th Marines, moved up to bolster the tattered line. These reserves had not been committed earlier because Vandegrift could not be sure they would not be needed even more urgently at some other spot. Although the total number of Marines on the island outnumbered Kawaguchi's 6,000 men by two-and-a-half-to-one, it was necessary for Vandegrift to protect the airfield on all sides. A breakthrough at any point would have thrown the perimeter into disarray. And if Kawaguchi could have managed to exploit such a breakthrough and consolidate his forces around the field, they would have been difficult to dislodge.

The Japanese general launched two more halfhearted attacks, the last at dawn. In the dim light, the battlefield seemed to be populated more by sprawled corpses than by men on their feet. As the scattered survivors advanced under a renewed hail of fire, at least one Marine was moved to say, "Those crazy bastards!" A mortar crew on the ridge spotted four men in a group, one carrying a flag and the others marching with heads bent forward and bayonets poised. The range was judged to be 200 yards; the tube's slant was adjusted and a shell dropped in. Making its characteristic plunk and leaping into its high arc, the missile scored a direct hit. When the smoke and dust cleared, according to one of the mortarmen, "there was no more flag and no more Japs."

This attack was shortly broken up, and the fighting diminished to sporadic exchanges of rifle, machine-gun, and mortar fire. During the night, some of the enemy had crept inside the perimeter and at dawn began sniping at behind-the-lines personnel. These plucky infiltrators were hunted down; some were shot from trees. A sword-swinging officer and two soldiers were killed while charging into Vandegrift's command-post clearing as the general stood reading his early morning messages. Behind the lines and also on the battlefield, a few prisoners were taken, most of them wounded. The first reaction of these men was to point to their bellies and say, "Knife! Knife!" But, as Dick Tregaskis noted, they seemed relieved when they were not accommodated. It was as though their request to be destroyed, or to be allowed to destroy themselves, fulfilled their obligation to Bushido. They were surviving through no fault of their own. Their concern for their honor was soon replaced by the desire for an American cigarette.

Kawaguchi's main force, leaving 600 dead on the field and carrying hundreds of wounded, drew off through the jungle under the harassment of Army planes firing shells from 37-millimeter cannon. Soon mercifully sheltered from sight, the pathetic procession made its way to Mount Austen. On a slope overlooking the battle zone, thereafter to be known as Bloody Ridge or Edson's Ridge, Kawaguchi bowed his head and whispered a prayer for the slain. That afternoon the sound of gunfire was finally heard from the west. It soon sputtered and died, and the general knew that Colonel Oka's attack, too, was a failure. Nothing had gone according to plan. Like all Japanese facing the Americans for the first time early in the war, Kawaguchi's troops had learned with astonishment that these supposedly effete men were formidable adversaries. And it was more than just a matter of superior firepower. "The Yankees have their own kind of spirit," stated one of Kawaguchi's men to a comrade, who nodded and said, "They love their country too. We're not the only ones."

Their part in the defense of the ridge had earned both Red Mike Edson and Kenneth Bailey the Medal of Honor. Edson came out of the battle with an increased respect for the Japanese. Although their tactics could stand some revision, they were superb fighters. "What they have done is to take Indian warfare and apply it to the twentieth century. They use all the Indian tricks to demoralize the enemy." The colonel added: "They're good, all right, but I think we're better."

Kawaguchi's first necessity after the battle was to get his troops to the coast, where they could be resupplied by the Navy and where the wounded could be cared for. The general did not go back the way he came, but headed westward to join Oka's detachment beyond the Matanikau River. He knew that his supplies in the east had been raided; moreover, the westward route was the shorter. The march was made with no attempt at order; the men simply struggled along in groups. By the second day many of the walking wounded were collapsing, and exhausted litter bearers were tearfully putting down their burdens. The casualties who remained with the march, a survivor recalled, "could not be given adequate medical treatment. There wasn't a wound without maggots." Hunger was rampant. Men chewed their leather rifle slings, grass, moss, roots, and bark, the luckier ones sometimes finding a few betel nuts. It was eight days before the survivors reached the coast, coming out at a coconut plantation, where the milk and white meat gave them the most delicious meal of their lives.

These ragged scarecrows were surprised to learn by radio that in Japan their defeat was being celebrated as a victory. It had been announced to the people that the Americans stranded on Guadalcanal, those victims of Roosevelt's foolish gesture, "had been practically wiped out," and 30,000 people gathered in Tokyo's Hinomiya Stadium for a roaring patriotic rally. The authorities who had released the report did not feel they were lying by much, since Guadalcanal was certain to be back in Japanese hands very soon. Holding a similar view was at least one of the wounded soldiers the Marines found among the battlefield's corpses. "Make no matter about us dead," he said in English. "More will come. We never stop coming. Soon you all be Japanese."

6

Vandegrift Reaches Out

======Japan's New Guinea campaign, even though poised for a climactic thrust at Port Moresby, was now suspended and sharp attention given to Guadalcanal. Assigned to the operation was a full division of reinforcements, the veteran 38th. These troops, however, had to be transported from the Dutch Indies and it would take time for them to arrive. Meanwhile, smaller numbers of men already standing by at Shortland were ferried down The Slot and put ashore in the night at Cape Esperance, thirty miles west of Henderson Field. At General Hyakutake's 17th Army Headquarters in Rabaul there were joint army-navy meetings aimed at better teamwork. "The operation to surround and recapture Guadalcanal," Hyakutake stated, "will truly decide the fate of the control of the entire Pacific." The general, chagrined at the failure of his two subordinates, Ichiki and Kawaguchi, decided to assume personal command in the field as soon as possible, taking with him the 17th Army's heavy artillery. He had made up his mind there would be no more rough-and-ready fighting. Thereafter, frontal assaults would be made only after the most careful preparation.

Upon leaving Guadalcanal on September 12, Kelly Turner had flown to Espíritu Santo in the New Hebrides, where the 7th Marine Regiment was awaiting disposition after being called from its camp in Samoa. This regiment belonged to Vandegrift's 1st Division but had been detached for Samoan garrison duty early in the year, while the general was still training the division in the States. Kelly Turner convinced a reluctant Admiral Ghormley that the 7th should be taken to Guadalcanal, regardless of the risk to the Navy, and the operation was launched. Cover for Turner's amphibious force was built around *Wasp* and *Hornet,* the only carriers Ghormley had available. Ghormley's concern proved to be well founded. The mission was costly. Japanese submarines demolished the *Wasp* (193 killed, 366 hurt) and disabled the battleship *North Carolina* and the destroyer *O'Brien.* This last vessel broke up and sank while being escorted to the States for repairs. But Kelly Turner, assisted by hazy skies and some first-class raids on Rabaul's airfields by Army bombers from MacArthur's Southwest Pacific Command, managed to get his amphibious fleet through to Lunga Point, arriving in the dawn of September 18 and putting ashore about 4,200 Marines, along with artillery, trucks, heavy engineering equipment, ammunition, and other supplies.

The Marines came in with all the usual curiosity of fresh troops enter-ing a combat zone, and were surprised to find the beach splotched with oil slicks and strewn with all kinds of debris, including broken boards, fuel drums, ammunition boxes, and spoiled provisions. Those Guadalca-nal veterans stationed along the shore, after their six tough weeks on the island, watched the regiment's arrival with lifted spirits but with a generally quiet demeanor. Only a few rushed forward to greet the newcomers effusively, pumping their hands and slapping them on the back. The contrast between the new men and the old was great, the new resembling parade-ground Marines, dungarees well scrubbed and features clean and sunny, and the old in dungarees soiled and worn, with most faces haggard and many bristling with whiskers.

Kelly Turner's unloading operations continued until evening, at which time the entire amphibious fleet left for safer waters. Turner's transports were carrying passengers from the island. Vandegrift had evacuated not only his wounded but also the 1st Parachute Battalion—or what was left of it. While performing its valuable work on Gavutu and Guadalcanal, the unit had suffered casualties of more than 50 per-cent.

The reinforcements Turner had landed at Lunga moved inland to bed down for the night. A few of the original troops had not heard about the new ones, and there was some confusion in the darkness. First Sergeant Harry D'Ortona, a newcomer, was poking around in a coconut grove when he was challenged, "Don't move, you son of a bitch, or I'll let you have it!" This led to a reunion, for the challenger was big, gruff, gray-goateed Master Gunnery Sergeant Leland "Lou" Diamond, whom D'Ortona had served with in several parts of the world, including Haiti and China. The fifty-two-year-old Diamond was an expert mortarman, a genuine "character," and a Marine Corps legend. It was a popular saying among Marines that "Old Lou" had been in the Corps since it was founded in 1775. The two men shook hands, but D'Ortona found himself unwilling to stay this close to his friend for very long. "Lou had been living in a foxhole for the past six or seven days, and . . . well, he smelled."

The reinforcements received a quick introduction to life on Guadal-canal. They were timed after spending a great part of the day as steve-dores, and only a few bothered to dig adequate foxholes. Some merely curled up on the ground. Ponchos were in general use as covers, for it had begun to rain. Mosquitoes buzzed about exposed faces. Soon after midnight a Japanese patrol plane throbbed through the clouds and dropped a flare. Eyes flicked open, to be almost blinded by the green brilliance. Then shells came swishing in from the sea, to crash and flare and shake the earth. Shrapnel whistled shrilly. Trees were denuded and shattered, and some toppled over. Many of the troops were on their knees now, making the dirt fly with entrenching tools, helmets, and bayonets. By the time the bombardment ended, a number of men had been killed or wounded. In the dawn light, the faces of many survivors wore new expressions. The anxiety of some was indicated by a fixed frown and narrowed eyes, while that of others appeared in the form of a blank look with eyes unnaturally wide.

Some 3,000 of Vandegrift's men were still occupying Tulagi against the possibility of a Japanese landing, but he now had more than 19,000 on Guadalcanal. Thus far his combat casualties had been moderate, the number not yet at 1,000. It was true that about 2,000 men were in poor shape, suffering from malnutrition, the residuals of dysentery, fungus infections, malaria, and exhaustion. But his strength was sufficient to give the general confidence. On September 19 he was approached by a visiting newsman, Hanson Baldwin of the *New York Times*, who had been surprised to learn that the Americans held so small a perimeter on this large island. The newsman knew of the growing Japanese threat, the severity of American naval losses, and the pessimism in Washington and at Ghormley's headquarters. Vandegrift admitted to the problems of the invasion but said he believed it had caught the Japanese off guard and had caused "mass confusion at high levels." As for losses, the enemy was taking them too, and very probably did not have the industrial capacity to replace his material losses as readily as the United States. Moreover, the general added, these early weeks of the campaign had given him a tremendous faith in American fighting ability. Baldwin then asked whether Vandegrift really believed he could maintain his beachhead. "Hell yes!" the general responded. "Why not?" The newsman left Guadalcanal with plans for a definitive series of articles on the campaign, and his efforts won him a Pulitzer Prize.

"The war in the South Pacific," Baldwin stated in one of the articles, "is a cold, hard, brutal war. The foe is supremely tough and supremely confident. But in the fighting on Guadalcanal he has shown at least one great weakness. Regardless of the circumstances, regardless of the hopelessness of a particular plan of action, regardless of the opposition, he has always strictly, stubbornly, face-savingly, fatalistically adhered to that plan; he has shown a definite inability to improvise a new plan on the spur of the moment in the midst of action. He will keep coming until he is dead. . . ." Paradoxically, the Japanese considered single-mindedness to be a strength, and their training manuals said of American fighting men: "They lack tenacity, and if they meet with one set-back they have a tendency to abandon one plan for another. We must not fail to hammer at this weakness."

Among the officers who arrived with the American reinforcements was a forty-four-year-old lieutenant colonel of medium stature: Lewis B. "Chesty" Puller, veteran of more than a hundred skirmishes in the Haitian and Nicaraguan "Banana Wars" and famous in the Corps as a man who loved to fight and was contemptuous of danger. The colonel was now commander of the 7th Regiment's 1st Battalion. Red Mike Edson and his staff had watched Puller step ashore, and Edson turned to his executive officer and said, "The Raiders will have some competition now." Puller and Edson were friends, and there was a hearty reunion. Then Puller asked, "Where are the Japs?" He was handed a map he could make nothing of, and said so, and several of the officers used their hands to make a general sweep of the jungle surrounding the perimeter. "Well," said Puller, "let's go get 'em!"

The pugnacious colonel soon got his chance. Since the Battle of Edson's Ridge, Vandegrift had confined his fighting to small patrol actions. Now he felt it was time to try something bigger. He had learned that the enemy was concentrating just beyond the Matanikau River, about five miles west of the perimeter, the information coming to him through his patrols, through aerial surveillance, and through Martin Clemens and his native scouts, including Jacob Vouza, who was already out of the hospital. If the Matanikau region could be cleaned out, the perimeter could be extended to include it. Vandegrift began the operation by sending Puller's battalion, which numbered about 800 men, on a two-day probe through the jungle south of the perimeter to make sure that no new threat was developing there. The battalion returned carrying a few dead and wounded, but had encountered only scattered patrols. Even these minor actions added to the Puller legend. Tales went around the perimeter of how he made a personal reconnaissance out ahead of his scouts, and how he walked about ignoring sniper fire to encourage his green troops. At dusk on the first day he located a Japanese machine gun by striking a match and lighting his pipe, then quickly moving away as the gun opened up. His own machine gunners fired at the weapon's muzzle flashes and knocked it out.

Puller was next instructed to patrol southwestward to the slopes of Mount Austen, then swing westward to the inland reaches of the Matanikau, his object to feel out the enemy's strength. Vandegrift believed that Mount Austen held an observation post with communications running toward the Matanikau concentration. According to the best information the general had, neither the observation post nor the concentration was formidable. Actually, the region held about 4,000 men. Although many were hungry and ill equipped, there were also fresh troops in full fighting trim, including elements of the crack 2nd (or Sendai) Division. Even the weaker troops, of course, were prepared to fight to the death.

Puller's 800 men moved out on September 23, slowly and cautiously, along a trail lined with tangles of brush and trees whose topmost branches were a hundred feet up and let in only a few mottles of sunlight. The jungle was noisy with curious-sounding birdcalls. It was not until the next day, when the patrol reached the grassy but rugged foothills of Mount Austen, that contact was made. About 500 of the enemy were surprised in their camp in the act of cooking their evening meal. A hot action developed, with Puller so far forward that he killed three men, one a major, with his .45 pistol. In the midst of the fighting the intrepid colonel paused for a few moments to eat some rice from a bowl he found. A machine-gun bullet knocked the bowl from his hand. The Japanese were scattered, leaving behind some thirty dead. Puller lost seven dead and twenty-five wounded, including eighteen stretcher cases.

The Marines dug in for the night on a nearby ridge. It rained, but there was no trouble from the enemy. Before nine o'clock the next morning Puller was joined by another battalion from the perimeter, the 2nd, 5th Marines. The colonel sent two of his own companies back with the wounded, and took his remaining company and the three new ones, about 1,000 men in all, westward toward the Matanikau, reaching the east bank of the brown stream during the morning of the twenty-sixth. Heading north along the east bank, the patrol was nearing the sea at about 2:00 P.M. when it was hit by mortar and small-arms fire from a ridge on the west bank. The river was shallow there and Puller led an attack across it, but was turned back when the surface began to churn under the impact of bullets and shells. Air support was called in, but the enemy fire remained heavy. By this time Puller had taken twenty-five casualties. Breaking off the action, he ordered the patrol to dig in at the mouth of the Matanikau. He radioed a report to Vandegrift.

Still underestimating the enemy threat, the general raised the number of troops in the operation to 2,000. He sent Red Mike Edson to Puller's position to coordinate a complicated three-pronged attack, with Puller acting as second-in-command. The depleted Raider Battalion, under Colonel Sam Griffith, was to start from the Matanikau's mouth and press upstream along the same route Puller had used to

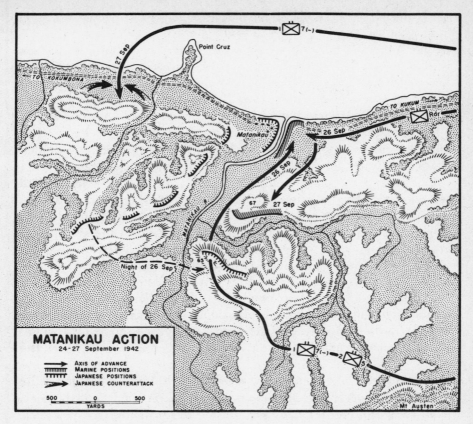

MATANIKAU ACTION
24–27 September 1942

AXIS OF ADVANCE
MARINE POSITIONS
JAPANESE POSITIONS
JAPANESE COUNTERATTACK

500   0   500
YARDS

come out, its mission to find a crossing and descend upon the right flank
of the Japanese concentration. As soon as he received word that the
Raiders were on the west bank, Edson planned to send the troops of
Puller's patrol, under Captain Joseph J. Dudkowski, attacking across the
sandbar at the river's mouth. At the same time, the two companies
Puller had sent back to the perimeter after the Mount Austen fight
were to be boated along the coast, supported by the seaplane tender
Ballard, for a landing in the enemy's rear. It was a good textbook plan,
but was made not only without enough knowledge of Japanese strength
and dispositions but also without enough regard for the problems posed
by the jungle. Conducted on September 27, the operation was a fiasco
from beginning to end.

The Raiders marching inland along the Matanikau's east bank were
brought up short by a body of Japanese that had crossed the river during
the night. Major Kenneth Bailey, who had won the Medal of Honor at
Edson's Ridge, was near the head of the column, helping to reconnoiter,
when the firing began. The men with him included Second Lieutenant
Richard E. Sullivan, who later recounted: "An enemy machine gun

opened up, and we all hit the deck. Ken went down on one knee, his head in his hands. The machine gun was going like mad. I hollered for him to get down. He didn't move. I reached out, grabbed his ankle, and pulled his foot out from under him. He was dead, hit right between the eyes." Major Bailey was farther forward than he should have been. Just a few days earlier he had told Dick Tregaskis: "You get to know these kids so well, and they're such swell kids, that when it comes to a job that's pretty rugged you'd rather go yourself than send them."

Leaving one company to hold the enemy's attention, Colonel Griffith led the rest of the battalion in a maneuver to get behind the position. The terrain was not only jungle-covered but was also split by sharp ridges, and progress was frustratingly slow. By the time the Marines got around, the Japanese were ready for them and laid down a new storm of fire. The colonel was seriously wounded and his men unable to close in. Both elements of the Raider attack were stalled on the Matanikau's east bank. And now, as explained by Griffith, "there occurred a communications muddle of major proportions. A series of garbled messages impelled both Division [i.e., Vandegrift] and Edson to conclude that the Raiders were indeed across the river and ready to jump off toward the sea."

From his command post at the river's mouth, Red Mike ordered the other two prongs of the operation to proceed as planned. Soon the boats from the perimeter went by just outside the surf, and Chesty Puller, tied to the command post as Edson's executive officer, chafed to see these men of his battalion, 500 of them, going into a fight without him. His concern shortly mounted, for the attack Edson launched across the sandbar came under heavy fire and was stopped; the few Marines who made it to the west bank were recalled. Then the truth about the Raider mission finally reached the command post. "Christ!" Puller exploded. "My men will be out there alone, cut off without support!"

The landing, led by Major Otho Rogers, a small, quiet man who had been a U.S. Post Office employee before the war, was made at 1:00 P.M. just beyond Point Cruz, about two miles west of the Matanikau's mouth. There was no opposition as the Marines ascended the beach and entered a coconut grove. Behind them, the landing boats drew away to join the support vessel *Ballard*. Major Rogers took the men inland about 400 yards, where they deployed on a grassy ridge that enabled them to look down a coastal road leading toward the river. They were surprised to see a large column of the enemy approaching, and Major Rogers said, "They told me the Jap strength here was no more than two or three hundred." Soon the enemy was moving to surround the position, and a desperate fight began. One moment Major Rogers was issuing orders, and the next he was lying in bloody segments, the victim of a heavy mortar shell that landed at his feet. His remains were wrapped in a blanket. Other Marines were killed or wounded. The Japanese tried to climb the ridge and were only barely held back. Now a plane from Henderson Field appeared overhead, and some of the Marines tore off their white undershirts and laid out a panel: HELP. The pilot, Second Lieutenant Dale M. Leslie, radioed word of the unit's plight to Edson's command post, and Edson radioed Vandegrift for reinforcements. The general was hastening to comply when an air raid from Rabaul knocked out his communications.

Fortunately, this was another occasion when Chesty Puller lived up to his reputation. The *Ballard* was off the Matanikau's mouth at this time, having resorted to evasive maneuvering as the air raid began. Puller hailed one of the landing craft riding the *Ballard*'s wake and was ferried on board. The vessel was soon off the coast where the Marines had landed, and Puller made them out on the distant hilltop. With the aid of signalmen, he began sending blinker and semaphore messages, and, in the circle of his field glasses, soon spotted a Marine standing tall amid the danger and answering with semaphore flags. Puller ordered the men to return to the beach and received the reply, "Engaged. Cannot return." Puller sent back, "Fight your way. Only hope." The colonel now had the *Ballard* use her guns to blast a path through the coconut grove right up to the ridge, and the trapped men began coming down.

There is a standing joke in the Corps that Marines never retreat but are sometimes obliged to "fight their way to the rear." Puller's men really did this, firing at Japanese who tried to close in from the flanks, and grenading patches of brush where others lurked in ambush. The Marines took casualties. A private was passing a thicket when an officer with a sword jumped out and lopped off his head, then quickly vanished. When his unit was hard-pressed from behind, Platoon Sergeant Anthony P. Malanowski, Jr., turned on the enemy with a BAR, calling to his squads to keep going, that he would catch up in a few minutes. The BAR was heard chattering for a time, and then stopped. Malanowski never reappeared. His deed was awarded the Medal of Honor.

Reaching the beach with their wounded and some of their dead, the Marines set up a defense line facing inland and also toward Point Cruz, jutting out just to the east, or to their left. The line came under a concentrated fire. As the Higgins boats in company with the *Ballard*, twenty-four of them, approached shore for the rescue, they were showered by bullets from the point. The craft had Coast Guard crews, and in overall command was Signalman 1st Class Douglas A. Munro, who, like Malanowski, earned the Medal of Honor, his citation reading, in part: "Munro, under constant strafing by enemy machine guns . . . daringly led five of his small craft toward the shore. As he closed the beach, he signaled the other craft to land, and then, in order to draw the enemy's fire and protect the heavily loaded boats, he valiantly placed his own craft, with its two small guns, as a shield between the beachhead and the Japanese [on Point Cruz]. When the perilous task of evacuation was nearly completed, Munro was instantly killed by enemy fire, but his crew, two of whom were wounded, carried on until the last boat had loaded and cleared the beach." By this time some of the enemy were closing in through the bushes near the water's edge.

Puller had gone in with the rescue flotilla, and when some of the coxswains had hesitated under the flanking fire from Point Cruz he bellowed orders that kept them going. The colonel was on the beach as the evacuation was concluded, and found his casualties to be twenty-four dead and twenty-three wounded. Back at the perimeter, he told the battalion's officers, "At least we've all been blooded now. Don't worry over things that are done, that we can no longer help. Concentrate on building a better combat unit."

Casualties for the operation as a whole were sixty-seven dead and 125 wounded. Archer Vandegrift was quick to admit he had made a serious mistake, and had been taught an important lesson: the danger of over-confidence. "Obviously the Matanikau area held a far stronger enemy than I suspected." The general did not give up the idea of clearing the river, but decided to move with more deliberation and in much greater strength.

Marine pilot Dale Leslie's vital aid during the Matanikau fighting was simply a continuation of the fine work done by the Cactus Air Force since its inception. As of September 22, the island's aviation personnel numbered 917 Marines, sixty-four Navy men, thirty-three Army. Henderson Field was not yet replete with planes; sometimes, in fact, the number the maintenance crew was able to keep operational dropped alarmingly low. But numerical deficiencies were always made up by the quality of the pilots. By early October they had amassed over 200 kills, and Marine Majors John Smith and Robert E. Galer had won the Medal of Honor for leading their squadrons, time and time again, in daring and aggressive clashes with superior numbers. Some impressive individual records had been piled up. Smith had made eighteen kills; Captain Marion E. Carl, sixteen; and Galer, eleven. Ace status came with five kills.

American planes went down, some in the jungle and some in the sea, but a good number of the pilots managed to survive and return to Henderson to fight again. On October 3, Second Lieutenant Kenneth D. Frazier's Wildcat was set afire by a Zero. Finding it difficult to rise from the cockpit to bail out, Frazier rolled the plane over and simply dropped free. On the way down under his chute a Zero fired at him, red-hot tracers cracking past his head. The enemy was driven off, smoking, by another Wildcat. Frazier made a safe landing in the water and was picked up by an American destroyer. Within a few hours he was back at the field, telling his story to his comrades. This was only one of many such adventures. Some of the downed fliers were rescued and helped home by friendly Melanesians.

By this time Commander Blundon's Seabees had Henderson in good operating condition and had even created an emergency strip about 650 yards from the main one. This was indistinct to the enemy's sight and proved a godsend to fliers coming in to land when the main strip was torn up by bombs or shells. Keeping the holes filled remained a critical job. The "crater crews" went into action the moment an air raid or a sea bombardment ended. "One hundred Seabees," Blundon said later, "could repair the damage of a 500-pound bomb hit in forty minutes. In other words, forty minutes after that bomb exploded, you couldn't tell that the airstrip had ever been hit." The Seabees were repeatedly endangered not only by bombs and shells but also by aerial small-arms fire. On October 3, during the same raid that sent Kenneth Frazier into the sea, Henderson was strafed by Zeroes. Seaman 1st Class Lawrence C. "Bucky" Meyer had set up a .30-caliber machine gun on the rim of his dugout and opened fire instead of cringing low. According to one of Bucky's comrades, a Zero came in "about 200 feet from the ground and shooting like hell." Bucky stuck to his gun and his bullets hit home. The watching Seabees raised a cheer as the plane crashed in flames at the end of the airstrip. Bucky was awarded the Silver Star but was killed two weeks later by a Japanese bomb.

Archer Vandegrift's disappointment over the Matanikau operation was partly assuaged by a dispatch he received shortly afterward from Washington. Army Chief of Staff George Marshall, who at first had been against a campaign in the Solomons and then had favored making such a campaign an Army operation under MacArthur, was now moved to say: "Heartiest congratulations from the Army on the magnificent job you and your men have done. I am filled with admiration for the way the task was carried through, the gallantry, the technique, the fortitude, and the general evidence of superiority over the enemy." The arrival of this message was closely followed by approval from another source.

Admiral Chester Nimitz, commanding the Pacific Ocean Areas with his headquarters at Pearl Harbor, flew in to Henderson—after a perilous interval in murky skies—and presented Vandegrift with the Navy Cross, at the same time decorating twenty-five other officers and men. The airstrip was slick with mud when the admiral returned to his B-17, and the craft nearly crashed on takeoff. Vandegrift heaved a sigh of relief when Nimitz was safely away. The general was encouraged by some of the things the admiral had said during his brief visit. Plans seemed to be under way for reinforcing Guadalcanal by land, sea, and air.

Japanese land reinforcements, a few hundred at a time, had continued coming ashore in the west, and with those troops that arrived during the night of October 3–4 was Lieutenant General Masao Maruyama, commander of the Sendai Division, now strongly represented on the island. This unit, organized in 1870, had a proud combat history and its members considered themselves to be looked upon with special favor by the Emperor. Their motto was taken from the writings of his grandfather, the great Meiji: "Remember that death is lighter than a feather, but that duty is heavier than a mountain." The division was superbly trained, and just recently, while at a camp in Japan, its 29th Regiment had taken up full combat gear and marched 122 miles in seventy-two hours, completing the last few miles at double-time.

Upon his arrival in the lines west of the Matanikau, General Maruyama was furious to learn that Kawaguchi and Oka had merged the advance elements of the Sendai Division with the demoralized remnants of the first campaigns. Maruyama's fears for Sendai morale were confirmed when he intercepted a letter in which one of his men wrote, "The news I hear worries me. It seems we have suffered considerable damage and casualties." The general reacted by pulling all of the original troops out of the lines, leaving the Matanikau zone in the hands of his 4th Regiment, wholly assembled after its piecemeal arrival from Rabaul. He told these troops: "From now on, the occupying of Guadalcanal is under the observation of the whole world. Do not expect to return, not even one man, if the occupation is not successful." To win, the Sendai must "hit their opponents so hard they will not be able to get up again."

Maruyama promptly began a limited operation intended to set the stage for a major attack planned by General Hyakutake, who was about to come down from Rabaul. The larger effort was to take place later in the month. To cover and protect the firing positions of the attack's artillery, and also to gain a safe crossing for its tanks, the Japanese had to secure and hold the Matanikau's east bank. Since all of the Marines involved in the unfortunate work of September 27 had retired, Maruyama's two advance companies met with no resistance when they crossed on October 6. One unit dug in along the bank just inland from the sandbar, while the other went up the river about 1,500 yards.

This maneuver was unknown to General Vandegrift as he planned another pincer movement aimed at clearing the west bank. This time he assembled five battalions, or half the perimeter's infantry strength, with Red Mike Edson commanding. Air support was arranged, and artillery fire from the perimeter was to be employed as called for. On October 7 Vandegrift sent the long column down the coastal road toward the river. The two leading battalions, Edson with them, were to deploy along the east bank, starting at the mouth, while the rear battalions were to swing 2,000 yards inland, cross to the west bank and attack toward the sea, three columns abreast. Edson was surprised

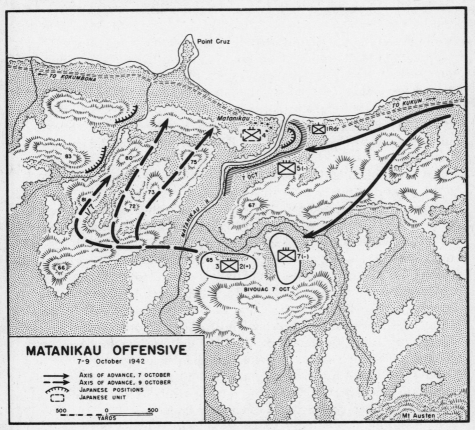

MATANIKAU OFFENSIVE
7-9 October 1942

➤ ➤ ➤   AXIS OF ADVANCE, 7 OCTOBER
     AXIS OF ADVANCE, 9 OCTOBER
ππππ   JAPANESE POSITIONS
⌐¯⌐   JAPANESE UNIT

500   0   500
YARDS

when his advance elements encountered resistance as they approached the river's mouth. Although only in company strength, the Japanese were well entrenched with their backs to the river, and they showed a definite unwillingness to withdraw across it. They hadn't even kept a flank on the sandbar, which would have ensured them a handy bridge. It was not consistent with their Bushido training for them to do much thinking in terms of retreat. Edson's deployment plans were not canceled but were altered. When he was set up, his coastal wing had a concavity respectful of the Japanese position. He did, however, seize the access to the sandbar, and his right flank touched the sea. As for the three battalions that moved inland, they bypassed the other Japanese company and by evening had reached their assembly area at a fork in the river. Vandegrift's plan called for them to cross over and begin their attack seaward the next morning.

There was a torrential rainstorm that night, and the lowlands at the river's fork became a vast swamp. Vandegrift ordered the attack delayed for twenty-four hours. But only the upriver Marines sat tight through the cloudy weather that continued through October 8. Those with Edson at the mouth kept busy harassing the resolute company entrenched there. From time to time, artillery and mortar concentrations were laid in. By sundown the Japanese had absorbed all the punishment they could take, and they determined to charge out and swing to their left in order to cross the sandbar to friendlier territory. Standing in their way was Company A of the Raiders, reduced during four previous fights to less than 100 men.

Twilight found one of the platoon leaders, Second Lieutenant Richard Sullivan, in the act of emplacing a few reserves he had obtained from company headquarters. "The Japs," says Sullivan, "broke from the jungle almost on top of us, charging in solid waves. I screamed the alarm as I began firing my Reising submachine gun. Corporal Joseph E. Connolly was cut down at my side by a sword or bushknife before he even had a chance to get his pistol out of its holster. The rest of the men were falling as I emptied two magazines. I reached for a third magazine while backing up to get to my foxhole, and was shot through the left shoulder by a .25-caliber bullet. As I reached my foxhole, I found another Raider there with two Japs standing over him, cutting him to pieces with swords. Sergeant Donald W. Wolf had a foxhole next to mine, so I turned and dived in on top of him. He and a nearby corporal killed three pursuing Japs who were almost upon me. Now it was pitch-black, and the Japs had completely overrun our lines."

One Marine surprised in his foxhole deflected a sword stroke with his left arm, and, even as he took a nasty gash in the back, reached out with his right hand and tore the enemy's windpipe away. A Raider with a BAR was charged by three men, and his weapon jammed. He pushed it broadside into the faces of two, and, stunned, they went down. Then he wrested a bayoneted rifle from the third man and used it to stab all three to death.

By this time Company A's commander, First Lieutenant Robert P. Neuffer, was phoning Red Mike Edson's headquarters in the rear. Neuffer recalls: "I reported our circumstances. Edson said, as only Edson could, 'Neuffer, you will hold your position.'" Anticipating this order, the lieutenant had already collared a number of retreating Raiders and set them up in a supporting line. The Japanese charge was swinging toward the sandbar, which was rigged with barbed wire and covered by heavy machine guns. One weapon accounted for fifteen of the enemy making the approach. Others were cut down as they became entangled in the wire. Those who got around the obstacle and were making a final dash across the bar to safety got a rude shock. A Japanese officer came running out of the jungle on the far side and screamed emphatic orders for them to go back.

The hottest part of the fight lasted for only forty-five minutes, but there were small-scale encounters all through the night. According to Neuffer: "I was told a reserve battalion was moving up the coast behind us, but the only additional manpower we received was one man, Major Lewis W. Walt. But what a man!" Known as "Silent Lew," the major had made a fine record for himself while on Tulagi and in other Raider engagements. He had his own remarkable adventure that night, spending ten minutes in a dark foxhole with a man he believed to be his runner but who was actually one of the enemy—a man who was killed by the real runner upon his return to the hole.

When dawn came, the Raiders were better able to distinguish friend from foe, and the last Japanese left alive on the east bank were killed. At a cost of twelve dead and twenty-two wounded, the Americans had destroyed fifty-nine of the enemy. Corpses were thick where the barbed wire spanned the sandbar. Later in the morning Vandegrift and Edson came forward, and the general surveyed the scene and asked, "Who did this job?" Edson's eyes misted as he said, "My Raiders, sir." Vandegrift shot back, "They're my Raiders now!" This was the 1st Raider Battalion's last fight of the campaign. Like the 1st Parachute Battalion, the unit had suffered heavy losses. Of its original 800 men, ninety-four had been killed, 200 had been wounded, and perhaps another 100 were malarial. In a few days the battalion would be evacuated to a rest camp in New Caledonia.

After the twenty-four-hour delay caused by the rainstorm, Vandegrift's three-column attack toward the sea developed as planned. But only the column on the left, Chesty Puller's 1st Battalion, 7th Marines, encountered the enemy in strength, an entire battalion bivouacked in a bowl-shaped depression among the ridges. The situation was an ideal one for Puller to strike a hard blow, and he called for artillery fire from the perimeter, at the same time putting his mortar crews to work. As the deluge began, accompanied by a thunder amplified by its confinement, and by shrieks of horror and pain, men clawed their way up the slopes in an effort to escape the trap, but the crests were covered by machine-gun and rifle fire, and few made it over. In less than an hour the bowl was red with corpses, nearly 700 of them. The proud Sendai Division's 3rd Battalion, 4th Regiment, had been wiped out.

Vandegrift's operation as a whole had afflicted the enemy with about 1,000 dead, the Marines losing sixty-five killed and 125 wounded. The battalions west of the Matanikau were recalled to the perimeter, but Edson was ordered to hold his position at the river's mouth. The region east of the perimeter remained of minimal concern. In a small operation Vandegrift launched along this coast on the same day the march to the west began, thirty-five of the enemy were killed and the few others present were driven into the jungle.

7 | *Defeat of the Sendai*

===== Before midnight on October 9, a Japanese convoy dropped anchor off Tassafaronga Point, about eight miles west of the Matanikau. Boated to the shadowy shore were General Hyakutake and other ranking officers, additional elements of the Sendai Division, and a variety of equipment and supplies, including bagged rice that was almost immediately stolen by lurking Ichiki and Kawaguchi survivors, now hardly more than walking skeletons. Hyakutake was met at the edge of the jungle by a messenger from Maruyama, who gave him the bad news: a Sendai battalion had been "massacred" and the Matanikau zone had been lost, with the Japanese front now two miles west of the river. This was the first retreat in the Sendai Division's long history. Hyakutake was troubled, and radioed Imperial General Headquarters in Tokyo: "Guadalcanal situation is far more serious than estimated." But the general had 15,000 men on the island, and also a good part of the artillery he needed; moreover, he knew that substantial reinforcements, equipment, and supplies were poised for transport down The Slot. So he decided to proceed with the October attack. The only real hitch seemed to be that, deprived of the Matanikau bridgehead, he would have to draw up a new plan.

Archer Vandegrift was about to get some of the fresh troops assigned him, these provided by the U.S. Army, a unit of Major General Millard F. Harmon's South Pacific Command. The "Americal" Division's 164th Infantry Regiment, about 2,800 men commanded by Colonel Bryant E. Moore, was on its way from New Caledonia, transported by Admiral Turner and assigned heavy protection by Admiral Ghormley. Another naval battle ensued. Off Cape Esperance during the night of October 11–12, Rear Admiral Norman Scott's Task Force 64 confronted a strong run of the Tokyo Express led by Rear Admiral Aritmo Goto. Scott lost a destroyer while depriving the Japanese of a heavy cruiser, a destroyer, and their admiral, who was mortally wounded. This American victory had little effect on the campaign except to increase the drag on the enemy's morale; heretofore, Japan's sailors had considered themselves to be invincible night fighters.

The U.S. Army troops began landing at Lunga Point as the sun rose on October 13. For the weary and ragged Marines, these 2,800 men were a morale factor beyond the aid they represented. Commitment of the GIs seemed to indicate that the United States was finally getting serious about holding the island. Moreover, the beginnings of an Army buildup portended at least the eventual evacuation of the Marines. The men of the 164th brought with them a large supply of candy bars, and that morning many a Marine gave up his most cherished Japanese souvenir in order to gratify his long-neglected sweet tooth.

If the day started well, it soon changed drastically. At noon a heavy air raid tore up Henderson Field, damaged several planes, and turned 5,000 gallons of aviation fuel into roaring flames. A second raid at 1:30 added to the destruction. Then, at 6:30 in the evening, a new element was added to the harassment. General Hyakutake had set up several of his long-range 150-millimeter howitzers, and the big shells began bursting at the field's western end. The Marines promptly dubbed this new weapon "Pistol Pete."

The daylight events were bad enough, but conditions became infinitely worse during the night. A large bombardment fleet that arrived off Lunga Point at 11:30 included two battleships, *Kongo* and *Haruna,* each armed with eight 14-inch guns. During a period of seventy minutes, the crews of the sixteen weapons dropped more than 900 of their heavy missiles on Henderson and its environs. Resistance was limited to harassment by four PT boats that had come to Tulagi Harbor a day or two earlier. The small plywood craft slipped from their new base, closed with the ponderous fleet, loosed their torpedoes, and fired their .50-caliber machine guns. It was a gallant effort, and the crews were certain they caused some damage before they retired, but the Japanese had no trouble making the bombardment one of the worst inflicted on American troops during World War II. The enemy sailors cheered ecstatically as Henderson was turned into a sea of fire. Ignited in addition to brush and grass were ammunition dumps, fuel drums, shacks, tents, aircraft. About fifty planes were destroyed or damaged, leaving only forty-two operational, and the main airstrip was badly pitted. Great masses of flying debris were silhouetted in the red glare. Combined with the rumble of the shellbursts was the shrieking of shrapnel, and the earth trembled as though undergoing a major quake.

The Americans huddled in dugouts and foxholes, even the bravest terrified. BAR man Andy Poliny of the 1st Battalion, 1st Marines, later recounted: "I do not believe there was a man who lived through that night who didn't wear out every prayer he knew. I was only a couple of foxholes away from our lieutenant, and I could hear him praying in the pitch black between the thundering shell explosions. The pathetic calls for corpsmen were heard everywhere. There was nothing we could really do except to dig our foxholes a little deeper. When a shell sounded as though it was going to land near, you would drop your entrenching tool and press your body as close to the earth as you could. About that time, one of those damn big land crabs that inhabit the island would grab you by the arm or leg. As dawn broke, all you could see was mounds of dirt and gaping holes. One mound to the left caught my eye. Protruding from its side were three pairs of legs and two pairs of arms."

Archer Vandegrift himself came close to disaster that night. Sitting on a bench in his headquarters dugout, he was knocked to the ground by concussion. Forty-one men died, and a large number were hurt; others were so shaken they would not recover for months. Asked later what he thought of men who suffered combat fatigue or shell shock, Vandegrift replied, "There but for the grace of God go I." It was not, he believed, a matter of such things as stamina, courage, or faith, but "a matter of man, and thus fortune."

Among the Marines who felt especially lucky on the morning of October 14 was Platoon Sergeant Philip L. Hardy, captain of one of the 3rd Defense Battalion's antiaircraft guns. During the days just previous to the fateful night, the battalion's weapons had been moved from positions around Henderson Field to Lunga Point. When Hardy paid a visit to the airfield after the bombardment, he was confronted by a sobering sight. "At the spot where my gun had been located, there was now a huge crater made by a 14-inch shell."

There was another punishing bombardment during the night of October 14–15, one dominated by 8-inch shells from the cruisers *Chokai* and *Kinugasa.* By morning the Japanese were so confident that Henderson had been knocked out that they began unloading troops and supplies from six transports anchored off Tassafaronga Point in broad daylight. In spite of a critical shortage of fuel, air commander Roy Geiger managed to get a few bombers and fighters off the field to contest the landing, and his efforts were augmented by Army bombers from the New Hebrides. The enemy was obliged to run three of the transports aground and withdraw the other three up The Slot. Nonetheless, about 3,500 troops and 80 percent of the supplies were landed.

General Hyakutake's numbers on Guadalcanal had been built to 20,-000, a mobilization at last strong enough, if used skillfully, to penetrate and overrun the American perimeter, presently manned by 23,000. At Japanese headquarters west of the Matanikau, Hyakutake and his staff completed their new plan with confidence, even discussing Vandegrift's surrender. The ceremony was to take place at the Matanikau's mouth, after which the general would be flown to Tokyo for parading through the streets. The attack would comprise three simultaneous moves, with a fourth to be added as these matured. While one column pressed across the river against the defenses Vandegrift had established on the east bank, a second would attack the perimeter from the south-west and a third from the south; the fourth segment would be boated along the Lunga coast for a landing at Koli Point, five miles east of the perimeter. The attack from the south would be the main one and would involve 7,000 men of Maruyama's Sendai Division. The operation as a whole would have strong air and sea support, with Admiral Yamamoto himself coordinating the naval efforts. General Kawaguchi, who helped Hyakutake make his plans and was to share in the leadership of the main thrust, injected a note of pessimism into the preparations, warning that not enough consideration was being given to the problems posed by the jungle. His words were not heeded. General Maruyama was even somewhat disdainful. The Sendai Division had been trained not only to fight but to endure.

During the night of October 15–16, a Japanese bombardment fleet made another attempt to finish off Henderson. There were casualties, and there was more destruction, but when dawn came General Geiger still had about thirty operable aircraft. That morning the seaplane ten-der *McFarland* got through from the New Hebrides with 40,000 gallons of aviation fuel. For the past few days, aerial transports had been bring-ing in an emergency supply a few drums at a time. Even while unload-ing her precious cargo, the *McFarland* began taking on casualties for evacuation; many of them were "war neurotics." Also sent from the New Hebrides on the sixteenth was Lieutenant Harold W. "Joe" Bauer, USMC, with reinforcements for Henderson, nineteen Wildcats and seven SBD dive bombers. As the planes were circling the field to land, nine enemy bombers began attacking the *McFarland*, still unloading its gasoline. The vessel cast off a barge filled with drums and began firing its antiaircraft guns, shortly accounting for one of the enemy. At the same time, Joe Bauer went into action. Although the tanks of his Wild-cat were nearly empty, he attacked the bombers, shot down four, and then, with his tanks drying up, made a safe landing. Out of the countless feats performed by Cactus fliers, this would stand as the most remark-able, and it earned Bauer the Medal of Honor. The *McFarland* had taken a hit that exploded its depth charges, and the fuel-laden barge also went up. The crew was able to save the vessel, but the heavy blasts and the wild burning of the barge sent the unfortunate neurotics stampeding and screaming along the passageways.

It was on the morning of this same day that General Maruyama and his 7,000 troops, including engineers, artillerymen, and medical personnel, got under way. They were obliged to march about twenty miles to reach the jumping-off place for their assault. A slender track swinging south of Mount Austen had been prepared in advance, and the general was pleased to consent when a subordinate suggested that this be named the Maruyama Road. Each soldier carried about sixty pounds of equipment, and the artillery had to be pulled along manually; but the first day's march, through coconut groves and over grassy ridges, was a fairly easy one. Using a walking stick, Maruyama strode in the lead, his white hair a beacon for the column. When they settled into a comfortable bivouac late in the day, the men were little more than pleasantly tired. But at midnight they were soaked by a rainstorm that left many of them chilled. The next day the column entered a dense and dark reach of jungle, where the trail wound over one steep ridge after another and where many of the low spots were soft with swamps. Now the individual loads grew heavy, and keeping the artillery moving became a strenuous struggle. By the third day even the strongest men were sagging, and progress was slowed until the column was moving by yards instead of by miles. It was a humiliating situation for men who, in training, had marched 122 miles in seventy-two hours. The frustrated Maruyama had no choice but to postpone his attack.

Although the general's march was a secret from the Americans, it was obvious by this time that the enemy had begun a major effort to retake the island. Several days earlier, Vandegrift had radioed Ghormley at his headquarters in Nouméa, New Caledonia: "Urgently necessary that this force receive maximum support of air and surface units." Ghormley radioed Nimitz in the Hawaiian Islands: "My forces totally inadequate to meet the situation." Ghormley asked for planes and ships from every possible source, the request including the submarines of MacArthur's Southwest Pacific Command. MacArthur was worried about his own survival, fearing that the fall of Guadalcanal would precipitate an all-out attack toward Australia. In Washington, a newsman asked Secretary of the Navy Frank Knox whether Guadalcanal could be held, and Knox responded, "I certainly hope so. . . . Everybody hopes we can hold on." Roosevelt himself was watching the situation with concern, limited in his ability to act by Allied plans calling for the mere "containment" of Japan until Germany and Italy were beaten.

As Admiral Nimitz worked on ways and means of aiding the effort on Guadalcanal, he decided that the situation required a more aggressive South Pacific Area naval commander. On October 18, Robert Ghormley was replaced by Vice Admiral William F. "Bill" Halsey (the admiral was never called "Bull" by anyone who knew him personally). News of the change was received with enthusiasm throughout the South Pacific Fleet and also among the Americans on Guadalcanal. Vandegrift was certain that the campaign would now get "the most positive form of aggressive leadership at the top." As for the Japanese, at least one radio commentator ventured the guess that Halsey had been appointed to preside over the U.S. Navy's abandonment of the South Pacific.

On October 21, Lieutenant General Thomas Holcomb, the Commandant of the Marine Corps, who was on a tour of the Pacific, flew in to Henderson to see Vandegrift. An expert tactician, Holcomb inspected the perimeter and listened to accounts of the fighting, afterward saying, "Vandegrift, I think you've done a good job." Unaware that a new Japanese attack was imminent, Vandegrift joined Holcomb in a flight to Nouméa to consult with Bill Halsey. Left in top command on Guadalcanal was Vandegrift's old friend, airman Roy Geiger.

General Hyakutake was receiving the air support he had been promised, but the results were not up to expectations. The Seabees and engineers had Henderson Field in respectable shape again, and the recently arrived pilots were eager to prove themselves. At noon on October 23, sixteen Betty-type bombers escorted by twenty Zeroes were met by twenty-four Marine and Navy Wildcats. Four of the Bettys and all twenty of the Zeroes were shot down, the heaviest toll taken of a single raid since the invasion began. Four of the Zeroes were destroyed by a cigar-smoking South Dakotan of rural origins, Captain Joseph J. Foss, who was fast on his way to becoming the campaign's greatest ace. Foss had taken to heart the advice of fighter commander Joe Bauer, who had knocked down four bombers on October 16: "Be aggressive. There is no way to make war safe. The thing for you to do is make it very *unsafe* for the enemy."

There were factors beyond the prowess of men like Joe Bauer and Joe Foss that were making it unsafe for the enemy's airmen. Whereas the Americans did their fighting close to home, the Japanese were obliged to make long trips, and these were full of strain, especially for the fighter pilots in their cramped cockpits. Fuel conservation was always a major concern, and a fighter's freedom for action was limited. When American planes were damaged, the pilots were usually able to set down on Henderson, but many of the enemy's cripples failed to complete their return, ditching in the sea. The Japanese bases were not only distant from the target but were also few in number, which made it impossible for top air commanders to assemble great armadas; they had to settle for hazardous piecemeal efforts. The whole situation was depressing for men who had spent years bringing themselves to peak

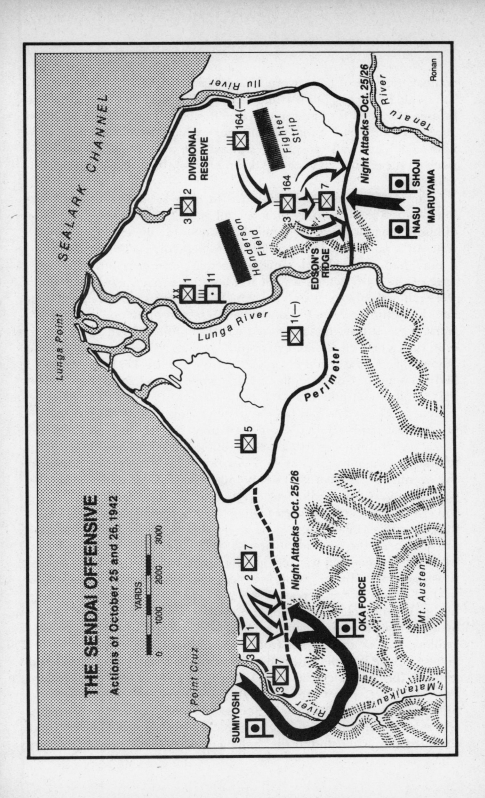

THE SENDAI OFFENSIVE
Actions of October 25 and 26, 1942

YARDS
0   100   2000   3000

SEALARK CHANNEL

Lunga Point

Point Cruz

Ilu River

Tenaru River

Fighter Strip

164

DIVISIONAL RESERVE

3 2

Henderson Field

3

164

7

Night Attacks—Oct. 25/26

NASU SHOJI
MARUYAMA

EDSON'S RIDGE

1 11

Lunga River

1 (—)

Perimeter

5

Night Attacks—Oct. 25/26

7

2

1

SUMIYOSHI

3

7

3

OKA FORCE

Mt. Austen

Matanikau River

Ronan

combat efficiency. They were being sacrificed to what they saw as "strategic blindness," to the inability of their nation's war planners to foresee the need for first-rate air facilities covering Guadalcanal. The fliers were sadly aware that this blunder—which Japanese military analysts would later call "one of the worst of the war"—operated as effectively in the enemy's favor as his destruction of their planes and personnel.

General Maruyama had continued to have serious trouble getting into position south of the perimeter. All of his artillery pieces and most of his heavy mortars were gone, abandoned one by one alongside the trail. After postponing his attack date from October 22 to the 23rd, the general had been obliged to make a second postponement, to the evening of the 24th, which was final. Messages concerning the changes were radioed back to Hyakutake at his headquarters west of the Matanikau. Unfortunately for the coordination of the operation as a whole, word of the last postponement did not reach the 2,900 men waiting to cross the river. This element was commanded by Major General Tadishi Sumiyoshi and was made up of Sendai troops of the 4th Regiment who had been out of Chesty Puller's reach during his attack of October 9, plus artillery and tank units.

General Sumiyoshi had been demonstrating against the Americans on the east bank—now the 3rd Battalion, 1st Marines, and the 3rd Battalion, 7th Marines—to keep attention diverted from the column marching around the perimeter. Sumiyoshi launched his main attack on the evening of October 23, twenty-four hours too early. He began the action with artillery and mortar fire that prompted the Marines to hug the ground but caused few casualties. During the shelling, Sumiyoshi's infantry units began massing on the coastal road in preparation for pressing over the sandbar behind nine eighteen-ton medium tanks. Although the massing was plagued by dive bombers from Henderson, it was achieved. In the gathering dusk, the column of tanks clattered to the bar and started across. The clumsy machines were immediately hit by 37-millimeter guns and 75-millimeter halftracks; and whistling over the Marines' heads came a deluge of shells from Pedro del Valle's artillery, these aimed at the troop concentrations. Only one tank survived to make it to the east bank, where it was first crippled by a hand grenade thrust into a tread, then knocked out by one of the halftracks. Perfectly targeted by the artillery and by mortars and small arms added to the effort, 600 of the massed Sendai were slaughtered, while many others were wounded; the rest scattered in dismay. At about midnight a few troops not affected by the shelling tried to force a crossing farther inland but were easily turned back. Sumiyoshi's attack was finished. At dawn the Marines overlooking the sandbar saw nothing but the quiet silhouettes of burned-out tanks and a scattering of corpses, some of which were shifting grotesquely in the jaws of crocodiles.

In one way, Sumiyoshi had succeeded; he had kept American attention riveted on the zone west of the perimeter. Maruyama's presence in the south was so little suspected that one of the perimeter's southern battalions, Lieutenant Colonel Herman H. Hanneken's 2nd, 7th Marines, was transferred to the Matanikau. This left Chesty Puller's battalion, its strength down to about 600 men, covering a front of a mile and a half extending eastward from the Lunga River past Edson's Ridge toward the troops of the 164th Infantry, U.S. Army, stationed along the west bank of the Ilu. It was south of Puller's thin line that Maruyama's 7,000 men were forming in the jungle, their aim to attack in two wings. Kawaguchi was to have commanded the right wing, but he had tried to influence Maruyama's plans with suggestions based on the futile fight for Edson's Ridge and was relieved of his command. His place had been taken by Colonel Toshinari Shoji. Commander of the left wing was Major General Yumio Nasu. It was at noon on October 24 that Maruyama issued his final attack order, which included the personal boast, "I intend to exterminate the enemy around the airfield in one blow." Under the circumstances, the boast was not an idle one. Although the Marines, as usual, had the advantage of firepower, it would be almost impossible for 600 widely extended men to prevent a breakthrough by 7,000 if the situation developed normally.

The attack did not come as a surprise. During the afternoon the smoke from many campfires was seen rising from the jungle about two miles south of Edson's Ridge. The Japanese were cooking their meager rations of rice. Farther to the west a column was seen crossing a bare ridge, and sighted on another high spot was an officer studying the perimeter through binoculars. Chesty Puller toured his lines to make sure that all of the machine guns and BARs were well sited and that the mortars were properly emplaced. When he bellowed his orders for changes, the colonel gestured with his stubby pipe, which was often cold. He had men use their bayonets to widen the fields of fire in the tall grass. Extra barbed wire was stretched, and it was hung with empty cans and fragments of shrapnel that would rattle when the wire was encountered in the dark. Puller phoned Pedro del Valle to arrange for artillery support and got the reassuring response, "Just call for all you need." The Army troops to the rear of Puller's left flank had 37-millimeter guns that could also be counted upon.

Maruyama's units began struggling through the jungle toward their lines of departure at 3:00 P.M. At the same time, as if to mark the movement, the sky released a cascade of rain. In a matter of minutes the jungle floor became mucky, and soon communications between units were washed out. Squads, platoons, and companies slogged about in confusion, and organization broke down. The attack had been scheduled to begin at five o'clock, but hours after that time, with the jungle in almost absolute darkness, the senior officers were still trying to get their commands into position. The right wing was not yet on line when the left began attacking at midnight.

Rain was pattering on American helmets, and this muted the approach, but the state of affairs became chillingly clear when the night was suddenly pierced by such cries as "Marine, you die!" and "Blood for the Emperor!" The line tensed for the onslaught, and some of the men responded with taunts of their own. "To hell with the Emperor! Blood for Franklin and Eleanor!" As the Japanese reached the barbed wire, the Americans loosed a storm of fire, and blood for Franklin and Eleanor spurted from hundreds of wounds. The first attack soon melted away, leaving a residue of dead and dying. Other attacks followed, and some minor breakthroughs were achieved, but the line held.

Chesty Puller phoned regimental headquarters for reinforcements and was assigned the 164th Infantry's 3rd Battalion, commanded by Lieutenant Colonel Robert K. Hall. The GIs had a mile to travel through the rainy darkness, and were led up by a Navy chaplain who had been to the front before. Puller divided the reinforcements into small groups and distributed them as needed all along the line. Although this was the first combat these "doggies" had ever seen, they took to the grisly work with courage and skill, and the Marines were profoundly glad to have their aid. The Army added something different to the line's firepower, since the riflemen were armed with the new Garand, or M-1, which loosed eight shots as fast as a man could pull the trigger. The Marines were still using the 1903 Springfield, with its manual bolt.

Attacking repeatedly through the night but never utilizing their full strength, the Japanese made only one serious penetration, and most of its perpetrators were soon disposed of. This attack was led by one of the proudest Sendai leaders, Colonel Masajiro Furumiya, commander of the 29th Regiment. Cut off from retreat, the colonel and his color guard hid themselves in the brush inside the lines, where they would remain for several days before shredding the colors—the emblem of many victories since 1870—and committing suicide. Furumiya left a written message he hoped would somehow reach Maruyama (but which fell into American hands): "I do not know what excuse to give. I apologize for what I have done. . . . I am sorry I have lost so many troops uselessly. . . . I am going to return my borrowed life today with short interest."

During the fighting in the rain, the Marines gained another Medal of Honor winner, Sergeant John Basilone, of Raritan, New Jersey, who was in charge of two machine-gun sections that "contributed in a large measure to the virtual annihilation of a Japanese regiment." Basilone did many things that night: moved guns around on his back, unjammed those weapons silenced by mud, dodged hand grenades thrown at his muzzle flashes, made trips under fire for belts of ammunition and spare barrels, fought infiltrators with his pistol. Basilone and his men were still fighting when the night closed. As the sergeant explained to a combat correspondent: "They kept coming, and we kept firing. . . . At dawn, our guns were just burned out. All together we got rid of 26,000 rounds."

With the coming of daylight the Japanese drew back into the jungle, leaving nearly 1,000 dead scattered along the American lines, their bloodstains turned pink by the rain. This number did not tell the whole story, for among the retreat's hundreds of wounded were many who were dying. Maruyama's aides, appalled at the decimation, urged the general to withdraw at once to the coast, but he refused to listen, issuing orders for the Sendai to spend the day regrouping for "a final death-defying night attack." At least a part of Maruyama's determination stemmed from his chagrin at learning that Furumiya had vanished with a Sendai flag.

After the dawn retreat, the Americans turned their attention to the evacuation of their wounded. Navy Lieutenant Edward Smith was one of the doctors who reported to a forward aid station to help with this work. At first there were no ambulances available. Standing alongside a road amid a number of stretcher cases, Smith flagged down a jeep coming from the front and asked for the use of the vehicle. "I'm sorry, Doctor," was the driver's reply. "I'm on my way back for ammunition. It's urgent. There may be another attack." The jeep went on, and several more passed with the same mission. Smith noted that the wounded men, some of whose lives depended on prompt hospitalization, made no protest. "They watched and understood." The needed ambulance vehicles soon came up from the rear.

It was now October 25, which the Americans came to call "Dugout Sunday," since they had to spend so much time under cover. During the early part of the day, Henderson Field was too muddy for planes to take off, and when the enemy's bombers and fighters came they had nothing to worry about but antiaircraft fire, which made them bolder than usual. Furthermore, from eight to eleven o'clock Pistol Pete shelled the perimeter, unhampered, from west of the Matanikau. That morning there was also action at sea when three fast Japanese destroyers entered the western end of Sealark Channel carrying the troops that General Hyakutake wanted set ashore at Koli Point, east of the perimeter. The destroyers sank two light vessels being used as ferries between Guadalcanal and Tulagi. One of the enemy ships was hit by 5-inch fire from a Guadalcanal shore battery. Then Henderson's fighters began getting off the sticky field for strafing runs, and the three vessels laid down a smokescreen and fled, the Koli landing aborted. Now flights of bombers from Henderson began attacking another small naval force northeast of Florida Island, scoring a hit on a destroyer and disabling the cruiser *Yura,* which was later given her deathblow by Army B-17s from the New Hebrides. That afternoon a large-scale air raid on Henderson was met by both Wildcats and antiaircraft fire, with twenty-six of the bombers and Zeroes going down. Four of the Zeroes were destroyed by fighter pilot Joe Foss, who had performed a similar feat just two days earlier. Henderson lost three planes but no fliers. Although Dugout Sunday had begun depressingly, it ended on an upbeat.

The day had been a searingly hot one, and the Japanese corpses littering the Puller and Hall front had putrefied, some of them bloating and bursting. A powerful stench hung over the area and it buzzed with bluebottle flies. This was the atmosphere that greeted Maruyama's Sendai in the evening as they began forming in the jungle opposite the line for their "final death-defying night attack." Such a move was anticipated by the Americans, yet it struck them as being tactically unsound. The Japanese must certainly be aware that they would be facing a reinforced line, one covered by even more heavy weapons than had been employed the first night. Later Puller would ask a prisoner why the Sendai had not shifted their attention to another spot in the perimeter. "That is not the Japanese way," the man responded. "The plan had been made, and no one would have dared to change it." The second night's series of attacks, accompanied by the same wild combination of sounds and illuminations as the first, resulted in nothing more than the lodgment of hundreds of new Japanese corpses among the old. These dead included many officers who, like Furumiya, had taken the lead in desperate attempts to overcome American firepower with spiritual inspiration.

And what of the remaining one-fourth of Hyakutake's master plan:

the attack on the southwestern rim of the perimeter, near the inland waters of the Matanikau? This was the responsibility of Colonel Oka, commanding two battalions of his own 124th Infantry and a battalion borrowed from the depleted Sendai 4th. Oka failed to get going during the rainy night, but jumped off the second night while Maruyama was taking his final beating in the south. Oka hit Herman Hanneken's 2nd Battalion, 7th Marines. The Japanese lost heavily while achieving only one breakthrough, which was thrown back at dawn by a mixed force, including headquarters troops, led by Hanneken's executive officer, Major Odell M. Conoley. During the night's fighting another machine-gun leader, Platoon Sergeant Mitchell Paige, won the Medal of Honor, he and his men accounting for 110 of the enemy. Paige manned several guns personally, at daylight cradling one in his arms and leading a charge that helped repel the breakthrough. When the fighting was over and the Japanese survivors had crept away, Paige realized that he was tired and sat down. "I was soaked with perspiration, and steam was rising in a cloud from my gun. My left hand felt funny. I looked down and saw through my tattered shirt a blister which ran from my finger-tips to my forearm."

The last act of Hyakutake's October offensive was his retreat, with about half the survivors heading eastward toward Taivu Point and the

Vice Admiral
Chuichi Nagumo.

rest making for the camps west of the Matanikau. Again men died of wounds along the trail, while the whole men grew weak from hunger. The campaign cost Hyakutake about 3,500 in dead alone. Maruyama's famed Sendai Division was virtually annihilated. The Americans had achieved their victory at the remarkably low price of less than 400 in dead and wounded. Seventy-eight of the casualties were sustained by the Army. Colonel Clifton B. Cates, commander of the 1st Marines, wrote a commendation for Colonel Bryant Moore of the 164th Infantry, saluting his men for "a most wonderful piece of work," and adding, "We are honored to serve with a unit such as yours."

On October 26, even as the land fighting ended, a new naval battle was beginning. Admiral Yamamoto had sent his formidable Guadalcanal Support Force cruising northeast of the island to intercept convoys bringing in reinforcements; or, as seemed a possibility when the October offensive was planned, to cut off troops trying to sail from the island to escape General Hyakutake's "righteous bayonets." The armada was composed of the 2nd and 3rd Fleets under the tactical command of Vice Admiral Chuichi Nagumo, and included four carriers, four battleships, twelve cruisers, and twenty-four destroyers. Sailing from the south came two slim American carrier forces under Rear Admiral Thomas C. Kincaid. In addition to the *Hornet* and the repaired *Enterprise,* Kincaid had two battleships, nine cruisers, and twenty destroyers. The American combination was decidedly outclassed, but when word reached Bill Halsey's headquarters in Nouméa that the enemy had been located, the admiral radioed, "Attack; repeat, attack."

The Battle of the Santa Cruz Islands was another that was fought entirely by aerial assault, the opposing fleets distant from one another. Kincaid lost the *Hornet,* one destroyer, and seventy-four aircraft. The *Enterprise* was again damaged. As the dying *Hornet* was being abandoned, a sailor shouted to a friend, "Are you going to reenlist?" The reply was decisive: "Goddamit, yes; on the new *Hornet."* And such a carrier would come to be. Naguma lost no vessels, although two of his carriers and one of his cruisers were heavily damaged. He lost about 100 aircraft. The Japanese claimed another great victory but had accomplished nothing decisive. Actually, the Imperial Navy could ill afford to lose so many planes and experienced pilots and crews.

8 | *Both Sides Gird Anew*

====In Washington and Tokyo the Guadalcanal campaign, now nearly three months old, had developed into something more than a contest for a strategic position. Its dimensions had grown until its progress was being followed by the world. The national honor of both belligerents was deeply involved. President Roosevelt was obliged to modify Allied global strategy, with its emphasis on Europe and North Africa, in order to meet the crisis in the Pacific. He informed the Joint Chiefs of Staff that he was so concerned about Guadalcanal that he wanted "every possible weapon" sent into the area. On the Japanese side, Emperor Hirohito told the Imperial Navy's Chief of Staff, Admiral Osami Nagano, "I hope the island will be recovered by our forces as soon as possible." This was not an order, but it carried the weight of one.

Hirohito's admirals and generals entered into their new plans with optimistic pronouncements, but their private outlooks varied. There were those leaders who maintained a spiritual belief in Japan's invincibility, who persisted in ignoring unpalatable facts, but the men of reason were distressed. At a staggering cost in blood and treasure, three offensives had failed. Could a fourth succeed? Disagreements marked the planning. Frontline officers, backed by certain men of the Navy, felt that no new attacks should be undertaken until Henderson Field had been obliterated by intensive aerial operations, even if this meant a delay while the necessary power was being assembled. The suggestion was brushed aside.

General Hyakutake had more problems than he knew. He made his plans with the belief that Yamamoto had been as successful against the American fleet as reports had claimed, and thought it should now be easier for the Navy to transport reinforcements and supplies down The Slot. Actually, the Navy had not only exaggerated its accomplishments but, to save face, had also concealed the true extent of its own losses even from the Army. Hyakutake was not without his detractors among naval officials, some of whom accused him of bungling the October offensive. "The Navy lost ships, airplanes, and pilots," a staff officer complained, "while trying to give support to the land assault, which was continually delayed." Perhaps it was true that Hyakutake had encountered terrible troubles in the jungle, but this possibility should have been thoroughly considered before he set his attack date.

In the end, the new plan called for the Navy to take the initiative. The

Tokyo Express would continue ferrying segments of troops and quantities of supplies down The Slot in the dark through early November. Then, on the nights of the twelfth, thirteenth, and fourteenth, Yamamoto's bombardment ships would hit Henderson Field, knocking it out once and for all. During this same three-day period the 38th Division and a special naval landing force, along with 10,000 tons of supplies, would be transported from the Shortlands by means of a single convoy. With his old units and his new ones combined, Hyakutake would have about 30,000 men on Guadalcanal, quite enough to overwhelm Vandegrift's perimeter, battered by the bombardment and deprived of air support. To strengthen his hold on the island, Hyakutake would soon be given another division and a mixed brigade.

As October closed, Archer Vandegrift was feeling good, for he was in the process of being reinforced from various parts of the Pacific. The troops included the 8th Marines, the 2nd Raider Battalion, detachments from the 5th and 9th Marine Defense Battalions, additional Army infantry, a large contingent of Seabees, and some Marine and Army artillery batteries, among them 155-millimeter howitzers, weapons strong enough to answer the vexatious Pistol Petes. Several new air units were also on the way. There was only one hitch. Admiral Kelly Turner, whom the Marines liked to accuse of having a penchant for "playing general," prevailed upon Bill Halsey to let him deposit a part of the reinforcements at Aola Bay, about thirty miles east of the perimeter, for the purpose of establishing a new airfield. This project, launched over Vandegrift's objections, would come to nothing. "Despite my loss," the general said later, the other reinforcements gave me riches beyond the dreams of avarice." When all of the fresh units arrived, American numbers would be more than a match for Hyakutake's 30,000.

But many of Vandegrift's original troops were in bad shape. Nearly three months of combat conditions, together with the heat, rain, and insects, and the diet deficiencies, dysentery, malaria, and fungus infections had taken their toll. According to a Navy doctor's analysis, the situation caused "a disturbance of the whole organism, a disorder of thinking and living" and, in some cases, "of even wanting to live." A bulletin dealing with the psychiatric cases reported: "The weight loss averaged about twenty pounds per man. Examination revealed marked dehydration as shown by dry skin and sunken eyes. Many of these patients reported being buried in foxholes, blown out of trees, blown through the air, or knocked out." While being treated, the bulletin continued, "many who had no anxiety in the daytime would develop a state of anxiety and nervous tension at night."

Carlson's Raiders landing at Aola Bay.

The number of psychiatric cases evacuated from the island was low. Only complete crack-ups gained the attention of the medical men. Minor emotional disturbances were common, and it became difficult for even the more stable to distinguish between normal and abnormal conduct. Men would stand on hills overlooking the jungle outside the perimeter and shout obscenities at a nonexistent foe. There were those who talked to imaginary pets, and some talked to themselves. One day a young second lieutenant donned a clean khaki uniform and stood in front of the division post office, telling men who approached him that he was waiting for the bus to Poughkeepsie. These men looked at him queerly, casting uncertain glances over their shoulders as they went on. As the afternoon passed, some came back carrying written messages they asked the lieutenant to deliver by phone to their families. By nightfall he had a pocketful of such notes. Finally he returned to his dugout and went to sleep. "It wasn't until the next morning that I convinced myself I wasn't on my way home."

The food situation had improved, but a shortage of working parties hindered equitable distribution. Marines stationed near the supplies that had been unloaded from the ships and piled up just inland from the beach tried to improve their fare by means of "midnight requisitions." The 3rd Defense Battalion at Lunga Point, according to gun captain

Philip Hardy, had a dump handy for pilfering. One night a Marine returned from a raid with a barrel on his shoulder, and his comrades crowded around eagerly as he pried off the top. The container was filled with shredded coconut. As it happened, the battalion was encamped near a coconut grove. "If there was one thing we didn't need," says Hardy, "it was more coconut meat." On another night a pilfering Marine was investigating a pile of canned foodstuffs when it was hit by a shell from a Japanese destroyer. The man returned to camp unhurt but somewhat dazed and thoroughly plastered with processed pumpkin. Soon afterward, the battalion was lucky enough to obtain, legally, an abundant supply of pancake ingredients. Phil Hardy consumed thirteen huge cakes at one sitting. "I was in agony from eating so much, but I was still hungry!"

On November 1, partly to keep the troops active as a stimulus to their morale and partly to drive Hyakutake's western forces farther from the perimeter, Vandegrift launched still another offensive across the Matanikau. Red Mike Edson commanded the 5,000 men involved: the 5th Marines, two battalions of the 2nd Marines brought over from Tulagi, and the 3rd Battalion, 7th Marines, allied with a scout-sniper unit. The attack had the support of the engineers, both Marine and Army artillery, the Cactus fliers and several bombardment ships. Near Point Cruz a body of the enemy was surrounded, its rear against the sea. The Americans shelled the position, compressed it with a bayonet charge, then systematically reduced it. "In this pocket," Vandegrift wrote in his report, "they killed to the last man 350-odd Japanese and captured three cannons, nine 37-millimeter guns, and thirty-two heavy and light machine guns."

Vandegrift was obliged to terminate his western offensive quickly because of new developments east of the perimeter. The general received word from Bill Halsey's intelligence section that the Tokyo Express, which usually made its night landings in the west, was planning one for the Koli Point area. Unknown to the Americans, those of Hyakutake's troops who had retreated eastward after the late October defeat —about 2,500 men under Colonel Shoji—had arrived on the coast near Koli, and the object of the eastern landing was to provide Shoji with supplies. Hyakutake was about to send Shoji new orders. As soon as the colonel's troops were resupplied he was to turn back into the jungle, swing south around the perimeter, and join the forces in the west. It was from the west that Hyakutake expected to make his new assault.

Vandegrift sent Colonel Hanneken's 2nd Battalion, 7th Marines, about 700 men, on a forced march eastward along the coast. On the

Bridge built by Marine engineers.

evening of November 2 the Marines made camp east of Koli on the Metapona River. Hanneken was unaware that 2,500 of the enemy were encamped less than a mile farther on. That night the Tokyo Express, five vessels, landed Shoji's supplies and a company of reinforcements. Hanneken could make out the convoy's silhouettes but was too far away to contest the landing. In the morning the colonel launched an attack but soon found himself involved with more of the enemy than he had expected. Threatened with encirclement, the Marines fell back three miles along the coast. By late afternoon they were digging in on the west bank of the Nalimbiu River, and Vandegrift was taking steps to relieve the situation. Aircraft from Henderson and the ships that had been supporting the Point Cruz action were dispatched to the area. The planes arrived almost at once, but unfortunately hit the American lines by mistake. At six o'clock Hanneken radioed division headquarters, "Request all planes stop bombing until things can straighten out."

On the following day Hanneken was reinforced by Chesty Puller's 1st Battalion, 7th Marines, and the 2nd and 3rd Battalions of the Army's 164th Infantry. Brigadier General William H. Rupertus, commander of the Marines occupying Tulagi, came over to take charge of operations but shortly contracted dengue fever and was replaced by the Army's Brigadier General Edmund B. Sebree, who had just arrived on Guadalcanal to prepare the way for new elements of the Americal Division. During a series of actions lasting for several days, the Americans failed in an attempt to pin Shoji against the coast, although they killed about 450 of his men. Among the American casualties was Chesty Puller, wounded for the first time in his long combat career. His legs and lower body were peppered with shrapnel. While the surgeons were digging out the fragments, they found one in the thigh that was too large for their limited facilities. Puller told them not to worry about it. "Hell, when I was a boy in Virginia half the old men in the county carried around enough Yankee iron in their bodies to open junkyards." Puller would make a good recovery but would fight no more on Guadalcanal.

On November 8, while the Koli operations were in full swing, Bill Halsey flew in to Henderson from Nouméa, a trip he had been eager to make ever since taking over the South Pacific Command. He came, according to Vandegrift, "like a wonderful breath of fresh air," showing enthusiasm for what had been accomplished and optimism for the campaign's outcome. The admiral told reporters that winning the war depended upon gaining control of the seas, and that gaining this control depended upon the capture of bases such as Guadalcanal. The Allies must continue sinking ships and must "kill Japs, kill Japs, and keep on killing Japs." Halsey's remarks were interpreted to mean that Japan's power must be rolled back island by island, the work coupled with a steady chipping away at her manpower and material resources. There was no shortcut to victory; an invasion of the home islands might well be necessary. Wrote newsman Ira Wolfert: "Observers fresh from the United States mainland regard these as very blunt facts indeed, but usually only one or two contacts with the Japs are necessary to convince them that the sooner Americans back home face these facts and stand up to them, the quicker the job will be done." It was during Halsey's visit to Guadalcanal that, halfway around the world, the Allies began their invasion of North Africa. They used amphibious techniques developed by the U.S. Marine Corps.

Eluding the American trap at Koli, Colonel Shoji and about 2,250 troops slipped southward through the jungle. But they had lost a good part of their new supplies, including rations. This was trouble enough as they began their long and arduous swing around Vandegrift's perimeter to join Hyakutake in the west, but more trouble came quickly. The struggling column was pursued by a fresh body of Americans: the Marines of the 2nd Raider Battalion, heroes of the Makin raid, under Evans Carlson. Newcomers to Guadalcanal, Carlson's Raiders had landed at Aola Bay (about twenty-five miles east of Koli) with the units assigned to Kelly Turner's injudicious airport project. Vandegrift had secured Carlson's release as the Koli affair began, and the Raiders had formed into a patrol and struck westward through the jungle. This was exactly

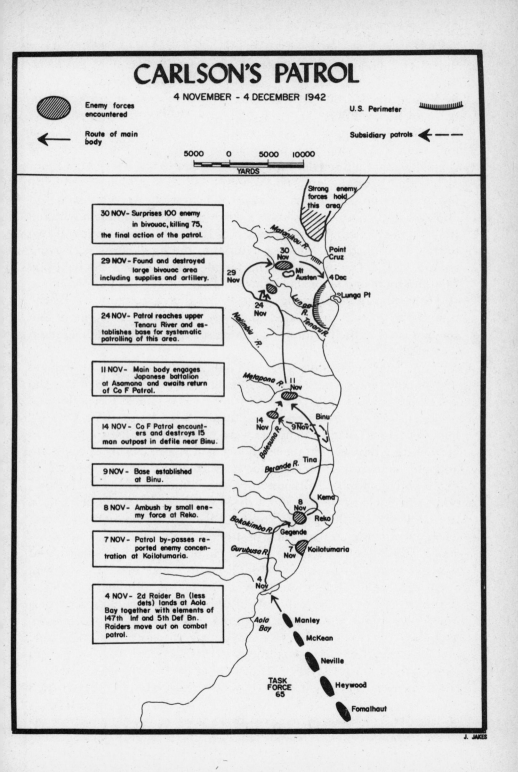

CARLSON'S PATROL

4 NOVEMBER – 4 DECEMBER 1942

Enemy forces encountered

Route of main body

U.S. Perimeter

Subsidiary patrols

5000   0   5000   10000

YARDS

30 NOV – Surprises 100 enemy in bivouac, killing 75, the final action of the patrol.

29 NOV – Found and destroyed large bivouac area including supplies and artillery.

24 NOV – Patrol reaches upper Tenaru River and establishes base for systematic patrolling of this area.

11 NOV – Main body engages Japanese battalion at Asamana and awaits return of Co F Patrol.

14 NOV – Co F Patrol encounters and destroys 15 man outpost in defile near Binu.

9 NOV – Base established at Binu.

8 NOV – Ambush by small enemy force at Reko.

7 NOV – Patrol by-passes reported enemy concentration at Koilotumaria.

4 NOV – 2d Raider Bn (less dets) lands at Aola Bay together with elements of 147th Inf and 5th Def Bn. Raiders move out on combat patrol.

Strong enemy forces hold this area

Matanikau R.

30 Nov

Point Cruz

Mt Austen

4 Dec

Lunga Pt

29 Nov

24 Nov

Lunga R.

Tenaru R.

Nalimbiu R.

Metapona R.

11 Nov

Binu

14 Nov

9 Nov

Bokosuna R.

Berande R.

Tina

Kema

8 Nov

Reko

Bokokimbo R.

Gegende

Gurubusa R.

7 Nov

Koilotumaria

4 Nov

Aola Bay

Manley

McKean

Neville

TASK FORCE 65

Heywood

Fomalhaut

J. JAKES

the sort of operation they were trained for. Sergeant Major Jacob Vouza, proudly wearing his sword scars and a Silver Star awarded him by Vandegrift, led the patrol's team of native scouts, of prime importance to the venture.* Fighting their own private war, far removed from the campaign's main events, the 600 Raiders stayed on Shoji's trail for a month, delaying his progress and whittling away at his numbers. Unable to maintain regular supply lines, Carlson's men were sometimes obliged to live off the land. This was especially difficult with the enemy trying to do the same thing, and gnawing stomachs were rampant. On one occasion a patrol came upon a dozen Japanese skinning a wild pig they had just killed. A concentration of BAR fire fatally wounded two of the enemy and sent the rest flying into the jungle, several leaving trails of blood. The hungry Marines made short work of the wild pig. Their marches and tactical maneuvering carried the Raiders 150 miles, and they engaged the Japanese in a dozen guerrilla skirmishes. By the time the game was abandoned, Shoji was short another 450 men. The Raiders entered the perimeter counting seventeen killed and eighteen wounded.

Even while the Raiders were still only starting out on their private mission, the tempo of the larger campaign was increasing. By night the Tokyo Express made its runs with troops and supplies, although some of the vessels were frightened into turning back by the bold little PT boats based on Tulagi, and others were hit by planes that caught them approaching the island in the last hours of daylight. During one of these aerial missions, squadron leader Joe Foss accounted for his seventeenth, eighteenth, and nineteenth enemy planes, then got lost in a rainstorm and went down in the sea about three miles off the island of Malaita, northeast of Guadalcanal. Darkness fell as Foss tried to swim for shore. "The current was so strong my best efforts only kept me in the same spot." Sharks gathered about him, their fins leaving phosphorescent wakes. Fortunately, a white islander, a planter, had seen Foss go down, and a party of whites and blacks in canoes managed to find him in the dark waters. He enjoyed the island's hospitality, including food of a quality he had not known for a long time, until the following afternoon. Then his friend Major Jack Cram brought a PBY over from Guadalcanal and took him home. "I went directly to the fighter ready-tent and had a grand reunion with my boys. They told me fifteen Jap planes had been shot down the day I got three." Before the Guadalcanal campaign

_____

*Jacob Vouza's war service made him a legend in the Solomons, and in 1979, at the age of eighty-five, he was knighted by Queen Elizabeth II. Sir Jacob was still alive at this writing (1982).

ended, Joe Foss would have twenty-six planes to his credit, a record matching that of Eddie Rickenbacker in World War I.

The American reinforcements and supplies continued to land by day. A large convoy entered Sealark Channel on the morning of November 11. The Marines on the vessels included the 1st Aviation Engineers, among them PFC Joseph M. "Pete" Kowal, who never forgot the convoy's arrival off Lunga. "It was November 10 in the States, the anniversary of the founding of the Corps. The captain of our transport, the *Zeilin,* gave us a speech on Marine history. Then General Quarters sounded and we were attacked by Japanese dive bombers." As the convoy's antiaircraft guns began their frantic firing, the planes roared in low, and the *Zeilin*'s hull was ruptured by near misses. The vessel was in no danger of sinking, but in the noise and confusion Pete Kowal saw a number of his comrades drop to their knees and start praying. Pete noted that among them, making their supplications with uncommon zeal, were two or three who had only recently been proclaiming themselves atheists.

The raid was over in a matter of minutes. Another came in the afternoon, but its main target was the airfield. The two missions cost the enemy about a dozen bombers and Zeroes, lost to antiaircraft fire, Marine Wildcats, and Army P-39s. During the afternoon action, a Marine pilot followed a burning bomber down, pulled abreast, and glanced over at the cockpit window. "The two Jap pilots looked at me, and their eyes were as big as coconuts." A few moments later the bomber smashed into the sea. This was not one of Henderson Field's happiest days; seven planes and five pilots were lost.

The next morning a second convoy, this one under the direct command of Kelly Turner, arrived off the Lunga coast. Its vessels brought in the Army's 182nd Infantry Regiment, Americal Division. Shortly, according to newsman Ira Wolfert, "at least four crap games were proceeding on Army blankets on the beach." The unloading activities were interrupted in the afternoon by twenty-five torpedo bombers and eight Zeroes. As the bombers swooped in over the shipping, even the spectators on the beach joined in the action, firing their rifles and revolvers. A cruiser and a destroyer were damaged, the former by a crashing bomber and the latter by misplaced antiaircraft fire. Only one bomber and three Zeroes survived the antiaircraft storm and the fighter-plane attacks. Cactus fliers returning to the island when the raid ended could see a dozen enemy bombers floating in Sealark Channel, some with crew members standing on the wings. Japanese fliers in predicaments like this usually refused rescue. On the approach of an

American vessel, they were apt to jabber in agitation and then shoot themselves.

All through the day on this busy November 12 Kelly Turner kept receiving alarming intelligence, gathered by aircraft and the Coast-watchers, concerning the movements of the Japanese Navy. Heavy forces were sailing to a convergence northwest of Guadalcanal, and by all signs the armada would visit the island that night. Turner made the correct assumption that the enemy's object was to bombard Henderson and the perimeter, that this was the start of Yamamoto's big push. At dusk Turner took his vulnerable transports, escorted by three destroy-ers and two minesweepers, out of the area and toward the New Hebri-des. He left behind two heavy cruisers, three light cruisers, and eight destroyers under the command of handsome, white-haired Rear Admi-ral Daniel J. Callaghan, a modest, deeply religious man known to his subordinates as "Uncle Dan." Although appraisals of the enemy's strength indicated that Callaghan was badly outgunned, the admiral had orders from Turner to contest the arrival. Regardless of the cost, Henderson had to be saved. Turner's decision precipitated the first act in the three-day Battle of Guadalcanal, one of the fiercest clashes in naval history.

As the night began, Vandegrift's troops knew the Japanese were coming and were uncertain of Dan Callaghan's ability to stop them. The Americans feared they were in for another pounding like that of the night of October 13, and they felt they might even be facing an assault by a large landing force thrown upon the Lunga beaches. After a bitter three-month struggle for this stinking island with its undeveloped air-port, nothing had really been decided, and personal security was as elusive as ever. Was the campaign, after all, to become another Wake Island or another Bataan? Depression gripped the perimeter. In the darkness, now rainy, now starry, the men stationed along the shoreline talked in low voices and frequently peered across the water toward Sealark Channel's western entrance, where the enemy was expected to appear.

Dan Callaghan's fleet was coming along the Guadalcanal coast from the east, and its wash began rippling against the Lunga beaches at about 1:15 A.M. At the same time, the Japanese fleet was entering the channel, unaware of Callaghan's approach. Commanded by Vice Admiral Hiroaki Abe, the enemy force was made up of two battleships, a cruiser, and eleven destroyers. The battleships measured three times the ton-nage of Callaghan's heaviest vessels, and their armament included 14-inch guns; Callaghan had no weapons of a bore greater than eight inches. Temporarily at least, the Americans had the advantage of surprise. Admiral Abe believed that Kelly Turner's entire support force had left with the transports, since Turner had no battleships and presumably had sense enough not to try to fight Japanese battleships with cruisers. Abe was anticipating an undisputed bombardment of Henderson, and he was stunned when his lookouts began to distinguish the American silhouettes. At about 1:45 A.M. the two fleets met head-on and were soon entangled and engaged in wildly tumultuous fighting.

"We want the big ones. Get the big ones first," Dan Callaghan instructed his captains from the bridge of his flagship, the cruiser *San Francisco.* The flagship herself did some good shooting, but within a period of minutes she was rocked by a number of heavy shells, and "Uncle Dan" was among those killed. Lieutenant Commander Bruce McCandless was the only able-bodied man left in the bridge area, and he found it "a weird place indeed in the intermittent light of the gunfire." Bodies, arms, legs, and gear lay in tangled and rapidly reddening masses. With a score of fires burning on her decks, the flagship was obliged to head for safer waters, but she retired with her undamaged guns blazing. A second cruiser, the *Atlanta,* was shelled and torpedoed into hopeless wreckage. Some of the shells, unfortunately, were American. Her dead included Rear Admiral Norman Scott, hero of the Battle of Cape Esperance. Two more cruisers, the *Portland* and the *Juneau,* took torpedoes. *Portland*'s stern was damaged, her steering crippled; *Juneau*'s forward fireroom was sundered, and from that moment she had to concentrate on staying afloat and getting away. By this time four American destroyers, pygmies that had moved bravely against the enemy's giants, had either been sunk with heavy losses or were aflame and in sinking condition. Admiral Abe's destroyers were suffering too. One had vanished in a fiery blast. The great battleship *Hiei,* Abe's flagship, was shuddering under the impact of salvo after salvo of shells.

For the Americans lining the shore, according to Ira Wolfert, the battle resembled "a door to hell opening and closing, over and over." The illuminations included brief shafts from searchlights seeking targets but loath to invite fire, muzzle flashes from the big guns, streams of tracers from the smaller ones, and shellbursts, explosions, and flames. The colors orange and yellow flickered on the dark waves and on the awed faces of the spectators, while the attendant noises swelled, subsided, then swelled again. Wolfert observed that "the sands of the beach were shuddering so much from gunfire that they made the men standing there quiver and tingle from head to foot."

The battle was brutal but brief, its main events lasting for less than half an hour. Although the Americans took a terrible beating and hundreds of them died, it was the Japanese who retreated, their bombardment of the airfield aborted. A drifting and burning destroyer was left behind, and the battleship *Hiei*, hit by more than eighty shells, could scarcely move. Admiral Abe feared he would not be able to get her out of range of Henderson's planes by daylight. The admiral had not only failed to complete his mission but was also in danger of losing one of his nation's most valuable warships. He prodded the repair crews and counted the hours till dawn.

Only one American vessel, the destroyer *Fletcher*, had escaped the holocaust unscathed, but six—three cruisers and three destroyers—were at least sound enough to begin retracing their course along the north coast of Guadalcanal, their aim to retire to the New Hebrides. Daylight found the battered force limping southeastward into the open sea. The vessels were soon spotted by a Japanese submarine. At eleven o'clock the cruiser *Juneau*, dipping along valiantly in spite of her torpedo-shattered fireroom, was torpedoed again. Watching from the deck of the *San Francisco* was Bruce McCandless. "The *Juneau* didn't sink —she blew up with all the fury of an erupting volcano. There was a terrific thunderclap and a plume of white water that was blotted out by a brown hemisphere a thousand yards across, from within which came the sounds of more explosions. When the dark cloud lifted from the water a minute or so later, we could see nothing of this fine 6,000-ton cruiser or the 700 men she carried." None of the surviving ships lingered to make a search for floating men. Their own situation was too perilous. A Flying Fortress drawn to the scene by the blast was asked by radio to relay a rescue request to Halsey's headquarters in Nouméa, but the message did not get through. Of the *Juneau*'s 700 men, about 100 hit the water alive. Only ten remained so. Three managed to paddle a life raft to a small island whose residents proved friendly, six on another raft were picked up by a PBY, and a week after the blowup a destroyer found a drifting raft that held the tenth. Among those who perished were five brothers, the Sullivans, a tragedy that prompted the Navy to end the practice of assigning more than one member of a family to a ship.

Back on Guadalcanal on the morning of *Juneau*'s death, the Americans at the waterfront beheld a scene that Ira Wolfert considered to be of even greater incredibility than that of the previous night, "if in a more subdued way." The waters of the channel were "like a basin filled with a bloody gruel simmering quietly in the tropical sun." Some 800 Americans were picked up by rescue boats, about a third of them suffering from wounds or burns, or both. A few had survived shark assaults and told of others who had been pulled below. Wolfert noted that many of the unhurt were laughing and joking as they stepped ashore, and he heard more than one man say, "You can't fight battleships with tin cans." As for the Japanese survivors, who had been paddling around in the dark without life belts, most refused rescue, entire groups killing themselves by diving and drowning. A few of the Americans in the cruising boats, who had come to hate the Japanese, partly because they sometimes tried to kill antagonists who offered them aid, used some of the bobbing heads for target practice. About twenty-five exhausted and oil-coated men were taken prisoner.

Some twenty miles northwest of the Lunga beach, just beyond little Savo Island, a column of black smoke sullied the bright blue sky. The source was the battleship *Hiei*, under attack by planes from Henderson, from the carrier *Enterprise* (making her return to combat in spite of incomplete repairs), and from the New Hebrides. Although the Japanese fought back with their antiaircraft guns, the huge vessel was kept in flames and was finally battered into helplessness. Late in the afternoon, Admiral Abe ordered her scuttled. The admiral and the crew, minus numbers of dead, boarded hovering destroyers and made their escape, and the burning *Hiei* went hissing under, her grave marked briefly by a cloud of steam.

Yamamoto was furious over Abe's failure, but the Japanese master plan was not changed. That night another bombardment force, three cruisers and four destroyers under Rear Admiral Shoji Nishimura, sailed into Sealark Channel. This time there was no American task force covering Henderson. The shadowy assailants trained their long-barreled weapons on the field and its environs for about forty minutes, the muzzles belching fire and the salvos whistling, shrieking, crashing, and throwing up debris. Again the battle-weary Americans, their numbers including the homeless sailors rescued from the sea, crouched in holes and prayed and swore. Damn the Japs! Damn the U.S. Navy's impotence! Damn this whole miserable, endless campaign! The bombardment might have lasted longer except for the intervention of two PT boats that sped over from Tulagi. Their six torpedoes accomplished little in the way of destruction but seem to have prompted the enemy to wrap things up and clear out. Although terrifying, the bombardment caused few casualties and did relatively little material damage. It demolished a few planes and afflicted a number of others with holes, most of which were reparable. The airstrips were cratered, but the Seabees and engineers had them usable again by dawn.

9 | The Issue Decided

=====Even though the enemy's blow was not a vital one, it had a deeply sobering effect on the war planners in Washington. They had hoped that Dan Callaghan's stand had put an end to Yamamoto's capacity for such measures. To compound the capital's gloom, word arrived that, simultaneously with the retirement of the night bombardment force during the early morning hours of November 14, a large fleet of Japanese troop transports was heading down The Slot unopposed by American surface forces. President Roosevelt himself was worried. The chances seemed strong that Guadalcanal would have to be evacuated.

It was air power that saved the situation. Even the enemy's retiring night bombardment vessels were hit before they got out of range. They had joined five other warships waiting near Savo Island, and planes from Henderson caught the twelve-ship force about 150 miles from Guadalcanal at 8:00 A.M. Torpedo planes punctured the hull of the heavy cruiser *Kinugasa*, while dive bombers blasted the decks of the light cruiser *Isuzu*. About two hours later, bombers from the *Enterprise*, now some 200 miles southwest of Guadalcanal, began working on the fleet. Their series of attacks finished off the *Kinugasa* and scored hits on other vessels. The fleet made it to the Shortlands, but not in good health.

Even while the raids on the bombardment vessels were winding down, a new succession of raids was beginning. The target was the Japanese transport group that was troubling Washington. These ships were not retreating but advancing, and they represented Yamamoto's grand attempt to reinforce General Hyakutake with 12,000 troops and 10,000 tons of supplies. Commanded by the able and tenacious Raizo Tanaka, the reinforcement group was made up of eleven transports escorted by eleven destroyers. The crews and the bodies of troops had begun their trip down The Slot with high hopes. "We were very happy," a destroyer captain told an American officer after the war, "because we thought that the bombardment groups had succeeded in destroying your planes the night before."

Tanaka's fleet had no protection but its antiaircraft guns and a few ineffectual Zeroes, and it was hit by raid after raid, with the fliers concentrating on the transports. The planes came from Henderson, from the *Enterprise*, and from the New Hebrides. Fighters strafed the crowded ships mercilessly; torpedo bombers holed their hulls; and Tanaka would never forget the sight of "bombs wobbling down from high-flying B-17s," of dive bombers roaring in low, releasing their missiles "and pulling out barely in time, each miss sending up towering columns of mist and spray, every hit raising clouds of smoke and fire." The admiral was obliged to witness "the tragic scene of men jumping overboard from burning, sinking ships." Destroyers went to the rescue, but many of the unfortunates were strafed as they struggled in the water, which was turned red by their blood. Some of the Americans sickened at the sight of the destruction and slaughter they were meting out, but none hesitated to do his best—or his worst. Every Japanese soldier killed was one less to threaten the lives of Vandegrift's troops. During each lull, the redoubtable Tanaka re-formed his remaining vessels and continued toward Guadalcanal. When darkness finally put an end to the assaults, the admiral had only four transports left. One, badly crippled, had turned back under destroyer escort; six others were either at the bottom of the sea or in flames and sinking in the convoy's wake. Perhaps 3,000 men were dead, while countless others were hurt. Hundreds of rescued troops were jammed on the decks of the four destroyers that had not turned back or had not been driven out of contact with the formation.

Although Tanaka was infinitely grateful for the protection of the darkness, his concerns were not ended. The aerial attacks had so delayed his progress down The Slot that he would be unable to reach Guadalcanal with what he later termed "the sorry remnant of the force that had sortied from Shortland" much before sunrise. He would have to unload by daylight. On the heartening side, Tanaka was about to receive some powerful aid. Ahead of him in The Slot, bearing down on Henderson, was a new night bombardment group. Led by Vice Admiral Nobutake Kondo, this force was made up of a battleship, two heavy cruisers, two light cruisers, and nine destroyers. Kondo's aim, like that of other commanders before him, was to shell the airfield into uselessness.

Waiting for Kondo near Savo Island was a task force rushed to the area by Bill Halsey. Commanding the two battleships and four destroyers was leathery-faced Rear Admiral Willis A. "Ching" Lee, a long-time friend of Archer Vandegrift's and one of the most intelligent and capable officers in the Navy. Lee had the considerable advantage of two battleships to Kondo's one, but he had no cruisers and was heavily outmatched in destroyers. Even those destroyers with Tanaka were near enough to function as a part of Kondo's force, if he needed them. The battle, which began at 11:17 P.M., was another that was watched with awe by the Americans on Lunga Beach. Vandegrift found it "a fantastic spectacle," and noted that "the heavy thunder of battleship guns drowned out the lighter destroyer fire."

Admiral Lee's destroyers entered the action boldly, but the *Preston* was soon sunk with 116 dead. At the same time, shells were rocking the *Walke*. Among the men on the bridge was Lieutenant (jg) John A. Walsh, who learned one of the age-old secrets behind creditable conduct in combat. "At first you're terrified, your feet frozen to the deck, your head ducking from every shell. And then suddenly you go past that point, and you know you're going to die. Convinced of death, that fear disappears. Your mind and body react mechanically, performing their duties from trained habit as swiftly and efficiently as when you're more conscious of your acts." The *Walke* was finished off by a torpedo from one of Kondo's destroyers. Seventy-five men died. John Walsh suffered both a broken neck and a smashed kneecap, but found himself swimming, with the aid of a life belt, when the vessel went under. He heard some of the other swimmers give a cheer for the flag as it disappeared. The destroyer *Benham* was also fatally hit by a torpedo. Of Ching Lee's four "tin cans," only the *Gwin* survived, and she was damaged. The enemy lost but one destroyer, the *Ayanami.*

Just before midnight the battleships *Washington* and *South Dakota* closed upon Kondo's main bombardment group, the battleship *Kirishima* and two heavy cruisers. A few hits were scored on the cruisers, but the enemy's return fire crippled the *South Dakota*'s radar and communications systems, leaving her in a state of confusion. The only unharmed vessel left to Ching Lee was the *Washington,* which happened to be his flagship. The *Washington* was enough. She poured fifty shells into the *Kirishima,* nine of which were 16-inchers. The battleship staggered away in flames, and the rest of Kondo's vessels joined in the retreat. The *Washington* was left mistress of the field. The *Kirishima* would not get far before her captain decided to scuttle her. She was the second battleship to be lost by Yamamoto in forty-eight hours. And still another of the admiral's attempts to smash Henderson had been thwarted.

While the ailing *South Dakota* left for the safety of a prearranged rendezvous area south of Guadalcanal, the *Washington,* a one-ship task force, moved a dozen miles up the dark waters of The Slot in search of Tanaka's transports. Lee failed to find them in the time available to him. He wanted to get out of range of the enemy's aircraft by dawn. While the *Washington* was swinging back, several destroyers that had come to oppose her launched torpedoes, which the battleship was able to dodge, some exploding in her tempestuous wake. Two of these plucky destroyers were sent by Tanaka, intent upon protecting his "sorry remnant" to the end.

According to Archer Vandegrift, the Americans who had watched the critical sea battle from Guadalcanal were not aware "as to the victor or vanquished until dawn showed the enemy gone." The same dawn illuminated a scene "now sickeningly familiar to the tired crews of the small boats and to the doctors who inherited the salvage." Along the coast about seven miles to the west, something else was visible. Raizo Tanaka had run his four surviving transports up on the beach, and they were busy unloading. The admiral himself had withdrawn his covering destroyers up The Slot, his mission concluded when the transports were delivered. It had been a remarkable achievement. But, as was the case with so many superhumanly courageous Japanese deeds, little was gained. The beached vessels were hit by aircraft, by artillery, and by the fire of a destroyer from Tulagi. Again the destruction and slaughter were ghastly. The Henderson pilots who participated called themselves the "Buzzard Patrol." The surf was reddened by blood and the transports were turned orange by flames. A long string of supplies piled on the beach was also ignited. While he watched from a spot on the Lunga coast, Ira Wolfert wrote, "We intend to keep that fire burning until there is nothing left to burn. It warms our hearts." In the end, out of 12,000 reinforcements and 10,000 tons of supplies that had started from the Shortlands, General Hyakutake received about 3,000 able-bodied men and five tons of supplies.

The three-day battle was over, and it was a disaster for the Japanese. A delighted Vandegrift, his perimeter saved from a new assault, radioed his thanks to Halsey for the major part played by the Navy. The general reserved his greatest praise for Dan Callaghan, Norman Scott, and their crews, "who with magnificent courage against seemingly hopeless odds drove back the first hostile stroke and made success possible. To them the men of Cactus lift their battered helmets in deepest admiration." Halsey himself was less poetic about the battle's outcome, simply grinning and announcing to his staff, "We've got the bastards licked." Back in the States, Roosevelt was greatly relieved. Now the news from the Pacific matched that coming from Africa and Europe. In Africa, General Bernard L. Montgomery was driving General Erwin Rommel after the German defeat at El Alamein, and the Allied forces under Lieutenant General Dwight D. Eisenhower were on the advance after their landings in Morocco and Algeria. In Europe, the Russians had stopped the Germans at Stalingrad. When he learned of the victory at Guadalcanal, the President told a newsman, "For the past two weeks we have had a great deal of good news, and it would seem that the turning point in this war has at last been reached."

Not to be left out of the picture, MacArthur's troops in New Guinea had turned the enemy threat to Port Moresby into a rout. This deepened the Japanese government's gloom over Guadalcanal. Hirohito's war planners, however, were not yet ready to admit that the campaign was a lost cause. They announced that the Navy had won another great victory, and met to discuss their options. The more objective leaders, of course, had no trouble seeing the handwriting on the wall. They favored evacuating the island and retiring this part of Japan's outer defense line to the Central Solomons. A colonel who attended the discussions confided to his diary that the "fake pride" of Imperial Headquarters was turning Guadalcanal into *the* decisive battle. "If we should be defeated at Guadalcanal, it is certain we will lose the Pacific war itself."

Pride won out, and still another offensive was planned, this one to be preceded by a strengthening of the campaign's air power. General Hyakutake, whose present numbers on Guadalcanal came to about 25,000, was notified that he could expect to be reinforced by two divisions for another offensive within a month. The general radioed back that he was already involved in new fighting on the Matanikau front and that his men were not only dying under the enemy's guns but were also starving. "By the time we get two divisions of reinforcements, it is doubtful how many troops here will be alive." This did not mean that Hyakutake was ready to quit. He planned to fight until his army was exterminated. The men in the ranks could not understand why so despised an enemy should be causing them so much grief, and many believed that as soon as reinforcements arrived the Americans would be made to surrender en masse. At least one soldier recorded in his diary that he was looking forward to avenging his dead comrades by "abusing a prisoner."

On the American side, even as the enemy was being pressed, reinforcements and supplies continued to pour ashore. To the gratification of Vandegrift's exhausted Marines, the Army's strength was mounting rapidly. Among the units that arrived off Lunga in the latter part of November were elements of the Americal Division's 247th Field Artillery Battalion. The troops in the first small boats to head for shore half expected to be challenged by enemy soldiers, but were met instead by a Seabee operating a bulldozer. The enemy did arrive shortly, but overhead, in three Zeroes. Private Lawrence C. Stix, Jr., was one of those who experienced this reception. "We scattered to find cover, and they made a pass at us, their guns yammering. Our own fighters appeared from nowhere, and the battle was on. It stretched over a five-mile area and ended with the downing of one Zero. He hit the water in flames, and there was a hiss as he sank. The entire incident took about five minutes. Then the first supply barge came in, and suddenly the beach was a beehive of activity."

During these moments, the artillerymen received a visit from the Americal Division's top commander, Major General Alexander M. Patch, the man who would take over from Vandegrift. Patch was highly popular with his troops, and his appearance on the beach, made for the purpose of offering both advice and encouragement, was inspirational. "We all felt ten feet tall," says Larry Stix.

"Material was really starting to move ashore now. Barges were making their runs with increasing rapidity. Trucks and guns had already been brought ashore, and drivers and gun crews had claimed them and immediately drove them inland a quarter-mile or so. The beach was soon piled high with ammo, food, and medical supplies. We worked like beavers to clear it by sundown. By this time the vessels that had brought us had weighed anchor and were out of sight." The artillerymen dug in near the beach for the night. Rumor had it that a Japanese bombardment fleet was expected, but the only attacks the newcomers suffered were those by mosquitoes. "They buzzed and stung, and we slapped and cursed." The next day the artillerymen were assigned to their place in the perimeter, several miles inland. They had no sooner got their guns set up and their foxholes dug than it began to rain. "In less than ten minutes we were ankle-deep in water, and it was still rising. Foxholes finally disappeared from view." An officer sloshed about advising the men to be careful not to fall into the invisible holes. He soon fell into one himself, vanished for a moment, then came up sputtering, "See what I mean?" This was the way the members of the 247th began arriving on Guadalcanal and settling in. Before the campaign ended, the battalion's 105-millimeter howitzers would blast Hyakutake's troops with 14,000 rounds of ammunition.

There was an abundance of ammunition for all weapons on the island by the latter part of November. There was plenty of food too, although not much of it was especially pleasing to the palate. There was one high spot. Bill Halsey saw to it that everyone had turkey and cranberry sauce on Thanksgiving. But the troops grew tired of the C-rations, the K-rations, the powdered eggs, the powdered milk. There was no bread, only biscuits, and they often had a peculiar aftertaste. Supplied in profusion were five-pound tins of corned beef. Some of the men used these to build dikes against the rain and mud, and they lamented profanely when the tins were stolen by the Melanesians. Another adaptation is explained by Marine PFC Pete Kowal of the 1st Aviation Engineers, who helped to maintain the airfield: "In emergencies we used the canned corned beef to fill bomb craters."

About this same time in late November, a young Japanese soldier recorded in his diary that he was weak from hunger. "I feel dizzy when

I move around." He added that he and his comrades spent much time talking about "our good old home dishes." Three days later the youth wrote: "I was told that we have to reduce our daily meals to one-third what we have now. This made me discouraged." The diarist would soon be dead.

For the Japanese high command at Rabaul, the first order of business was to try to find a way to alleviate Hyakutake's emergency. The job was left to Raizo Tanaka and his Tokyo Express. If anyone could solve the problem, Tanaka could. The admiral secured about 1,350 large metal drums and filled them with basic foodstuffs and medical supplies, leaving enough air space so that the drums would float. Sealing them tightly, he loaded them on the decks of six destroyers, about 225 on each, and linked them together with strong rope. Tanaka's intention was to make a run past Hyakutake's beaches in the darkness, pushing the drums into the sea. Small power boats from shore were to dart out and tow the chains in. Tanaka started his trip from the Shortlands on November 29, warning the captains of his fleet of eight destroyers—six with drums and two serving as escorts—that the after-dark approach to Guadalcanal on the following day might well be contested by the U.S. Navy. "In such an event, utmost efforts will be made to destroy the enemy without regard for the unloading of supplies."

Another of Bill Halsey's task forces was indeed waiting for Tanaka, this one commanded by Rear Admiral Carelton H. Wright and made up of four heavy cruisers, one light cruiser, and six destroyers, enough power to blast Tanaka's eight destroyers to smithereens. The only thing in the Japanese admiral's favor, other than his singular resolution and skill, was that Wright had little experience in the Guadalcanal arena. Incredibly enough, Tanaka not only won the Battle of Tassafaronga, but won it smashingly. Using torpedoes alone, his destroyers left the heavy cruiser *Northampton* in sinking condition and damaged the heavy cruisers *Pensacola, New Orleans,* and *Minneapolis* so severely they would be out of action for nearly a year. While performing this prodigious feat, Tanaka lost one destroyer. If the debacle held a bright side for the Americans, it was that Tanaka returned to the Shortlands without delivering a single drum of supplies and that his victory had no material effect on the campaign's outcome. There was no deep discouragement for Bill Halsey in the damages, since his South Pacific Command was now receiving additional warships in handsome numbers.

Tanaka's destroyer squadron made several other runs with cargoes of drums; but, as the admiral's chief of staff recorded, trying to supply "that cursed island" was "a strenuous and unsatisfying routine." The vessels were harassed both by aircraft and PT boats, the "Petes" now on hand in formidable strength. Some of Tanaka's runs were turned back, and even when the destroyers managed to complete their passes, many of the released drums were sunk by PT machine-gun fire while the starving Japanese watched from the beach. During one of the admiral's trips, the Petes torpedoed his flagship and he was wounded and knocked unconscious. He was evacuated from the doomed vessel and taken to Rabaul for hospitalization. His wounds were painful but not dangerous, and he was soon back on his feet. Perhaps 30 percent of Tanaka's drums reached Hyakutake, actually a good showing under the circumstances, but this was not enough to be of substantial help. Rabaul added some airdrops and submarine deliveries, but their effect on the situation was equally disappointing.

During this same period, the Japanese were working with frantic haste on a new air base at Munda on New Georgia Island, about 175 miles northwest of Guadalcanal. This would, at long last, put planes within easy striking distance of Henderson Field; but the measure was coming too late to help save the campaign. Henderson was emerging as a strong base, its number of aircraft approaching 200, an array that included Wildcats, Dauntlesses, Avengers, Airacobras, Lightnings, Hudsons, Flying Fortresses, and PBYs. The Munda field was scouted and photographed during the first week in December, and was subjected to its first full-scale bombing on the ninth.

The ninth was also the day when Archer Vandegrift turned his command of the Guadalcanal operation over to the Army's Alexander Patch. Vanguard elements of Vandegrift's 1st Marine Division, after four months on the island, stumbled out of the lines and prepared to embark for Australia, where the division would be rehabilitated before being reassigned. The ragged, thin, and sickly men first paid a solemn visit to the perimeter's cemetery, with its hundreds of mounds, each neatly covered by a palm frond; then they boarded landing craft that ferried them to the waiting transports. Many of the veterans were so weak they could barely make it to the top of the cargo nets draped at the vessels' sides, and these men submitted gratefully to being helped over the rail by robust sailors with tear-filled eyes.

It would be nearly four weeks before all elements of the 1st Marine Division were evacuated. Remaining with the Army, and under General Patch's command, were the 2nd and 8th Regiments of the 2nd Marine Division, along with some of the defense battalion men and their antiaircraft guns. The 8th Regiment had arrived from Samoa in early November and had been committed to the Matanikau fighting almost at once. The 2nd Regiment had been a part of the campaign since D-day. Although less battered and debilitated than some of the other D-day units, the regiment had seen its share of action. Its men were to achieve the distinction of serving in the Tulagi-Guadalcanal area longer than any other rifle troops. The 2nd Marine Division was rounded out with the arrival of the 6th Marines from New Zealand on January 4, 1943. By this time the Army's Americal Division had been joined by the 25th Infantry Division from Hawaii. Including the personnel of Henderson Field, General Patch now had about 50,000 men, and he pressed the campaign.

General Hyakutake's forces were all in the west, the lines swinging from Mount Austen across the Matanikau and along the northern coast. In addition to the unrelenting combat deaths, hundreds of Japanese were dying of sickness and malnutrition. Some of the desperately hungry had resorted to eating the flesh of the dead. As early as December 23, Hyakutake had radioed his superiors that he and his men wanted permission "to break into the enemy's positions and die an honorable death rather than die of hunger in our own dugouts." The request was not granted, and Hyakutake had managed to hold on. The tenacity of his resistance, in fact, had given the Americans second thoughts about the nearness of their victory. Were the Japanese bracing for another offensive in spite of their recent setbacks? This seemed a distinct possibility, since it was learned that Japanese naval activity around Rabaul had increased again. Actually, the high command in Tokyo, after some agonized soul-searching and some explosive Army-Navy debates, had finally abandoned all plans to try to retake the island. The Emperor himself, deeply concerned over the way Hyakutake's men were suffer-

Marines leaving Guadalcanal.

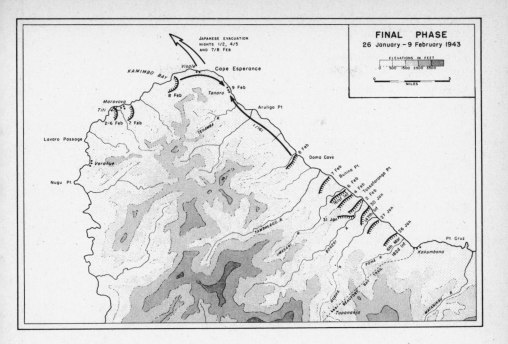

ing, had sadly concurred in the decision. A new and surprising set of orders reached the general on January 14. He was to prepare for evacuation; a series of destroyer runs would ferry his army out.

Cooperation between the Imperial Army and Navy was excellent during the evacuation period, and this very difficult maneuver became one of the most brilliant of its kind ever executed. The Americans had no inkling of what was happening, believing until the end that the renewed activities of the Tokyo Express meant that Hyakutake was being reinforced. Late in January the general's troops began falling back toward Cape Esperance, moving mostly at night, their rear-guard units keeping up a fire out of proportion to their numbers. The Americans reacted cautiously. During the three runs of the Tokyo Express that took away nearly 12,000 men—runs made on February 1, 4, and 7—the large fleet of destroyers was exposed to the usual attacks by planes and PT boats, but each run was eminently successful. The operation's good fortune as a whole, according to one Japanese officer, was "a rare miracle." Commander of the Express at this time was Rear Admiral Tomiji Koyanagi, since Raizo Tanaka had gone to Japan to complete his recuperation.

When on February 9 Alexander Patch realized that the only Japanese soldiers still on the island were the dying, who had necessarily been abandoned, he was astonished. This outcome was not altogether an American triumph, for thousands of the enemy had escaped to fight again, but Patch was nonetheless happy to be able to radio Bill Halsey:

"Total and complete defeat of Japanese forces on Guadalcanal effected 1625 today." Halsey responded: "When I sent a Patch to act as tailor for Guadalcanal, I did not expect him to remove the enemy's pants and sew it on so quickly. . . . Thanks and congratulations." As for Japan's reporting of the news, Radio Tokyo informed the nation that Hyakutake's army had been evacuated after closing the campaign "by pinning down the Americans to a corner of the island."

The struggle was finally over. It had lasted for six months. The first Americans had landed on August 7, 1942, and Koyanagi's destroyers came for the last evacuees on February 7, 1943. The cost of the campaign in blood and treasure had been heavy. Sealark Channel and the lower regions of The Slot held so many sunken American and Japanese hulls that they affected the compass needles of the sound vessels passing above. Strewn over this same murky and restless bottom were the bones of thousands of men. The exact number cannot be told, for neither navy ever calculated its personnel losses. On land, some 24,000 Japanese were either killed or died of sickness or starvation. Only about 1,000 became prisoners, and most of these were laborers. The Marine Corps ground forces lost about 1,200 dead and 2,800 wounded, the Army about 450 dead and 1,900 wounded. Hundreds of others of both services fell victim to serious illness or combat fatigue. The Americans lost several hundred aircraft, the enemy probably well over 1,000. A particular drain on the Empire's war effort was the death of more than 2,300 experienced airmen. Efficient rescue operations and the handiness of Henderson Field kept fatalities among Marine, Navy, and Army fliers low. Less than 100 of the Marines died, and some of these were killed on the ground by enemy bombs or shells.

For the "tenacity, courage, and resourcefulness" that enabled him to win a vital victory over "a strong, determined, and experienced enemy," Archer Vandegrift was awarded the Medal of Honor. Summing up the campaign in later years, the general explained: "We struck at Guadalcanal to halt the advance of the Japanese. . . . We were as well trained and as well armed as time and our peacetime experience allowed us to be. We needed combat to tell us how effective our training, our doctrines, and our weapons had been. We tested them against the enemy, and we found that they worked." The general might have added that the victory bolstered American morale, enhanced the security of Douglas MacArthur's position in New Guinea, removed Guadalcanal as a threat to the lines of communication between the United States and Australia, and gained the springboard the Allies needed for further operations against the enemy's cordon of island defenses.

10 | *Up the Solomons Ladder*

======The next Allied objective was Rabaul, the mighty Japanese base in the Bismarck Archipelago, nearly 600 miles northwest of Henderson Field and about 350 miles northeast of MacArthur's New Guinea lines. Early plans called for the base to be captured and occupied, but the final decision was that it be neutralized and bypassed, which would be less costly. Rabaul and its immediate environs held nearly 100,000 Army and Navy troops. In charge of the Allied campaign were MacArthur and Halsey, with the theatrical general and the down-to-earth admiral striking up a harmonious partnership. "We had arguments," Halsey said later, "but they always ended pleasantly."

During this period, the war planners in Washington worked out the Pacific strategy that would be followed for the remainder of the conflict. The Japanese mainland would be attacked from two directions, with the Army under MacArthur proceeding through New Guinea and the Philippines, and the Navy under Nimitz, after the Solomons were tied down, moving across the islands of the Central Pacific. Over MacArthur's objections, the Navy's campaign would gain priority, with the war planners reasoning that the central islands, all relatively small, would be easier to subdue than the islands in MacArthur's path. Nimitz would have strong Army support, but his Marines, as a result of their concentrated amphibious training, would be required to bear the heaviest load in the perilous work of establishing the beachheads. The Fleet Marine Force in the Pacific was rapidly building toward 110,000 men serving in three divisions, three air wings, and a variety of supporting units. The majority of the combat troops were in the South Pacific under Halsey's command.

The enlisted Marines, along with the enlisted men of the Army and Navy, were at this time generally optimistic that the Pacific war would soon be won and they would be going home; but the senior officers, the long-time students of warfare, knew better. Wrote General George C. Kenney, head of the Allied Air Forces in the Southwest Pacific: "I'm afraid that a lot of people who think the Jap is a pushover as soon as Germany falls are due for a rude awakening. We will have to call on all our patriotism, stamina, guts, and maybe some crusading spirit or religious fervor thrown in to beat him. No amateur team will take this boy out. . . . You take on Notre Dame every time you play!" The fact that Japan's more astute and realistic leaders had already glimpsed the

THE SOLOMON ISLANDS

Spring 1943

☐ Enemy Bases

○ US Bases

100   0   100   Nautical
                  Miles

MAP #1

THE SLOT

PACIFIC OCEAN

N

ST. MATTHIAS ISLANDS

EMIRAU

ADMIRALTY ISLANDS

NEW HANOVER

KAVIENG

NAMATANAI

BORPOP

RABAUL

NEW IRELAND

BISMARCK ARCHIPELAGO

HOSKINS

GASMATA

NEW BRITAIN

CAPE GLOUCESTER

ARAWE

LAE

HUON GULF

SALAMAUA

NEW GUINEA

PORT MORESBY

SCHWIMMER AIRFIELD

BUNA

HORANDA AFLD

NORTH BORIO AFLD

GOODENOUGH BAY

MILNE BAY

D'ENTRECASTEAUX ISLANDS

TROBRIAND ISLANDS

WOODLARK ISLANDS

LOUISIADE ARCHIPELAGO

CORAL SEA

GREEN ISLANDS

BUKA

BONIS

BOUGAINVILLE

BUIN-FAISI

SHORTLAND

TREASURY ISLANDS

KAHILI

BALLALE

SOLOMON ISLANDS

SOLOMON SEA

ONTONG JAVA ISLANDS

REKETA

NEW GEORGIA ISLANDS

RUSSELL ISLANDS

RUSSELLS AIRFIELDS

SANTA ISABEL

MALAITA

FLORIDA

TULAGI

CARNEY AIRFIELD

HENDERSON AIRFIELD

GUADALCANAL

RENNELL

SAN CRISTOBAL

specter of defeat in no way impaired the Empire's will to fight. It had taken the Americans six months of bitterly punishing work to take Guadalcanal. A few more such experiences among Japan's island outposts, Tokyo reasoned, might well prompt Washington to settle for a negotiated peace.

The first element of a strong assist to pending Allied operations—twelve F4U Vought Corsair fighter planes—reached Henderson Field on February 12, 1943. The "gull-winged" Corsair, which was to become identified with Marine Corps aviation, could not only range twice as far from its home base as the Wildcat but could climb about 3,000 feet per minute. It was faster than any aircraft the enemy possessed. Many Japanese fliers considered the Corsair to be the best fighter in the Allied service.

There were Marine Corsairs among the planes in the air over the Solomons on February 21 when the 3rd Marine Raider Battalion, commanded by Lieutenant Colonel Harry B. "Harry the Horse" Liversedge, along with elements of the Army's 43rd Infantry Division and other units—about 9,000 men in all—began landing in the Russell Islands, about fifty miles northwest of Henderson. This was the first step up the Solomons ladder toward Rabaul. The operation was unopposed, since the Japanese had moved out. Some of the invaders were met by grinning Allied Coastwatchers and their native assistants and were offered a cup of tea. The Russells soon became a major Allied forward operating base and staging area.

In April, Admiral Yamamoto, then at Rabaul, launched a massive air attack on Guadalcanal and on MacArthur's positions in New Guinea. Although the Japanese fliers believed their efforts to be highly successful, nothing of telling consequence was accomplished in either zone. The armada that hit Guadalcanal provided the opportunity for a greenhorn Marine aviator to earn an instant reputation. Lieutenant James E. Swett, flying an old Wildcat in his first aerial combat, shot down seven Val-type carrier bombers in fifteen minutes. Swett had to be fished from the sea when his damaged Wildcat crashed, but his injuries were minor. His feat won him the Medal of Honor and set hundreds of other young fliers dreaming of doing something as impressive.

The renowned Japanese admiral had conducted his last operation. On the morning of Sunday, April 18, he and his staff left Rabaul by air to tour the upper Solomons for the purpose of inspecting defenses and bolstering troop morale. Yamamoto wished to stop first at Kahili airfield, on the southern coast of Bougainville, where he planned to board a launch to visit the nearby isle of Ballale, at that time base of the remnants of the Sendai Division, recuperating after the nightmare of Guadalcanal. Yamamoto wanted to thank these men personally for their service and sacrifice. The admiral and his party traveled in two Betty bombers, covered by nine fighters, with no one suspecting that the mission was known to the Americans. A coded message giving the time schedule had been intercepted and deciphered. As the Bettys came in for a landing at Kahili, they were met by sixteen U.S. Army P-38 Lightnings from Henderson Field, Major John W. Mitchell commanding. Both bombers were shot down, and Yamamoto perished in a flaming crash in the jungle. Five or six other top officers were also killed.

When it was announced in Japan that the nation's most trusted and admired military figure "had met a gallant death in a war plane," the populace was stunned. In Tokyo, a million citizens turned out to watch the funeral procession. Among all branches of the Japanese service, morale was dealt what one officer called "an almost unbearable blow." There was exultation among the Americans. On first hearing the news, Nimitz broke into a beaming smile, Turner whooped and applauded, and an equally happy Halsey shot off a wire congratulating Major Mitchell's squadron for conducting a duck hunt that bagged a peacock. Since Yamamoto was the best naval brain in Japan, the neatly managed execution was the equivalent of victory in a major battle.

For two months after Yamamoto's death the waters of the central Solomons were a kind of amphibious no-man's-land between the Russells and Bougainville. While the Allies prepared for their next advance, the enemy built up his bases. As before, Japanese destroyers and transports throbbed down The Slot at night, but now the naval leaders at Rabaul withheld their heavier vessels, for the Allied fleet in the Guadalcanal area had been materially strengthened. On the Allied side, this growth did not breed rashness. When elements of the fleet entered the central Solomons at night to lay mines and bombard installations, the commanders proceeded cautiously, for the enemy's Navy had earned their abiding respect. By day, the skies of the disputed waters were ranged by the aircraft of both sides, with the monotonous drone of the bombers often dimmed by the anguished shriek of maneuvering fighter planes and the clatter of gunfire.

The primary Allied targets were the enemy's airfields. But neither aerial attacks nor naval bombardments could put these installations wholly out of commission. As Rear Admiral Walden L. "Pug" Ainsworth stated in a report: "We may destroy large quantities of gasoline and stores, and we may render the fields unusable at critical times, but the only real answer is to take the fields away from them." An added consideration was that the Allies needed the fields for their own use, the better to pound Rabaul.

Bill Halsey's next offensive, timed to coincide with fresh operations by MacArthur in New Guinea, was directed against the New Georgia group of the central Solomons. The group, composed of a half-dozen large islands and many small ones, was occupied by about 15,000 Japanese under Rear Admiral Minoru Ota and Major General Noboru Sasaki. The approximate center of the group was Munda airfield on the largest island, New Georgia itself. The field, about 175 miles northwest of Guadalcanal and 110 southeast of Bougainville, was Halsey's chief objective. Kelly Turner, in the Solomons aboard the *McCawley*, planned the assault. Turner's ground forces were made up largely of Army men: the 25th, 37th, and 43rd Infantry Divisions. The chief Marine Corps units involved were the newly organized 1st Raider Regiment, commanded by "Harry the Horse" Liversedge (recently of the 3rd Raider Battalion), and the 4th, 9th, 10th, and 11th Defense Battalions. All of the usual Army, Navy, Coast Guard, and Marine support, service, and supply units were on hand, as were the vitally important Seabees, who had the assignment of revamping captured installations and creating new ones.

The operation, dubbed "Toenails" by Halsey and his staff, began with a preliminary landing at Segi Point, New Georgia, on June 21, 1943, when two companies of the 4th Marine Raider Battalion, unopposed, rescued a Coastwatcher the Japanese were hunting down. The main landings, made on the islands of New Georgia, Rendova, and Vangunu, were begun on June 30. The weeks of fighting—the same period that saw the Allies in Europe victorious in Sicily and on the Russian front— included both sea and air engagements. Drawn out of obscurity were such names as Kula Gulf, Vella Gulf, Rice Anchorage, Wickham Anchorage, Viru Harbor, Bairoko Harbor, Enogai Inlet, Zanana Beach. In all, some 30,000 Allied land troops were committed. The outnumbered Japanese fought fiercely as usual, often from well-prepared defenses; and that other enemy, the jungle, was almost as troublesome. But by August 5, the Munda airfield was in American hands. Mopping up went on for another six weeks. Meanwhile, on August 15, a lightly contested landing was made on Vella Lavella, the northernmost island of the group. One major island, Kolombangara, was simply bypassed. The capture of Vella Lavella asserted Allied dominance in the central Solomons.

It was during the closing weeks of the New Georgia campaign that Major Gregory Boyington, destined to become the Marine Corps' best-known flier, came roaring into the fray. Not a tall man but stocky and strong, the major was brash, boisterous, and bellicose and had an obsession for flying. As a prewar Marine who had resigned his commission to join Claire Chennault's Flying Tigers in China and Burma, Boyington accounted for six enemy planes before returning to the States and rejoining the Marines in 1942. While the New Georgia campaign approached its climax, the major was in the New Hebrides putting together a squadron made up of casuals, replacements, and greenhorns, men who referred to themselves as "black sheep." Because their commander was all of thirty-one years old, they began calling him "Pappy," and he preferred this to his formal title. During less than a month of training, Boyington instilled in his Black Sheep Squadron his own brand of cunning and daring.

Transferring to a base in the lower Solomons, the squadron, with all of the men flying new Corsairs, went into action for the first time on September 16, escorting a formation of bombers in a strike on the airstrip at Ballale, off southern Bougainville. As the bombers began their runs, the raid was challenged by some forty Zeroes (or Zekes, as official Allied jargon now termed them). In the fighter-plane actions that ensued, Boyington shot down five of the enemy, while his men accounted for seven more. The effect on the squadron's morale and confidence was tremendous. Within a month the Black Sheep, while losing only two of their own men, had fifty-seven kills to their credit. The major's share was fourteen, which, added to his six kills as a Flying Tiger, made him four times an ace. This wasn't enough to satisfy him, but the time had come for the squadron to pull back for a rest.

Although it gained its ends, the New Georgia campaign suffered from more than its share of mismanagement. The Army, Navy, and Marines were still learning the vital lessons of interservice cooperation. The cost of the campaign was higher than it should have been: about 6,000 men in killed, wounded, captured, or missing. Of this number, 726 were Marines. The Raiders were badly hurt during an attack on the defenses at Bairoko Harbor. American material losses included 141 aircraft and eight vessels, among the latter Kelly Turner's flagship, crippled by a torpedo from a Betty bomber, then accidentally finished off by an American PT boat whose commander believed the *McCawley* to be Japanese.

The enemy's personnel losses, though never precisely calculated, were high, the dead alone numbering in the thousands. As at Guadalcanal, the survivors were evacuated. Listed with Japanese material losses were nineteen substantial vessels, dozens of barges, and several hun-

Memorial services at a cemetery in the Russells.

dred aircraft. The planes, in particular, were sorely missed. To compound the Empire's woes, during this same period the Allies ousted the Japanese from Alaska's Aleutian Islands. In Tokyo, a perturbed Hirohito had begun to ask his war ministers, "Can't we repulse the enemy *somewhere*? How is this war going to turn out?"

By the autumn of 1943, each of the three Marine Corps divisions in the Pacific was training for a particular landing: the 1st for Cape Gloucester at the western end of New Britain, the 2nd for Tarawa in the Gilberts, and the 3rd for Bougainville, the largest of the northern Solomons. As the last step in the climb toward Rabaul, Bougainville was the priority target. The island, 130 miles long and thirty miles wide, was not marked for complete conquest, since this would not be necessary. All the Allies wanted was a beachhead about 200 miles from Rabaul where an air base could be established and fortified against counterattack. There was a need for strips from which fighters could be sent up to fall in with the heavy long-range bombers and escort them to and from Rabaul, and from which the smaller, short-range Dauntless dive bombers and Avenger torpedo planes could be dispatched. Getting such strips into operation would be a long step toward rendering Rabaul ineffectual while MacArthur advanced in New Guinea and Nimitz attacked across the Central Pacific.

It was Bill Halsey's job to establish the Bougainville beachhead. He had a new amphibious commander, Rear Admiral Theodore S. Wilkinson. Kelly Turner had moved over to the 5th Fleet in the Central Pacific, his eye on Tarawa. Archer Vandegrift, now a lieutenant general, was in charge of the Bougainville ground troops, a large portion of which were trained on Guadalcanal. In addition to the three rifle regiments of the 3rd Marine Division, the invasion forces included the 12th Marines (artillery), the 19th Marines (engineers), units of Marine Raiders and Paratroopers, the 3rd Marine Defense Battalion, five battalions of Seabees, Navy small craft and communications men, the 8th Brigade Group of the 3rd New Zealand Division, and the U.S. Army's 190th Coast Artillery Regiment, Antiaircraft. The Army's 37th Infantry Division would be in reserve, with the Americal Division also available as needed.

Vandegrift would be facing his old Guadalcanal adversary, Haruyoshi Hyakutake, still commanding the 17th Army. The Japanese general's forces were not in the best of shape. His Sendai Division had been ordered to the Philippines for reorganization, and his 38th Division, after heavy losses on Guadalcanal, had been further battered in the New Georgia campaign. Only two regiments of his remaining division, the 6th, were in real fighting trim; the third was another casualty of the central Solomons actions. Hyakutake also had detachments from several Special Naval Landing Force units, plus various remnants of infantry that were still arriving on Bougainville after fleeing the islands below. In all, the general had about 15,000 men. Added to these, however, were perhaps 20,000 Army and Navy troops that made up the garrisons of the half-dozen air bases in the Bougainville area.

On the part of the Allies, the move against Bougainville required considerable daring. There was no chance of gaining a strategic surprise; Hyakutake could safely assume that the northern island was next on the Allied list. The invasion forces would be entering a hornet's nest of air power, and their success would depend to a great degree on the strength and prowess of their own air. Moreover, the Navy must be ready to confront surface resistance from the direction of Rabaul and also of Truk, the base in the Carolines. The Allies *did* have a tactical advantage. Since Bougainville was big, Hyakutake could only guess at the site of the landing. His numbers were greatest on the southern coast, the region of the principal bases.

The spot chosen for the landing was Cape Torokina in Empress Augusta Bay, about halfway up the island's western coast. Allied intelligence had learned that this area was only lightly defended. Once securely ashore, the invaders would have time to set up strong positions before the enemy could bring heavy reinforcements against them. The landing was scheduled for November 1. In order to keep Hyakutake guessing, the main event was preceded several days by two diversionary landings on islands within thirty miles of Bougainville's southern coast. The 2nd Battalion, 1st Marine Parachute Regiment, under Lieutenant Colonel Victor H. "Brute" Krulak (a small, wiry man who received his nickname while serving as a coxswain at Annapolis), was boated to Choiseul, and the New Zealand troops to the Treasury Islands. Both incursions were accomplished with minimum losses. After throwing several hard jabs at Choiseul's superior numbers, Krulak's men were evacuated—with Lieutenant John F. Kennedy, future President of the United States, skippering one of the PT boats that assisted. The New Zealanders were able to remain in the Treasurys, the enemy's attention shifting from them as Vandegrift's main landing force headed for Cape Torokina, covered both by aerial and surface missions against those bases whose planes might interfere.

November 1, 1943, dawned clear over Bougainville's western coast, although a light mist lingered on Empress Augusta Bay. First Lieutenant John A. DeChant, in a twin-engined Marine Ventura night fighter that had been patrolling above the invasion force for the past four hours, watched the vessels take form on the gray water, with the transports pointing like an arrow at Cape Torokina. "Hovering around this line at dawn, as they had been during the moonless night, were the naval forces which started shelling the beach area at 0601." As the transports themselves prepared to join in the firing, the combat-loaded Marines on the decks peered toward the island and were awed by what they saw. Behind the white surf and the coastal lowlands rose a jumble of jagged hills culminating in a lofty peak that was an active volcano, complete with an ominous trail of smoke. On board the *Hunter Liggett*, Coastguardsman Robert B. Pero noted that the Marines were tense as they boarded the landing craft that were to be lowered to the water by davits. The men "looked strangely alike in their deep helmets and camouflaged uniforms." At this point, Pero asserts, "everyone won-

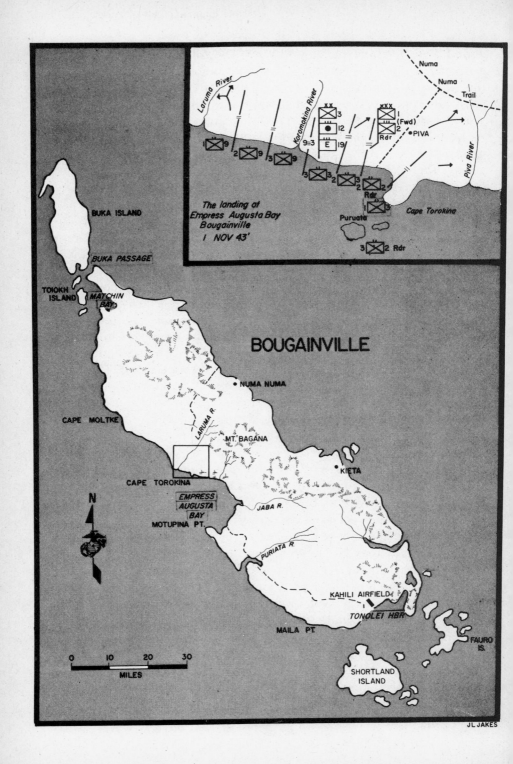

The landing at
Empress Augusta Bay
Bougainville
1 NOV 43'

BOUGAINVILLE

BUKA ISLAND

BUKA PASSAGE

TOIOKN
ISLAND

MATCHIN
BAY

NUMA NUMA

CAPE MOLTKE

LARUMA R.

MT. BAGÁNA

KIETA

N

CAPE TOROKINA

EMPRESS
AUGUSTA
BAY

JABA R.

MOTUPINA PT.

PURIATA R.

KAHILI AIRFIELD

TONOLEI HBR

MAILA PT.

FAURO
IS.

SHORTLAND
ISLAND

0   10   20   30
MILES

JL JAKES

dered whether this was going to be a surprise to the Japs."

It was. Although there seemed to be a remote possibility that the Allies would try to land in the Empress Augusta Bay area, the spot they had picked, just north of Cape Torokina, was an unlikely one, since the terrain there was inhospitable to such a venture. The beaches were rough and the coastal ground swampy. Manning the site were only 300 Japanese, the 2nd Company, 1st Battalion, 23rd Regiment, together with a regimental weapons platoon. And even this detachment was divided, perhaps 250 men on the cape and the rest on the nearby islands of Puruata and Torokina, with only a very few on the latter. But the defenders were well trained and well armed, and had all of the usual Japanese fighting spirit. After their first shock at seeing the Allied armada, which obviously held thousands of troops, the men retired to their quarters, donned their best uniforms and their campaign ribbons, took a last look at photos of loved ones at home, then went to their defenses and prepared to fight to the death.

11 | *Bougainville*

══════ The eastern sky was turning a brilliant orange as scores of Allied landing craft took to the water and began circling in groups, awaiting the signal to form into waves for the run to the designated beaches that stretched four miles leftward from the cape. Shells arcing from the warships were landing along the shoreline, the explosions raising geysers of mud and pulverized vegetation. In the sky were dozens of light bombers and fighters, including P-40s flown by New Zealanders. At 7:20 the naval gunfire was lifted to targets immediately inland, and about forty Navy planes bombed and strafed the beach. By this time the first waves of landing craft were making their approach. Huddled in the plywood shells were 7,500 Marines: two regiments of Major General Allen H. Turnage's 3rd Division and two battalions of Lieutenant Colonel Alan Shapley's 2nd Raider Regiment.

Even as the invasion began, enemy planes from Rabaul made for the offshore shipping. During the ensuing dogfights and bomber runs, the transports engaged in evasive maneuvering toward the open sea. When the Japanese departed, their own damages greater than those they inflicted, the transports nosed back to the beach area and were met by groups of landing craft that had disgorged their Marines and equipment and were ready to take on additional troops and such items as ammunition and rations. But a full ninety of the small craft had not returned from shore. Eighty-six had fallen victim to the shoals and rough surf that characterized the leftward beaches, where the 9th Marines had landed unopposed. The other four boats were lost on the extreme right, where the 1st Battalion, 3rd Marines, had encountered heavy fire from the determined Japanese on the offshore islands and Cape Torokina. The battalion's route carried it past the islands and toward the cape's main defenses, made up of twenty-seven bunkers, most of which had not been harmed by the preliminary bombardment. Set low in the ground, these were composed of ironwood and coconut logs bulwarked by sandbags, and they were camouflaged with earth and tangled underbrush. Armaments included a 75-millimeter artillery piece, and it was this weapon that sank the four small boats, also damaging ten others.

There is no dread connected with amphibious assaults greater than that of getting hit on the way in. The landing craft are highly vulnerable, and unless a man is one of those who believes in the power of prayer he feels utterly defenseless, unable to do a single thing to enhance his security. While maintaining his footing in the closely packed crowd, and while listening to the booming of shore batteries that he knows may well be aiming at him, he can do nothing but steel his nerves and wait out the long minutes until the boat's prow grinds up on the beach. Although this means he has simply exchanged one form of peril for another, he has now regained at least a partial control over his fate.

One of the 1st Battalion's boats took three shells as it was nearing shore, and, according to an occupant, was rendered "an awful mess." The Navy coxswain was blown overboard and a number of Marines fell amid the deck's muddle of feet. Several of the men were immediately still in death, while others writhed and screamed. One had been shorn of a large section of his back muscles, while another was bleeding profusely from the head. The boat, leaking through a number of holes, glided into shallow water, but its ramp was jammed in a closed position. The able-bodied men, along with most of the blood-soaked wounded, began to throw themselves over the side into the surf. Exhausted by the exertion, the critical cases were dragged ashore by buddies, some of whom were bleeding from wounds of their own. Even as the men on their feet began to prepare for action, a few turned back and, aided by a surviving sailor, tried to salvage the boat in order to send the wounded out to the fleet. Two or three of the limp corpses on deck were stuffed into the larger holes, and the wounded were hoisted on board and fitted with life jackets. Although the boat was able to churn out of the shallows, it shortly sank. The floating men were returned to shore and placed behind fallen coconut trees to await the arrival of a sound vessel, and now all of the samaritans turned their full attention to the assault.

These men, along with the rest of the 1st Battalion, 3rd Marines, and the 2nd Raider Battalion operating on their left, had hit the single area along the four-mile landing zone that held formidable fixed defenses. The Japanese on Puruata Island, which had been bypassed by the two units and was under assault by the 3rd Raider Battalion, were scattered through the jungle. The 1st Battalion, 3rd Marines, had the toughest job, since its area held twenty-five of the enemy's twenty-seven bunkers. Moreover, the unit was on its own, cut off from the Raider Battalion on its left by a swampy inlet. The situation was unique. Although the Japanese company was ridiculously outnumbered by the invasion force as a whole, the only Marines actually opposing it were the three rifle companies of the 1st Battalion, 3rd. This made for a textbook confrontation: the Japanese had the advantage of their defenses, while the Marines had the required superiority in numbers. In the larger sense, the Japanese situation was worse than hopeless; but, viewed by itself, the developing fight was a fair one.

The Japanese artillery piece had made a shambles of the 1st Battalion's landing plan. While maneuvering frantically to avoid the shells, the boats had disrupted their approach formation, and only one company was set ashore in its prescribed place. The other two landed not only out of position but with their platoons intermixed. Confusion was heightened as the enemy opened up with mortars and small arms. At first the Marines could do nothing but sprint across the narrow strip of beach and take cover in the edge of the jungle. The battalion's commander, Major Leonard M. Mason, soon suffered a severe wound. Scorning the concerned attention of his aides, the colonel ordered his executive officer to take over and "get the hell in there and fight!"

The troops had seen no previous combat and were getting their baptism in the toughest way possible. What saved the day was their intensive training in small-unit tactics against fortified positions. Rifle groups began forming under ranking men, and all along the line these units pressed toward the menacing bunkers. While BAR men, together with riflemen using the new M-1, poured fire into the dark embrasures, other Marines circled around and dropped hand grenades through the ventilators or blasted the rear entrances with grenades or TNT. One by one, the defenses were silenced. When a Marine was killed or wounded, there was always another to take his place. Sergeant Robert A. Owens won the Medal of Honor in an assault on the big bunker that held the 75-millimeter gun. According to the citation, "Sergeant Owens unhesitatingly determined to charge the gun bunker from the front, and, calling on four of his comrades to assist him, carefully placed them to cover the fire of two adjacent hostile bunkers. Choosing a moment that provided a fair opportunity for passing these bunkers, he immediately charged into the mouth of the steadily firing cannon and entered the emplacement through the fire port, driving the gun crew out of the rear door and insuring their destruction before he himself was killed."

Soon the 1st Battalion radioed the fleet: "Old Glory flies on Cape Torokina. Situation well in hand." Most of the bunkers were subdued before noon. Meanwhile, on the battalion's left, across the inlet, the men of the 2nd Raider Battalion—after their regimental executive officer was killed consolidating the attack—had overcome the few defenses that opposed them and were edging inland. Over on Puruata Island the 3rd Raider Battalion had run into unexpectedly tough resistance from the Japanese platoon fighting from concealment in the jungle. When Gunnery Sergeant John R. Leyden was cut down by a sniper, the medical corpsman who went to his aid was shot in the leg. As recalled by PFC M. W. "Dutch" Doornbos: "Leyden was dying, but he kept training his field glasses around, trying to locate the sniper." Minutes later, a dozen of the enemy approached and were met by M-1 fire and hand grenades. "The gunny," Doornbos explains, "lived long enough to see the Japs get theirs."

Another flight of Japanese bombers and fighters appeared over the bay at about 1:00 P.M. This raid, too, was frustrated by alert Allied airmen. Marine Lieutenant Robert M. Hanson shot down three of the enemy craft before his Corsair was hit in turn and he went down in the sea. Unhurt and able to inflate his rubber raft, the lieutenant presently sighted an American destroyer and paddled toward it singing a line from a popular song, "You'd be so nice to come home to"! Hanson was picked up and was soon enjoying what he called "swell chow." Three months later, then a leading Marine Corps ace and a Medal of Honor winner, the lighthearted lieutenant would crash in the sea again, this time explosively and fatally, his plane failing to pull out of a strafing run.

By late afternoon on D-day, all of the bunkers on Cape Torokina had been reduced and the Marines counted 153 enemy dead. Resistance from the survivors, who had been driven into the jungle, amounted to little more than sporadic sniper fire. The 1st Battalion, 3rd Marines, had

A trek through the mud.

suffered the greater part of the day's total American casualties, which came to thirty-nine killed, thirty-nine missing, and 104 wounded. About 14,000 men were now ashore, and the invasion's second echelon was loading at Guadalcanal. That evening, as it began to rain at Empress Augusta, working parties made up of Seabees, engineers, artillerymen, signalmen, and even medical personnel struggled to sort the supplies that had been dumped on the beach. Just inland, the rifle troops slogged around cursing the swamps and the twisted underbrush as they tried to bring a semblance of order to their four-mile beachhead. When the men finally settled down for the night, some were in foxholes half filled with mud and water. A total blackout was imposed, and soon a roving Japanese tumbled into a hole on top of a Raider. As the Marine grabbed for his combat knife, the enemy soldier shrieked in English, "I'm too young to die!" These were the last words of his short life.

During the hours just after midnight, while the Marines were coping with infiltrations that were nerve-racking but minor, a storm broke over the western sea, well beyond the horizon. The murmuring men standing in a drizzle on the beach soon came to the conclusion that the flashes were not lightning and the rumblings not thunder, and they were right. A Japanese naval force commanded by Rear Admiral Sentaro Omori— two heavy cruisers, two light cruisers, and six destroyers—had come down from Rabaul to contest the invasion and had been intercepted by four light cruisers and eight destroyers under Rear Admiral A. Stanton "Tip" Merrill. Although Omori had the greater firepower, his fleet got the worst of it, his casualties one light cruiser and one destroyer sunk and several other vessels damaged. Seaman 1st Class James J. Fahey was among those who watched American guns turn an enemy vessel into "a mass of flames and red-hot steel," with many of its crew ending up "roasted and blown to bits." When Omori fled the field, Merrill counted his own damages as one destroyer knocked out of action and one cruiser and one destroyer hit but not seriously harmed. The next morning, a flight of some seventy Japanese planes approached Merrill's force to "finish off the cripples." While making light hits on the cruiser *Montpelier,* the enemy lost about twenty planes to aggressive fighter pilots and antiaircraft fire. James Fahey saw some of the shipboard gunners engage in a practice that the Japanese were accused of initiating. Several enemy fliers who parachuted from disabled planes were targeted by 20-millimeters and hit the water in the form of "meat cut to ribbons."

That morning the Marines began pushing their beachhead inland. Only two relatively dry trails, both on the right, led toward the higher ground, which meant that most of the patrols had to thread their way through the swamps. This often involved wading in deep water. Soon a joke made the rounds that one Marine, seen moving along with only his head showing, protested that his situation was even worse than it looked; that he was actually standing on a bulldozer driven by a Seabee. In truth, the Seabees were then trying to make a decent road along the beach, at the same time plotting canal routes by which the swamps might be drained into the sea. The bright spot in the terrain mess was the knowledge that if enemy reinforcements chose to attack by way of the high country, their routes of approach would be limited. Resistance was slight as the Marines expanded, although the sound of firing carried across the water from Puruata Island, where the Raiders were hunting down the last of the jungle fighters. As for tiny Torokina Island, its few defenders were still firing on targets of opportunity. By the time the island was invaded by a small force the next day, it had been abandoned.

On the mainland, the development of the beachhead, along with plans for the first air facilities, continued on succeeding days. Air raids interfered from time to time but, thanks to friendly air cover, were largely ineffective. At first the only vehicles able to move about freely were LVTs, or amphibian tractors, equally at home on land and water. Maps carried by the officers were poor, and the terrain held few identifying features. It was almost impossible to mark the maps with the troop dispositions. Colonel Edward A. Craig, commander of the 9th Marines, resorted to an ingenious expedient. "I had each company on the line put up small weather balloons above the treetops in the jungle and then had a plane photograph the area. The small white dots made by the balloons gave a true picture, finally, of just how my defensive lines ran in a particularly thick part of the jungle. This was the only time during the early part of the campaign that I got a really good idea as to exactly how my lines ran."

Those Marines who had known the jungle of Guadalcanal found that of Bougainville even worse. Some of them swore that the vines in the underbrush made deliberate attempts to strangle them. There were birds that dived at their heads with shrill cries, bats that darted about with whistling wings, and a remarkable variety of insects, lizards, and snakes. A platoon leader reported that one night "snakes ten feet long, with brown and sickly yellow markings, came out of the jungle to be our bedfellows." At dawn the platoon area resounded with cries of "Snakes! Snakes!" and with thuds and thumps as the creatures were beaten to death. On another night Corporal Carroll DeVaurs saw a smaller snake come over the rim of a foxhole he was sharing with two buddies, who were asleep. DeVaurs lost track of the snake while he was fumbling for his bayonet. "I thought I saw it at the front of the hole, and I started chopping. The other guys woke up, plenty startled. They thought a Jap had climbed in with us. The snake got away. All I managed to do was chop up the poncho we were sleeping on."

Unknown to the Marines on Bougainville, Bill Halsey had learned at his headquarters in New Caledonia that a Japanese naval force built around seven heavy cruisers was assembling at Rabaul, its obvious purpose to storm Empress Augusta. Halsey hadn't a single heavy cruiser of his own, since all of the capital ships in the Pacific Fleet had been assigned to the upcoming invasion of Tarawa and Makin in the Gilberts. The admiral did have the carriers *Saratoga* and *Princeton.* Although he knew it would be risky to send their planes against such a strong base as Rabaul, he could do nothing else, so he ordered the task force commander to "go to it." On November 5, the planes, nearly 100 of them, swarmed in for a surprise attack. They came through with moderate damage and handsome results. No sinkings were achieved, but the warships were hit so hard that several were seriously disabled. The more enthusiastic American fliers returned to their carriers claiming they had avenged Pearl Harbor. What they had managed to do was to eliminate the enemy's heavy vessels as a threat to the Empress Augusta beachhead.

Although the Allies were not aware of it as yet, the move against Bougainville was working out beautifully. General Hyakutake, at his headquarters in Rabaul, was in a quandary. He was apprehensive that the landing in the west would be followed by others against his main bases, around Buin in the south and at Buka and Bonis in the north. Because of this possibility, the general felt he must keep these bases heavily garrisoned, that he could not employ their troops in a major counterattack at Empress Augusta. Japanese naval leaders at Rabaul, fearing the establishment of an Allied air base at Empress Augusta, urged Hyakutake to move in force, and as quickly as possible, against the beachhead. But the general, with some justification, persisted in maintaining the strength of the Buin and Buka-Bonis bases. This left him severely limited in troops for offensive measures, and he began repeating the mistakes of Guadalcanal.

Estimating American numbers at 5,000 (when they were now closer to 18,000), Hyakutake planned his first counterattack with approximately 2,500 troops. This was to be another combination effort, a pincer attack involving two teams. While the main body, composed of elements already in the bay area plus reinforcements from the south, closed in from the high country by way of the Numa Numa Trail on the perimeter's right, a 500-man diversionary force, in barges, was to creep down the west coast for a landing on the left. As was so often the case with Japanese plays like this, coordination was poor. During the night of November 5–6, with the diversionary force still on destroyer transports at Rabaul, advance elements of the main force jumped the gun.

Alan Shapley's Raiders had set up a defense line at the spot where the two narrow tracks from the sea, the Mission and Piva Trails, came together and joined the Numa Numa coming down, and the Japanese launched probing attacks on the position, with the result that it was reinforced. The daylight hours of the sixth and the ensuing night were relatively quiet. In the dawn of November 7 the 500-man diversionary force came down the west coast in its barges, and, remarkably, made it ashore and into the jungle on the perimeter's left, under the eyes of the fleet and units of Marines on the beach. The barges were mistaken for friendly ones. After the truth was known, these Japanese hadn't a chance, although they fought valiantly against the three battalions sent against them.

One of the battalions was the 1st, 3rd Marines, which was called out

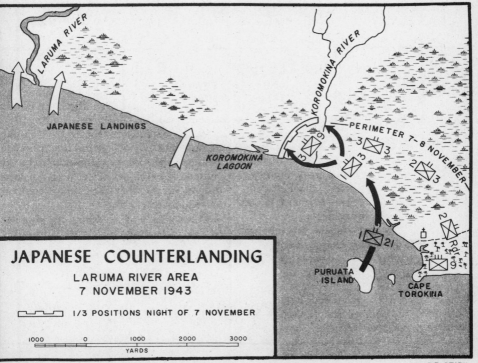

R.F. STIBIL

of the reserve spot it had occupied since its assault on Cape Torokina's bunkers. Captain Gordon Warner, a company commander in the 1st, made a name for himself by committing his unit expertly in the difficult terrain, and at the same time fighting his own personal war against the enemy's Nambu machine guns. Carrying a helmet filled with hand grenades, Warner would instruct one of his BAR men or several of his riflemen to pin down a nest while he circled in and blew it up. The captain once made his company's job a little easier by shouting, in fluent Japanese, "Fix bayonets and charge!" About thirty enemy riflemen obeyed and were immediately cut down by small-arms fire. At last Warner, while beside a tank directing its fire, had his knee smashed by one of the Nambus. His men dragged him to safety and rushed him to a field hospital, but the leg could not be saved.

It took two days for the Marines, aided by artillery fire and air strikes, to silence the last of the enemy's guns. Scattered through the jungle were 377 corpses. In areas where artillery shells and aerial bombs had done their work, parts of the bodies, including strings of entrails, were hanging from the trees. Marine losses were seventeen killed or missing and thirty wounded.

The fighting on the right of the perimeter, at the trail block, began during the afternoon of November 7 and remained a stalemate until the ninth. Early that morning both sides pitched in with special determina-

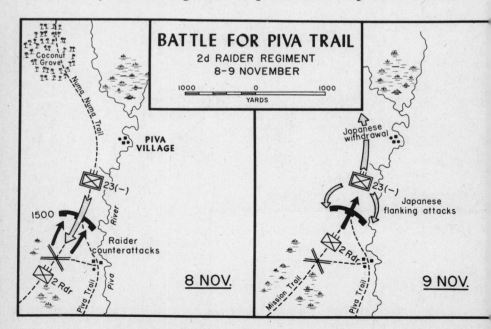

tion. Lieutenant Colonel Fred D. Beans, commander of the 3rd Raider Battalion, soon won the Navy Cross. When word reached him at the rear that his leading troops were pinned down, Beans "unhesitatingly advanced his command post to the front lines without regard for his own personal safety, rallied his men, and immediately launched a furious counterattack." Now the fight developed into a malevolent slugging match, during which the sounds of small-arms fire and the explosions of hand grenades and mortar shells were punctuated by oaths and shrieks from both sides. Early in the afternoon the Japanese, their ranks decimated and their nerves frayed by the foe's superior firepower, began to withdraw. When the Raiders moved forward, warily, to the Japanese bivouac area, they found it deserted. More than 100 dead were counted along the way. The forty-eight hours of fighting had cost the enemy perhaps another 200 men killed. The Raiders had lost twenty-one killed and fifty-seven wounded.

On the morning of November 10, after some noisy artillery and aerial preparation, two battalions of the 9th Marines passed through the Raiders and swung up the trail. They came upon clusters of abandoned arms and equipment and thirty or forty of the enemy killed by the preparation, but they were not resisted. That evening they dug in around the village of Piva. On November 13 the 2nd Battalion, 21st Marines, commanded by Lieutenant Colonel Eustace R. Smoak, took over at the front. Moving past the 9th Marines at Piva, Smoak's men pushed toward the junction of the Numa Numa and East-West Trails. The enemy made a stand there, and the result was a two-day affair known as the Battle of the Coconut Grove. Although plastered by small arms, mortars, tanks, artillery, and aircraft, the Japanese managed to give the Americans plenty of trouble. But at last dazed and weary, their numbers diminished by another forty men, the defenders retreated. By the night of the fourteenth the Marine battalion, at a cost of twenty killed (including five officers) and thirty-nine wounded, had full control of the junction.

It was now two weeks since the initial American landings, and the circumference of the perimeter had been expanded to 16,000 yards, or about nine miles, and was held by nearly 35,000 men, including elements of the Army's 37th Infantry Division. The soldiers assumed responsibility for the leftward half of the position, which faced few of the enemy and where the clashes were limited to patrol actions. The top Marine command had changed, with Roy Geiger, formerly of Guadalcanal, taking over from his friend Archer Vandegrift, ordered to return to the States to become Commandant of the Marine Corps. When the

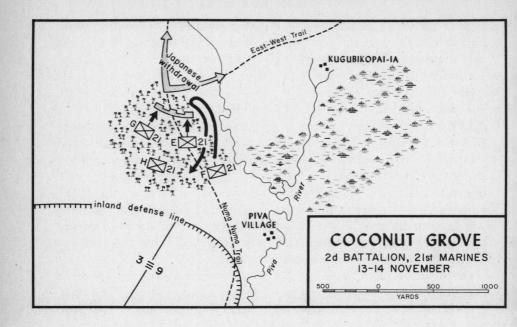

COCONUT GROVE

2d BATTALION, 21st MARINES
13–14 NOVEMBER

500   0   500   1000
YARDS

Japanese withdrawal

East-West Trail

KUGUBIKOPAI-IA

G 21

E 21

H 21

F 21

inland defense line

Numa Numa Trail

PIVA VILLAGE

Piva River

3 III 9

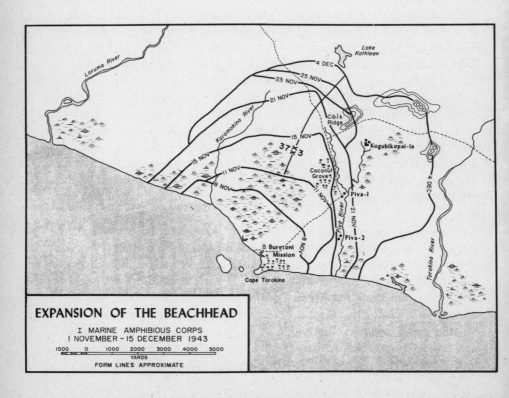

EXPANSION OF THE BEACHHEAD

I MARINE AMPHIBIOUS CORPS
1 NOVEMBER – 15 DECEMBER 1943

1000   0   1000   2000   3000   4000   5000
YARDS
FORM LINES APPROXIMATE

Laruma River

Lake Kathleen

4 DEC

25 NOV

23 NOV

21 NOV

Koromokina River

15 NOV

15 NOV

11 NOV

8 NOV

8 NOV

Cibik Ridge

Kugubikopai-ia

37 X 3

Coconut Grove

Piva-1

21 NOV

Piva-2

Piva River

4 DEC

Torokina River

Buretoni Mission

Cape Torokina

two men parted, Geiger told Vandegrift he would find his job in Washington hectic, and Vandegrift soon wrote back that Geiger had been right. "Many times have I longed, even in this brief space of time, for the peaceful calm of a bombing raid on Bougainville."

After the Battle of the Coconut Grove, contact with the main body of the enemy was temporarily lost, but there were patrol actions in the jungle. The Marines took casualties, and the helpless wounded had to be carried back to the lines on stretchers. One torrid, overcast, drizzly afternoon two Marines with a stretcher case came slipping and staggering back through the mud of a narrow trail that took them near the artillery command post. They stopped and set down their burden to catch their breath and to free a hand to fling the beaded moisture from

Evacuating the wounded.

their foreheads. Lieutenant Colonel John S. Letcher, executive officer of the 12th Marines, noted that the man on the stretcher, who was covered with a blanket, was white-faced and had his eyes closed. One of the stretcher-bearers called to the artillery group, "Which way to the medical company?" Someone pointed down the trail toward the rear and gave instructions, and the two men lifted the stretcher and started off, again slipping at every other step. About half an hour later, John Letcher was surprised to see the pair come struggling from the front through the wet jungle in the same way as before, carrying the same white-faced casualty. At the colonel's request for an explanation, one of the men said, "We lost our way and did not find the medical company." Letcher exclaimed, "Well, Great Lord, let's take him to our sick bay right here. He'll die while you are wandering around looking for the medical company." The stretcher was set down outside the medical tent and a doctor knelt beside it. After examining the man for a brief time, the doctor rose and said. "He's been dead for at least an hour, maybe two."

Letcher wrote later: "This incident of the stretcher-bearers staggering along the muddy trail through the dark woods in the drizzling rain, losing their way and carrying a man, on and on, long after he was dead epitomized for me the miserable conditions under which men lived and fought and died in this campaign. There were other campaigns where the fighting was harder and the casualties greater than at Bougainville, but the oppressive heat, the continuous rain, the knee-deep mud, the dark overgrown tangled forest with the nauseous smell of the black earth and the rotting vegetation, all combined to make this one of the most physically miserable operations that our troops were engaged in during the war."

By this time the campaign was counted a success, for the perimeter could be endangered by nothing less than a massive sea, air, and land effort by the Japanese, and it was becoming clear that they were either unable to mount such an operation or were unwilling to expose their ships, planes, and manpower to the major risks that such an operation would entail. The limited number of enemy planes sent to Bougainville did little damage, since the raids were usually frustrated by airmen from the bases in the Solomons to the south. Also a threat to the Japanese were the Marine and Army antiaircraft batteries. The American planes from down the island chain included Ventura night fighters. They were pioneering craft and few in number, so the enemy's night bombers had some success at harassing the perimeter.

Japanese airmen also tried to disrupt American shipping. Before dawn on November 17 a fleet of destroyers and transports was hit while approaching Cape Torokina. The destroyer transport *McKean* took an aerial torpedo. She shot down the offending plane, but, exploding and burning, soon sank. The holocaust took the lives of sixty-four Navy men and fifty-two Marines. With the Marine passengers on another vessel was Private K. Sterling Felton, who would recall: "We were below deck, near the fantail. Amidst the reverberating noise of the antiaircraft guns, we heard a loud thump directly overhead, and this was followed by the sound of something metallic rolling across the deck. When the raid ended, we learned that the ship had been hit by a bomb, but that it was a dud. So we lived to reach the beachhead."

During the lull in the Bougainville ground fighting, American efforts were centered on the improvement of supply routes and the construction of the airstrips, both tasks kept difficult by the nature of the terrain. It rained almost daily, and there were sometimes thunderstorms that felled trees. One tree crushed a Marine, breaking his back. The luckier men were encamped in what they called "dry swamps," which meant that the water reached only to the tops of their shoes. The single road that was developed inland, starting near the mouth of the Koromokina River on the left and cutting toward the Numa Numa Trail on the right, was at first a makeshift affair. The streams were bridged by handhewn timbers and the reaches of mire were corduroyed with fallen trees. By dint of long hours of frantic, hot, and enervating labor on the part of engineers, Seabees, and combat personnel, the road reached the Numa Numa Trail on November 16. This eased the supply problems of the Marines up the trail at the front, and they were now ready to seek heavier contacts with the enemy. It was especially important that the perimeter be further expanded in the vicinity of Piva Village and the coconut grove, for the ground was being developed for two of the air strips. The security of air facilities begun by the Seabees and engineers at Cape Torokina was already assured.

Until this time the Bougainville campaign had been getting good coverage in the news periodicals and on the radio in the States, but it was about to be eclipsed by events in another theater. Admiral Nimitz had launched his drive across the Central Pacific, and an invasion force was heading for the Gilbert Islands, which held Tarawa. D-day had been scheduled for November 20.

On November 19 the Marines at the Bougainville front initiated a series of actions that became known as the Battle of Piva Forks. Although heavily outnumbered, the Japanese resisted stoutly, and even counterattacked. In the beginning they had one advantage: they knew

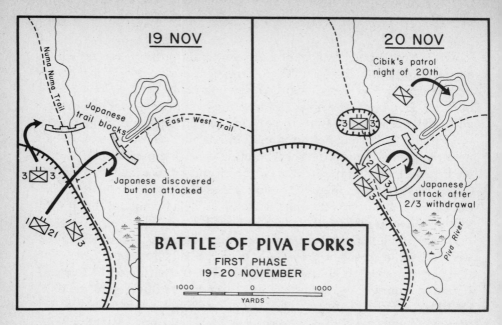

BATTLE OF PIVA FORKS

FIRST PHASE
19–20 NOVEMBER

1000   0   1000
YARDS

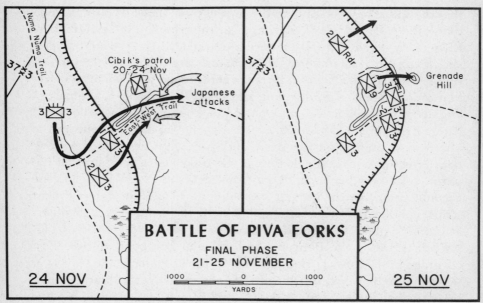

BATTLE OF PIVA FORKS

FINAL PHASE
21–25 NOVEMBER

1000   0   1000
YARDS

the terrain better than the Marines. But even this was soon taken from them. On November 21 a combat patrol from F Company, 2nd Battalion, 3rd Marines seized a ridge that, according to First Lieutenant Steve J. Cibik, was "an oasis in a sea of mist-covered jungle, the only high ground for miles around." Cibik and his men could see a vast region between the sparkling bay and the inland mountain range, with its smoking volcano. In practical terms, the Marines had gained a fine position from which to assess the battle zone, to look for enemy concentrations and artillery sites, and to call down their own artillery fire.

"Cibik's Ridge" was held against the enemy's counterattacks, and on November 23 it was utilized by artillery forward observers in the plotting of a barrage to precede a general attack by the infantry the next morning. The artillery effort involved seven battalions: the four that made up the 12th Marines and three from the Army's 37th Division, which was holding the leftward portion of the beachhead, where things had remained relatively quiet. When the guns opened up at 8:35 A.M. on the twenty-fourth—Thanksgiving Day—they fired for twenty minutes and laid more than 5,600 75-millimeter and 105-millimeter howitzer shells on a region that covered half a square mile. Mortars and machine guns joined in, but they were scarcely heard amid the greater din. The Japanese, all of whom should have been cringing in holes, managed to get off an alarmingly accurate artillery counterbarrage, but only a brief one. At nine o'clock when the 2nd and 3rd Battalions of the 3rd Marines jumped off in their attack, the terrain before them was still. According to the regiment's Captain John Monks: "For the first hundred yards both battalions advanced abreast through a weird, stinking, plowed-up jungle of shattered trees and butchered Japs. Some hung out of trees, some lay crumpled and twisted beside their shattered weapons, some were covered by chunks of jagged logs and jungle earth. . . ."

But as the advance proceeded, the Marines learned that not all of the Japanese were dead. Gradually the stunned survivors began to rally, and they were joined by fresh troops from bivouac areas outside the shattered zone. Resistance that began with a few scattered rifle shots soon swelled to a storm of fire that included machine guns, mortars, and artillery. Marines went down, but, aided by the counterfire of their support weapons, including some of the Army's 155-millimeter howitzers, the rest continued the attack, their rifles cracking as they moved from tree to tree. The few fixed positions encountered were tackled by engineers with flamethrowers.

The slain and helplessly wounded Marines were carried back on stretchers. Waiting to receive the dead was a Catholic priest. At one time he was kneeling beside a row of corpses, writing down the names and serial numbers taken from the dog tags, when a stretcher team passed bearing a man who was covered with a poncho, his head included. "Hold up a minute," the priest called after. "Is that a body there?" The top of the poncho flipped back. "Yes, it is, Father." The casualty grinned. "But you ain't going to bury it!"

By the end of Thanksgiving Day the disputed zone belonged to the Marines, and some of them were able to celebrate by eating turkey sent to the front by their company cooks. Next day, most of the action occurred to the left of the zone, as the 2nd Raiders and the 1st Battalion, 9th Marines, moved up from the rear to come abreast of the new line. The men of the 1st had trouble with a small rise they dubbed Grenade Hill, which was not occupied until the following morning. This ended the Battle of Piva Forks. It had cost the Japanese about 1,300 dead; the Marines lost 162 dead and wounded.

Again there was a lull in the action, occasioned by the need of the Americans to improve their supply lines to the expanded front. The remaining Japanese, some few hundred of them, had fallen back, and Marine patrols made only minor hostile contacts. Artillery officer John Letcher and forty of his men joined one of the patrols in order to investigate an abandoned Japanese gun position on a hilltop to the east. It was discovered that the enemy artillerymen had buried the parts of three weapons before retreating, and the parts were dug up. The Americans decided to destroy two of the guns with TNT and carry the parts of the other back to their lines to assemble as a trophy. A number of the strongest men picked up the tube of the trophy gun and started down the trail. The tube weighed nearly a thousand pounds, and the men began slipping and stumbling; several barely escaped having a leg crushed. The idea of saving the gun was soon abandoned. John Letcher was astounded by the enemy's capacity for physical labor. "They had not carried *one* gun. . . . They had manhandled a whole battery with ammunition thirty miles through the jungle from their base on the coast, and had then carried the parts of the guns up the steep, rain-soaked, jungle-covered, muddy, slippery side of the mountain where they had assembled them and put them in firing position. It was a Herculean task. . . ."

One of the enemy's smaller coastal bases was as close as Koiari, ten miles south of Cape Torokina. During the predawn hours of November 29, Major Richard Fagan's 1st Parachute Battalion, along with a company of Raiders, about 600 men in all, were boated to Koiari, their mission to raid the base, destroying supplies and disrupting communications. It was Fagan's intention to land on the objective's flank and attack it from the rear, but, as the result of faulty intelligence, he came ashore directly in its face. In the dim light, a Japanese officer who believed the Marines to be friends greeted them on the beach, a mistake that was instantly fatal. Fagan's troops made it inland nearly 200 yards while the garrison was recovering from its surprise. Then they were hit by mortar, machine-gun, and rifle fire. Backs to the sea, they were surrounded on three sides and outnumbered two-to-one. Unable to withdraw because of artillery pieces trained on the offshore waters, they dug in and began a desperate defense. By late afternoon the detachment had suffered 121 casualties, about 20 percent of its number, and ammunition was running low. Then, under cover of long-range artillery fire from Cape Torokina and the fire of three destroyers and an LCI gunboat that had reached the scene, the survivors made it back to their boats. Although the Japanese were hurt, the raid was a dismal failure. The only thing Fagan's troops could feel good about was that they had squeezed out of a mighty tight spot.

About 2,000 yards ahead of the Marine front at Piva Forks was a hill mass that had to be occupied in order to expand the Bougainville perimeter to its final inland defense line. This would make the perimeter about four miles deep and five miles wide, which was as much ground as the Americans had to hold to protect their airstrips. Once this final line was established the Army would assume responsibility for the entire perimeter and most of the Marines would leave the island. The greater part of the advance was made on December 6. There was little trouble from the enemy, but Nature was responsible for an interruption that, although brief, was startling enough. Bougainville was hit by a severe earthquake. According to Private Sterling Felton: "At first it seemed like a heavy artillery bombardment without the noise." The ground trembled and rolled, and the jungle trees swayed. Felton was flipped off his feet. "I landed hard, right on my butt." Many other Marines went down as abruptly.

The hostilities of the next three days, as the Marines maneuvered to secure the main elevation, Hill 1000, included numerous patrol actions. A member of one of the patrols conducted by I Company, 3rd Parachute Battalion, was PFC Jack Charles, who found the terrain frustrating. "Everything was the same; nothing but jungle, jungle, jungle. Looking up, you could not see the sky. We were told that we were not to engage the enemy unless there was no alternative. Our task was to try to learn his location, his strength, his dispositions. The task seemed impossible. To find the Japanese we would have to get close enough to shake their hands. As we proceeded, we occasionally came upon a path we knew had been used by the enemy, and we saw places where he had bivouacked, but that's all. On the second day, we were ambushed. Sergeant Banks Tucker and Corporal Mort Mills were hit by shrapnel,

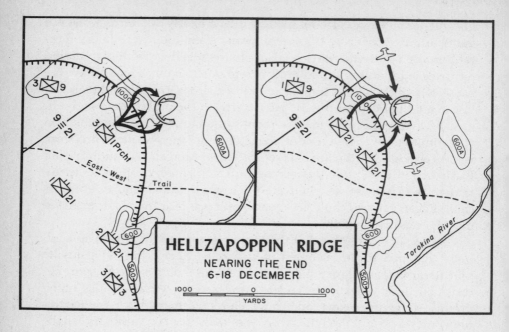

HELLZAPOPPIN RIDGE
NEARING THE END
6-18 DECEMBER

1000   0   1000
YARDS

probably from hand grenades. Although we could see no one, we opened up with everything we had. After a few minutes we stopped firing and listened intently for evidence of the enemy. The jungle was completely quiet." The patrol returned to the lines with its wounded and reported its meager findings.

On the afternoon of December 9 a Japanese counterattack was broken up by artillery fire, and on the tenth the Marines completed their advance to the final defense line. But a serious problem remained. The counterattack had originated on a spur extending from Hill 1000. Although the Marines were on the hill, they did not have the spur, which loomed ahead. A natural fortress, the position was occupied by a reinforced company, about 235 well-armed and decidedly stubborn men. The Marines spent a week fighting for the spur, which they came to call Hellzapoppin Ridge. The heroic holdouts were finally pulverized by artillery fire and by bombers flying from the new strip at Cape Torokina, and the 21st Marines occupied the spur on December 18. On December 24 an outpost was established on Hill 600A, about 300 yards ahead of the final defense line. With this, the Marines completed their Bougainville mission. Their relief, begun on December 27, was effected by their old friends from Guadalcanal, the Army's Americal Division.

During the two months of fighting, the Marines had sustained 1,841 casualties—423 killed and 1,418 wounded. The Japanese had left about

2,500 dead on the field. Twenty-five prisoners were taken. An interpreter asked one of these men what he thought of the Marines as jungle fighters and got the response, "I don't know what kind of jungle fighters you are, for you don't fight us in the jungle. You either blow the jungle away with shells and bombs or push it back over us with bulldozers and make us fight you in the open." One of the Japanese was captured inside the American lines, where he had been lurking for a month. The Marines got a laugh out of his reply when he was asked how he had managed to subsist. At first, he said, he had lived on the large snails that abounded in the jungle. Then he began eating the American C-rations he found along the trails. After two weeks of this, however, he returned to eating snails. As a steady diet, he explained, he found them preferable to C-rations.

The Bougainville perimeter was not permanently secured when the Marines turned things over to the Army. In March 1944, General Hyakutake finally got around to counterattacking with a major force, some 15,000 men strongly supported by artillery. It required sixteen days of fighting by the two infantry divisions and their artillery, aided by the 3rd Marine Defense Battalion, naval gunfire, and flights of bombers and fighters, to send the Japanese reeling in retreat, their numbers halved. This work by the Army put the final seal on the doom of Fortress Rabaul. The tentative seal had been administered as early as December 17, 1943, while the Marines were still fighting. It was on that day—thanks to the almost miraculous work of the Seabees and engineers—that Rabaul was first subjected to aerial efforts staged on the Bougainville strips. The seventy-six-plane fighter sweep was led by the flamboyant Pappy Boyington. Results were less than anticipated, but this was only the beginning of the short-range aerial work that would help to keep the key base neutralized until the end of the war.

After returning to Guadalcanal, General Roy Geiger received a message sent from Washington by Archer Vandegrift. "I want to congratulate you on the splendid work that you and your staff and the Corps did on Bougainville. . . . Those of us who know the constant strain, danger, and hardship of continuous jungle warfare realize what was accomplished by your outfit. . . ." Vandegrift was regretful that this important campaign had been "kind of put off the front page" by the spectacular assault on Tarawa.

12 | "Operation Galvanic"

Tarawa, in the Gilbert Islands, provided the first real test for the amphibious procedures the Marines had adopted shortly after the First World War and had spent two decades propounding, rehearsing, refining, and, finally, applying in a limited way. Betio, the isle at the southwestern extremity of triangular Tarawa atoll, which held many other fragments of coral and sand, was classically fortified. The Japanese officer in command, Rear Admiral Keiji Shibasaki, boasted that a million Americans could not take Betio in a hundred years.

Only about half a square mile in area, this flat, narrow birdwing of an isle was scarcely able to accommodate its airfield yet also held barracks for nearly 5,000 troops: 1,497 men of the 7th Sasebo Special Naval Landing Force, 1,122 men of the 3rd Special Base Force, the rest airfield personnel and laborers, most of whom had been assigned combat responsibilities. Betio's armaments included twenty heavy cannon, twenty-five field pieces, seven light tanks, thirty-one machine guns of the 13-millimeter type (similar to American .50-calibers), an unknown but large number of lighter machine guns, numerous mortars, scattered land mines, plus weapons such as rifles, pistols, and hand grenades. Regions of the isle that were not smoothly covered by the airfield were lumpy with bunkers and pillboxes, some made of reinforced concrete, some of coconut logs, and some a combination of both; most had sand piled over them, and all showed dark slots that were firing ports. Many of the structures were mutually supporting, which meant that a team of attackers moving against one would come under fire from others. Betio was also provided with trenches and with larger excavations designed as tank traps.

During the buildup, which was undertaken in earnest after Carlson's Raiders made their hit-and-run raid on nearby Makin in August 1942, the Japanese on Betio lived an agreeable life. The Tarawa atoll was tropically beautiful, with its expansive lagoon, its chain of white beaches, its coconut palms, breadfruit trees, and casual tangles of mangroves. The garrison had to work hard, but there was time enough for fishing, swimming, and boating or for just sitting around talking, playing cards, or writing letters home. Rations were decent, and there was at least enough *sake* to enable the drinking men to get pleasantly high now and then. The radio news from Tokyo was always encouraging: Japanese forces were defeating the Americans everywhere. If, as broadcasts from San Francisco seemed to indicate, it was really true that

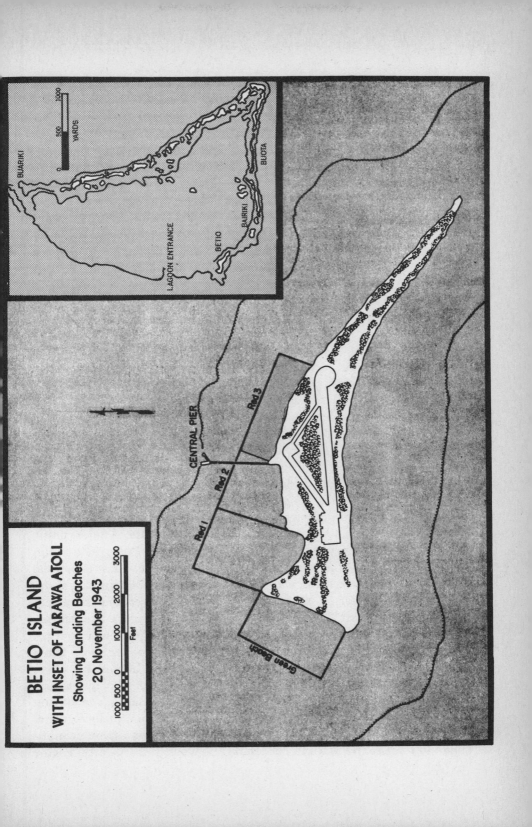

BETIO ISLAND
WITH INSET OF TARAWA ATOLL
Showing Landing Beaches
20 November 1943

Feet
1000 500 0 1000 2000 3000

CENTRAL PIER

Red 1
Red 2
Red 3
Green Beach

LAGOON ENTRANCE
BUARIKI
BETIO
BAIRIKI
BUOTA

YARDS
0 500 1000

Japan had withdrawn from the southern and central Solomons, there was doubtless a good strategic reason for this. The islands probably weren't worth holding.

There was no hint of trouble for Betio until American B-24 Liberators began paying occasional visits to the isle, droning over at such heights that some of their bombs did nothing more than land in the water and kill fish. Then on September 18, 1943, Betio was bombed and strafed by carrier planes. Twenty men were killed, and a number of aircraft were destroyed on the strip. During the weeks that followed, the garrison's hours of recreation were few. Work on the defenses was accelerated, and there were more lectures on weapons and tactics, and more training exercises. Complaints were rare; morale actually flourished. As the state of readiness culminated, the consensus was: Let the Americans come. As Admiral Shibasaki kept saying, Betio was impregnable. And even if the admiral was wrong, the isle was surely strong enough to hold the Americans at bay until Truk or Rabaul sent an armada of ships and planes to smash them.

What Betio's garrison did not know was that, as a result of the Bougainville campaign, there was no such armada in fighting trim. The area fleet had not only suffered serious damage to some of its major vessels but had also lost a crippling number of carrier planes. Without adequate air cover, it would have been foolish for the healthy warships to venture forth. The impending campaign would come to include some Japanese submarines and aircraft, and they would manage to inflict some damage, but they would have no effect on the campaign's outcome. The men of Betio would defend their isle in virtual isolation.

In overall command of American operations was the slender, natty, and somewhat august Admiral Raymond Spruance, who had begun making a reputation at Midway. Kelly Turner, who was fast becoming an expert on work like this, was in charge of the amphibious part of the fleet. Under Turner, commanding the landing forces, was sixty-one-year-old Holland M. "Howlin' Mad" Smith, who had played a vital role in bringing the Marine Corps to its present status. Now a major general, Smith had gained a few pounds with maturity and looked more like a benign grandfather than a Marine, but the eyes behind his steel-rimmed glasses held a glint that suggested he had kept all of his old fire. He was, in fact, as ready as ever to champion Marine causes; and, during their planning sessions, he and Kelly Turner, who was equally forceful, had many a blistering argument. Now one of the Corps' top men, Smith liked to refer to the Marines chosen for the work in the Central Pacific as "my Marines."

Commander of the 2nd Marine Division, the unit that would assault Betio, was Major General Julian C. Smith, who seemed even less like a typical Marine than Holland M. Also bespectacled, Julian was mild-faced, quiet, and modest. He was nonetheless a determined man capable of decisive action. After its service in the Guadalcanal campaign, the 2nd Division had sailed to Wellington, New Zealand, for recuperation and further training. The New Zealanders opened their doors in welcome, and many a rough-and-ready Marine learned to sit down to "morning tea" at eleven o'clock and "afternoon tea" at four. The Americans had excellent luck with the New Zealand women, large numbers of whom were lonely because their men were serving in distant war zones. Some 500 Marines took New Zealand wives. When the division prepared to ship out, the men were not told they were sailing for the Gilberts. In order to deceive the enemy's spies, Julian Smith passed the word that the division was going on an amphibious training exercise and would return to Wellington shortly. The convoy sailed on November 1. One of the unmarried Marines said later, "We may not have left many broken hearts in New Zealand, but we left an awful lot of broken dates."

"Operation Galvanic," as the campaign for the Gilberts was called, included a reinforced regiment of the U.S. Army's 27th Infantry Division, the 165th Regimental Combat Team, under the division's commander, a *third* major general named Smith, this one Ralph C., who was subordinate to Holland M. and Kelly Turner. While the Marines assaulted Betio, the Army was to take Makin, held by 284 Special Naval Landing Force troops, about 100 aviation personnel, and 446 laborers. The Army team trained in Hawaii, and Holland Smith was present at its invasion rehearsals. The Marine general was not enthusiastic about what he saw, but he was willing to concede that part of the trouble was that Army troops were not as familiar with amphibious techniques as Marines. After completing the rehearsals, the team sailed for the Gilberts, its transport convoy escorted by warships and designated the Northern Attack Force.

The Marines from New Zealand, the troops of the Southern Attack Force, tarried in the New Hebrides for two invasion rehearsals, then headed for a rendezvous with the Northern Attack Force in the open sea east of the Gilberts. The two convoys met on November 18, and the agitated pilot of a Japanese search plane soon radioed his base: "Enemy fleet sighted. Several carriers and other types too numerous to mention." The news was quickly relayed to all of the Japanese bases in the Central Pacific. On Betio, Admiral Shibasaki informed his troops that the enemy was approaching in superior numbers. "We will lure him within range of our fixed defense installations, and then, using all our strength, destroy him."

D-day in the Gilberts was still forty-eight hours away. The two attack forces had scarcely rendezvoused before they separated again, one heading for the northerly island of Makin, and the other bearing toward Tarawa in the south. The islands were about 100 miles apart.

By this time the Marines had been aboard ship, except for their brief departures during the landing rehearsals, for eighteen days. Some of the men had slept a lot, in their canvas bunks below or, to escape the stifling heat and the fusion of body emanations, in out-of-the-way places on the steel decks. Others did the usual things: gathered for bull sessions, played cards, smoked heavily, drank coffee they begged from the Navy messmen, cleaned their rifles with oiled rags, put a sharper edge on their bayonets and knives, read paperback books, washed their clothing by letting it bounce along on the waves at the end of a rope secured to the rail. Sometimes there was group singing, and a particular parody was especially popular. Whereas their fathers in World War I had sung, "It's a long way to Tipperary," this generation of fighting men sang, "It's a long way to Yokohama." The Marines also wrote letters— thousands of them—addressed not only to the States but to New Zealand, and the junior officers who were obliged to act as censors were overloaded with work. One lieutenant lamented that he had to put up with a lothario who wrote "five identical letters to five different girls every day."

Included with the troops on the transports was a unique group of specialists. Attached to 2nd Division headquarters was a photographic section whose job was to make as complete a pictorial record as possible of the Tarawa campaign—not so much to gain publicity for the Corps as to obtain material for study during planning and training for future operations. The section's commanding officer was Captain Louis Hayward of Hollywood, star of several popular motion pictures, including *The Man in the Iron Mask.* Hayward told his men, who numbered about a dozen: "I know all of us are fed up with hearing about the *marvelous* photography coming out of the European war. This time let's really give 'em something to talk about—from the Marines in the Pacific." The captain and his crew were unaware of the golden opportunity they would be granted—nor would the knowledge have been altogether welcome.

The troops revealed few indications of apprehension, although the majority naturally felt it. A news correspondent asked a rifleman whether he was scared and got the reply, "Hell no, mister, I'm a Marine." But hardly a man, underneath, was really that sure of himself. The experienced troops remembered the horrors of Guadalcanal, while the replacements who had seen no action wondered what they were getting into and could not be altogether certain they would measure up. But the customary *esprit de corps* was there. They were all Marines, and they were in this thing together, and they would do the best they could to uphold the Corps' reputation and sustain one another. Few men talked in terms of "death before dishonor," but the ancient code applied.

Through their shipboard briefings, the Marines learned a lot about Betio. The intelligence had been gleaned largely from aerial photographs and from a remarkable set taken by the submarine *Nautilus* during a bold run along Tarawa's coasts. A novel method was used to calculate the number of troops on Betio. The aerial photos showed latrines on rickety platforms out over the water. These structures were counted, and an estimate made as to how many bottoms each would be likely to accommodate. The total arrived at by simple multiplication came very close to the island's actual garrison of 4,836 men.

The photographs also revealed the extent of Betio's defenses. It was comforting for the Marines to learn that the campaign's planners had included softening-up operations by long-range Army bombers, carrier bombers and fighters, and naval gunfire vessels. The ships alone expected to lay 2,700 tons of hot metal on Betio before the Marines landed. General Julian Smith had been present during some of the Navy's gunfire planning sessions. Hearing the captains of two warships, a battleship and a cruiser, agree that the strength of their armor would enable them to move in close to do their shelling, the general urged them to do a good job. "When the Marines go in," he said, "the only armor they'll have is their khaki shirts." Smith was skeptical when he heard Rear Admiral Howard F. Kingman, commander of the gunfire group, speak of "obliterating" Betio's defenses. Although the general felt that the Navy deserved praise for its unfailing readiness to help the Marines solve their landing problems, he found that naval officers tended to be "unduly optimistic as to the results obtained from bombardments."

Their shipboard briefings acquainted the Marines with all aspects of the invasion. The transports would heave to about three miles west of Tarawa atoll, and the troops would board their landing craft and pass eastward through a channel into the atoll's vast triangular lagoon. After forming into waves, the craft would head south toward Betio's northern shore, another three miles away. About 500 yards from the beach was a reef, and this created a nagging worry. Tarawa's tides were unpredictable, and no one could be sure the reef would be covered with enough water to float the Higgins boats. They needed 3.5 feet, and chances were strong that there would be less. The only comforting thing about the situation was that the first three waves of troops would not be in Higgins boats but in amphibian tractors (officially LVTs but now better known as amtracs), and these would have no trouble churning over. The hundreds of Higgins boats coming behind would be in danger of getting hung up. The men assigned to them were warned they might have to wade, under fire, the last 500 yards to the beach, somehow manhandling their equipment, artillery pieces included. It was a sobering prospect.

There were many optimists, however—men who believed that the preliminary bombardment would prove as devastating as the Navy had predicted. Some went so far as to say they hoped there would be at least a few of the enemy left alive to fight. There were also men who were convinced that the survivors of the bombardment would evacuate Betio before the assault. Among those who expressed full confidence that the Marines would be able to handle the situation at its worst was the handsome, mustached commander of the 2nd Battalion, 2nd Marines, Lieutenant Colonel Herbert R. Amey, Jr., who told his men, "We are very lucky. This is the first Marine landing against a well-defended beach, and the first one over a coral reef. And it will be the first time the Japs have had the hell kicked out of them in a hurry!"

On D-minus-1, a special message was read to the troops on the transports. It was from their division commander, Julian Smith, who said: "A great offensive to destroy the enemy in the Central Pacific has begun. American air, sea, and land forces, of which this division is a part, initiate this offensive by seizing Japanese-held atolls in the Gilbert Islands which will be used as bases for future operations. . . . Army units . . . are simultaneously attacking Makin, 105 miles north of Tarawa. . . . Garrison forces are already en route to relieve us as soon as we have completed our job of clearing our objectives of Japanese forces. . . . What we do here will set a standard for all future operations in the Central Pacific Area. Observers from other Marine divisions and from other branches of our armed services, as well as those of our Allies, have been detailed to witness our operations. Representatives of the press are present. Our people back home are eagerly awaiting news of victories. . . . Your success will add new laurels to the glorious traditions of our Corps. Good luck, and God bless you all."

That evening many Marines attended religious services. One chaplain passed around mimeographed copies of a page of selections from the Scriptures. The page was entitled: "Spiritual Ration for D-day." In the western sea, the sun went down a flaming red.

The hours of rest were brief that night. Shipboard buglers blew reveille at 12:45 A.M. Some of the listeners wondered how many men were hearing the call for the last time. As the troops rose, so did a bright half moon, and the weatherdecks were well illuminated in spite of the blackout conditions. Breakfast consisted of beefsteak, eggs, potatoes, and coffee. This was the traditional pre-invasion meal, but some of the Navy surgeons protested that it was too substantial for men whose innards might soon require emergency stitching.

By two o'clock the fleet's gunfire support vessels were taking up positions three or four miles west of shadowy Betio. It was from here the warships would begin their pre-invasion bombardment, resorting to maneuvers as necessary. Plans called for the troop transports to group themselves several miles to the north, well away from the isle's guns; but as the result of a navigational error these vessels drew up on the northern fringe of the warships, even closer than they to the island. Unaware of the mistake, the transports began their unloading operations at once. Boatswains' whistles sounded, then davit winches whined as the Higgins boats were lowered to the water, empty except for their crews. The craft began circling near their respective ships, awaiting the signal to pull alongside and receive the Marines as they climbed down the cargo nets. The amtracs that would make up the first three waves entered the water through the bow doors of LSTs.

The preparations in the moonlight were accompanied by many a private prayer, not only by Marines but also by Navy and Coast Guard personnel who were going in as landing-craft crews, medical teams, shore parties (workmen in charge of unloading and organizing supplies), or in other capacities. One of the Coast Guardsmen, Boatswain's Mate 2nd Class Carl Jonas, found himself mumbling nervously, "Now I lay me down to sleep; I pray the Lord my soul to keep." He knew this wasn't appropriate, but what bothered him more was that he couldn't remember how the childhood prayer ended.

Until this time Betio had remained a still, dark strip in the moonlit sea. Some of the combat-loaded Marines on the decks of the transports began making jokes about the isle being inhabited not by enemy troops but by native girls in grass skirts, easy of conquest. Then a searchlight beam sprang from shore, swept the transport area, and snapped out. The Americans strained their eyes toward the light's point of origin, but could make out nothing. All was again dark and quiet, and it remained so. The incident, however, put an end to the jokes.

Although Admiral Shibasaki was as yet uncertain which of the beaches the Americans planned to use for their landing, he and his troops were ready, both in terms of defense and psychology. Some of the men had donned the *hachimaki*, the white headband that had symbolized defiance and acceptance of death for Japanese warriors down through the centuries. At the same time, there were others wearing the *sennimbari*, the "belt of a thousand stitches" made by the women at home, a charm to ward off the enemy's bullets. As friends separated to report to their respective defenses, they promised one another that if death found them they would meet again at Tokyo's Yasukuni Shrine. It was there that the spirits of Japan's illustrious war dead were believed to dwell as deities—as equals of the Emperor himself.

At 4:40 A.M. Betio sent up a red star-shell cluster that put a weird glow on the isle, the water, the widely scattered vessels, the uplifted American faces. Nothing more happened for nearly half an hour. Then the crew of an 8-inch Vickers gun (obtained when the Japanese took Singapore from the British) opened up in the direction of the warships. As the first boom rent the predawn stillness, many Americans jumped. A young sailor said, in something like amazement, "Why, they're firing on us!" The first shell, and those that followed, exploded in the water. Two or three were near misses that caused casualties.

The battlewagon *Maryland,* flagship of the Southern Attack Force, enlisted the support of two of her sister vessels and returned the fire, the heavy missiles looking like red comets as they arched in. One of the guns soon made a direct hit on a magazine filled with 8-inch shells. A sheet of flame rose 500 feet into the air, and the isle was rocked by an explosion whose shock waves came rolling out toward the fleet. After a moment of silent awe, the Americans began cheering. Some believed that a fuel dump had been hit, among them Coast Guardsman Carl Jonas, who was waiting to board a landing craft. "We shouted as though we were already in battle and had set the dump on fire ourselves." The blow gave special satisfaction to the crew of the *Maryland;* they and their vessel had gone through the Japanese attack on Pearl Harbor.

By this time, with the eastern sky turning gray, the transports were moving northward toward their proper position west of the channel leading into Tarawa's lagoon. The Higgins boats and amtracs, some filled with troops and some still carrying only their crews, bobbed along behind. Enemy guns harassed the movement, shells erupting in the water, some alarmingly close. In the confusion, a number of the small craft became separated from their transports.

Counterbattery fire from the warships was hammering Betio, the shellbursts flashing vividly, raising gushers of debris, turning into mushrooms of smoke. Flames and columns of sparks flared among some of the island's wooden buildings. From the mangrove thickets, panic-stricken birds rose in flocks, shrieking and floundering.

At 6:13, with daylight expanding across the sky, the warships desisted as bombers from the carriers *Essex, Bunker Hill,* and *Independence* swarmed over Betio, their plummeting missiles duplicating the drumbeats of the shells. Even though the isle was now almost entirely screened by smoke, the Grumman Hellcat fighters making up the escort bore in low for strafing runs, their .50-caliber machine guns loosing hundreds of rounds a minute. Through a mix-up in their orders, the carrier fliers had arrived half an hour later than expected. A scheduled strike by long-range Army bombers, whose crews were inexperienced in operations such as this, failed to materialize. This was a keen disappointment to the Marines, since the B-24s had been slated to blanket Betio with 2,000-pound bombs.

The carrier raid was completed in seven minutes, with the bombers and fighters winging off as a colorful sunrise portended a beautiful day. As the warships resumed their bombardment, the transport group to the north made its final preparations for the invasion. Covered by two destroyers, two minesweepers nosed eastward through the milky blue channel, not only to make a check for mines and other obstacles but also to use flags on buoys to mark a route for the landing craft to follow into the lagoon. All four of the vessels were fired upon by batteries on Betio's northern coast, and all four fired back. The two destroyers entered the lagoon and moved down close to the isle. "The Japs," one sailor would recall, "could have hit us with rocks." The *Ringgold,* as a matter of fact, was hit by two 5-inch shells, both duds. One smashed into the after engine room at the waterline. The ship's engineer officer, Lieutenant W. A. Parker, had nothing at hand to stuff into the spurting hole. In a move somewhat reminiscent of the boy at the legendary dike, Parker thrust his shoulder against the spot until his men found a suitable plug. The destroyer continued in action, soon blasting an ammunition dump out of existence.

Even as Betio and its encircling waters trembled under the heaviest naval bombardment ever laid on a target of this size, the landing craft —all of them now filled with their allotted troops—left the transport area and filed through the channel into Tarawa's lagoon. The craft began forming into waves about three miles north of the objective. According to United Press correspondent Richard W. Johnston, "The long, flat island was canopied in smoke, its splintered palms looking like the broken teeth of a comb. At many points, orange fire studded the haze, and at dead center a great spiral of black smoke curled up from a pulsing blaze. . . ."

The landings were scheduled to be made over a mile-long stretch of beaches starting at Betio's western extremity, or, viewed from the north, at the isle's extreme right. Moving leftward from this point, the beaches had been designated as Red 1, Red 2, and Red 3. In almost the exact center of the landing zone, a pier made of logs and crushed coral jutted out 500 yards to the reef. This was how the Japanese had solved the problem of the barrier, with its shallow covering of water, for their own landing purposes. The pier would have been a convenient route ashore for the Americans, except that it was, of course, thoroughly covered by the enemy's guns. It was even manned by a few machine gunners and snipers who were prepared to deliver enfilading fire both right and left as the Marines went by on their way to the beaches.

The first three waves of the assault—about 1,500 Marines in 100 amtracs—crossed the line of departure at 300-yard intervals. Several hundred yards ahead of the leading wave were two Higgins boats whose occupants had the commando-type mission of landing at the end of the pier and cleaning out the structure's troops. These Marines belonged to a reinforced scout-sniper platoon commanded by twenty-nine-year-old Lieutenant William D. "Hawk" Hawkins, commissioned in the field during the Guadalcanal campaign. Although he had grown up hating war and was opposed to the nation's entry into World War II, Hawkins had enlisted shortly after Pearl Harbor because he felt it was his duty. Now a specialist in slaughter and totally dedicated to his job, he did not expect to live to return home.

In the sky above the formation of landing craft was a spotter plane that had been catapulted from the flagship *Maryland*. The pilot, Lieutenant Commander Robert A. MacPherson, swooped low to examine the reef and was shocked by what he saw. There was so little water on the coral that some expanses were high and dry.

The naval gunfire, except for that of the destroyers *Ringgold* and *Dashiell* in the lagoon, was lifted at 8:55, and was followed at once by a brief air strike along the landing beaches. By this time the two boats carrying Lieutenant Hawkins and his scout-snipers had reached a ramp leading up to the end of the pier. Thanks to the thunderous distraction along the shoreline, 500 yards away, Hawkins was able to tackle his ticklish job without risking his entire force. He and five others, one man with a flamethrower, climbed the ramp and crept along the pier, first burning out an equipment shed and destroying a machine-gun crew, then flaming a partly submerged launch that held several snipers. Still farther on, Hawkins personally grenaded a machine-gun crew perched, unsuspecting, on a platform attached to the pier's pilings. Once they were unable to spot any more of the enemy, the six men hurried back to their boats, with bullets from shore snapping around them. It was the scout-sniper platoon's next mission to land with the early waves of the invasion.

The preliminary work of the warships and planes was now over. The pounding had done considerable damage, knocking out most of the big coast defense guns and various other positions, as well as killing hundreds of the enemy. Accomplished by luck was the destruction of Shibasaki's communications. Fragments of shrapnel were scattered over Betio almost as densely as lumps of ice after a hailstorm. But even many of the bunkers and pillboxes that had been hit were still fully operational, saved by their absorbent sand and thick walls and ceilings. Added to the defenses, now that the shelling had ended, were many light machine guns, brought from cover and emplaced in the isle's network of trenches.

The Japanese were shaken by the bombardment, by this unexpectedly violent introduction to the enemy's capabilities. But when the big guns fell silent and Betio stopped trembling, the able-bodied survivors rallied, to a man, and faced the looming crisis.

13

===== Patches of smoke from the smoldering isle drifted up the lagoon toward the three waves of amtracs as they labored toward the reef. Shells began bursting in the air above the widely spaced craft, and machine-gun bullets began raising small splashes in the water about them. This early fire was ineffectual. As the first wave of tractors clambered over the coral barrier, the gunners in the craft opened up with their .50-caliber machine guns.

Thousands of Americans were watching the show from a distance, among them Quartermaster 3rd Class Walker M. Gunter of the battleship *Colorado*. "I had a panoramic view of the invasion. As the waves of craft approached Betio, a shore battery opened up. You could see its flash as it fired. Sometimes the big shell splashed in the water; at other times you could see the black smoke of a direct hit. Fortunately, a destroyer soon moved in and put the gun out of action." But now, as the tractors began closing on the beach, the distant observers saw the Japanese loose a shower of missiles from antiboat and antitank guns. A Marine in one of the scores of Higgins boats still out beyond the reef said in surprise, "Why, they're shelling the hell out of them!"

Riding in one of the tractors of the first wave was PFC Richard M. Larsen, who would recall: "An antiboat gun stopped our craft about thirty yards from shore. We were in the midst of all kinds of fire. We jumped out into the shallow water and ran around to the back of the craft. A bullet hit me in the left side of the back of my neck and came out my right cheek. Another bullet just skinned the back of my neck. There were four of us behind the tractor, and we were trapped there. They threw mortar shells, machine-gun bullets, and rifle bullets at us."

Another tractor that was nearing shore made a sudden lurch as its driver was shot dead. A nearby passenger, a young lieutenant, yanked the body away and grabbed the controls, only to take a bullet himself a moment later. Then a shell found the range, bursting inside the craft, evoking a chorus of lamentations. The concussion alone was brutal; the flying shrapnel killed or wounded about ten men. Among those hurt but able to rise to their feet was Private N. M. Baird, an Oneida Indian who had been operating one of the tractor's machine guns. Dazed and deafened, Baird looked around. Bleeding comrades were "sprawled all over the place." Baird's assistant, who had been feeding a belt of ammunition into the gun, had slumped down, his pack and helmet blown away. "In the back of his head was a hole I could have put my fist in." Another Marine was lying on his back, a hand clasped over a bloody face. "He was mumbling something." The craft was now aground in the shallows, and a pillbox just in from shore was spraying it with machine-gun bullets, some of which tore through the thin armor. Baird yelled, "Let's get the hell out of here!" He and a dozen others went over the side, bullets pouring at them "like a sheet of rain." Only a few completed their splashing run to the beach, where they dropped behind a four-foot seawall made of coconut logs. Panting and trembling, some of them bleeding, the survivors were safe at least for the moment.

Crouching among the Marines in a first-wave tractor coming in over another stretch of water was one of Captain Louis Hayward's photographers, Corporal Obie E. Newcomb, Jr., formerly of the Associated Press. During the approach, Newcomb's companions threatened him with reprisals if their pictures did not appear in *Life* or *Look*. Five of these men were killed by bullets or shell fragments as the tractor neared shore, and a sixth died in a shellburst that disabled the craft on the narrow beach, at the very end of its journey. The twenty survivors, including Newcomb, jumped out under fire and took cover behind the seawall. Newcomb learned quickly what it meant to be a *combat* photographer. He had left his camera in the smoking tractor, and now picked up a BAR from beside a dead Marine in order to join the others in firing over the wall at the dark apertures of the area's pillboxes. "Brother, I was scared. Lifting my head above that wall to take aim the first time was the toughest job I ever had in my life." Later, Newcomb would return to the tractor for his camera and would spend the rest of the day taking 192 pictures under conditions as hot as any combat photographer has ever endured.

Most of the 100 amtracs that made up the first three waves were menaced by some kind of fire, with many casualties resulting. Among those killed was the top commander of the amtracs, Major Henry C. Drewes, shot through the head while joking about the stiffness of the opposition. But the majority of the craft made it to the beach—to this narrow, mile-long strip of coral sand, with its lacings of freshly killed fish, its acrid odor of smoke and gunpowder, its appalling background of rattling, booming, and flashing defenses, and—fortunately for the Marines—its coconut log seawall.

By 9:22 A.M. there were Americans on all three beaches: elements of the 3rd Battalion, 2nd Marines, on Red 1; of the 2nd Battalion, 2nd Marines, on Red 2; and of the 2nd Battalion, 8th Marines, on Red 3. But

An early moment at the seawall.

the American line was discontinuous and thin. Many men were pinned down behind the seawall, while those who had begun attacking were only as far as shellholes a few feet inland. On the beach along the wall, doctors and corpsmen were already moving among rows of white-faced wounded, rows that kept lengthening and were a hovering-place for Death. Even as they worked, some of the medical people themselves, crying out in alarm, became units in the grievous progression.

During these early moments, an engineer of the 1st Battalion, 18th Marines, Staff Sergeant William J. Bordelon, provided an example of courage and aggressiveness that was an inspiration to his comrades. Using demolitions in the form of satchel charges, Bordelon made successful assaults on three pillboxes, shattering them, turning them into tombs for their gunners. Although wounded during the work, the sergeant was not satisfied with his record. Obtaining a fresh charge, he moved against a fourth pillbox. This time the enemy shot him dead. Bordelon never knew it, but he had earned the Medal of Honor.

Everybody was well aware that many more Marines were needed

ashore if this infernal isle was to be taken, and anxious glances were turned out over the lagoon. The view that presented itself was almost enough to turn anxiety into despair. The Higgins boats of the support-ing waves were not approaching the beach but were grinding up on the reef in a long row, which made them sitting ducks for a storm of fire sent over the heads of the beached Marines. Some of the boats were bursting apart under the impact of shells. Others, their ramps lowered, were disgorging clusters of troops who were trying to wade ashore but were being decimated by shellfire and machine-gun bullets.

In a boat that reached the reef at the western end of the line was Coast Guardsman Carl Jonas and his shore-party associates, as well as a number of Marines. During a lull in the enemy's fire, the occupants emerged down the ramp into the shallow water and paused to scan the Red 1 shoreline to get their bearings. The entire leftward two-thirds of this beach was bare of Marines. Heavy fire from a strongpoint on the zone's left flank had sent the amtracs veering rightward toward Betio's western tip. It was there that the surviving craft had set down their surviving occupants.

Looking toward this point, Jonas was puzzled. There were groups of Marines wading out from shore, moving laboriously toward the reef and its boats. "Suddenly we realized with a shock that they were some of the wounded." One of the larger parties approached Jonas and his comrades. The first man to draw near, his brow tight with pain, had a bullet in the leg. The next two, one with a useless arm and the other with a chest wound, were helping each other, stumbling every few steps. Many more arrived, one with a curious network of bloody lines on his cheek and neck. Jonas and the others helped the unfortunates into the boat, easing some to sitting positions and placing others supine. All were exhausted and breathing heavily. The man with the chest wound had pink foam on his lips and his face was greenish. Jonas winced to note that some of the dying "were reaching up, like the men in the Italian primitive paintings of the damned in hell."

The Higgins boat backed off the reef, and the original occupants started wading toward the ominous-looking isle, spreading out to keep from presenting too solid a target, and soon losing contact with each other. To his right front, Jonas saw several silver geysers go up. Mortar shells. Even more worrisome, he was approaching an area of smaller and paler splashes made by a crossfire of machine-gun bullets. The Coast Guardsman scanned the shoreline, trying to determine where the fire was coming from, but learned nothing. On the right flank were several disabled amtracs, two of them burning. This spot, at least, seemed the one to head for. The course angled him away from the thickest machine-gun splashes. He saw other men—strangers all—plodding in the same direction. In about three feet of water now, Jonas squatted down so that only his nose, eyes and helmet were above the surface. He began the difficult job of "duck walking," digging the butt of his rifle into the coral and sand to help push himself along, vaguely troubled because one was supposed to protect one's weapon against even a *sprinkle* of salt water. The Coast Guardsman passed two or three dead Marines bobbing gently in the waves. His legs aching, he finally reached a sandbar only about fifty feet from shore. Sprawled over it were fifteen or twenty dead or wounded men. Working his way around the bar, Jonas continued toward the beach, once tumbling into a deep channel, but at last crawling up under the seawall near a knocked-out gun emplacement. He dropped prone, unhurt but dead weary. Jonas was so relieved at having reached shore safely that for the moment the perils ahead meant nothing to him. He just wanted "to lie there forever without moving a muscle."

Only two or three hundred Marines of the 3rd Battalion, 2nd Regiment, had made it ashore here at Betio's western end, the right flank of Red 1. These men were isolated; there was a 600-yard strip of hostile coastline between them and the Americans on Red 2. To make matters worse, the battalion's commander, who was supposed to be following the early waves with his reserves, was holding these men in their Higgins boats outside the reef, the craft circling while he scanned the beach with his binoculars. Growing more agitated over the carnage with each survey, the major could not bring himself to lead the reserves into the caldron. He radioed the Higgins boat that held the invasion's central command post: "Unable to land all. Issue in doubt." He was ordered to "land Red 2 and work west," but could not force himself to obey. Not completely paralyzed, the major spotted some tank-carrying LCMs nosing along the reef and ordered the Shermans unloaded and sent to his unit's aid. Six tanks came down the ramps, lumbered over the nearly dry reef, and plunged into the water, their tracks throwing up twin fountains behind them. Guided by men on foot, all managed to reach the surf safely; but then, while seeking a place to go ashore where they would not crush wounded men, four tumbled into potholes. The two surviving Shermans reported to Major Michael P. Ryan, who had landed as a company commander, but, in the battalion commander's absence, had quickly assumed the larger responsibility. Ryan was losing men at an alarming rate while trying to get an attack going, and the tanks were a godsend.

Off Red Beach 2, the commander of the 2nd Battalion, 2nd Marines, Lieutenant Colonel Herbert Amey, came over the reef in an amtrac he had commandeered. Amey had made the shipboard speech in which he termed himself and his unit "very lucky" to have been chosen to take part in this significant assault. Among the men in the craft with Amey was Associated Press correspondent William Hipple, to whom the colonel turned, flashing a grin under his well-shaped mustache, and said above the engine's roar, "I guess you get your story. Looks as though the Japs want a scrap." While the tractor was still some distance from shore it became entangled in a patch of barbed wire and bogged down. Amey ordered the occupants over the side into water that was about waist-deep. According to Hipple, they were caught in a crossfire laid down by rifles and machine guns, with automatic weapons of a heavier caliber making an occasional contribution. "The bullets hissed in the water." As the depth diminished, most of the men got down and began crawling on their hands and knees. Hipple's head was knocked back. "I felt the top of my steel helmet, and it was red-hot where a bullet had creased it." The colonel had remained on his feet. Now he gestured toward the beach with his .45 pistol. "Come on!" he shouted. "Those bastards can't stop us!" He began running, his feet raising great splashes. A burst of machine-gun fire caught him squarely in the chest and he went down, dead almost at once, his blood forming a pink cloud in the surf.

One of the officers from Amey's tractor who reached shore safely was Lieutenant Colonel Walter I. Jordan, a modest man with quiet ways who was acting as an observer for the newly forming 4th Marine Division and had no official combat responsibilities. To his astonishment, the colonel suddenly found himself to be the senior officer on Red Beach 2, and it became his duty to assume leadership over a battalion of strangers. He set up a command post in a shellhole and, with the aid of a volunteer runner, assessed the situation, which was not encouraging. The battalion's organization was badly disrupted. Platoons were out of position, their squads and fire teams intermixed. The killed and wounded included many officers and noncoms. Surviving leaders were trying to put together groups to attack the defenses, but the enemy's volume of fire made the job almost impossible. Jordan sent out a message requesting reinforcements.

The situation was only slightly better on Red 3, the eastern beach, where the 2nd Battalion, 8th Marines, had come in. It was off this coastline that the two destroyers had operated just prior to the landing, and their fire had kept these defenders off-balance for some minutes longer than those on Red 1 and Red 2. A Japanese in the Red 3 zone who survived the battle would remember the point-blank blasts of the destroyers as "most terrifying," a reaction that would have surprised those Marines who believed that all Japanese military men were relatively fearless because they were eager to die and gain eternal glory. Commander of the assault team on Red 3 was Major Henry P. "Jim" Crowe, a sturdy redhead with a booming voice. The major, who had the unqualified respect and devotion of his men, had waded ashore with the same kind of bravura as Amey, and had got away with it, although he drew fire and was once knocked down by the blast of an underwater mine. Now Crowe was trying to broaden his hold on the narrow strip of sand in preparation for his attack inland. Each time a unit moved, it drew streaks of bullets from the looming mounds that were bunkers and pillboxes, and from camouflaged machine-gun nests in the connecting trenches. The maneuvers left trails of dead and wounded. On Red 3, as elsewhere, reinforcements were needed.

Crowe was encouraged by the arrival of several Sherman tanks on his beach early in the fight. The top commander of the invasion's Sherman tank battalion tried to land at this time but did not succeed. Falling badly wounded in shallow water, Lieutenant Colonel Alexander B. Swenceski was obliged to drag himself atop a tangle of dead Marines in order to keep from drowning. With the corpses starting to decompose beneath him, the colonel would lay there all day, all night, and well into D-plus-1 before being found and treated.

Although the invasion's opening hours offered the Marines no opportunity to land their artillery, a few 75-millimeter halftracks soon rolled from the ramps of lighters grounded on the reef. Only one made it as far as the surf. It fired several times, then tried to change its position and bogged down. A pair of 37-millimeter guns laboriously manhandled through the shallows had better luck, arriving on Red 3 and settling down to steady work, a boost to the morale of the riflemen who saw them recoil and heard them bark.

These were anxious and uncertain moments for the invasion's high brass, Rear Admiral Harry W. Hill, in overall charge of the Southern Attack Force, and the 2nd Division's Julian Smith, both of whom were on board the *Maryland*, southwest of the isle. (Kelly Turner and Holland Smith had sailed with the Northern Attack Force to Makin, where the Army was landing against light opposition.) Smoke hanging over Betio obscured the view from the *Maryland*'s deck, and the battlewagon's radios were malfunctioning; not every message from shore was being picked up. For the conduct of the assault, Harry Hill and

Julian Smith had to rely heavily on the command post then operating from a Higgins boat in the lagoon, outside the reef. Top man in this mobile center was Colonel David M. Shoup, thirty-nine years old, stocky, ruddy-faced, serious-eyed, something of a paradox. Hard-boiled and profane, Shoup used grammar like that of an undereducated sergeant, yet he had graduated from college with high grades and found pleasure in composing poetry. The colonel had absolute faith in the Marine Corps' ability to achieve its goals, however difficult. Today both the Corps and Shoup's talents as a leader were being put to the ultimate test. Among those in the boat with Shoup were former Raider Evans Carlson, another observer for the 4th Division; the commander of an artillery battalion, Lieutenant Colonel Presley M. Rixey; a regimental surgeon, Commander Donald Nelson; Shoup's operations officer, Major Thomas A. Culhane; and several enlisted men, including a sergeant with a radio on his back.

Shoup had no intention of directing the fight from afar, and soon flagged down an amtrac that was carrying casualties from the beach to the transports. The colonel had the pathetic cargo transferred to the Higgins boat, established his CP in the tractor, and ordered the driver to head back over the reef toward the left half of Red 2. The first resistance came in the form of aerial shellbursts that showered the men with a granular shrapnel that was nearly impotent, though "it was strong enough," as Shoup said later, to go through your dungarees and cut you." Soon afterward, "a kid named White was shot, the LVT was holed, and the driver went into the water. At that point I said, 'Let's get out of here,' moved my staff over the side, and waded to the pier."

The men of the CP were still about 400 yards from shore as they gathered under the pier, among its trestles, which gave them at least a measure of protection. Now they paused to look back, up the shimmering lagoon, to watch two reserve battalions approaching the reef. Shoup had ordered Major Wood B. Kyle's 1st Battalion, 2nd Marines, to land on Red 2, west of the pier, and Major Robert H. Ruud's 3rd Battalion, 8th Marines, on Red 3, to the east. Kyle's men were in amtracs that had survived the first round-trip run, while Ruud's were in Higgins boats.

The tractors came under antiboat fire before they reached the reef. One took a hit at its forward end, spinning it like a top, and its occupants were thrown into the water. Two or three lay still. The sputtering survivors shed their gear and began swimming, some toward the reef, others back up the lagoon. PFC John G. Behm was among those in the latter group. "The lagoon was full of circling landing craft, and a Higgins boat picked us up and took us out to one of the transports, where we obtained new gear. We were shortly on our way in again." Behm and most of his comrades made it ashore, but had trouble finding their platoon. As Major Kyle's amtracs had crossed the reef, the enemy's fire increased, and the formation was disrupted. The majority of the surviving tractors maneuvered their way to their prescribed beach just west of the pier, but a number veered to the right and landed on Red 1, at the isle's western tip. Major Kyle's loss was Major Mike Ryan's gain. Ryan was more than glad to receive these unexpected reinforcements.

Major Ruud's battalion, in Higgins boats that came down the lagoon east of the pier, fared worse than Kyle's. The Japanese in this sector had managed to get one of their coast defense guns back into action, and as the boats of the leading wave churned up on the reef, first one, and then a second disintegrated with a dazzling flash and a reverberating clang. In both cases, the dark-hued debris that settled on the shallow, sunlit water of the reef was interspersed with fragments that were a brilliant red. From his position under the pier, Dave Shoup used his radio to call down naval gunfire, and the big weapon was soon silenced for the second time. But as the occupants of the other first-wave boats began wading toward Betio, the butchery was taken up by antiboat guns and machine guns. Two out of three of these Marines did not make it ashore.

As succeeding waves of waders, true to their training, began to follow gamely, some of the men passed within a hundred yards of Shoup's CP, and the colonel snapped to his aides, "Get those damn fools over here to the pier, or they'll all be killed!" The aides began shouting, but their voices merely merged with the din from shore. Better results were obtained by a pistol shot fired into the air by Evans Carlson. Urgent gestures brought some of the waders over, and Carlson led them along the pier to the beach. Returning unharmed to the CP, the colonel picked up another group and took it in. This time a bullet passed between his thighs, leaving one with a painful abrasion, but he made it back again.

Major Ruud's fourth wave, Ruud with it, tried to come in at the end of the pier. The boats received so hot a reception that Ruud withdrew them to reappraise the situation. Orders soon came down from regimental headquarters, on board one of the warships, for the major to "land no further troops until directed." The survivors of Ruud's earlier waves, completely disorganized, were absorbed by Jim Crowe's battalion.

As small-arms fire chipped away at the trestles about them, Dave Shoup and his men worked their way along the pier toward the beach. The party made the last leg of the trip in another commandeered amtrac. When nearly in, Shoup noticed several Marines cringing behind one of the wrecked craft. Calling them "yellow sons of bitches," he jolted the men into following him ashore. Shoup was no sooner on the beach than a mortar shell exploded near him, peppering his legs with shrapnel and knocking him to his knees. He was momentarily sickened. Then, ordering his concerned aides to keep away, he got back on his feet and was again vigorously functional except for a limp. When the aides headed into a large shellhole, Shoup followed and said, "Okay, let's get going. If we don't secure a piece of this island by nightfall, we're in a spot." It was then about noon. The indomitable colonel soon had his CP set up behind a long, low air-raid shelter about fifty feet inland. While busy establishing his communications, he was told there were live Japanese in the shelter and that it could not be blown unless he moved. Shoup simply ordered the apertures plugged with debris and the entrances watched by guards. Thus he began running the battle for Betio almost within arm's length of a number of the isle's able-bodied defenders.

Shoup's first act was to radio Julian Smith, on board the *Maryland*, the location of his command post. Enormously relieved that the work ashore had gained a base of operations, the general turned to Red Mike Edson, who was serving as his chief of staff, and said, "Well, they've done it!" Edson's response was reserved. His own estimate of the situation was that it was still critical—which it was. The Japanese, however, were already somewhat less confident of victory than they had been at first. In spite of the punishment the Americans had been handed, their assault had not been smashed in the surf as anticipated. Too many hundreds of these unexpectedly determined men, advancing past their dead comrades, had established themselves on shore. Had the Japanese known of Dave Shoup's arrival, their apprehensions would have increased, for he was exactly the kind of leader the American crisis required. When at 12:30 he decided to send Evans Carlson out to the *Maryland* to explain the situation to Harry Hill and Julian Smith, Shoup said, "Tell the admiral and the general that we are going to stick and fight it out."

Shoup had been somewhat encouraged by his first impressions of the fighting. There was less demoralization among the Marines than he might have expected. "A surprising number," he said later, "displayed a fearless eagerness to go to the extreme for their country and fellow

Making the break inland.

men." These Marines were attacking the deadly mounds by firing at apertures, dropping hand grenades through air vents, and using flame-throwers and demolitions against the low, dark entrances in the rear. Muffled screams were often heard, and these were nothing less than the sweetest music. Marines, too, were crying out as they were hit by bullets or mortar fragments. A man had only about a 50 percent chance of coming through this early work whole.

Fighting on Dave Shoup's left was Crowe's battalion, bolstered by remnants of Ruud's. An observer in this area was Time-Life correspondent Robert Sherrod, who had waded in with the fifth wave, undergoing his share of fire but reaching shore unhurt. He was now sitting alongside the seawall with several Marines, feeling relatively safe. A dead man lay near, and Sherrod heard someone say, "His name was Cowart. He married a girl in Wellington." Then two more corpses were brought and placed with Cowart, and Sherrod found that "already the smell of death under the equator's sun could be detected faintly." The correspondent soon noticed a Marine coming along the beach at a brisk walk. As he reached Sherrod's position, the man spotted a buddy sitting with the group and grinned and waved. At that instant a bullet thudded into his temple. He spun around and fell dead, his body coming to rest in such a way that his eyes, wide open and bulging, looked squarely at Sherrod and his companions. Of the many things he saw during his combat tours, the correspondent would remember this as "the most gruesome."

The shot had been fired by a rifleman concealed in a coconut log pillbox only about fifteen feet in from the seawall. Major Crowe was on the scene, and he shouted, "Somebody go get that son of a bitch!" With Sherrod and his group rising cautiously to watch, three Marines climbed the wall, the first carrying several small blocks of TNT, and the other two with a flamethrower, one bearing the heavy tank on his back, one handling the hose and nozzle. The two or three blocks of TNT that were exploded in the structure's entrance did not kill the Japanese but prompted him to come running out. Sherrod saw him "flare up like a piece of celluloid" as the flamethrower stream hit him. The man collapsed into a charred heap, and his executioners began ducking as the bullets in his cartridge belt exploded like a string of firecrackers. Sherrod and the other observers ducked too, since "nobody wanted to be killed by a dead Jap."

Looking westward along the beach toward the base of the pier, Sherrod saw several Marines set up an 81-millimeter mortar and begin lobbing shells inland. Shortly two of the crew fell, one dead and the other wounded, shot from another pillbox. Again the men with the TNT and flamethrower went into action. This time the demolitions man used a heavy charge, and the pillbox went up with a roar, some of its parts rising for fifty feet. The flamethrower men turned the remains into a furnace. Four of the enemy perished.

Sherrod was impressed by the coolness affected by the Marine officers he observed, but felt that at least one was carrying his bravura a bit too far. Captain Aubrey K. Edmonds strode around nonchalantly, wearing no helmet, refusing to duck even when snipers were shooting at him. Edmonds, however, had already proved himself to be more than a man of reckless courage; he had shown some effective leadership. On the way down the lagoon, as his amtrac crossed the reef, the captain had noted enemy fire coming from the pier, which had been reoccupied after William Hawkins and his scout-snipers cleared it. Edmonds promptly headed for the pier and led several of his men in a successful replay of Hawkins's exploit.

As for Hawkins and his platoon, they had been busy inland ever since coming ashore, attacking pillboxes and machine-gun nests, suffering losses but remaining potent. Sherrod got a glimpse of Hawkins during one of the lieutenant's trips to the beach for more ammunition. Some-one said, "Get down, Hawk, or you'll get shot." Hawkins answered, "Aw, those bastards can't hit anything." Actually the lieutenant's jacket was bloodstained, but the wound didn't seem to bother him. He was soon back over the seawall and in action again.

In the early afternoon, no part of the front on Red Beaches 2 and 3 was more than 200 yards inland, and most parts were decidedly less, but the Marines were at least gaining a toehold. They had some forcible and noisy aid. Ahead of the front lines, carrier planes came down bombing and strafing. Destroyers in the lagoon fired on the long tail that made up eastern Betio, beyond Red 3. From their positions in the sea south-west of the isle, the other warships lobbed shells at targets on the southern shore, opposite the beachhead. Dave Shoup's biggest worry at this time was that, as the result of faulty radio communications, he was not in contact with the Marines on Red 1, at Betio's western end. He had no idea of what was happening there. Actually, Mike Ryan was handling the situation well, was fighting to gain a toehold of his own.

Coast Guardsman Carl Jonas found the scene on Ryan's beach "highly theatrical," suggestive of a dozen motion pictures he had seen. The sand was a gleaming white, the knocked-out gun emplacement just in from the beach burned and blackened. Along the beach to the left a mortar crew was operating, and on the right was a gathering of wounded and a Navy doctor who was moving about silently, giving injections of mor-phine and adjusting bloodstained battle dressings. In the pendular surf, several corpses were gliding in and out, in and out.

Jonas teamed up with another Coast Guardsman, and the two began making themselves useful, helping to unload the occasional amtrac that managed to make it ashore with supplies, and carrying wounded men from the front on a litter, a job they found strenuous because they had to move at a crouch to reduce their chances of being shot. When there was nothing to do, the men lay in their foxholes on the beach and rested. Once they saw a Marine come walking from the front and drop to a sitting position against the seawall. There was a bullet crease in his helmet, and he was in a mild state of shock. Arms clasped around his knees and head bent forward, he kept murmuring about the men who had been killed near him. At last he stood up, took a deep breath, climbed the seawall, and went back to the front. Said Carl Jonas's buddy: "You can say what you want about the Marines, but they got guts."

At another time Jonas was helping to unload .50-caliber ammunition from an amtrac when he heard rifle fire that sounded closer than it should have been; the Marines at the front seemed to be retreating toward the beach. The Japanese on the southern shore had opened up with a heavy-caliber gun and with mortars, which raised the possibility they were planning a counterattack; the Marines were pulling back and setting up a defensive position. A runner from the front reported the news to an officer on the beach, who shouted to the men in the area, "Okay, let's form some kind of line!" The line was established on a crest of sand just inland from the seawall, and the Coast Guardsman was part of it. As he lay there nervously awaiting the expected counterattack, he again found the setting suggestive of a motion picture. "But," he thought, "it isn't supposed to end this way." To Jonas's great relief, the situation was saved by a combination of naval gunfire and aerial bombing and strafing. "The whole Jap side of the island seemed to rise in splinters and flame." It was an example of the kind of punishment that often convinced Japanese fighting men that all was lost and prompted some of its survivors to kill themselves. One of the paradoxes of Japan's philosophy of war was that such suicides were considered heroes even though they achieved nothing in passing and actually made the enemy's task easier.

The Marines were soon advancing again. These men of Red 1, in fact, were on their way to making the best gains of the day. Mike Ryan continued in charge. The original battalion commander, unable to muster his spirit, remained afloat in the lagoon until midafternoon. Then, receiving stern orders from Julian Smith to go ashore and regain control of his unit, he went in. But he followed the earlier order, and landed on Red 2. Since there was still 600 yards of enemy-held territory between these lines and those on Red 1, the unhappy officer was simply left at loose ends.

The destruction inflicted on Betio's defenses was not yet great enough to have a significant effect on the fire sweeping the waters of the landing areas, and the Marines who filtered ashore during the afternoon had as tough a time as their predecessors. According to one, every man who made the trip was "an American fish in a Japanese rain barrel." Like the morning's landing operations, those of the afternoon were inhibited and kept in a state of confusion, but were not stopped. A particular problem was that of supply. The aid stations were short of medical necessities, and not enough ammunition and water were reaching the front. Ship-to-shore radio communications remained poor. Compounding the malfunctions of the *Maryland*'s gear was the damage done by salt water to many of the small sets taken ashore.

On the Japanese side, thanks to the preliminary work of the U.S. Navy, communications were almost nonexistent. Inland from Red 3 stood Admiral Shibasaki's command center, a concrete blockhouse large enough to hold two or three hundred men. With his telephones useless, Shibasaki's ability to command was limited. He hadn't been able even to consider organizing a coordinated counterattack that might have driven the first Marines from the beaches. Illuminated by lanterns and candles, his blockhouse was a gloomy, compartmented place, its air stale and smelling of perspiration. Late afternoon found the rooms bustling. Staff personnel were rummaging through stacks of papers, selecting those that must be burned lest the enemy learn damaging war secrets. Unit commanders and runners from the front were hurrying in and out, and wounded men were being carried in and placed along the walls. Amid these activities, a wild-eyed officer ran in waving a bloody *samurai* sword and boasting that he had just killed a dozen Americans. He gathered several volunteers for a new mission, and the group rushed out. Although Shibasaki's phones were dead, there were still radio communications with Tokyo. But this gave the admiral little solace. He received no word that help was on the way. At one time a radio officer

Corpses and wrecked amtracs at seawall.

called for silence in the room and read a message he claimed had been sent by Hirohito. "You have all fought gallantly. May you continue to fight to the death. *Banzai!*" Perhaps the message was composed by Shibasaki. It was an inspiration to the Bushido stalwarts, merely an edict of doom to the others.

As the sun neared the sea west of Betio, the sounds of battle diminished, although Japanese machine gunners and riflemen continued to pepper the pier and its waters, which had become the chief landing route for both reinforcements and supplies. Nature was indifferent to the day's bloodshed, and the tropical sunset was one of exceeding beauty. Betio and its wreckage were bathed first by a mellow amber and then by a rich violet. Shortly afterward, except for its smoldering fires, the isle was cloaked in darkness.

By this time, some 1,500 Americans had been killed or wounded. The able-bodied Marines on shore numbered about 3,500, which was nothing like the three-to-one edge over the enemy that such a situation called for. Shibasaki, in fact, probably had almost as many effectives as the Marines, if his combat-trained labor troops were to be included in the count. Fortunately, the Americans had additional reserves available. Bobbing around in Higgins boats in the lagoon were the men of the 1st Battalion, 8th Marines, while still aboard ship were the three battalions of the 6th Marines. These last had come to the Gilberts under the control of Kelly Turner and Holland Smith, who felt they might be needed to support the Army on Makin; but as the situation on Betio grew critical, Julian Smith had obtained their release to him. While his request was pending, the enterprising general had begun organizing his headquarters people into an emergency landing party that he planned to lead ashore himself should his request be refused.

The Marines digging in on Betio for the night occupied two separate fronts, one in the center fanning out from the pier, and one in the west. Mike Ryan's men had pressed down the west coast about 500 yards, but toward the end of the day the major pulled the line back 200 yards in order to set up a tight defense, a 250-yard semicircle with a flank on either shore of the isle's tiny northwestern peninsula. The central holdings, which embraced a part of the airfield, were about 700 yards wide and about 300 yards inland at their deepest point. In all, the Marines held only one-tenth of the objective.

Stationed in the darkness on either flank of the interrupted beachhead was a single Sherman tank, *Colorado* on the left with Crowe, and *China Gal* on the right with Ryan. *Colorado*, although dented and blackened by enemy fire, had come through the day in pretty good shape. *China Gal*'s 75-millimeter gun had been ruined, but her bow machine gun was still operating. Most of the other tanks were out of commission. Ironically, two had been disabled by American aircraft.

Unaware that Japanese communications had been disrupted, the Marines braced for a general counterattack. Betio's commander may have missed his opportunity during the day, but he would surely act now. Night attacks were a Japanese tradition. Correspondent Robert Sherrod, in a foxhole near the seawall, found the situation "worse than wading into the machine-gun fire, because the unknown was going to happen under cover of darkness." As the slender moon volunteered a measure of light, the Americans at the front peered anxiously at the clusters of unassaulted pillboxes and trenches. The maze of shadows remained still. On board the *Maryland,* Julian Smith and his aides stood at the rail and listened for the crash of gunfire that would herald the dreaded action. Some sporadic shooting was heard, but the wider crash never came.

14

Victory at a Price

══════ Although the night of November 20–21 saw little movement on the part of the Marines at the front, there was plenty of American activity along the pier and on the beach to the right and left of its base. An important achievement was the landing of Presley Rixey's howitzers, some in amtracs or rubber boats, others borne in pack loads by wading artillerymen. Also landed were ammunition, water, and other supplies, many of the items carried in from the end of the pier by shore-party personnel. This work was supervised by the assistant division commander, Brigadier General Leo D. "Dutch" Hermle, sent from his shipboard headquarters by Julian Smith. Moving outward from shore were casualties on stretchers. Some were placed on rubber rafts and pushed to the reef, while others were carried there. Sometimes the Americans tried to use the pier as it was meant to be used, but this only made them clearer targets for the enemy's fire.

Removing the wounded by rubber raft.

A good part of this fire, the Americans discovered, came not from the island but from totally unexpected spots on the water—from the wrecked landing craft scattered between the beach and the reef. Small parties of the enemy had stolen out from shore and were using the machine guns that had been left on their mounts. As tracers from the weapons crisscrossed in the darkness, those Americans watching from the beach gaped in wonderment. Thought Robert Sherrod: "Clever, courageous little bastards!" Almost equally surprising was the fire coming from another offshore source, the hull of the *Saida Maru,* a Japanese derelict on the reef northwest of the pier. Curiously, however, the Japanese on shore missed out on an opportunity that would have meant more than the offshore efforts. As a Marine officer put it: "Why didn't the Japs use mortars that first night? People were lying on the beach so thick you couldn't walk. All the Japs had to do was fire at the water's edge and they would have killed hundreds of Marines."

Even as it was, the night saw an increase in deaths and maimings. Some of the badly wounded were cared for in an emergency hospital that had been set up in a reduced bunker soon after the invasion began. The operating was done by a slender, bespectacled, black-bearded Navy doctor, Lieutenant Herman R. Brukardt. He was assisted by three corpsmen, one of whom said later, "We used up four flashlights the first night." The able Brukardt was much admired by his patients, and he, in turn, found them to be "the bravest youngsters" he had ever seen. "When our anesthetics gave out, I had to perform some painful operations, but very few of the men let out a whimper." Of the 125 patients Brukardt treated, only four died.

The night was long and worrisome for the Marines at the front. Only toward morning did they begin to realize that no counterattack was coming. At about five o'clock a new apprehension developed as several Japanese planes were heard approaching across the sea. But the craft dropped only a few sticks of bombs—on territory held by their friends —and went on, their drone soon fading. Then the darkness in the east gave way to silver and pink and the sun came up, its dazzling rays portending another clear day, at the same time spotlighting the isle's many unassaulted defenses. In more ways than one, Betio promised to be very hot again.

But the Americans who were to draw the enemy's earliest fire that day were not on shore. They were in Higgins boats out beyond the reef, where they had spent the night awaiting orders to land. In this battle that was excessive with unlucky Marine units, none had a more terrible time than Major Lawrence C. Hays's 1st Battalion, 8th Regiment. It wasn't enough that communications failures had caused these men to receive their orders only after spending many hours packed in bobbing boats, and that they had been assailed with discouraging reports on the battle's progress; worse yet, the breezes from the beach kept bringing them the smell of their dead comrades.

It was shortly after six o'clock that Hays's men began wading in from the reef, their destination the central beach. They were hit not only by fire from shore but also from the *Saida Maru,* and many of them fell, some quietly in instant death, others giving the involuntary cry of "Oh, my God!" that is so common among a battlefield's stricken. Men thrashed in the water as they tried to regain their feet, and some of the badly disabled drowned. Among those lucky enough to escape unhurt was PFC James Collins, who was shocked to see patches of water that were red with blood. "I never prayed so hard in my life. Only three men out of twenty-four in my boat ever got to shore that I know of." While Sergeant Gene Ward was making the trip, he was acutely conscious of plaintive cries of "Corpsman! Corpsman!" He saw one man, already burdened with a machine-gun tripod in addition to his personal gear, struggling to lift a helpless buddy. When about halfway in, Ward found himself in a very shallow stretch of water and dropped prone. "I wormed along on my belly. Recalling that coral cuts badly, I kept looking at my hands and wrists. They were bloody but I couldn't feel anything." The sergeant soon passed a wounded friend who was creeping in the opposite direction, and he asked him how badly he'd been hit. "I'll make it," the man said, and he kept going. Some of the bullets from shore, Ward noted, skipped lightly along on the water, raising several small splashes before sinking. Those coming from the *Saida Maru* seemed to be of a heavier caliber.

Not everyone was aware of the gunners in the shadows of the wrecked vessel. An amtrac loaded with casualties from the beach was passing near it when a voice cried in English, "Hold up a minute. We're stranded here and need a lift." The driver of the tractor shouted back, "Sorry, Mac. I've got to get these wounded to a hospital ship right away." As the craft sped on, a burst of machine-gun bullets rattled across its stern. The driver exclaimed, "What the hell?" and then added, "Those tricky son of a bitches!"

At 7:30 A.M. the *Saida Maru* was bombed and strafed by American carrier planes. The Japanese guns were not silenced, even though four bombs and hundreds of machine-gun bullets struck home. Some of the bullets carried among the wounded Marines dotting the reef, and they screamed in protest. Equally unsuccessful at reducing the guns of the

Saida Maru were Rixey's shore-based pack howitzers and a party of engineers with explosives. The job was finally accomplished by naval gunfire, which left the hulk a mass of twisted steel, its occupants torn to pieces.

While Major Hays and his men were struggling ashore, with more than one out of three becoming a casualty, Dave Shoup tried to help by directing assaults on the chattering and booming emplacements ashore. Rixey and his pack howitzers performed ably at this time. So did William Hawkins and his scouts and snipers. But the lieutenant's luck had run out. His posthumous Medal of Honor citation explains that he began the morning by "personally initiating an assault on a hostile position fortified by five enemy machine guns, and crawling forward in the face of withering fire, boldly firing point-blank into the loopholes, and completing the destruction with grenades. Refusing to withdraw after being seriously wounded in the chest during this skirmish, he steadfastly carried the fight to the enemy, destroying three more pillboxes before he was caught in a burst of Japanese shellfire and mortally wounded. His relentless fighting spirit in the face of formidable opposition and his exceptionally daring tactics were an inspiration to his comrades during the most critical phase of the battle." After Betio was secured, the captured airport was named Hawkins Field.

Betio's long eastern tail, where no Marine had yet set foot, was given strong attention during the Hays landing. Howitzer shells and 81-millimeter mortars were rained upon it, and scores of carrier planes assailed it with bombs and bullets. From his position westward along the beach, Robert Sherrod could feel the isle trembling. The show was an impressive one, but the correspondent found himself wondering, "Are we knocking out many of those pillboxes?"

One of Louis Hayward's photographers, Marine Gunner John F. Leopold, made his landing at this time. The day happened to be Leopold's forty-first birthday, and he was sure it would be his last. But he felt he might be able to take some good pictures before he died. "It really didn't matter which way I aimed the lens. There was action in every direction. It was a photographer's paradise—in hell!"

Dave Shoup's plans for the second day called for Crowe and Ruud, on Red 3, the eastern beach, to attack to their left toward Betio's tail. Jordan and Kyle, on Red 2 in the center, were to press across the isle's airport to the southern coast. Hays, who in spite of his losses soon had several hundred men on Red 2, was ordered to attack to the right, in an attempt to link up with Ryan in the Red 1, or western, zone. Ryan was making an independent attack down the 800 yards of Betio's west coast, which had been designated as Green Beach.

Shoup felt that the attack plans were well conceived but was far from sure they would succeed. At 11:00 A.M. he consulted with Julian Smith's command post on the *Maryland*. Those observing the colonel noted that the hand that held the phone was trembling slightly. Shoup had been running this difficult battle for thirty-six hours without rest. Moreover, his leg wounds were paining him. "We're in a mighty tight spot," he informed the shipboard CP. Asked whether he needed more men ashore, he said he did. He was told that the 6th Marines would be landed as soon as possible.

Shoup was still operating from behind the air-raid shelter just in from the beach, and the structure still held live Japanese. At noon the scout-sniper platoon, now commanded by Gunnery Sergeant Jared J. Hooper, was sitting around the CP awaiting new orders from the colonel when one of the Japanese chose to act. He thrust his rifle through a ventilator and fired a random shot. It struck Corporal Leonce "Frenchy" Olivier in the leg. The scout-snipers got their new orders at once. "Hooper," Shoup yelled, "get those Japs out of there!" Hooper and two or three others pulled the debris away from an entrance and emptied their rifles into the dark interior. They ducked back as a rifle cracked in response. Next the scout-snipers began tossing in grenades and blocks of TNT. One of the men was audacious enough to make quick appearances at the entrance to try to learn if any of the occupants were still capable of firing. Nothing happened, so the Marines went in with flashlights. They found a scattering of torn bodies, all of them very still.

The general attack that Shoup had ordered was under way. Ryan's independent efforts in the west faced only moderate opposition, but the going was tough in the other zones. Under a torrid sun, small groups of Marines inched forward from shellholes, from behind fallen trees, from spots among wrecked buildings and jumbles of broken concrete. Closing with the enemy in his blazing pillboxes and trenches, they fired their rifles and pistols, they threw hand grenades, and they used demolitions and flamethrowers. They were supported by mortars, machine guns, artillery, tanks, 75-millimeter halftracks, 37-millimeter guns, and aircraft. Although the Japanese died by scores, Marines fell too, victims not only of the ground defenses but of fire from the tops of coconut trees. These snipers were hard to spot. Their gunpowder was smokeless, and some of them wore hats made of coconut hulls as a part of their camouflage.

The Marines gained some encouragement from the Japanese themselves, who, not wanting to risk being captured, were beginning to kill themselves in growing numbers. Attacking units came upon groups of these bloody suicides. One man would have a knife or a bayonet in the midriff. Another would be lying parallel with his rifle, a big toe on the trigger and his forehead shattered. Still another would have a gouged-out chest cavity and a missing hand, which indicated he had held a grenade to his stomach. Under the circumstances, these sights were more agreeable than horrifying. These Japanese had killed or maimed their last Americans.

Crowe and Ruud made only minor progress in their attack eastward, and Hays was frustrated in his attempt to reach Ryan in the west. But by midafternoon Ryan was wrapping up his conquest of Green Beach. At the same time, Jordan and Kyle were establishing a perimeter defense on Betio's south coast. From his Navy spotter plane high above the island, Robert MacPherson noticed activity on the southern beach and dipped low to take a better look. The men on the beach grinned and waved, and MacPherson was elated. When he entered the incident in his log, he wrote: "There is no mistaking the smile of a grinning Marine."

Things were improving. In addition, two battalions of the 6th Marines were preparing to land. The coming of this regiment was viewed with mixed feelings by at least one of Dave Shoup's aides, who protested that these men were cocky enough as it was. "Now they'll come in and claim they won the battle." The regiment's reputation went back to the First World War. Along with the 5th Marines, the 6th had fought brilliantly in France and had helped to create some Marine Corps legends. Arriving at the Château-Thierry front as the French lines were collapsing under German attacks, the brigade was urged by a French officer to retreat at once. "Retreat, hell!" a young captain responded. "We just got here!" More recently, the 6th had helped to clean up Guadalcanal. As if to confirm the aide's belief in the unit's cockiness, some of its men debarked from their transport singing lustily, "From the halls of Montezuma . . ."

The 2nd Battalion, 6th, under Lieutenant Colonel Raymond L. Murray, landed not on Betio but on Bairiki, about 3,000 yards to the southeast, a move made to keep Betio's surviving defenders from wading and swimming to that isle. Bairiki held only fifteen of the enemy, and they were roasted to death in a gasoline fire ignited by strafing aircraft. Major William K. Jones's 1st Battalion, 6th, landed on Green Beach, Betio, where Ryan's troops had prepared the way. The landing was attended by some confusion, and an amtrac was blown out of the water by a mine, but there was little or no resistance from the enemy ashore. Many of Ryan's grimy, ragged, and exhausted Marines greeted the fresh troops with tears in their eyes. They had a good chance of staying alive now.

Upon receiving a message from Dave Shoup, Jones ordered his men to dig in for the night and be prepared to attack eastward in the morning.

In a report on the second day's fighting made to Julian Smith, Shoup spoke of the Marines as "dishing out hell and catching hell." The report ended with a terse summary: "Casualties many. Percentage dead unknown. Combat efficiency—we are winning." Late that evening the dog-tired colonel was relieved by Red Mike Edson, who came in from the *Maryland* wearing a holstered revolver and cartridge belt reminiscent of the Old West. After helping Edson plan the next day's fighting, Shoup was finally able to stretch out on the sand and get some rest. He did not know it yet, but he had won the Medal of Honor. Out of the four awarded for service in this battle, Shoup's was the only one that wasn't posthumous.

Most of the Marines who had landed on D-day shared Shoup's weariness. They'd had little sleep during their last night on the transports, and the threat of a counterattack had kept most from sleeping during the first night ashore. The second night was far from free of worry about the enemy's intentions and capabilities, but few men at the front could maintain their alertness. As recalled by Major Kyle: "In this little perimeter we had set up on the far side of the island, I was sitting in an antitank ditch with Major Hal Thorpe. It was during the latter part of the night, and we talked to each other to stay awake. And then we both went to sleep. I woke up maybe an hour later and looked around. Everyone near me was asleep. I woke them and started walking up the ditch toward the beach. I found no one awake. I kept going and walked around the entire perimeter, waking people as I went. I finally found the company commanders and a few other officers and got them to help. At the time I began my tour, there wasn't a man awake in the whole outfit!"

Betio's skies were visited by four Japanese planes at about 5:00 A.M. on November 22. They were impartial with their bombs, dropping half of them on the Americans and half on their friends. One exploded with a bright flash on the thickly crowded northern beach. Robert Sherrod was in a foxhole in this area, and he heard a Marine shout, "There are a lot of men hurt bad up here. Where are the corpsmen and the stretchers?" One Marine was dead, and seven or eight had been wounded. While the wounded were being treated, another clear dawn arrived.

Inside his huge command post just east of the front lines on Red 3, Keiji Shibasaki began the day by making preparations for his death, which was now inevitable, either at the enemy's hands or his own. The admiral's final message was radioed to Tokyo: "Our weapons have been destroyed, and from now on everyone is attempting a final charge. May Japan exist for 10,000 years!"

American efforts for the day opened with another general plastering of Betio's eastern tail by carrier planes, naval gunfire, and land-based artillery. Some of the artillery fire came from Bairiki, where a battery of howitzers had just been landed. The forward observer for this work was on Betio, which put him in the novel position of directing the fire of the guns while looking down their muzzles. This situation had been anticipated and rehearsed during training exercises in New Zealand.

The attack plans for the third morning involved three simultaneous efforts. Hays was to continue trying to reduce the pocket of defenses that had been keeping the Marines on Red 2 from making contact with Ryan in the Red 1 zone. Crowe and Ruud were to resume their eastward pressure against the equally stubborn defenses, which included Shibasaki's command post, that barred the way to the tail. The troops under Jones that had landed on Green Beach in the west the previous evening were to advance along the southern shore to Kyle's perimeter. Jumping off early, Jones made good progress, reaching the perimeter at 11:00 A.M. At the same time, Green Beach received the last Marines to be landed, the 3rd Battalion, 6th, under Lieutenant Colonel Kenneth F. McLeod. These troops moved eastward in Jones's wake. Across the isle, Hays was having the same kind of trouble with the pocket that he'd had the day before, his progress bitterly slow. The most dramatic work of the morning was done in the Crowe-Ruud zone.

Most formidable among the defenses facing these Marines were three that were mutually supporting: the command post, a steel pillbox, and a coconut log bunker. Through a happy combination of skill and luck, a mortar shell touched off the ammunition stored in the bunker, and the structure dissolved with a mighty blast. As the debris was settling, a cheer went up among the Marines. Next, the medium tank *Colorado* clattered forward and, firing its 75-millimeter gun, knocked out the steel pillbox. This left the command center, which was crowded with men, Shibasaki among them. Additional troops lurked in pillboxes and trenches behind the structure.

The Marine line edged forward, the men firing their rifles as they went. Return fire from machine guns and rifles snapped and whined about them, some of the bullets scoring. Accompanying the rifle platoons was a team of assault engineers led by First Lieutenant Alexander Bonnyman, a Princeton graduate and the owner of a silver mine in New Mexico. Covered by the riflemen and several machine-gun crews, Bonnyman and his group rushed at the massive center, with its multiple

Marines swarm over a bombproof shelter.

entrances and firing ports. They assaulted the nearest entrance with demolitions and a flamethrower, leaving it smoking. Then, while moving against other openings, the Marines were counterattacked by a number of Japanese from the defenses in the rear. There was a short, hot fight, with Bonnyman in the fore of his team, firing his carbine. The enemy was bested, but not before the lieutenant was fatally wounded.

At this point, scores of Japanese from inside the command center, reduced to panic by the assault on the western entrance, came running out of the southern and eastern sides in an attempt to flee toward Betio's tail. But now the whole Marine line was semicircling the structure, and a tempest of small-arms fire and canister from a 37-millimeter gun struck the fugitives. More than a hundred fell in a matter of minutes. Soon a bulldozer was summoned, and sand was heaped against all of the center's entrances. Gasoline was poured down the air vents, and hand grenades were dropped in. Muted screams were heard as a fiery death claimed the occupants, at least 150 of them, many of whom had sought safety in the center after being wounded. Shibasaki himself probably died at this time. The most troublesome set of defenses in the Red 3 zone had been reduced, and Alexander Bonnyman had won the Medal of Honor.

The practice of Japanese in hopeless situations to fight until they were slaughtered en masse was ever a source of wonderment to Americans, to whom it seemed unnecessarily costly for both sides. On this third day on Betio, Associated Press correspondent Bill Hipple remarked: "I'm asking the home office for a transfer to the European theater the first chance I get. At least they surrender over there."

As was always the case in battles between the Marines and the Japanese, all of the action was not at the front. Bypassed defenders caused many problems for those Americans behind the lines. This included the Seabees, who were now ashore and were already busy converting the airfield to American use. Every now and then a crew was obliged to stop working because of interference from a sniper. These Japanese were usually hunted down by the crews themselves, for Seabees prided themselves on their ability to fight as well as work.

Also troubled by snipers was a Military Police unit that landed on Green Beach. Serving as pinch hitters for demolitions engineers who were busy elsewhere, these men were engaged in the tricky job of digging up enemy land mines, and the singing bullets were especially nerve-racking. It was soon learned that the snipers were concealed in a series of pillboxes that had been knocked out and then reoccupied. The enterprising MPs obtained some demolitions, and a charge they set off against the rear slope of one of the structures had an unexpected effect. Eight of the enemy—most of them Korean labor troops—stepped out of the entrance, their hands held high. They were taken prisoner, and one of them quickly became a valuable ally. He could speak English, and he told the Marines that the pillbox held four more men. Another charge was exploded against the mound, and the four came out, three with their hands up and one who began firing his rifle and had to be shot down. The collaborator now began going into the other pillboxes, advising the occupants to surrender. Many did, some coming out with handkerchiefs tied across their eyes, expecting instant execution and preferring not to see the weapons aimed at them. Soon these men were smiling and asking for American cigarettes. In a few instances the collaborator emerged from the pillbox warning the Marines that some of the occupants intended to come out shooting, and these men were killed as soon as they showed themselves. In the end the MPs had about eighty prisoners, mostly Koreans. Ordinarily it was the job of the MPs to *guard* prisoners, not to capture them.

Unlike the Japanese, the Koreans were often willing to surrender. If they performed their combat duties well, it was usually because they had no choice. Unfortunately, many were killed before they could give up. To the Americans, the Koreans looked like the Japanese. In attitude, the two peoples were entirely different. Japan annexed Korea in 1910 but had never gained the nation's loyalty. The Koreans were treated more like slaves than wards. Some of the men in the Japanese labor battalions were enlistees who had been motivated by poverty and hunger, but many more had been conscripted, sometimes simply taken from their homes with no advance notice. One of the Koreans captured on Betio told an interpreter that when American bombs and shells began hitting the isle he and his countrymen were happy, even though some of them were dying. "Every victory for the Allies means that freedom for Korea will come that much sooner." Another prisoner said that he was troubled by the way the Americans looked at him. "They think I am Japanese. I wish they understood that I hate the Japanese as much as they do."

Also busy behind the lines on the third day were burial parties supervised by the regimental chaplains. This work had become urgent, for the stench of the dead hung over the island so thickly it permeated the hair and the clothing of the living and could almost be tasted. Numerous men had been driven to spells of vomiting. Marine bodies were especially thick on the boundary between Red 1 and Red 2, and a shore-party commander asked that they be removed, since they were hindering movements to and from the pier, which had been repaired by the engineers and was in full use. While collecting the corpses, members of the burial parties came upon men who had been their friends. On seeing the remains of Herbert Amey, who had been shot down while leading his battalion ashore, Chaplain W. Wyeth Willard mused upon the colonel's hearty spirits at a recent party in New Zealand. The bodies brought in from the shallow, sun-heated waters inside the reef were in especially bad shape. Some were grotesquely bloated and blistered, others had patches of hair missing from the head. There were faces whose features were shapeless pulp, the eyes merely jellied blobs. A bulldozer operator, dodging the inevitable sniper fire, scooped out three long trenches. The bodies were laid in, side by side, just as they'd been found. Then the dozer pushed sand over them. As always at times like this, the dead reminded the living of their own mortality. One witness of the proceedings recalled something he had read, a quote on putrid corpses by a Civil War officer: "This is essentially what we are, and what all of us will soon become."

It was on the third day that Julian Smith came ashore from the

Maryland. He and his ten-man command group landed first on Green Beach in the west, then reembarked in an amtrac to swing around the north shore to the pier and Red 2. During this trip the tractor was fired upon from the pocket of defenses that Hays was working on; the craft was disabled, its driver wounded. Another amtrac was summoned and the trip was completed without further trouble, with the general and his aides establishing themselves with Edson and Shoup behind the air-raid shelter.

By the end of the day the Marines, now numbering approximately 7,000 effectives, controlled about two-thirds of the objective. In the west, the defenders in the pocket were still holding out. The rest of the Japanese survivors, who made up the majority, had withdrawn to the isle's tail. In all, there were probably no more than 1,000 of the enemy left alive. The coming of darkness found the three companies of Jones's 1st Battalion, 6th Marines, along with elements of the 8th under Crowe and Ruud, established in a line facing the Japanese on the tail, a line that spanned Betio from the south shore to the north. The Japanese were trapped. Segments of them responded by counterattacking in the night. The numbers involved were small, but they caused much trouble. In spite of the Marines' superiority, the front line was thin. Men at the front are seldom thickly emplaced, for this merely makes it easier for the enemy's weapons to find targets. A night attack, even by a minor force, is something to be dreaded, especially by troops who have been fighting all day and are much in need of rest.

The first attack, made by about fifty men at 7:30, achieved a penetration between two of Jones's companies. These Japanese were wiped out, some in hand-to-hand encounters, with the help of the battalion reserve, made up of men belonging to the headquarters and weapons units. Now the Marines began pounding the tail with artillery fire, and salvos were added by a destroyer. The fireworks were both noisy and brilliant, but the shrapnel they produced failed to keep the Japanese in check. At eleven o'clock about 100 of them made another try. "They came at us," recalled one of Jones's company commanders, First Lieutenant Norman K. Thomas, "with grenades and light machine guns and rifles with fixed bayonets. Their officers were swinging swords." Most of these men went down under mortar and small-arms fire, but a few entered the lines. Thomas himself warded off a bayonet thrust by the biggest Japanese he had ever seen, managing to knock the man to the ground and kill him with a pistol. The final attack, also against Jones's battalion, was made by some 300 jabbering and shrieking men at 4:00 A.M. Again, most were destroyed, scores by shellfire alone, before they could close in; but there was another round of savage hand-to-hand fighting with those who made it. Finally at five o'clock Lieutenant Thomas phoned battalion headquarters: "It's over. We stopped them. Please send stretcher-bearers to evacuate the wounded." The battalion's wounded numbered 128; forty-five had been killed. There were about 200 enemy dead lying in or near the Marine lines, and about 125 farther out, where the pack howitzers and destroyer fire had got them. The zone was at last blessedly quiet.

Then the Marines began cocking their ears at a new sound coming from far down the tail. There was no mistaking it. Somewhere amid the rubble created by American gunfire, a Japanese rooster was crowing his usual salute to the dawn.

Beginning at 7:00 A.M. the tail was subjected to a new barrage by carrier planes, naval gunfire, and the Marine howitzers. For an hour the zone rumbled and shuddered and gave rise to billowing smoke and dust. At eight o'clock McLeod's 3rd Battalion, 6th Regiment, the freshest unit ashore, passed through Jones's battered lines and began heading for Betio's eastern tip. At the same time, the Marines in the west resumed their work against the knot of defenses that made up the pocket. The attacks were supported by light and medium tanks, 75-millimeter halftracks and 37-millimeter guns. Progress was excellent and Marine casualties light. Most of the remaining Japanese were blasted and burned to death. Some obligingly committed suicide. Symbolically, victory came at noon when the first American carrier plane, cheered by the Seabees, set down on Betio's airfield. Officially, the isle was secured at 1:12 P.M. It was the fourth day of the battle, November 23, seventy-six hours after the first Marines had landed.

There was still mopping up to be done. The few live defenders scattered about the isle had to be ferreted out to end the sniper threat. This went on through the rest of the day. Other Marines were organized on the beaches for the possibility of a counterinvasion from other Tarawa isles. At the same time, burial parties roamed Betio, attending to both friendly and enemy dead. Some of the Japanese were buried in mass graves; others were taken out to sea and dumped overboard. Conditions had improved for giving more careful attention to the American dead, and cemeteries were developed. Some of the men took time to mark certain graves with little signs saying such things as A GOOD BUDDY AND A GREAT MARINE. The remarkable Dave Shoup was sufficiently composed and clear-minded that afternoon to write a poem memorializing an officer who had been a friend.

When Betio's Marines got word that a mail plane would be leaving the area within twenty-four hours and that the rules of censorship had been temporarily eased, men hastened to scribble letters home, mostly brief ones telling their families they had come through the battle okay. A few employed the impressive device of writing on Japanese stationery. (At least one mother was impressed in the wrong way; at first sight of her son's note she thought he had been taken captive and was writing from Japan.)

Searching for souvenirs was another of the afternoon's occupations. Marines were famous for this. The story was told that during the fight for Betio a Marine shouted at a pillbox, "Come out, you Jap son of a bitches!" and was answered, "Come in and get us, you souvenir-hunting Yankee bastard!" Betio abounded with swords, knives, handguns, field glasses, flags, paper money, coins, and a thousand other choice objects. One man found a Japanese news magazine whose cover featured a drawing of Roosevelt and Churchill, dressed as American Indians, swinging tomahawks and pouncing upon a tent that bore the symbol of the International Red Cross. A more modest item, a roll of undeveloped film, was picked up by PFC Howard R. Ditzler of the 3rd Battalion, 6th. He had the film processed later and found the photos to be of barracks scenes, of small groups of smiling men in casual uniform, some holding dogs or cats. These men were obviously the photographer's buddies, and he doubtless planned to send the pictures home. Ditzler discovered something that many Marines failed to realize. The enemy was human.

Of the 4,836 men of Betio's garrison, only seventeen Japanese and 129 Koreans were taken prisoner. As for American casualties, the final count was 984 dead and 2,072 wounded. Former Raider Evans Carlson called the battle the damnedest he had ever seen. Actually, it was the damnedest that *any* Marine had seen in the entire history of the Corps.

On the same day the Marines secured Betio, Army General Ralph Smith released the message "Makin taken." Marine General Holland Smith, who, along with Kelly Turner, had been watching over this operation, had found the Army's progress "infuriatingly slow." Ralph Smith's 165th Regimental Combat Team (Reinforced) numbered 6,500 men, whereas the enemy had little over 800, more than half of them laborers. Holland Smith felt that the conquest should have been completed by dusk on D-day. "Any Marine regiment would have done it in that time." The Army's slowness, Howlin' Mad concluded, was not so much the fault of the men as of the officers. "Had Ralph Smith been a Marine general, I would have relieved him on the spot." There was to be more trouble between the two Smiths later in the war.

The Army's casualties on Makin were sixty-six dead, 152 wounded.

Elements of the Navy supporting the Makin operation suffered to a far greater degree. As early as D-day, an accidental explosion in a turret of the battleship *Mississippi* killed or wounded sixty-two men. At dawn on November 24, the escort carrier *Liscome Bay* was torpedoed by a Japanese submarine. The aircraft bombs stored in the hold were detonated, and the vessel burst apart with a mighty roar. Fifteen hundred yards away, the battleship *New Mexico* was showered with fragments of steel, human flesh, and other debris. The fiercely burning carrier went down with a prolonged hiss in twenty-three minutes. Only 272 men were plucked from the oily, flame-ravaged waters; 644 perished.

Even as this tragedy was playing itself out, the transports in the sea west of Tarawa made a slow and majestic passage through the channel into the lagoon, where they hove to and prepared to pick up the battalions of the 2nd and 8th Regiments. The Marines of the 6th were to remain behind, temporarily, to finish cleaning up Betio and the atoll's other isles.

Holland Smith came down from Makin by seaplane that morning. He was saddened not only by the sight of the unburied dead but also by the aspects of the living. Dirty, unshaven, hollow-eyed, and haggard, they "looked older than their fathers." They had survived the fight, "but it had chilled their souls." The general arrived in time to attend the official flag-raising with Julian Smith. A topless palm tree had been rigged with a pulley and rope. There was a delay as the ceremony began. The bugler who stepped forward to sound "to the colors" was wearing a white Japanese uniform, a replacement for his own impossibly dirty dungarees. Julian Smith snapped, "Take those damn things off, and keep them off." The bugler undressed and borrowed the clothes of a nearby buddy, who was presumably left in his underwear. As the bugle's clear notes sounded over the devastated isle and the flag was run up, the Americans around the pole and in adjacent areas came to attention and saluted, some with tears running down their smudged cheeks. Wounded men struggled to their feet to join in the homage. The helpless men on litters merely watched, eyes wide. The Marines who were shuffling along the pier toward the reef for embarkation turned and looked back, catching sight of the flag as it began to flutter at the top of the pole, and at least a part of their weariness was replaced by pride. Almost simultaneously with the raising of the American colors, the British Union Jack was run up another tree. The Gilbert Islands had been British mandates before they were seized by Japan.

While the flags were unfurling over Betio on November 24, Murray's 2nd Battalion, 6th Regiment, the unit that had occupied Bairiki, was launching a campaign for Tarawa's other isles, a chain that ran eastward for ten miles, then made a turn to the northwest and continued for another eighteen. These tropical gems, which held about 180 of the enemy, were connected by reef waters that could be forded at low tide. The Marines encountered no resistance as they began their march but were joined by groups of fine-looking natives, male and female, both sexes bare-breasted—people who were eager to see what happened when the Japanese were cornered in the north. The fight occurred on the morning of November 27, and the Japanese were wiped out. The natives were happy to help bury the riddled corpses. But the affair had not been altogether one-sided. Marine casualties were thirty-two killed and fifty-nine wounded. Many of the wounded found their situation quite tolerable, since the bare-breasted girls helped attend them. Next day the battalion was picked up by landing craft and taken to Betio.

Conducted simultaneously with the campaigns for Tarawa and Makin was the conquest of a third Gilbert atoll, Apamama, "Land of Moonlight," about seventy-five miles southeast of Tarawa. Robert Louis Stevenson had resided on Apamama for several months in 1889 and called it "a treasure trove of South Sea Island beauty." The atoll was profaned only slightly by the Marine invasion. An advance unit—a reconnaissance company numbering eighty men—was landed there on November 21 by the submarine *Nautilus*. The defenders, no more than twenty-five in all, were easily disposed of. Most, in fact, disposed of themselves. The Marines were soon enjoying the hospitality of beaming natives, including a party of pretty girls (topless) who approached them singing "Brighten the Corner Where You Are," learned from missionaries. When, on November 25, General Hermle arrived from Betio with the main landing force, there were no Japanese to fight—merely a host of natives to fraternize with. The festivities included singing by the light of campfires. In their rich, melodious voices, the natives contributed sedate chants, and the Marines responded with such classic pieces as "The Beer Barrel Polka." The two groups cheered each other with gusto. Early in December, on the evening before the Marines left the atoll, the two choruses combined to sing "Silent Night." Combat correspondent Jim G. Lucas reported: "It was one of the most stirring and touching scenes I have ever witnessed. It was brought home suddenly to all of us that we were about to spend another Christmas thousands of miles from home."

The Marines of the 2nd Division spent Christmas of 1943 at a camp of their own construction—they named it Camp Tarawa—in the Hawaiian Islands. It was on the largest island, Hawaii itself, and it utilized a part of the great Parker ranch. The veterans of Betio found no pleasure in the way the news of their sacrifice and heroism was received in the States. Few people seemed to understand the importance of the campaign for the Gilberts. It had gained Admiral Nimitz a foothold in the Central Pacific and had furnished four new airfields for the Army Air Forces to use in raids farther west. As for the Betio assault, it had proved the basic soundness of Marine Corps amphibious doctrine and had provided a textbook example for officers to study. Lessons had been learned and mistakes had been pinpointed, assuring that improved procedures would be applied to forthcoming operations. It was Betio's cost the American people could not accept—3,000 casualties in just three days of fighting. So far, these were the highest American losses of any three days of the war, Pacific or European. There were cries for a Congressional investigation. Editorial writers referred to "tragic Tarawa," and compared the assault to the Charge of the Light Brigade. Who, they asked, had blundered? Some critics believed that Betio should have been bombed and shelled into submission. At this point, many civilians did not realize that bombing and shelling alone could not cope with the ingenuity of Japanese fortifications, that in the end ground troops would always have to go in and dig the enemy out. All of the criticism stunned the battle-scarred 2nd Division. A sergeant lamented: "If the Marines could stand the dying, you'd think the public could at least stand reading about it." In Washington, Archer Vandegrift stated, "No one regrets the losses more than the Marine Corps itself. No one realizes more than does the Marine Corps that there is no Royal Road to Tokyo." At another time the general quoted Joseph C. Grew, the nation's former ambassador to Japan: "The Japanese will not crack. They will not crack morally or psychologically or economically even when eventual defeat stares them in the face. Only by utter physical destruction or utter exhaustion of their men and materials can they be defeated." The American people, Vandegrift pointed out, must be steeled to the realities of the situation.

Washington's efforts in this direction got some able assistance from Louis Hayward and his photographers, who had left Betio with hundreds of still shots and thousands of feet of movie film, much of the footage in color. Hayward got his wish: the world had something to talk about. The pictures, some of which he had taken personally, were hailed as the finest and most startling records of combat ever obtained. Staff Sergeant Norman Hatch made photographic history by catching both Marine and Japanese combatants in the same frames of film. The color footage was edited and produced as a twenty-minute documentary, *With the Marines at Tarawa,* and it won an Oscar while performing its task of educating the public.

After *Tarawa* had made the rounds of the nation's theaters, Robert Sherrod asked Brigadier General Robert Denig, chief of Marine Corps public relations, what kind of effect the film had on the Corps itself. "A strong one," Denig replied. "Enlistments are down thirty-five percent."

15 | *The Rains of New Britain*

======= At the time of the Tarawa fight, which opened the Navy's island-hopping attack across the Central Pacific, the Marine Corps was not yet through with its participation in the operations around Fortress Rabaul. Western New Britain remained to be secured, with Cape Gloucester the point of assault. New Britain is the island in the Bismarcks, northwest of Bougainville, on which Rabaul is located. An east-west crescent, it is 370 miles long and from forty to fifty miles wide, and much of its terrain is rugged mountains and trackless jungles. Rabaul is at the island's eastern extremity, Cape Gloucester at its western. In this assault the Marines—the 1st Division, which came to fame on Guadalcanal—served under Douglas MacArthur, whose forces were moving along the north coast of New Guinea toward the Philippines. The assault was initiated to protect MacArthur's right flank.

When the men of the 1st left Guadalcanal for Australia at the close of the campaign, they were a tattered, emaciated, and sickly bunch. MacArthur, who was short of troops at the time, welcomed the division's assignment to his sphere, partly because he wanted his own amphibious specialists and partly because of the extra security the men would provide; Australia was still a possible target for Japanese invasion. Two officers of MacArthur's staff came to the docks at Brisbane to watch the Marines disembark and were shocked by their appearance. Many were so weak they kept stumbling and falling. The Army men exchanged glances. A Marine officer told them with bitter humor, "Well, here are your defenders of Australia." At first as many as 7,500 men at a time were racked with malaria, and there were countless other disabilities, including malnutrition. Men given liberty in Brisbane were known to pass out on the street. Then, after being transferred to a set of salubrious camps at Melbourne, the division began regaining its vitality. It was reinforced and reequipped, with the old Springfield rifle replaced by the new semi-automatic Garand. A heavy training schedule was resumed. All the while, the Marines got royal treatment from the Australians, who regarded them as the continent's saviors, which they almost literally were, since their invasion of Guadalcanal had turned back the enemy's advance and had preserved Australia's communications with America. Melbourne's newspapers referred to the men of the 1st as "Our Marines." When certain of the Americans took advantage of their savior status with rambunctious acts in public, they were forgiven. Right from the start, the young women played an eager role in the rehabilitation program, and, as had happened during the 2nd Division's stay in New Zealand, engagements and marriages resulted. Finally a team of officers from Lieutenant General Walter Krueger's 6th Army inspected the division, which was now commanded by General William Rupertus, and gave it this rating: "[It is] well equipped, has a high morale, a splendid esprit, and approximately 75 percent of its personnel have had combat experience. . . . The combat efficiency of this division is considered to be excellent."

In the autumn of 1943 the Marines, about 19,000 strong, sailed for the north coast of eastern New Guinea, the region held by MacArthur, where they did some additional training. It was on this coast, just south of New Britain, that the forthcoming campaign was staged. Information on the coveted western part of the island was obtained by means of aerial photography and daring missions by scouts in small boats. The Army's 5th Air Force did the softening up, laying in a whopping total of 3,926 tons of bombs in thirty-eight days. Allied bombers and fighters also hit Rabaul to limit its capacity for responsive action. The campaign was launched on December 15 by the Army's 112th Cavalry Regiment, which made a diversionary landing at Cape Merkus, or Arawe, a small base on the objective's southern coast.

Ten days later, on Christmas morning, Rear Admiral Daniel E. Barbey led the Cape Gloucester assault force out of New Guinea's Buna Harbor. As the convoy moved northward along the coast under a punishing sun, a Marine on one of the transports tried to get the men to sing Christmas carols. He started with "Silent Night," but got little response. A switch to "O Come, All Ye Faithful" was equally unproductive. "Somehow," one man recalled, "those songs seemed out of place that day." Next the singer broke out with "Pistol-Packin' Mama," and soon half the Marines on the ship were belting out the lively lyrics. On another vessel a former divinity-school student assembled a number of men and read them the Christmas story from the Bible. Nearby, indifferent to the proceedings, several Marines sat on the deck around the edges of a blanket, playing poker.

The Japanese were aware that the Marines were on the way. Announced Radio Tokyo: "Our soldiers are fully prepared to repulse this insolent attempt. The jungles will run red with the blood of the butchers of Guadalcanal." Manning western New Britain, stationed at bases scattered along its coastal rim, were about 9,500 men of the 65th Brigade under Major General Iwao Matsuda. Because its original mission had been the maintenance of supply routes to New Guinea, the unit

FIRST MARINE DIVISION
STAGING AREA

OCTOBER-DECEMBER 1943

NAUTICAL MILES

was top-heavy with transportation personnel. For defense purposes, these men had been attached to the brigade's two infantry regiments, the 53rd and 141st. The Japanese were not as combat-ready as Radio Tokyo claimed. Their own supply routes had been disrupted by American aircraft, and they were on half rations. Moreover, many of their shelters had been blown out of existence, and the monsoon season was starting; the men were forever wet. Large numbers were coming down with malaria, dysentery, and serious fungus infections. Only about 4,000 of the defenders were in the Cape Gloucester area, but Matsuda himself had his headquarters there. The general was considerably more comfortable than his men, his well-concealed cottage made up of a bedroom

with a double-width four-poster bed and a kitchen that was both convenient and adequately stocked. His furnishings, mostly imported pieces,
included a pink wicker easy chair, and he had a phonograph and an
assortment of records. He was well supplied with *sake* and beer, and
had even obtained a few bottles of Coca-Cola. A ladder dropping from
a trapdoor in his kitchen floor led to an air-raid shelter lighted by
candles and stocked with extra rations.

The American assault called for two simultaneous landings, the main
one about six miles east of the cape, and a secondary effort at Tauali,
about seven miles to the west. During the night of December 25–26 the
attack force passed through Vitiaz Strait and swung to the right around
Rooke and Sakar Islands in order to come upon the cape from the
northwest. At 4:22 A.M. the Tauali group broke off. It will not be necessary to follow the progress of this landing, made by the 2nd Battalion,
1st Marines, reinforced. Although well executed, the effort involved
only minor fighting and had no important effect on the campaign. Its
chief contribution to Corps lore was that it produced a clash that gained
a unique name: the Battle of Coffin Corner.

It was still dark on December 26 when the main force drew up east
of the cape. The support vessels—two cruisers, eight destroyers, and
two LCI rocket ships—opened fire at 6:00 A.M., and the first flight of 5th
Air Force bombers reached the scene an hour later. Smoke was thick
over the jungle and along the beaches when the bombardment ended
and the boated Marines churned shoreward at 7:45. There was little
resistance. General Matsuda had not expected an attack at this spot,
since its vegetation was nearly impenetrable and its floor watery. Had
the Marines known as much about the terrain as Matsuda, they probably would have landed elsewhere. As it turned out, their landing was
a tactical gem. The Japanese were deployed to the right and left of the
tangled swamps. The landing was made in such a way as to cut the
defending force in two.

It was Colonel Julian N. Frisbie's 7th Marines that spearheaded the
assault, the battalions coming in over beaches designated as Yellow 1
and Yellow 2. There was only about six feet of sand between the surf
and the edge of the jungle. In some places the Marines had to use
machetes to get through the rim of underbrush. Those men on the right
soon found themselves in a zone their maps called "damp flat." The
"dampness" extended as high as their armpits. Time and again, men fell
into sinkholes and had to be pulled out. As the perimeter was expanded,
the only resistance came in the form of sniper fire. It wasn't a bullet that
caused the first American fatality; it was a falling tree, its roots jarred
loose by the bombardment.

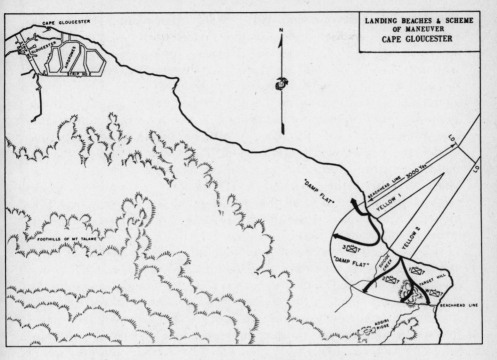

A half-hour after the initial landing, elements of the 3rd Battalion of Colonel William J. Whaling's 1st Marines came in on the right, their mission to swing westward along the enemy's coastal road to the airport. These men soon came up against a roadblock consisting of four machine-gun bunkers and a system of rifle trenches. Company K, in the lead, quickly lost both its commander and its executive officer. In the ensuing confusion, the Marines found everything going wrong. Their bazooka rockets failed to detonate in the soft earth piled over the bunkers, and their flamethrowers malfunctioned. An amtrac on the scene as an ammunition vehicle tried to double as a tank and became wedged between two trees. Some of the Japanese swarmed from cover and killed the amtrac's machine gunners. The driver, however, managed to work the tractor free and ram the nearest bunker. At this, the Marines of K Company rushed forward with rifles and hand grenades and reduced the entire position. As recalled by a participant: "A German shepherd dog serving as a sentry for the Japanese died with his master in this encounter. I noticed our own scout dog smelling his dead contemporary. . . ."

The fighting at the roadblock was the sharpest of D-day. Elsewhere the Marines expanding the perimeter continued to have more trouble with the terrain than the enemy. At noon the troops on the left, the 1st

Battalion, 7th Marines, occupied Target Hill, a key point on their maps. By this time the division commander, William Rupertus, had come ashore. Scattered along the surf line, their ramps lowered to the beach, were seven LSTs. The bulldozers they had disgorged were chewing up the margin of the jungle. Scores of supply-laden trucks were parked along the narrow strip of sand, and, stripped to the waist, sweating shore-party personnel were unloading priority items such as ammunition, rations, and water. Tanks and artillery pieces were lumbering inland, the guns towed by amtracs or TD-9 tractors equipped with bulldozer blades. According to an officer of the 4th Battalion, 11th Marines, "One of the guns and its TD-9 tractor bogged down while crossing the swamp, and all that remained above the mud was five inches of the gun shield and the driver's seat, exhaust pipe, and a few levers of the tractor."

At 2:30 P.M. the beachhead and its shipping were raided by twenty-five carrier bombers and some sixty fighters, the bulk of Rabaul's diminished striking force. The planes roared in low, bombing and strafing. As the Americans reacted, there was a blunder among the antiaircraft gunners aboard a newly arrived echelon of LSTs. A formation of Army B-25s happened to be coming in at treetop level for a strike on Matsuda's positions, and two were shot down, two others seriously damaged. Thrown into confusion, the crews of the remaining B-25s bombed and strafed a Marine artillery position at Silimati Point, on the perimeter's left flank. One man was killed, fourteen wounded. The Japanese planes made their strongest effort against the offshore shipping. They were challenged by 5th Air Force fighters, and the sky buzzed with dogfights, trails of smoke marking the last moments of the vanquished. The enemy's bombers hit several vessels, including the destroyer *Brownson,* which took two missiles at the base of her after stack. "I rushed out of the pilot house," recalls the ship's skipper, Lieutenant Commander J. B. Maher, "and saw that the entire structure above the main deck, and the deck plating from the center of Number 1 torpedo mount aft to the Number 3 five-inch mount, was gone." The *Brownson's* back had been broken, and she folded in the middle, soon going down, some of her depth charges exploding as she vanished, her demise marked by swirls of bloody water. More than 100 of her crew were dead, while many of the rescued had painful wounds. When the air raid ended, the Americans were short several planes and the Japanese had lost a good part of their precious number. This was Rabaul's first and last large-scale aerial strike against the American forces at Cape Gloucester.

That afternoon, as the Marines began digging in for the night along a perimeter extending about 1,000 yards inland, the sky turned somber and the men on the beaches watched a gray deluge come racing across the inky, white-capped Bismarck Sea. Soon the wind-driven water was slashing into the jungle in such quantities as the Americans had never known. Men at the front who thought they had found dry spots for their foxholes were soon immersed to their necks. The water even found its way into the canopied jungle hammocks of those farther back, soaking their sagging rumps. The storm notwithstanding, Matsuda counterattacked during the night, sending Major Shinichi Takabe's 2nd Battalion, 53rd Infantry, against the center of the perimeter, held by the 2nd Battalion, 7th Marines.

Throughout the fighting, a Marine officer explains, "the wind roared in from the Bismarck Sea at hurricane velocity, bringing down giant trees with rendering, splintering crashes." Men were blinded by lightning, and "deafening thunder drowned out the noise of the gunfire." According to the commander of the Marine battalion, Lieutenant Colonel Odell Conoley, the foxholes were now overflowing and "men were forced to get on top of the ground. It was a choice of drowning or getting shot. . . . Rifles refused to work on account of the water and mud, as did numerous other weapons. Eighty-one- and 60-millimeter mortar fire through the tree tops, laid 'by guess and by God,' was invaluable in these attacks." Toward the end of the action, Conoley's battalion was reinforced by the men of Battery D of the regiment's Special Weapons Battalion, who did a praiseworthy job of fighting as infantrymen. It was well after the coming of daylight when the Japanese finally withdrew, leaving about 200 dead sprawled in the muck before the American lines. Marine casualties were few.

The enemy returned to attack the same spot, the perimeter's center, in the afternoon, and was again repulsed. He continued trying on succeeding days, never to any advantage. Although there was little expansion of the perimeter inland during this time, the right was pushed steadily along the coast toward the airfield. All the while, the rains continued. As recorded in the division action report: "The ground became a sea of mud. Water backed up in the swamps in the rear of the shoreline, making them impassable for wheeled and tracked vehicles. Amphibian tractors were the only vehicles able to transport ammunition and food to troops in the forward areas. The many streams that emptied into the sea in the beachhead area and along the route of the advance toward the airfield became raging torrents and increased the difficulties of transportation. Troops were soaked to the skin and their clothes never dried out. . . ." The report might have added that most of the men discarded their canvas leggings because they did not repel the water but held it in, that leather wallets turned green with mold, that pocket-knife blades rusted together, that "waterproof" watches corroded and stopped, and that cherished letters from home sometimes fell apart while they were being read. About the only combustibles available for heating coffee were the waxed cardboard and paper of the K-rations, and these humble items became like gold. Many Marines would remember this campaign more as a struggle with the monsoon jungle than as one with the Japanese. No one, of course, had more trouble with conditions than the Seabees and engineers who were trying to build roads.

The heaviest clash during the march of Whaling's 1st and 3rd Battalions along the coast toward the airport occurred on December 28 at a spot the Marines dubbed Hell's Point. As recalled by Lieutenant Hoyt C. Duncan, Jr., the commander of K Company, 3rd Battalion: "We encountered twelve huge bunkers with a minimum of twenty Japs in each. The tanks would fire point-blank into the bunkers. If the Japs stayed inside, they were annihilated; if they escaped out the back entrance, the infantry would swarm over the bunkers and kill them with rifle fire and hand grenades." One of the charging Marines came upon a live Japanese who was buried in a collapsed trench, only his head showing, his eyes round with dread. While the Marine was trying to decide what to do about this novel situation, an intelligence officer came up and ordered the Japanese dug out and made prisoner. Although wounded in the shoulder, the man was able to enjoy a chunk of K-ration cheese and an American cigarette, and he cheerfully answered an interpreter's questions about Matsuda's dispositions. Imperial soldiers were not supposed to be captured; therefore, no one ever told them that, if they were, they should give only their name, rank, and serial number.

Landed as reinforcements for Whaling's 1st Regiment on December 29 were the Marines of the 5th Regiment under Colonel John T. Selden. On the same day, against only minor resistance, the combined forces enveloped the airport. One company's advance was led by a cavorting, merrily barking dog, a Japanese deserter. The next day there was some clean-up fighting around two bypassed hills, Razorback and Nameless. This ended the first part of the campaign, the fight for the airport. It had cost the Japanese about 1,000 dead; the Marines had lost about 250 in killed and wounded. General Rupertus radioed the 6th Army's General Krueger in New Guinea: "1st Marine Division presents to you as an early New Year's gift the complete airdrome of Cape Gloucester." Krueger responded that he was "delighted." Rupertus received a more effusive message from Krueger's illustrious superior, Douglas MacArthur: "Your gallant division has maintained the immortal record of the Marine Corps and has covered itself with glory." Since the victory had been a relatively easy one, the Marines were somewhat embarrassed by this lavish praise. They were not sure they had covered themselves with glory, only that they had covered themselves with mud.

General Matsuda, commanding from his snug cottage about five miles inland from the American perimeter, had reacted ineptly to the invasion. True, he had been surprised by the landing between the two wings of his Cape Gloucester defense force. But he had employed neither wing in a concerted manner. Part of the fault was that his intelligence team had made the common Japanese mistake of underestimating the enemy's numbers, arriving at the incredibly low figure of 2,500. Now Matsuda assigned a subordinate, Colonel Kenshiro Katayama, the task of counterattacking the perimeter at Target Hill, adjacent to Borgen Bay. Katayama, commander of the 141st Infantry and its attached units, decided to use only about 1,000 men in the assault, which was to be spearheaded by a single reinforced company. The Americans themselves happened to be planning a movement here on their left. As soon as their right had been anchored at the airport,

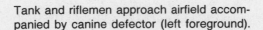

Tank and riflemen approach airfield accompanied by canine defector (left foreground).

General Rupertus had ordered his assistant division commander, Brigadier General Lemuel C. Shepherd, Jr., "to conduct operations to the southeast in order to extend the beachhead perimeter and clear the enemy from the Borgen Bay area." Created for Shepherd's use was a task force built around the 7th Marines and the 3rd Battalion, 5th. The general's front lines extended from Target Hill about 3,000 yards to the west.

Shepherd attacked first, but not at Target Hill. He held fast on this flank while swinging his right wing toward a steep-banked but fordable stream that meandered through the jungle. The Marines who made this advance (on January 2) were not aware that the innocent-looking waterway was a moat before a long line of interlocking defenses, masterfully concealed in the undergrowth. Manning the ambush were the survivors of the series of attacks on the original perimeter's center. These men of Major Takabe's 2nd Battalion, 53rd Infantry, were waiting to exact their revenge. When those Marines leading crossed the stream and climbed the bank, according to combat correspondent Asa Bordages, "the jungle exploded in their faces." The Americans dropped prone and tried to fight back, but could fire only blindly. "Marines died there . . . cursing because they couldn't see the men who were killing them." At last the survivors stumbled in retreat across the creek, dragging their helpless wounded. Other units began probing up and down the bank, looking for a soft spot, but found none. Platoons would work their way across, come under fire, and fall back with their casualties. The attack was stalled. Late afternoon found the Marines digging in on their own side of the waterway, which they had begun to call Suicide Creek. At dusk some fifty Japanese sneaked over and charged the line. About twenty of the intruders were killed, several in hand-to-hand encounters. The rest faded back.

Just before dawn the next day, Colonel Katayama launched his one-company attack on Target Hill, a measure covered by artillery, 20-millimeter machine cannon, mortars, and machine guns. The fire was largely ineffective, although a mortar shell hit the machine-gun position that was the key to the defense. Two men were killed, but the gunner was able to continue firing. He put 5,000 rounds through the weapon, all the while supported by Marines making effective use of rifles and hand grenades. Lieutenant Shinichi Abe, a brave and able officer who was idolized by his men, was the attack's leader. But, as explained by Captain Marshall W. Moore, in command of the defense, "There was an officer other than Lieutenant Abe driving the men on. He was screaming and yelling at the top of his lungs. He was off to the right of the assaulting troops in heavy jungle. We located the officer's approximate position and poured heavy fire into the area. His screams ceased, and then the attack stopped." The retiring enemy left forty dead on the slope, among them the gallant Lieutenant Abe. According to a Marine officer who saw Abe's body: "He appeared to have all of his worldly possessions with him. . . . He had on two pairs of pants, two or three shirts, a raincoat, and was carrying a heavy pack with a coat strapped to the pack. This was in addition to his sword, pistol, and entrenching tool. He carried all this equipment while leading the attack up this steep hill."

Colonel Katayama reported the attack to General Matsuda in this way: "By the desperate struggle of the officers and men of the regiment, Sankoku Yama [Target Hill] had been captured and the enemy were forced to the water's edge, but, owing to the enemy's counterattack with superior forces we have relinquished it again with much regret." Knowledge of this message would have surprised Captain Moore's Marines. Katayama had not only failed to drive them back; he had cost them but three dead and ten wounded.

During the same dawn that saw Katayama defeated, the Japanese in the defenses along Suicide Creek lobbed mortar shells across at the Marines whom they had stalled and compelled to dig in. At the close of one of the flurries, a sergeant ran along the front to learn if anyone had been hit. "A kid was sitting there in his foxhole. He didn't have any head. He just had a neck with dog tags on it." This was another frustrating day for the Marines at the creek. The enemy held to his concealed defenses and continued to punish the platoons that probed them. Tanks were on the way from the rear to help but were creeping almost literally like snails. The terrain was swampy, and the machines had to be preceded by engineers laying a corduroy road, log by log. At 2:00 P.M. morale rose at the front when Chesty Puller, now serving as executive officer of the 7th Marines, came forward from regimental headquarters, sent by William Rupertus to try to get things moving. One of the first things Puller did was to order the officers to prepare for a general attack to take place the next morning. "We have enough power here to drive," he said, "and we are going to drive." The tanks arrived late in the day. A bulldozer came too, since the creek was a natural tank trap; a section of its banks had to be fashioned into a crossing. Puller supervised the work, which was hazardous. Two drivers were shot from the dozer's seat. A third, PFC Randall Johnson, got the job done by staying on the ground and operating the controls with a shovel and an ax handle, keeping the machine between himself and the enemy.

The next morning, after a fifteen-minute artillery preparation, the tanks, followed by a pair of 75-millimeter halftracks, spearheaded the attack Puller had ordered, and it was successful. Numbers of the Japanese were killed in their defenses; the rest retreated into the jungle. The forty-eight hours of action at Suicide Creek had cost the Marines about forty dead and 200 wounded.

General Matsuda now began to realize that he was fighting a much larger force than he could handle. He had perhaps 2,000 effectives left in the Cape Gloucester area. The rest of his troops in western New Britain were either too distant for expeditious transfer to the cape or were tied down by the invader's diversionary landings. The Marines at Tauali were about to be withdrawn, but this would free only a handful. There were about 1,000 Japanese at Cape Merkus, where the Army's 112th Cavalry Regiment had landed on December 15. Even if Matsuda could have gained these troops they would have been of small help, for they were in poor shape. On January 5 their commander, Major Shinjiro Komori, wrote in his diary: "Our losses to date are 65 killed, 57 wounded, and 14 missing. Ten men have perished from fever. Malaria is our main problem, with dysentery a close second. I do not know of

The advance across Suicide Creek.

a man who does not have one or the other, or both. Air drops become less frequent, possibly because of the loss of our airfield at Cape Gloucester. Most of our supplies are coming in under cover of darkness by barges. I am sending our most critical hospital cases of sick and wounded out with these barges. The enemy has been shelling us continually now for the last two days."

On the day Major Komori made this entry, Lemuel Shepherd's task force was preparing for the last phase of the conquest of the cape. The Marines made their plans around information obligingly provided by the enemy. Taken from the pocket of a platoon leader who died on Target Hill was a field dispatch he had received from Lieutenant Abe just before the attack was launched. The translators found the message to be composed mainly of battle instructions, but it included a statement that intrigued General Shepherd: "It is essential we conceal the fact that we are maintaining positions on Aogiri Ridge." The general did not know which of the elevations south of Target Hill the Japanese called Aogiri Ridge, but he determined to find out.

Preceded by an artillery barrage and a strike by Army B-25s, Shepherd's attack jumped off at 11:00 A.M. on January 6. It spanned a front of about 2,500 yards, the terrain swampy, its jungle undergrowth thick. The companies on the left, next to Borgen Bay, met with only minor resistance while pressing toward a knob on their maps called Hill 150. These Japanese were overrun with the aid of tanks and halftracks that were keeping up with the advance by means of a fairly solid coastal road. Shepherd's right had trouble mostly with the terrain. The troops in the center, however, were soon stopped by heavy fire from an unseen enemy. During the next two days, while the flanks held fast, the central troops probed their opponents, whose position was difficult to assess because of the thickness of the vegetation. On January 8, according to the division action report, the men of the 3rd Battalion, 5th Regiment, were inching forward when "it became apparent that the advance elements were ascending a gently rising ridge. . . . The maps showed no high ground in the vicinity, but as the advance continued the ground rose precipitously and terrific machine-gun and sniper fire covered every avenue of approach." Leading the battalion at this time was Lewis "Silent Lew" Walt, now a lieutenant colonel, who had taken over after the original commander and his executive officer were wounded. While moving up the slope on the eighth, Walt once sought cover amid a set of banyan roots. "During a burst of machine-gun fire, I felt a sharp and painful blow on my lower spine. I was momentarily stunned and unable to move." Chesty Puller happened to be present, and he exam-

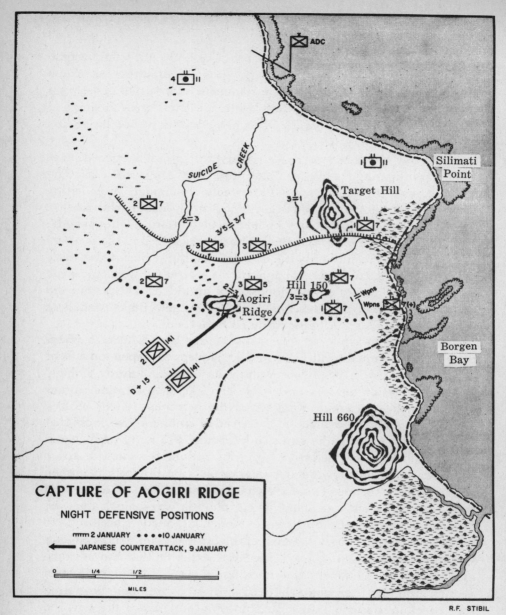

CAPTURE OF AOGIRI RIDGE

NIGHT DEFENSIVE POSITIONS

ㅠㅠㅠ 2 JANUARY   • • • • 10 JANUARY

◀━━━ JAPANESE COUNTERATTACK, 9 JANUARY

0   1/4   1/2   1

MILES

R.F. STIBIL

ined Walt, finding nothing at the painful spot but a reddening lump. Walt now noticed that "a spent machine-gun bullet lay on the ground. I was very grateful that the banyan root was three inches thick instead of two; otherwise, the bullet would have severed my spinal cord." As the day waned, Walt ordered the battalion to pull back and dig in for the night. He informed regimental headquarters that he believed he'd found Aogiri Ridge.

When the attack was resumed the following afternoon it was preceded by the customary artillery preparation from the rear. At the front, Lew Walt had only one heavy support weapon, a 37-millimeter gun. The tanks and halftracks had been unable to make it because of the swamps, which kept filling with new rains. As Walt's battalion started forward in direct assault, elements of the 7th Marines tried attacking the ridge from the left flank but were soon stopped. The flanking troops and Walt's battalion alike suffered casualties inflicted by a largely invisible foe. "The undergrowth," states the division action report, "was so thick that the men could not see ten yards in front of them. The Jap machine guns had been cleverly concealed among the roots of trees and were well protected by snipers." At dusk, Walt's leading troops, dragging and pushing the 900-pound gun, managed to win a hold on the slope; but, as the action report explains, "the situation was desperate. The assault elements had reached the limit of their physical endurance. It was a question of whether or not they could hold their hard-earned gains." Lew Walt saved the day. Calling for volunteers to continue attacking with the gun, he took hold of a wheel himself. The sweating and panting group edged the weapon toward the summit. "Every few feet a volley of canister would be fired. As members of the crew were killed or wounded, others ran forward to take their places. By superhuman effort the gun was finally manhandled . . . into position to sweep the ridge. The Marine and Jap lines were only ten yards apart in some places. As night came on, the Marines dug in where they were."

It was indeed Aogiri Ridge that Walt's battalion had occupied, vital to the Japanese because it masked their main supply trail from Borgen Bay to their inland bivouac areas. Early in the night the defenders were heard moving around on the reverse slope, and the Marines surmised correctly that they were reinforcing for a counterattack. Walt called down the artillery of the 1st and 4th Battalions, 11th Regiment, but the Japanese were not deterred. At 1:15 A.M., in a driving rain, they came up the slope chanting, "Marines, prepare to die!" Walt's line responded with mortars, machine guns, rifles, and grenades, the flashes shimmering weirdly in the deluge. The war chants were replaced by screams of anguish, and the attack soon receded. Three times more the Japanese advanced and were turned back. At the close of the fourth attack the Marines found themselves nearly out of ammunition. Even as the enemy was massing for a fifth charge, a battalion headquarters detail made it to the front and distributed the crucial belts and bandoliers. At the same time, Walt requested that the artillery fire be pulled in closer.

As the Japanese surged forward, the shells began bursting among them, as near as fifty yards to the Marines firing from their foxholes. At the height of the action, a Japanese major broke through the line and, sword in one hand and pistol in the other, charged toward Walt's hole, fifty yards back. A short round of artillery—the kind of mistake that is often a terror to front-line troops—exploded in a tree above the officer, and he went down. Walt said later: "He actually died three paces from where I crouched, .45 in hand, waiting for him." This attack was the final one. The survivors drew back and slunk away, leaving about 150 corpses on the slope. Walt's casualties were gratifyingly few, but dawn found most of the men glassy-eyed with fatigue and shock. General Shepherd soon came forward to congratulate the battalion and announce that he was giving Aogiri Ridge a new name. From now on, he said, it would be known as Walt's Ridge.

There was still a pocket of the enemy in the lowlands between Walt's Ridge and Hill 150, where Matsuda had a supply dump. Elements of the 1st Battalion, 7th Marines, aided by tanks and halftracks brought up on a corduroy road, reduced the pocket on January 11, robbing the Japanese general of materials critical to his operations. After this fight the division totaled the losses incurred since D-day. They came to 180 dead and 636 wounded. Nearly 600 sick and wounded had been evacuated to hospitals in New Guinea. The sick who were not disabled remained at the cape. Private Charles Doolittle would recall: "Jungle rot or fungus, plus malaria, were common. Like many others, I had malaria. It was painful, with headaches, high fevers, chills, and sweating; and it lasted three or four days or even longer." Thanks to the development of a yellow pill called Atabrine, malaria was not the scourge it had been at the beginning of the war. But the medicine was impossibly bitter, it turned the skin yellow, and rumor claimed it could make a man sterile.

About 1,000 yards south of the newly established American line was the campaign's last objective, Hill 660. The job of taking the position was assigned to the 3rd Battalion, 7th Marines, commanded by Lieutenant Colonel Henry W. Buse, Jr. The battalion was supported by a special weapons task force under Captain Joseph W. Buckley, a team composed of tanks, halftracks, 37-millimeter guns, a rocket-mounted Army DUKW, a bulldozer, and two platoons of infantry from the 1st Battalion, 7th. The three-day fight ended on January 16, the retiring enemy leaving behind more than 200 dead. Marine losses were some fifty killed or wounded.

The Japanese in western New Britain were now about finished. At Cape Merkus, in the Arawe region of the south coast, where the U.S.

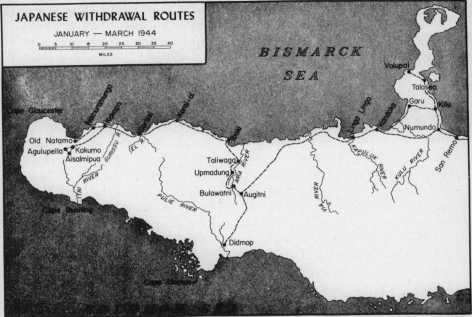

R.F. STIBIL

Army's diversionary operation had been harassing the garrison, Major Komori was finding it increasingly difficult to record anything cheerful in his diary. On January 17 he wrote: "Tonight I was in touch with 65th Brigade headquarters. The battle for Cape Gloucester does not look good. Our troops have been beaten back, and losses are heavy. There is no longer any hope of reinforcement." January 22: "Was notified today that my unit is being held as standby for a rear-guard mission should the brigade be forced to withdraw from its positions at Cape Gloucester."

The major would be on standby for a month. Already, however, General Matsuda was starting the depleted 65th Brigade on a march eastward through the jungle, his aim to avoid all further contact with the Marines and escape along the north coast toward Rabaul. General Rupertus expected the Japanese to flee the cape and tried to intercept them with combat patrols. But at first the Marines were uncertain of Matsuda's chosen route and consequently did their most vigorous patroling to the south. This netted them nothing but minor actions with stragglers and with elements of a rear guard commanded by Colonel Jiro Sato. As a secondary mission, the Americans helped repatriate the area's Melanesians, who had left their villages to escape the Japanese.

The largest patrol southward was led by Chesty Puller, who spent long days hiking even though he was still troubled by the Guadalcanal shrapnel in his thigh. Sato's rear guard had headed eastward in the wake of Matsuda's main body, and Puller's Marines met only sickly stragglers, some of whom they bayoneted. "The pig-sticking," Puller said later, "was fine." Other than helping to restore some 1,700 Melanesians to their villages, the patrol accomplished little of importance; but it gave rise to a new Puller anecdote. The patrol was supplied by air drop, and one day Puller radioed division to send him several hundred bottles of mosquito lotion as soon as possible. "The delivery," one of the supply officers recalled, "was made within a few hours, although there were those in the division CP who privately wondered why the colonel, who had often expressed contempt for what he considered the luxuries of campaigning, had changed his mind about mosquito lotion. A patrol member queried at a later date was somewhat amused. 'Hell, the colonel knew what he was about. We were always soaked, and everything we owned was likewise, and that lotion made the best damn stuff to start a fire with that you ever saw.' "

Puller reported back to the perimeter on February 18. The next day Major Komori penned in his diary: "I have decided to get all of the wounded out of our hospital right away. They are being evacuated over

Marine patrol fording a stream.

the trail [toward the north coast] at this moment. It will take a good portion of our able-bodied soldiers, yet it is a thing that must be done if we are to save the lives of these men." February 24: "At last the news I have been waiting for has come. We have been ordered north to join up with Colonel Sato's rear guard. I suspect that the 65th Brigade is being withdrawn to the eastern end of the island. With the airfield at Cape Gloucester in enemy hands, only our base at Rabaul has any value. . . . I am happy to be leaving this place."

By this time American patrols, some in boats, were moving along the north coast twenty or thirty miles behind Sato. "The coastal track," a Marine officer recalled, "presented an increasingly gruesome sight as the withdrawal continued. Men unable to shift for themselves had been provided with hand grenades and instructed to blow themselves up at the approach of the enemy. Many did not prolong their agony to that extent. Many others died of illness or sheer starvation before the Marines came up with them. The stench of death hung over New Britain's north coast like a miasma."

At Iboki, sixty miles east of Cape Gloucester, the coastal track swung twenty miles inland, or southward, around marshlands at the mouth of the Aria River. At the point of deepest penetration was the village of Augitni, where Komori, coming up from the south coast, met Sato on March 5. "He greeted me with bad news. The enemy has landed at Iboki. . . . We will have to withdraw before we are cut off." The combined forces, including stragglers from the 65th Brigade, numbered about 1,000 men. "Several of our officers," wrote Komori, "suggested that we stay and make a fight of it, but Colonel Sato pointed out that our primary mission is to cover the withdrawal of our main army, not to expend ourselves in a useless action."

The stronger survivors of General Matsuda's Cape Gloucester force, plus the garrisons of several bases on the north coast, had already achieved safety in eastern New Britain. Of the original 9,500 troops manning the west, perhaps as many as half escaped. Matsuda himself, gathering up some of his sick and wounded, had gone out by boat, leaving the mouth of the Aria River and swinging northeastward around the Willaumez Peninsula for a landing at Cape Hoskins, about 150 miles from Rabaul.

The rear guard was on its own. Colonel Sato divided the troops, sending Major Komori ahead with 300, following the next day with the remainder. Komori wrote of passing many starving stragglers. "They were a pitiful sight, but we could do little for them. We have only the few provisions we carry on our backs." The next supply depot was

Kandoka, at the western base of the Willaumez Peninsula, some forty
miles away. Komori's radio soon brought him bitter intelligence. Marines in large numbers were landing on the peninsula, at Volupai Plantation, only twenty miles north of Kandoka. This news also reached
Sato, farther back along the trail. One of the colonel's lieutenants later
told his American captors: "Sato pointed out quite honestly and frankly
the seriousness of the situation. He had no words of encouragement for
his officers but expected them to carry out their duties in the traditional
manner."

Progress was painfully slow for both groups. There were countless
detours to be made around swamps, and the swifter streams had to be
scouted for crossings. "Many men," Komori recorded on March 10, "are
weak from fever and dysentery and the daily rains." Reaching the
coastal track at their separate times, Sato and Komori never saw each
other again. Their troops ran out of food, grew hourly more debilitated,
and lost most of their will to fight. The Marine patrols were not opposed
but were eluded by toilsome off-trail marches. Men fell out, unable to
go on. There were drownings in the rampaging streams. The survivors
of the Komori groups staggered into Kandoka on March 24. "What was
expected to be a joy has become tears. The post is evacuated, and all
the food and supplies are gone. It is a terrible blow. Already, three of
the men have wandered off into the jungle. My problem now will be
to maintain a semblance of sanity among the troops I have left. I am
determined to continue the march. We must somehow reach Rabaul."
The men trudged on, heading through the jungle at the base of the
peninsula. They managed to keep alive by eating coconuts and vegeta-
bles rifled from Melanesian gardens. By March 29 the party was halfway
to the peninsula's eastern base. "We crossed the Kulu River this morning. Five men were drowned in the swift current. Several others
refused to try. They simply turned and walked back into the jungle."

Sato and his remaining troops, perhaps 200 in number, had reached
Kandoka on March 26, when they had a brush with a Marine patrol,
making a creditable showing but soon drawing off. On the following day
the keeper of the party's operations journal recorded that the men were
"physically and spiritually worn out." They had resorted to eating tree
buds. On the twenty-ninth the column came upon some taro fields, and
the men feasted on the tuberous roots. While they were plodding along
the next day, with Sato now on a litter, the Marines caught up with
them and closed in, making a surprise attack. The colonel had scarcely
time enough to leap to his feet and unsheathe his sword before he was
riddled. During the moments of tumultuous firing, most of it from the

American side, many of the Japanese fled. But a heavy toll was taken. Second Lieutenant Richard B. Watkins led the party that examined the field. "We counted fifty-five dead, including three officers. It was quite easy to believe that perhaps twenty more died in scattered positions throughout the dense underbrush." This ended the Sato group's existence as a cohesive force.

As for Komori, he made his last diary entry on March 31, saying simply, "We are very tired and without food." At this point the major came down with malaria, which compounded his weakness. Instructing his column, except for three of his headquarters people, to continue the march, Komori took refuge in a Melanesian village. Growing somewhat stronger in a few days, the indomitable major returned to the trail. The four bedraggled fugitives made it to San Remo Plantation, at the eastern base of the peninsula, and were within twenty miles of safety when, in their stuporous condition, they blundered into an American trailblock. There was a flurry of fire, and the four went down. Only one, Corporal Isamu Kozuki, was alive when the Marines approached, and he was taken captive. The corporal identified Komori, and the Americans searched the major's pack. They found his diary, which was turned over to intelligence and became a valued item in the Corps' archives —which, had Komori known it, would doubtless have pleased him.

It was April 9 when the Japanese major met his fate, and the campaign was ending. One of its more bizarre aspects was that among the Japanese who had died early in the retreat, not only their flesh but also their clothing had already disintegrated. As recalled by Private Harry A. Dearman, who accompanied one of the last Marine patrols in the Aria River region: "Leaving a native village, we pushed down a broad trail and soon came upon a camp that held a scattering of bare skeletons. It was the beginning of an eerie patrol. A little farther on we came to a camp with two or three hundred skeletons, all bare. There was nothing of value present except the gold teeth in some of the skulls, and we began collecting these. Every half-mile or so along the trail we came to another camp with more such skeletons, sometimes many. During that entire patrol we didn't see a living thing in that damned jungle except the trees, vines, and brush. I don't remember hearing the call of a single bird. There wasn't even a whisper of wind. It was as if the jungle was in mourning."

On April 22 there was a final clash with retreating survivors on the trail near San Remo. Twenty of the enemy died, together with one Marine, the last to lose his life in New Britain's incredibly wet jungle, where twenty-five men had been crushed to death by falling trees.

After this last encounter, the few hundred wretched Japanese hiding in the west were left at the mercy of the elements, the Melanesians, and the U.S. Army's 40th Division, now arriving.

On April 17 the cruiser *Nashville* had appeared off Cape Gloucester, the largest vessel seen in the area since the December landings. Douglas MacArthur was on board, and he came ashore to pay a visit to the division command post. The general shook hands with everyone. "He was very affable," an observer reported, "and gave you the impression he was very glad to see you again—even though he had never seen you before." The hand-shaking and picture-snapping took only a few minutes, where-upon MacArthur and his party returned to the beach to reembark. A week later the Marines themselves began trooping to the beach, and by mid-May the last unit, the 12th Defense Battalion, had left the island. The campaign's toll was only 310 killed and 1,083 wounded, which, the officers pointed out, was an indication that the Marines could keep their casualties down when there was room to maneuver.

Military historians, with the benefit of hindsight, were to call the New Britain campaign unnecessary, asserting that the Japanese at Cape Gloucester were not really a threat to MacArthur's flank as he moved along the New Guinea coast. The general, however, has never been faulted for ordering the action, since he planned it around intelligence he had at the time. The official Marine Corps estimate of New Britain came to be this: "Few if any operations in the Pacific were more soundly planned in detail or more efficiently executed. However 'useless' the campaign may have proved strategically, it taught many useful lessons and served as the standard on which General MacArthur modeled his subsequent jungle operations to and through the Philippines."

MacArthur was so pleased with the 1st Marine Division that he wanted to keep it, but Nimitz reclaimed it. The general, however, did acquire control over some of the Corps' air units. Conspicuously missing from the list of squadron leaders was the celebrated Pappy Boyington, who had been shot down and captured during a fighter sweep over Rabaul on January 3. The major's luck ran out just after he had ac-counted for his twenty-eighth Japanese plane, which made him the Corps' leading ace. Just behind him were Joe Foss, with twenty-six planes shot down, and Robert Hanson—who crashed and died on Feb-ruary 2—with twenty-five. Boyington's imprisonment in Japan was a tough one, but he survived to be liberated and to take possession of the Medal of Honor he had been awarded *in absentia*.

Even before the 1st Marine Division left Cape Gloucester, the ring around Rabaul had been completed by other Allied forces. As early as

Exhausted campaigners display Japanese flags.

February 15, the 3rd New Zealand Division landed in the Green Islands, north of Bougainville. The U.S. Army's 1st Cavalry Division invaded the Admiralty Islands, northwest of New Britain, on February 29. Emirau Island, east of the Admiralties, was occupied by the 4th Marine Regiment, made up of former Raiders and Paratroopers, on March 20. The Allies now had enough air facilities to keep Fortress Rabaul neutralized, by means of unrelenting raids (in which Marine fliers would play a prominent part), for the remainder of the war. The base was bypassed both by MacArthur on his way to the Philippines and Nimitz attacking across the Central Pacific.

It hadn't been necessary for the admiral to wait until Rabaul was ringed to press his campaign. Only two months after his forces had taken Tarawa, Makin, and Apamama in the Gilberts, he sent Raymond Spruance, Kelly Turner, and Holland Smith to invade the Marshalls.

16 | *Quick Win in the Marshalls*

========The Navy's long drive toward Japan was something unique in warfare, its success dependent upon the bold employment of the modern weapon of carrier air power. Above all else, it was this cover that enabled the Marine and Army amphibious troops to assault the enemy's fortified islands. Japan's sea and air power had to be kept neutralized. The main purpose of capturing the islands was to gain bases ever closer to the enemy's homeland, and the most important aircraft using the bases were the Army's long-range bombers, their mission to neutralize or soften up objectives still farther on. Nimitz was looking toward the day when his assault troops would win islands far enough westward to enable the Army bombers to begin clobbering Japan itself. Douglas MacArthur persisted in opposing the Navy's view of the war. He still believed that his advance toward Japan by way of the Philippines should be given priority. The Navy was simply perpetrating a "stunt," said the general and his supporters. Japan could be bombed, as originally planned, from bases established in China. But Washington continued to favor the Navy's campaign, with MacArthur advancing in a supplementary way, as promising the quickest results at the lowest cost.

It was now two years since Pearl Harbor, and the Navy had been greatly strengthened. The vessels available for the Marshalls operation —Admiral Spruance's 5th Fleet—made a formidable array. The carriers alone numbered six heavies, six lights, and eight escorts, and among the battleships were eight new ones capable of doing thirty knots. There were nearly 300 vessels in Kelly Turner's attack force, including eleven of the carriers, seven battleships, eight heavy and four light cruisers, sixty-three destroyers, twelve destroyer escorts, twelve improvised gunboats, seventy-three troop and cargo transports, fifty landing ships, and about the same number of auxiliaries such as minesweepers, tugs, oil tankers, and water tenders.

The expansion of the Navy in ships and men had been paralleled by a strengthening of the Marine Corps, which now numbered five divisions and four air wings. There was also a Women's Reserve, which would soon grow to 1,000 officers and 18,000 enlistees, their commander Colonel Ruth C. Streeter. The clerical and other noncombat duties the women performed would release enough men for the formation of still another division before the war ended. At the start of 1944 the Corps totaled 390,000 men and women.

For the work in the Marshalls, Kelly Turner and Holland Smith were given the new 4th Marine Division, commanded by Major General Harry "The Dutchman" Schmidt, which came directly from California, and an independent regiment, the 22nd Marines, which had been performing garrison duty on Samoa. The Army was represented by Major General Charles H. Corlett's 7th Division, whose men were veterans of Attu in the Aleutians, and the 106th Regiment of Ralph Smith's 27th Division, a sister regiment to the one that had captured Makin. With the Seabees and other special-service units included, the invasion force came to nearly 85,000 men.

The Marshalls, which lie about 2,000 miles west of Pearl Harbor, are made up of thirty-four atolls scattered over 350,000 square miles of water and comprising only sixty-six square miles of land. Top commander in the Marshalls was Rear Admiral Monzo Akiyama, and his troops were the 6th Naval Base Force, the 61st Naval Guard Force, the 4th Special Naval Landing Force, the 1st Amphibious Brigade, the 23rd and 24th Air Flotillas, and the 1st, 2nd, and 3rd South Seas Detachments. American reconnaissance revealed that six of the atolls were fortified, the strongest being Wotje, Maloelap, Mille, and Jaluit in the east, facing the Allied line of advance. These bases held a total of more than 13,000 men. Majuro, a fifth eastern island of some strategic value, was undefended. The plan approved by Nimitz was that Majuro be seized but that the others be neutralized by air strikes and bypassed in favor of an attack on Kwajalein in the central Marshalls, to be followed—three months later—by the conquest of the western island of Eniwetok. Kwajalein held about 8,500 of the enemy, Eniwetok about 3,500.

American intelligence personnel were convinced that Kwajalein would be hard to crack. "The Japanese," asserted one officer, "have had control of this atoll for some twenty-five years and have had ample time to prepare the base against assault." In order to warn the American people what could be expected, the intelligence evaluations were released to the press, and while the expeditionary armada steamed toward the Marshalls late in January 1944, the Stateside newspapers carried announcements such as: "We are invading a part of the Japanese Empire. This will be the most audacious attack attempted in this war. We expect Kwajalein to be tougher than Tarawa."

But the operation had been so well planned and the preliminary work so well executed that such pessimism was unwarranted. For the past two months the Marshalls had been mightily assailed by land-based air (with the bombers of the Army's 7th Air Force scoring steadily), by carrier planes, and, finally, by close-in naval gunfire. Said one observer (paraphrasing Winston Churchill): "Never in the history of human conflict has so much been thrown by so many at so few." Most of the defenses—not as strong as believed—were turned to rubble. Interfering aircraft were whittled away. The Japanese fleet, although still a powerful force, never ventured near. It would take no risks to protect the Marshalls. Tokyo had decided to pull the Empire's Central Pacific line back to the Marianas. The troops in the Marshalls had been instructed to fight a delaying action until they were overwhelmed. One man wrote in his diary: "When the last moment comes, I shall die bravely and honorably." By the time the invasion loomed, a great many of the defenders were already dead.

Kwajalein is the world's largest atoll, its ninety-three isles grouped in a rough triangle around some 650 square miles of lagoon water. Making up the atoll's northern extremity are the Siamese-twin isles of Roi and Namur, while the southern extremity is Kwajalein isle. About fifty miles apart, these two points were the American objectives, with the Marines scheduled to take Roi-Namur, and the GIs, Kwajalein. January 31 was D-day, and it was an unusual one. While a Marine reconnaissance company seized undefended Majuro, elements of the 4th Marine Division landed on several tiny isles adjacent to Roi-Namur, and elements of the Army's 7th Division did the same at Kwajalein. The purpose of these operations was to set up artillery to pound the main objectives, which were to be invaded the following day. That night, for the first time in the Pacific war, Navy underwater demolitions teams, men who called themselves "half fish and half nuts" and were popularly known as "frogmen," swam in to investigate the assault zones, checking on surf and beach conditions and searching for mines and other obstacles the enemy might have emplaced. The approaches to both Roi-Namur and Kwajalein were declared to be safe for the next day's work.

The landing on Roi was made by the 23rd Marines, that on Namur by the 24th. The beaches of both isles were found to be strewn with decomposing fish thrown up by bombs and shells that had burst in the surf. Nearly every palm tree had lost its top. The ground was a carpet of shredded fronds, broken concrete, twisted pieces of steel, and myriad other debris. Dead and mutilated Japanese lay about in grotesque positions. The usually aromatic tropical air was horribly foul. At first it seemed that the only living creatures were a few stunned pigs, chickens, dogs, and birds. On Roi this impression was not far from the actuality. The isle fell to the Marines in six and a half hours.

Namur was tougher. In addition to the fire of the die-hard defenders, the Marines encountered a staggering misfortune. A large concrete structure they assumed to be a bunker was really a storehouse for heavy munitions, including torpedo warheads. A satchel charge thrown inside caused an explosion of Vesuvian proportions. "Great God Almighty!" cried an observer in a carrier plane overhead. "The whole damn island has blown up!" The plane was tossed about a thousand feet farther aloft. As the brown and white mushroom expanded and billowed, according to an officer on one of the offshore destroyers, "debris and bodies could be seen spinning round like straws in a gale." The entire island was quickly enveloped, and a Marine approaching shore in a small boat saw "trees and chunks of concrete flying through the air like matchsticks." A piece of the concrete killed a Marine in another boat. Within the next half-hour, the arsenal was the source of two more explosions. When it was all over, twenty Marines were dead and 100 were hurt. One man who survived had been blown off the isle and out into the lagoon. The catastrophe slowed the attack, and the fighting carried over into the second morning.

As affairs were winding down, one of the battalion commanders,

On the beach at Namur.

Lieutenant Colonel Aquilla J. Dyess, won the Medal of Honor. "He was constantly at the head of advance units, inspiring his men to push forward until the Japanese had been driven back to a small center of resistance and victory assured. While standing on the parapet of an antitank trench directing a group of infantry in a flanking attack against the last enemy position, he was killed by a burst of machine-gun fire." It was 1:18 in the afternoon when Namur was declared secured. The date was February 2.

Roi-Namur had cost the 4th Marine Division 313 killed and 502 wounded. About 3,500 of the enemy—victims either of the bombardment or the assault—were buried, and the engineers began working on Roi's rubble-strewn airfield, a job shortly taken over by the Seabees. During this same period the Marines occupied about fifty additional islets in the atoll's northern group. Down at the Kwajalein end of the atoll the Army finished its work, which included some supplementary occupations that involved stiff fighting, on February 5. Losses were 173 killed and 793 wounded. About 5,000 Japanese were buried.

One of the few Roi-Namur Japanese taken captive. A comrade lies dead beside him; another, alive but wounded, peers around base of wall.

All in all, the conquest of the world's largest atoll went much better than most participants had expected. As a result, the expedition's top commanders changed their thinking about Eniwetok. Instead of delaying three months to reorganize, they initiated the new operation at once. The assault plan was much the same as that for Kwajalein. Eniwetok is another extensive atoll, although circular rather than triangular. It is made up of forty isles, some of them hardly more than dots, and its lagoon measures 388 square miles. As at Kwajalein, the Americans had northern and southern objectives: Engebi isle in the north and Eniwetok and Parry isles in the south. The one big difference in the plan was that the invasions would be covered by a massive naval attack on Truk, the base in the Carolines, 670 miles southwest of Eniwetok.

The objective isles had already been bombed in connection with the assault on Kwajalein, and now, as the preparatory strikes began, a Japanese defender on Engebi recorded in his diary: "When such a small island is hit by about 130 bombs a day, and, having lost its ammunition and provisions, lies helpless, it is no wonder that some soldiers have gone out of their minds." The diarist explained that the men were obliged to subsist on a single ball of rice a day. He thought of his family seated at dinner in Japan. "Their joy helps me to bear these hardships, when I realize that it is because of just such hardships as these I am now suffering that they are able to eat their rice cakes in peace." Conditions on the southern isles were not quite so bad. There was a little *sake* left to go with the reduced rations. But these defenders, too, were aware that death was near. On February 12, even as bombs were falling, the men on Parry celebrated the anniversary of the coronation of Jinmu, Japan's first emperor. Grasping at a straw, a diarist wrote, "There must be some meaning for us in that."

On February 17, as the 22nd Marines and the Army's 106th Infantry Regiment began their work among Eniwetok's isles, Rear Admiral Marc A. Mitscher's fast carrier forces launched a two-day air and surface attack on Truk. The big ships of the base had been withdrawn to calmer waters, but some forty lesser vessels were destroyed, along with at least 250 aircraft. With rare candor, Radio Tokyo informed the Japanese people of the attack, going even further: "The enemy is constantly repeating powerful raids with several hundred fighters and bombers. . . . The war situation has assumed unprecedented seriousness. . . . The tempo of enemy operations indicates that the attacking forces are already pressing upon our mainland."

The assaults on the Eniwetok objectives went well, although the survivors of the small garrisons made some heroic last-ditch stands.

Engebi, where the Marines landed on February 18, was overrun in one day and mopped up in one more. The work on Eniwetok isle, begun on the nineteenth by a combination of GIs and Marines, stretched out to four days. Parry, another target reserved exclusively for the Marines, was assaulted on the twenty-second and secured on the twenty-third. This ended the major fighting; minor landings followed. While wiping out Eniwetok's defenders (except for sixty-six men taken prisoner), the Marines lost 254 killed and 555 wounded; the Army, ninety-four killed and 311 wounded. There was some profane grumbling among the 22nd Marines about the 106th Infantry; the "doggies" were accused of lacking offensive spirit. The complaint would have been of small significance, except that it involved a part of Ralph Smith's 27th Division, previously blasted by Holland Smith for its sluggishness on Makin. The association between the Marines and the 27th would continue, and deeper trouble would result.

The main part of the campaign for the Marshalls was now over, but minor landings and investigations throughout the group continued for another two months. By the end of April the surviving Japanese, about 13,000 of them, held only the bypassed islands of Wotje, Maloelap, Mille, and Jaluit. Much of the work of keeping these bases neutralized for the rest of the war fell to Marine Corps airmen flying from Marshalls strips. There was also Army and Navy air participation, and an occasional Navy shelling. The enemy's resistance was limited to antiaircraft fire. Over a period of a year and a half, the Marine fliers alone poured in nearly 7,000 tons of bombs and rockets. About 2,500 Japanese were killed, and another 5,000 died of starvation or disease. One day 200 of Mille's men were bombed and strafed to death while trying to dynamite fish in the sea. Rats were eaten, and so was human flesh. A few Japanese, lured by surrender leaflets and canned salmon dropped on the islands, survived by swimming out to American vessels. As always in cases like this, most of the Japanese who died could have lived; all they had to do was surrender. While performing their "milk run" duties, the Marines lost a number of planes, along with twenty-two dead and twenty-six wounded. Several of the deaths occurred only after the victims had parachuted into the hands of an extremely bitter enemy.

The victory in the Marshalls—although gained quickly and at a low cost—was one of profound significance to the Navy's Central Pacific campaign. From his foothold in the Gilberts, Admiral Nimitz had made a leap that carried him almost halfway to the Marianas. These islands —chiefly Guam, Saipan, and Tinian—were the admiral's next target, and they were only 1,500 miles from Tokyo. Once air bases were estab-

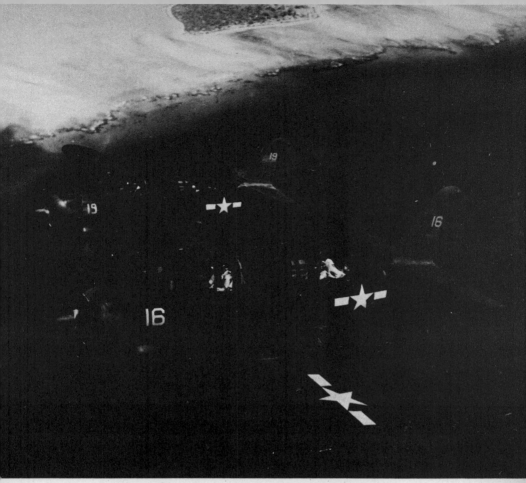

Marine dive bombers flying from Marshalls bases.

lished in the Marianas, America could use its newest weapon, the B-29 Superfortress, against Japan itself. This huge silver plane—too proud, it was said, to resort to camouflage—could carry a bomb load of 10,000 pounds, and it had a greater range than any other aircraft in the world.

Whereas the assault on Tarawa had shocked the American people, the capture of the Marshalls and the raid on Truk raised their morale. Certain news analysts saw the victories as having a meaning beyond their military implications. The nation had been suffering from a spiritual uncertainty since the close of World War I, had struggled through a depression, had been militarily crippled at Pearl Harbor. Now at last—as the result of industrial cooperation, good leadership at all levels, and the determination and courage of the men at the front —something of capital importance had been achieved. "We need doubt no longer," wrote Walter Lippmann, "the capacity of the nation to meet its tests and to fulfill its destiny."

As far as the Marines were concerned, the war was about to assume a new ferocity. The bases ahead were large ones, the foe in heavy numbers. And the terrain was different. Until this time the fighting had occurred either in heavy jungles or on islands of flat coral. The remaining objectives held many hill systems interlaced with caves, both natural and created. Only the relatively few Marines who had fought on Tulagi, Gavutu, and Tanambogo had encountered cave systems. The rest of the Pacific veterans had to learn some new tricks. And there was another consideration. With their homeland threatened, the Emperor's soldiers, sailors, and airmen were prepared to fight harder than ever.

17 | *On Southern Saipan*

══════ In early June 1944, the Marshall Islands became the rendezvous area for nearly 800 ships of the U.S. Navy's 5th Fleet. Steaming into the blue lagoons of Majuro, Kwajalein, and Eniwetok came aircraft carriers, battleships, cruisers, destroyers, gunboats, troop and cargo transports, landing ships, and all of the usual auxiliaries. The atolls where the ships anchored were in the hands of garrison troops now, their camps marked by tall motion-picture screens. The beach at Eniwetok was dotted with gaudy umbrellas which, during the heat of the day, sheltered Navy nurses in swimsuits, the target of many a set of shipboard binoculars. Even while Raymond Spruance's vessels were gathering, an even greater fleet—a combination of American and British ships—began the invasion of Normandy, halfway around the world. In both theaters of the war, the period was one of decisive events. Spruance was preparing to invade the Marianas, a part of Japan's inner defense line. His vessels held a total of 350,000 men representing all branches of the service. The amphibious troops—Marines and GIs—had been brought from training camps in the Hawaiian Islands and on Guadalcanal. The top amphibious commanders were again Kelly Turner and Holland Smith.

Saipan was the first objective. An island of some seventy square miles, it was a fueling and supply station for the Imperial Navy, and held a seaplane base and two airfields. Vice Admiral Chuichi Nagumo had his headquarters there. Nagumo, who had led the attack on Pearl Harbor and had also commanded Japan's carrier striking forces at Midway and Santa Cruz, was now in charge of the newly created and still insignificant Central Pacific Fleet, and of a shore outfit known as the 5th Base Force. The admiral's chief troop units were the 55th Naval Guard Force and the 1st Yokosuka Special Naval Landing Force. Saipan was also headquarters for the 31st Army, and forming the garrison were the 43rd Division and the 47th Independent Mixed Brigade, plus numerous attached units. The island's Army commander was Lieutenant General Yoshitsugu Saito, a man of mature years and uncertain health. Saito was not on the best of terms with his co-commander, Nagumo, for the admiral was unable to deal with the American submarines that were stalking the troop and supply ships approaching the Marianas. One out of three of these ships was being sunk, a second damaged. Saipan's reinforcements were drowning, and there was a shortage of cement, lumber, steel, and barbed wire needed to strengthen the defenses. The

Army and Navy troops on the island, however, totaled 30,000. And there was a large civilian populace whose support could be counted upon. These people, many of whom were connected with Saipan's thriving sugar industry, included Japanese, Okinawans, Koreans, Formosans, and native Chamorros and Kanakas. The majority of the civilians had been taught not only to hate the Americans but to fear them as barbarians. Tokyo had ordered the evacuation of the older people and the women and children, but it proved just as difficult to get these civilians out as it was to get the military in. One of the outgoing ships torpedoed and sunk with tragic losses was carrying 1,700 people belonging to the island's leading families.

Chosen to make the assault on Saipan were the 2nd and 4th Marine Divisions and their attached elements—about 50,000 men. Making up the floating reserve was the Army's 27th Division under Ralph Smith. The forces were none too strong for the job; they did not represent a three-to-one ratic. Intelligence estimates had placed the enemy garrison at a number considerably lower than its true size. But the American edge in firepower was greater than ever. For one thing, the Marines had reorganized their rifle squads. Whereas the earlier ones had a single BAR each, they now had three. This upped a division's automatic-rifle strength from 558 to 853. Each platoon had a special assault squad armed with a bazooka, demolitions, and two flamethrowers. The number of flamethrowers in a division had been increased from twenty-four to 243. Moreover, there were twenty-four long-range flamethrowers for mounting on light tanks. Each tank battalion now had forty-six medium Shermans. It had been found expedient to reduce a division's number of pack howitzers, but the weapons platoons had been given additional mortars.

Also continuing to grow was the power of the sea and air support provided for an invasion. The preparatory work for Saipan was begun on June 11 by the planes of Marc Mitscher's Task Force 58. A junior Japanese officer, Tokuzo Matsuya, explained in his diary that, as the first air-raid siren sounded, he led his men into a trench. "Scores of enemy fighters began strafing and bombing Aslito Airfield and [the town of] Garapan. For about two hours the enemy planes ran amok, and finally left in a leisurely manner amid unparalleledly inaccurate antiaircraft fire. All we could do was watch helplessly." Either in the air or on the ground, about 150 planes had been destroyed, which gave the Americans mastery of Saipan's skies. There was another strike the next day, and a Japanese soldier with a ringside seat on the nearby island of Tinian was disappointed to see that not a single Zero went aloft. "The planes which cover the sky are all the enemy's. They are far and away more skillful than Japanese planes. . . . Enemy planes overhead all day long, some 230 in number. They completely plastered our airfields. . . . Our antiaircraft guns spread black smoke where the enemy planes weren't." This same Japanese wrote gloomily, "Now begins our cave life."

On June 13, Tokuzo Matsuya recorded: "At 0930, enemy naval guns began firing in addition to the aerial bombing. The enemy holds us in utter contempt." The Japanese had a particular dread of these naval bombardments, and for good reason. The Imperial Army's high command had calculated that a single American battleship, firing only half its main batteries, had "a casualty-producing potential equal to the firepower of five Japanese ground divisions or 1,250 light bombers." In the present case, however, the naval fire was more blusterous than effective. Saipan's land area was extensive, and too few of the enemy's installations were pinpointed.

The invasion's preparatory work was not limited to Saipan. Tinian and Guam were hit, as were numerous other islands within supporting distance of the objective. Although Truk, the once-feared base in the Carolines, had been given what amounted to its death blow by Mitscher's forces as early as April 29, there were lesser stations that retained the capacity to send aircraft to Saipan. The most venturesome American move was made on June 14, when two fast carrier groups broke away from Task Force 58 and attacked Iwo Jima, Haha Jima, and Chichi Jima in the Bonins, only 700 miles from Tokyo. The Navy's activities were not challenged by the Japanese fleet, but this situation would not last. Tokyo had its own plans regarding the assault on Saipan. While Admiral Nagumo and General Saito destroyed the invaders on the beach, the Combined Fleet, commanded by Admiral Soemu Toyoda, would strike at the American naval forces. The combination effort, designated "A-Go," was viewed by the more realistic men at Imperial General Headquarters as Japan's last chance to turn the tide of the war. "The fate of the Empire," Toyoda informed his subordinates, "rests on this one battle." The public, through Radio Tokyo, was addressed more positively: "It has been announced here that the Imperial Navy in the near future will win a great victory in the Pacific. We are all waiting for the news." Tokyo Rose broadcast to the Marines that they were expected on Saipan. "She told us," recalled Private Joseph V. Drotovick, "that we would be annihilated." Rose played some American records, advising the men to enjoy the music while they could. This silky-voiced propagandist never affected American morale the way she was supposed to. She was merely amusing and entertaining.

She did make the Marines realize, however, that the restrictions placed on their letters home, which cramped their self-expression, were overdone. They were not allowed, for example, to tell where they were encamped, even if it happened to be in the Hawaiian Islands. The Japanese, through their civilian spies and military intelligence personnel, usually knew where the different Marine outfits were located and what they were up to—often, in fact, knew more about an impending operation than the Marine letter-writers themselves.

As the bombardment of Saipan heated up, Tokuzo Matsuya, unaware of the A-Go plan, penned in his diary: "Where are our planes? Are they letting us die without making any effort to save us? . . . Wouldn't it be a great loss to the Land of the Gods for us all to die on this island?" Matsuya himself wanted to stay alive "for the sake of the future."

At dawn on June 15, the aggregation of American ships carrying the invasion forces arrived several miles off Saipan's western coast, which stretched for about fourteen miles between Agingan Point in the south and Marpi Point in the north. From his position at the rail of one of the troop transports, Time-Life correspondent Robert Sherrod saw the island as "a shadowy land mass, purple against the dim horizon." Fires caused by the previous day's bombardment illuminated several spots in the woods, fields, and towns. As the rising sun put a red tint on the clouds behind Saipan's volcanic hills, the American naval guns began sending in their pre-H-hour missiles. At seven o'clock, with the Marines preparing to land, the air strikes began. Amid the clatter and the thunder, the target zones flashed and twinkled and gave rise to heavy smoke. "Within a very few minutes," Sherrod noted, "the whole of the area in back of our landing beaches was obscured by these columns." The correspondent was thrilled by the show but doubted that many of the enemy were being killed. One clear indication that the Japanese were surviving was that the Navy's gunfire vessels were receiving counterbattery fire, some of which was hitting home and causing damage.

While a detached group of transports made a pretense of unloading troops off the northern half of the island (a ruse that caused the defenders only a few moments of uncertainty), the real invasion got under way in the south. It covered a four-mile front, with the 2nd Marine Division on the left and the 4th Marine Division on the right. Leading the way were twenty-four LCI gunboats firing rockets and 20-millimeter and 40-millimeter guns. Next came two battalions of amphibian tractors, about 135 vehicles in all, armed with 75-millimeter howitzers and machine guns. Of these "amtanks," half belonged to the Marine Corps and half to the Army. The Marine vehicles ran interference for the 2nd

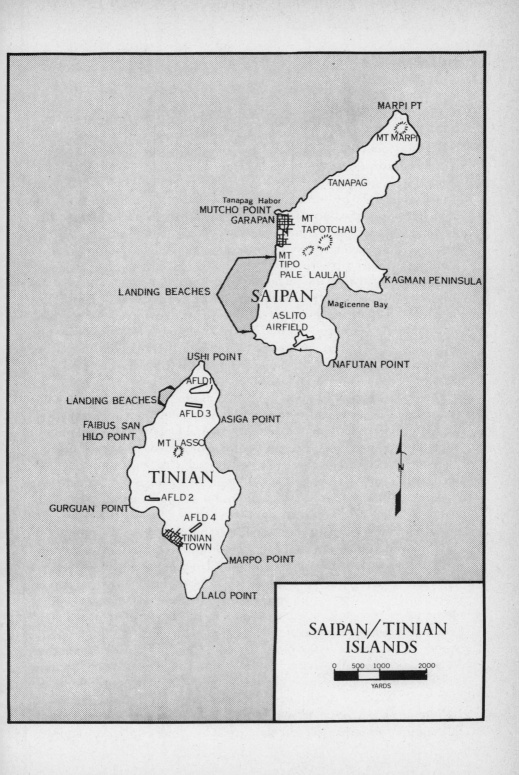

MARPI PT

MT MARPI

TANAPAG

Tanapag Habor
MUTCHO POINT
GARAPAN

MT
TAPOTCHAU

MT
TIPO
PALE LAULAU

KAGMAN PENINSULA

LANDING BEACHES

SAIPAN

Magicenne Bay

ASLITO
AIRFIELD

NAFUTAN POINT

USHI POINT

AFLD 1

LANDING BEACHES

AFLD 3

ASIGA POINT

FAIBUS SAN
HILO POINT

MT LASSO

TINIAN

AFLD 2

GURGUAN POINT

AFLD 4

TINIAN
TOWN

MARPO POINT

LALO POINT

N

SAIPAN/TINIAN
ISLANDS

0   500   1000   2000
YARDS

Division, those of the Army for the 4th. The men of the assault waves were riding in some 700 regular amphibian tractors. Half of these vehicles, too, were manned by Army crews.

As at Tarawa, there was a reef to cross, but, with everyone in amtracs, this posed no problem; the waves simply lumbered over. As those in the lead began bobbing through the deeper pools inside the reef, a Marine remarked above the churn of his tractor's engine, "Well, it looks as though we'll get in okay." His words were punctuated by a shellburst, a near miss that brought shrapnel and water slamming against the vehicle's side. Now both artillery and mortar shells came plummeting down along much of the four-mile line. At the same time, the amtracs began rattling under the peck of machine-gun bullets. Shouted another Marine, a veteran of Tarawa, "The same old dish of soup, warmed over!" American aircraft, darting in from the sea to attack the gun and mortar positions, unintentionally added to the general dismay. They began firing their machine guns while roaring low over the Marines, and the shell casings came down like rain, plopping into the water and into some of the amtracs. At least momentarily believing they were being strafed by their own planes, the affected Marines howled with dismay.

There was a genuine reason for dismay as the enemy made telling hits on some of the crowded tractors. Shellbursts felled men in groups, their blood forming rivulets on the deck among the feet of comrades stunned but still standing. Tractors spun round as their drivers were shot from the controls. Here and there, one of the vehicles went under, half its occupants dead or wounded, all of the living struggling to shed their packs and other gear and stay afloat until they could be pulled from the water by men in other tractors. If no help was near, the swimmers began paddling toward shore, some leaving pink wakes. A number of the armored vehicles in the lead were knocked out either in the surf or almost as soon as they crawled up on land. Segments of the assault were thrown into confusion. Japanese antiboat guns firing from Afetna Point, in the center of the four-mile front, were a factor in causing elements of the 2nd Division to veer to the north of their assigned beaches, where some became enmeshed with units landing in their proper places. But the assault as a whole was far from being another Tarawa, for it began to succeed quickly, and almost as planned. By nine o'clock, twenty minutes after the designated H-hour, Saipan's shoreline held 8,000 Marines. And thousands more were on the way in.

Watching the invasion from a hillside some distance inland was Admiral Nagumo, who marveled at the display of American power and was particularly impressed by the number of heavy warships in the monstrous armada. After using binoculars to study the battleships, the admiral turned to an aide and explained that several of those his airmen had sunk at Pearl Harbor were back in action. There was a note of admiration in his voice. Even now, some of the fleet's guns were booming, and a shell happened to land at a spot in the hills where the elderly General Saito was holding an outdoor staff meeting. Half the group was killed; the general was dazed but soon rallied. At this stage in the battle, both Saito and Nagumo tended to be optimistic. They knew that the Combined Fleet, itself a large and potent force, was on the way. If they could not stop the invasion at the shoreline, they could fight a delaying action until the fleet came to the rescue. They had enough troops to put up a strong fight. It was Saito who assumed top responsibility for the defense, and this morning, with the foe thick on the beach, the general was placing strong reliance on artillery batteries set up behind the inland ridges. These batteries had the aid of a spotter in a unique position. Near the center of the American landing zone was the devastated coastal village of Charan Kanoa, and it held the smoldering ruins of a sugar refinery whose tall smokestack was still standing. The spotter was secreted inside the top of the stack, and he had a fine view of the beachhead.

The undulating coastal lowlands the Marines were facing were made up largely of farms, cane fields, brush patches, and woodlands. There were palm trees, but few of the woodlands could be classified as jungles. Just inland from Charan Kanoa lay a swamp-rimmed lake. The preliminary bombardment had torn up the terrain and blackened it with fires, and most of the farmhouses and their utility buildings had been destroyed or damaged. The residents had fled to the hills, but the fields were populated with oxen, cows, goats, and chickens. This area held few heavy fortifications but was amply furnished with mortar and machine-gun positions, together with riflemen in ruined buildings, in trenches, in clumps of brush, and behind rises in the fields. The terrain was well suited to defense. Once again the Marines, although superior in numbers and firepower, knew the terrifying disadvantage of having to advance in the open against a concealed and deadly enemy. They had to initiate each encounter by pitting their flesh against steel.

Casualties mounted alarmingly under the sustained artillery fire from the hills and the mortar and small-arms fire from just inland. At two spots along the landing zone there were Japanese at the water's edge: at Afetna Point in the center, which the 2nd Division's incoming craft continued to avoid by swinging north; and at Agingan Point in the extreme south, near the 4th Division's right flank. One of the 2nd Division units that had landed too far north—the 2nd Battalion, 8th Marines—began moving down the beach and attacking Afetna from the flank. Some of the Marines carried shotguns, which proved remarkably handy for disposing of defenders who rose from their holes and charged. One of the battalion's early casualties was its redheaded leader, Jim Crowe, of Tarawa fame. He was first shot through a lung, near the heart, and then peppered with the fragments of a mortar shell that killed a corpsman and wounded a doctor who were helping him. Crowe's life was despaired of, but he would make a good recovery.

While Crowe's men were struggling to clear the Afetna area and the other 2nd Division units were inching their way inland, the 4th Division was fighting an equally difficult battle in the southern zone. One platoon leader, Second Lieutenant Fred B. Harvey, was leading his platoon up the beach when he was rushed by a Japanese officer with an upraised sword. Harvey, a former Harvard athlete, parried the blow with his carbine, jumped back, and shot the man dead. Incidents like this were uncommon, but the danger from shellbursts and bullets was constant. The weapons aimed at the division's right flank from Agingan Point compelled the men of the 1st Battalion, 25th Marines, to hug the beach, many pouring their blood into the dancing and churning sand, until naval gunfire and aircraft strikes put a temporary end to the menace. The help was especially timely, since the Japanese were preparing to counterattack. Just to the left of the 1st Battalion's zone, amtracs carrying elements of the 2nd Battalion, 25th, climbed the beach and transported their occupants about 600 yards inland, to the shelter of a railroad bank. The battalion's commander, Lieutenant Colonel Lewis C. Hudson, gave much of the credit for the success to the Army amtanks that covered the move. They "took more than their share of punishment" and "diverted enemy attention from the tractors carrying troops."

The Marines on the 4th Division's left, Lieutenant Colonel John J. Cosgrove's 3rd Battalion, 23rd Regiment, came ashore at Charan Kanoa, the ruins of which were brightened by bougainvillea vines in full bloom. There were only a few snipers in the town, and three amtanks and eight amtracs rolled on through, the troops setting up a line on a rise some distance inland. Here they were subjected to heavy fire and were also harassed by moves against their flank. Approaching Charan Kanoa over the same waters a little later was the regimental reserve, and in one of the tractors was a Marine Corps combat correspondent, Sergeant David Dempsey. As his vehicle neared shore, Dempsey poked his head up and took in the view. He saw several amtracs that "had been hit and were flipped over like pancakes on a griddle." The only people in evidence were a Navy beachmaster who was waving the tractors in, and a group of bandaged wounded awaiting transport to a hospital ship. The reserve troops remained in their amtracs and took the road through Charan Kanoa, passing what Dempsey thought should have been the town square but was actually an American-style baseball diamond. Nearby stood a Buddhist temple. Debarking while still inside the town limits, the troops began moving toward the front on foot. For a time their zone was quiet and the sun "lay over the town like a soft blanket." Then the spell was broken by whooshing and crashing shells. Dempsey and a Marine scout jumped into a Japanese stand-up foxhole, which, by means of their entrenching tools, they began enlarging. To their surprise, they unearthed a case of port wine. Tested, the beverage was found to be mild and sweet. The pair drank one bottle and passed the rest around. Meanwhile, shells were shaking the area and making hits. Finally, Dempsey and his companion returned to the beach, where they found the shellfire even hotter. The correspondent began to help with the wounded, whose number kept growing. "One man was brought in with his leg almost blown off between the hip and the knee. The doctor amputated without removing him from the stretcher." Some of those brought back from the front were psychiatric cases, men who had cracked under the relentless artillery and mortar fire. "They hid behind trees and cowered at each new shellburst. Some could not remember their names."

Up in the 2nd Division zone the Marines at the front were beginning to experience minor thrusts by enemy tanks, machines of a design that, by American standards, was peculiar. On the extreme left of the beachhead was the 1st Platoon, F Company, 6th Marines, commanded by Lieutenant James R. Ray. The unit was positioned on the coastal road about a mile south of the town of Garapan, an enemy stronghold. Prior to bringing his men ashore, Ray had warned them that they must be prepared for the worst, that the Japanese would probably hit them with everything they had, "including the kitchen sink." Shortly after noon, PFC Nestor Sotelo, who was watching the road, saw two of the odd-looking tanks drawing near, and he shouted, "Pass the word to Mr. Ray that the Japs have arrived from Garapan with the kitchen sink." The two machines were quickly knocked out with bazookas and antitank grenades.

Robert Sherrod, traveling in an amtrac with the 2nd Division's assistant commander, Red Mike Edson (now a brigadier general), came ashore on the left at 2:30 in the afternoon. For the first twenty minutes the correspondent was obliged to huddle in an abandoned Japanese tank trap while artillery and mortar shells walked up and down the beach and also splashed in the waters offshore. The trap held five dead Japanese and an American aid station. Sherrod heard a corpsman say, "Hell, I'm going back up front; it's safer." When Sherrod was able to leave the trap and take a look around, he decided that Saipan might be a nice place "if it were properly fixed up by the Seabees and the engineers." During his investigations up and down the coast, the correspondent counted about twenty enemy and 100 American dead. One Marine "had the top of his head neatly carved out, evidently by a shell fragment, and his brains had run out on the sand." Sherrod saw a tangle of human parts in a shellhole where six Marines had taken cover, only to be found by one of the enemy's larger guns. "No more than half of any one man was left." There was a live Japanese in the area, "a gold-toothed little fellow with a bullet hole in his leg," who was being interrogated by two intelligence officers. A truly heartening sight was a group of tanks, "one medium and eighteen lights," lumbering in from the reef through a span of shallow water. At this time, a company of fourteen medium tanks was already helping the Marines who were attacking Afetna Point.

The 4th Division's tanks, as a result of unfavorable surf conditions and enemy shellfire, had trouble getting in; some never made it. A number of those that did proved a godsend to the Marines on the far right, near Agingan Point, who needed the support to deal with a two-company counterattack. In a short but convulsive action, the charging Japanese were massacred. Along the entire beachhead, the presence of the tanks raised morale—even though there was peril in getting too close to them, since they drew enemy fire. Almost equally encouraging was the sharp cracking of the artillery pieces that were now ashore and supporting the attack, a strong supplement to the Navy's guns and aircraft. In addition, it was good to know that supplies were pouring ashore, that dumps were building up at points just inland.

By the end of the day, Saipan was host to 20,000 Marines. But casualties had been high: more than 2,000 men dead or wounded, one out of ten. Some of the units that landed early in the day suffered one out of three, a ratio high enough to raise the threat of panic. As at Tarawa, the fact that panic did not occur had to be attributed to the physical and moral toughness of Marine Corps training. The beachhead—about 10,-000 yards long and 1,500 yards deep—was only half the planned D-day goal. Conditions remained harrowing both at the front and on the beaches, and there was no prospect of a quick victory. The Marines, however, were confident that they had come to Saipan to stay. In spite of the new dangers the coming of dusk presaged, there were men who could pretend to be lighthearted. While using his shovel to dig a fox-hole, a private sang out, "My father always told me that if I didn't finish high school I'd end up digging ditches!"

Making the rounds among the men of both divisions at this time was the welcome news that the commanding generals had landed. Harry Schmidt was still in charge of the 4th, while the 2nd was now being led by Major General Thomas E. "Terrible Tommy" Watson, a former enlisted man. Watson had trouble getting settled. He tried a spot on the beach, but it was so hot with shellfire he decided to move. "The sun had already set; the distant night was alive with fires, and the shelling from enemy artillery and mortars was unremitting. . . . Our headquarters group moved northward along the beach, then struck inland across the beach road, and, moving in the shadows of the road, finally reached the wooded area which had been selected for the new command post. . . . We were delighted to find trenches and shelters already dug by the Japanese. Our joy was soon dispelled, however, when we discovered that these not only contained dead Japanese who had to be moved, but dynamite and other explosives. The dangerous materials were moved out . . . and the area served as an excellent divisional command post . . . although . . . it was located only a few yards behind our front lines."

If the night was a bad one on the beach, it was even worse at the front. All along the perimeter the Japanese made probes and counterattacks, approaching both in small numbers and in large. American destroyers off the coast sent up star shells that burst over the island and descended slowly under silk parachutes, their brilliance making the enemy easy to discern, at the same time producing flickering shadows among the trees and shrubs that made for some false alarms. The Marines spent most of the night either anxiously scanning the terrain for hostile movement or fighting to save their lives and their lines. The clashes involved not only multikeyed sounds but also vivid pyrotechnics: gun muzzles flashing yellow, tracers leaving red streaks, shells and grenades creating orange arcs with jagged edges. For the Americans watching from the vessels offshore and for the Japanese reserves and the civilians looking down from their commanding hills, the combination of sound and color was a fascination, even had a kind of wicked beauty. For the combatants, of course, the setting was simply hellish.

There was a gap between the two Marine divisions, the result of the landing problems caused by the Japanese guns at Afetna Point, and the spot was probed repeatedly through the night. Most of the infiltrators were fired upon and stopped, but some made it all the way to the beach. The zone's shore-party people, who had been busy dodging shells and unloading and organizing supplies, were obliged to meet the threat by doubling as infantry. Many were Army men. A Marine observer later referred to this beach as "a hotbed" where the Army "fought and worked and did a good job."

At one time during the night, the Marines of the 25th Regiment, at the 4th Division's front, were surprised to see a large body of civilians —men, women, and children—approaching across the fields, hands aloft as though coming in to surrender. While waiting to receive the throng, the Marines suddenly realized they were being tricked. The shout went up, "There are Jap troops behind them!" With their compassion replaced by the will to survive, the Marines lashed out with all of the firepower they could muster—with rifles, machine guns, mortars, 37-millimeter guns, 75-millimeter halftracks, and 105-millimeter howitzers. The zone became an inferno, the detonations and flashes constant, the roar permeated by shrieks and wails. Remarkably enough, the Japanese troops almost achieved a breakthrough. A shell from their side hit one of the halftracks, turning it into a sheet of fire and exploding its ammunition, and a part of the American line drew back. In the end, however, it was the surviving Japanese who drew back to stay, leaving the zone littered with dead and dying, at least some of which the Marines did not like to contemplate. It was not known whether the civilians were coming in willingly and were followed by the troops, or if they were driven.

The heaviest attack of the night developed on the perimeter's extreme left, the 2nd Division flank that lay on the beach road a mile south of Garapan. Serious trouble had been expected at this spot. During the afternoon, units of Japanese had been seen coming down from the inland hills and entering the town. An American air observer discovered the streets growing busy with what seemed to be patriotic rallies. Some of the men were grouped around gesturing speakers, others were waving flags, or marching to and fro, or drinking from tilted bottles. Soon after dark the attack troops—about 1,000 in all—gathered in the town's southern outskirts, some on foot, some in trucks or tanks, some even in barges in the surf. The approach to the perimeter was made with all the secrecy of a circus parade, motors throbbing, tank tracks clanking, and voices unmuted. At ten o'clock an advance party made a probing attack, which the Marines turned back. Several other small-scale actions followed. Finally, at 3:00 A.M., the entire assault force formed. The Marines were obligingly—and somewhat unbelievingly—warned what was about to happen by an enemy bugler, who blew "charge," the notes sharp on the night air. Waving swords and flags, and shouting and shrieking, the Japanese came on at a trot. "Flares! Flares!" the Marines cried, and an officer put in a fast call to the Navy: "Illumination requested." Three destroyers complied, and in a few moments the area was starkly bright, the Japanese taking on a white cast that made them look like moving statues. Caught in a maelstrom of fire, with even the battleship *California* joining in with some of her secondary batteries, the statues began tumbling, shattering, turning crimson. The attack was stopped. But, with all of their usual persistence in pressing lost causes, the Japanese soon came on again, and the Marines took casualties from the supporting mortars and from small arms and grenades. Where positions were overrun, the fighting came to hand-to-hand. Not until five Sherman tanks rolled forward, their howitzers and machine guns raging, was the action ended. As the surviving Japanese fell back up the coastal road, they were pursued by fire from land and sea. The attack force had suffered some 700 killed. When daylight came, Marines poking around among the clusters of human debris noticed the sun reflecting on a brass object: the Japanese bugle, dented and torn by bullets.

Down in the 4th Division zone, the period just before dawn found the enemy's counterbattery fire from the hills beginning to exact a particular vengeance on the 105-millimeter howitzers of the 5th Battalion, 14th Marines. There were a dozen of these guns, four to a battery. As reported by the battalion commander, Lieutenant Colonel Douglas E. Reeve: "By 0430, all of Baker Battery's guns had been knocked out; 0500, two guns in Able Battery knocked out; 0545, one gun in Charlie Battery knocked out; 0630, the other two guns in Able Battery knocked out; 0730, one more gun in Charlie Battery knocked out. . . . When I say *knocked out*, I mean just that—trails blown off, sights blown off, recoil mechanisms damaged, etc. By 1000, with the help of division ordnance and by completely replacing one or two weapons, we were back in business, full strength, twelve guns." The battalion had sustained eight men killed and more than fifty wounded.

That morning Raymond Spruance, commander of the 5th Fleet, boarded his admiral's barge and paid a visit to Kelly Turner and Holland Smith on Turner's flagship, the *Rocky Mount*. Spruance had learned that Japan's Combined Fleet, which was being tracked by American submarines, was plowing eastward from the Philippines and would be near enough to the Marianas to do battle in about forty-eight hours.

Admiral Jisaburo Ozawa.

Task Force 58 would intercept, but Turner's assault shipping might be imperiled. Spruance informed Turner and Smith that they must complete the critical phase of their unloading operations by the following evening, at which time Turner would have to take the bulk of the shipping on a temporary retreat eastward, out of the danger zone. Smith did not object to the order. "I realized it was essential and that we must hang on like good Marines until the fate of the Japanese fleet was decided." But Smith would have to make a change in his plans. His floating reserve, Ralph Smith's 27th Division, U.S. Army, would have to be landed at once. As Spruance was going back to his barge, Smith asked him whether there wasn't a possibility the enemy would turn and run. The admiral was certain this would not happen. "The attack on the Marianas is too great a challenge for the Japanese Navy to ignore." Actually, the commander of the Japanese strike force, Admiral Jisaburo Ozawa, believed he had a good chance of achieving the smashing victory Radio Tokyo was predicting. It was true that his intelligence officers judged the American fleet to be nearly twice as strong as his own, but he expected to get heavy support from aircraft stationed on strips in the Marianas. About 500 planes had been sent to these islands within the past two months. With this support, Ozawa figured, his air power would be a match for that of the foe. Unfortunately for the admiral's plans, a large number of the land-based planes had already been destroyed by American strikes. Also working against Ozawa was the limited experience of most of his airmen. The majority of the veterans had died in previous fights.

At Saipan on the second day, American plans called for the accelerated unloading of troops, equipment, and supplies; for the 2nd Division to mop up and consolidate its positions on the assault's left; and for the 4th Division to begin pushing across the southern end of the island toward Aslito Airfield. The enemy's shellfire continued, even though its sources were avidly sought by Marine artillerymen, by the gunners on battleships and cruisers, and by the pilots of diving aircraft. The hills were kept smoky with the American counterfire. The Japanese shells were placed with particular accuracy in the Charan Kanoa area, where the spotter still held his place in the sugar-mill smokestack. (This mettlesome fellow would manage to operate for another two or three days before his discovery and capture.) In spite of the shellfire on the beaches and in the surf, the unloading operations proceeded efficiently. The supplies were handled by soldiers, sailors, Coast Guardsmen, Seabees, and Marines. A member of one of the parties, Marine PFC S. G. Silcox, had never seen men "work so hard and willingly." He mused upon what a blessing it would be for the world "if everyone suddenly behaved and acted as these men did." Silcox adds a somber note: "We worked with dead all around us, both friend and enemy, and had to move them to stack the ammo and supplies." There were also groups of wounded, Marines brought from the front, and these men were placed on board empty landing craft for delivery to the hospital ships. By this time it was clear, as Robert Sherrod noted, "that Saipan was becoming a very expensive operation."

That morning, while he was walking the beach, the correspondent saw his first civilians, three women and four children. Two of the children were crying. The other two were babes, and their mothers were nursing them even as shells shook the area. Sherrod heard a Marine lieutenant say, "God damn! Does war have to come to this?"

The 4th Division opened its attack at 12:30 in the afternoon and found the going tough. Almost at once, a mortar shell killed the commander of the 1st Battalion, 24th Marines, Lieutenant Colonel Maynard C. Shultz. The colonel was only one of a number of high-ranking officers hit since the invasion began, a situation the Marines were able to adjust to without serious impairment to their efficiency. On the right of the attack, the 3rd Battalion, 25th, led by Justice Chambers, veteran of Tulagi and the Marshalls and now a lieutenant colonel, worked with tanks to destroy two howitzers, five machine guns, and about sixty of the enemy. Tanks were equally active along other sections of the front.

Fourth Division men hurling hand grenades.

When the Sherman commanded by Gunnery Sergeant Robert H. McCard, 4th Tank Battalion, was disabled by enemy fire, McCard ordered the men of his crew to safety and died covering their escape, a deed that won him the Medal of Honor. Although the 4th Division spent the afternoon moving mostly by inches, losing men all the while, it did manage to secure a hold on the ridge overlooking Aslito Airfield. An indication that the invasion was not proceeding according to expectations was that preliminary plans called for this ridge to be fully occupied on D-day. As for casualties, by the end of the second day the two divisions had sustained a total exceeding 3,000.

That night the 2nd Division's left sector was the target of another spectacular counterattack, this one coming down the interior slopes and including some forty tanks and 500 infantry troops. There was no surprise involved. American air observers operating late in the day had discovered the Japanese assembling, so the Marines had ample time to ready every weapon, light and heavy, in their titanic arsenal. Plagued by communications failures and problems with the terrain, the Japanese milled about behind their covering ridges for hours before completing their organization. These hours were filled with the whooshing, rumbling, and flaring of artillery duels, and several Marine guns took disabling hits. Finally at 3:30 A.M., under a moon dimmed by lacy clouds, the Japanese tanks came squeaking and rattling out of the mouth of a ravine and started down across the open fields. Some of the infantrymen were perched on the machines, while the rest were walking behind them. The Marines called for illumination, something the enemy had come to dread. Already a diarist had written, "Every time we try a night attack, they turn the night into day." It was no different this time. As the fields brightened, the Marines opened up with howitzer and mortar fire and other prepared concentrations. According to Major James A. Donovan, Jr., executive officer of the 1st Battalion, 6th Marines, "The battle evolved itself into a madhouse of noise, tracers, and flashing lights. As tanks were hit and set afire, they silhouetted other tanks coming out of the flickering shadows to the front. . . ." The starkly lighted foot soldiers were cut down by scores. Particularly effective against the tanks were the 37-millimeter guns and bazookas. Donovan noted that the bazooka "was verified as a superior tank-buster." Also helping with the destruction were booming American Shermans. But the Japanese kept coming, and a number of the tanks soon reached the front-line Marines. These veterans of Tarawa held their ground and threw grenades or fired their rifles or machine guns at point-blank range, the bullets ricocheting wildly, a few finding weak spots in the enemy's armor. Two or three of the tanks rolled directly over Marines in deep, strong-walled foxholes, and warm oil dripped down on the hunched figures. As soon as the clattering hulks were past, these men rose up and began throwing grenades or shooting at the broad back ends. Other Marines found themselves fighting at bayonet range with aggressive foot soldiers.

By this time some of the Japanese tank crews, having lost their infantry guides, were becoming confused. One machine came to a halt. Its hatch was thrown open and a head was thrust up. Hit by a bazooka rocket, the head exploded like a melon. A Marine came running with a satchel charge, which he dropped down the hatch. As the confined burst crushed and seared the crew, the hatch produced a pillar of fire. Another tank was finished off by a Marine who jammed one of its tracks with a plank, then stood by with a grenade until the driver opened the hatch to learn what had happened. As Donovan watched, several tanks "ambled on in the general direction of the beach, getting hit again and again until each one burst into flame or turned in aimless circles only to stop dead, stalled in its own ruts or in the marshes of the low ground." Those machines that kept shooting were knocked out by the clanging fire of halftracks.

The coming of dawn found tanks burning everywhere. The few surviving machines, along with most of the surviving infantrymen, were retreating back up the slopes. The foot soldiers who remained behind to lie in holes and snipe were being finished off by rifle and machine-gun fire. One machine-gun crew that had fought with special fury was now completing the expenditure of 10,000 rounds. When the battle zone fell quiet, it held 300 enemy dead besides those in the tanks. The melee had cost the Marines about 100 in killed or wounded, a few of whom had doubtless been hit by friendly fire. At seven o'clock the last Japanese tank to leave the area was sighted on a road winding over a distant hill. Its turret was moving among a small group of buildings on the crest. Naval gunfire was called in, and the spot was blanketed. "The tank," says Donovan, "sent up an oily smoke and burned for the rest of the day."

It was a day during which the Americans improved their situation in both divisional zones. The men of the 2nd expanded north toward Garapan and east toward the center of the island. The 4th Division, with the Army's 165th Regiment now manning the right flank, continued working across the southernmost region. By evening the lower attack was halfway to the east coast, and the 165th was at the western edge of Aslito Airfield. The Americans, north and south, had more casualties to count, but the enemy's coastal defenses were broken. Along the landing beaches, the day saw reserve troops, equipment, and supplies flowing in from the transports under easing resistance from Japanese guns. The shore and beach parties had some new help, a number of young Chamorros who had come out of hiding and volunteered their services. Eager to please, the youths did a lot of smiling and laughing. To everything that was said to them they had but a single response, "Okay," and they pronounced the word in tones that were curiously musical. S. G. Silcox noted that the Americans enjoyed the novel company. "Soon everyone was saying 'okay' and trying to make it sound like the Chamorros."

Holland Smith came ashore from the *Rocky Mount* that afternoon and established his headquarters in Charan Kanoa, the streets of which were now heavy with dust created by the marching invaders and their vehicular traffic. The point had been reached where the passage of a single jeep raised a cloud that dimmed the sunlight. While one of the general's aides was digging a foxhole he turned up a human skeleton of another time. The spot chosen for the command post happened to be an old cemetery rendered indistinguishable by shellfire.

In agreement with Admiral Spruance's orders, Kelly Turner's amphibious shipping began sailing away at dusk. The situation was far different from the time on Guadalcanal, nearly two years earlier, when Turner was obliged to desert Archer Vandegrift and the 1st Division. Holland Smith was left with 78,000 men, and they had 33,000 tons of cargo to sustain them until the problem of Japan's Combined Fleet was resolved. As Turner's ships were leaving, a number of enemy aircraft from nearby islands appeared overhead, and American antiaircraft fire laid a bright pattern against the darkening sky. The Japanese paid the price of three planes in order to damage one LST. The raid was followed by a rainstorm that turned the island's dust to mud, flooded foxholes, and made the Americans generally miserable.

Saipan's Japanese realized that the departure of the enemy's amphibious shipping meant that their own fleet was nearing. General Saito had been obliged to admit to Tokyo that he had failed to annihilate the Americans on their landing beaches, but he was not castigated. The response came from Japan's Prime Minister, Hideki Tojo, who exhorted Saipan's commanders to "inspire the spirit of officers and men" and "continue to destroy the enemy gallantly and persistently." Hirohito must be relieved of his anxiety. "The fate of the Japanese Empire depends on the result of your operation." Tojo did not mention something else that was at stake: his position as prime minister. Saipan's high command radioed back: "By becoming the bulwark of the Pacific with 10,000 deaths, we hope to requite the Imperial favor." But the tiring General Saito had grown doubtful that a sacrificial delaying action, linked with the efforts of the Combined Fleet, would result in the defeat of so powerful and tenacious an adversary, and he began burning his secret papers.

On the fourth day, June 18, the 2nd Marine Division, although encountering some pockets of resistance, generally improved its positions and achieved a salient that extended halfway across the island. The 4th Division, operating in the low and less difficult southern terrain, made it all the way across to the shores of Magicienne Bay—or, as the enlisted Marines chose to call it, Magazine Bay. On the division's right, the Army's 165th Regiment, now teamed with the 105th, with Ralph Smith in overall command, overran Aslito Airfield.

It was a day when scores of civilians were flushed from caves, gullies, and brush patches where they were hiding. Some of these grimy and hungry people had lost their homes to shells or bombs, or to flames created by such missiles; others had simply fled when their district was threatened. A mixture of immigrants and people native to the island, they ranged from wrinkled oldsters to smooth-faced babes strapped to their mothers' backs. Most of the Christian Chamorros seemed happy to be taken into protective custody. Some of the Japanese were belligerent. But none was of the faction that had an excessive hatred and fear of the Americans. Those people were making every effort to keep within Japanese-controlled territory. The refugees were fed and placed in barbed-wire enclosures on the beach. They were allowed to wander out, and the first desire of many was to go down to the sea and bathe.

Holland Smith was pleased with the day's progress, including that of the Army, and during a visit to Ralph Smith's command post the Marine general voiced this approval. The meeting left Ralph Smith in a cheerful mood, and he told an Army public relations man of his satisfaction with the "perfect teamwork" that had been established by the Navy, Marines, and Army. The general said he was pained by the fact that many of the people back home believed that "because a soldier and a Marine get in a fight in a saloon the relations between the services are at cross-purposes. Nothing could be farther from the truth out here in the field." Unfortunately, the spirit of June 18 would not endure.

The Americans now had Saipan spanned, and they controlled about one-third of its total area. A remnant of the Japanese garrison had been cut off in the southeast and was holding the peninsular Nafutan Point. The main body was in the north. General Saito, assisted by Admiral Nagumo, hastened to establish a new front along a line starting at Garapan and running inland over the central hills and down to the shores of Magicienne Bay. That evening the commanders received a message from Hirohito himself. After offering his congratulations to the garrison for "fighting splendidly" up to this point, the Emperor stated: "If Saipan is lost, air raids on Tokyo will take place often. Therefore, you will hold Saipan." Whether or not this would be possible was about to be decided by the Battle of the Philippine Sea.

Fought on June 19 and 20 in the skies over Guam and in waters to the west, the "Great Marianas Turkey Shoot" was a decisive American victory. The Japanese lost 476 planes and 445 airmen, many of them trainees only seventeen or eighteen years old. American submarines sank two carriers, and the fliers a third. Two other vessels were sunk, several badly battered. Damages to American vessels were easily sustainable, but 130 aircraft were lost. Only fifty of the planes went down in combat; the rest splashed into the sea while trying to return to their carriers after dark. In all, seventy-six airmen died. Admiral Ozawa, whose great flagship carrier *Taiho* was sunk beneath him but who managed to survive, glumly ordered a retreat to Okinawa, south of the home islands. Ozawa's log bore the report: "Surviving carrier power: 35 aircraft operational."

A-Go had failed miserably. When the news reached the Japanese commanders on Saipan, they were not surprised. Their forces, reduced to less than 20,000 effectives, were now stripped of all hope of receiving aid, were surrounded by a fleet of infinite strength, and were facing three heavily armed land divisions. General Saito sighed and did the only thing a Japanese commander in such a position could do—prepared his garrison for a fight to the last man.

Junior officer Tokuzo Matsuya stopped thinking in terms of staying alive "for the sake of the future." He recorded in his diary what he intended to do when he came face-to-face with the enemy: "I will take out my sword and slash, slash, slash at him as long as I last, thus ending my life of twenty-four years."

18 | **The Drive Northward**

══════ On Saipan, while the battle of the fleets was raging out of sight and hearing, Holland Smith changed the direction of his attack from east to north, the left-flank battalion of the 2nd Division, on the coast below Garapan, serving as a pivot for the rest of the Marine units, both 2nd Division and 4th. The 4th Division, with the longer way to go, moved with its right flank on Magicienne Bay. Things proceeded auspiciously: the 2nd took Hill 790 on June 19; the 4th took Hill 500 on the twentieth. Not initially a part of the northward attack, Ralph Smith's Army troops continued their work against the Japanese cut off in the southeast, at Nafutan Point. The Seabees and engineers were already Americanizing the captured airport, which would be named Isely Field in memory of Commander Robert H. Isely, a naval aviator killed during a pre-invasion strike. The first American plane, a Navy torpedo bomber, landed on the field on the evening of June 20. This was one of the Pacific war's fateful moments, portending bad times for Japan's home islands.

Prior to launching his all-out push against Saito's cross-island front, Holland Smith set aside June 21, D-plus-6, for the two Marine divisions to reorganize, bring up supplies, mop up bypassed positions, and send out reconnaissance patrols. The 27th Division spent the day pressing the holed-up Japanese at Nafutan Point. It was a day that saw the beginning of trouble between the Marine and Army generals. Holland Smith, as the assault's top commander, issued a set of orders regarding the control and disposition of the Army units that Ralph Smith did not follow. It was probably more a matter of misinterpretation than deliberate disobedience, but Holland Smith was angered. Moreover, the Army's work at Nafutan Point was proceeding too slowly to suit the Marine general's overall plans. In this criticism he had the support of an Army observer, Lieutenant Colonel John Lemp, who noted that on June 21 the 105th Infantry Regiment showed "a certain amount of inertia." It was an instance, according to Lemp, when the 27th Division "might be censured for its lack of offensive spirit."

By this time the American invasion forces had suffered nearly 6,500 casualties: 3,628 in the 4th Division, 2,514 in the 2nd Division, and 320 in the 27th. The cemeteries that were being created had become a dire necessity, since the older corpses were in advanced stages of decomposition. The ones that had to be fished out of the surf were soggy and bloated, and as they were dragged up on shore they emitted nauseous gases. The handlers were obliged to poke about in the gelatinized flesh to find dog tags or other means of identification before burial could be made. An officer supervising the work at the 2nd Division cemetery remarked to Robert Sherrod: "If the people back home could see the condition of these bodies when they are brought in here, I wonder if they would want to keep on fighting."

The night of June 21–22 found the Japanese resorting to minor infiltrations along several parts of the front, the tactic that, all through the war, did so much to keep their adversaries edgy and overtired. On this particular night, a lone infiltrator achieved a success of stunning consequence, using an incendiary bullet to touch off a 2nd Division ammunition dump near the beach. In the wake of a dazzling eruption that sent hot metal flying in all directions, Captain Carl A. Nielsen led a team of Marines toward the flames to try to keep them from spreading. The men were met by a second blast. "To the best of my knowledge," the captain said later, "this explosion killed, or was the cause of the death of, my entire detail, with the exception of myself and one other." The fireworks continued through the night, shrapnel from artillery and mortar shells hitting many more men. Just after one o'clock, a new element was added, if only briefly, to the nightmare of noise and color. A dozen Japanese bombers, survivors of American raids on the nearby islands, droned overhead, dropping missiles both on the Marine positions and the offshore shipping. The strike was ineffectual.

The 2nd and 4th Divisions began attacking northward, after a brief but earth-rocking artillery preparation, at 6:00 A.M. Proceeding over rugged terrain but encountering resistance only in pockets, the Marines generally made good progress. The 2nd reached Mount Tipo Pale, southeast of Garapan, while the 4th advanced about 2,000 yards beyond Hill 500. In the middle of the afternoon the attackers received some welcome new support, that of rocket-armed Army Air Force fighters, P-47 Thunderbolts, brought to the Marianas on escort carriers and already flying from the captured airfield. The day's casualties were relatively light: 157 in killed or wounded. But the wounded included the legendary ex-Raider Evans Carlson, a 4th Division staff officer. Carlson was shot through the arm and thigh while helping to carry a wounded enlisted man to safety. The old guerrilla fighter, who had made the Chinese term *gung ho* (work together) a part of Marine Corps jargon, had seen his last combat.

The Marines were now facing the enemy's first cross-island defenses, a maze of caves, dugouts, and trenches in terrain that abounded with hills, cliffs, and ravines. Here in the center of the island and to the north

Truck-mounted rocket launchers blast Japanese positions on northern Saipan.

were some 15,000 able-bodied Japanese troops and an even greater number of civilians. Many of the caves served not only as defenses but also as shelters, with troops and civilians often intermixed. Some of the wounded, of which there were thousands, were in the caves, but most lay on the ground in ravines, where they were exposed to the elements and to American shells, bombs, and rockets. The overworked medical teams were able to provide only a fraction of the care needed. Operations were performed hastily, the "table" a stretcher elevated on two boxes. Commonly, there was no anesthetic. Sanitation was poor, and many wounds seethed with maggots. The delirious victims murmured of home, and the lucid talked of it wistfully. There were still men, wounded and whole alike, who told themselves that reinforcements were coming and that they would see Japan again. Those resigned to death wrote last letters and last testaments they hoped would reach their families. At least one such composition became an American souvenir.

"TO MY FATHER AND MOTHER: I have been more than resolved from the beginning that my bones shall bleach on this field of battle, that I may receive life eternal at the right hand of his Majesty the Emperor. This is the true desire of the soldier. I approach death cheerfully and with peace of mind, only, more than anything, I cannot bear the shame of having been unable to render more satisfactory service. For twenty years it has cost you, my parents, much trouble and anxiety to bring me up into my present splendid body of over five feet, and I have absolutely no excuse for not knowing of some way to requite you. There is no way now but to thank you, very deeply. I have laid aside, bit by bit, the savings which have been my one pleasure, and they have now reached the sum of 200 yen. If this money can be of aid to our country, I ask you to use it with that purpose in mind. When I left for the front, there were two debenture bonds, ten yen and five yen, in the desk; please look them up. And please dispose of the things in my clothes chest as you think best. I ask my relatives and everyone in the neighborhood to forgive me for having neglected to write. I hope that our village Production Guild Chief and all the employees will remain in robust health and will work hard for the development of the guild and the village. In closing, I hope that you, my honorable parents, and my brothers and sisters . . . will always remain in good health. Especially because you are now aged, my parents, please take good care of your venerable bodies. As I think about it now, my only regret is that I have not been able to see the home which you have worked, heart and soul, to build. Otherwise, I have no regrets. Although it seems that there are still things for me to write, I feel a lump in my throat and cannot call them to mind. Well, take care. TATSUO."

June 22 ended with further trouble arising between the two Generals Smith. The GIs had made no progress against the Japanese holdouts at Nafutan Point. Ralph Smith, an intelligent and fair-minded man, conceded Holland's right to be displeased over this. Holland believed that the 27th was facing a mere handful of the enemy, which wasn't quite true. There were about 1,000 soldiers and civilians at the point, which comprised irregular ground with numerous caves. Now the Marine general decided he needed the 27th at the northern front. Ralph Smith was ordered to leave only one battalion, about 1,000 men, at Nafutan, the unit's mission either to clean out the Japanese or contain them until a stronger force could be spared from the more important northern fighting. Ralph warned of the possibility of a Japanese breakout that could endanger the airfield and its personnel. While preparing for the move north, the Army general sent the detached battalion orders that Holland Smith considered to be in contravention of his own. It was a minor matter, but the discord between the two commanders was growing.

Holland Smith chose to use the 27th Division in the center of his attack, the unit's flanks protected by the battle-hardened Marines, the 2nd Division on its left and the 4th on its right. Saipan was much wider in this region than in the south. Only with extra troops in the center would the 4th Division be able to fan out to the east and take Kagman Peninsula. But the three-division attack had scarcely begun on the morning of June 23 when Ralph Smith's troops, the 106th Regiment on the left and the 165th on the right, encountered stiff opposition. The dominating features of the zone were soon dubbed Hell's Pocket, Death Valley, and Purple Heart Ridge. Because the 27th made scant progress during the day, it was the interior Marine flanks that were left unprotected. The 2nd was compelled to interrupt its attack on 1,500-foot-high Mount Tapotchau, and the 4th was unable to go as far as it could have in the east. Holland Smith grew very unhappy, and he conferred with Major General Sanderford Jarman, the senior Army man on the island, slated to become military governor when the battle was won. Jarman recalled: "He stated that if it was not an *Army* division and there would be a great cry set up, more or less of a political nature, he would immediately relieve the division commander and assign someone else. . . . He asked me to go see General Ralph Smith and see what I could do in helping this division to move forward. . . . I found that General Smith had been up in the front lines all afternoon and was thoroughly familiar with the situation. I explained the situation as I saw it and said that I felt from reports . ... that his division was not carrying its full share. He immediately replied that such was true; that he was in no way satisfied with what his regimental commanders had done during the day and that he had been with them and pointed out the situation. He further indicated to me that he was going to be present tomorrow, June 24, with his division when it made its jump-off, and he would personally see to it that the division went forward. I explained that my interest in the matter was that I was senior Army commander present and was anxious to see that the Army did its job as it should be done. He appreciated the situation and thanked me for coming to see him and stated that if he didn't take his division forward tomorrow he should be relieved."

The evening's events did nothing to raise the spirits of Ralph Smith's GIs, for they were twice hit by Japanese tanks, six in the first group and five in the next. Both attacks were stopped, with most of the tanks being knocked out, but during the second attack one of the machines broke through the front, spraying fire into men lying helpless in an aid station, and also igniting an ammunition stockpile, which drove a part of the line back until the tempest subsided.

As a bright moon rose, the 4th Division experienced its own tank attack, while a 2nd Division artillery position was heavily shelled. The usual alarms over infiltrations began occurring in all zones. Just before one o'clock there was a small-scale air raid on the shipping off Charan Kanoa. The island presently quieted down, and the weary Americans were able to get some snatches of sleep.

As he had promised, Ralph Smith was at the front when the three-division attack was resumed in the morning. Unfortunately, the general was unable to get his regiments moving through Death Valley. The failure was probably as much a matter of fate as of impotent leadership. If there were times when the 27th hesitated in the face of light resistance, this was not one of them. Death Valley was held by determined troops in commanding positions. But the Army was made to look especially bad by the fact that the Marines on both flanks were able to jump off on schedule and to keep moving. Soon the cross-island front was sagging in the middle. Howlin' Mad Smith decided it was high time he acted. (Later, Archer Vandegrift wrote him: "You showed more forbearance than I could possibly have shown under similar circumstances.") Holland boarded a landing craft and went out to the *Indianapolis* for a consultation with Admirals Spruance and Turner. "Ralph Smith," said the Marine general, "has shown that he lacks aggressive spirit, and his division is slowing down our advance. He should be relieved." The two admirals accepted the judgment.

Holland Smith's task was not an agreeable one. He had known Ralph Smith for some years and considered him to be "a likable and professionally knowledgeable man." If there was any satisfaction at all for Holland in this affair, it was that he seemed vindicated in his opinion of the National Guard system. The 27th was a New York National Guard unit. Its officers were long-time friends, and Holland believed them to be more concerned with one another's feelings and reputations than with running a tight outfit. The Marine general never doubted that there were many brave men in the 27th, but he felt that the unit's effectiveness was crippled by slack leadership and soft training. He had said at the outbreak of the war that all National Guard units should be split up so that the debilitating circles of friendship would be broken. If what Holland believed was true, if the 27th was indeed afflicted with a cronyism that made for bland attitudes and sluggish tactics, it was a considerable misfortune for the unit to have been thrown in with the Marines, who made a religion of rigid discipline and a style of fighting aimed at keeping the foe off balance. "Our casualties," Holland liked to say, "are actually lower when we push forward than when we stand still." Although it was Raymond Spruance who authorized Ralph Smith's relief, the storm stirred up by the Army's high command—a storm that lasted through the war and for years beyond—fell upon Holland. By the time it subsided, Holland's reputation was more tarnished than Ralph's. There were other high-ranking officers relieved during the war, most of the time with minimal publicity; but in this case an Army general had been relieved by a *Marine*, and the Army's high brass, perhaps not altogether unreasonably, found this intolerable. An unfortunate result of the furor was that it put a critical spotlight on the 27th, which did incalculable harm to its morale.

Holland Smith never doubted that he had done the right thing, explaining in his memoirs, "There was no question of animus against an Army general. I would have relieved a Marine general under the same circumstances, only sooner." Robert Sherrod saw Holland on the afternoon the relief was effected and General Jarman was placed in temporary command of the 27th. Holland was low in spirits, but justified himself. "I've got a duty to my country. I've lost 7,000 Marines. Can I afford to lose back what they have gained? To let my Marines die in vain?" His conscience, he added, was clear.

As for the matter of Marine casualties, protests about them were beginning to be raised in the States. News analysts with an imperfect understanding of the Central Pacific drive accused the Marines of making another "reckless charge" into a Japanese stronghold. It was pointed out that the Army was achieving important gains all over the world at a reasonable cost. Criticisms and comparisons like this always confounded the Marines, who accepted their high casualties as a part of their specialized job. It was necessary for them to "do the impossible well," and this was bound to be costly. Some of the Stateside newspapers of this period reached Saipan. Along with the moans about the Marines were stories lauding the Army's triumphal march into Rome on streets strewn with flowers and past sidewalks crowded with cheering citizens, including thousands of women with love in their eyes. Some of the Marines began to believe they had picked the wrong war.

General Jarman accomplished little in his new role during the remainder of June 24, but the Army began edging forward on the twenty-fifth. That was the day the Marines on the right overran Kagman Peninsula and elements of those on the left climbed and fought their way to the summit of Mount Tapotchau, gaining an observation post of great value; it commanded an unobstructed view of the island's northern reaches. That night a Japanese staff officer wrote a gloomy report. "The fight on Saipan as things stand now is progressing one-sidedly. . . . In the daytime, even the deployment of units is very difficult, and at night the enemy can make out our movements with ease by using illumination shells." There was a serious shortage of weapons and equipment, he said, and communications were breaking down. "Moreover, we are menaced by brazenly low-flying planes, and the enemy blasts at us from all sides with fierce naval and artillery cross fire. . . . Even if we move units from the front lines and send them to the rear, their fighting strength is cut down every day." In closing, the report alluded to the ferocity of the enemy's frontline attacks: "Step by step he comes toward us and concentrates his fire on us as we withdraw, so that wherever we go we are quickly surrounded by fire."

Everything this officer said was well known to General Saito, and he radioed Tokyo that there was no hope of victory. "Please apologize to the Emperor that we cannot do better than we are doing." Saito was handed an added discouragement during the night when eleven barges filled with reinforcements tried to approach from nearby Tinian and were turned back by American destroyers.

The Japanese knew they were beaten but, as always, kept fighting. And among the various American forces—land, sea, and air—that comprised the offensive, it was, as always, the foot troops who continued to bear the heaviest responsibility for gaining the victory. General Thomas Watson, commanding the 2nd Division, said later: "The rate of progress was determined by the willingness and ability of the individual front-line Marine and soldier to dig out and kill the stubborn and skillful Japanese defenders." Americans fell, but the work was pressed, much of it done with rifles, hand grenades, flamethrowers, and demolitions. Sometimes not only enemy troops but civilians were slain, caught in cross fires or incinerated in caves. Other civilians were captured, hundreds of them. It was strange to see the Americans in one zone engaging in the most brutal kind of slaughter and cursing the intransigence of the foe, while those in a nearby zone were bringing civilians out, leading children by the hand, even carrying babies and trying to allay their fears with soft words.

Also captured were numerous Japanese fighting men, most made helpless by wounds. Among the prisoners was a medical officer who was surprised to learn that about fifty of the most serious cases—men who were blinded, or were legless, or had broken backs—were being sent to

Honolulu. The officer asked Holland Smith why the American government wanted to saddle itself with these useless men. Smith responded by
asking what the Japanese would do with them, and got the reply, "We
would leave them a hand grenade apiece, and if they did not use the
grenades it would be a simple matter to slit their jugular veins."

The ways of the Japanese would never cease to baffle the Americans.
At the front one day, S. G. Silcox was with a group of Marines who
spotted an enemy soldier leaning against a tree, chewing on a section
of sugarcane, his rifle leaning against the tree beside him. A Marine with
his own rifle at the ready began walking toward the man, who did not
even look up from his snack. Using some of the Japanese words he had
learned, the Marine called out a surrender request. There was no reaction. Silcox found it "unbelievable that he actually seemed to ignore our
existence completely. The Marine let go three or four rounds, and he
dropped dead."

The unfortunate 27th Division acquired another demerit in the eyes
of the Marines during the night of June 26–27. It happened down at
Nafutan Point, where a single Army battalion—hardly an abundance of
troops for the job—had been fighting the isolated holdouts. Unknown
to the GIs, an enterprising Japanese captain (his name has survived only
as "Sasaki") had spent the daylight hours of the twenty-sixth completing
plans to take 500 men, a mixture of soldiers and sailors, through the
American lines. Sasaki intended to attack the airfield and then charge
northward, hopefully making it far enough to link up with friendly
forces. The captain wrote a set of orders that ended: "Casualties will
remain in their present positions and defend Nafutan Point. Those who
cannot participate in combat must commit suicide. We will carry the
maximum of weapons and supplies. The password for tonight will be
'Seven lives for one's country.'" Launching his move soon after midnight, Sasaki lost twenty-seven men while pushing through the Army.
Four Americans were killed and twenty wounded. Toward morning the
Japanese burst upon the airfield, where they blew up one P-47 and
damaged two or three others before they were hastened on their way
north by the field's Seabees, Marine engineers, and Air Force personnel. Heading toward Hill 500, Sasaki and his band soon began running
into units of reserve-area Marines and GIs. A few of the Americans were
caught asleep and were killed, but the rest rallied with weapons blazing. The fighting continued until noon, with Sasaki and all of his men
dying—some, as usual, by their own hand. That same day the Army
finished its job at Nafutan Point, overrunning the last enemy ground,
encountering few troops but numerous civilians, who were taken into

custody. Found in a cave were the men Sasaki had ordered to kill themselves; they had obeyed. With the close of the southern fighting—except for the inevitable mopping up—about one-half of Saipan was in American hands.

On June 28 a Japanese report said of the northern fighting: "In our frontline units, the troops have been three days without drinking water but are hanging on by chewing tree leaves and eating snails." That was the day the 27th Division was taken over by the permanent replacement for Ralph Smith, Major General George W. Griner, flown in from Hawaii. On the twenty-ninth and thirtieth the Army broke through Death Valley. "No one," said Marine General Harry Schmidt, commander of the 4th Division, "had any tougher job to do." Schmidt's troops had made good gains along the east coast, and the 2nd Division had moved forward from Mount Tapotchau to the "Four Pimples." Most of Central Saipan was now under American control, and the second phase of the campaign had ended. The Japanese began withdrawing toward their final cross-island defense line in the north. American casualties had reached 10,778, with 4,488 in the 2nd Division, 4,454 in the 4th, and 1,836 in the 27th. Most of the Army's had been taken during its week in Death Valley.

The climactic American offensive was launched on July 2. While the 27th and the 4th Divisions began pressing up the island's thinning northeastern section, the 2nd Division concentrated on Garapan and Tanapag Harbor. It had been necessary to proceed cautiously against Garapan until Tipo Pale, Tapotchau, and other heights overlooking the town were secured. Even now, the advance through the streets was coupled with an attack on Sugar Loaf Hill, in the eastern environs. By this time Garapan, Japan's Central Pacific capital and until recently the home of 15,000 people, had been rendered a shambles by naval shells and aerial bombs and rockets. Hardly a building was left intact; some lay in piles only a few feet high. Sheets of corrugated metal, a primary roofing material, were scattered about like confetti. A sight the Americans found curious was that of dead cows, bloated and stiff-legged, on the lots behind many of the wrecked houses. The remains of delicate Japanese gardens held ponds with muddied waters on which tropical fishes floated, stomach up. Only a few live enemy troops remained in the town, but these holdouts were dangerous, resisting the Marines with rifles, machine guns, and mortars. One group of six Japanese in a machine-gun nest, coming under heavy fire, began waving a white flag. When the fire was lifted, five of the men stole away, leaving a sniper to cover their retreat. Only the sniper was slain. Once cleaned out,

Garapan proved to be a souvenir hunter's paradise. The wreckage held all sorts of fascinating things: colorful garments, wooden shoes, china-ware, silverware, books, photo albums, toys, musical instruments, phonographs, and records. Although most of the records were oriental and not particularly pleasing to the Western ear, albums of Bach, Wag-ner, and Beethoven were also discovered, and these were played on a street corner at top volume. In the ruins of the town's bank, according to PFC John Behm, the vault was found intact. "We blew it open with bazooka rockets and took out big bundles of Japanese currency." The loot was given the most casual treatment and was passed around freely. Groups of Marines played poker with it, making huge bets with foot-high stacks in front of them. Others used it as toilet paper. "We had no idea at the time that when we got to Japan this would have been very useful to us. It was, of course, perfectly good money."

The 2nd Division completed its work at Garapan and Tanapag Har-bor on July 4, and went into reserve. By this time the unit had been pinched out by the 27th Division advancing on its right. The 27th and the 4th, moving abreast, had pushed to a line that gave the invasion forces control of three-fifths of the island. Highly pleased with every-one, including the Army, Holland Smith issued a congratulatory mes-sage: "It is fitting that on this 4th of July you should be extremely proud of your achievements. Your fight is no less important than that waged by our forefathers who gave us the liberty and freedom we have long enjoyed. . . . To all hands, a sincere well done!"

General Saito had withdrawn to his sixth and final headquarters cave. Admiral Nagumo, the hero of Pearl Harbor, was in a cave nearby. The location was a ridge overlooking the newly nicknamed "Valley of Hell," a receptacle for American barrages that shook the earth and showered the cave entrances with debris. A Japanese officer who saw Saito on the fourth recalled that he "was feeling very poorly because for several days he had neither eaten nor slept well and was overstrained. He was wearing a long beard and was a pitiful sight." Saito explained to his staff: "We can continue fighting our withdrawing action, which will end in our complete annihilation at the northern tip of the island, or we can attempt to muster our crumbling forces for an all-out attack." The latter course was decided upon, and on the morning of July 6 the old general issued his last order: "For more than twenty days since the American Devils attacked, the officers, men, and civilian employees of the Impe-rial Army and Navy on this island have fought well and bravely . . . but now we have no materials with which to fight, and our artillery for attack has been completely destroyed. Our comrades have fallen, one after another. . . . The barbarous attack of the enemy is being continued. . . . We are dying without avail under the violent shelling and bombing. Whether we attack or whether we stay where we are, there is only death. . . . We must utilize this opportunity to exalt true Japanese manhood. I will advance with those who remain to deliver still another blow to the American Devils, and leave my bones on Saipan as a bulwark of the Pacific. . . . Here I pray with you for the eternal life of the Emperor and the welfare of our country, and I advance to seek the enemy. Follow me!"

Actually, General Saito was too far gone in health and strength to lead the attack. He and Admiral Nagumo decided to commit hara-kiri. For the once-proud Nagumo, this ending was without a shred of glory. The few ships of his Central Pacific Fleet had been sunk during the enemy's preliminary raids, and he had been trapped on Saipan with no essential duties, merely confirming Saito's judgments and retreating from cave to cave. Nagumo had been very quiet most of the time, apparently brooding over his shattered career and ignominious doom. Now, accompanied by aides with pistols, Nagumo, Saito, and Saito's chief of staff left the headquarters cave and walked to one that was smaller and more private. Stepping inside, the three men turned toward the entrance and made bows in the direction of Japan and the Emperor, then seated themselves on the ground, cross-legged, side by side, the aides behind them. The commanders drew their swords and made a salute to the Emperor, then used the points of the weapons to draw ceremonial blood from their bared midriffs. At that moment the aides shot them through the head. The bodies were burned.

That evening about 3,000 Japanese—soldiers, sailors, and male civilians—filtered down the ridges toward Makunsha, a village on the west coast, selected as the *banzai* assembly area. Along with the able-bodied were hundreds of walking wounded, variously bandaged, some using canes and a few even swinging along on crutches, a leg missing. Armaments included mortars, machine guns, rifles, pistols, hand grenades, swords, clubs, and spears (knives or bayonets lashed to the end of sticks). A few tanks—all that had survived—joined the movement. The groups of men on foot, who reminded one saddened officer of sheep being led to the slaughter, left thousands of empty *sake* and beer bottles in their wake, a mute record of the moment that would remain visible for decades. As a result of communications problems and American shellfire, preparations for the attack consumed most of the night. The effort was to be launched down the coastal plain, and patrols were sent to probe this flank of the enemy's line, which happened to be manned by the star-crossed 27th Division. The three battalions of the 105th Regiment were about to gain the dubious distinction of undergoing one of the heaviest *banzai* attacks of the Pacific war. The 3rd Battalion, farthest inland, was on a height that lent it security, but the 1st and 2nd, whose lines stretched to the coast, were dug in on relatively flat terrain.

The enemy's patrol actions, which increased in size as the night wore on, were in themselves nerve-racking to the GIs. Covered by machine-gun tracers and incendiary bullets that filled the moonlit night with red, yellow, green, and blue streaks, the Japanese approached singing and chanting. A probe witnessed by 1st Sergeant Mario Occhinerio was accompanied by the "damnedest noise" he'd ever heard, sounding much like the buzzing of a large hive of bees. "It kept getting louder and louder. All at once a couple of Japs burst through the bushes in our front. Someone shot them." The purpose of these curious tactics was not only to gain information but also to keep the Americans from resting. The efforts were successful on both counts. The patrols secured a good knowledge of the Army's dispositions, discovering a 300-yard gap that could be exploited, and kept nearly everyone at the front from sleeping a wink.

Not until dawn approached did the main rush get under way. Raising a great hubbub, the Japanese came down the plain in columns, one aimed at the 3rd Battalion on the high ground, the others heading for the vulnerable 1st and 2nd. Nearly every American, of course, was tense with dread. One who was *not* was Private Celso Flores of the 1st Battalion, an eighteen-year-old who had been complaining since he landed that he hadn't been able to get a really good shot at the enemy. Now as the jabbering columns approached, Flores watched from his foxhole and exclaimed, "Holy cow! Look at 'em! Just look at 'em! Oh boy! Oh boy!" He readied his rifle in happy anticipation of good shooting at last.

The 3rd Battalion had little trouble holding off the assault on its heights. The Japanese there soon swung to their right and poured through the gap in the line, their new target the support troops dug in about 1,500 yards to the south. At the GI front, some 1,100 men of the 1st and 2nd Battalions, strongly outnumbered and hit head-on, were plunged into a furious struggle for their lives. The Japanese, according to Major Edward McCarthy, commander of the 2nd, charged like stampeding cattle. "They just kept coming and coming. It didn't matter if you shot one; five more would take his place." The melee was one of exceptional barbarity and involved much more than shooting. Hand-grenade fragments ruptured flesh and fractured bones. Bayonets on

Garand rifles clattered against improvised spears as one or the other was thrust home. Skillfully wielded swords lopped off heads, sliced away shoulders, and bared intestines. There was kicking, fist-fighting, clawing, and incidents of strangulation. The victors in the duels cried out with relief at surviving; the losers gave shrieks protesting their fate. Men on both sides fell by scores, and the ground became a patchwork of bloodstains. The Americans held for half an hour, then began to fall back, carrying their helpless wounded and shielding those who could walk. Brave men died covering the retreat. The commander of the 1st Battalion, Lieutenant Colonel William J. O'Brien, had been fighting with a pistol in each hand, had continued to fire even when seriously wounded. His Medal of Honor citation explains: "After his pistol ammunition was exhausted, he manned a .50-caliber machine gun mounted on a jeep. When last seen alive he was standing upright and firing into the Jap hordes who were then enveloping him." The remnants of the two battalions headed for the coastal village of Tanapag, about 1,000 yards behind the front. It had occurred to the surviving officers that the houses would provide cover for the establishment of a new perimeter.

By this time the Japanese who had passed through the gap in the original front were south of Tanapag and heading for the first of the support troops, which happened to be a Marine artillery unit, the 3rd Battalion, 10th Regiment. The Marines had heard the firing at the front, and one had said, "Somebody up there sure is trigger-happy." As the Army began its retreat the sound of the firing grew louder, and the Marines became apprehensive. They were ill equipped for face-to-face encounters, since artillerymen usually did their work with frontline troops between themselves and the enemy. As recalled by Lieutenant Arnold C. Hofstetter of Battery H: "It began to appear that we might be attacked, and the gunners were told to cut their fuses to four-tenths of a second for close-in fire." In the early light, about 500 Japanese were spotted approaching in column-of-fours, officers in dress uniforms marching in the lead, three tanks in support. Battery H opened up with its 105s. They took a toll, but the survivors simply scattered and kept coming, many of them screaming, singing, and chanting. To at least one Marine, they seemed to be "all *sakied* up." This may have been true, but they still could shoot straight, and the gunners began falling. Additional Japanese were blown off their feet, and a tank was destroyed, but the fire could not be maintained. Hofstetter relates: "We fell back about 150 yards from the howitzers, across a road, and set up a perimeter defense in a Japanese machinery dump. This was about 0700. We held out there with carbines, one BAR, one pistol, and eight captured Jap rifles." Other rear-area units came under attack and formed similar defense lines.

Up at Tanapag the few hundred survivors of the 1st and 2nd Battalions of the Army's 105th Regiment had set up a new perimeter, utilizing some of the town's buildings and a set of trenches dug by the Japanese garrison. Here, with their backs to the sea and surrounded by a fanatical foe who outnumbered them two-to-one, the GIs made a heroic stand. The enemy poured in mortars and machine-gun and rifle bullets. Small groups crept close enough to hurl grenades, and a few men infiltrated into the town, but the main body was held at bay. Taking an enthusiastic part in the defense was young Private Flores, who was getting in many fine shots and was exclaiming repeatedly, "Oh boy! Oh boy!" During the rampant exchanges of fire, both sides suffered severely. The Japanese who were only wounded killed themselves with grenades. The American wounded, dragged into trenches or into buildings, got little attention, since most of the medical corpsmen had been killed. Some men bled to death. Others went into shock for want of plasma. Most suffered from acute thirst.

At about 11:00 A.M. Major McCarthy, the perimeter's highest-ranking survivor, got together about 100 volunteers, most of them walking wounded, whom he instructed to try to make a break down the coast to seek help. As the men left the southern outskirts of the village they were sighted by Army artillery observers on the inland heights, who mistook them for a group of the enemy. The gunners, who had done a fine job of harassing the Japanese during their nocturnal preparations in the north and had been firing on targets of opportunity all morning, now laid a concentration on their hapless friends, inflicting heavy casualties. The distraught survivors began racing down the coast, only to encounter the horror of a second concentration. Again, the carnage was fearful, some of the men receiving direct hits. This time the survivors made a wild rush for the surf, and some swam out to the reef. The mission was totally thwarted. Nor was this the end of the tragedy. Two artillery concentrations were also poured into the town, with equally terrible results.

On the bright side, early afternoon found the Japanese attack losing some of its steam. In the south, American reserves from the rear, the GIs of the 106th Regiment, had launched a counterattack and were beginning to recover the lost ground. The going was slow, however, and the front did not reach Tanapag that day. The perimeter's survivors were rescued by another method. In the evening, Army amphibian tractors and DUKWs streamed up the coastal waters and took them off.

One of the last men to leave his position in the lines was Private Flores. Although wounded, he had continued fighting with all of his original enthusiasm. The youth entered his amtrac with a certain reluctance, saying, "I'll never get this many shots again." Most of the other survivors had got a far greater number of shots than they figured a soldier was entitled to. During the day, many men had been reminded all too often of General Custer's fatal stand against the Sioux Indians, and the experience would cause them nightmares for a long time to come. The two battalions had suffered a total of 918 killed or wounded. Out of the eight companies that had participated, only 189 men were able to answer the next roll call. Credited with killing more than 2,000 of the enemy, the soldiers received a Distinguished Unit Citation stating that they had "contributed materially to the defeat and destruction of the Japanese forces at Saipan." They really had—the hard way.

During this action on the left of the American front, the 4th Division on the right had been making excellent progress northward. On July 8, with the 2nd Division taking the place of the 27th on the left, the front was pressed toward Marpi Point, the island's northern tip. There was

Flame tank incinerates holed-up defenders.

an occasional hot action as a group of defenders charged from hiding, and a few machine gunners and snipers remained active, but in many areas the Japanese chose to die meekly in their holes. It was, as a Marine officer said, "just like killing rats." Saipan was declared secured on July 9, although there was still much mopping up to be done. Moreover, Marpi Point, which included a high plateau with seaside cliffs, had not been thoroughly investigated.

It was at Marpi Point that the campaign's crowning horror occurred. The seaside cliffs were honeycombed with caves, the last refuge of some hundreds of troops and thousands of civilians, and these people now began killing themselves. The Americans peering over the edge of the plateau or watching from small naval craft offshore could do little to stop the slaughter. Pleas by loudspeaker, even when made by Japanese in American custody, were largely ignored. Attempts to move in were apt to hasten the grisly work, or to be met by bullets from the caves. There were Americans who died trying to save these people from themselves. The scenes on the ledges and along the shoreline were not only ghastly but hard to credit. Families gathered in tight circles and exploded grenades in their midst. Some parents, before finding a way to kill themselves, strangled their children or stabbed them or cut their heads off. There were cases of babies being taken by their feet and their brains dashed out. Groups of men, women, and children gathered on shelves hundreds of feet high, joined hands, and leaped with prolonged screams to jumbles of jagged rocks. Others jumped from a lower cliff directly into the lashing surf. There were women who picked their way down to this spot, carefully combed their splendid black hair, then waded out and drowned themselves. The water here was clogged with bodies. Some of the civilians who hesitated to kill themselves were shot by Japanese soldiers or sailors, who followed soon after by shattering their chests with grenades. The Americans could accept the sight of the military deaths, but the others made even the toughest shudder, and many a grimy face was troughed with tears.

The number of civilians who died at this time and previously can only be guessed at. About 15,000 were interned; probably at least that many perished. Some 1,700 military personnel were captured; the remainder of the garrison's 30,000 men were killed, or obligingly killed themselves, many during the mopping up that continued for months. Saipan, which *Time* magazine called "one of the bloodiest battles in U.S. military annals," cost the Americans 16,525 in killed or wounded—12,934 Marines and 3,591 soldiers. But the strategic gains were enormous. The United States had breached the enemy's inner defense line and had won its first B-29 airfield. Moreover, the campaign had precipitated a naval engagement that had crippled the enemy's fleet. In Japan, Hideki Tojo was forced to resign as prime minister, and Fleet Admiral Osami Nagano, supreme naval advisor to the Emperor, lamented, "Hell is upon us."

19 | *Taking Out Tinian*

Saipan was the main objective of the Marianas campaign, but Guam and Tinian remained to be taken. Because it lay only about three miles southwest of Saipan, Tinian was a threat to the Americans. Furthermore, it happened to have a good deal of level land suitable for airfields. As early as 1742 the chaplain of a visiting British naval vessel wrote of the island: "The soil is everywhere dry and healthy, and being withal somewhat sandy is thereby less disposed to a rank and overluxuriant vegetation; and hence the meadows and bottoms of the woods are much neater and smoother than is customary in hot climates." As for Guam, located about 150 miles southwest of Saipan, it had to be assaulted not only to secure it as a base but also to salve national pride. The United States had held the island from the time of the Spanish-American War in 1898 until the Japanese seized it in 1941, making prisoners of its American garrison and oppressing its Chamorro populace. Washington had vowed to take Guam back. Both secondary missions were tackled during the latter part of July 1944, Guam on the twenty-first and Tinian on the twenty-fourth. Since Tinian was an extension of the work on Saipan, this assault seems to merit first consideration.

There were some 9,000 Japanese troops on Tinian, the 50th Infantry Regiment, a battalion of the 135th Infantry Regiment, the 56th Naval Guard Force, plus various smaller army, navy, and air units. There were civilian militia groups also, but these men had been given no weapons except grenades to use on themselves if necessary. Their families became their chief concern. In charge of the defense was Colonel Keishi Ogata, recently transferred from a station in Manchuria. Top naval commander was Vice Admiral Kakuji Kakuda, who was more than six feet tall and weighed over 200 pounds. There would be no command disagreements between Ogata and Kakuda. After failing in half a dozen attempts to leave the island by submarine, the admiral went into seclusion and was heard from no more. The naval command devolved upon Captain Goichi Oya.

Roughly diamond-shaped, Tinian measured twelve miles from north to south and about six miles across the center. Although the island was so gently contoured that ninety percent of its area was in cane fields, its shoreline was made up largely of coral ledges and cliffs rising from six to 100 feet. There were only three spots where an amphibious landing was possible: Tinian Town Harbor in the southwest, Asiga Bay in the northeast, and a pair of small beaches in the northwest, one sixty yards wide and the other 160, with 1,000 yards of coral ledges between them. Ogata had set up his main defenses to cover Tinian Town Harbor, with secondary attention going to Asiga Bay. The colonel considered it extremely unlikely that the enemy would attempt a major landing over the tiny beaches in the northwest.

Had Kelly Turner's views prevailed, Ogata's judgment would have been proved correct, for the admiral dismissed the northwestern beaches as not large enough for consideration. Holland Smith, however, argued strongly for the use of the two passages. Aerial intelligence had revealed Ogata's plans to receive the Americans at the other spots. There was a discussion between Turner and Smith that, according to the general, "generated considerable unprintable language," but nighttime investigations by Marine reconnaissance people and Navy frogmen showed the small beaches to be practicable for landing, and Smith had his way. His plan was "to sneak in the back door while the Japanese waited at the front door." Smith would not command at Tinian, but would go to Guam. The Tinian invasion would be made by the 2nd and 4th Marine Divisions, still on Saipan. These units were given only two weeks to recuperate from the fierce physical and psychological battering they had received. Only a few replacements were available for scattering among their depleted ranks. Harry Schmidt was moved up from commander of the 4th to take charge of the new landing, his place with the 4th assumed by Clifton Cates, now a major general. The assault would be unusual in that parts of it would be conducted from shore to shore rather than from ship to shore.

Never in the Pacific war had the Japanese been obliged to prepare for an invasion under harsher conditions. Tinian had been taking regular poundings by sea and air ever since the softening up of Saipan had begun. Now, with the assault looming, thirteen battalions of American artillery, 156 guns, were firing from the south coast of the captured island. Making things more hellish, the Americans had added a new aerial weapon to their arsenal: a bomb composed of napalm powder mixed with aviation fuel that burst into a sea of flame. The chief purpose of this weapon was to eliminate the cane fields and brush patches as hiding places, but the flames were also proficient at roasting troops. As for the naval vessels that ringed the island and lobbed in shells, they included three battleships, five cruisers, and sixteen destroyers. Some of the destroyers were able to send phosphorus incendiary shells into cave entrances.

Early on the morning of D-day (or Jig-day, as it was called), the Japanese subjected the fleet to a measure of revenge, directed against a group of vessels lying off Tinian Town. As recalled by Quartermaster 3rd Class Walker Gunter of the battleship *Colorado:* "We were completely dead in the water. I was the helmsman with nothing to helm. We were lobbing in 16-inch and 5-inch shells one after the other. Soon an enemy shell went over the ship; next one dropped short; and then all hell broke loose. We took twenty-two 6-inch shells in a very short time. Being at anchor, we could not get under way immediately. Had it not been for the other ships, which soon silenced the Japanese battery, our topside would have been leveled." The destroyer *Norman Scott* was also hit at this time, taking six shells that killed or wounded sixty-six men; the vessel's skipper was among the dead. On the *Colorado,* Walker Gunter was struck from behind by a sliding door that jumped its track. Momentarily numbed, Gunter thought he felt blood pouring down his back and legs, but it turned out to be perspiration. Many of Gunter's comrades were not so lucky. "When the first shell burst on the signal bridge, a sailor was standing near the railing. His headless body was found where he had been standing, his head on the fantail about 400 feet away. Four of our ship's barbers had been on station at a 20-millimeter gun position, three sitting on an ammunition ready-box and one sitting on the deck, leaning against the box. A shell burst in front of them, severing both legs of each of the men on the box and decapitating the one sitting on deck. A Marine gunnery sergeant and his crew had been manning one of the 5-inch antiaircraft batteries. A shell burst at this position, destroying the gun and killing the entire crew. The sergeant was blown into hundreds of small pieces. These were scooped up, put in a trash can, and the whole thing thrown over the side." In all, there were 241 men killed or wounded, forty-two of them seagoing Marines.

This mayhem occurred in connection with a maneuver designed to confuse the enemy. While the 4th Marine Division—riding in amtracs, some of them Army—headed for the small northwestern beaches (White 1 and White 2), the 2nd Marine Division made a pretense of landing from transports off Tinian Town. When the demonstration ended and the warships and transports drew off, a Japanese soldier took a moment to record the event in his diary, closing with, "Maybe the enemy is retreating." The 2nd was actually swinging northwest to make its real landing behind the 4th, an operation planned for D-day evening and the next day. The Marines of the 4th received only light fire as they approached the White Beaches, but there was trouble on White 2 with land mines the Japanese had implanted in the sand. PFC Daniel G. Carns, of the Army's 534th Amphibious Tractor Battalion, was nearing the beach in a third-wave craft when he saw one in the second wave, just ahead, bounce upward. "We felt the concussion of the explosion as the tractor was turned into a pile of trash. There were no survivors. I was surprised to find that I myself had taken a small piece of shrapnel in the hand." Two additional amtracs hit mines. Many of the rest veered from the danger zone, which made it necessary for their occupants to climb the coral ledges to get ashore. But the landing was supremely successful. Resistance remained relatively light all day as 15,600 4th Division Marines, along with artillery, tanks, halftracks, 37-millimeter guns, and supplies, flowed in as though through a funnel and spread out over a beachhead two miles wide and a mile deep. Casualties were 240 killed or wounded—about one-eighth of the first-day toll on Saipan. All in all, it had been a heartening invasion for these still-weary veterans, who had dreaded the possibility of another tough one.

The first night on shore, however, was filled with all of the old horrors. Although Colonel Ogata was taken unaware by the landing, he had wasted no time organizing countermeasures. Little had been achieved during the day because American shells, bombs, and rockets had made it too difficult for the troops to maneuver. Many brave men had remained glued to their cover because of the new fire bomb. But when night fell, the assigned units—perhaps 2,500 men in all—began getting into position, star shells and harassment notwithstanding, and they made their series of attacks during the early morning hours. Covered by artillery and supported by tanks, the howling hordes hit the Marines on the left, on the right, and in the center. Most of the attackers were cut down as fast as they came, their tanks destroyed, but in the center about 200 managed a breakthrough. Half headed toward the beach and ran into an artillery battery that opened up with both howitzers and .50-caliber machine guns. These Japanese, according to one observer, "were literally torn to pieces." The other group was stopped by a torrent of small-arms fire from a support platoon of the 3rd Battalion, 25th Marines. A few survivors ran into a woods within the lines, and Captain Thomas S. Witherspoon ordered K Company's mortar section to lay in a barrage. The section leader hesitated, reminding the captain that the woods were known to hold a Japanese torpedo dump. Sending in mortars might be dangerous. "Damn the torpedoes!" Witherspoon yelled. "Fire away!" There was no catastrophe, except for the trapped enemy soldiers.

Just before dawn, with the strife dying down, the Marines heard a strange racket all along the front. The Japanese were removing their helpless wounded on stretchers made of corrugated tin, which crackled with every undulation. Daylight came before all of the disabled men could be carried away, and the Marines of the 2nd Battalion, 23rd Regiment, beheld a singular sight. As reported by the battalion operations officer, Major J. W. Sperry: "Jap bodies began to fly ten to fifteen feet into the air in the area in front of our lines. We knew that hand grenades did not have the power to blow a man's body that high, and we could not figure out what was happening. It turned out that about half of the Japs had been carrying magnetic mines and had obviously been ordered to break through our lines and destroy the tanks to the rear of us. The Japs who were wounded and unable to flee were placing the tank mines under their bodies and tapping the detonators."

During the morning mop-up, there were two tank mishaps. One Sherman ran over a dead Japanese who was clutching a bangalore torpedo. Six blocks were blown off the machine's left track, but the crew escaped unhurt. Another Sherman incurred minor damage when a death-feigning Japanese jumped up and slapped a magnetic mine against its side. A volley of rifle fire dropped the man in almost the same spot from which he had risen. When it was all over, the number of enemy dead was counted at 1,241. About 750 had been wounded. Perhaps 500 had got away whole. Reports of the action and its casualties depressed Colonel Ogata. Nothing had been accomplished, and he had lost a large portion of his best troops.

Ogata might have been heartened at least slightly had he known that one of his 75-millimeter gun crews got in a telling blow that morning. A shell made a square hit on the fire direction center of an artillery unit, the 1st Battalion, 14th Marines. Ten men were killed: the battalion commander, the operations officer, the intelligence officer, and seven of their assistants. Fourteen other headquarters people were wounded. This was a remarkable score for a single 75-millimeter shell.

Encountering only moderate resistance, the Americans captured the northern end of Tinian—about one-fifth of its land mass—by the close of July 26, Jig-plus-2. This part of the island held the Ushi Point Airfield, the spot from which, in a little over a year, B-29s would carry atomic bombs to Hiroshima and Nagasaki.

Now the Marines began pressing southward on a cross-island front, the 4th Division on the right and the 2nd on the left. There was little fighting, for the foe was kept battered, staggered, and on the run by the support fire laid down by ships, aircraft, and artillery. Particularly useful in spotting for the artillery and scouting for the infantry were small OY observation planes flown by Marines. Some segments of the advance turned out to be nothing more than hot and tedious foot-slogging through cane fields that held only occasional nests of troops or frightened civilians. At one point the 3rd Battalion, 23rd Marines, captured a warehouse stacked to the rafters with beer and liquor. The battalion commander, Major Paul S. Treitel, found that "it took a great deal of leadership and persuasion by platoon leaders and company commanders to get their men to continue the attack without stocking up."

The weather turned stormy and the Marines grew soggy and miserable, and their supply lines were threatened by high seas. When it became impossible to get the wounded out by water, action was taken by aircraft based on Saipan. As explained by a combat correspondent, Sergeant James J. McElroy: "Seabees on Tinian cleared the airstrip of debris in anticipation of the planes, and by midafternoon of July 30 two combat-painted Curtiss Commando transports skidded cautiously down at Ushi, their interiors fitted out with flying litters. Seven minutes after the planes took off again, their wheels touched ground at Saipan. The first of the Tinian wounded were on their way to the ample facilities of the base hospitals there." The aerial transports, McElroy adds, were also used to provide Tinian's invaders with "urgently needed food, rockets, bomb fuses, medical supplies, and other freight."

Resistance increased, although not greatly, as the Marines began herding the surviving Japanese into the island's southern sector. Growing numbers of hungry and thirsty civilians were taken into custody, most quite willingly, even those of Japanese blood. Many of these people were carrying suitcases filled with clothing and were wearing their "Sunday best." American propaganda efforts, primarily the distribution of surrender tickets by airdrop and shellfire, were having an effect. "The bearer," said one of these cards, "has the special right to be aided by American forces. According to international law, we will give you fair treatment and will grant you sufficient clothing, food, and shelter, as well as tobacco and medical treatment. American troops will make every effort to preserve the lives of persons who desire aid." There was a special card for the Japanese enlisted troops: "Your officers have been lying to you," it said. Then it listed all of the Pacific battles the Americans had won. "Your officers told you that the Japanese Navy and Air Force would come to your aid in all of these places. . . . Why do you go on fighting for officers who lie to you? It is not necessary to fight to the last man or commit suicide. . . . You do not gain anything by dying." This card had little effect. Ironically, Japanese morale was undergoing a temporary rise as the result of a rumor that the Imperial Navy had regrouped and was approaching at full speed.

Colonel Ogata had issued his final order on July 29, Jig-plus-5. The surviving troops, perhaps 2,500 in number, were to make their last stand on the wooded ridges on the southern coast. By the afternoon of July 30 the Americans were closing in on this rugged region. That night the lines of the 24th Marines were hit by a one-company, tank-supported *banzai,* which was easily stopped. The next morning the cornered Japanese were clobbered with 615 tons of naval shells and 69 tons of explosives from the air. Prisoners later described the barrage as "almost unbearable." But enough of the enemy kept their senses to put up a bitter resistance from caves, dugouts, and trenches as the Marines ascended the ridges. Although the island was declared secured on August 1, Jig-plus-8, the fighting went on. Colonel Ogata, along with 123 others, was killed in a *banzai* attack on the 2nd Division's lines during the night of August 2–3. A burst of machine-gun fire draped the colonel's body on the division's barbed wire.

In an effort to save lives on both sides, the Americans set up amplifying equipment both ashore and afloat, and surrender appeals were addressed to the troops and civilians who had crowded into the seaside caves. Thousands of civilians responded, some wearing bright silks to dignify the occasion, and they were joined by a few disillusioned military men. The other survivors either clung to the temporary security of their hiding places or turned to orgies of murder and suicide. Soldiers shot civilians or blew them up in groups, then used grenades on themselves. Parents threw their children from the cliffs to the rocky surf, then jumped after. Mothers made the leap with babies in their arms. Some of the soldiers also jumped. Unfortunately, the cliffs were not high enough to ensure death, and, although many did die, others merely broke their backs or necks or limbs and lay writhing in the shallows or on the beach. PFC Glenn Zettlemoyer saw something he would never forget. "A young mother was lying there dead. The baby she had jumped with was trying to breast-feed." The Americans saved the baby and as many of the injured as they could.

By August 6, all 4th Division units had been phased out of the operation, with the 2nd taking over full responsibility for the mop-up. As the 4th prepared to sail for its camp in the Hawaiian Islands, a doctor given to punning wrote in the surgeon's log, "Here today and gone to Maui." Some hundreds of the enemy remained alive at this time. There were 252 military prisoners, and 9,000 civilians had been placed in camps. American casualties, including those of the *Colorado* and *Norman Scott* on Jig-day, came to 389 killed and 1,816 wounded, which was considered a very reasonable price for this valuable island. It was the 8th Marines of the 2nd Division, under the assistant division commander, Red Mike Edson, that did the final mopping up. The last elements of the regiment did not join the division at its camp on Saipan until January 1, 1945; this was nearly five months after the operation's official end. Another 542 of the enemy had been killed. The 8th lost thirty-eight killed and 125 wounded.

Holland Smith called Tinian "the perfect amphibious operation of the Pacific war." These were days of fulfillment for the general, who, along with a few other American military leaders, had so early foreseen the nation's need for amphibious specialists and had pressed for their creation against public apathy, governmental skepticism, and limited finan-

Second Division howitzer fires into cave during Tinian mop-up.

cial appropriations—officers who had refused to be frustrated by the fact that a democracy, in its zeal to keep the military under restraint, makes it difficult for even the most perceptive students of war to apply their expertise. Smith and his associates had proved the value of persistence under the system, for it was becoming quite clear that America's amphibious preparations were the key to victory over Japan.

Guam Repossessed

======The largest of the Marianas, Guam, roughly peanut-shaped, measures about thirty miles between its southwestern and northeastern extremities, and is from four to eight miles across. It has an area of 225 square miles and is encircled by a coral reef ranging in width from twenty-five to 700 yards. Although replete with arable areas, the island has more than its share of hills, cliffs, ravines, and thick rain forests. When, at the close of World War I, Japan received the other Marianas as mandates, Guam was left an American island in Japanese waters. This worried only the military experts, for in 1919 no one else was thinking in terms of war with Japan. In 1923, when the Empire was rocked by one of the worst earthquakes in history, Americans were generous with their assistance. Guam, which served the United States as a minor naval station, had no heavy fortifications, and the Navy and Marine Corps anticipated its fall to Japan long before the Pacific war even began. By 1936, five years before Pearl Harbor, officers attending the Marine Corps schools at Quantico, Virginia, were studying ways of effecting Guam's repossession.

In July 1944, the island was held by 18,500 Japanese troops, including the 38th Infantry Regiment, the 48th Independent Mixed Brigade, the 10th Independent Mixed Regiment, and the 54th Naval Guard Force. Lieutenant General Takeshi Takashina, another Manchuria veteran, was in overall command. The civilians were nearly all Chamorros, or Guamanians, as they preferred to be called. Their partisanship for the United States had brought these people much grief at Japanese hands. The gentlest fate that befell them was to be conscripted for hard labor. There were public floggings, emasculations, beheadings. People condemned to death were forced to dig their own graves. It was treatment reminiscent of that given the islanders by their Spanish masters of earlier centuries. In the spring of 1944, with an American invasion imminent, most of the Guamanians were placed in concentration camps on starvation rations.

Designated the 3rd Amphibious Corps, the forces assigned to the assault were Allen Turnage's 3rd Marine Division, the 1st Provisional Marine Brigade under Lemuel Shepherd, all of the usual attached units, and a strong array of Corps Artillery led by Pedro del Valle, now a brigadier general. In reserve but slated for an early landing was the Army's 77th Division, under Major General Andrew D. Bruce, an outfit

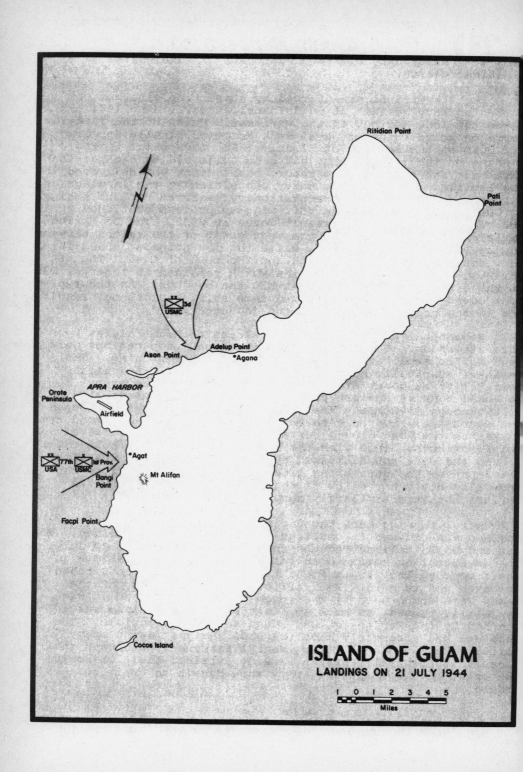

Ritidian Point

Pati Point

3d
USMC

Asan Point

Adelup Point
•Agana

APRA HARBOR

Orote
Peninsula

Airfield

77th   1st Prov.
USA   USMC

•Agat

Bangi
Point

⚡ Mt Alifan

Facpi Point

Cocos Island

ISLAND OF GUAM
LANDINGS ON 21 JULY 1944

1 0 1 2 3 4 5
Miles

that was well trained but had never seen action. The total number of troops was 54,891. Accountable to Kelly Turner and Holland Smith, Roy Geiger was in top command. Those ships of Spruance's Central Pacific Task Forces involved in the operation were the responsibility of Rear Admiral Richard L. "Close-in" Conolly.

The first carrier planes lashed at Guam on June 11, forty days before the landing, and the first naval gunfire was boomed in on June 16. Early in July, the bombardment was stepped up, and Spruance's flagship, the heavy cruiser *Indianapolis,* participated. One of the ship's ensigns, Herbert L. Brummel, recalled a unique moment: "We were busy blasting the island on the Fourth of July when we suddenly pulled out of the battle line to eat a filet mignon dinner. Then we went back." During the two weeks previous to the invasion the fleet fired nearly 28,764 shells of all sizes between 5-inch and 16-inch. A Japanese officer admitted that this caused "scattered outbreaks of serious loss of spirit." Along with the other damage, the bombardment leveled the beautiful old capital town of Agana, site of the governor's palace built by the Spanish nearly three centuries earlier. Only the brick gateway leading to the gardens was left standing.

During this period of the bombardment, on the evening of July 10, a pair of destroyers that had moved in close to shore spotted a man high on a cliff waving semaphore flags. He was an American, Radioman First Class George R. Tweed, who had been hiding from the Japanese ever since they captured the island. A number of Guamanians, including a revered young priest, had been beheaded on charges of aiding Tweed, but he had never been betrayed. The islanders viewed him as a symbol of better days, and of days they hoped would come again. The Japanese had told them that America was losing the war and would never return. Tweed's presence seemed a refutation of this. Rescued by motor launch in the dusk, the shaggy "Robinson Crusoe" gave the fleet much valuable information on the enemy's installations.

During the three days before D-day (or W-day), July 21, American airmen blanketed the island with 1,131 tons of explosives, losing sixteen planes to antiaircraft fire. An audacious part of the preparations was that performed by the Navy's frogmen, who cleared nearly 1,000 improvised obstacles from the waters of the chosen beaches, mostly palm log cribs and wire cages filled with coral. No underwater mines were found. The doughty swimmers left a sign on the reef:

WELCOME MARINES.

The assault was planned to make simultaneous use of two beaches, six miles apart, on Guam's western coast. The 3rd Marine Division would land just north of Asan Point; the spot where Ferdinand Magellan probably first set foot in 1521, while the 1st Marine Provisional Brigade, followed by the Army's 77th Division, would land at Agat, just south of Orote Peninsula. At dawn on D-day the bullhorns of the troop transports blared a brief speech by General Geiger: "The eyes of the nation watch you as you go into battle to liberate this former American bastion from the enemy. Make no mistake; it will be a tough, bitter fight against a wily, stubborn foe who will doggedly defend Guam against this invasion. May the glorious traditions of the Marine *esprit de corps* spur you to victory. You have been honored." The speech was followed by a rousing rendition of the "Marine's Hymn." It was a moment of special meaning for some of the older officers and men, who had been stationed, at one time or another, at the Marine barracks on Orote Peninsula. They had friends among the 150 Guam Marines who had been taken captive and were even now enduring hardships and indignities in Japanese prison camps.

As the Marines prepared to land, the Navy began to bombard the beaches and the regions behind them. Throughout W-day, the battleships, cruisers, destroyers, and rocket-armed gunboats would unleash 27,386 shells—very nearly as many as had been fired during the entire record-breaking barrage of the previous two weeks. At 6:15 A.M., with the sunrise flaming on a misty horizon, the first carrier planes reached the scene, and scores of others were on the way. The combination of bombing, strafing, and shelling would not only demolish fortifications, disrupt communications, and cause many deaths but would also reduce numbers of the untouched defenders to trembling, wild-eyed incompetence.

One American who had a panoramic view of the southern part of the invasion was Technical Sergeant William K. Terry, a combat correspondent with the 1st Marine Provisional Brigade. Terry was in a DUKW, or "duck," with an artillery reconnaissance party that was scheduled to land and seek out a site for its guns as soon as the infantry had cleared the enemy from the beach. "We could see our planes bombing and strafing defense-studded Orote Peninsula and the beach where we were to land. Bombers alternated with warships in pouring in tons of steel. At times parts of the island were so enshrouded in smoke that we could not see Mount Alifan in the distance. American ships of all types were around us as far as the eye could see. Major Alfred M. Mahoney, commanding officer of the artillery outfit, pointed out that a light rain had brought out a rainbow in our rear. By now we could see the assault waves lining up to go in, the craft looking like tiny water bugs. The beach was heavily peppered before they landed, and explosions like gigantic firecrackers could be heard. The Japs were shooting back at our small boats, either with mountain guns or depressed antiaircraft batteries. Some of the shells whizzed over our heads and landed in the water several hundred yards farther out. As our planes and ships shifted all of their fire to Orote Peninsula, we could see large fires and huge columns of smoke this caused.

"After the first wave landed, the Japs laid a heavy mortar barrage on the beach, and they continued firing at landing boats still in the water. We saw several in flames, and some wrecked ones on the beach. Others were stranded on the reef. Our craft got stuck on the reef, and Major Mahoney said, 'We walk in from here, boys. Into the water!' Holding my carbine overhead, I dropped into water which reached to my shoulders. We scattered so that if a shell landed in our midst our casualties would be at a minimum. Jap shells continued to come our way as we waded in, and we could hear machine-gun bullets zinging overhead. We saw signs that the infantry was advancing quicker than we had expected. We could see three tanks up in the hills, firing at enemy positions. To the left, one of our planes went down while bombing Orote Peninsula. When we hit the beach we were pinned down temporarily by machine guns and small-arms fire from a coconut palm grove that fringed the beach. The reconnaissance party reorganized under the protection of a slight ridge. Major Mahoney led the artillerymen along the beach and then inland, closely following the assault infantry. The enlisted men in the major's party killed two machine gunners in a trench and a sniper in a cave entrance. As soon as the artillery locations had been selected, the guns and their crews were called in. They had been floating around in the bay in landing craft. The guns were set up quickly and efficiently."

As revealed by Terry's account, the southern assault was progressing well in spite of stiff resistance. Things were about the same in the north, where the 3rd Marine Division went in three regiments abreast. A sidelight to the landing of the 9th Marines is related by the regimental commander, Colonel Edward Craig: "I was in a free boat, with permission to go anywhere I desired. My 3rd Battalion had already landed and was cleaning out Asan Point. My 2nd Battalion was also ashore. So I told the free boat commander to land. The ensign refused to carry out my orders. He said he was assigned to a certain wave, which was then coming in, and could not change his orders. I told him that if he didn't carry out my orders he'd go over the side. One of my sergeants jumped up and said, 'I'd be delighted.' So this ensign decided to change his

Third Division assault troops on beach near Asan Point.

orders. I finally got ashore and was in a shellhole with my adjutant watching the attack on the ridge in front when he was shot through the neck."

Meeting their heaviest resistance at a seaside cliff and a set of ridges on their left flank, the Marines in the north spent the day carving out a beachhead about 2.5 miles wide and, in some spots, nearly a mile deep. In the south, just below Orote, the area gained was about the same size, but the inland progress had been more uniform. American casualties for the day were 1,037 in killed, wounded, and missing. During the afternoon, advance elements of the Army's 77th Division had come ashore over the southern beaches.

That night the Japanese counterattacked both beachheads. They were repulsed with heavy losses, but only after hours of fighting that was also punishing to the Marines. Those in the south were the harder hit. Perhaps no American on the island had a rougher time than PFC Rudolf G. "Rudy" Rosenquist, a machine gunner with the 4th Marines who was stationed on the extreme right of the southern beachhead.

Things began innocently enough. At about eleven o'clock the star-shell light revealed a small Japanese dog making its way along in front of the lines. Rudy and his buddies tried to coax the animal in, but it kept going and disappeared into a rice paddy. A little later a single Japanese shot rang out, and a BAR man slumped soundlessly from his sited weapon. There was nothing moving out in front; the Japanese were pressed against the shadowed ground. Soon two ominous clicks were heard: two of the enemy were arming hand grenades by tapping the buttons on their helmets. These missiles burst brightly just short of the hole Rudy was occupying with another machine gunner. The pair had ducked, and although fragments rattled against Rudy's helmet they did him no harm. Now the Marine opened up with the machine gun, hosing down the entire front. When he stopped, nothing more happened for about twenty minutes. Then more clicks were heard and six or eight grenades came flying; but all fell short and merely tore up the ground. Rudy's gun chattered again as he gave the front another hosing. For a few minutes after he stopped, the shadows were silent and still. Then a line of the enemy rose up shouting and came in at a trot. Rudy swept the line and the men went sprawling. A second line rose and charged, and Rudy scythed it down. By this time Japanese mortar crews were in action, and the shells whoomped along the Marine positions, throwing up debris. Ignoring the blasts, Rudy kept knocking down new waves of attackers until his partner cried, "Dammit, let me have some!"

Another attack was beginning as the partner took over, and some of these Japanese got through. Rudy heard a shriek on his left and looked up to see a bayonet on the end of a rifle being shoved down at him. He tried to roll away, but the blade went through his side and pinned him to the ground. As the enemy soldier pulled out and stepped over him, Rudy reached up and grasped the man's canteen strap and was yanked to his feet. The Japanese tore loose and rushed on. Now a second enemy soldier came running, and Rudy took a bayonet wound in the stomach. By this time he had got out a .38 pistol, which he emptied into the man, who fell back upon the Marine at the machine gun. Seconds later, a third Japanese crashed into Rudy, and the pair went down grappling, the Japanese screaming the same few words over and over. This time Rudy used his combat knife. The two were face-to-face in the star-shell light, and even as he plunged the knife home Rudy thought, "How young he looks." The Marine was trying to get back on his feet when something—he never learned what—struck him on the head and he passed out.

When he regained his senses, Rudy pulled himself into a sitting position against the trunk of a palm tree. Except for scattered American and Japanese bodies, he seemed to be alone on the battlefield, which was a mixture of shadows and illuminated spots under the star shells. He was still holding his combat knife; and, as he said later, "it felt as though it had been dipped in glue." His midsection was soaked with blood, but he felt little pain. Sheathing the sticky knife, he took his fatigue cap from his jacket pocket and stuffed it under his belt and over one of his wounds in an effort to stop the bleeding. Rudy heard the sound of firing from along the lines to the left and from the enemy's positions across the rice paddy. He summoned his strength and got up and began walking toward the rear. Passing through a woods and emerging into an area of low brush, he was challenged to give the password by a group of Marines occupying a large shellhole. Coming to a halt at the challenge, Rudy found himself thinking in anger, "I can't remember the damn password!" He explained that he was wounded and needed help. Just then he grew weak and fell to his knees. "I was sure they would shoot me for moving so suddenly, but then I remembered the password and they let me crawl into their shellhole." A corpsman stripped Rudy to the waist, put sulfa powder and battle dressings on his wounds, and gave him a shot of morphine.

Rudy's nightmare of perils was not over. Shortly a squad of Japanese, voices conversational and gear rattling, came marching toward the shellhole over the same route Rudy had just used. The men with Rudy took positions on the rim and opened fire with their rifles. Some of the enemy were killed, while others took cover. There was a brief period of complete silence. Then two or three clicks were heard. As the grenades landed in the shellhole, all of the Marines but Rudy scrambled out. Rudy was too weak and morphine-numbed to move that fast, but there was a small radio near him and he pulled it across his groin. The grenades roared and the radio was wrecked. Rudy had grenade fragments in both legs, one in his chest and one in his right hand. By this time the other Marines were throwing grenades of their own. Rudy decided to try to make it to the rear on his hands and knees. "I hadn't gone thirty feet when I came face-to-face with a wounded Jap, also on his hands and knees. He jabbed at me with what looked like a short spear, and he stuck me between the fingers of my injured right hand." The Japanese turned tail, and Rudy crept back to the shellhole. His friends had won their battle by now, and they told Rudy to stay in the hole, that they would see that he got help. He lay down on his back and passed out. "When I came to, I was alone and the flares were coming at longer and longer intervals." Rudy's senses slipped away again, and

Riflemen engaged in firefight during expansion of Guam beachheads.

next time he awoke the sun was high and he was sunburned on the face, chest, and arms. He raised up and called for a corpsman, then thought, "Oh, hell, the Japs will hear me." Settling back down, he was soon unconscious again. This time when he awakened he saw, through blurred eyes, two figures looming above him, and he thought they were Japanese. "But then my wits returned and I realized they were Navajo Code Talkers working stretcher detail."* Rudy was taken by truck to a tent near the beach, where a Navy surgeon was working. While he was lying on his litter, awaiting his turn for attention, Rudy heard two Japanese bullets rip through the top of the tent. The surgeon continued working, and Rudy got the preliminary help he needed. He was soon on board a hospital ship, scheduled for evacuation to Honolulu.

*The regular work of the Navajo Code Talkers was a great asset to American efforts in the Pacific. As communications personnel, these native American Indians transmitted messages among each other: between aircraft and the ground, between ships and stations on shore, between frontline tanks or artillery and the rear, and among the various infantry command posts. The code employed, based on the Navajo language, was absolutely undecipherable to the Japanese.

American efforts of the next few days were aimed at strengthening the two beachheads and pushing them toward each other. The Japanese on the left-flank heights in the north remained particularly stubborn, killing or wounding 815 Marines of the 3rd Regiment during one forty-eight-hour period. On the right flank, however, the northern beach-head was speedily extended down the coast to embrace the ruins of the former United States Navy Yard at Piti and the offshore isle of Cabras, which made it easier for the fleet to unload supplies. It was the primary object of the southern troops to expand northward to Orote Peninsula, which was slated for early capture. By the evening of July 25, a line had been established across Orote's base, and patrols from the two beach-heads had made contact along the coast above Orote; but the beach-heads themselves were still about two miles apart.

Alarmed by the rapid erosion of his manpower under the assaults by land, sea, and air, General Takashina now launched his major counter-blow, a nocturnal effort involving thousands of men. While the naval troops on Orote Peninsula attacked the line that the southern invaders had thrown across the peninsula's base, six battalions of infantry swarmed down from the inland hills and hurled themselves against the 3rd Division in the north. The night was a rainy one. Many of the Japanese were saturated also with beer and *sake*, which swelled both the volume and the hysteria of the war cries—some of which sounded suspiciously like wails of despair—and added to the impetus, if not to the precision, of the charges.

On Orote Peninsula, scene of the lesser of the efforts, the enemy's naval troops were met by the roar, concussion, and jagged shrapnel of 26,000 artillery shells that sent bodies, parts of bodies, and shattered equipage in all directions. "Arms and legs," reported one observer, "flew like snowflakes." The Japanese who got through the inferno gave the 22nd Marines some bad moments in hand-to-hand encounters, but were soon annihilated. The attack cost the enemy 400 dead. Numbers of wounded were carried, or managed to walk, back up the peninsula. Marine casualties were light.

Takashina's assault on the 3rd Division was a 4,000-man tidal wave. Although there were spots where it dashed itself into an ebbing trickle, there were others where it swept away entire platoons. In the center of the torrent, Lieutenant Colonel Robert E. Cushman's 2nd Battalion, 9th Marines, managed to stand against seven major charges but lost half its men killed or wounded.

Among the Americans in support back near the beach was artillery officer John Letcher, who contemplated events from his foxhole: "The fighting along the front lines increased steadily throughout the night. The star shells fired by the warships kept the hilltops continuously lighted, and the noise of rifle and machine-gun fire never ceased. Our batteries were firing at their maximum rate. I was awake during most of the night, and I realized that a terrific battle was raging on the tops of the hills a quarter of a mile up the valley from us, but when I heard shots fired nearby or heard explosions of grenades my only thought was that they were the result of the men being nervous and imagining that they saw Japanese."

Letcher dozed off shortly before daybreak, but was soon awakened by a Marine who ran up, flung himself on the ground beside the foxhole, and shouted, "Colonel! Colonel! We are being attacked!" Letcher heard several bullets crack in the air over his head as he asked, "Where are they?" The Marine pointed to a nearby machine-gun nest and said, "Right there!" The colonel asked incredulously, "Are you sure?" He was answered, "Yes! Yes! They drove us out of it a minute ago!" Finally aware that a crisis was at hand, Letcher said, "Well, Great God, give me a grenade!"

The colonel relates: "Two or three grenades appeared from somewhere, and, seizing one, I crawled forward towards the nest, still scarcely able to believe that the enemy could have gotten in so close to us without my knowing it. A small ridge of earth was between me and the emplacement, and when I had crawled a dozen feet and had come up to it I pulled the pin from the grenade and raised up to throw it. In the nest I saw a Japanese soldier pointing the machine gun at me as he fumbled at the breech in an attempt to fire it. I threw the grenade and dropped to the ground behind the ridge. I heard it explode as I looked back over my shoulder and called for more grenades. These were tossed to me and I threw another one, but the first one had done the work; for when I raised up to throw the second I saw that the Jap who had been pointing the gun was crumpled across the breech. Two others were lying behind him and one was crawling slowly along the ditch away from the nest. I learned that the Marine who had awakened me had had the presence of mind to take the bolt out of the machine gun before he left the nest, and that was why the Jap had not been able to fire the gun." Letcher's experience was the beginning of a skirmish around the artillery command post that lasted for several hours. When it was over, seventeen of the enemy were dead; the Marines had lost six killed and seventeen wounded.

There were many other behind-the-lines skirmishes. The security of the division hospital, a cluster of tents filled with men on cots, was disrupted at dawn when a Marine rushed in from the direction of the front crying, in a manner reminiscent of Paul Revere, "The Japs are coming! The Japs are coming!" Men naked except for their bandages jumped up and headed for the beach, some of the more serious cases reopening their wounds and dripping blood as they hobbled along. Other patients, some in their underwear, grabbed their Garands. Corpsmen dropped their instruments of mercy and took up their carbines. Although the international rules of warfare called for medical personnel to go unarmed, it would have been idiocy for American corpsmen in the Pacific to follow this regulation, since many of the enemy took special pleasure in shooting them down. These particular Japanese soon appeared at the hospital—which they *knew* to be a hospital—and began shooting and throwing grenades. In the surgery tent, a doctor continued with a critical operation as shrapnel tore through the canvas. Outside, one of the corpsmen got seven of the raiders with his carbine. Reinforcements soon arrived from division headquarters, and all of the Japanese were killed.

According to Technical Sergeant Alvin M. Josephy, Jr., a combat correspondent with the 3rd Division, every Marine and Seabee on the beach was now mobilized and squads were formed to hunt down the survivors of the breakthrough. "All normal activity behind our front lines ceased. Cooks, drivers, clerks, telephone operators, unloaders on the reef—everyone available—went into the hills that morning to eliminate the threat to our beachhead."

By the time the counterattack was completely stopped, both behind the lines and at the front, about 3,500 Japanese were dead. By far, the larger number had been killed at the front. The Americans had lost some 600 killed, wounded, and missing. As always, the fate of the missing was a matter for apprehensive speculation. It is probable that at least some fell into Japanese hands, were dragged into caves, and met death by torture. A report went to Tokyo describing the attack and regretfully conceding defeat, and also offering sympathy to the families of the men who were slain. Tokyo responded by ordering the resistance continued, since it was "a matter of urgency for the defense of Japan." The resistance was continued, much of the time with true Bushido spirit, but its only effect was to make the American victory more costly. Actually, this was the idea behind the order. Japan might yet secure a face-saving peace settlement if America decided that completing its Pacific drive would take too many lives.

The Marines of the southern beachhead had the situation on Orote Peninsula well in hand by July 29, W-plus-8. As "to the colors" was sounded on a captured Japanese bugle, the American flag was raised beside the wreckage of the old Marine Barracks at Sumay. In the presence of a gathering that included Raymond Spruance and Holland Smith, Lemuel Shepherd delivered a brief but apt address: "On this hallowed ground, you officers and men of the First Marine Brigade have avenged the loss of our comrades who were overcome by a numerically superior enemy three days after Pearl Harbor. Under our flag this island again stands ready to fulfil its destiny as an American fortress in the Pacific."

By this time the two beachheads were in firm contact, and the enemy's main body was withdrawing inland to take up its final positions. General Takashina was killed as the retreat began, shot down by a machine gunner on a Sherman tank. U.S. Army patrols sent to scour the southern half of the island found only a few Japanese, which indicated that the main body had swung northward through the rough terrain of the rain forests. The American pursuit was made with the Army on the right and the Marines on the left, the front stretching across the island. Only minor resistance was encountered at first, but the Army soon reached a clearing that held a concentration camp filled with Guamanians, about 2,000 ragged, emaciated, and sickly people who began laughing, crying, cheering, and singing. Their opening song was the "Marine's Hymn," but the GIs did not complain. Later, after the plight of the internees had been eased, there was a ceremony during which the Stars and Stripes was raised over the camp and the schoolchildren sang "God Bless America" and "America the Beautiful." When the camp's young women saw American photographers approaching they ran into their huts and came out with their hair combed and beribboned. A Guamanian man explained that the girls thought a movie scout might see the pictures. "They all want to go to Hollywood."

The drive northward liberated thousands of other Guamanians. Some of the stronger young men took up machetes or begged firearms and joined the pursuit. It is doubtful that many of the enemy stragglers they found wounded or sick along the trail survived to become prisoners. Although the healthy Japanese were badly disorganized, they managed to make a few stiff stands against the Marines and GIs. During this campaign the Army earned the admiration of Holland Smith, who said later that the raw 77th Division "showed combat efficiency to a degree one would expect only of veteran troops." The Marines and GIs reached the north coast on August 10, W-plus-20, and on that day Guam was declared secured.

Winning back the island had cost the Americans 7,800 in killed or wounded: 6,716 Marines, 839 soldiers and 245 sailors. About 11,000 of the enemy were dead. Another 7,500 were concealed in scores of caves, ravines, and dense patches of vegetation scattered over the island's 225 square miles. Many died of starvation, while the others were sought by the garrison troops, mainly the 3rd Marine Division. The Marine camps were surrounded by skulking Japanese, most of them nonbelligerent.

As recalled by PFC Harold H. Schwerr: "One day we were going about our camp duties when into camp walked a rather imposing person in Japanese uniform. He was quite tall and regal-looking. We suddenly realized that this was the enemy walking among us. There was no trouble, for the man had come in to give himself up." Schwerr tells of another incident: "We were in our tents late one night when we heard noises outside, and someone got up to investigate. Several Japs were trying to steal the clothes off our line. The thieves were routed and took off with machine-gun fire chasing them. No one was killed, but I think the road was wet with Jap urine." There were also enemy soldiers who tried to steal food, and there were even a few who crept in at dusk to watch the American movies on the outdoor screens.

Marine patrols that roamed the island did the mopping up. Although

Civilian refugee camp behind American lines.

Airstrip on Orote Peninsula as it appeared ten days after Guam was secured.

Pressing the drive northward.

they fought back, the Japanese were systematically destroyed by gunfire, demolitions, and flamethrowers. The Marines had the help of war dogs, Doberman pinschers and German shepherds trained to sniff out the enemy and to keep him from making surprise attacks. Not all of the last defenders fought to the death, died of starvation, or killed themselves. By the end of August the Americans had 1,250 prisoners. Other Japanese eluded the Marines, somehow kept themselves in food, and finally surrendered when the war was over. A few individuals refused to accept Japan's capitulation and hid out for years afterward.

The repossession of Guam had the expected effect of elating the people back in the States. They could understand this conquest better than they could some of the others. As for the island's importance to the war effort: it became a vast supply depot, a major naval station, a troop-training area, and, like Saipan and Tinian, a base for Army Air Forces B-29s, the craft whose bombs were intended for the Japanese homeland.

21 | **Blunder in the Palaus**

In latter July 1944, while the conquests of Guam and Tinian were in progress, Franklin Roosevelt, Douglas MacArthur, and Chester Nimitz met in Honolulu to discuss the next phase of the two-pincer drive toward Japan. By this time MacArthur's forces had completed their series of leaps along the north coast of New Guinea to the Vogelkop Peninsula and were looking northwest toward Morotai, an island about halfway between their position and the southern Philippines. The general came to the conference with a strong recommendation that his campaign now be given priority over that of Nimitz in the Central Pacific. When he fled the Philippines at Roosevelt's order just before these American possessions fell to the Japanese, MacArthur had vowed to return at the earliest possible moment. His failure to redeem this pledge, he argued, would not only have an adverse psychological effect on the suffering Filipinos but would also seriously diminish America's prestige among her friends in the Orient. Moreover, he added, an early move into the Philippines would also be sound strategy. The general was persuasive and won his point, even with Nimitz. The admiral was more sympathetic toward MacArthur's cause now that the problem of the B-29 bases had been solved. Opening plans called for MacArthur to make his jump from New Guinea to Morotai on September 15. For the second time, the 1st Marine Division was called upon to protect the general's right flank. On the same day his troops landed on Morotai, the Marines, backed by the Army's 81st Division, were to make a landing about 500 miles to the northeast, their objective the island of Peleliu in the southern Palaus.

Bill Halsey, as commander of the Western Pacific Task Forces, was in overall charge of the supportive operation, which utilized some 800 ships—lately the 5th Fleet of the Central Pacific and now designated the 3rd Fleet. The admiral exercised direct control over the covering forces, and while the amphibious groups were plowing toward the Palaus he made a carrier cruise that included strikes on the southern and central Philippines. While inflicting heavy damage on aircraft, ships, and installations, the raids were only lightly contested, which indicated that the Philippines were not as strongly held as had been surmised. On September 13, two days before the scheduled assaults on Morotai and Peleliu, Halsey radioed his superiors an urgent recommendation that they scrap the current campaign in favor of an early jump all the way to the central Philippines. The war planners readily agreed to advance the Philippines timetable, but Morotai and Peleliu were not called off. This made little difference to MacArthur's troops, for Morotai held few defenders; but the Marines were plunged into a savage fight that was not essential to the progress of the war.

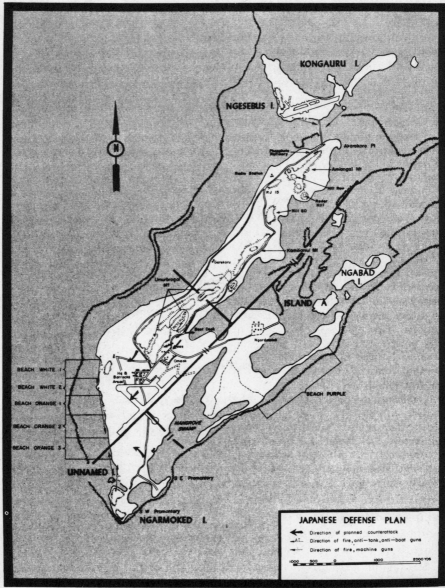

E. L. Wilson

One of the reasons Peleliu was not canceled was that Admiral Nimitz believed the island would be easy to take and would be useful as a base during MacArthur's ascent of the Philippines. The trouble was that little was known of the Palaus. Marine Corps spy Pete Ellis had died on the Palau island of Koror under puzzling circumstances in 1923, and the group had remained a mystery to the Americans ever since. Even the Navy's pre-invasion reconnaissance by aircraft, submarine, and underwater demolitions teams failed to produce a true picture of Peleliu and its defenses. Often described as resembling an open lobster claw reaching toward the northeast, the island is six miles long and roughly two miles wide. The Japanese had an airfield at its southern end. The Americans believed Peleliu to be wholly flat, but its scraggy jungle vegetation concealed a set of coral ridges running north from the airport and containing hundreds of natural caves that had been interconnected by tunnels and otherwise developed for defense. Some of the entrances held artillery pieces protected by sliding steel doors. Others offered perfect concealment for machine gunners, riflemen, and grenadiers. Vertical pits had been fashioned into mortar emplacements, and there were crevices housing rocket launchers. The coral's rigidity made many of the defenses impervious to bombs and shells, reducible only at close range by flamethrowers, demolitions, and grenades.

To compound the problems facing the Marines, Tokyo had ordered all Pacific island commanders to change their tactics against amphibious assaults. Every attempt to "annihilate the enemy at the beach" had failed. From now on the defenders were to confine their work at the beach to simple delaying tactics. The main line of resistance and its backup positions were to be established inland so as to be less vulnerable to naval shells and more difficult to reach. The headlong and life-wasting *banzais* were to be replaced by counterattacks judiciously planned and executed.

Commanding the defense of Peleliu was Colonel Kunio Nakagawa, whose garrison numbered some 10,500 men: the 2nd Infantry Regiment, two battalions of the 15th Infantry Regiment, a battalion of the 53rd Independent Mixed Brigade, a naval guard force, a tank battalion, artillery and antiaircraft units, air-base personnel, and a combat-trained labor force. Many of the troops were crack veterans of the fighting in China.

On the American side, Roy Geiger, lately of the Guam campaign, commanded the Marine and Army forces. The 1st Marine Division, still under William Rupertus, had been brought from its camp on Pavuvu in the Solomons, near Guadalcanal, where it had gone after New Britain. This was a wet, muddy, stinking, rat-ridden place the Marines called a "hog lot." Supposedly there for rest and rehabilitation and a new training program, they had to struggle long and hard just to create camp conditions that were passably endurable. Morale sank, many sickened, and some became psychologically unsettled, or, as it was termed, "Asiatic." One evening a man ran from his tent and began beating his fists against a coconut tree, crying, "I hate you! Goddammit, I hate you!" From inside a nearby tent came a shout, "Hit it once for me!" Out of contact with women, the Marines howled at the sight of the seductive female images on the camp movie screens. Pinups, photos of sweethearts, and pornographic pictures became objects of worship. Eyes popped when Frances Langford and Patti Thomas flew in with Bob Hope and Jerry Colona to put on a show, which became the camp's main topic of conversation for days. Most of the Marines were glad to leave Pavuvu, even though they knew they were returning to combat.

The division had been expanded to 28,500 men, although most of the reinforcements were support troops rather than infantry. As for the Army reserves, Rupertus was convinced he would not have to ask Geiger for their aid. Rupertus was optimistic about the operation and told his men, "We're going to take some casualties, but let me assure you that this will be a short one. Rough but fast. We'll be finished in three days. It might take only two."

During the three-day preliminary bombardment, the island kept its secret. As the naval shells and the aerial bombs and rockets tore up the tangled vegetation, numerous cave entrances were laid bare, but no one gave them much thought. At the close of the show the evening before D-day, the man in charge, Rear Admiral Jesse B. Oldendorf, reported jubilantly, "We have run out of targets." In the morning, many of the Marines preparing to head for shore in their amtracs found the pre-H-hour bombardment altogether reassuring. "I wondered how many Japs would be left alive to fight," recalled Private Harry Dearman. "Battleships, cruisers, destroyers, and rocket ships were blasting away, and airplanes were bombing and strafing. The island was so heavy with smoke and dust it was obscured from sight."

One of the men who did not share the general optimism was Chesty Puller, commanding the 1st Regiment. As the colonel prepared to debark from his transport, a naval officer assured him he'd be back on board in time for supper, that Peleliu had been smashed by the bombardment. "Well, sir," said Puller, "all I can see is dust. I doubt you've cleaned things out. I've been boning up on the maps for weeks, and I believe we'll be running into fortifications like we've never seen before.

They've been at it for years." It was unlike Puller to be pessimistic before a fight. As a precaution against the obliteration of his headquarters group, he divided it, taking half the men with him in a third-wave tractor and assigning the other half, under his executive officer, to a craft farther back.

With the tropical sunrise portending a hot day, the 1st Marine Division headed for Peleliu's southwestern beaches with its three regiments attacking abreast, Puller's 1st on the left, Colonel Harold D. Harris's 5th in the center, and Colonel Herman Hanneken's 7th (less its 2nd Battalion, held back as the division's reserve) on the right. More than a mile in width, the front was everywhere covered by Japanese artillery and mortar positions that had scarcely been touched by the Navy's bombardment. As the weapons opened up, many of them twinkling in the thinning smoke and dust, Admiral Oldendorf was "surprised and chagrined." Marines who had been singing confidently in competition with the roar of their amtracs stopped abruptly. Some began praying.

Harry Dearman relates: "We were half a mile from the beach when a shell landed twenty yards behind us. I knew they were plotting our range and I held my breath while waiting for the next shell. It came so close it sent spray all over us in the amtrac. They had our range now, and I figured the third shell would be fatal. For some reason, it never came." Most of the landing craft made it as far as the reef, about 500 yards from shore, before their peril grew critical. An aerial observer soon reported, "There are amtracs burning on the reef."

Chesty Puller had drilled it into his men that they must leave a landing craft and get off the beach with all possible speed. Now, as the colonel's tractor nosed up on the white sand, he himself bounded over the side and "ran like hell for at least twenty-five yards" before dropping prone. The sprint caused him pain in the thigh that held the chunk of Guadalcanal shrapnel. When he looked back at the amtrac, Puller saw several shells smash into it at the same moment. Most of the men had got out as fast as he, but a few had dallied and were killed. One officer, his leg blown off, still moved but was dying. Puller looked up and down the beach. "Every damn amtrac in our wave had been destroyed in the water or shot to pieces the minute it landed." Most of the craft were sending up flames and black smoke.

Puller's regiment landed on the northernmost beaches, its left flank under enfilading fire from the Point, a jagged, fissured, boulder-strewn coral mound about thirty feet high, the natural defensive features of which had been augmented by concrete pillboxes and spider holes dug with dynamite. The suicidal job of tackling this coastal minifortress went to the 235 men of Captain George P. Hunt's K Company. The captain saw a large part of his unit turned into "human wreckage." Initially, this bewildered him. "Then it made me hot with anger; but finally my feelings cooled to accepting a gruesome inevitable fact." To balance the score, many of the enemy were killed in their defenses; and soon Hunt and thirty of the company's survivors were atop the Point. Just to the south, Chesty Puller and his other units were working their way inland, through a shell-shattered wood, toward the southern end of the Umurbrogol ridges.

Landing on Puller's right, over the central beaches, the 5th Regiment had its own share of terrible moments. Most of the amtracs were hit by small-arms fire at least, and some took shells. PFC Charles Doolittle saw one blown apart: "Arms, legs, heads, guts, and brains went flying." While the Marines scrambled to get off the beach, according to PFC Eugene B. Sledge, "shells crashed all around." There was also machine-gun and rifle fire, and Sledge and his comrades found their world "a nightmare of flashes, violent explosions, and snapping bullets." Leaving a trail of casualties, the units of the 5th began fighting their way inland toward the airfield, their first objective.

It was the mission of the 7th Regiment, whose companies landed over the southernmost beaches, to clean out the island's southern end. These Marines encountered antiboat barriers, antiboat mines, antitank mines, antipersonnel mines, artillery and mortar fire, and barbed-wire entanglements covered by machine guns. Casualties among both landing craft and personnel were heavy, and serious disorganization resulted.

Life magazine artist and correspondent Tom Lea came ashore in this zone at a time when the first wave was only about twenty-five yards inland. Gunfire was rattling and crashing, and Lea was conscious of the pungent smell of the oil burning in the shattered amtracs. Half bent over, he tried to run up the beach. Losing his balance, he fell on his face just as a mortar shell landed near. "A red flash stabbed at my eyeballs." The shell cut down four men from Lea's tractor, tearing one to pieces, a scene the artist witnessed "with terrible clarity." He made another dash, jumping into a small shellhole as a second mortar splashed dirt over him. Looking up, he saw a wounded Marine staggering past him toward the waterline. "His face was half bloody pulp, and the mangled shreds of what was left of an arm hung down like a stick." Shortly the man pitched forward and lay still, his blood forming a garish pattern on the white sand. Lea soon made it to the brush line, where he took cover against a three-foot ledge. Mortar shells whooshed overhead, and the artist looked back toward the surf just in time to observe a direct hit on an incoming tractor. "Pieces of iron and men seemed to sail slow-motion into the air." Now the shellbursts, at intervals of a few seconds, began climbing the beach toward the spot where Lea was lying. In the wake of a "flat cracking flash," he was nearly buried by sand, his left shin burned by a small piece of shrapnel. He shook himself loose, brushing grains of sand from his sweating eyelids. The bursts continued, walking out toward the reef, then returning to the beach. Another combination of sounds, "a shuddering explosion" followed by "the wild popping of .50-caliber shells," issued from the brush ahead as an amtrac was destroyed by a mine.

As if all of this weren't about as much as men could stand, the area came under additional shellfire, that of a battery of 75-millimeter guns on a promonotory to the south. Five or six amtracs were hit as they crossed the reef, and a shell dropped among a group of Marines wading ashore. Other men sloshing in from damaged tractors were swept by machine-gun fire, some of them falling "with bloody splashes into the green water." Happily, the 75-millimeter guns were soon knocked out by dive bombers flying from a carrier. At about the same time, the mortar and small-arms fire subsided. Lea and those around him were

Stretcher team places casualty on amtrac for trip to offshore hospital ship.

infinitely grateful for the lull. They sat up and lit cigarettes and savored "the sheer joy of being alive."

William Rupertus, on board the division command ship, was worried by the reports that reached him from shore. Moreover, from his canvas deck chair the general could see the burning amtracs. Rupertus was presently on crutches, having broken an ankle during the operation's training period. Now he was tempted to go ashore early, crutches or no, but his aides talked him into waiting until D-plus-1. The assistant division commander, Brigadier General Oliver P. Smith, went in with a skeleton staff at 11:30 A.M. on D-day, setting up in a Japanese antitank ditch just inland from the central beaches, near a leg of the airport. Smith was soon followed ashore by the operation's top commander, Roy Geiger, who could have legitimately remained on board ship until the beach was safe. Smith, astonished to see Geiger come sliding down into the ditch, said, "Look, General, according to the book you're not supposed to be here at this time." The nonchalant Geiger responded, "I wanted to see why those amtracs were burning," and then added, "I'd like to see the airport." Smith told him, "That's simple. All you have to do is climb this bank, and there it is." Both officers crawled up.

Smith narrates: "While we were up there, the telephone rang. It was for me, and I slid down the bank to talk. About that time the Japs put over in rapid succession what must have been rockets, not mortars. They made a horrible screech and sounded as though they were just clearing your head. Well, they put three of these over, and General Geiger slid down the bank. I asked him if he'd seen the airport, and he said yes, he'd seen it. Then he went down the beach to visit the 5th and 7th CPs."

Smith was glad to see Geiger go, for it relieved him of responsibility for the corps commander's safety. But Geiger was soon back, saying, "Now I'm going up to see Puller." Smith protested, "Now, look, General, there is a gap of 800 yards above here, and we don't know who's in there, and you just shouldn't go up there." Geiger took the advice and presently went back on board ship. Rupertus, sitting on his deck chair with his foot in a cast, fumed when he learned that his superior officer had beaten him ashore.

Geiger would have been extremely unsafe in Puller's zone, for the colonel's regiment was in precarious straits. Only the units on the right had been able to reach the first objective, the 0-1 phase line Rupertus had designated on the map. On the left, the invasion's northern extremity, the thirty men of George Hunt's company were still atop the sun-baked Point at the water's edge, where it was urgent they stay to protect this flank against a counterattack. South of the Point, in the regiment's center, the push inland was meeting with heavy opposition, not only in the form of shellfire from the southern end of the Umur-brogol ridges but also from defenses in the lowland brush.

One of the Marines fighting in this zone was Private Harry Dearman, who had observed the pre-H-hour bombardment with reassurance, and was then rudely awakened to reality by a spray of water from a Japanese shell. Dearman's platoon, commanded by Lieutenant Roy G. Pucci, had been badly hurt getting across the beach. One of the victims fell by Dearman's side, his head nearly torn from his shoulders by a single bullet that passed through his neck. Dearman's assigned job was that of runner, or messenger, but Pucci soon ordered him to help with the assault on a pair of adjoining concrete pillboxes, a task that had been launched under the initiative of PFC Victor L. Case, who had already managed to get a hand grenade into the long, horizontal firing slot of one of the twin defenses, killing most of its crew. As Dearman ap-proached to assist, he noted that Case was in a perilous position, stand-ing with his back pressed into a fissure between the structures and holding a grenade he was trying to slip into the slot that was still active, its machine gun chattering. The weapon was keeping the supporting Marines at bay, and its gunner was also traversing as far as he could toward Case, and bullets were cracking past him. Dearman and the others fired their rifles at the dark aperture and managed to cause interruptions in the machine gun's work. But Case was unable to use his grenade from where he stood. Suddenly he dropped down and scrambled under the slot and along a path that led around to the em-placement's rear. "He disappeared, and the enemy fire kept us from following." Utilizing the cover offered by the terrain, Dearman and four or five others edged toward the flank, looking for a way around. None offered itself.

"Finally, a big Marine named Pack stood up and went forward. I don't know what stopped the Japs from killing him, unless they stayed back from the slot because of the threat of our fire. Another man, I think it was Junior Ekins, went forward and around the pillbox. Then a little Italian who had been with the platoon a long time tried it. He got as far as the path leading around the pillbox, where he was shot down. I was never so scared in my entire life as I moved to where he was sitting. I asked where he'd been hit, and he said in the leg. The blood was beginning to run into his shoe, and I started to call for a corpsman, but he told me to go on and join the other three, that he was a bleeder and was done for. There was no way I could drag him back to Pucci and the rest of the platoon without crossing directly in front of the machine-gun slot, so I stood up and started around the rear. A rifle shot sounded from inside, and I just knew I was hit. But miracles do happen, and I wasn't touched. Behind the pillbox, I found Case, Pack, and Ekins, who were trying to open its door. I moved to help, but they told me to stand back and cover them with my BAR. They were so intent on their work that they did not see five Japs come out of the woods toward us. The one in the lead, an officer or an NCO with a shaved head and wrap-leggings, had a pistol and began firing as he came. The others had rifles. I knew that if any of them stopped long enough to aim, Case would get it, for he was in an exposed position on the stoop at the door. From where I was crouched, I fired a BAR burst from the hip and got the first two men behind the officer. A second burst cut down the other two. By this time the officer was closing in on Case, still firing and missing. At short range I got off a single fast shot that caught the man in the head. His skull was cleft and I could see light through it. The shaved head resembled a ripe watermelon that had been split open, revealing the rich red interior."

The unflappable Case continued to work on the pillbox door until he was able to get a grenade inside and the crew was killed. Dearman now made an urgent suggestion that the little team fall back upon the platoon. Case had a different idea. Armed with a couple of grenades, he went on to another pair of pillboxes. "I didn't follow him, and no one else did. We just kept him covered as well as we could from where we were. He returned in a short time, telling us that the pillboxes were taken care of. With this, Case was willing to take a break, and we filed back toward the platoon. As we came to the spot where I had left the little guy with the leg wound, we found him dead. He had bled to death as he said he would."

During the afternoon the 5th Regiment, operating in the center of the invasion, pushed its right flank across the southern end of the airfield to the island's east coast, forming a salient in the beachhead. At about 5:00 P.M., Marines looking northward across the still-unoccupied part of the field toward the base of the Umurbrogol ridges saw a group of vehicles moving rapidly westward and raising a cloud of dust. "Nip tanks!" said one observer, and he was right. Thirteen of the machines, supported by shellfire that arched over them, were heading for the joint between the 5th and 1st Regiments. Some of the tanks had snipers riding atop them, and a company of infantry was following on foot. In accord with their new tactics, the soldiers were not charging wildly but were moving from shellhole to shellhole. They were soon far behind the tanks. The Americans had been expecting a counterattack in this area.

Although many of their own tanks had been hit while coming ashore, a number were on hand to open up with their 75s. Other weapons covering the juncture were artillery pieces, 37-millimeters, bazookas, grenade launchers, and heavy machine guns. The snipers were shot from their perches, and, one by one, the tanks—all of light construction —were knocked out; some burst into oily flames and others exploded, hurling pieces of metal and parts of bodies in all directions. A Navy dive bomber swooped down and added to the devastation with a 500-pound bomb. A few of the tanks broke through the lines, and two Marines were turned to red pulp by steel tracks.

Private Jay C. Blakely found one of the machines bearing down on him and managed to put a rifle grenade through its shell. The turret cover was thrown open and the commander popped up. Shortly the tank ground to a halt and went into reverse. Blakely ran forward and climbed aboard. The commander slashed at him with his pistol, and the barrel scraped harshly across his left eye. "I pushed the Jap off the tank," Blakely recalled, "and another Marine killed him." Blakely then dropped two hand grenades through the opening, and the rattling blasts finished off the crew. Only two of the tanks survived to retreat.

Marines inspecting shattered Japanese tank
whose crewmen lie dead on the ground.

The Japanese infantrymen, who had never closed in, faded away as the tank attack failed. There was soon a lesser probe in the same area, and another farther south. Both were easily repelled.

But it had been a bad day for the 1st Marine Division. Casualties numbered 1,111 in killed, wounded, and missing. There were also numerous cases of combat fatigue and heat prostration. General Rupertus was troubled not only by the high casualties but also by the fact that the beachhead embraced less than half the southern part of the island, when he had expected to take the entire region by nightfall. He began to rue his prophecy that the campaign would be a brief one.

The warm tropical night was filled with the whining and crashing of shellfire from both sides, along with small-arms fusilades and the popping of hand grenades at spots where the Marines stood against minor counterattacks and infiltrations. Illuminating the scenes were American star shells, some of which gave everything a greenish hue. In a hole with Private Russell Davis was a black man, an ammunition and water carrier from the beach, who looked at Davis and said, "I knew people came in black and white, but I never expected to see any green ones." Davis was not directly involved in the night's various actions but was aware of much that was happening. Sometimes a local fight was preceded by a hot exchange of words. A Japanese would holler, "American pigs and dogs! You die! You die!" And the Marines would respond with profane insults or with jibes such as, "Come on in and see what we did to your tanks!" Finally the shouts would give way to shots. Once there was firing to Davis's rear, and he and his comrades swung in that direction, their weapons ready. Soon the word was passed that no Japanese were involved, that a young Marine had cracked up and started running around and had been shot by mistake. At another time, Davis was jolted from a light sleep by a cry so piercing and so prolonged that it sounded above the combinations of gunfire. He was relieved to learn that it was only "The Screamer, back at the CP," a Marine who was subject to vociferous nightmares every time he made an invasion.

On the left flank of the beachhead, Captain Hunt and his men were still on the crest of the Point at the water's edge. They were out of contact with the rest of Chesty Puller's units but were tied in with an amtrac supply line that, at dusk, had brought them extra ammunition and water. Harassed by enemy fire through the night, these Marines were counterattacked at dawn. The action, according to Hunt, was "a vicious melee of countless explosions, whining bullets, shrapnel whirring overhead or clinking off the rocks, hoarse shouts, and shrill-screaming Japanese." The attackers were decimated and driven back, but

Hunt was left with only eighteen able-bodied men. When an amtrac arrived with additional supplies and fifteen reinforcements, the captain was not greatly heartened. "We were still out on a limb."

The island had cooled only slightly during the night, and even the sun's earliest rays caused heat waves to radiate from the patches of coral. *Life* artist Tom Lea noted that the Marines met the new day "whiskery, red-eyed, and dirty." Because of the temperature, many now discarded their canvas leggings and their underwear, and some used their combat knives to shorten their trousers—being careful, however, to keep their knees covered, for much of the coral was sharp. Camouflage cloths were loosened from helmets and suspended in back as neck shields. Blanket rolls and gas masks were discarded. In general, ponchos, knapsacks, and entrenching tools were retained. But outside of their weapons, the only items of gear the men deemed truly indispensable on this battlefield were their two canteens.

William Rupertus came ashore on his crutches that morning and set up his command post in a tarpaulin-covered antitank ditch a few yards inland from the center of the landing beaches. In shaded spots like this, the temperature was 105 degrees. The general's plans for the second day called for Puller's 1st Regiment to head for the southern end of Bloody Nose Ridge, as the Umurbrogol heights had already been dubbed; for Harris's 5th Regiment to complete its capture of the airfield; and for Hanneken's 7th Regiment to secure the island's southern end. The goals were largely the same as they had been on D-day.

Following a thunderous preparation by the Navy's guns and planes, all units jumped off as ordered. Gains were made in spite of strong resistance, heavy casualties, and a water shortage that left many Marines with swollen tongues and split lips. But the attack again fell short of its goals. The promontories at the southern end of the island remained untaken. In the center, most of the airfield was overrun but the success could not be nailed down. In the north, Puller made little progress toward Bloody Nose Ridge. The colonel's casualties now numbered about 1,000 in killed, wounded, and missing; he had lost one out of every three men he had brought ashore. Rupertus found it necessary to give him the division reserve, the 2nd Battalion, 7th.

The Japanese were elated over the grief they were causing the Marines, and, employing an American device, put out a propaganda leaflet that was read in the stricken lines that evening: "American brave soldiers! We think you much pity since landing on this ileland. In spite of your pitiful battle, we are sorry that we can present only fire, not even good water. We soon will attack strongly your army. You have done

A firefight near Peleliu's airfield.

bravely your duty. Now, abandon your guns and come in Japanese military with white flag or handkerchief, so we will be glad to see you and welcome you comfortably as we can well."

The coming of darkness found George Hunt still concerned with holding the Point, which remained the key position on the invasion's left flank. Hunt's situation had improved during the day. His right was now tied in with the rest of Puller's units and he had been reinforced, chiefly by elements of his own K Company who had lost contact with him early in the landing. They had been lamentably shot up but added a new strength to the thin line. The captain had also gained artillery support. When some 500 Japanese began attacking at 10:00 P.M. the Marines, although heavily outnumbered, were ready for them. As the battle broke, according to Hunt, it was as though the doors of hell had been shattered, subjecting human ears to "the horrible turmoil which bawled and writhed within." The captain found himself shouting at the top of his lungs, "Give 'em hell! Kill every one of the bastards!" The Marines were busy with rifles, machine guns, and mortars, and the summit's team of artillery spotters was calling down salvos by radio. Japanese mortar fragments and bullets whirred and zinged among the rocks. Men on both sides let out howls, some of defiance and some of pain and fear. For the next four hours the sounds and flashes and their attendant violence waxed and waned. Then the Japanese retreated, leaving 350 shattered bodies scattered through the woods at the Point's base. This was the last attack on the commanding elevation. The next morning K Company was relieved. Of the 235 men George Hunt had led ashore, seventy-eight were still on their feet.

It took another two days for Hanneken's 7th Regiment to clean out Peleliu's southern promontories, which were studded with pillboxes and laced with trenches. No single Marine contributed more to the success of the work than PFC Arthur J. Jackson, who won the Medal of Honor by "boldly taking the initiative when his platoon's left flank was held up by the fire of Japanese troops concealed in strongly fortified positions, unhesitatingly proceeding forward of our lines and, courageously defying the heavy barrages, [charging] a large pillbox housing approximately thirty-five enemy soldiers. Pouring his automatic fire into the opening of the fixed installation to trap the occupying troops, he hurled white phosphorus grenades and explosive charges brought up by a fellow Marine, demolishing the pillbox and killing all of the enemy. Advancing alone under the continuous fire from other hostile emplacements, he employed similar means to smash two smaller positions in the immediate vicinity. Determined to crush the entire pocket of resistance although harassed on all sides by the shattering blasts of Japanese weapons and covered only by small rifle parties, he stormed one gun position after another . . . and succeeded in wiping out a total of twelve pillboxes and fifty Japanese soldiers."

This happened on September 18, during the afternoon of which Hanneken was able to report to Rupertus that the first mission of the 7th Marines on Peleliu was completed. Hanneken's regiment had fought not only with skill but with remarkably good luck. While accounting for 2,609 of the enemy, the unit lost only forty-seven dead, 414 wounded, and thirty-six missing.

By this time the men of the 5th Regiment had finished their conquest of the airport and were moving against the eastern pincer of the Peleliu lobster claw. Although harassed by shellfire from the Umurbrogol heights, or Bloody Nose Ridge, which was on the larger western pincer, they were lucky enough to be moving away from the menace. Puller's 1st Regiment, at the cost of another 500 casualties, had fought its way into Bloody Nose's first series of hills.

Only now did these Marines begin to see the objective in its true perspective. "Along its center," explains a regimental report, "the rocky spine was heaved up in a contorted morass of decayed coral, strewn with rubble, crags, ridges, and gulches thrown together in a confusing maze. There were no roads, scarcely any trails. The pock-marked surface offered no secure footing even in the few level places. ... Into this the enemy had dug and tunneled like moles; and there they stayed to fight to the death." The Marines themselves, according to the report, were unable to entrench in the hard terrain. "The best they could do was pile a little coral or wood debris around their positions. The jagged rock slashed their shoes and clothes and tore their bodies every time they hit the deck for safety. Casualties were higher for the simple reason it was impossible to get under the ground away from the Japanese mortar barrages. Each blast hurled chunks of coral in all directions, multiplying many times the fragmentation effect of every shell."

With the help of the 2nd Battalion, 7th, and with his own units reinforced by headquarters personnel and support troops drawn from the rear, Chesty Puller resumed his attack on schedule the morning of September 19. Tanks, some of them mounted with flamethrowers, were worked among the ridges; also employed were portable flamethrowers, demolitions, bazookas, mortars, grenades, and small arms. Many of the

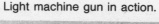

Light machine gun in action.

enemy were blasted to death in their caves, but Marines fell in equal numbers, some to the enemy's guns and some to thirst and heat. The temperature reached 115 degrees, and there was precious little shade.

Back at his CP—which was much closer to the front than it should have been—Puller fretted over his continuing losses. He was in pain, for his Guadalcanal shrapnel had become a serious irritation, causing his thigh to swell and throb. But, stripped to the waist and chewing on a battered pipe which he sometimes replaced with a cigarette, the colonel managed to maintain his aggressive and confident demeanor. A reporter from *Time* paid him a visit during this stage of the fight, and the result was a Stateside article entitled "Man of War." This shocked Puller's wife, Virginia, for it depicted him as hard-boiled and profane, when she knew him best for what she called his "fine and gentle side." His letters to her were always couched in tender, affectionate terms.

(Had all of the other Marines in the Pacific been written up as Puller had been, their vernacular faithfully quoted, large numbers of Americans would have shared Virginia's shock. Many a youth who had left home with a polished deportment and without a single cussword in his vocabulary had reverted to rough language, not only profane but also obscene. This was not the result of the strains of military life. The men simply believed that such talk was necessary for them to be accepted as real Marines—just as many believed they must learn to drink, whether they liked booze or not. Reporters of the time often mentioned the profanity but rarely alluded to the obscenities. These were carried to remarkable lengths, were strengthened and colored by talented improvisors, and often entered the realm of entertainment. Few men intended to take the practice home with them. Most did not want their families to know of their lapse from decorum. Incredulity would have been general if the Marines had been told that their worst language would be explicitly presented by many postwar military authors.)

As his attack inched northeastward, Puller's left flank was on Peleliu's west coast, which meant that some of his men were moving in the lowlands between Bloody Nose and the sea. Among these troops was Harry Dearman. He and the venturesome Victor Case were now serving as platoon scouts. "On September 19, Lieutenant Pucci ordered Case and me to cross a large open space that had been cleared by our shellfire. After crossing, we sat down on a coconut log to wait for the platoon. Around us were five dead Japanese soldiers in various stages of decomposition. While sitting there, we heard someone holler, 'Hey, Marines, don't shoot!' I looked back toward the platoon area in time to see a man in a white undershirt duck down out of sight. He soon raised up again and repeated, 'Hey, Marines, don't shoot!' We hollered back at him to come on up, and as he got closer we saw that he was carrying a large silver container of some sort. It turned out that he was a cook on one of the naval vessels, and had brought steaming wieners and whole corn ashore to pass out to the Marines. Pucci had sent him up to us. We held out our steel helmets, the liners removed, and he poured in our portions. The man, who was wearing kitchen whites, was un-armed. As he left us, he said, 'Good luck, Marines!' I knew a lot of brave sailors, but this one had done something unforgettable. Case and I ate in the presence of the Japanese dead, and in spite of the way they smelled, that food was delicious.

"After we finished eating we talked for a while, and Case suddenly turned morose. He had been fighting with exceptional daring for the past five days, taking many chances with his life. Now he said, 'Dear-man, send my gear home.' I pleaded with him to quit talking that way, but it did no good. He said, 'Send my gear home to my mother,' and showed me his watch and billfold. Soon the men from the platoon began to holler for us to come back, as the day was growing late, and we went back. I spent the night on the sharpest coral bed imaginable, and be-tween that and the shellfire I got little sleep. The next morning Case and I recrossed the open area. As we came to the log and the five dead Japs I was reminded of what Case had said about sending his gear home. He kept on going past the log and entered a draw, and I had to hurry to keep up with him. We shortly ran into some heavy brush on either side of a huge shellhole, probably made by one of our battlewagons. Case went around one side and I the other, and I lost sight of him. Hearing a shot fired by a Jap rifle, I called across the hole. Case did not answer right away, and I called several times. Finally he answered that he had been shot and that I should stay away from him, as the Japs were watching him and waiting for me to come over. I asked him how bad he'd been hit. He told me he'd got it below the belt and that I should send his gear home. I couldn't get to him, and it was the most agonizing, demoralizing time of my life. I talked with him until he died, and the last thing he said was 'Send my gear home.' "

Dearman could not see the Japanese but could hear them talking, and he began throwing grenades through the brush. This drew volleys of rifle fire, but he was not hit. He shouted back toward the platoon area for help. A lone Marine brought up a new supply of grenades but did not stay. Resuming his single-handed fight, Dearman managed to keep the enemy at bay until a party from the platoon came up and carried Case's body back. Dearman himself returned to the platoon area, arriving there in a state of nervous collapse. He was taken to an aid station by four Marines serving as stretcher-bearers. Dearman would be okay after a few months of rest and rehabilitation. Case's deeds were awarded the Navy Cross.

Case was killed on September 20, D-plus-5. Lieutenant Pucci's platoon was down to about ten men. As for Puller's regiment as a whole, its casualties stood at 56 percent. The survivors were exhausted, and the attack on Bloody Nose was stalling. The next day Corps Commander Roy Geiger and his staff paid a visit to Puller's CP. "It became rapidly apparent," recalled one of the staff officers, "that the regimental commander was very tired. He was unable to give a very clear picture of what his situation was, and when asked by the corps commander what he needed in the way of help he stated that he was doing all right with what he had."

Geiger and his party left Puller and proceeded to the division CP to consult with Rupertus. "The 1st Marines," said Geiger, "are finished." He added that he felt the unit should be replaced by a regiment of the 81st Infantry Division, the invasion's Army reserve. Rupertus protested, saying that he expected to complete his capture of the island in another day or two and did not need help from the Army. Geiger overruled the division commander and ordered the 1st Marines relieved by the Army's 321st Regiment.

The 81st Division had not been idle while the Marines were fighting on Peleliu. On D-day the unit had supported the Marines by making a feint against the large northern Palau island of Babelthuap, which held a major Japanese garrison but was to be bypassed. Two regiments of the division had gone on to invade smaller Angaur, ten miles southwest of Peleliu, while the third regiment was presently poised for an assault on Ulithi atoll, northeast of the Palaus, wanted as an advance naval base. The 321st was on Angaur when Geiger's call came on September 21. Leaving the remainder of the Angaur campaign to its sister regiment, the unit began embarking for Peleliu on the morning of the twenty-second and by noon of the twenty-third was coming ashore over the same beaches the Marines had used.

Like William Rupertus, Chesty Puller was not too pleased to see the Army arrive. The colonel told his men that they were being relieved only for a rest period and would be going back into action in three days. The men themselves were happy to learn that this was not true, that Roy Geiger had ordered their return to their camp in the Solomons. Puller himself was in no condition to resume fighting. He was not only overtired but also in dire need of an operation on his thigh. The shrapnel was successfully removed in the sick bay of the ship that took Puller out. As for the men, more than one was heard to say, "I never thought I could be this glad to be going back to Pavuvu." Puller's reputation as a fighter did not suffer through the removal of his regiment from the Bloody Nose front. The 1st was credited with capturing ten defended coral ridges, three blockhouses, twenty-two pillboxes, thirteen antitank guns, and 144 caves. Said Assistant Division Commander Oliver Smith: "It seemed impossible that men could have moved forward against the intricate and mutually supporting defenses the Japanese had set up. It can only be explained as a reflection of the determination and aggressive leadership of Colonel Puller." Peleliu was Puller's last World War II campaign.

During the night of September 23–24, a fleet of barges carrying Japanese reinforcements came down from Babelthuap. The effort was met by naval gunfire, artillery fire from shore, and a counterattack by amtracs, and most of the craft were sunk. Several hundred of the enemy survived to wade ashore and disappear into Peleliu's cave system. This was all that was accomplished from the large island, which the Navy kept under harassment.

It was actually the 7th Marines who took over in the zone evacuated by Puller's regiment. The Army's 321st Infantry pressed up along the west coast past Bloody Nose in order to begin attacking the position from the north. The 5th Marines, with their mission on the eastern claw completed, were pulled over to the west coast and were sent beyond the Army to clean out Peleliu's northern tip. On September 28 the 3rd Battalion of the 5th—supported by naval gunfire, artillery, and Marine Corsairs flying from the newly captured airfield—took the isle of Ngesebus, just off Peleliu's north coast. The beginning of October saw the northern sector secured.

From then on the fight centered upon Bloody Nose, and a long and bitter fight it was. After making some essential gains among the hellish ridges, the 7th Marines exhausted their combat efficiency on October 5. They were replaced by the already weary 5th Marines, who carried on doggedly, winning ground but taking further punishment. On October 12 the battle's assault phase was declared ended, with the Japanese survivors confined to a shrinking area called the Umurbrogol Pocket. Additional Army troops reached Peleliu on October 14, and the final relief of the Marines began the next day. Responsibility for the campaign passed from William Rupertus to the Army's Major General Paul J. Mueller, but the last Marines did not leave the lines for transport to Pavuvu until the latter part of the month. The Marine Corps airmen stayed on to support the Army.

By this time events in the Pacific had left Peleliu behind, and even some of the lower-echelon officers connected with the campaign began to wonder at its necessity. MacArthur was already established on Leyte and the great naval battle of Leyte Gulf had been won, which meant that the general's conquest of the Philippines was firmly begun. Peleliu, launched as an auxiliary to MacArthur's operations, had played no part in them. It began to appear as if Bill Halsey had been right: Peleliu should have been called off.

Toward the end of the Peleliu fight, the surviving Japanese were sorely tempted to end their lives by means of the traditional *banzai* attack, but were cautioned by the Palau high command on Babelthuap: "It is easy to die but difficult to live on. We must select the difficult course and continue to fight because of the influence on the morale of the Japanese people. Saipan was lost in a very short time because of vain *banzai* attacks, with the result that the people at home suffered a drop in morale."

It wasn't until November 24—ten weeks after D-day—that a Japanese radio operator in the constricted Umurbrogol Pocket informed the

Marine Corsair bombs Umurbrogol defenses.

Babelthuap garrison that the end had come on Peleliu. The few unas-saulted caves became settings for the usual flag-burnings and suicides. Three days later General Mueller was able to report that all organized resistance had ceased. The campaign had caused the death of well over 10,000 of the enemy; only 302 were captured. Marine casualties totaled 6,265—1,124 killed, 5,024 wounded, and 117 missing. The Army had 277 killed and 1,008 wounded.

When, after the war, the Marine Corps' official historians summed up the campaign, they concurred in this statement: "Except for those who participated in it, Peleliu largely remains a forgotten battle, its location unknown, its name calling forth no patriotic remembrance of self-sac-rifice or gallant deeds. . . . For the Marines who stormed ashore on Peleliu, however, the strategic value of the island may not have been clear, but duty was. They had been given a job to do, and they went ahead and did it."

22 | *The Approach to Fortress Iwo*

====== The only Marines who participated directly in MacArthur's conquest of the Philippines—aside from those serving aboard the supporting naval vessels—were the 1st Aircraft Wing and elements of the 5th Amphibious Corps Artillery. It fell to the Marine infantry divisions to resume their assault across the Central Pacific. The Corps had been built to six full divisions and was now the largest, best trained, farthest ranging, and most consistently victorious body of amphibious troops in history. The next target was tiny Iwo Jima, halfway between the Marianas and Tokyo. It had become necessary for American forces to capture, occupy, and defend this island in order for them to maintain unremitting pressure on Japan. Specifically, Iwo had to be taken to eliminate its air threat to the Marianas; to use as a base to help cover naval operations in Japanese waters; to equip with a fighter escort service for the new very long range bombers, the great silver B-29 Superfortresses, which began hitting Japan on November 24, 1944 (even as the fight for Peleliu was ending); and to provide these bombers with an emergency landing place. The conquest was to be history's classic example of this kind of operation, the ultimate test of Marine Corps amphibious tactics. Destined to be tougher than Tarawa, Saipan, or Peleliu, it would call into full play all of the amphibious constituents the Americans had developed during twenty years of peacetime training and three years of war.

Iwo Jima was in the Nanpo Shoto, a chain of island groups starting at the entrance of Tokyo Bay and stretching in a southerly direction for 750 miles. The chain was governed as a part of the Japanese homeland. Iwo was in the southernmost, or Volcano group, and, as this name implies, was of volcanic origin. Composed chiefly of rocks, gray sand, sulfur, and areas of scraggy vegetation, it had an area of only 7.5 square miles, and, viewed from the air, resembled a pork chop, with the shank extending toward the southwest. The island held two airfields and the beginning of a third. Even before the Americans invaded the Marianas, Japan had marked Iwo for a major military buildup. Things began rolling in May 1944. By the end of that month the garrison numbered 7,000 soldiers, sailors, and airmen, and their equipage included 200 aircraft and a burgeoning arsenal of weapons, including heavy coastal guns. The defenses under preparation, many of which were ensconced in rugged hill systems, were much like those of the Umurbrogol ridges on Peleliu.

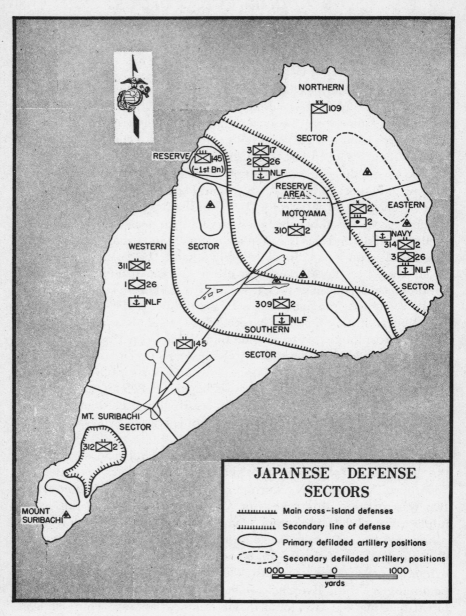

JAPANESE DEFENSE SECTORS

NORTHERN SECTOR
109

RESERVE 45 (-1st Bn)

3 17
2 26
NLF

RESERVE AREA

MOTOYAMA

310 2

2 2

EASTERN

NAVY
314 2
3 26
NLF

SECTOR

WESTERN SECTOR

311 2
1 26
NLF

309 2
NLF

SOUTHERN

1 45

SECTOR

MT. SURIBACHI SECTOR

312 2

MOUNT SURIBACHI

Main cross-island defenses
Secondary line of defense
Primary defiladed artillery positions
Secondary defiladed artillery positions

1000   0   1000
yards

In early June, stocky and neatly mustached Lieutenant General Tadamichi Kuribayashi came from Tokyo to assume the garrison's top command. He was met not only by a delegation of officers but also by schoolchildren waving tiny flags and singing patriotic songs. There were 1,100 civilians on the island, all of Japanese descent. They would soon be evacuated. Kuribayashi's arrival boded ill for the Marines. Experienced, intelligent, and capable, he was exactly the man for the task assigned him. His first impression of Iwo's defenses was that they were still much too weak, and he ordered work on them accelerated. At the same time, he trained the men in the new defensive concepts handed down by Tokyo, adding ideas of his own. Kuribayashi expected to lose the battle and to die, for he understood America's power. After making a tour of the nation in the 1920s, he had written home: "The United States is the last country in the world that Japan should fight." The general's intention now was to make the conquest of Iwo Jima so costly to the invaders that Washington would think twice before ordering another assault in Japan's home waters.

Kuribayashi's command included some first-rate officers. The island's senior naval leader was Rear Admiral Toshinosuke Ichimaru, an airman who had been crippled in a crash and who walked with a limp. Like many other Japanese officers (including Kuribayashi), the admiral wrote poetry. In an ode he penned to his transfer to Iwo, he expressed joy at the chance "to fight on the foremost front," and said he desired only to "fall like the flower petals" in his garden at home. Among Kuribayashi's army officers was Lieutenant Colonel Takeichi Nishi, commander of the 26th Tank Regiment. Nishi was a baron, the scion of an old and wealthy family. A horseman of international reputation, he had taken part in the 1932 Olympics in Los Angeles and won for Japan the gold medal for the individual jumping event. The baron was popular in America and had made some friends there, and he regretted the war. He had no wish to die and considered his assignment to Iwo ironic. Kuribayashi's staff officers included Major Yoshitaka Horie, who was not stationed on Iwo but on Chichi Jima, about 150 miles to the north. Most of the troops, arms, and supplies on the way to Iwo from Japan passed through Chichi, and it was Horie's job to control this traffic. He was Iwo's "emergency supply officer." The major would survive the campaign to become its chief Japanese chronicler. Thanks to him, the world knows more of the Japanese side of Iwo than of any of the other island battles.

The Americans did their best to hinder Iwo's development as a fortress. Submarines stalked the ships coming down from Tokyo Bay, taking their toll. (The convoy bearing Baron Nishi had been hit, and twenty-eight of his tanks went under.) Carrier planes from out at sea and Army bombers from the Marianas visited the island, blowing up buildings, destroying aircraft, and pocking the strips. Nonetheless, the month of September saw the work on the defenses swing into high gear. Iwo now held about 15,000 men. The basic army unit was the 109th

Infantry Division, and its chief components were the 2nd Mixed Brigade, the 145th Infantry Regiment, and the 3rd Battalion, 17th Mixed Infantry Regiment. Attached were several independent tank units and an air group. Navy personnel consisted of air groups, a Naval Guard Force and the 204th Naval Construction Battalion, which included Koreans.

Among the island's heavier armaments, in addition to the coast defense pieces, were artillery, antiaircraft guns, rockets, and mortars. Built close to the surface with sand piled over them were concrete pillboxes, bunkers, and blockhouses. Many of those in clusters were connected by trench systems. Under the ground were living quarters, some of the chambers capable of holding only a few men, and others large enough to accommodate three or four hundred. Included were hospital wards with surgical instruments and operating tables. There was room for the storage of food, water cans, ammunition, and other supplies. The lighting ranged from electricity to oil lamps and candles. To guard against entrapment, the chambers were provided with multiple entrances and exits. Those on levels one above the other were linked by stairways. Some of the chambers were made of building blocks cut from the volcanic rock, while others were utilizations of the island's caves. This network was augmented with miles of tunnels, much of the system interconnected. The surface openings were designed as fighting positions.

The men of the garrison began calling themselves "the underground troops." Their construction work was difficult, hot, and tedious. Drinking water was in short supply, for the island had no fresh water except that gathered in cisterns. In areas where sulfurous steam emanated from cracks in the earth, gas masks had to be worn, and the shifts kept short. Although progress everywhere was well maintained and morale remained generally good, now and then a man would stop digging, mop his brow, and lament, "Why are we working so hard? We're all going to die anyway."

General Kuribayashi himself often mentioned his impending death in his letters to his family in Tokyo. He wrote his son, Taro, who was nearly twenty, "The life of your father is like a lamp before the wind." The message went on to urge the youth to try to quit smoking. In a letter to his wife, Yoshii, the general said, "I am sorry to end my life here, fighting the United States of America. But I want to defend this island as long as I can." On another day he wrote her: "I am very sorry for you, because too many heavy duties will fall upon your shoulders." If it should prove possible, he promised, he would watch over her from his place in the other world. "Thank you," he closed, "for your kind care of me for such a long time."

In October Iwo Jima began to receive increased attention from Army B-24s based in the Marianas. The Japanese working on the island's surface had to run for cover at least once a day, huddling there while the earth boomed and trembled. The Liberators came also at night. Most of the troops slept on the surface to escape the heat and foul air of the underground chambers, and their rest was disrupted. Wailing sirens set them stumbling for shelter, often half asleep, and some of the sluggish were maimed or killed.

American aircraft joined the submarines harassing Iwo's supply lines from Japan. The planes struck at Chichi Jima and at tiny Haha Jima, a way station about halfway between Chichi and Iwo. The loss of vessels was high, and Major Horie was hard-pressed to keep the troops and supplies moving with dispatch. The major noted that when units of troops survived the hazardous trip from Japan to Chichi, only to learn that the remainder of the trip would be even more hazardous, their faces became "pale with uncertainty and tension."

The Americans lost a few planes to Iwo's antiaircraft fire. Japanese fighter planes had dwindled under the raids and were not much of a menace. However, on October 21 a B-24 met its match in a single Zero. The Liberator had just moved in over the island when the enemy craft dived into its tail assembly, tearing it away. Both planes plunged into the sea, the bomber exploding on impact. The encounter left no survivors. Early in November Iwo was the target of two strikes by B-29s. These were ineffectual, since the crews were new to their job, but the Japanese were awed by the sight of the huge craft, gleaming silver in the sunlight.

The prevalent color displayed by the Americans on November 12 was a dull gray as a naval task force moved along Iwo's shores, laying down a bombardment and gathering intelligence. Some of the enemy's coast defense guns opened up but did no damage. First Lieutenant Robert K. West, of the Marine detachment aboard the heavy cruiser *Salt Lake City*, one of the first Marines to see the fateful island, found it "bleak and ominous-looking." At the end of November a secret visitor arrived off Iwo, the USS *Spearfish*, a submarine on reconnaissance. The vessel prowled about at periscope level, her commander keeping his eye at that instrument and giving a running account of what he saw: an armored car in motion, a variety of construction work, some completed blockhouses, numerous caves. At one of the cave entrances he glimpsed "a dejected-looking individual sitting right in the entrance sunning himself." Photos were made of the beaches, and some of the island's sounds were recorded.

On December 8—December 7 in the United States—a gathering of American forces gave Iwo a special clobbering in commemoration of Pearl Harbor Day. First twenty-eight P-38 fighters roared in strafing and bombing. Then sixty-two B-29s rained down more than 600 tons of bombs. After another fighter sweep, about 100 somber-looking B-24s droned over and added nearly 200 tons of bombs to the deluge. In the afternoon the fleet of cruisers that had been there on November 12 moved in for a seventy-minute bombardment. If the target had been a town, it would have been leveled, but Iwo was mostly open terrain and the damage was minimal. Such assaults, however, were nerve-racking, and they were to worsen. The Army's 7th Air Force led off by launching the longest sustained aerial effort of the Pacific war. Some of the night flights were scheduled so that the bombers assaulted Iwo singly, every forty-five minutes, all night long.

In a letter to his wife, Baron Nishi called the bombings "psychological warfare." Colonel Kaneji Nakane, an infantry officer, was one of the few men who seemed undisturbed by the worst the Americans delivered. In mid-December the colonel wrote his wife that the big bombers were arriving ten times each twenty-four hours on a schedule so regular that "if they don't come we miss them." For one thing, he said, when the bombs failed to hit the island and exploded in the water, many choice fish were thrown upon the beach. Everybody around him, he added, seemed to be very happy. "We are gladly waiting for the enemy." At least a part of the cheer Nakane's letter radiated was doubtless intended as a boost to his wife's morale. She might better be able to accept his death if she believed he had approached it in high spirits, surrounded by equally spirited men.

Bright faces were not lacking on Iwo, but behind them was a weight of serious thought. The men carried a burden beyond a concern for their own safety. They all knew of the B-29 raids on Japan, which meant that their families were in danger. They were tied to Iwo at a time when they were needed at home. General Kuribayashi himself was among the deeply troubled. He wrote Yoshii that he was very sad to learn of the mounting attacks on Tokyo. He listed ways for her to improve the air-raid shelter in their yard. "Make the covering of earth thicker. Did Taro make a thick board door for the entrance?" Since Tokyo was now a kind of battlefield, he told her, she must be as strong as a warrior; but she should be sure to wear plenty of warm clothing, including her belly band, and she must dry her hands and feet carefully after her bath so they would not chap and crack; and she had better take a hot water bottle into the shelter during the raids for extra heat. Having already accustomed Yoshii to the idea of his death, the general did not spare her the news of his own trials. His schedule, he explained, was often interrupted by enemy bombs, the effects of which defied description. Incendiaries created seas of fire even where there was nothing to burn, and the regular bombs shook the island on its foundations. He added that not enough rain was falling to keep up with the garrison's freshwater needs. "Every day we look at the sky and sigh."

Despite the assaults on Iwo and its communications with Japan, supplies and reinforcements kept making it through and the work of building the fortress continued. The officers told the men that "every blade of grass and every grain of sand must be armed with death for the Yankees." Time was also found for intensive training in the new defense tactics. Kuribayashi issued a general order in which he explained: "The Japanese spirit is based upon 3,000 years of history and a respect for God and our ancestors. We must purify our mental condition and increase this spirit, destroying the enemy that is trying to overrun it, and making the spirit known to the world. We are now in the front line of the national defense. We must do everything we can for the Emperor, for the personnel already perished in the war, and for the people of the homeland." A set of "courageous battle vows" was mimeographed and posted in almost every cave, pillbox, and bunker: "Above all, we shall dedicate ourselves and our entire strength to the defense of this island; we shall grasp bombs, charge enemy tanks and destroy them; we shall infiltrate into the midst of the enemy and annihilate them; with every salvo we will, without fail, kill the enemy; each man will make it his duty to kill ten of the enemy before dying; until we are destroyed to the last man we shall harass the enemy with guerrilla tactics." There was no mention of the time-honored *banzai* attack.

Although the island's unhealthful conditions caused considerable sickness and debilitation, the majority of the men were determined to fight as Kuribayashi ordered. If there were complaints about the shortage of *sake* and beer and the absence of women, there was also singing. A group of officers and men composed a patriotic piece they called "The Song of Iwo Jima." This became the garrison's theme song, and copies were sent to Japan.

Baron Nishi, wearing boots and carrying a riding whip as a swagger stick, strode about the island, drawing attention wherever he went. The troops had grown up listening to tales of his horsemanship. The baron was preparing his tanks for battle, and he wasn't pleased. They were not to be used in their mobile capacity but were being buried with only their turrets and guns showing; they were becoming metal pillboxes. During a trip to Japan to secure more tanks and other weapons for the defense, Nishi was given a rare opportunity. He wasn't looking his usual vigorous and healthful self, and influential friends hinted that this could be used as a basis for pulling strings; he could secure orders to remain in Japan. This kind of thinking, the baron sighed, would not do; his men were waiting for him. Observing the pain on the faces of his wife and children as he prepared to leave, Nishi tried to cheer them by saying that he might not be required to die. "I will try as hard as I can to live."

A few of Iwo's enlisted men persisted in telling themselves that the garrison would gain a great victory and that they would see home again. In diary entries they conjured up visions of affectionate reunions. One man wrote his family that he expected to return home soon, but that the actual time of his arrival was "really uncertain." Many of the men used ammunition boxes as tables to write their letters on, and also as receptacles for their writing materials. One soldier who sought out his box after an air raid found that it had been penetrated by a bullet. His next letter home was on stationery with a hole in the center. "This made my mother aware of how serious things were on Iwo Jima."

As the fortification of the island and the training program continued, the American attacks became worse. Powerful naval forces came over the horizon more often now, brazenly approaching to close range and lobbing in their shells. A few fighter planes were still getting off Iwo's airstrips to meet the B-24s and their escorts, and the island's antiaircraft positions were now numerous, but the damage inflicted was easily absorbed. The bombers were relentless. They destroyed grounded planes and blasted innumerable holes in the airstrips, keeping the repair crews perpetually busy, and changed the island's contours again and again. They struck antiaircraft positions and radio and radar installations, damaged cave entrances, and blew the camouflage and covering sand from bunkers and pillboxes. Almost by habit now, the Japanese ran for cover when the air-raid siren sounded, and returned to their work or training exercises at the "all clear." The nights remained a trial, and getting enough sleep continued to be problem. Increasing numbers of men were showing the strain. Deaths occurred both from illness and from American missiles, and the bodies were quickly but solemnly buried.

The submarine and aerial damage to Iwo's supply lines, especially in the areas around Chichi Jima and Haha Jima, had become critical. Supply losses had risen to hundreds of tons, and 1,500 lives had been lost. Marine Corps fliers stationed in the Marianas had joined this effort.

Making night flights in B-25 medium bombers, and using radar and rockets, they reported knocking out twenty-three vessels. To counter their losses, the Japanese had begun using air freight for many items usually sent by ship—things such as foodstuffs, automotive parts, and munitions. The trips required good timing, since the planes had to arrive at hours when Iwo did not have hostile visitors. Such hours were getting fewer. On February 1, 1945, the Army assigned "every available aircraft in the Pacific" to the Iwo operation. Only eighteen days remained before the invasion of the "stinking pork chop," as the island was called by airmen who had sniffed its sulfurous fumes. During the previous six months, the fliers had taken thousands of photos while over Iwo, and these had been studied by intelligence personnel. Repeated comparisons were made with earlier photos, and it was known all along that the island's strength was growing. The air raids and naval shellings were called "softening-up" measures, but Iwo had become "harder."

The garrison now numbered about 21,000 men, and the great labyrinth of fortifications was ready to receive the landing forces. The biggest weapons were the coast defense guns, their broad muzzles jutting from heavy concrete bunkers. Hundreds of other gun positions distributed about the island in five defense sectors were mutually supporting, and almost every square yard of the terrain could be brought under fire. Artillery pieces of various weights were poised in cave entrances and bunkers. Rocket launchers and mortar tubes stood in scattered pits. The turrets of the buried tanks pointed their light cannon from commanding spots. Many of the antiaircraft guns were dual-purpose; their long barrels could be cranked down so that they paralleled the ground. Slender machine-gun muzzles peered from the dark apertures of pillboxes; numberless cave entrances, tunnel openings, and other holes had been allotted to snipers, who were also armed with hand grenades. Antipersonnel mines had been prepared for shallow burial on the beaches, and heavier mines were concealed along the routes it was believed American tanks would travel, routes also lined with deep antitank ditches. For extra measure, the island had been provided with networks of trenches, and some of the ditches and trenches had been rigged with mines and booby traps. Working under tremendous difficulties, the Japanese had succeeded in turning Iwo Jima, an obscure bit of volcanic rock and sand, into what was probably the most ingenious fortress the world has ever seen.

General Kuribayashi had established himself at the island's northern end, where he believed the Americans would come last. Above the ground was a huge communications blockhouse built of reinforced con-

crete, its walls five feet thick, its roof ten. It held about twenty radios
and the necessary personnel, whose job was to maintain contact not
only with the defense sectors on the island but with Chichi Jima and
Imperial Headquarters in Tokyo. Seventy-five feet below the floor of
the radio room was a system of caves and tunnels in which Kuribayashi
and his staff had their personal quarters, small concrete rooms illuminated by candles. Sitting in his shadowy cubicle, the general wrote
his last letters to Yoshii, about whom his worries had increased. He was
about to sacrifice his life in an attempt to help protect the people on
the mainland, but already the effort had begun to seem futile. General
MacArthur, with his strong hold on the Philippines, was getting too
close. Moreover, the B-29s from the Marianas were raiding Japan with
increasing boldness and in growing numbers. The damage they inflicted, Kuribayashi knew, would soon be horrendous. From his small
cell, all the condemned general could do to help Yoshii and the children
was to write to them and implore them to be careful of their health and
safety. He advised Yoshii to listen to the radio reports and read the
newspapers and use them as a guide for her actions. It might be a good
idea if she left Tokyo. No, he said in answer to one of her questions,
there was no possibility he would be transferred. He was soon to die,
and she must accept the fact. Not even his remains would return home.
But that did not matter; he would live on in her and the children.
Writing on February 3, 1945, Kuribayashi lamented that Yoshii's letters
were not getting through. Was she all right? Had she left Tokyo? He
reported that he was well and needed nothing from Japan. She should
not trouble herself to send any gifts by the air transport service. He
urged her to be careful not to catch cold and to have herself massaged
frequently to help combat her fatigue. And she should tell Taro to lead
a punctual life. "The plane is about to leave. I must close this. Good-
bye." This was the last letter Yoshii received.

February 11 was a Japanese holiday, the birthday of Emperor Meiji,
grandfather of Hirohito. The celebration was tied in with Japan's long
national history. Between air raids, Iwo's troops, with even the healthi-
est showing signs of fatigue after months of labor with insufficient sleep,
conducted ceremonies honoring the present emperor, and also tapped
their dwindling stock of beer and *sake*. Since this was a popular family
holiday, the observance gave many an intense longing for home. Then
home was heard from in an unexpected way. Tokyo broadcast "The
Song of Iwo Jima" in the garrison's honor. Listening by means of the
island's loudspeakers, the troops were seized with fervent patriotism.
Eyes brimmed everywhere, and the cry went up, *"Banzai! Banzai!*

Banzai!" That night a soldier wrote in his diary, "We are proud that we are going to fight to the end."

The assault on Iwo Jima was another operation run by Raymond Spruance, Kelly Turner, and Holland Smith. Harry Schmidt commanded the invasion troops, the 5th Amphibious Corps, made up of the 3rd, 4th, and 5th Marine Divisions. The 3rd, which had fought at Bougainville and Guam, was at its camp on the latter island, cleaning out the last pockets of resistance, when it received its orders to prepare for a new campaign. The 4th was at its camp on Maui in the Hawaiian Islands, following its service on Roi-Namur, Saipan, and Tinian. Iwo would be the division's fourth operation in a little over a year. The 5th, encamped on the island of Hawaii itself, had seen no combat as a unit but was formed around a 40 percent nucleus of Pacific veterans, most of them former Marine Raiders and Paratroopers, outfits now disbanded. These elite forces had established a fine record, but had at last been deemed unnecessary to the performance of a corps whose ordinary members were themselves elitists. The Paratroopers had never had occasion to make a jump in combat, always going into action by boat, which was the final reason for their disbandment.

In the latter part of December 1944, the 4th and 5th Divisions received orders to rendezvous at Pearl Harbor. The 3rd Division, still on Guam and 3,000 miles closer to the objective, would not embark until later. This unit had been designated as the invasion's floating reserve. Even as the 4th boarded its transports at Kahului, Maui, Tokyo Rose mentioned the fact in one of her nightly broadcasts. The men of the 4th, who knew little of their destination, listened to her more carefully after that, figuring they might very well learn more about upcoming events from her than from their own officers. This was a time when rumors and "scuttlebutt" flew about everywhere. But even the most naïve Marine and sailor had learned that such information could not be trusted. According to Signalman 2nd Class Robert L. Collyer, of the attack transport *Sibley,* a piece of scuttlebutt was usually "a modified version of a revised revision with qualifications and additions."

Pearl Harbor was a busy place in mid-January 1945. Either tied up at its docks or anchored in its expansive waters were nearly 500 vessels. Some were formed into convoys from time to time as the Marines, Navy, Coast Guard, Seabees, and a few attached Army amphibious units went out among the islands for invasion rehearsals. In the harbor, gigs and landing craft hurried among the anchored vessels or performed missions from ship to shore. Oil tankers and water tenders slipped about performing their servicing duties. Barges laden with stores from the docks saw to it that the various cargo vessels were brought to full supply. It had taken the usual months of work by Army, Navy, and Marine supply units to gather the vast amount of materials necessary to the operation. Nearly all of the assault troops knew that the supplies included cigarettes and liquor, but few were aware of the burial equipment and the myriad wooden crosses.

The men were given liberty in Honolulu, 25 percent of the total force each day. With thousands at a time on shore, the city deemed it wise to keep its bars closed. This was deplored by some, but the rest were content to swim at Waikiki and to visit the curio shops, tattoo parlors, shooting galleries, photo booths, and refreshment stands. There were hula shows too, but some of these were a disappointment, the dancers a mixture of thin schoolgirls and stout matrons. Among the officers, the Pearl Harbor period saw some of the off-duty hours devoted to the traditional prebattle parties. Colonel John Letcher attended one that was graced by a number of Navy nurses, WAVES, and air-raid-warden girls, and it included dancing. Letcher regarded the evening in a romantic light. "Perhaps the most famous occasion of gay festivity before a battle was the Duchess of Richmond's ball in Brussels the night before Waterloo. We could not have our party the night before our battle, and her ball was a considerably larger and more elaborate affair than ours; but under the circumstances we did pretty well towards upholding the warrior tradition of revelry before battle and no long faces."

On the duty side at this time, the officers attended briefings concerned not only with Iwo Jima's defenses but also with its personnel. Ensign G. Edward Metcalf was impressed by a bound volume he was given to peruse. "It contained biographical sketches of what seemed to be most of Iwo's officers. I marveled at the intelligence involved in collecting this information, and was surprised to learn that the enemy officers were pretty much like us."

Late in January the various elements of the fleet moved slowly out of the harbor and formed for the long trip westward. On the second day out, the enlisted troops finally learned where they were going. Maps of Iwo made from aerial photographs suddenly appeared everywhere. They were surprising in their detail. Gathered in groups with the maps as centerpieces, the troops were briefed on all aspects of the invasion. Many grew sober as they began to realize what they were up against.

The days allotted to briefings soon gave way to a day on which there was a great piece of horseplay. Early in February the fleet crossed the 180th meridian, or the international date line, and all men making their first crossing were subjected to humbling initiation ceremonies at the hands of those who had crossed before. No one was exempt. One enlisted Marine ran belowdecks and tried to hide, but several strong men went after him. As they dragged him up the last gangway, he was heard to shout, "I demand to see my commanding officer!" He saw this man very soon; he was on deck being initiated.

During this part of the voyage the Marines were advised they would be allowed to send notes home stating that they were going into battle but giving no details. Thousands of men sat on the decks of their ships in the sun and wrote these messages, many saying no more than something like this: "Am at sea, headed for combat. In case I am not able to write again for a while, don't worry. I'll be okay. Will write as soon as I can." Many parents and wives who received these notes never heard from their young Marines again. The next message they received was from Marine Corps Headquarters in Washington.

From February 5 to 7 the convoy anchored and refueled in the lagoon at Eniwetok in the Marshalls. Swimming call was sounded each day, and hundreds of men bobbed about in the milky waters. Then the fleet moved on to Saipan in the Marianas, coming to anchor on February 11. The men of the 4th Division were surprised to see a destroyer move in and shell a rocky area where some die-hard defenders had been spotted. It had been eight months since the 4th had been part of the assault here. Saipan had changed dramatically. In place of the burnt cane fields strewn with Japanese dead were long white airstrips. Nearby Tinian, also well known to the 4th, had similar strips.

Each morning during their stay in the area, the men of the convoy were treated to the sight of the giant B-29s taking off for their runs to Japan, one after the other in a seemingly endless stream. More than once the men's fascination turned to horror as a bomber failed to lift its great load and crashed into the sea, exploding for half an hour afterward, its crew lost. Unknown to the shipboard spectators, the morale of the B-29 crews was dragging at this point. They were developing an obsession about Iwo Jima, a perpetual threat to their missions and their lives. All were aware that if America took the island it would be converted from a dark peril to a glistening asset.

The invasion's assault troops, the first ten waves of Marines, were now placed on board an array of LSTs with amtracs in their holds, and a final rehearsal was conducted, with Tinian the objective. No one was actually landed; the amtracs merely made a run toward the beach and then drew off. The sea was rough and the men were glad to get back aboard their LSTs. Just before the departure for Iwo Jima everyone was dusted with DDT powder as a defense against the island's insects, and this was done with a generosity that would have dismayed later generations. "We probably had enough DDT in our systems," recalled Lieutenant George Stoddard, "to kill Iwo Jima's insects by spitting at them."

By this time the campaign's various elements were beginning to function in accord with prearranged plans. Marc Mitscher's Task Force 58 was on its way to Japan to deliver a powerful diversionary and covering attack, and an amphibious support force under Rear Admiral William H. P. Blandy was headed for Iwo Jima for a three-day preliminary bombardment. Holland Smith had argued with the Navy for a longer bombardment period but was told that this would throw the campaign's timetable out of order and was probably unnecessary anyway. Smith was disturbed by the decision. "I could not forget the sight of Marines floating in the lagoon or lying on the beaches at Tarawa, men who died assaulting defenses which should have been taken out by naval gunfire."

The American submarine service was a part of the operation, its vessels on special assignments. B-24s and other aircraft from the Marianas continued their work against Iwo, Chichi, and Haha. The air forces in the Southwest Pacific and even Allied air commands in India were helping, their mission to pound bases, on islands southwest of Japan and on the Asian mainland, that might send air reinforcements to the home islands or to Iwo.

The assault shipping left Saipan in sections. Leading off on February 15, four days before D-day, were the LSTs carrying the Marines of the 4th and 5th Divisions who were to land with the first ten waves. Some of the smaller men-of-war provided the escort. The main body of the vessels followed on the sixteenth. On board the troop transports, along with the rest of the men of the 4th and 5th, was a regiment of the 3rd, that division having joined the convoy from its camp on Guam. Bringing up the rear on February 17 were the transports carrying the remainder of the 3rd and its attached units. A certain optimism was evident among the men of the 3rd. As the assault's floating reserve, they might not be landed. And even if they were, it would not be until the beachhead was established and things had cooled down a bit. They congratulated each other on their luck. The feeling, however, was not unanimous. Said a veteran sergeant, "The trouble with luck is that it runs out."

During the 700-mile trip, the Marines spent much of their time on deck. Out on the sunlit sea, porpoises and flying fishes gave pleasing performances. Coastguardsman Chester B. Hack, a crewman on one of the convoy's twenty-four LSTs, noted that the Marines stayed busy.

"They were briefed repeatedly, and they exercised to keep in shape. They were forever taking their rifles apart and cleaning them. They were given guard-duty assignments that weren't really necessary but kept them active. There was a chaplain aboard our ship whom the Marines thought the world of, who had been in action with them before. He held services every day, and as we got closer to Iwo the attendance grew larger and larger." One day, according to Hack, a Marine on an LST sailing up ahead fell overboard. "We turned to port to avoid hitting him and threw him a life preserver, but had orders not to stop. We could not hold up twenty-four ships for one man. Looking back, we could see him waving his arms, and it broke our hearts that we couldn't help him. We hoped that one of the destroyers or other small men-of-war that were cruising around to protect us would pick him up, but we never heard that one did."

While the several divisions of the assault force plowed toward Iwo, the island had the attention of William Blandy's support force, which moved in on the southeast during the dawn of February 16. At the same time, Mitscher's task force launched its planes against Japan. Mitscher intended to swing back to Iwo in time to help support the landing. The Japanese on Iwo observed the arrival of Blandy's armada with awe. They had never before seen such an assemblage of naval power. To an ensign named Toshihiko, "the sea looked as though a thick layer of black ink had been spread over its surface." Many of the men decided that the situation was hopeless, and the word went around, "Let us all die happily together." General Kuribayashi broadcast this announcement: "All shout *banzai* for the Emperor! I have the utmost confidence that you will all do your best. I pray for a heroic fight." On the previous evening, Kuribayashi had radioed Tokyo he had learned the Americans were approaching and that now was the time for the Imperial Navy to do what it could to help him. The Navy sent back word that it would not come out now but would wait until April 1, at which time it would drive the Americans all the way back to their mainland. It was the kind of reply the general had expected. All he could hope for was some aerial support. Otherwise he and his men would have to fight their battle in isolation. The island's officers had given the troops their final briefing on the way the Americans were to be received. The early assault waves were to be allowed to land relatively unmolested; then, with the beaches crowded, all commanding weapons on the heights were to begin raining down fire.

The workhorses of Admiral Blandy's force were its six battleships and five cruisers. Each had been assigned its own sector of the island, and

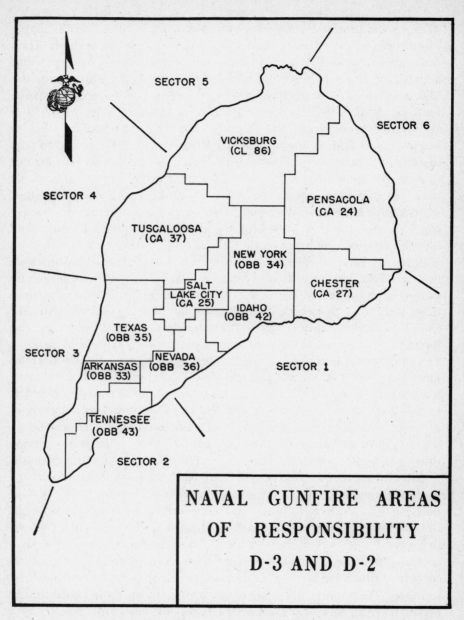

SECTOR 5

SECTOR 6

SECTOR 4

VICKSBURG
(CL 86)

PENSACOLA
(CA 24)

TUSCALOOSA
(CA 37)

NEW YORK
(OBB 34)

SALT
LAKE CITY
(CA 25)

CHESTER
(CA 27)

IDAHO
(OBB 42)

TEXAS
(OBB 35)

SECTOR 3

NEVADA
(OBB 36)

SECTOR 1

ARKANSAS
(OBB 33)

TENNESSEE
(OBB 43)

SECTOR 2

NAVAL GUNFIRE AREAS
OF RESPONSIBILITY
D-3 AND D-2

the firing began at about 7:00 A.M. Spotter planes were catapulted from the vessels to help seek out targets and to report on the hits. Unfortunately, the day soon turned cloudy, and the bombardment's effectiveness was severely curtailed. Minesweepers operated with little interference along the coasts, but the carrier planes that went in during breaks in the overcast found antiaircraft fire heavy. Forty-two B-24s from the Marianas, arriving over the island at a time when the clouds were thick, turned back without releasing their loads. At 6:00 P.M. the fleet withdrew seaward for the night. Among the hundreds of targets marked for destruction, only a very few had been accounted for. When informed of this, Holland Smith was appalled. Only two days of the bombardment period remained.

The next morning the weather was clear and visibility good. A dozen minesweepers sailed to within 750 yards of the coast, and soon several of the big support vessels, lying about 3,000 yards out, opened up over them. The Japanese answered this fire with their shore batteries, and the battleship *Tennessee* took a hit that wounded four men. The sweepers found no mines, reefs, or shoals, but they drew both small-arms and 40-millimeter fire. The cruiser *Pensacola* moved in to provide close support, and a heavy gun got her range. Within three minutes she took six hits and was forced to draw off with her crew fighting fires and plugging holes near her waterline. Her casualties numbered seventeen dead, including her executive officer, and 120 wounded. *Pensacola* might have fared even worse if the Japanese gun hadn't been dismounted by its recoil. Watching the cruiser retreat with smoke pouring from her decks, the crew chief lamented, "We could have sunk her! We could have sunk her!"

At 10:30 A.M. Blandy's vessels deployed for a special event; it was time for the Navy's frogmen to go to work. The bombardment diminished during this deployment, and some of the Japanese surfaced to see what was going on. They were surprised to note than many of the enemy sailors were hanging over the rail and scanning the island as though they were on peacetime tour boats; and across the water came the unmistakable sound of popular music from record players. The heavy gunfire support vessels began a slow and deliberate barrage. Inside their position, about 2,500 yards from the island, seven destroyers formed a line that paralleled the eastern beaches, which stretched for nearly two miles. Twelve LCI gunboats, armed with rockets and both 20-millimeter and 40-millimeter guns, passed through the destroyers and eased toward shore. In small boats racing shoreward along the two-mile front were more than 100 swimsuited frogmen coated with camouflage grease and also with cocoa butter to cut the water's chill. Now carrier aircraft joined the activities, making crashing rocket runs along the beach. Additional rockets were poured in by the LCIs.

It all began to seem to the Japanese, who were unaware of what was really happening, that the assault was beginning. They believed the twelve LCIs to be filled with Marines. The craft loomed as easy targets for the artillerymen in the bunkers at the base of Mount Suribachi at the island's southern tip, and for those concealed in the cliffs at the northern extremity of the beaches. These Japanese were naval personnel over whom General Kuribayashi did not have absolute control. They knew they were supposed to remain quiet until the Marines were jammed up on the beach, but the targets were too tempting, and they opened fire. Caught up in the excitement, some of the Army's mortar crews, machine gunners, and riflemen joined in.

The LCIs fought back with their rockets and guns, and the small boats containing the swimmers, who looked like marble statues in their grease, continued their run for the shoreline. As mortar shells and small-arms fire began to strike around them, some of the men managed to grin and make jokes. "What the hell," said one, "it all counts on twenty," meaning that it was just another part of the trek toward retirement. As the boats neared the beach, they suddenly swerved into courses parallel to it, and one by one the swimmers flopped out. As soon as a boat had dropped its last man, it began zigzagging seaward at top speed. The abandoned frogmen launched their investigations, seeking safety under water when shells or bullets splashed too near. Glancing toward the terraces that made up the beach, they sometimes saw the riflemen who were shooting at them.

By this time the LCI gunboats, only about 1,000 yards offshore, were in serious trouble. All twelve were hit; nine were put out of commission, one so badly damaged it had to be abandoned. The officers and men remained at their stations as long as possible. Forty-seven were killed and 153 wounded. One skipper, Lieutenant Rufus G. Herring, wounded three times, earned the Medal of Honor, and ten other skippers the Navy Cross. Of the destroyers that were involved in this action, one was hit with a loss of seven killed and thirty-three wounded.

The carrier planes continued active, and the heavy support vessels kept up a steady fire, also laying a smokescreen along the shoreline to facilitate the recovery of the frogmen by the same boats that had taken them in. The daredevils had completed their mission, finding the water free of obstacles and of a good depth right up to the beaches. Some of the men even brought back sand samples in tobacco pouches. Only one swimmer had been lost, presumably the victim of mortar fire. One boatman died of a bullet through the head. That afternoon fresh teams, with similar sea and air support, examined the second-choice landing area, the beaches in the west. There was enemy resistance, but the operation came off well. One mine was discovered and detonated. The western approaches were otherwise clear and would be suitable for landing if necessary.

The Liberators from the Marianas had a clear view of the island that day, and the crews amassed an excellent record of hits in the airfield areas. By this time Iwo's air forces were about finished. At one time during the day, two surviving Zeroes took off valiantly, their pilots ordered to ram warships, but while clearing Mount Suribachi the planes were caught in the Navy's gunfire and were tumbled into the sea.

General Kuribayashi could not be too unhappy with the unauthorized firing on the LCIs. He believed that a landing attempt had been repulsed, and reported the action that way to Imperial Headquarters in Tokyo. Admiral Ichimaru and his men were radioed a commendation. But the attack on the LCIs had been a mistake. Many gun positions hitherto invisible to the Americans were spotted, and that afternoon some of these were destroyed.

That night, however, the atmosphere on board Admiral Blandy's flagship, the *Estes*, was grim. Only one more day of the bombardment remained, and not even the landing area had been neutralized, let alone the other sectors of the island. The Marine gunfire officer working with the Navy, Lieutenant Colonel Donald M. Weller, urged that the last day's bombardment be concentrated on the fortifications overlooking the eastern or preferred landing beaches, and Blandy was quick to agree to this. By dawn on Sunday, February 18, the weather had turned gray again, with visibility only fair. At 7:45 the admiral ordered his vessels to "close beach and get going." He specified that the heavy batteries at the base of Mount Suribachi and those overlooking the landing zone from the north absolutely had to be destroyed. The ships approached to within 2,500 yards of shore and began laying in their shells. Carrier planes operated as the weather permitted. Again the visiting Liberators had to turn back without dropping their bombs. The work of the gunfire vessels had its effect. When the bombardment ended at 6:30 P.M., a study revealed that out of 200 prime targets in the landing area, nearly half had been destroyed or heavily damaged. Broken down, this amounted to eleven coast defense guns, twenty-two dual-purpose guns with five-inch bores, sixteen large blockhouses, and about forty-five pillboxes.

That evening one of the underwater demolition teams that had survived the hazardous beach reconnaissance of the previous day came to disaster in an unexpected way. The men were sitting in the mess hall of their vessel, the APD *Blessman*, some writing letters home while others played cards, when a Japanese plane winged over and dropped two heavy bombs. One merely churned up the water, but the other made a direct hit on the mess hall, which burst into flames. Eighteen members of the team were killed and twenty-three were wounded or burned. Similar casualties were suffered by the *Blessman*'s crew.

With the scheduled three-day bombardment over, William Blandy sent a message to Kelly Turner, whose flagship was approaching Iwo with the assault shipping: "Though weather has not permitted expenditure of entire ammunition allowance, and more installations can be found and destroyed with one more day of bombardment, I believe landing can be accomplished tomorrow as scheduled if necessary." Blandy had permission from his superior, Raymond Spruance, who had accompanied the task force that went to Japan, to delay the landing one day if he thought an additional day's bombardment was needed; but Turner felt that the original plan should not be modified, that a sufficient amount of added destruction would be accomplished by the two-hour bombardment arranged to precede H-hour, the time of landing. Holland Smith made no objection. He had wanted the bombardment to start earlier, not to run over its planned closing date. That night the general, seized by what he called "a deep emotional surge" occasioned by the imminence of action, sought the consolation of his Bible and solitary prayer.

On this eve of the battle, Tokyo Rose was especially informative. She named many of the vessels connected with the operation, identified the participating Marine Corps units, and disclosed the ports where they had been picked up. Rose told the Americans that however tough they had found their previous landings, all had been easy compared with the one they were facing.

23 | *From Dawn to Dusk on D-day*

══════ The dawn of February 19 found Kelly Turner's assault shipping anchored several miles east of Iwo Jima; the vessels had eased in and joined William Blandy's armada during the night. At first the combat-laden Marines on the weatherdecks saw the island as a gray shadow with faint green tracings. In silhouette Iwo resembled an encased mummy. Rising 550 feet at the southern tip, Mount Suribachi formed the feet. The land running northward from the base of the extinct volcano rose gradually to a height of 380 feet in the chest area, then tapered off to the head end on the northern coast. When the pre-H-hour bombardment began, the somber image was altered by fiery explosions and dust and smoke.

Soon nearly 500 amtracs were bobbing around in a sea now glimmering with warm sunlight. The warmth was welcome, for Iwo was not in the tropics but the subtropics. In one of the craft, a Marine sang: "Happy D-day to you! Happy D-day to you! Happy D-day, dear Marines; happy D-day to you!" In one way, it *was* a happy D-day. Iwo had a treacherous surf, and bad weather would have made the landing extremely difficult, even without the enemy's fire. Today the sea was relatively calm. From Kelly Turner's flagship came the announcement: "Boating, excellent; visibility, excellent." The breeze was just brisk enough to set the fleet's hundreds of flags and pennants waving proudly, their colors bright in the sun.

The Japanese peering from cave entrances and apertures in bunkers and pillboxes were incredulous at the size of the fleet after its augmentation during the night, not only by the assault shipping but by several of the men-of-war that had been to Japan. A radio operator informed Imperial Headquarters in Tokyo, "We are doomed. The enemy is firing on us from both seas." Even as the island shook under the bombardment, some of the Japanese could not help but admire the fleet's majesty and the symmetry of the landing preparations. Watching from a cave on Mount Suribachi, PFC Kiyomi Hirakawa found himself thinking, "How systematic and beautiful!"

The amtracs loaded with Marine rifle companies had formed into slowly circling groups and were awaiting the signal to head for the line of departure, where they would form abreast for the dash to shore. Equipment and supply vessels of various sizes were also standing by. H-hour had been set for nine o'clock, and the gunfire support vessels,

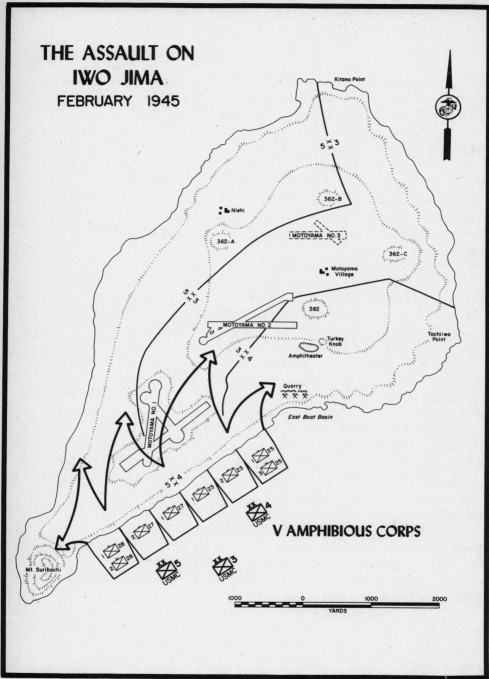

THE ASSAULT ON IWO JIMA

FEBRUARY 1945

Kitano Point

5 × 3

362-B

Nishi

MOTOYAMA NO. 3

362-A

362-C

Motoyama Village

5 × 3

382

MOTOYAMA NO. 2

Turkey Knob

Tachiiwa Point

3 × 4

Amphitheater

Quarry

East Boat Basin

MOTOYAMA NO. 1

1 25
3 25

2 23

5 × 4

1 23

4
USMC

2 27

1 27

V AMPHIBIOUS CORPS

1 28
2 28

5
USMC

3
USMC

Mt. Suribachi

1000   0   1000   2000

YARDS

K.W.WHITE

some lying only about 1,000 yards offshore—much closer than the circling landing craft—were not losing a moment. They were laying down the heaviest pre-H-hour bombardment in history, the explosions coming with the rapidity of drumbeats. Smoke and dust hung over Iwo in great white, yellow, and gray clouds, blotting out its sunlight.

One of the American newsmen watching from shipboard was Robert Sherrod, whose campaigns included Tarawa and Saipan. He wrote in his notebook: "Though I've seen this many times, I can't help thinking, 'Nobody can live through this.' But I know better." Among the other observers, the most distinguished was the Secretary of the Navy, James V. Forrestal. Raymond Spruance, bearing top responsibility for the operation, was back from Japan, on the *Indianapolis*. Ensign Herbert Brummel, on the bridge with the admiral, marveled at how calm he looked.

At 8:05 the naval gunfire was temporarily lifted, and seventy-two carrier bombers and fighter planes sped to the attack. Suddenly the operation's motif was blue—blue sky, blue water, blue planes. Rockets, bombs, and machine-gun bullets were showered on Suribachi, the beaches, and the rugged high ground that overlooked them from the north. Then forty-eight additional fighters, including twenty-four Marine Corsairs, flashed in and hit the same areas with napalm and more rockets and machine-gun bullets. As soon as the last planes droned away, the gunfire support ships, having maneuvered into their final positions, opened up with renewed fury. "Everything is coming off like clockwork!" thought Gunner's Mate 2nd Class Louis Berard of the crew of the attack transport *Missoula*. And the same satisfaction was felt by thousands of others who were backing up the Marines and had been working for months toward this critical moment. Now fifteen B-24s from the Marianas appeared over the island and added nineteen tons of bombs to the Navy's deluge of shells and rockets. Another thirty Liberators had been assigned to this strike but had been delayed by bad weather between the Marianas and Iwo.

At 8:30 a division of rocket ships, sailing abreast at wide intervals, began moving toward the island. After loosing a storm of missiles against the beach defenses, they veered off to the right and left to make way for nearly seventy armored amtracs now heading shoreward along a two-mile front, their mission to cover the waves of troop-carrying craft that were beginning to follow at 250-yard intervals. Some of the troop-filled tractors passed close by battleships and cruisers firing at point-blank range. Viewed from the tiny craft, hardly more than corks on the water, these vessels looked amazingly huge. Their gray plating rose clifflike toward the decks that held the big guns. Sailors stood along the rails looking down, some waving coffee cups and others making victory signs. One Marine thought he heard a sailor shout, "Go get 'em, you damned glory hounds!" The amtrac in which Corporal Bill B. Faulkner was riding passed directly beneath a set of the big guns as they were booming. "The fire rings came out over us, and we could see the projectiles starting off. And that concussion! For a moment we thought our little tractor would be driven under."

At 8:57, a few minutes before the armored amtracs were scheduled to reach the island, the naval gunners lifted their landing-zone fire and began to train their weapons on inland targets. It was part of the general plan that they support the landing with a rolling barrage. During this interval the Marine Corsairs returned to strafe the beach. They roared in from the south past Suribachi, dropped close to shore as they fired, then peeled off over the sea. Additional runs were made 500 yards inland.

For American purposes, the two-mile stretch of beach had been divided into seven segments. Starting at the base of Suribachi on the left, they were: Green Beach, Red Beaches 1 and 2, Yellow Beaches 1 and 2, and Blue Beaches 1 and 2. The initial landing was being made by the 27th and 28th Regiments of the 5th Division on the left, and the 23rd and 25th Regiment of the 4th on the right.

The armored amtracs climbed out of the surf at 9:02. They had been firing their 75s and their machine guns on the way in, but now they were hindered by a sandy terrace that ran parallel to the water's edge and ranged up to fifteen feet in height. Some of the craft were able to churn their way up the terrace front, while others found it necessary to back off into the water to resume an effective fire.

Until this time the Japanese had sent only a few shells and some scattered small-arms fire toward the assault waves, most of the defenders abiding by General Kuribayashi's orders to permit the Marines to establish a crowded beachhead before beginning to hit them. But one troop-filled tractor was sunk and a number of its occupants lost. A few other craft experienced near misses. Supply Sergeant Raymond A. Dooley, heading shoreward near Suribachi, heard the crack of bullets going over just above his helmet. This was Dooley's first time under fire, and he found himself thinking, "They say a miss is as good as a mile. I'll take the mile."

The enemy's antiaircraft crews were busy against the dive bombers, fighters, and two-man observation planes. Major Raymond W. Dollins, the 5th Division's chief air observer, was over the island, and the men of the fleet who were tuned to his radio frequency heard him sing, "Oh, what a beautiful morning; oh, what a beautiful day. I've got a terrible feeling everything's coming my way!" It was a colorful touch, and the listeners laughed in appreciation. A few minutes later the major's plane, trailing flames and smoke, plunged into the sea near Suribachi. Both Dollins and his pilot were killed.

It was 9:05 when the first wave of troop-carrying amtracs sloughed through the lacy edge of the surf and came to a stop. The ramps at the rear of the craft rattled down, some splashing into the water, and within moments nearly 1,400 Marines, scores with soggy feet, were spread along the two-mile front. The smell of cordite from the last friendly fire on the beach was still heavy, but making a deeper impression on many was the freshly washed sand, sloping from the waterline, which held no footprints—an effective reminder that they were the first Americans ashore. The men hurried across the wet ribbon and threw themselves against the face of the first terrace. There were three of these, one above the other, created by a violent storm two years earlier, and they led up to a plateau that held the first airfield. The sand, or volcanic ash, was light and loose, and those men whose first thought was to dig a foxhole found the stuff flowing back in almost as fast as they scooped it out. The job was like trying to dig a hole in a bin of wheat.

In accord with General Kuribayashi's plan, resistance was still light. The gunners on the American vessels believed that their rolling barrage, hitting the island in a semicircle around the landing zone, was responsible for this. An occasional mortar shell whoomped along the beach, and sporadic small-arms fire snapped and whined about. There were a few casualties. On the extreme left, the Marines of the first wave noticed an armored tractor standing quietly in the surf, two men hanging grotesquely over the sides of its gun turret, their arms dangling.

The first-wave troops did not linger near the surf. Other waves were coming in behind, and it was necessary to start the inland movement at once. Defenses were light on the terraces, since the Japanese had anticipated the hammering this area would get. But the sand itself was a formidable deterrent to progress. The Marines had been trained to make movements like this on the run, but now they could only plod, sinking ankle-deep at every step and leaving elephantine footprints.

The Japanese, except for the twisted and bloody remains of a few who had been caught in the bombardment, were not in evidence. Iwo looked uninhabited. But the Marines, recalling their shipboard briefings, knew that they had been thrust into the worst possible situation. On their left loomed Mount Suribachi, ostensibly an extinct volcano but in reality a fortress. Up ahead, on that long, sandy plateau with the many contours, was a maze of half-buried bunkers and pillboxes. On their right was a rugged ridge and cliff area that looked down on the beaches in the same manner as Suribachi. The Americans could make no unobserved moves; they were like ducks in a shooting gallery.

Among the thousands of Japanese who were standing by their weapons was Seaman 1st Class Tadayoshi Koizumi, an antiaircraft gunner in the high ground north of the beaches. He could see the wide lines of Marines plodding inland, and noted that when the foremost groups were about 200 yards from the water, "any and all Japanese weapons commenced firing." This included artillery, mortars, rockets, machine guns, and rifles, a new and busy combination of noises added to the rumbling fire from the American naval vessels. As scores of shells raised sand spouts among the Marines, stopping them, Koizumi cast his eye to the beach and out over the water, the nearer reaches of which were filled with a variety of small craft, heading in. Shells had begun to land among them, too, and some were taking hits. But the general picture, Koizumi noted, did not change. "The enemy continued the landing. To my regret, there were no Japanese naval vessels, nor aircraft."

Initially, the hottest beaches were those of the 4th Division on the right. When Private Charles Bagnole landed, the terraces were already covered with Marines, and Bagnole and his comrades had trouble finding a route inland. "Some of us began moving down along the beach to our left, where the first terrace tapered off to meet the water. We had barely got going when we heard the whistle of a Jap shell. We hit the sand as the shell exploded in a Higgins boat that was just beaching. There was a tremendous secondary explosion; the shell apparently set off some demolitions the boat was carrying. A huge mass of black ash and debris went up and came raining down: equipment of all kinds, clothing, parts of the boat, and parts of men. After everything settled, we got up and continued on our way, and we passed close by the littered spot. The boat was practically in toothpicks. Marines were floating in the surf. One was decapitated, another was all but cut in two, and there was an arm bobbing around by itself. At the water's edge was a pile of debris: a mixture of equipment, clothing, men, flesh and blood—just a horrible sight. Some of the boat's occupants had already run up on the beach when the shell hit, and a few of these had been lucky. But there were a lot of calls for corpsmen, and one Marine was lying there with his clothing on fire, and we could smell his flesh burning. I thought I had a good stomach. I had worked for a funeral director as a teenager, and I had seen bodies in the morgue that had undergone complete postmortems; they were all apart, their organs laid around them on the table. That hadn't bothered me much, but this was different. These men had been torn apart *alive.* I had to swallow a few times to keep my breakfast down."

Bagnole was with the 3rd Battalion, 25th Marines, commanded by veteran officer Justice Chambers, by this time well known as "Jumpin' Joe" because of his bouncing stride. The 3rd was on the invasion's extreme right flank, directly under the guns of the ridge and cliff area. This unit had been in tough spots before, and its members called themselves the "Ghouls of the 3rd Battalion." They had made up a kind of humorous dirge they sang to the tune of Chopin's "Funeral March." It dealt with the cheapness of their lives and the comfort of having government life insurance. Each time one of them died, the dirge proclaimed, "ten thousand dollars went home to the folks." Now, during the early moments of D-day on Iwo, Jumpin' Joe Chambers and his 3rd Battalion ghouls swung northward, and, with the 1st Battalion, 25th Marines on their left, began a dogged advance toward the bristling high ground.

Immediately to the south of these two battalions of the 25th, the 1st and 2nd Battalions of the 23rd, also of the 4th Division, were trying to reach the first airfield but had been slowed by a storm of shells and bullets from bunkers, pillboxes, ditches, and trenches that stood in the way. Sergeant Darrell S. Cole led a machine-gun squad against a set of sand-covered pillboxes blocking his platoon's progress. From the dark slits came both small-arms fire and hand grenades. When Cole and his men cut loose at the slits, the enemy action stopped. Then the machine gun jammed, and the Japanese pinned down not only the squad but the whole platoon. Armed with grenades, Cole dropped back and circled around to the rear of the pillboxes. He tossed his missiles through the low entrances, and each muffled explosion, accompanied by escaping debris, told of occupants destroyed. Cole returned to his platoon's lines for more grenades and repeated his performance. Making the rearmament circuit again, he was completing his third attack, convinced that most of the Japanese were dead, when a survivor flipped out a grenade that exploded at his feet. Cole died instantly, unaware that he had earned the Medal of Honor.

Cole's battalion, the 1st, 23rd, was the southernmost unit in the 4th Division zone, its left flank touching the right flank of the 1st Battalion, 27th Marines, 5th Division. One of the men in this battalion was Gunnery Sergeant John Basilone, who had won the Medal of Honor on Guadalcanal. Basilone had got a lot of publicity and could have had a commission and the choicest duty in the Corps, but he chose to remain an enlisted Marine with the field troops. He landed on Iwo with one of the earliest waves. Now, as he was leading his machine-gun platoon toward the southern end of the first airfield, Basilone was killed by a mortar shell.

On the left of Basilone's battalion, trying to swing around the airfield's southern tip, was the 2nd Battalion, 27th Marines. Completing the two-mile line were the 1st and 2nd Battalion, 28th Marines, 5th Division, their left flank only about 400 yards from the base of Mount Suribachi. The men of the 1st, who were closest to the volcano, had been assigned the most dramatic mission of the day. The island was only 700 yards wide in this area (the southernmost part of the pork chop's shank), and it was their job to isolate Suribachi by pushing across with all possible speed. When the far coast was reached, the entire 28th Regiment was to place itself on a line across the neck and attack the volcano. The 550-foot eminence had to be taken quickly, for it was a key position, commanding not only the beaches but about two-thirds of the island, and functioning not only as a fortress but also as an observation post. As long as the enemy held it, the movements of the bulk of the landing force could be clearly observed and the information relayed to the gun crews of widely scattered emplacements. General Kuribayashi had foreseen the attention that would be paid to Suribachi and had made it a semi-independent defense sector. It was held by about 2,000 men under Colonel Kanehiko Atsuchi. Kuribayashi had ordered the colonel and his troops simply to stand fast and to kill as many Marines as they could before they themselves were annihilated. They were told, in direct terms, to make Suribachi their tomb.

With its brushy approaches, ashen dome, and fissures and shadows, the volcano impressed the Marines as a forbidding sight. The naval bombardment was causing it to smoke in spots, but in others it was twinkling in retaliation. It was honeycombed with caves and tunnels right up to its summit, but its heaviest defenses were in a semicircle on the landward side of its base. The bombardment had given these special attention, but many were still strong. In their rapid push across the neck, the Marines bypassed the base defenses, their left flank remaining about 400 yards out. They were concerned mainly with the defenses in front of them, which began in earnest about halfway across the neck and continued thick to the opposite shore. As the men advanced, Suribachi looked down on them and its occupants peppered them with the fire of both light and heavy weapons. They also took punishment from their right flank, since they exposed it by pushing ahead of the

Marines operating against the airfield. This part of the invasion had all the aspects of a suicide mission.

The battalion tried to maintain a uniform two-company front, but this field-manual formation was quickly disrupted. Shellbursts ripped up and down the lines, and small-arms fire zigzagged everywhere. Dozens of men fell dead or wounded. Whole squads were pinned down, while others managed to slog on through. Some of the bunkers and pillboxes were assaulted; others were bypassed. Soon the companies were strung out in two battered columns. The dead remained where they fell. The wounded were dragged into holes, treated by corpsmen, and then left. The helpless had a worry beyond their wounds. The Japanese, although mostly unseen, were everywhere: in the bunkers and pillboxes and in trench systems and antitank ditches. It meant death—quite possibly a slow one—to fall into their hands. Even areas in which all of the enemy had been killed could not be considered permanently cleared. "When we secured a pillbox," recalled Sergeant Al C. Eutsey, "we would put up a white flag to signify it had been taken care of. I looked into several of these and saw no sign of life. A little later these same pillboxes opened fire again. The Japs could maneuver everywhere by means of underground passageways." Eutsey soon learned something that Marines all over Iwo were learning, much to their dismay, at about the same time. "The Japs had their mortars zeroed in on some of the trenches they had dug, and on some of the shell craters. When these trenches and craters were filled with Marines, they would open fire, killing and wounding many."

Both company commanders became casualties. One was shot through the knee; the other, who had unholstered his .45 pistol and joined the men in the assault, received a fatal wound in the throat. One of the company executive officers was also hit, taking a disabling crease in the back of the neck.

Despite the resistance, the losses, and the disorganization, the island's isthmus was crossed. The first Marines to reach the cliff overlooking the western beach were six members of B Company under Lieutenant Frank J. Wright. The time was 10:30 A.M., only ninety minutes after H-hour. These men were quickly joined by a fragment of C Company under Lieutenant Wesley C. Bates. The crossing had been completed so fast that an American destroyer firing at the western cliffs, unaware the Marines were there, sent in two rounds that struck just below the spot where three men were digging in.

By this time the 1st Battalion's A Company, which had landed in reserve but was right behind the first two companies, had been commit-

ted to the attack. Before the company got off the beach, its radio operator went down with a shattered foot. Setting up the radio where he fell,
the man used it to good advantage until he passed out. There were
other early casualties. A platoon leader who pushed up on the first
terrace ahead of his men turned around and shouted, "You'd better get
the hell up here if you want to win this war." A moment later he was
lying dead. One A Company man, Corporal Tony Stein, quickly set
about winning the Medal of Honor. Armed with an aircraft machine
gun he had secured in the Hawaiian Islands and made into a hand
weapon, Stein exposed himself fearlessly to seek out enemy positions,
and he covered his platoon's advance with torrents of fire. His single-
handed attacks accounted for at least twenty of the enemy.

More and more Marines filtered through to the west coast, and by
noon the operation to isolate Mount Suribachi was assured of success.
The fighting and mopping up, however, would continue for the rest of
the day.

The Marines to the north had continued to suffer as they worked their
way inland, and conditions along the beaches were worsening. Beach-
masters and their crews, which included Seabees, were striving to get
things organized, but a chain of destruction was forming at the water's
edge. Useless landing vessels, trucks, jeeps, and other pieces of heavy
equipment were settling haphazardly into the surf-soaked sand. Hostile
shellfire was not the only cause of this rapidly mounting congestion. As
jeeps and trucks emerged from their landing craft they often bogged
down in the sand before clearing the ramp. Unless a tractor was on hand
to tow a stranded vehicle free at once, the landing craft, its bow pinned
to the beach, usually broached and swamped. To further complicate
matters, the sea was beginning to rise. One of the enemy's most spectacular achievements against the beach activities centered upon a 5th
Division rocket section. As the four truck-mounted launchers rolled
from their vessels they were brought under artillery fire, and three
were quickly blasted out of commission. The survivor, however, soon
loosed a ripple into the slopes of Suribachi and caused a monstrous
explosion. The Marines on the beach, assuming that one of the enemy's
ammunition dumps had been destroyed, gave a long cheer.

The invasion's artillery was only now preparing to land, but the tanks
had been coming in since midmorning. In spite of the stability provided
by their tracks, some of the machines had trouble clearing their landing-craft ramps. Once ashore, all were plagued by congestion, land
mines, the soft sand of the terraces, and antitank fire. A man on the
beach in the 4th Division zone who watched one of the tanks start

inland explained later: "It was trying to edge over the first terrace when it was hit by a mortar that blew off its right tread. Marines began trying to get out of the turret. Another mortar lit right on the turret. The tank spread apart a little. All the Marines were killed." A number of tanks were lost, but some waddled into action.

Conditions on the beach were a serious impediment to the landing of supplies. Only such high-priority items as ammunition, communications equipment, medical supplies, rations, and water were being brought in. Amphibian tractors and amphibian trucks (some of them Army) and "weasels," which were small boatlike tracked vehicles without ramps, proved invaluable at this time. Instead of unloading on the beach, many took their precious cargoes directly to the front, often bringing back casualties.

The Navy doctors and corpsmen had set up their aid stations on the beach against the first terrace, a place of scant security. These teams themselves suffered casualties, and the Marine casualties from the front were sometimes wounded again or killed. In the 5th Division zone, Navy Lieutenant Paul Bradley, a regimental chaplain, moved among the wounded men, stopping beside each to utter a few words of comfort. He knelt by one Marine just as a stray bullet entered the man's side. Father Bradley did not flinch, but the words of comfort he had begun were supplanted by the administration of last rites. As usual, the Marines who died were gathered in groups and shrouded with their ponchos.

General Kuribayashi was following the progress of the battle from the headquarters blockhouse above his living quarters at Iwo's northern end. He was in contact with all of the units on the island, and also with Imperial Headquarters in Tokyo. In one of his first messages to Japan, the general stated that the Iwo Jima garrison was donating 125,000 yen to the national treasury. As soon as the invasion had become a fact and the men had no more use for their currency, they had burned it. Kuribayashi also reported on the garrison's bravery, citing individuals for special acts and recommending them for posthumous promotion. The general would continue this policy throughout the battle.

Early afternoon found the attack progressing only a yard or two at a time. The island's isthmus had been crossed, but this had done nothing to weaken the territory extending northward. The first airfield, about 700 yards in from the beach, was still in enemy hands, and the 25th Marines had not taken the ridge and cliff area that overlooked the landing zone on the right. Japanese shellfire remained the chief deterrent to the advance. Although bullets were thick and punishing, the

Japanese from whose weapons they came could be spotted and destroyed. The origins of the artillery and mortar shells and the shrieking rockets were more of a mystery, many coming from far off.

When the fleet began landing the first reserve battalions at about 2:00 P.M., they got a hotter reception than the assault troops. Among the watchers from the sea at this time was Colonel John Letcher, corps artillery commander and coordinator of all the invasion's support fire. Letcher was aboard Harry Schmidt's command ship, the *Auburn*, and he had been called on deck by Colonel Edward Craig, the corps operations officer, who said, "Look at that artillery fire falling on that beach. Did you ever see anything like it?" Letcher was duly awed, and he later recounted: "The Japanese were raining shells of all sizes upon the beach which were sending geysers of dust and sand into the air. Several fires had been started in piles of ammunition and supplies, and flames and smoke were pouring upward from these. Numbers of boats and vehicles had been hit and their wreckage was strewn along the beach and in the water. The enemy on top of Mount Suribachi were looking right down on the beach and could give explicit directions to their artillery in regard to where our forces were presenting the best targets, and the artillery was certainly making good use of the information. The enemy shelling which I had seen in other operations was as nothing compared to this and I wondered if any of our people on the beach were going to survive."

Fourth Division troops pouring ashore on D-day.

Similar thoughts were entertained by other shipboard observers, among them nearly a hundred news correspondents—American, British, and Australian—representing wire services, radio networks, and magazines. Some of these people had covered other invasions, both in the Pacific and in the war's European theater, and they found this battle unique not only in its fury but also in its setting. All areas of the field could be taken in with one sweeping glance. They watched America's first penetration of Japan's home territory as they might have watched a football game. Of course, the correspondents themselves were located within the battle's arena; they were part of the fleet that was lobbing in shells, and whose aircraft were making darting attacks on Suribachi and the northern cliffs toward which elements of the 25th Marines were fighting.

Between the viewers and the shoreline plied innumerable landing craft, some heading in with troops and equipage, others coming out with cargoes of wounded. The wreckage on the beach was outlined against the first terrace, and one observer thought the scene looked like a long line of frame houses that had been hit by a tornado. The shore parties and other men on the beach could be discerned, the latter including artillery crews who were trying to get their weapons into position for firing. Tanks looking like beetles moved about behind the lines and at the front. The frontline troops were harder to see, but some could be picked out with good glasses.

Not all of the news people were content to watch from a distance. Robert Sherrod started for shore at about five o'clock. He had been preceded by a few others, among them Keith Wheeler of the *Chicago Times.* Wheeler was returning to the fleet to write his D-day story at the same time Sherrod was starting in, and they met. "I wouldn't go in there if I were you," said Wheeler. "There's more hell in there than I've seen in the rest of this war put together." But Sherrod went in. Later he tried to analyze what made men, military personnel included, expose themselves to battlefield perils voluntarily. He concluded that the impulse had little to do with lofty ideals such as the desire to help preserve liberty but was largely the product of pride, mutual sympathy, a sense of duty, and the instinct for self-defense. "The most important of these was pride—personal pride, pride of unit, and pride of country (the latter seemed quite remote, it had to be added)." Sherrod landed in the 4th Division zone at dusk, and while hurrying inland to seek a site for his foxhole he passed about twenty slain Marines. "The smell of death was wafted lightly through the cool evening air."

On the extreme right of the 4th Division zone, Jumpin' Joe Chambers and his 3rd Battalion ghouls were now among the defenses on the high ground they had been fighting toward all day. Their ranks had been thinned both by casualties and disorganization until only 150 effectives were left of the 900 that had begun the trek. Nineteen of the battalion's officers had been felled. As the ghouls fought to hold the heights, their weapons flashing in the gathering darkness, they continued to suffer. But soon relief troops came up behind, and the weary, dusty, dry-mouthed men, some wearing bandages over light wounds, began with-drawing a hundred yards to the rear, where perhaps they would be a little safer than at the front. The battalion's losses in dead had not been tallied, but the survivors knew they were high, and that many a ten-thousand-dollar check would "go home to the folks."

The fleet had landed additional 4th and 5th Division reserves late in the day, and about 40,000 Americans were now ashore. Although the beachhead was relatively secure, it was less than half as deep as the landing plan called for. Casualties for the day were about 2,500 killed, wounded, or missing, plus another hundred combat-fatigue victims.

24

A Flag for Suribachi

======As always, the Marines fretted to see night settle over terrain that was completely unfamiliar to them and known intimately to the enemy. Many a man who had spent the daylight hours hoping and praying he would survive the battle was now concerned only with getting through the hours of darkness. The temperature soon dropped to about sixty degrees and seemed lower to the Americans after their months of duty in warmer climes. Those who had laid aside their packs and blanket rolls to enhance their mobility now regretted the act; their thin dungarees did not keep out the chill. The rations in the packs, however, were missed by few; there was little craving for food in stomachs heavy with apprehension. Even some of the reassurance provided by the fleet had been lost; many of the vessels had withdrawn to night stations, and the carriers had reclaimed their planes. Remaining behind was a scattering of hospital, supply, and gunfire support ships. Mortar-armed gunboats concentrated their fire on the high ground dominating the 4th Division beaches, while destroyers with searchlights looked for targets on Suribachi and along the coasts. The destroyers also kept the island illuminated with star shells, which had the usual effect of making it easy for the Marines to spot the enemy's movements but also caused false alarms by making inanimate objects seem to move.

Holland Smith, at this time on board Kelly Turner's flagship, had notified his subordinates on the island to be prepared for a large-scale counterattack this first night. "We will welcome a counterattack. That is generally when we break their backs." But Kuribayashi's orders prevailed, and there was no big attack. There were infiltrations only, accompanied by a continuation of the shellfire, with pyrotechnics added. Most fearsome of the missiles were the 675-pound spigot mortars that screeched as they wobbled through the air and burst so heavily they shook the earth over a wide area. Hardly less jarring were the 550-pound rockets launched in the north from crude wooden troughs. Neither of these giant projectiles was very accurate, and the enemy's supply of both was limited. Most of the smaller missiles—rockets, mortars, and artillery shells—were amply stocked and were used at night almost as effectively as in the day.

Numbers of men were hit as they lay in their holes. Some were tormented for a time by near misses before the big one dropped in with them, the power of its burst increased by the confines of the hole. One of the shells struck the command post of the 1st Battalion, 23rd Marines, instantly killing the battalion commander and his operations officer. There were hundreds of narrow escapes. One Marine literally had his hair parted by a mortar shell; a large fragment sliced through his helmet from front to rear, almost halving it. Sergeant Howard T. Olson, an unscathed survivor, later wrote home: "All we could do was huddle in our foxholes and pray. And when I say pray, I mean exactly that. This went for enlisted men and officers alike. The fire provided my foxhole with scalloped edges."

The enemy gunners did not neglect the shoreline, where the landing of supplies continued amid the wreckage. On the Yellow and Blue Beaches, the fire became so heavy that they were closed at eleven o'clock. Farther south, a limited number of landing craft still operated, and bulldozers went on with their work of freeing bogged equipment, digging revetments, and making roads. The landing craft exchanged their supplies for wounded men lying on stretchers at the base of the first terrace, blankets over them and their faces white in the star-shell light. Among the landing craft were amphibian trucks, or "ducks," some of which belonged to the Army. One of these vehicles churned up on the beach just north of Suribachi and encountered Marine Supply Sergeant Ray Dooley. The driver suggested that the load of supplies be taken inland and added, "You lead us, Sarge!" Dooley climbed aboard and the duck clattered up the terraces and made a sweep behind the front lines, with Dooley and the crew tossing out rations, water, and ammunition as they went, leaving the materials in a long trail across the sand. Back on the beach, Dooley helped the crew load the duck with wounded, and it headed out toward a hospital ship.

As for the growing supply dumps on the beach, they were imperiled by more than shellfire. Kuribayashi had organized "wolfpacks" of three or four men each, their mission to slip through the Marine lines and blow up the fuel and ammunition deposits with hand grenades. One of these teams reached a 4th Division dump that held two boatloads of ammunition, gasoline, and flamethrower fuel. The pile went up with a great roar accompanied by a sheet of fire that could be seen all over the island and far asea, and the concussion collapsed foxholes for yards around. A Navy doctor and a Marine major sharing a hole were buried, and they nearly suffocated before managing to crawl free amid the red glare of the flames and the din and debris of the secondary explosions.

The strongest attempt at infiltration in the customary way was made in the zone occupied by the 27th Marines, at the southern end of the first airfield. A hundred or more Japanese started down the runway and were met by a hail of rifle and machine-gun bullets, augmented by a barrage from the artillery of the 13th Marines. Those Japanese not killed or disabled slipped back into the holes that had produced them.

In other areas, infiltrators came by water as well as by land. A Seabee on watch at the shoreline was looking out over the surf when a log came floating down from the north, borne past by the current. It seemed harmless enough, but then it made a sharp turn. The Seabee opened fire, and a dead Japanese rolled off, later washing up on the beach. Those Marines on the cliff overlooking the western shore near Suribachi were surprised to see a barge full of enemy soldiers push out from the volcano's base and come northward along the coast. The vessel nudged up on the beach just below the Americans, and the infiltration attempt was summarily ended. In numerous spots about the beachhead, there were the usual hand-to-hand encounters, with all of their characteristic noise, confusion, and bloodshed.

Not all of the infiltrators had destruction and slaughter on their minds. There were those like Tadayoshi Koizumi, whose job was reconnaissance. He had spent a long day at his antiaircraft gun north of the landing beaches, and had retired to his night shelter only to be ordered to "take three men and reconnoiter the enemy around the southern coast." Exchanging solemn farewells with comrades, the patrol picked its way among rocks, sand ridges, and patches of brush, trying to avoid the light of the star shells and the searchlights of the destroyers. The four men were amazed at how the terrain had been changed by the enemy's naval shells since they had last seen it. With a few bullets cracking over their heads and an occasional shell from their own forces falling near them, they managed to slip through the American lines to a spot on one of the terraces overlooking the southern beach, where the landing activities had continued. Inching closer, they neared a hole in which a black Seabee was standing guard. The man was armed with a BAR, whose trigger he fingered nervously as he studied the shadows about him, his ebony features highlighted by a star shell. He did not see them. "We were armed with hand grenades," Koizumi recalled, "but it was our duty to return to our own lines without challenging the enemy." They eased away, making it safely to the edge of home territory. Here an American shell exploded near them, and one man was badly injured. The others carried him to a shelter that held a doctor, then went to their own shelter, where they reported on the landing activities and received the congratulations of their comrades for making it back alive.

For the Americans, the night dragged wretchedly. Between the repeated alarms and the chilly temperature, many men were often obliged to grit their teeth to keep them from chattering. It was nearly dawn before a degree of quiet settled over the island. Robert Sherrod, whose personal trials included a near miss by a half-pound piece of hot shrapnel that invaded his foxhole, reported that "the first night on Iwo Jima can only be described as a nightmare in hell."

With the coming of the blessed daylight, the Marines were encouraged to see the fleet reassembling in full strength in the waters offshore, and the renewed movements of the smaller vessels indicated that the landing activities were being pressed in spite of enemy fire and a high surf. But the debris along the two-mile landing zone had thickened to such an extent that incoming vessels had serious trouble finding places to beach. Lying every few yards was a wrecked or bogged Higgins boat, amtrac, tank, halftrack, or jeep. Some had been flipped over by mines or heavy shells. Bulldozers and tractors sat crippled on roadways they had been building, and cranes brought in to unload cargo lay on their sides or reached up at impossible angles. Also scattered about were water cans, ammunition boxes, rifles, gas masks, packs, blankets, ponchos, toilet articles, and letters and photos from home. Many of these things were torn by shrapnel or riddled by bullets, and, commonly, they were splotched with bloodstains turned brown. Some of the surf-washed dead were now almost wholly covered by sand. Here and there, all that showed of a corpse was a foot or an upstretched hand. Most of these bodies would be retrieved; those lost would help swell the total of "missing in action." At dawn special efforts were launched to evacuate casualties it had not been possible to take out during the night. In spite of the many problems, a system was being established. Several LSTs doubling as hospital ships lay about 2,000 yards offshore to receive emergency cases and serve as control centers. The regular hospital ships were farther out. Auxiliary facilities were provided by some of the troop and cargo vessels.

The morning of February 20 saw the battle for Iwo Jima develop into two distinct operations. In the extreme south, the three battalions of the 28th Marines, 5th Division, occupied a line across the island facing southward toward Suribachi. Just to their north, or behind them, the 26th and 27th Regiments of the 5th were arced across the southern tip of the first airport, in preparation for a drive northward. On the right, or northern, flank of these regiments, the three regiments of the 4th Division—the 23rd, 24th, and 25th Marines—were also set for a northerly swing, their left at the airport and their right anchored in the cliff area near the eastern beach. The 3rd Division, made up of the 3rd, 9th,

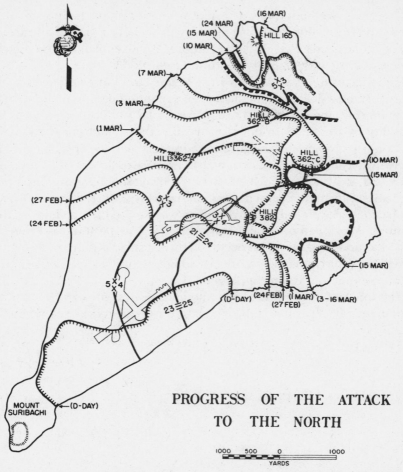

(16 MAR)

(24 MAR)
(15 MAR)
(10 MAR)

HILL 165

(7 MAR)

5 X 3

(3 MAR)

HILL
362-B

(1 MAR)

HILL 362-A

HILL
362-C

(10 MAR)

(15 MAR)

(27 FEB)

5 X 3

(24 FEB)

3 X 9

HILL
382

21 ≡ 24

(15 MAR)

5 X 4

(D-DAY) (24 FEB) (1 MAR) (3 - 16 MAR)
(27 FEB)

23 ≡ 25

MOUNT
SURIBACHI

(D-DAY)

PROGRESS OF THE ATTACK
TO THE NORTH

1000   500   0   1000
YARDS

and 21st Regiments, was still in floating reserve. Kelly Turner and
Holland Smith hoped that the 3rd Division would not be needed on
Iwo, that it could be saved for the Okinawa operation, scheduled to
follow.

The artillery, naval gunfire, and air preparation for the attack on
Suribachi and the drive northward began soon after daybreak. The
front lines were marked with panels of white cloth so the airmen would
not bomb and strafe the Marines, an idea that worked well except in
those areas where the enemy sneaked out and stole the panels. Even
during the bombardment, some of the Japanese managed to fire back.
On the Suribachi front, Platoon Sergeant James Elmore and Corporal
Jack Charles were standing in a hole watching the bursts on the volcano
when Charles remembered that his legging strings needed tightening

before he moved out. "Just as I bent over to make the adjustment, an enemy shell exploded within a few feet of the hole. I looked up and saw that the blast had killed Sergeant Elmore." Charles had to overcome his shock in short order, for it was time to get going.

The attacks north and south were begun simultaneously at 8:30 but were instantly slowed as the Japanese responded with a deluge of artillery, mortar, and small-arms fire. A particular problem at first was the inability of the tanks to operate because their maintenance sections were not yet ashore. According to the special action report of C Company, 5th Tank Battalion, attached to the troops attacking southward: "We had eight tanks to place in action, but no fuel or ammunition was available. Salvaging from knocked-out tanks was started. A heavy mortar barrage was placed upon us and we were forced to move to another position. Work had no sooner started in the new position and the barrage was upon us again. This occurred three times, as there was no place which we could move where we would not be under direct observation by the enemy on Mount Suribachi."

The left half of the line facing the volcano was in open sand, while the right half threaded through patches of ragged vegetation. The

37-millimeter gun firing on Mount Suribachi.

terrain leading to the base was a wasteland of sand, broken rocks, and extensions of the stunted brush. Although the heaviest defenses were in a fringe of green at the base, the cave and tunnel entrances scattered up the barren slopes held some light artillery pieces, mortars, and machine guns. Each entrance was also a fine observation post. The Marines could be seen even when they jumped into shellholes. Tactically, the problem at Suribachi was a simple one. Lieutenant Colonel Robert Williams, executive officer of the 28th, expressed it this way: "A frontal attack; surround the base; locate a route up; then climb it!" The hard part was the frontal attack.

It was being made with the 2nd Battalion on the left and the 3rd on the right, the two units spanning the neck from coast to coast. The 1st Battalion, which had made the dash across the neck the previous day, was in reserve but was not idle; it was mopping up behind the lines. At the front, the tanks joined the fight at about 11:00 A.M. In firing positions not far behind them were the 37-millimeter guns and 75-millimeter halftracks of the regimental weapons company. From the rear, artillery missions were fired in close succession by the 3rd Battalion, 13th Marines. Ships on both flanks lobbed in shells, and the carrier planes continued their runs. Suribachi rumbled, quaked, smoked, and spewed up debris; but the Japanese managed to keep firing back, and by noon the attack had gained no more than seventy-five yards. Only about 125 yards would be added during the afternoon.

Better progress was made by the 5th Division units attacking northward, their left flank on the west coast and their right about 1,000 yards inland. Much of this terrain was relatively open. Although it led to the main cross-island defenses, it was not amenable to heavy fortification. Scattered bunkers and pillboxes, however, took their toll, as did artillery and mortar barrages. Land mines were also encountered. These Marines shed their share of blood, but gained 800 yards by the day's end.

Attacking up the center of the island on the 5th Division's right, the 4th Division's left wing suffered heavy casualties but by noon reached the north end of the first airport. This wing now faced the southern tip of the second airport and the first line of cross-island defenses. The 4th Division's right wing, having come ashore on the beaches farthest north, was already facing the first of the cross-island defenses when the attack opened at 8:30. On the eastern shore, these began on the cliffs Jumpin' Joe Chambers and his ghouls had reached the previous evening. The nature of this coastal ground was regarded with astonishment by Captain Frederic A. Stott of the 1st Battalion, 24th Marines, the unit that had bolstered the battered ghouls during the night: "At the water's

Artillery spotters at work in shellhole near first airfield.

edge were giant rocks which, after a short space of level terrain, rose in a cliff line to the table land on top. This lower shore area was sufficiently rugged with a plentiful supply of caves, small canyons, and fixed fortifications. But atop the cliff the terrain almost defied passage. Trees and vines twisted in confused fashion over an area in which erosion and excavation had created cuts, dips, rises, and pinnacles which made direct-line progress impossible. Rock piles and dirt mounds jutted everywhere, and no man could be certain that the ground ten feet to his front was devoid of Japs." This wing of the attack made few gains.

Unknown to most Americans ashore, the day saw efforts made to reinforce them with the 21st Marines of the 3rd Division. The high brass had decided that this regiment, at least, was needed in the present fight and could not be saved for Okinawa. The men were boated, but a rising wind, coupled with the nearly impossible conditions on the beach, caused the operation to be canceled.

Not canceled was the landing of additional artillery units; their support had been urgently requested by the officers at the front. The 105-millimeter howitzers of the 3rd and 4th Battalions of the 14th Marines, an arm of the 4th Division, had come to Iwo in ducks sitting in the holds of LSTs. All of the 3rd Battalion ducks made it off the ramp and into the rough water safely, but the 4th Battalion was less fortunate. Eight of its ducks swamped and sank, and a dozen men were lost with the guns. During the landing the ducks were menaced by enemy fire and beach congestion, and the unlucky 4th lost two more by broaching. Of its original twelve guns, only two remained to go into action. LST 779 took four heavier guns—155-millimeter howitzers of John Letcher's corps artillery—directly ashore, ramming its bow through the wreckage of Red Beach 1. The vessel's huge doors creaked open, its ramp rattled down, and tractors with cables not only pulled the 2.5-ton weapons out on the beach but also managed to work them up the terraces and across the island to the 5th Division zone near the west coast.

The day's gains, which gave the Americans control of about one-fourth of the island, had cost them nearly another 1,000 men in killed or wounded. An added detriment to morale was that no one knew how many of the enemy had been slain, since only a few hundred bodies were visible for counting.

The second night of the battle was a repetition of the first. Star shells floated down under their silk parachutes and created their ghostly light, and artillery, rocket, and mortar barrages from both sides screeched and roared and rumbled; sometimes the entire island seemed to be shaking. Either by a Japanese shell or by infiltration, a large ammunition dump on the beach was ignited, setting off another spectacular fire-works display. The explosions and waves of flame rose and fell for perhaps an hour, bathing the island with a flickering redness that, more than ever, made it resemble the popular conception of hell.

Japanese infiltrations amounting to minor counterattacks were repulsed in both the 4th and 5th Division zones, one with the aid of fire from the destroyer *Henry A. Wiley*. Individual infiltrators, often illumined by the star shells, were busy everywhere. A 4th Division Marine was appalled to see a spectral figure rushing toward his foxhole, a rifle with fixed bayonet thrust forward. The Marine did not have his own rifle ready, but he had a hand grenade. There was no time to pull the pin. He simply threw the missile with all his might. It caught the charging Japanese squarely on the chest, and he drew up with a loud grunt, threw his rifle at the Marine, and turned and fled. Even more unnerving was the experience of another Marine in the same area. An enemy soldier slipped into his hole and was so near he had to react with his bare hands. Getting a grip on the man's throat, he started to shut off his air. The result was a scream that so startled the Marine he let go, and the Japanese darted away. Some of the infiltrators were successful at inflicting harm, as were many of the enemy's shells. Medical corpsmen risked their lives hurrying about in answer to cries for their help, aid station personnel piled sandbags higher around the revetments that held rows of the wounded on stretchers, and bone-tired doctors rose from their sandy night berths to minister to new cases as they were brought in.

Dawn of February 21, D-plus-2, found the Marines on both fronts preparing to renew the attack. The push northward was falling into a pattern, a simple but painful one. The Marines were required to main-tain a dogged frontal advance against heavy resistance, with no indica-tion that conditions would soon change. In the south, however, a climax was fast approaching; the American lines were now only about 200 yards from Suribachi's main defenses. At this distance the volcano loomed up ponderously, and some of the debris from the pre-attack bombardment winged toward the men in their foxholes. This morning all three battalions of the 28th were on the line; the 1st had been assigned a one-company front on the far right. As the bombardment ended with a forty-plane strike against Suribachi's base, rockets slammed into the defenses and into the rocks and brush with such a terrific noise and concussion that the Marines in their holes were tem-porarily deafened. The volcano was hidden by clouds of smoke, dust, rocks, banyan branches, and shreds of enemy equipment. When the planes darted away across the water, a relative silence fell. Some of the Marines stood up and began looking anxiously toward the rear for the attack's tank support, but no tanks were in sight. Once again these important machines had been delayed by refueling and rearming diffi-culties.

It was 8:25, time for the Marines to jump off. All along the 700-yard front they began to leave their holes. Those on the beaches, east and west, simply started walking toward Suribachi's flanks. On the brushy western half of the island the men threaded forward cautiously, while on the open eastern half they trotted from shellhole to shellhole. For a few moments the hulking fortress remained still. Then it began to react. First came the crack of rifles and the chatter of machine guns. This quickly grew to a heavy rattle, and bullets snapped about in wild patterns, the ricochets whining. Then the mortars started coming, some of them visible as they made their high arcs, and shortly much of the front was being blanketed by roaring geysers of steel and sand. It was as though the volcano's ancient bowels had come to life.

Some parts of the line were staggered, but most kept edging forward. The resistance on the western beach proved the most manageable, and the 1st Battalion, with its one-company front, soon picked up momentum on its way to Suribachi's right flank, its intention being to swing around the base at the shoreline. All along the rest of the front the enemy's resistance remained savage. Caught up in some of the heaviest fighting on the open sand just left of the attack's center was the 2nd Battalion's E ("Easy") Company under Captain Dave E. Severance. First Lieutenant J. Keith Wells and the 3rd Platoon, on the company's right flank, had moved out first, and Second Lieutenant Edward S. Pennell and the 2nd Platoon, on the left, had started very soon afterward.

The men under Keith Wells had no sooner jumped off than four were wounded, one fatally. Corpsman Clifford R. Langley hastened to aid the casualties and was himself peppered with mortar fragments. Up ahead, some of the company's hole-hopping groups soon neared the belt of defenses in the brush fringe, and they found a degree of hope in the sight of the destruction that had been wrought by the Navy's guns and planes. But as the men began to rush the first defenses they discovered there were still plenty of live Japanese among them.

Sergeant Henry O. Hansen and PFC Donald J. Ruhl, who had been charging in the lead with Wells, ran to the top of a silent, sand-covered pillbox and promptly clashed with several of the enemy in a network of trenches behind it. While the two Marines were emptying their rifles at these men, a demolitions charge came flying through the air and landed on the sand in front of them. Shouting, "Look out, Hank!," Ruhl dived on the charge and absorbed its full blast. Hansen, who had recoiled back off the mound, was spattered with blood and bits of flesh. With the mound between him and the enemy, the sergeant reached up and grasped Ruhl by the foot. Wells, who was crouching nearby, quickly ordered, "Leave him alone. He's dead." The lieutenant had seen Ruhl's arm fly back and reveal a gory cavity where his chest had been. The sacrifice earned Ruhl the Medal of Honor.

Wells's 1st Squad, led by Sergeant Howard M. Snyder, was moving up on the left flank of the pillbox now, and these men took up the fight. The Japanese had begun to scurry back and forth through the trenches, talking excitedly, and one man seemed to be issuing commands as though trying to organize a counterattack. Snyder and Corporal Harold P. Keller began to lob grenades into the trenches, while PFC James A. Robeson and PFC Louie Adrian, the latter a Spokane Tribe Indian, took turns firing with their BARs. One man would stand up and shoot until he had emptied his weapon; then the other would jump up and the first would duck to reload. After Snyder and Keller had thrown all the grenades the squad had, Wells tossed them his own and ordered more passed up to them. The combination of grenades and bullets took their toll, and no counterattack developed. But now Louie Adrian, while standing erect and firing into the trenches, took a bullet through the heart. His BAR kept chugging as he crumpled to the sand.

By this time the platoon's 2nd and 3rd Squads were moving in among the leading attackers, and BAR man PFC Leo Rozek took Adrian's place. A Marine carrying a light machine gun entered the platoon's zone, and Wells placed him on the line. He began to make it hot for the entrenched Japanese but was soon shot dead. Several others who tried to man the gun were shot away from it, and the gun itself was knocked out. During these moments a bunker just ahead of the platoon began emitting a profusion of hand grenades. Many of the men were pinned down by the blasts, and not much could be done about them. Rifle fire was ineffective, the platoon was out of grenades of its own, and Corporal Charles W. Lindberg's assault squad, with its flamethrowers and demolitions, had not yet made its final break through the fire being laid on the sand to the rear. Wells sent two volunteers back for grenades, but they hadn't gone far before they were fatally shot, one taking a dum-dum bullet that tore up his insides.

Several members of the assault squad had got through with demolitions now, and Henry Hansen told Wells he thought he could get to the bunker with a satchel charge. "I told him to try it," the lieutenant recalled, "because we weren't getting anywhere trying to dodge those damned grenades. He took a large demolitions satchel and put in a time fuse. Then he ran at the bunker. But instead of placing the charge at an aperture, he threw it—and missed. We all had to duck, because when that C-2 went off it rocked the whole area. The dirt had hardly settled before grenades were flying like mad."

Making things worse, the volcano's mortarmen had begun to pull in some of their fire, and shells were starting to burst alarmingly close. A direct hit was soon scored on an amtrac clattering forward with supplies. Next the barrage closed in on Easy Company's 2nd Platoon, engaged in its own heavy fighting on the 3rd Platoon's left. BAR man Private Arthur J. Stanton was lying on his stomach on the sand when a shell exploded close to his feet. "The powder flash went up the legs of my pants, burning large patches of skin off my hips, and the concussion threw me about ten feet in the air." Stanton gathered his senses, ignored the pain of his burns, and stayed in action. He was about to run forward to join two of his comrades, who were lying side by side on the sand, facing the front, when he saw a shell explode between their heads, killing them instantly. The same barrage wounded Lieutenant Pennell, making it necessary for Platoon Sergeant Joseph McGarvey to take over. For his vigorous leadership during this first part of the attack, Pennell was awarded the Navy Cross.

The mortar fire was still registering only near misses in the 3rd Platoon area. One of Easy Company's communications men came running up to Keith Wells with a telephone whose wire trailed across the sand toward the rear. The lieutenant, lying in a depression with several of his men, made a report of the platoon's situation to Captain Severance. Wells looked rearward while phoning and noted that the battalion commander, Lieutenant Colonel Chandler W. Johnson, was standing conspicuously on a knoll watching the action through binoculars. "Chaney" Johnson, a heavyset, hard-driving man, was not one to worry about his security. The colonel had trained his troops to take every advantage of a battlefield's cover, but ever since coming ashore he had disregarded his own counsel. This was something the men found both paradoxical and inspirational.

In the 3rd Platoon area, Charles Lindberg shortly arrived with the rest of the assault squad, and Wells was preparing to direct the two flamethrower men against the bunker and the other busy defenses when the Japanese mortarmen got the platoon's range. One of the shells soon scored a bull's-eye, bursting among Wells and four others, wounding all five. The lieutenant, who had been lying on his stomach facing forward, was hit along the back of both legs. "My clothes were nearly all blown off me from the waist down and I was full of shrapnel." But Wells did not relinquish his command. By the time Corpsman John H. Bradley had given him first aid and injected him with morphine he learned that his legs were still usable, and he turned his attention once more to the platoon's problems. The unit had lost one-third of its number in about forty-five minutes, and the survivors were being taxed to the limit of their endurance and had only a precarious hold on the section of line they had hit.

But then the situation began to change. Braving the mortars, hand grenades, and small-arms fire, Charles Lindberg and Private Robert D. Goode moved against the bunker and the other defenses with their flamethrowers. The platoon's riflemen covered them by shooting at the menacing apertures. Sending streams of fire into every opening they could find, Lindberg and Goode began destroying dozens of the enemy. As the concealed men died amid flames and exploding ammunition, the Marines could smell them roasting, and the circumstances made the odor seem ambrosial. For his work at this point, which a comrade called "a remarkable example of cool-headed fighting," Lindberg earned the Silver Star.

Tanks were soon working along much of the regiment's front. Also moving up were the unit's halftracks and 37-millimeter guns. Farther back, the artillery and the rocket trucks sought targets up the volcano's gray slopes. Ammunition and other supplies were coming forward in amphibious vehicles, each one unloading in a hurry, picking up a group of wounded and retiring to the beach. Stretcher teams roamed the terrain just behind the front lines looking for casualties in obscure holes and taking great risks to get them to safety. The efforts at the front were becoming generally more effective. The reserve platoons had been committed, and as mortarmen, tank crews, riflemen, machine gunners, flamethrower operators, and demolitions experts of the 5th Engineer Battalion, all working together, drove wedges into the belt of mutually supporting bunkers and pillboxes, the system was disrupted and its resistance began to diminish.

During this phase of the action Keith Wells, wearing little in the way of trousers except bloody bandages, was still hobbling around directing his platoon's attack. In a lunge for cover when a Japanese machine gun fired at him, the lieutenant got sand in his wounds and they grew very painful. Corpsman Bradley gave him a second shot of morphine and made an attempt to clean and re-dress the injuries, admonishing him to head for the rear at once and have himself properly treated. But Wells remained at the front for another half-hour. Then, at last deciding he was no longer fit to command, he turned his unit over to Platoon Sergeant Ernest I. Thomas and crawled to the rear on his hands and knees. Like Edward Pennell, Wells had earned the Navy Cross.

Around noon, minor counterattacks were broken up in both the 2nd and 3rd Battalion zones, and the semicircular advance continued. First to reach Suribachi's base, soon after three o'clock, was Ernest Thomas and a few men of Easy Company's 3rd Platoon, who had been working with one of the tanks. Thomas climbed to the top of a silent bunker and waved his helmet in triumph, his blond hair gleaming, the sight a heartening one for a host of Marines to whom the past few hours had brought nothing but feelings of terror and impending doom. Chaney Johnson was watching through his binoculars, and his weatherbeaten face cracked into a smile. Suribachi's lines had been breached, and one of his companies had done it! The unit was strengthening its hold on the base defenses when the colonel came up, chewing on an unlit cigar. To Ernest Thomas he said, "Son, you've won yourself the Navy Cross. Hang on to command of that platoon." By this time Corpsman John Bradley had also earned the Navy Cross, having done a heroic job of caring for the unit's wounded. Easy Company's 3rd Platoon had established a Marine Corps decorations record. In about eight hours of fighting, its members had won a Medal of Honor, three Navy Crosses, a Silver Star, and seventeen Purple Hearts.*

The attack was now succeeding in all zones of the regimental front. The companies advancing along the east and west beaches were moving around the volcano's flanks. Although the companies of the 3rd Battalion, operating on the right of Johnson's 2nd, had not yet got through to the base, they were not far out. Their best efforts to the day's end, however, did not take them all the way in.

The attack northward had seen the best gains made by the 5th Division Marines moving up the west coast. The going had been rough enough, but only now were these men approaching the heavy cross-island defenses the right wing of the 4th Division had been struggling against since it landed. One man of the 5th, Captain Robert H. Dunlap, and two of the 4th, Captain Joseph J. McCarthy and Sergeant Ross F. Gray, joined Donald Ruhl in winning the Medal of Honor. These men, however, managed to stay alive. The high decoration was awarded with unusual frequency in this battle. The day's gains on all fronts increased American holdings to a strong one-third of the island. Again approximately 1,000 casualties had been sustained, bringing the total for the three days to about 4,500.

It began raining in the evening, but that did not stop twenty-five *kamikaze* planes from hitting the invasion fleet. They managed to bomb or ram five vessels, inflicting varying degrees of damage. The worst casualties were two of the aircraft carriers. The *Saratoga* suffered more than 300 killed or wounded, and was so badly damaged she had to head for Pearl Harbor. The *Bismarck Sea*, swept by fires that could not be contained, exploded and sank, and over 200 of her crew were lost in the dark, rain-swept waters. All of the enemy planes were either shot down or destroyed themselves in ramming. Not a single pilot survived. At this stage of the war, Japan's *kamikaze* corps was becoming a formidable weapon. It was in a class by itself. Ordinarily, when a nation develops a new weapon it is soon copied by other nations, but Japan's new weapon was to remain unique. As one American naval officer put it: "Nobody else is going to get the *kamikaze* boys, because nobody else is built that way."

It was still raining when dawn came on February 22, D-plus-3. Suribachi's peak was cloaked in a restless fog, portions of which rolled down over the crater's rim and gathered in the higher fissures. Inside the volcano, and in the base defenses not yet overrun, were some eight or

*The author was a corporal in this platoon and the recipient of one of the day's Purple Hearts.

nine hundred Japanese, many bearing flamethrower burns and other wounds, all aware the end was near. Some squatted near candles to make final entries in diaries or to write letters they hoped might in some way reach their families. Colonel Atsuchi sent a radio report of conditions to General Kuribayashi, requesting permission to take the survivors out in a grand *banzai* charge. In his reply, the general ignored the request, saying curtly, "I had imagined the first airfield would be overrun quickly, but what has happened to cause Mount Suribachi to fall in only three days?" Kuribayashi would have been surprised to know that Holland Smith, headquartered offshore, was dissatisfied with the American performance and was starting to send corps commander Harry Schmidt, also still afloat, messages such as, "Should somebody be relieved?" The Marines at the front would have been surprised too. They had a tremendous respect for Howlin' Mad, but this was one occasion when they would not have appreciated being pushed.

That day the three battalions of the 28th Regiment tightened their grip on Suribachi's base, with the 3rd doing the heaviest work. The rain continued, and the low-hanging clouds amplified the roar of battle. At one time during the bloody activities a Marine officer who could speak Japanese took a loudspeaker into the front lines and called upon the surviving defenders to surrender; but, as usual, the appeal was ignored. By the end of the day the fight for the volcano was largely won. The network of caves in the dome still held a few hundred live defenders, but the front and flanks of the base had been occupied in strength, while patrols from the flanks had met at the water's edge in the rear. That evening a message from Holland Smith filtered down to the commander of the 28th, Colonel Harry Liversedge: "You must take Mount Suribachi tomorrow. The success of the whole operation is hanging in the balance." Liversedge told his staff, "Tomorrow we start climbing."

The day had been an especially bad one for the regiments attacking northward, all of which were now either enmeshed in, or approaching the fringe of, the main cross-island defenses. By midmorning the settling clouds made it impossible for the carrier planes to operate, and rain and patches of fog also caused visibility problems for the tanks. Several were crippled by land mines or gunfire. As the infantry started forward, bullets streaked from sodden mounds and misty hillside caves and crevices, and artillery and mortar shells accompanied the rain from the clouds. Along most of the line, casualties were far out of proportion to gains, and the loss among officers was particularly high.

The 21st Regiment of the 3rd Division, after failing in its attempt to land on D-plus-1, had come in on D-plus-2 and had been emplaced in the center, between the two original divisions. These men were on a heavily fortified slope leading to the southern end of the second airfield. Their best efforts in their uphill fight advanced their irregular front from fifty to 250 yards and cost them dearly. One company was so badly battered it had to be relieved. The 21st was facing some of the best troops on the island, the 145th Regiment under Colonel Masuo Ikeda, whose defenses included artillery bunkers with guns sited to fire straight down the runways the Marines were trying to take.

The day did see a heartening development in the zone occupied by the 25th Marines near the east coast. Jumpin' Joe Chambers and his 3rd Battalion ghouls, still in action in spite of the heavy casualties they had suffered on D-day, caught about 200 of the enemy in the open, men driven from their hillside defenses by a shattering rocket barrage. The ghouls shot down many of them as they scrambled for new cover. This was doubtless the heaviest blow struck against a group of Japanese in the open since the battle began. But a few hours later Jumpin' Joe himself took a bullet through the collarbone. The wound was serious, but the colonel was another Marine who won the Medal of Honor and kept his life.

Supply operations as seen from the bow of an LCI rammed up on the beach.

The day's surf conditions made it extremely hazardous for the smaller landing craft to operate, and the evacuation of casualties was impeded. Scores of the unfortunate men were obliged to spend long hours lying on their stretchers in the rain, ponchos tucked about them and helmets tipped over their faces. But the landing of equipment and supplies from the larger craft, which rammed up on the beach and were unloaded through their bow doors, was accomplished at a good pace, and the work was continued after dark. That night the number of heavy support vessels lying off Iwo diminished as Task Force 58 left for another strike against Japan, to be followed by one against Okinawa.

February 23, D-plus-4, dawned clear. The sunshine would not last, but the encroaching overcast would at least be thin. This was the morning that Harry Liversedge wanted the 28th Marines to "start climbing," but there was a problem. Although Mount Suribachi was only 550 feet high, its slopes were so steep that a cooperative move could not be made. There seemed to be only one practical route up. It lay on the northeast side, which the 2nd Battalion was facing, and so it was Chaney Johnson who got the order to "secure and occupy the summit." The colonel decided to send up an assault patrol from Easy Company, which was holding a position around the volcano's east side. Captain Dave Severance gave the job to the 3rd Platoon, led originally by Keith Wells and now by Ernest Thomas.

At about 8:00 A.M. Easy Company's executive officer, Lieutenant Harold G. Schrier, assembled the platoon, its thin ranks bolstered to forty men by a machine-gun section, and led it back around the volcano to 2nd Battalion headquarters near the northeast base. Chaney Johnson was found standing outside an improvised pup tent sipping from a steaming cup of coffee. In accord with the colonel's contempt for enemy shells and bullets, the tent was not in a sheltering hole but at ground level. While Johnson and Schrier consulted, the men were issued a replenishment of ammunition and water, and were joined by a radioman, two teams of stretcher-bearers, and a photographer, Staff Sergeant Louis R. Lowery of *Leatherneck* magazine.

Johnson gave Schrier a folded American flag that the battalion adjutant, Lieutenant George G. Wells, had brought ashore in his map case. Johnson's orders were that Schrier take his patrol to the summit, secure the crater, and raise the flag. Since he had already sent smaller patrols probing to the summit and they had returned safely, the colonel was confident the mission would succeed. The men themselves had serious misgivings as they headed for the volcano's base through flame-blackened rubble past scattered corpses, some of them Marines. But nothing happened. According to Corporal Harold Keller, the climb up the rock and ash of the slope, in spite of the caves that were passed, was "about as dangerous as a Sunday school picnic." It was a hard climb, however, and some areas had to be negotiated on hands and knees. From below, the Marines semicircling the northeast base watched the struggle, and one said, "Those guys ought to be getting flight pay." Also watching, many with binoculars, were hundreds of men of the fleet.

The patrol reached the outside of the crater's rim sometime before ten o'clock. Although the men were tensed for action as they filed over and fanned out along the inside edge, the cave entrances they spotted remained dark and silent. While half the patrol held to the rim, the other half began to press down the crater's ashy slope to probe for resistance and to look for something that could be used as a flagpole. Harold Keller, moving in the lead with his rifle ready, made the first hostile contact: "A Jap started to climb out of a deep hole, his back toward me. I fired three times from the hip, and he dropped out of sight." Now several grenades arced from nearby caves. The Marines responded with grenades of their own, some of which came flying back out of the entrances before exploding.

Even as this action continued, Corporal Robert A. Leader and PFC Leo Rozek discovered a long piece of pipe, apparently the remnant of a rain-catching system, and passed it to the summit. Waiting with the flag were Harold Schrier, Ernest Thomas, Henry Hansen, and Charles Lindberg, and they lashed it to the pole. The flag was planted at 10:20; and, seized by the wind, it began whipping proudly over the volcano. The incident had a particular significance: Mount Suribachi was the first piece of land under the direct administration of Tokyo to be captured by American forces during World War II.

Leatherneck photographer Lou Lowery put the great moment on film as the tired and unshaven observers below began pointing and shouting, "The flag's up! The flag's up!" Some men wept, while others cheered and clapped one another on the back. Chaney Johnson lifted his cap and yelled, "Hurrah! Hurrah! Hurrah!" The sensational news began spreading at once to the units all around the base and to those fighting the main battle to the north. At the water's edge near the center of the two-mile landing zone, a Navy beachmaster, Lieutenant Commander Gordon A. Hebert, turned his public-address system to its highest volume and announced the event up and down the shore and to the nearer vessels of the fleet, some of whose crews had been too busy with unloading activities to watch the patrol's ascent. Cheers were already rising on the ships near Suribachi's base and on those farther

First flag raising on Mount Suribachi as captured by *Leatherneck* photographer Lou Lowery.

out, and the growing chorus was joined by a medley of fog horns, whistles, and bells. To Gordon Hebert, the demonstration sounded "like the applause after a touchdown at a football game." Coastguardsman Chet Hack was equally impressed: "Talk about patriotism! The uproar almost shook the sky."

On the volcano's summit, which commanded a view of most of the

Americans on the island and most of the encircling ships, a few Marines waved in response to the tribute. But the flag's security was not yet assured. A set of caves near the site suddenly came to life. First a rifleman stepped out of an entrance and opened fire. Hitting no one, the man was felled by a burst from James Robeson's BAR. Next an officer charged out swinging a broken sword. Several Marines fired, and the charge became a headlong tumble. The entrances now produced a flurry of hand grenades. One landed near photographer Lou Lowery, and he was obliged to leap down the outside of the volcano. Tumbling for fifty feet before catching hold of a bush, he broke his camera but saved its film. The patrol moved against the caves with grenades and a flamethrower. By this time groups of Marines from below were arriving on the summit to assist with the mopping up, and the entrances were soon blown shut with demolitions. Scores of the enemy, some of them bearing wounds from the fighting at the base, were sealed in alive. Work of a similar nature had been started on the volcano's outer slopes.

Standing at his headquarters near the northeast base, Chaney Johnson tipped his head for another look at the banner snapping at the summit, then addressed his adjutant: "Some son of a bitch is going to want that flag for a souvenir, but he's not going to get it. That's our flag. We'd better get another one up there." The colonel had a second reason, one that was wholly practical, for replacing the first flag. It measured only fifty-four by twenty-eight inches, which restricted its morale value. At Johnson's order, Second Lieutenant A. Theodore Tuttle went to the beach looking for a bigger flag; and from LST 779 he obtained one that was eight feet long and four feet, eight inches wide. The new flag was carried up the volcano by PFC Rene A. Gagnon, formerly of Easy Company but now a battalion runner. During the climb, Gagnon met several men of Easy Company's 2nd Platoon, including Sergeant Michael Strank; and when the group reached the summit Strank took the flag, approached Lieutenant Schrier, and said: "Colonel Johnson wants this big flag run up high so every son of a bitch on this whole cruddy island can see it."

A second piece of pipe was secured, this one from partway down the outside of the volcano's north side. When the new flag was fastened, Schrier ordered that it be raised at the same moment the small one was struck. The new raisers were Michael Strank, Rene Gagnon, Navy Corpsman John Bradley, PFC Ira Hayes, Corporal Harlon H. Block, and PFC Franklin R. Sousley—all of Easy Company, although Gagnon had been detached.

It was at this time that Joe Rosenthal of the Associated Press got his classic photograph, which has been criticized by some as having been

Joe Rosenthal's shot of the second flag raising, taken for the Associated Press.

"posed," or "staged," or as depicting a "reenactment," all of which is nonsense. Rosenthal photographed the authorized replacement of a small flag with a large one, and under combat conditions. He himself described his great piece of military art as the product of a set of accidental circumstances. "The sky was overcast, but just enough sunlight fell from almost directly overhead, because it happened to be about noon, to give the figures a sculptural depth. Then the twenty-foot pipe was heavy, which meant the men had to strain to get it up, imparting that feeling of action. The wind just whipped the flag over the heads of the group, and at their feet the disrupted terrain and the broken stalks of the shrubbery exemplified the turbulence of war."

The raising of the big flag could be seen by the Marines fighting toward the north. "It made us feel good," recalled Private Donald L. Puff, "because it meant that the Japs would no longer be looking down on our backs." Approaching the beach at the time the flag went up was a landing craft carrying Holland Smith and the Secretary of the Navy, coming in for a brief visit. The sight of the colors flashing vividly on the gray peak filled both men with the deepest pride, and Forrestal said, "Holland, the raising of that flag means a Marine Corps for the next five hundred years." Captain Arthur H. Naylor, leader of one of the companies at the base, climbed the volcano with a congratulatory message from Smith and Kelly Turner. A Catholic chaplain was already preparing to say Mass at the summit, and several Marines were helping him build an altar of rocks. Nearby, Easy Company's Robert Leader found himself talking with a correspondent from the London *Times*. Down in the crater a BAR chattered. There was still considerable mopping up to do, but the Suribachi saga, which had cost the 28th Marines more than 900 men killed or wounded, was ending. Holding its present positions, the regiment was about to become the corps reserve.

Communion during Mass on Suribachi's summit.

25 | *On to Kitano Point*

══════Although D-plus-4 was a red-letter day for the Marines in the south, it was simply another harshly punishing one for those fighting northward. This front, which stretched across the island from east to west, was now about two miles from Suribachi, with the land between in American hands, though it still held numbers of live Japanese. Between the front and the northern sea was another two miles, the broader part of Iwo, which held Kuribayashi's main defenses. The terrain itself, described by an American newsman as looking "like hell with the fire out," was made up of barren plateaus, craggy hills, cliffs, twisting ravines and gullies, crumbling boulders, and struggling brushwood. February 23 closed with both the left and center of the American lines in about the same position they had been in when the attack began in the morning. On the right the 4th Division had gained from 100 to 300 yards.

At dawn on February 24, Colonel Ikeda's lines protecting the second airfield became the target of the main thrust of the American effort. This was a critical moment in the battle, since a great part of the attack had been virtually stalled for two days. A breakthrough by the 21st Regiment of the 3rd Division here in the center would aid the advance of the divisions on the right and left. The 21st placed a fresh battalion at the front, the 3rd under Lieutenant Colonel Wendell H. Duplantis, who told his company commanders, "We have got to take that field today."

The preparatory work for both the special attack and that of the rest of the cross-island front began at eight o'clock. Heavy-caliber naval guns spoke from the flanking waters, artillery batteries sent their salvoes sizzling from behind the lines, and carrier planes raced in with bombs and rockets. In the 3rd Division zone, two columns of tanks rolled forward. Unfortunately, this advance was staggered by mines and antitank fire and had not yet recovered when it was time for the infantry to move out. Wendell Duplantis and his 3rd Battalion were about 800 yards south of the center of the airfield, the spot where its two runways crossed. The low ridge these Marines had to reach in order to achieve their breakthrough lay on the other side of the junction. Even if the tanks had made it up on time, many of the men would have considered the goal entirely beyond reach; but the battalion jumped off as ordered, Companies I and K abreast, their front stretching about 400 yards.

As so often happened, the support weapons did not crush the enemy's capacity for resistance. Rifle fire came zipping, machine-gun bullets made tiny geysers in the sand, and mortar shells walked back and forth with their fearsome giant steps. Bullets thudded home and jagged shell fragments took ghastly courses; but the two companies kept going, assaulting some of the defenses and bypassing others, their primary aim to reach the objective. The din and the confusion intensified, and the trails of green-uniformed dead and wounded grew longer. At 10:13 the commander of K Company, Captain Rodney L. Heinze, was wounded by grenade fragments, and Lieutenant Raoul J. Archambault took over. At 10:17 the commander of I Company, Captain Clayton S. Rockmore, was killed by a bullet through the throat. Within minutes afterward, the lieutenants commanding three of the platoons went down. The attack was maintained even when the enemy's fire was swelled by artillery, and observers in the rear were reminded of things they had heard about Pickett's charge at Gettysburg.

At 11:45 a handful of Raoul Archambault's K Company Marines, running in short spurts, managed to plunk themselves on the southern edge of the runway junction. "This," thought Archambault, "is like fighting on a pool table." Lieutenant Dominic Grossi's platoon, down to the size of a squad, led the race across the junction, the men falling on their stomachs at the foot of the fifty-foot elevation that was the objective. Another depleted platoon made it across and the Marines joined forces, gritted their teeth, and started up the slope. Heartbreakingly, their own artillery began falling on the summit and they were forced back. They had the fire called off and started up again. This time they were pushed back by the Japanese, some of whom emerged to fight in the open. The Marines made a third attack and were again unsuccessful. Realizing they were taking enfilading fire because their flanks were exposed, they picked up their wounded and fell back across the junction to re-form with the other elements of the battalion. The morning's gains were consolidated.

At 1:30 in the afternoon, following a second period of preparatory fire, the two assault companies, badly hurt but reorganized, resumed the attack. K Company was again first to reach the foot of the objective. Less than 200 strong, the men formed a line and began another ascent. As they neared the summit, a wave of Ikeda's troops, shouting lustily, rose up from the other side and charged over at fixed bayonet, the officers flourishing swords. The Marines were not caught unaware, but the rifles of some were clogged with sand, while those of others were quickly emptied. In the frenzied hand-to-hand fighting that ensued, the Marines augmented their weak firepower with grenades, bayonets, knives, clubbed rifles, and even entrenching picks and shovels. It was all over in a few minutes, the Marines the victors, their losses few. Around them, dyeing the ground with their blood, lay about fifty Japanese. I Company soon moved up abreast, and the two units tied in securely. Lending support to the conquest were tanks now operating at the junction, firing at every defense in sight. The vital ridge had been won, and the breakthrough was a fact. Wendell Duplantis was delighted with his battalion's work. "It was the most aggressive and inspiring spectacle I ever witnessed."

The day also saw considerable progress made by the 26th Marines, 5th Division, operating just to the left of the central zone; one battalion came close to matching the Duplantis advance. On the west coast the 27th Marines, 5th, were slowed by a well-defended valley. As for the 4th Division on the right, its coastal flank remained entangled in the extremely difficult terrain on the cliffs; but elements of the 24th Marines operating inland spent the day shooting, burning, and blasting their way to a spot called Charlie-Dog Ridge.

Among the afternoon's wounded was Lieutenant Colonel Alexander A. Vandegrift, Jr., son of the Commandant. Casualties for the entire landing force soared to 7,758, but the sixth day of the campaign was one of general encouragement for the Americans. Complementing the progress at the front, the operation's overall organization had greatly improved. A second regiment of the 3rd Division, the 9th, had landed to take its place with the 21st in the center. (The 3rd Division's last regiment, the 3rd, would not be called in.) More than 50,000 Americans were now ashore. Corps commander Harry Schmidt had landed, as had all three division commanders. The replacement drafts were handy, working as beach parties until needed at the front. Supplies were pouring ashore, and the southern end of the island was becoming a busy military city. Last but far from least, the Seabees were starting to reconstruct the first airfield.

When operations in the north were resumed on the morning of February 25, the 5th Division, in its zone on the left, simply consolidated its gains of the previous day. Its front was about 400 yards ahead of that of the 3rd Division in the center, and it had to hold up until the 3rd came abreast. The consolidation was attended by numerous minor actions. During the afternoon, Acting Corporal R. Travis Canon, Jr., became involved in one of these while he and several other Marines were occupying a broad sandbagged hole formerly belonging to the enemy. The men noticed Japanese activity in some rocks and brush to their front and began spraying the area with their rifles and a light machine gun. Canon, a BAR man, emptied two or three clips, then put aside his weapon to assist the machine-gun crew by dusting sand from their belts of ammunition. Suddenly, out of the corner of his eye, Canon saw two pairs of Japanese leggings flash past the hole. Having burst from some rocks a few yards off to the side, these men were followed by others, some of whom stopped to fight. Two of them, one with a bayoneted rifle and the other carrying a Nambu machine gun, loomed on the entrenchment's rim. The unarmed Canon, in a sitting position, threw up his feet as a barrier against the bayonet he saw coming toward him. At that instant a Marine just in back of Canon swept up the BAR Canon had set aside and shot both of the Japanese dead. But even though the man with the bayoneted rifle collapsed, his weapon kept coming. The blade cut through the edge of Canon's boot sole, tore along the inside of his trousers leg, and lodged in his groin. The Marine had been bayoneted by a dead man. To compound Canon's moment of horror, the enemy soldier with the Nambu fell across him. At the same time, the Marine felt a sharp blow on the head as a live Japanese jumped into the hole behind him and swung his rifle barrel as a club just before someone shot him down. Canon was wearing only the liner of his helmet, and the blow not only dazed him but left him temporarily blind in one eye.

The Marine's good fortune was that the fight ended as quickly as it had begun, and his comrades were able to give him immediate aid. A Japanese jacket was used as a combination compress and bandage for the groin injury, which included a nipped artery but was not critical. Canon, the only Marine casualty, could not be evacuated at once, and his friends would have to leave him. To help ensure his safety they employed a gruesome but practical artifice. Hanging down over the rear rim of the entrenchment was a dead Japanese with blood dripping from his nose. The Marines dragged Canon to this spot, placing him just beneath the corpse. Then they fetched the dead man who had fallen across Canon and laid him across him again. Now the Marine himself looked like a corpse among corpses. All he had to do was to lie quietly after his friends left, which he did. The nose above him soon stopped dripping. "Crazy at it sounds," Canon said later, "I felt very secure with these two enemy dead protecting me." The Marine was not evacuated until well after dark. The Japanese jacket attached to his groin went with him aboard the hospital ship, and he would keep the souvenir for life.

In the center that day, the 9th Marines replaced the 21st and continued the 3rd Division's attack on the defenses north of the second airfield. The regiment was assisted by the 3rd Tank Battalion under

Major Holly H. Evans. "We were hit by antitank weapons, machine-gun cannon, five-inch guns and 150-millimeter mortars, as well as mines of all descriptions. They knocked hell out of us for a while." Evans lost nine of his twenty tanks, but his support helped the 3rd Division's rifle companies, in spite of their own losses, to obtain a firmer hold on the airport's northern environs. One of the day's special heroes was PFC Ralph H. Crouch, a runner for B Company, 9th Marines. On his way from headquarters with a message for one of the platoons, Crouch took a bullet through the stomach. Instead of lying where he fell, he crawled to the platoon and delivered the message, dying soon afterward.

On the right of the three-division attack, the coastal units of the 4th Division remained entangled in the cliff defenses while the inland units began struggling with a set of fortifications harboring troops of Major General Sadasue Senda's 2nd Mixed Brigade, including elements of Baron Nishi's 26th Tank Regiment. This latter defense system, to become known as the Meat Grinder, comprised Hill 382, a shallow bowl named the Amphitheater, a bald rise called Turkey Knob, and the ruined village of Minami. Hill 382, the name indicating its height in feet, was the main objective.

On February 26 and 27, the eighth and ninth days of the assault, the 5th Division on the left and the 3rd Division in the center made significant gains. The 4th Division on the right continued its debilitating contest with the Meat Grinder and the cliff defenses. On the first day,

On February 26, tiny OY becomes first American plane to use Iwo's air facilities. Marine perched on strut is guiding pilot out of range of enemy shellfire.

elements of the 3rd Battalion, 23rd Marines, managed to reach the
Meat Grinder's Hill 382, an advance in which the work of a single man
played a major part. Using a bazooka, PFC Douglas T. Jacobson
knocked out sixteen positions and destroyed about seventy-five Japanese, a performance that earned him the Medal of Honor. A follow-up
attack on the hill was unsuccessful.

The day was another grueling one for the Marines atop the coastal
cliffs. Among these men was PFC Donald Puff, who had begun the
battle an ordinary rifleman but was now a squad leader. The promotion
had not been sought, nor even wanted. Puff's decimated platoon had
lost so many of its NCOs that he was drafted. The unit had been in a
reserve spot, but was ordered to return to the front that morning. "We
began to hear fighting ahead. The terrain was a series of ridges, each
one slightly higher. As the firing became heavier we formed a skirmish
line. We were supposed to attack through the platoon we were relieving. Lieutenant Joe Daniels shouted 'Follow me!' and we started over
the last ridge behind the front. Daniels was hit almost at once, and the
rest of us scooted for cover." A new plan was devised: the platoon would
swing leftward and use the cover of a draw to reach the front. "We
hustled along the defilade and turned up through the draw. We were
well spread out and I was running full tilt when I went down like a
stone. I thought I was hit. My face was bloody and I hurt all over. I was
alone. Slowly it came to me that I had only tripped over a wire." But
Puff was in a state of acute anxiety. Totally certain he was a goner if he
went to the front, he wanted to shoot himself in the foot or smash his
hand with a rock. Then the platoon guide came back looking for him
and asked, "Are you hit, Puffy?" The spell was broken. Puff answered,
"No, I'm okay," and got up and continued forward.

As the platoon replaced its counterpart in the entrenchments along
the frontline ridge, Puff noted that the area held numerous American
bodies. The fighting at present, however, was limited to sporadic exchanges of fire. Soon Puff's attention was drawn to a comrade down the
line to his left. Private James E. Reynolds had been shot through the
hand and was waving the bloody member and laughing. "I'm hit!" he
rejoiced. "I've got the million-dollar wound!" Climbing out of his hole
to head for the rear, Reynolds called, "I'll see you in Philadelphia,
Puffy!" Puff waved a farewell and looked away, only to hear PFC Robert
Noyes cry, "My God! He's dead! Shot in the back of the head!" It
occurred to the shocked and saddened Puff that Jimmy Reynolds "had
gotten four or five steps toward Philadelphia."

Now Noyes began to gesture busily. "He pointed out two sheared-off trees six or seven yards to his front and ten yards to my left. There was a big rock between the trees, and it seemed to have a loophole cut through it. Noyes said, 'Fire about two or three feet back of that rock.' I pumped off four rounds, and a Jap came up on the side to return my fire. Noyes shot him the instant his head appeared. I'm sure we got the Jap that killed Jimmy Reynolds."

That evening Puff was wounded by a mortar shell. "There was a blinding flash about ten yards to my front. I didn't really feel anything until someone said, 'Puffy, you're hit!' I put my hand up to the side of my face, and blood was streaming from my ear. I became aware that I couldn't see out of my right eye. The same voice said, 'You'd better get your ass out of here.' " Puff was luckier than Jimmy Reynolds. He got back to the beach and was soon evacuated to a hospital ship, his recovery only a matter of time. As for Robert Noyes, he was killed later in the battle.

The nights at the front continued to be terrifying, especially for the helpless wounded awaiting evacuation. At dusk on February 27, Private Charles Bagnole found himself lying alone among some rocks out ahead of the lines, partly patched up after a close-range encounter in which he shot two of the enemy, then took a bullet in the chest and hand-grenade fragments in the head, groin, and leg. Bagnole lay on his back with a bandage about his head, a section of his undershirt gathered into a lump over the hole in his chest, and his left hand pressing a pair of socks to his bleeding groin. "It was soon dark, and the first flares started coming down. They caused the rocks to cast shadows, and at times it appeared that people were moving around me." Bagnole thought of one of his comrades whom the Japanese had captured and gutted, and was glad he had his carbine. He believed himself to be fairly well concealed but was made edgy when the enemy's night calls began sounding up and down the lines. He heard the usual things like "Marine, you die tonight!" and also something a little different: one man shouted obscene defamations of American actress Betty Grable. Some of Bagnole's concern gave way to anger, and he cursed the Japanese under his breath. He was bitter about his injuries, especially the one in his groin, and he kept wondering how bad this was. Finally his platoon leader, a lieutenant named Willis, came up with a corpsman whose first move was to determine whether Bagnole's bleeding had stopped. It had. The coverings were stuck to his wounds, and his left hand was firmly glued to the pair of socks at his groin. The corpsman gave him some sulfa tablets and water, used the precious carbine to splint his injured leg, and covered him with a poncho.

Soon the Marine was alone again, awaiting a stretcher team. "I lay there all night under the star shells, listening to the Japanese catcalls, sometimes dozing, often jumping at the sound of explosions. It was one hell of a night, but it finally passed. The last time I woke, it was to the sound of Japanese gamecocks crowing. Totally miserable and aching everywhere, I slowly eased over on my right hip and shoulder. Soon I noticed a little bug making its way over the ground—over what, for him, must have been very rough terrain. Sometimes he moved around a stone; at other times he crawled over, tumbling down the far side but quickly righting himself and going on. I was very impressed with that little bug. He was overcoming every obstacle and going on his way. It may sound ridiculous, but I suddenly felt better; I acquired a more positive mood. That little bug did a lot for me that morning."

It wasn't long until a stretcher team arrived and Bagnole was carried —past spots still only half subdued and through areas where shells were falling—to an aid station on the beach. Much irrigation was required to soak his left hand loose from the groin he was so concerned about. After a preliminary going over, Bagnole was taken to a hospital ship. He was destined to make a good recovery from all of his wounds and would marry and raise a family.*

On February 28, D-plus-9, the 4th Division in the east managed to gain a precarious hold on Hill 382 of the Meat Grinder, while the 5th Division in the west began assaulting Hill 362A. In the central zone, the 21st Regiment was back at the front. By this time, according to combat correspondent Alvin Josephy, these 3rd Division Marines "were bearded and hunched over. Their clothes were dirty and torn, their eyes watery and distant, their hair matted, their lips puffed and black; and their mouths were open as if they were having trouble breathing." But they had not lost their will to fight. That day Wendell Duplantis and his 3rd Battalion, with the aid of the invasion's supporting arms, advanced about 1,000 yards, the drive reminiscent of the breakthrough at the second airfield. This put the 3rd Division entirely through the enemy's main cross-island defenses and on the high ground overlooking the uncompleted third airfield. As before, the 3rd Battalion bypassed many installations that required mopping up, but these were the tactics favored by division commander Graves Erskine; he considered them to be the quickest way to victory at the lowest cost. When Colonel Hartnoll Withers, commander of the 21st, radioed division headquarters in a light vein, "Shall we keep going?," he was answered in the same spirit:

---

*Bagnole mailed the author his story on tape, commenting on the irony that the cassette was manufactured in Japan.

"Go ahead. We'll send an LCI around to the north shore so you won't have to walk back." About half the island was now in American hands.

On March 1 the 3rd Division occupied a part of the unfinished airfield, while the 4th Division strengthened its hold on the Meat Grinder. In the 5th Division zone on the west coast, the 28th Marines went back into action for the first time since the fall of Suribachi and succeeded in taking Hill 362A. The next day the 4th Division overran the whole of Hill 382, but the Amphitheater, Turkey Knob, and Minami Village remained unconquered. The 3rd Division, now only about 1,500 yards from its coastal objectives, was able to make progress on its left but not on its right. In front of this wing was a sector soon to become known as Cushman's Pocket.

The sector's most distinguished defender was Baron Nishi, who had his headquarters in a large cave complex on three levels, now filled with wounded from the front. The air was hot and fetid. A curving entrance passageway on the top level had some fifty blankets hanging from the ceiling, one behind the other, an expedient Nishi hoped would diminish the heat of a flamethrower assault. The baron approached this stage of the battle with outward resolution but inward sadness. No Japanese on the island had more to live for. In addition to his family, he had affluence, social stature, and an international reputation. He was in his prime and eager to continue his fulfilling way of life. Like many educated Japanese, Nishi questioned the Bushido code even as he followed it to the letter. Fighting without quarter and to the death may have had its place on feudal battlefields, but victory in modern warfare depended as much on material superiority as on personal valor. General Kuribayashi had summed it up when he asserted that he was not afraid of three Marine divisions but that no amount of dedication and sacrifice was going to triumph over America's ever-growing number of ships, planes, tanks, and other armaments. One of Nishi's own lieutenants took exception to an ancient poem that proclaimed, "Bushido is to die." While admitting that the lines had an inspirational ring, he argued that the theme did not apply to a place like Iwo Jima. Here, on the modern world's most dismal battlefield, the Japanese were facing "heartless iron."

On the west coast, March 2 found the 5th Division assaulting a ridge about 300 yards ahead of Hill 362A. "The trouble with this place," an officer complained, "is that there are too damned many ridges. You take one ridge, and then you've got to take another. There's always another ridge."

March 2 was the day the 2nd Battalion, 28th, lost its esteemed com-

Fifth Division Marines attacking up west coast. Japanese shell has set tank afire.

mander, Chaney Johnson. Easy Company had reached the ridge and the action had lulled when the colonel came forward. As he moved into the company area he was hit by a heavy shell, perhaps a misplaced American round, that blew him to pieces. Three of the men on their feet near Johnson when the shell exploded were PFC Virgis C. Anglin, Private Shelby C. Roundtree, and Private Tony G. Salicos. "I thought I was killed," Virgis Anglin recalled. "The blast and the shrapnel and the flesh from Johnson's body that hit me knocked me down. When the dust settled, the only part of the colonel in sight was his chest section, and that was split apart. Other men in the area were killed or wounded. Roundtree was okay, but Salicos was down with a foot wound. I believe that the shrapnel I received went through Johnson's body. A big piece glanced off my tailbone, a smaller piece lodged in my left arm, and a long thin sliver penetrated my right wrist. The last was easily pulled out, and Roundtree dug the piece from my arm with the point of his K-bar. Although my tailbone pained me, I was able to stay in action. We were a bloody mess from Johnson's flesh and had to scrape it from our dungarees."

March 3, the thirteenth day, found the 5th Division pushing several hundred yards farther up the west coast at the high cost of 518 in killed or wounded. Although the 3rd Division's right wing made little progress against Cushman's Pocket, its left wing reached a point only 1,000 yards from the sea. The remaining Meat Grinder defenses continued to frustrate the 4th Division, which reported that its combat efficiency was down to fifty percent, that its men were "tired and listless" and had lost many of their leaders. The Marine landing force as a whole, now in control of two-thirds of the island, had sustained about 16,000 casualties, with the death toll topping 3,000. General Kuribayashi, who had begun the fight with about 21,000 men, estimated that he had only 3,500 effectives left. There were doubtless twice that many able Japanese still alive, but communications and organization were breaking down. So far the Americans had taken only about eighty prisoners, more than half of them Korean laborers.

The Seabees and engineers now had a 1,000-yard strip of the lower airfield in operation, and March 3 saw the landing of the first planes from the Marianas. The next day was an even bigger day for Iwo's American air facilities. *Dinah Might,* a B-29 Superfortress returning from Japan in a crippled condition, unable to get its reserve fuel flowing, landed on the field, using up almost every inch of the runway. As the silver craft came to a stop at the northern end, shellfire began hitting near it. The Japanese wanted that first B-29 badly. But *Dinah Might* swung around and taxied out of range toward Suribachi. Hundreds of Seabees and Marines cheered as the sixty-five-ton plane stopped and cut its engines. One of the witnesses was Field Music 1st Class Frank L. Crowe of Easy Company, 28th Marines, who had come south from the front to have an eye infection treated. "The hatch opened, and four or five members of the crew jumped down and fell to their hands and knees and kissed the runway. What a contrast! Here were men so glad to be on the island they were kissing it. A mile or two to the north were three Marine divisions who thought the place was hell on earth, its ground not even good enough to spit on." The crew of *Dinah Might* soon had the faulty valve working and left for the Marianas. Ten of the eleven men saved by Iwo Jima that day were lost during later missions. But the island had begun to function as intended; this was what the battle was all about.

General Kuribayashi radioed Tokyo that everything would soon be over, but he was wrong. His remaining defenses were considerably stronger than he believed. Moreover, American combat efficiency was continuing to decline. Casualties among the frontline troops exceeded 50 percent, and the survivors were critically fatigued.

Corps commander Harry Schmidt set aside March 5, the fifteenth day of the battle, for rest, reorganization, and resupply. All along the front, groups of replacements came marching in. A controversy had arisen over the failure of Kelly Turner and Holland Smith to land the 3rd Regiment of the 3rd Division, the last unit in floating reserve. Their reasoning was that another regiment would only add to the congestion. It was true that Iwo had become one of the most heavily populated areas of its size in the world, but one place that wasn't congested was the front; the lines were thin. Every weary and nerve-strained combat Marine on the island would have rejoiced to see a fresh regiment come in. The corps operations officer, Edward Craig, said later: "Commitment of this well-trained and experienced regiment would have shortened the campaign and saved us casualties."

The Navy's role in the campaign was tapering off. March 5 saw Raymond Spruance, commander of the 5th Fleet, head his flagship toward Guam. Some of the gunfire support vessels had left earlier, as had the empty supply transports. Task Force 58 had not returned to Iwo after its second trip to Japan and its raid on Okinawa.

Just after sunrise on March 6, artillery commander John Letcher climbed to the summit of Suribachi to witness "the greatest preparation for an attack that Marine Corps artillery had ever fired. One hundred and thirty-two guns of eleven battalions opened fire. I saw the first volley of shells fall, but in a matter of seconds the dust raised by the explosions formed a cloud that masked everything below it." Holland Smith watched the work from shipboard and was certain it was devastating the Japanese compressed into the upper third of the island. But they were deeply dug in, and most survived. When the earth stopped shaking and the smoke and dust cleared, these troops surfaced and laid down a blistering fire they maintained throughout the day. Marine gains were minimal and losses were high.

There were, of course, enemy casualties too. Colonel James P. "Phil" Berkeley witnessed a unique local drama. "I saw a bazooka man watching a rock. Every now and then a Jap would put his head over the rock and the Marine would get the bazooka all lined up, only to have his target disappear. Finally he got the Jap out long enough to pull the trigger and blew him to smithereens. I said, 'An expensive way of killing a Jap, isn't it?' He answered, 'It did the job, didn't it?' " Incidents like this were only momentary morale raisers. All in all, the Americans found the day deeply sobering. The lack of progress surprised Holland Smith. General Kuribayashi had become "the most redoubtable" of his Pacific adversaries.

Especially unhappy about March 6 was 3rd Division commander Graves Erskine, whose troops had been making some spectacular advances up the center of the island until their right wing hit Cushman's Pocket. Even so, their left wing had been pushed abreast of the pocket and was within sight of the sea. Getting there was important, for this would divide Kuribayashi's surviving forces, becoming the final disaster for their organization and communications. Erskine won permission from Harry Schmidt to resume his attack in the darkness before the next dawn, with no heavy-support weapons preparation to warn the enemy he was coming. This offbeat measure was successful on the left, where Lieutenant Colonel Harold C. Boehm's battalion of the 9th Marines overran Hill 362C and reduced the distance to the coast. On the right, however, a supplementary move into the fringes of the pocket by the battalions of the 9th under Major William T. Glass and Lieutenant Colonel Robert Cushman (after whom the pocket was named) proved painfully expensive. Baron Nishi and his troops remained firmly positioned.

On the west coast, roughly abreast of Erskine's lines, the 5th Division spent March 7 driving to within 1,500 yards of Kitano Point, Iwo's extreme northern tip. In the 4th Division zone in the east, the strength of the remaining Meat Grinder defenses was being whittled down and the regiments were readying their own assault to the sea. During the two weeks in which the right flank had been inching its way through the impossible terrain north of the coastal cliffs, the rest of the division had been using this flank as a kind of hinge, the attack moving at first northward, then eastward toward the coast. The Japanese commanders in this narrowing strip were the army's General Sadasue Senda and the navy's Captain Samaji Inouye. During the night of March 8–9, these officers disregarded Kuribayashi's orders and launched a large-scale *banzai* attack. This achieved nothing and cost the Japanese about 800 killed. Inouye was among the slain, but Senda survived.

In the south, this period saw U.S. Army troops coming ashore from newly arrived transports and setting up tent camps. Army aircraft flying from the lower field were replacing the carrier planes helping the Marines. Many of the naval support vessels that had stayed on were now departing, Kelly Turner with them, his attention swinging to the forthcoming invasion of Okinawa. A modest force under Harry Hill would continue at Iwo.

On March 9, elements of the 3rd Division broke through the center to the sea, despite the fact that part of the division's right wing was still heavily engaged with Baron Nishi's command in Cushman's Pocket more than 1,000 yards to the rear. By nightfall the division was holding about 800 yards of bluffs overlooking the coast, and the defenses on northern Iwo were cut in two. This was the 3rd Division's proudest moment, and a canteen of salt water with the tag "Forwarded for inspection, not consumption" was sent back through channels to Harry Schmidt's command post, causing rejoicing wherever it went.

That night the United States launched its first great fire raid against Japan. Well over 300 B-29s from the Marianas hit Tokyo with 1,665 tons of incendiary bombs, destroying sixteen square miles of buildings and killing at least 72,500 people, perhaps many thousands more. Two damaged B-29s landed on Iwo Jima. Before the war ended, the island would prove a haven for 2,251 distressed Superfortresses carrying 24,761 crewmen.

The twentieth day of the battle, March 10, was a propitious one for General Cates and the 4th Division. The Amphitheater, Turkey Knob, and Minami Village, which had been holding up a section of the line for nearly two weeks, were at last subdued and left behind. The entire front now linked up for a drive to the eastern sea. Largely because of the enemy's losses during the nocturnal *banzai*, the day's gains were excellent. Some units advanced as much as 700 yards, which placed them little more than 300 yards from the coast. The division's right wing faced a final pocket, the one holding General Senda. As for the 5th Division on the other coast, it was now nearing the Gorge, a defense system about 500 yards south of Kitano Point, its mouth on the water and its other extremity about 700 yards inland. In and around the Gorge were about 1,500 Japanese under the direct command of Kuribayashi and Admiral Ichimaru. Kuribayashi's huge headquarters blockhouse was at the inland end of the Gorge. Even when he laid out the island's defenses, the general had foreseen how the American attack would develop and had intended to use this region to make his last stand.

The Marine units in all zones were now only shadows of their original strength. Combat efficiency was probably nowhere greater than 40 percent and experienced troops were scarce. Cooks, mechanics, and other behind-the-lines personnel had been called to the front to augment the regular replacements. Junior officers were commanding companies, and corporals and first-class privates had become platoon leaders. Some of the companies were hardly larger than platoons. The top commanders of both the Navy and Marine Corps were becoming impatient to bring the battle to at least an official conclusion. It had dragged on beyond all estimates, and the casualties were far higher than expected. Back in the States, people were protesting again. One woman wrote the Navy Department: "Please, for God's sake, stop sending our finest youth to be murdered on places like Iwo Jima." There was a

Fourth Division patrol pushes toward eastern sea.

flag-raising ceremony at Harry Schmidt's headquarters on March 14, but it was not possible to aggrandize the event by declaring the island secured.

The architect of the unparalleled American misery remained safe, at least for the time being, in his headquarters complex, which was under heavy bombardment but hadn't been reached by the foot troops. Still in radio contact with Japan, the general experienced a poignant moment when the schoolchildren of Tokyo made a special broadcast dedicated to the surviving defenders. They sang "The Song of Iwo Jima," which began: "Where dark tides billow in the ocean/A wing-shaped isle of mighty fame/Guards the gateway to our empire/Iwo Jima is its name. . . ." The song went on to glorify, in the name of the Emperor and the nation, the hardships necessary to the defense; and the final verse spoke of relegating "the hated Anglo-Saxons" to a place in the dust. The program closed with the children praying for victory. Kuribayashi radioed back his appreciation to the Japanese people.

Both the 3rd and the 4th Divisions finished their work on March 16. The 3rd not only extended its hold on the coast leftward to Kitano Point as an assist to the 5th (unable to get there because the Gorge stood in its way), but also took Cushman's Pocket, where Baron Nishi had held out for so long. The 4th Division overran the pocket near the east coast held by General Senda. The general killed himself, but Nishi remained alive in his three-tiered headquarters cave. Its entrance, however, had been assaulted by the Marines as they passed. According to one of the baron's lieutenants: "Colonel Nishi suffered burns in his eyes. He had no trouble walking, but after that his adjutant was always with him." Late in the afternoon of the sixteenth Kuribayashi radioed Tokyo that the battle was now indeed nearing its end. He appended the report with one of his "poor poems." It expressed his deep sadness over the loss of the battle, and closed with the line "I worry about what Japan's future will be when weeds cover this island."

That evening the American high brass declared Iwo Jima secured, news that astonished the Marines of the 5th Division, who had barely begun their work against the Gorge. It was an evening never to be forgotten by Pharmacist's Mate 3rd Class John R. Simms, a corpsman with the division. "We were under one of the heaviest mortar barrages I had ever experienced when our radioman yelled, 'Simms, I just got word the island is secured!' I yelled back, 'Somebody forgot to tell the Japs!'"

The next evening Kuribayashi's defeat was announced by radio in Japan, with Prime Minister Kuniaki Koiso admitting that the loss of Iwo Jima was "the most unfortunate thing in the whole war situation."

Even as Koiso was speaking, a curious drama was being enacted by lamplight in Admiral Ichimaru's cave headquarters deep below the surface of the Gorge. "The loss of this island," Ichimaru told the fifty or sixty survivors of his command, "means that Yankee military boots will soon be treading upon our motherland." After urging the men to continue their brave fight to the end, the admiral had one of his aides step forward and read a message he had addressed to President Roosevelt. The American leader was accused of defaming Japan as a "yellow peril" when her cause was righteous. "Why is it that you, an already flourishing nation, nip in the bud the movement for the freedom of the suppressed nations of the East?" There was much more in a similar vein, the conclusion of the message predicting the eventual downfall of the "barbaric world monopoly" the United States was establishing. Nothing was said about the barbaric measures Japan had been using while trying to establish a monopoly of her own. The admiral left an English version of the letter in the cave, hoping it would be found by the Americans —which it was. Late that night Ichimaru and Kuribayashi moved from the headquarters complex to a set of caves farther down the Gorge toward the western sea. This had become urgently necessary, for the Gorge was now surrounded, except at its mouth on the coast, and the Marines in the east had begun driving down its length toward the big blockhouse.

Until this time Baron Nishi had remained in his bypassed cave complex in Cushman's Pocket. No other officers of high rank were with him; all of those still alive were with Kuribayashi in the Gorge. On the night of March 18 the baron decided to lead his decimated command in a final attack, his scorched eyes notwithstanding. The badly wounded and the sick who crowded the caves were given pistols and hand grenades and a three-day supply of bread, but no extra water. "We took much time," one man recalled, "in saying good-bye to them." Finally all of the troops still on their feet, many wearing bandages and some limping, went out into the night. Nishi had to rely on his adjutant to guide him over the stygian terrain. The baron took the pathetic force north toward the Marine lines on the coast. As they neared these lines the Japanese were pinned down by mortar and small-arms fire, and at dawn a deluge of grenades was added. Nishi ordered the survivors to assemble, and those able to crawl to him were told to take refuge in caves along the beach. The baron's last moments are not a matter of record. It is believed that he stood by the sea, facing Japan, and shot himself in the head with his pistol.

On March 19 the 4th Division left Iwo Jima for its camp in the Hawaiian Islands. On Iwo, elements of the 3rd took over the occupation of the vacated zone, and were soon joined by the 147th Infantry Regiment of the Army, slated to garrison the island and finish mopping it up after all of the Marines were gone. In the 5th Division zone, the chief accomplishment on March 19 and 20 was the reduction of Kuribayashi's blockhouse and its cave complex. Blowing the blockhouse alone required four tons of explosives. Succeeding days saw the work against the Gorge wearily pursued, with the Japanese being squeezed into an ever-decreasing compass. On March 21 Kuribayashi reported that he had only 400 men with him. "The enemy suggested we surrender through a loudspeaker, but our officers and men just laughed and paid no atten-

Prisoner taken near battle's end.

tion." By the next day, all food and water were gone. "But our fighting spirit is still running high. We are going to fight resolutely to the end."

The Marines, too, were going to fight to the end, but they were making no claims about their resolution and fighting spirit. Just to keep going required all of the will they could muster. The average battalion, which had landed with thirty-six officers and 885 enlisted men, was down to about sixteen officers and 300 enlisted men—and this included the replacements brought up from the rear. To cite a specific example: The flag-raising company had come ashore with about 235 officers and men, and had received about seventy replacements. By March 23, according to records kept by First Sergeant John A. Daskalakis, the company had suffered 240 casualties, more than 100 percent of its original number. In addition, numerous men had been hurt but were still in action. The majority of those connected with the two flag-raisings were either dead or had been evacuated with wounds. The only officer still with the unit was its commander, Captain Dave Severance.

For the few Marines who had managed to escape death or injury since D-day and were in the middle of their fifth week of this special hell, these were some of the worst moments of all, every man hoping desperately to stay lucky for a few more days. By this time Joe Rosenthal's flag-raising picture was being published widely in the States and the battle was considered to be over. "It makes me mad," PFC H. C. Hisey, Jr., of the 28th Regiment's Headquarters and Service Company, complained in a letter, "when I think that the people back home believe this island was secured a week ago and that all the Marines have left. These people would think differently if they saw the wounded still being brought in."

March 23 was the last day that Kuribayashi's radioman got through to Major Horie's relay station on Chichi Jima. At about five o'clock the station received the message "All officers and men of Chichi Jima, good-bye." A weeping Horie ordered the radioman to stand by, just in case something further came through. "But there were no more messages from Iwo Jima. Ah!"

Two days later the 5th Division completed its capture of the Gorge. Remnants of all three regiments, some of the men so weak they were staggering, teamed up to overcome the last flurries of resistance. So ended the fifth week of the battle, which the high brass had expected to take no more than ten days. Even now, there were about 3,000 Japanese survivors scattered about the island, and Kuribayashi and Ichimaru were still alive somewhere in the Gorge. But every part of Iwo's 7.5 square miles had been overrun, and the Marines could finally claim the accomplishment of their mission.

As if to mock them, several hundred of the enemy formed near the northernmost airfield in the darkness of the early morning hours of March 26, slipped through the Marine lines to the west coast, moved southward over a trail known only to them, and, before dawn, quietly infiltrated a cluster of tent camps housing Army Air Force units, Seabees, and Marine Pioneers and shore-party personnel. A number of the airmen had their throats cut in their sleep before the alarm was raised. In the ensuing battle, which lasted into the daylight hours, the Seabees employed their training as infantrymen, the Army brought up flame tanks, and the Marines first formed a defense line and then counterattacked. One of the Marine units was made up of blacks who had seen no previous action, and they gave an excellent account of themselves. In the end, more than 250 of the enemy lay dead and eighteen had been taken prisoner. The rest disappeared into the earth. On the American side, fifty men had been killed and well over 100 wounded. Among the slain was Lieutenant Harry L. Martin, 5th Pioneer Battalion, who won the Medal of Honor that morning. This was the last of twenty-seven such awards earned by Iwo participants, an incredible number for a

Camp of the 62nd Seabee Battalion *(Photo by Henry Bogenrief)*

small-island campaign. Sixteen of the medals came to the 5th Division, which had traveled the longest route, from Suribachi to Kitano Point, and had also suffered the heaviest casualties.

It was on the morning of the day following the last attack that General Kuribayashi, sitting in a cave with a number of his officers and men, decided it was time he ended his life. Limping from a leg wound acquired in the Gorge fighting, the general went to the mouth of the cave, faced north toward the Imperial Palace, knelt down, bowed three times, and plunged a knife into his abdomen. An aide finished the job for him by lopping off his head with a sword. Kuribayashi died worrying over the future of his country and that of his wife and children, having no way of knowing that Japan would prosper in a friendship with America and that his family would fare well. The other ranking officers who had remained alive in the Gorge died on the same day as Kuribayashi, most by suicide. It appears that Admiral Ichimaru was cut down by machine-gun fire while leading a handful of naval survivors in a *banzai*.

During its mopping up, the Army killed 1,602 Japanese and took 867 prisoners. In all, only 1,083 of the defenders were captured. About 20,000 died violently or perished slowly in their caves. The final casualty figures on the American side were 6,821 dead, 19,217 wounded, and 2,648 cases of combat fatigue, a total of 28,686. This was the only time in the Pacific offensive that the number of American casualties exceeded those of the enemy. Newsmen began calling the campaign "the worst since Gettysburg." Holland Smith was moved to tears by the losses; yet the old general found in them a positive military lesson. "Iwo Jima," he said, "proved the falsity of the theory that regiments or battalions that are decimated can never win battles."

Third Division cemetery on Iwo, with gateway built by 133rd Seabee Battalion. *(Photo by Henry Bogenrief)*

26 | Convergence in the Ryukyus

══════ Chosen by Allied war leaders as the point of convergence for the Southwestern Pacific and Central Pacific drives, Okinawa lies in waters about 350 miles south of Japan. The largest of the Ryukyus, the island measures sixty miles from its northern to southern extremities and is from two to eighteen miles wide. The Allies planned to use Okinawa as the staging area for an invasion of the Japanese homeland itself. This was an unhappy development for the Okinawans, some 435,000 in number, who were mostly peace-loving farmers. A small-statured people who were a complicated mixture of Chinese, Japanese, and other Asian strains, the islanders had been under Japanese domination since 1879. Even earlier than that, in 1853, the first American Marines paid Okinawa a visit as part of the expedition led by Commodore Matthew Calbraith Perry that opened Japan to trade with the West. The Marines donned their dress uniforms and paraded before the people, who, according to a contemporary account, "clustered thickly on the sides of the road to gaze at the glittering novelty" and "evidently were pleasantly excited." Perry advised the United States to establish a military presence on the island, but not until the spring of 1945 was such a course undertaken.

Japanese preparations anticipating the American invasion had been launched the preceding year, after the fall of the Marshalls. At that time the 32nd Army was activated at the Okinawa port of Naha. With some of the earliest troops to sail into the ancient harbor was Captain Tadashi Kojo, who was impressed by the beauty of the water. "It was so clean and clear we could see the bottom." Okinawa's patchwork of farms and its green hills and ridges, Kojo noted, "looked very peaceful." When he landed and scouted around, the captain decided the island was defensible. "At that time I did not know that Japan's naval forces were already mostly destroyed. My fighting spirit was high. Of course, in the back of my mind was a slight feeling of uncertainty." Kojo had nothing but praise for the 32nd Army's commander, Lieutenant General Mitsuru Ushijima. "He was always quiet, leisurely, and smiling, and was respected by any and all of the officers and men." Ushijima's troops grew to number well over 100,000, nearly a fourth of them native Okinawans, both volunteers and conscripts. The civilian masses, like the military, had a high regard for the general, since he considered their welfare. When he told the civil governor that the people need not die

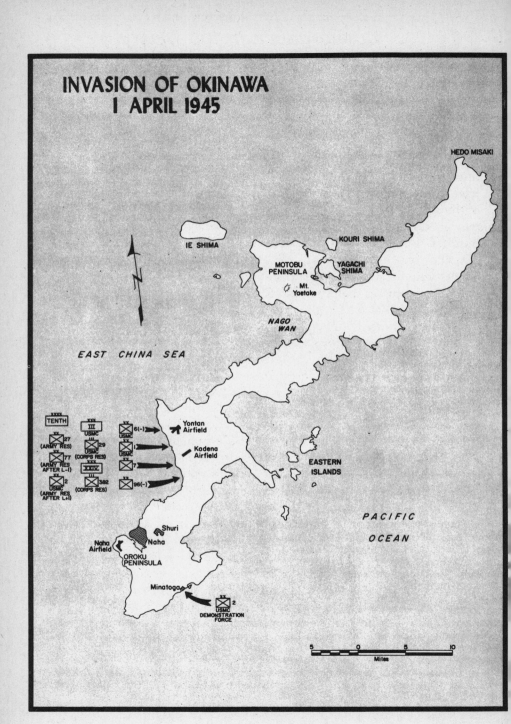

INVASION OF OKINAWA
1 APRIL 1945

HEDO MISAKI

IE SHIMA

KOURI SHIMA

MOTOBU
PENINSULA

YAGACHI
SHIMA

Mt.
Yaetake

NAGO
WAN

EAST CHINA SEA

TENTH

III
USMC

27
(ARMY RES)

29
USMC
(CORPS RES)

77
(ARMY RES
AFTER L-1)

XXIV

2
USMC
(ARMY RES
AFTER L+1)

382
(CORPS RES)

6(—)
USMC

Yontan
Airfield

1
USMC

Kadena
Airfield

7

96(—)

EASTERN
ISLANDS

PACIFIC

OCEAN

Shuri

Naha

Naha
Airfield

OROKU
PENINSULA

Minatoga

2
USMC
DEMONSTRATION
FORCE

5   0   5   10
Miles

during the American invasion but could surrender, he was answered, "There is no difference between the troops and the inhabitants." The governor, however, fell in with Ushijima's plans to evacuate some of the aged and the very young. On August 21, 1944, 1,000 of the aged and 700 children were placed aboard the transport *Tsushima Maru*. The fathers and mothers came to the wharf to see the youngsters off and to watch the vessel fade over the horizon toward Japan. The next night the *Tsushima Maru* was torpedoed by an American submarine. With the screams of her passengers ending in gurgles, the transport plunged beneath the black waters. Her death toll was 1,473. Only 168 of the old people and fifty-nine of the children were saved.

Ushijima's 32nd Army included two divisions, a brigade, a naval base force, a tank regiment, and a heavy concentration of artillery. The general chose to emplace most of his strength in a series of cave-riddled ridges at Okinawa's southern end, the island's most defensible terrain. Only about 3,000 troops were assigned to the vast northern sector, and no attempt would be made to defend the beaches at Hagushi, on the west coast, where the invasion was expected to come, nor the belt of land extending across the island from that region. Ushijima's unorthodox defense plan, prompted in part by Okinawa's size, would keep this campaign from rivaling Iwo Jima as history's classic amphibious operation.

Lieutenant General
Mitsuru Ushijima.

Disregarding the tenets of Bushido, the general told his men: "You must realize that material power usually overcomes spiritual power in the present war. The Americans are clearly our superiors in weaponry. Do not depend upon your spiritual power to overcome this enemy. Devise combat methods based upon mathematical precision, and then think about displaying your spiritual power." Ushijima's situation was critical but not hopeless. His defense was to be coordinated with flights of *kamikaze* planes sent against the invasion fleet by Imperial Headquarters. In addition, there were some 700 explosive-laden suicide boats secreted among the smaller islands around Okinawa. The mission of these boats, like that of the planes, was to ram the enemy's ships. If the great fleet could be crippled and driven away, the American landing force would soon be impotent through a lack of supplies. The concept was something more than the wild invention of desperate men; it had a chance of succeeding.

If the American assault on Okinawa, coded "Iceberg," was not a classic operation, it was certainly a massive one, outmatching all previous Allied efforts in the Pacific. Before it ended, the campaign would

Japanese suicide boats.

involve nearly 550,000 men, about 1,500 ships, including a British component, and myriad aircraft, some hundreds of them flown by Marines. Raymond Spruance, commander of the 5th Fleet, was again top man. Kelly Turner headed the amphibious forces. This time Holland Smith was not present, for the assault was Army-led. In charge of the ground troops was Lieutenant General Simon Bolivar Buckner, Jr., son of the well-known Confederate leader. Buckner's force of 182,112 men, 81,165 of whom were Marines, was designated the 10th Army. The GI divisions, all Marine-trained, were the 7th, 77th, and 96th, with the 27th (of prominent but controversial service on Saipan) in floating reserve. The Marines involved, Roy Geiger's 3rd Amphibious Corps, were the 1st and 6th Divisions, with the 2nd going along to make an offshore demonstration on D-day, or, as it was called, L-day.

The softening-up period, begun even before D-day on Iwo Jima, included all of the usual elements: long-range strikes by Army bombers, carrier raids, aerial photo reconnaissance missions, submarine cruises, coastal scouting by rubber boat at night, work in the surf by underwater demolitions teams, and ship-to-shore bombardments. It was still early in the aerial campaign when a Japanese soldier wrote in his diary: "The ferocity of the bombing is terrific. It really makes me furious. . . . What the hell kind of bastards are they? They bomb us from six to six!" L-day was scheduled for April 1, 1945, which happened to be both Easter Sunday and April Fool's Day. The main event was preceded by landings in the Kerama Retto, a group of small islands about fifteen miles off Okinawa's southwestern coast. These operations, conducted by the Army's 77th Division and begun on March 26, destroyed the lairs of many of the enemy's suicide boats, practically eliminating this threat to the fleet. The men of the 77th also gained the invasion forces some good harborage, a supply base, artillery positions from which to shell southern Okinawa, and a station for Marine Air Warning Squadron Eight. There were more of these radar-equipped squadrons on the way to Okinawa, their mission to provide early air-raid warnings for the fleet and the invasion troops, to lead Navy and Marine night-fighter planes to enemy aircraft, and to guide straying American airmen home. Radar Technician Carl Mahakian, who landed in the Kerama Retto on March 27, said later: "Our squadrons got little publicity, yet they played a vital part in the campaign."

Japan's *kamikaze* planes got busy as soon as the Allied fleet began massing in the Okinawa region. Between March 26 and 31, six vessels, including Spruance's flagship, the *Indianapolis*, were crashed into and damaged. Radio Tokyo reported: "Ten battleships, six cruisers, ten destroyers, and two transports have been sunk." The actual record was enough to cause the invaders concern, but their efforts proceeded on schedule. In addition to the naval shellfire rained upon Okinawa, some 3,000 air sorties were launched from the carriers. The enemy's antiaircraft fire was mostly sporadic and ineffectual, but a few planes were lost.

On the morning of March 31, a Navy Avenger torpedo bomber flying from the *Intrepid* had just unloaded its bombs when it was hit by flak and was obliged to ditch in the sea. The pilot and the gunner in the upper level had little trouble stepping out into the rubber boat, but the third crewman, Aviation Radioman 3rd Class Lawrence M. Hebach, who was in the lower compartment, found himself in serious trouble. "Water was pouring in on me. I was dazed from a bump on the head and my wrist was badly gashed, and I couldn't get the side door open. I finally managed to kick it open, and, fighting the wall of water, made it to the surface and into the boat." The three airmen were soon picked up by a destroyer. Their trip back to their home carrier was a circuitous one. Three days after their rescue they were shifted to the carrier *Hancock*, where they spent six days and shared the perils of a *kamikaze* attack that left seventy-two dead and eighty-two hurt. Then, during a two-day period, the airmen boarded a second destroyer, a third destroyer, an oiler, and a fourth destroyer, the last vessel taking them to the *Intrepid*.

L-day, April 1, dawned pleasantly cool, with the sunlight filtered by transient clouds. As four divisions of ground troops—two Marine and two Army—prepared to land over the western beaches at Hagushi, the 2nd Marine Division feinted toward the southeastern coast. The morning was still very new when the demonstration convoy was menaced by *kamikazes*, with one of the planes doing severe damage. Signalman 2nd Class Bob Collyer, of the transport *Sibley*, had a good view of what happened. "To port, an LST flamed up after being hit by a bomb. The same plane that dropped the bomb approached us to port, but either by intent or through the force of our antiaircraft guns it veered up, skimmed our rigging, and dived into the transport *Hinsdale*, to our starboard. Her engine room's port side was hit just at the waterline. She slowed abruptly and began listing to port. Flames, oil, men, and debris covered the sea on both sides of us. Boats from ships in the vicinity were lowered to pick up survivors. All available fire hoses were directed at the stricken vessels. It took some time, but both were saved." Casualties came to about 100 killed or hurt, fifty-three of whom were Marines of the 3rd Battalion, 2nd Regiment. It was ironic that the invasion's first casualties—and, indeed, the worst Marine casualties of L-day—were incurred by a unit not scheduled to land. On the plus side, the demonstration encountered no further trouble.

The operations at Hagushi were covered by a storm of fire from 500 carrier planes, ten battleships, nine cruisers, twenty-three destroyers, and 177 gunboats. Japanese return fire was light and nearly harmless. The amtracs went in on a front of eight miles, with the Army's 7th and 96th Divisions on the right and the 1st and 6th Marine Divisions on the left. Outside of the confusion that naturally attends an assault of this scope, there were no problems on the way in. The men kept their heads raised, noting that the farm-covered terrain sloped up gently from the shoreline. PFC Eugene Sledge, of the 5th Marines, found the island "beautiful except where the ground cover and vegetation had been blasted by shells." The amtracs lumbered up on the beach, the ramps in back clattered down, and the men simply walked out, formed their units, and began strolling inland, or eastward. Sledge, who had landed on Peleliu, was incredulous. "I neither saw nor heard any Japanese fire directed against us." There was fire in a few areas of the front, but nothing substantial.

The Marines everywhere became jubilant, many shouting, "Happy Easter!" To others the lack of resistance seemed a delightful April Fool's joke. The communications men ran around laying their telephone wires without the usual need to keep ducking. At the aid stations that were soon established the surgeons merely sat around smoking, some looking a bit frustrated. The casualties that came in had nothing to do with the enemy. One battalion provided two: one man had accidentally shot himself in the foot, while another had come down with appendicitis. The advancing troops encountered few of the usual fortifications, and most of those that were spotted were still. A major addressed a sergeant: "See that pillbox over there? Secure it!" The sergeant gathered six men, and the group walked over and emplaced a machine gun atop the structure. The sergeant shouted to the major, "Pillbox secured!" A young captain scanned the rolling ground ahead and said with a grin, "What a shame! This is the prettiest fighting country I've seen this side of Gettysburg. There should be a hell of a battle going on here." A lieutenant responded, "It's all so disappointing, I enjoy it."

At ten o'clock, Time-Life correspondent Robert Sherrod, whose campaigns included Tarawa, Saipan, and Iwo Jima, wrote in his notebook, "This is hard to believe." Sherrod felt more like a tourist than an imperiled invader. He joined the Marines in their investigation of the keystone-shaped burial vaults that dotted many of the lower hillsides. Constructed of coral blocks, the tombs measured about ten-by-ten feet and were about six feet high. Each sheltered a set of steps lined with large urns filled with skulls and other bones. Sherrod soon learned that the invasion route also held live Okinawans. First only a few at a time, and then hundreds began passing through the American lines. The small, dark figures were generally miserable-looking and "undernourished beyond description."

Everywhere were habitations the frightened people had abandoned. Sergeant James Finan, a Marine Corps combat correspondent, came to a quaint-looking bamboo barn that a number of other Americans had reached a little earlier. "Inside, two dozen black pigs were squealing with hunger. Two Marines were feeding them sweet potatoes from a sack. In the yard, a Marine was struggling with a nanny goat, milking her into his helmet." The nanny's kid was browsing nearby, its new legs still unsteady. "It jumped every time the naval guns went off, then nibbled the grass again." A little farther on, Finan came to a row of simply constructed homes that had been serving the enemy as a battalion headquarters complex. Inside one of the dwellings the correspondent found several Americans trying to get music out of a Japanese phonograph. Someone had scrawled on the battalion commander's blackboard, "The Marines have landed."

Conditions were similar in the Army's zone, joining that of the Ma-

Okinawan refugees.

rines on the right, or to the south. All day long Marines and GIs kept coming ashore, with their supplies and equipment. The fields near the beaches grew heavy with stacks of ammunition, rations, cans of water, and artillery pieces, trucks, and jeeps. The tanks, as usual, reached the front early, but they were largely unneeded. By the end of the day the beachhead was about nine miles wide by three miles deep, and it embraced two precious airfields. Including Seabees and other service troops, 75,000 Americans were ashore. Casualties for the entire landing force were twenty-eight killed, 104 wounded, and twenty-seven missing.

That evening the fleet was attacked by a few more *kamikazes,* who were met by "the mightiest night display of antiaircraft fire" that Robert Sherrod had ever witnessed. One of the planes that got through crashed into the battleship *West Virginia*'s galley and laundry, killing four men and wounding twenty-three. The fleet would have received much heavier attention from suicide planes on L-day except for American Task Force 58, which had plastered Japan's southern airfields two weeks earlier. The *kamikaze* squadrons were still reorganizing.

The Marines and GIs on Okinawa, with no certain knowledge of the enemy's dispositions, were uneasy as they settled down for the night. Many believed that the lines would be subjected to a great *banzai* attack. But, except for some minor local actions, nothing happened. General Ushijima, of course, was fully aware of the American presence. His first line of cross-island defenses was about five miles south of the Army's right flank. The Japanese were watching the assault plan develop. They knew that the invaders would first push to the eastern shore and would then divide to attack northward and southward. It was the Marines who were scheduled to make the swing to the north, where the terrain was vast but the defenders relatively few. The Army would swing directly into the heavily manned defenses concentrated at Okinawa's southern end.

Already on L-plus-1, the first American airplane, a small Marine artillery spotter piloted by Lieutenant Frank A. Milliken, sputtered in from its shipboard berth and landed on one of the captured fields. As always, these little planes would perform essentially, not only as artillery spotters but as general observation and photo reconnaissance craft. Major General Francis P. Mulcahy, USMC, was the island's tactical air commander, and his forces would grow from this first "grasshopper" to some 700 Marine planes, chiefly fighters and bombers, plus several fighter and photo reconnaissance squadrons provided by the Army. Although the prime mission of Mulcahy's armada was to support the ground troops, it became heavily involved in the struggle with the *kamikazes*.

The Marines and GIs spent L-plus-1 and L-plus-2 bisecting the island. Only a few pockets of resistance were encountered. "By God," exclaimed a Marine officer, "this is very mysterious." He said this, according to civilian newsman John Lardner, while his troops "looked around desperately for something to shoot." By the afternoon of April 3 many of the Americans were swimming in the eastern sea. Lardner was with the 4th Regiment, 6th Marine Division, which occupied the deserted coastal village of Ishikawa. That evening the newsman wandered around "looking at the lights of a dozen barbecue fires that were beginning to flicker in the dusk. Pigs were roasting, and chickens. Assistant chefs were going up to the fires with handfuls of onions, garlic, and radishes." Moving on to visit regimental headquarters, Lardner found the commander, Colonel Alan Shapley, wearing "a sprig of blue flowers in the buttonhole of his shirt." Several enlisted men in the headquarters area were gathered around an old woman in a black kimono who was eating from a C-ration can with chopsticks.

By this stage of the campaign the top Marine commander, experienced Roy Geiger, was shaking his head and saying, "This is the damnedest battlefield I've ever seen!" In a few days the honeymoon would be over for the Army, but not for the Marines. The 2nd Division, after repeating its offshore demonstration on L-plus-1, was circling around in the sea and would soon return to its camp on Saipan. The Marines of the 1st Division were assigned to cleaning up and occupying the cross-island belt of land already almost wholly overrun, with no other work looming. Along with their patrolling, they set up comfortable camps, complete with mess halls and showers. There was even an outdoor motion-picture screen. The men had ample time to sit in the sun and write long letters home, to harmonize around their campfires, and to play with their pet rabbits, ponies, and goats. Their chief enemies at this time were mosquitoes and itinerant goat fleas. Not as lucky as the 1st was the 6th Marine Division, given the job of securing the island's northern sector, although at first these men had more trouble with the mountainous terrain than with the Japanese.

There was no honeymoon for the Navy. The *kamikazes* kept coming, with the first full-scale attack occurring on April 6 and 7, the force including about 700 planes, 355 of them suiciders. Also a part of the operation was a famed battleship, the great *Yamato*, the largest and most powerful warship in the world. She left Japan with an escort of one light cruiser and eight destroyers. The three admirals and most of the thousands of others on the vessels realized that their situation was nearly hopeless, but the officers made grandiose battle plans. There was talk of breaking through the enemy's fleet, of perhaps even destroying it, and of grounding the *Yamato* on Okinawa and using its mighty batteries to pulverize the American positions. On the practical side, the planners believed that their advance would aid the *kamikazes* by drawing away a part of the enemy's carrier-plane screen.

The two days of *kamikaze* attacks—a furious melee of aerial actions, antiaircraft barrages, bombings, and crash dives—resulted in the sinking of three destroyers, an LST, and two ammunition ships. At least a dozen other vessels were crippled. The number of dead and wounded was high, with much of the damage in the form of burns.

As for the *Yamato* and her escort, they were still nearly 300 miles from Okinawa when the sky around them began to fill with American carrier planes, many of them torpedo bombers. The proud battleship, the cruiser, and four of the destroyers were shattered and sent to the bottom, the death toll exceeding 3,500. The American fliers, counting their losses to antiaircraft fire at ten planes and twelve men, had virtually finished off the Japanese Navy. This happened on April 7. Back in Tokyo that day, newly appointed Prime Minister Kantaro Suzuki began looking for a way to get Japan out of the war.

It was on April 8 that the struggle between the two land forces on Okinawa finally began to warm up. In the south the U.S. Army's 7th and 96th Divisions encountered the first of General Ushijima's cross-island defenses. In the north the Marines of the 6th Division reached the base of Motobu Peninsula, the western headland—ten miles long and from four to eight miles wide—on which the main body of the northern enemy was established.

Staff Sergeant Elvis Lane, a combat correspondent with the 29th Marines, was soon writing: "Motobu Peninsula is filled with rugged mountains, pastoral valleys, and sudden death. Here the fighting is like that of the Indian wars—stalking the enemy, ambushes, long periods of waiting. The Japs may be hidden on the next hill, or the following one. There is no definite front. There may be two Jap snipers firing from a hillside in the rear, three enemy machine guns ahead, and Japanese mortars somewhere on the ridge on the right. There's not a sound. Suddenly the air is filled with rifle fire, clattering machine guns, and exploding mortar shells.

"As quickly as it started, the noise ceases. A runner emerges from the brush. 'A Jap machine gun 300 yards ahead. We lost three men—one killed, two wounded.' The commanding officer orders another patrol up an adjoining hillside. The patrol disappears, Indian-file, into the heavy woods. 'Say, Mac,' a youthful Marine edges close to the runner, 'who was killed?' The tired runner replies, 'Tommy.' The news passes up and down the ranks. 'Tommy's been killed.' Yesterday it was Willy-Nilly, the freckle-faced youngster from Georgia. The day before, the husky lieutenant from Pennsylvania, and Charley, the growling sergeant, died in an enemy ambush.

"American fighter planes hover overhead, waiting for word from the ground forces that there's a concentration of Japs on a particular hill. Offshore, Navy destroyers keep their guns leveled on the mountainous coast, ready to fire the moment the Marines say where.

"Rifle fire, then the explosion of hand grenades. A communications corporal picks up a telephone. 'Enemy machine gun destroyed. Eight Japs killed.' Then a message from the patrol on the left that enemy mortars are set up behind the next village. A few minutes later American fighter planes dive low, strafing the spot. The planes leave, and Navy ships shell the area. 'Two enemy mortars knocked out. One crew escaped up the hill,' reports the patrol. The patrol is ordered to pursue the Japs.

"Sunset, and the hills turn darkish green. The hills look like those in Kentucky and the Missouri Ozarks. But the valleys with their rice paddies and straw-roofed huts are foreign. The Marines dig foxholes and open canned rations. 'Cigarettes out in fifteen minutes,' an officer yells. The Leathernecks try to make themselves as comfortable as possible. 'Joe!' someone calls. 'Don't have a nightmare tonight. I almost tossed a hand grenade in your foxhole last night when you screamed.' Soon it's dark and there's not a sound. Then a snap of a twig, and a machine gun lets loose two bursts. Then quiet until midnight. Enemy mortars explode nearby. A few seconds later our flares light up the hillside. Our artillery rumbles. Thirty minutes later silence has returned. Dawn comes. Another day. More patrols, a few more miles progress. Maybe Motobu Peninsula will be secured in a few days."

As it happened, progress slackened when the Marines reached Mount Yaetake, 1,200 feet high, rocky, gnarled, brush-covered, laced with caves. The uphill fight, under the gunsights of an enemy who could not be seen and whose positions had to be tackled one by one, was both costly and enervating.

The Marines at the front had trouble keeping themselves in supplies. "One evening," recalls Corporal John R. "Moe" McCormick, "we needed ammunition, food, and water. Sergeant Frank A. 'Andy' Anderson and I and a dozen other volunteers went back down that miserable hill about two miles to the spot the supply jeeps could reach. We made the return climb with each man carrying a case of .30-caliber ammunition, or two five-gallon water cans, or two cases of C-rations. It was after dark when we got back to our defense area, and we were exhausted. Andy and I shared a foxhole, and we alternated at taking watches an hour long. Sometime well past midnight Andy woke me. I reached for my automatic rifle and took the watch. In fifteen seconds he was asleep. For a while all was quiet. And then Andy began to snore. Have you ever heard a jackass bray, an owl hoot, or the dismal bellow of a fog horn on a lost ship? That was Andy's snore.

"The situation filled me with anxiety. The Japs were close. They had been quite close all day and quite dedicated to killing us. The firing here and there along the line meant that scattered groups of them were trying to infiltrate. If Andy's snoring didn't scare them to death, some of them might decide to drift in our direction to ascertain the source of this remarkable symphony. I shook Andy awake. He reached for his rifle and asked, 'Is it time already?' I whispered back, 'No, you still have a half-hour. You've been snoring.' He muttered, 'Okay, I'll stop,' and

105-millimeter gun in cave on Mount Yaetake.

went immediately to sleep—and started snoring again, louder than
ever. I began to see shadows, ghostly figures moving in front of us.
Perhaps it was my imagination. I woke Andy again. This time he
reached for his .45 and stuck the barrel under my chin. It was not a
gentle act. 'God damn you, Moe,' he hissed, 'If you wake me one more
time I'll blow your head off!'

"I had known Andy as a man of monumental patience, had never
seen him lose his calm. It was not like him to take the Lord's name in
vain. I had never heard him swear before. As a matter of fact, I had
never had him shove a .45 under my chin before either. 'Okay, Andy,'
I said, 'but I'm getting out of this hole.' There was a bit of shrub about
the size of a tumbleweed a yard or two to the right of us. I crawled over
and slid under the bush. I was more vulnerable there than I had been
in the foxhole, but I felt a whole lot better about it. In thirty seconds,
Andy was snoring once more.

"A few minutes passed. Suddenly there was a pop in front, and a hand
grenade exploded only yards away. Dim figures rushed toward us. I let
go with my automatic rifle. There were screams, more figures rushing.
Then they were gone past, through the line, crashing down that steep
hill behind us. From a hundred yards back came the explosions of
grenades, shots, and a long burst of automatic-rifle fire. One of our
machine guns opened up to our right. The firing spread all up and down
the line. Star shells bloomed overhead. Our mortars came to life, and
a salvo of 105-millimeter shells hit several hundred yards ahead of us.
It was one magnificent hullabaloo. A dozen Japanese soldiers who had
been trying to get at our 60-millimeter mortars were blasted as they hit
the defensive perimeter the mortar platoon had set up a hundred yards
behind us.

"As the firing died down, I crawled over to check on Andy. He was
lying with his pistol clutched in his right hand, still asleep and snoring
as before. It was almost daybreak. I decided not to disturb him."

It took nine days for the 6th Division to secure Mount Yaetake. With
considerable help from the sea and from the air, the Marines accounted
for more than 2,000 of the enemy. Their own casualties came to nearly
1,000—207 killed, 752 wounded, and six missing.

There were fewer native Okinawans in the north than in the south,
but during the work against Motobu's caves the Americans found themselves killing numbers of civilians along with the holed-up troops. The
efforts of a concerned Marine to do something about this had a bizarre
outcome. Correspondent Elvis Lane hunted up the top official of one
of the villages, intending to ask him to spread the word that it was safe

for the Okinawans to leave their cover and surrender. "When I located the SOB, all he wanted me to know was that he was a geisha master. Our colonel overheard his bragging and ordered me to round up his nine geishas. 'We'll open a whorehouse for the men of headquarters,' the colonel decided. The Protestant and Catholic chaplains protested bitterly, and the colonel instantly transferred them out of the regiment. I, too, protested that geishas aren't whores, but the colonel growled, 'Aw, shut up! I don't want to transfer *you*.' I shut up." And so it developed that for a few days a unit of Marines in combat, following a practice common to the enemy, had its own group of "comfort girls."

Marines share foxhole with young Okinawan whose parents have died in the fighting.

1442

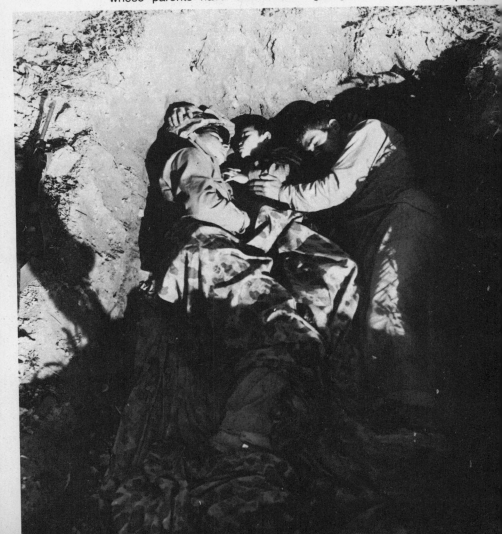

Elvis Lane was part of another affair involving a northern civilian, and its outcome left him deeply affected. There was a leper colony in this region of Okinawa, and the Marines had been warned they might encounter some of these unfortunates, perhaps being driven toward their lines by the Japanese in an effort to make men abandon their cover and thus become easy targets. The Marines were told not to panic, for leprosy, except in rare cases, was not contagious. The reassurance had little effect, for most of the Marines were convinced that leprosy was *highly* contagious. It was only a day after the warning was issued that Lane and his comrades saw their first leper, a tiny old man. "He wore filthy rags, there was a dark hole where his mouth should have been, and he had black stumps instead of fingers. He was wide-eyed with terror and so skinny he appeared to be starved." The Marines threw cardboard boxes of K-rations toward the man, and he stared at them with astonishment. The Marines next "made sympathetic sounds and motioned how he was to open a box and stuff the contents into his mouth. The pathetic leper, thinking none of us would harm him, ran with outstretched arms to embrace nearby Marines. He was probably laughing, because gurgling sounds emerged from what had once been his mouth. The Marines broke ranks and fled from him. It was a ridiculous sight. Tough, mean Leathernecks, one after another, running away from a tiny, unarmed old man! And forgetting that the hills which enclosed us might contain Japanese soldiers waiting for the opportune moment to open fire! There was no alternative. I raised my carbine." But the shot that rang out came from another weapon, that of a nearby captain. When the officer saw Lane with his raised carbine, he shouted in anguish, "If I had waited one second, just one second, you would have done it! Not me! Not me!" Lane said, "The leper died happy, Cap'n," and the officer, looking as though he were about to bawl, shot back, "What makes you think that?" Lane replied, "He thought he was among friends."

While the 6th Division was cleaning out the north, things were happening elsewhere. On April 9 General Buckner's floating reserve, the Army's 27th Division, came ashore—minus the 3rd Battalion, 105th Regiment, withheld temporarily for a special mission. The unit landed on tiny Tsugen Shima, off Okinawa's southeastern coast and knocked out a set of Japanese guns that threatened an anchorage Kelly Turner wanted to use for establishing east-coast unloading activities. With the landing of the 27th, Buckner's forces ashore comprised five divisions: three Army and two Marine.

On April 12 the fleet was hit by 380 Japanese aircraft, 185 of them *kamikazes.* A large number of the planes were destroyed by Navy and Marine airmen and by antiaircraft fire, but two ships were sunk and about fifteen damaged, some so badly they would have to go home. There were heavy losses, attended by many terrible moments, among the fleet's personnel. When the destroyer *Abele* went down a few minutes after being struck by two suiciders, the survivors flailing around in the sea awaiting rescue were bombed and strafed. One of the swimmers was Ensign David Adair. "A bomb exploded close enough to lift me out of the water. I heard several around me scream from pain caused by the blast." It was becoming clear that this was a campaign in which the violence at sea would rival that of the fighting on land. During the hours of darkness following this second large-scale *kamikaze* raid, General Ushijima's southern forces hurled a counterattack at the encroaching U. S. Army. The GIs hurled it back.

At dawn on April 13 the public-address systems of the vessels off Okinawa blared an announcement that spread rapidly among the Americans ashore: President Roosevelt was dead! The Commander in Chief had succumbed to a cerebral hemorrhage at his Little White House at Warm Springs, Georgia. The troops ashore and afloat reacted with stunned disbelief, and Kelly Turner was obliged to issue a confirmation. To many of the servicemen, Roosevelt was like a trusted father. They had been so young when he was elected to the first of his four terms that he was the only President they had known. There was consternation among troops of all ages about the effect Roosevelt's death —which many knew was analogous to that of another great wartime President, Abraham Lincoln—would have on the present conflict and their lives. Everywhere, men asked, "What do we do now?" The general concern would have been even greater had the troops known that the United States was in the final stages of developing the most powerful military weapon the world had ever seen, a bomb whose ownership would require the wisest of decision-making—and one whose progress toward maturity Harry S. Truman, as Vice President, had not even been apprised of. But the Allied course that Roosevelt had done so much to chart was not endangered. Germany was tottering; a mixed Allied force had enfeebled the last of the Japanese in Burma; and Douglas MacArthur, stating "It has been a long way back," had raised the American flag over Bataan and Corregidor in the northern Philippines.

On the night of April 13 the GIs on southern Okinawa were counterattacked again, and repelled the enemy as before. On the fourteenth the two Army divisions reported having killed 6,883 Japanese since coming ashore two weeks earlier. It was the Navy's turn to step into the limelight again on April 15. Admiral Spruance launched a two-day fighter sweep against Japan's southernmost airfields, knocking out a great many planes. But the Japanese were still able to get off a 165-plane strike of their own. They sank a destroyer and crippled eight other vessels, including the carrier *Intrepid.* By this time the Japanese, with their customary optimism, were referring to the ships off Okinawa as the "U.S. Sea Bottom Fleet."

On April 16 the Army's 77th Division, which had been marking time aboard ship since securing the Kerama Retto, assaulted the small island of Ie Shima, west of Motobu Peninsula, wanted for its air facilities. Ie Shima was thick with Japanese, all skillfully entrenched, many of them occupying a dead volcano much like Mount Suribachi on Iwo Jima. The 77th took the tough little island in six days, destroying 4,706 of the enemy and losing 1,137 in killed, wounded, or missing. Among the Americans who died during the fighting of April 18, shot through the head, was civilian war correspondent Ernie Pyle, viewed with admiration and affection by GIs the world over.

On Okinawa, Simon Buckner's southern front, stretching for five miles between the east and west coasts, now incorporated three Army divisions, the 7th on the left, the 96th in the center, and the 27th on the right. The GIs were approaching what became known as the Shuri Line. This part of the island was not as high as the north; it was rolling, hilly country broken by terraces, natural escarpments, and ravines. Although largely under cultivation, the region also held Okinawa's largest towns: Shuri, Naha, Itoman, and Yonabaru. The rural slopes and ridges abounded with caves and burial vaults the Japanese had developed into firing positions. Running generally east and west, the ridges provided for the establishment of successive defense lines extending toward the southern sea. The one thing the area lacked was good military roads. Most of the traveled ways were country lanes that were chokingly dusty in dry weather and deep with mud when it rained.

The Army's Major General John R. Hodge, in direct command of the southern troops, launched a general attack on the morning of April 19. In earthquaking support were twenty-seven battalions of artillery, the guns of twenty warships, and 650 Navy and Marine aircraft. Although well conceived, the attack was soon stopped by punishing Japanese counterfire. The GIs had come up against their own Iwo Jima. That day the 27th lost twenty-two of its tanks to an enemy trap, another smudge on that hapless division's record. A regimental commander was relieved. This time the dissatisfaction with the 27th did not come from the Marine Corps but from the Army.

During the remainder of April, John Hodge's GIs fought doggedly but with scant optimism. Men were killed or wounded in shocking numbers, and most of the going was slow. The officers of the fleet began complaining about the pace of the campaign, for they wanted to take their ships out of *kamikaze* range as soon as possible. These dreaded planes kept coming even though the powerful B-29s from the Marianas were now helping with the Navy's assaults on the bases that produced them.

Admiral Nimitz, who had moved his headquarters from the Hawaiian Islands to Guam, paid a visit to Okinawa at this time, bringing with him Marine Corps Commandant Archer Vandegrift, who had shaken free of Washington for a few weeks and was touring the Pacific. During a meeting with the Army's Simon Buckner, Vandegrift urged that the 2nd Marine Division be called back from Saipan and used to make a landing in the enemy's rear. The idea of a second beachhead was favored by Kelly Turner and Roy Geiger and also by certain Army officers, but Buckner rejected it, feeling he could win the fight quicker and at the lowest cost by continuing to slog straight ahead. Nimitz had the power to intercede but let Buckner have his way. This was basically an Army campaign. Moreover, the admiral wanted to avoid all possibility of a Marine-Army controversy such as had developed on Saipan.

There is no proof that Buckner was wrong, but by the time Okinawa was secured American newsmen would be asking such questions as: "Did the Army officers who handled the campaign adopt a slow course?" "Were there other landing places that could have been used?" "Why were the Marine Corps generals with far greater experience in amphibious operations not given the opportunity to carry on another type of campaign that might, perhaps, have meant larger land casualties at the outset, but in the end a quicker all-around result for the armed forces as a whole?" General Buckner did make one change in his operation. All of northern Okinawa had been taken by April 20, and he ordered Roy Geiger to bring the 1st and 6th Marine Divisions south to join the GIs in their attack.

Buckner now had 170,000 troops on the island: four Army divisions and two Marine. On April 29 the general began reorganizing his cross-island front, except that he left the 7th Division in its position on the left, or in the east; this unit had not been tested as severely as the others. In the center the 77th, brought over from Ie Shima, passed through the 96th, badly in need of rest after its month of action. Three days later the 1st Marine Division moved down to the right of the line, which flanked the west coast, and began relieving the 27th, ordered by Buckner to go north to mop up and perform garrison duty. On the line for two weeks, the 27th had taken 2,661 casualties. In keeping with its usual luck the unit had been thrust into some especially tough situations. It had not always measured up. Buckner said publicly that these GIs had "paid heavily" and had shown "lots of guts," which was certainly true; but the Marines heard it rumored that the general relieved the division because he was less than satisfied with its overall performance, which seemed the final vindication of Holland Smith's complaints about the 27th on Saipan. As for the 6th Marine Division, Buckner at first kept it as his reserve.

On May 1, as the 1st Marine Division took over the right of the line, cool and cloudy weather heralded the start of Okinawa's rainy season. The next day, as the Marines and GIs began their cooperative advance, a driving rain set in. This limited the attack's air support but did not inhibit Japanese counterfire. Casualties were high and gains disappointing.

On the evening of May 3 the enemy's *kamikazes* began another series of damaging raids, work that was coordinated with a Japanese land attack of massive proportions. The preliminaries were launched during the night, with small forces in barges and canoes sailing up the east and west coasts, their mission to confuse the Marines and GIs and do what damage they could behind the lines. Neither of these diversionary attacks was successful. Both forces were spotted by the Navy, illuminated, and fired upon. The Japanese in the west hurried toward shore and plunged right into the arms of the Marines, who blasted them out of existence. Those in the east who survived the Navy's fire were slain by the GIs.

At dawn, after a thunder-and-lightning artillery preparation, Ushijima threw a heavy frontal assault at the Army, its aim to smash

entirely through the lines and then take care of the Marines by swinging left and attacking them from the rear. Every bit of power that
Ushijima could muster was put into the effort, but it failed. Although a
battalion-sized breakthrough was achieved, it could not be exploited.
The Army, supported by naval gunfire and aircraft, stopped the rest of
the attack cold, then spent two days breaking up lesser forays and
mopping up the battalion that had broken through. In the end the GIs
held more ground than when the counterattack began. The Marines
were not involved in this affair. Even as its noises rumbled across the
hills to their ears, they were busy fighting at their own front, losing men
to a concealed enemy but making some heartening gains.

Ushijima's senior operations officer, Colonel Hiromichi Yahara, considered the great clash "the deciding action of the campaign." The
general himself saw the defeat as a total disaster, and he was left in tears
at his headquarters in a cave system beneath ancient Shuri Castle,
where Matthew Perry had been entertained in 1853. More than 6,000
Japanese had been killed, while additional thousands of wounded had
staggered back, or had been carried back, to the lines. Moreover, half
of Ushijima's precious artillery had been lost to counterbattery fire,
naval gunfire, and aerial attacks. From now on, the general knew, he
would have to fight as Kuribayashi had done on Iwo Jima. Ushijima had
scarcely more than half his original strength left—about 60,000 men.
He would be obliged to use these forces defensively, employing only
minor counterattacks, keeping most of the men fighting from concealment with orders to destroy as many of the advancing Americans as
possible before they themselves were annihilated.

It was at this time that the 6th Marine Division was ordered to take
its place at the front, alongside the 1st. These troops came part of the
way by truck over a road sticky with mud and snarled with traffic. At
one point the procession topped a rise that gave the Marines a view of
much of the battlefield that stretched for five miles between the two
seas. The once-green terrain was now mostly brown with shell scars and
mud—a quaking, rumbling, rattling, smoking, twinkling, and flashing
hodgepodge of lowlands, hills, ridges, and crumbling cliffs.

The scene reminded Sergeant William Manchester of photos he had
seen of World War I battlefields. "This, I thought, is what Verdun and
Passchendaele must have looked like." Manchester was awed as he
contemplated the two great armies "locked together in unimaginable
agony." While he watched, an American observation plane took a burst
of antiaircraft fire and disintegrated.

It wasn't long before the sergeant and his comrades were a part of the infernal landscape. The 6th took over the flank on the west coast, the 1st making room by sidestepping toward the center of the island. The two Marine divisions now covered the western half of the front, the Army divisions the eastern. The Marines had come late to the brutal southern fighting; the GIs had been knocking heads with Ushijima's main forces for a month. From now on, however, the struggle toward the south coast would be a fifty-fifty proposition.

On the morning of May 8, with the Americans bogged down in a quagmire caused by heavy rains, word came that the war in Europe was over, that Germany had surrendered. The Marines and GIs were too preoccupied with the perils and discomforts of their own situation to be as elated as they should have been, but, according to Kelly Turner, "many ships conducted divine services in thanksgiving for victory in Europe. At exactly twelve noon one round from every gun ashore accompanied a full-gun salvo from every possible fire-support ship directed at the enemy, as a complimentary and congratulatory gesture to our armed forces in Europe."

By this time Turner was putting new pressure on Simon Buckner to accelerate his campaign. Although the *kamikazes* were less often as thick as they had been at the start, and although Navy and Marine airmen and shipboard antiaircraft crews were doing some spectacular work against them, the fleet was still being sorely cudgeled. Vessels were going down, others being damaged; sailors and seagoing Marines in frightful numbers were being drowned, blown to pieces, horribly burned. On May 11 Buckner responded to the admiral's urging by launching a general offensive against the bastions of the Shuri Line. The GIs on the extreme left headed for an elevation called Conical Hill, while those toward the center marched on the city of Shuri itself. In its location west of the center, the 1st Marine Division approached two ridges, one behind the other, that covered Shuri's western environs; and on the right flank the 6th Marine Division attacked toward the coastal city of Naha by way of Sugar Loaf Hill.

The struggle for the Sugar Loaf complex was to be the 6th Division's severest test. Already, to get into position for the attack, the 22nd Marines, who would lead it, had fought their way across the Asa River, a move that had the essential aid of the 6th Engineer Battalion, whose members, working at night but nonetheless endangered by enemy fire, spanned the waterway with both a footbridge and a bridge strong enough to carry tanks. Only two or three companies got across before the enemy blew the footbridge by means of "human demolitions charges," but the larger bridge remained intact. Watching a column of tanks start rolling across on the morning that Buckner's general attack opened, a short, red-headed engineer shouted, "We'll do it again whenever you need us. Blast them all to hell!" One of the jobs assigned the tanks was to help C Company, 1st Battalion, 22nd Marines, to take a small but heavily fortified rise called Charlie Hill near the center of the regimental lines. The position was not completely subdued until the end of the next day, and by that time C Company had lost 103 men killed or wounded out of its original 256. This was a sample of things to come.

While C Company was cleaning out Charlie Hill on May 12, the rest of the 22nd had tried to move on. Some progress was made by the Marines working along the coast, but the inland flank was soon slowed by fire from the Sugar Loaf complex, three ugly piles of coral and volcanic rock. In the fore stood Sugar Loaf itself, perhaps seventy-five feet high and 300 yards long. The other two rises, the Horseshoe and the Halfmoon, were just to the south and the southeast of Sugar Loaf. This triangle, the western anchor of the Shuri Line, was one of the strongest defense systems on the island. Each elevation was a fortress in itself, a swiss cheese of caves and tunnels, and the three were interconnected by trenches and underground corridors. To attack one would be to invite fire from the other two as well, for the rises were mutually supporting. Moreover, the system was covered by guns on the

Sugar Loaf Hill.

heights in the 1st Marine Division zone just west of Shuri. Perhaps worst of all, there was no covered avenue of approach; the assault would have to be made by men and tanks moving entirely in the open.

Unaware of the extent of Sugar Loaf's strength, the 22nd made its initial attack on the brown and gray mound that first afternoon. Stepping out in the lead, accompanied by four tanks, were the men of G Company, 2nd Battalion, commanded by Lieutenant Dale W. Bair, a big man of great strength. Only a patter of enemy fire sought the Marines until they began closing in. Then 47-millimeter antitank shells and mortars began coming, raising their black puffs and spewing their shrapnel and broken rocks. At the same time, machine guns began producing their rattling crisscross patterns. One of the 47-millimeters clanged against a tank and knocked it out. Casualties were taken by the Marines on foot, and soon two-thirds of them were pinned down, their bodies tense against the quaking earth. Dale Bair led the rest in a tank-supported charge. The Marines began clawing their way up the cave-spotted slope, and a handful, Bair included, made it to the top.

But now both mortars and hand grenades, the latter coming from the reverse slope, began bursting on the barren crest. Bair's handful of Marines became a palmful. One man near death began shouting for his parents, "Mother! Mother! Dad! Dad! Please help me!" Shortly the shouts subsided to a low wail. There was no way that the few survivors could hold the summit. Bair called for a smokescreen, then covered the removal of the helpless wounded by firing a machine gun from his hip, the ammunition belt thrown over his shoulder. He reminded one witness of "Victor McLaglen in one of those movies from the thirties." Some of the wounded made the return trip riding on the tanks. Bair himself got out alive, but he was bleeding from three serious wounds. He had won the Navy Cross. The lieutenant and his men did not know it, but they had established a pattern of fighting that would continue for a week.

The 29th Marines were brought in on the left of the 22nd to put pressure on Halfmoon while the 22nd maintained its attack on Sugar Loaf. On May 14, F and G Companies were ordered to take Sugar Loaf at any cost, but when evening came the hill was still in enemy hands, the attackers diminished by 100 men and several tanks. Dusk found forty-four Marines commanded by Major Henry A. Courtney, Jr., huddled at the foot of the slope, mortars and grenades coming down on them. The Japanese seemed about to *banzai.* "It's time," said Courtney, "we make a *banzai* of our own. Who's coming with me?" At that point the major started off, on his way to earning the Medal of Honor, its

Tank taking stretcher case to rear.

citation explaining: "Inspired by his courage, every man followed without hesitation, and together the intrepid Marines braved a terrific concentration of Japanese gunfire to skirt the hill on the right and reach the reverse slope. Temporarily halting, Major Courtney sent guides to the rear for more ammunition and possible replacements. Subsequently reinforced by twenty-six men and an LVT load of grenades, he determined to storm the crest of the hill and crush any planned counterattack before it could gain sufficient momentum to effect a breakthrough. Leading his men by example rather than by command, he pushed ahead with unrelenting aggressiveness, hurling grenades into cave openings on the slope with devastating effect. Upon reaching the crest and observing large numbers of Japanese forming for action less than one hundred yards away, he instantly attacked, waged a furious battle, and succeeded in killing many of the enemy and in forcing the remainder to take cover in their caves. Determined to hold, he ordered his men to dig in; and, coolly disregarding the continuous hail of enemy shrapnel, he rallied his weary troops, tirelessly aided casualties, and assigned men to more advantageous positions."

Suddenly, around midnight, some of the enemy shrapnel the major was disregarding turned his Medal of Honor into a posthumous one. His disconcerted men covered his remains with a poncho as a cold rain began sweeping in from the western sea. A few reinforcements climbed Sugar Loaf at 2:30 A.M., and another group came up through the mists of the early hours of daylight. But as the 22nd and the 29th were preparing to consolidate the night's gains with an attack, the Japanese began counterattacking, and Sugar Loaf, absorbing a new outpouring of American blood, was lost again.

With some tumultuous help from their supporting arms, the two regiments stopped the counterattack and then struggled to regain their balance. The 29th made some advances during the day, but the 22nd, longer at the front and diminished in combat efficiency, was unable to get going. The next day, however, the 22nd again struck out against Sugar Loaf while the 29th attacked Halfmoon. Resistance was ferocious. General Ushijima had replaced the system's dead and wounded with some of his crack reserves, and had also ordered heavy fire laid on the Marines by the artillerists and mortarmen in the Shuri sector. Leaving scores of dead and wounded in their wake, both regiments reached their objective, but neither could hold. In the evening, under cover of smoke, the tired and discouraged Marines staggered back, carrying as many of their helpless wounded as they could. For the 6th Division, this was the worst day of the campaign.

The fight for the Sugar Loaf complex produced at least one extraordinary experience for every Marine who participated. PFC Sigurd Carlson astonished his comrades and made medical history by surviving three dumdum bullets that caught him squarely in the abdomen. The invasion of a man's midsection by just one of these mushrooming missiles is often enough to kill him.

Corporal John A. Spazzaferro, hit six times by rifle and machine-gun fire, fought on until the enemy weapons that got him were silenced, only then collapsing. Near him was his platoon leader, Lieutenant Edgar C. Greene, who fell wounded at nearly the same time. The two were in Japanese territory, and four of the enemy soon approached. The Marines slowed their breathing and played dead. One of the Japanese took Greene's wristwatch, then thrust a hand into the lieutenant's jacket pocket, only to recoil in disgust as his fingers made contact with warm, sticky blood. After the group had left the area, Greene raised his head and called, "Spazz!" He was relieved when the other raised his own head and grinned. Greene decided that Spazzaferro was the toughest man he had ever known. The two Marines lay in their harrowing position until the next day, when they were rescued by tanks.

A flamethrower man, Private James J. Lore, nearly met his end when his weapon malfunctioned. After incinerating four Japanese machine gunners in a cave entrance, Lore turned his hose on three more but was barely able to ignite their clothes before the stream of fluid lost its flame. Screaming with rage, the trio started for Lore, who turned to run but immediately tripped and fell. The Marine spun on the ground and met the attack with the only thing he had—flameless fluid. Since the trio's clothes were burning, this was all he needed. The Japanese writhed and died in what the relieved Lore saw as "a blaze of glory."

The fighting of May 16 had left the 22nd Marines with a combat efficiency of only about 40 percent, and the division commander, Lemuel Shepherd, shifted the zones of responsibility so that the full burden of the Sugar Loaf complex fell upon the 29th. The assault of May 17—although preceded by a land, sea, and air preparation of titanic proportions—was another costly and unsuccessful one. By the end of the day the 29th had won and lost Sugar Loaf four times. One battalion, however, was able to dig in and hold only a short distance from Halfmoon. At dusk a Japanese counterattack from behind Halfmoon and Horseshoe was blown to bits by artillery fire. By this time the pummeled defenders had lost much of their strength and spirit, and Sugar Loaf was ready to fall. It was Captain Howard L. Mabie's D Company, 2nd Battalion, attacking around the flanks with strong tank support, that gained the blood-drenched hill for keeps on May 18.

Since crossing the Asa River nine days earlier, the 6th Division had lost 2,662 men killed or wounded, while another 1,289 had been evacuated because of combat fatigue or exhaustion. Fortunately, the 6th still had the 4th Marines to bring up, and this unit relieved the now shattered 29th on May 19. One company of the 4th seized the western end of Halfmoon, while another enveloped its eastern flank. The north slope of Horseshoe was also taken, and was held against a counterattack. This clinched the 6th Division's grip on the complex.

Combat correspondent Elvis Lane, with the 29th Marines near Sugar Loaf, wrote in his notebook: "This must be the bloodiest triumph in Corps history. . . . Thank God there are no signs, none whatsoever, that the enemy is again rushing troops forth to try and recapture this hill. I've lost count of how many times Sugar Loaf was seized by us, by them, and how many days we've been here. The silence convinces us that Sugar Loaf really does belong to the 29th. No longer do artillery and mortar shells explode in our midst. There are no shrill clackings of machine guns. No whines or whiffs of bullets zooming by. Nor the dull thuds of bursting grenades. And no Japanese voices! We couldn't understand them but we knew they were cursing us. Just as we were cursing them. . . . For the first time we can see all of Sugar Loaf. Its crest. Its edges. Its bottom. If we want to, we can stagger to the top and look down the other side. We can also see the horrible havoc of war. Corpses litter the gray, muddy landscape. There are numerous severed arms and legs. And an occasional head. There's also the overpowering odor of death. A sweet, sickening stink which hurts the nostrils and settles nauseously in the lungs. The smell sticks to our hands. To our dungarees. To our weapons. I wonder how many besides me are trying not to look at the dead. Some of the corpses seem to be grinning. The flesh has rotted away from the skull and the teeth are bared. I am afraid that if I stare, one of these grinning dead might ask: 'Don't you belong with us?' And another might make this monstrous prediction: 'The war isn't over! You'll soon be joining us!' So I pretend to be oblivious of the dead who surround us. . . . None of us wanted to die. A wry jest emerged to contradict the famed Marine Corps call to charge during World War I. Then, Leathernecks were asked, 'Do you want to live forever?' They answered by attacking the enemy. When we asked ourselves if we wanted to live forever, we replied, 'Yes! Yes! Death has no future!' . . . At this moment I feel, and I'm sure the other Marines do also, somewhat humble. We know we are not supermen. In fact, we're quite ordinary. Well, a fraction or more above average. . . . Many others are now here for a look at Sugar Loaf. A group of Army officers are not far from us. Numerous Marines, of all ranks and none whom we know, are moving all around us. 'We'll soon be told to leave,' a sergeant quips. 'That we're trespassing.' Another asks, 'Where were all these bastards when the Japs were here?' It's quiet. But in the distance there is the rumble of artillery. We can't see them because the sky is overcast, but we hear the buzz of U.S. planes overhead. The war goes on even though Sugar Loaf has been captured."

On the left flank of the 6th Marine Division, the men of the 1st Marine Division had spent the days since May 11 making a slow, bloody, and debilitating journey through the defenses of Dakeshi Ridge, Dakeshi Town, and Wana Ridge, and into bristling Wana Draw, which led to Shuri's western environs. Moving against equally stubborn enemy units, the GIs just east of the 1st Marine Division had entered Shuri's northern environs, while those inching over the ridges nearer the coast had taken Conical Hill, the eastern anchor of the Shuri Line, a position of the same status as Sugar Loaf.

On May 22 the cross-island attack began bogging down under rains that created a new sea of mud. Along the entire front, the period since

May 11 had been the toughest of the campaign. The Japanese in all sectors had made the Americans pay a staggering price for every yard of captured ground. The break in the enemy's belligerence came with the fall of Sugar Loaf and Conical Hill. Now Shuri itself, the core of the line, was imperiled not only from the front but from both flanks.

It was the southern part of the city that held Shuri Castle, painstakingly built in medieval times and rapidly turned to rubble by American shells and bombs. During the night of May 22, as rain lashed the toppled ramparts and the water in the debris-cluttered moat, General Ushijima and his staff sat in the damp, dimly lighted headquarters room below and planned their next move. Ushijima felt that a retreat was necessary in order to prolong the battle and do the enemy the most harm. Several officers objected, at least one out of compassion for the many wounded who would have to be left behind unattended.

Actually, the condition of the wounded was already deplorable. In one cave, according to a survivor, "there were almost ninety men lying on the ground in the mud in pitch-darkness, except when a doctor or corpsman would come around with a light and ask them how they felt. Medical supplies were very low, so very little could be done to care for the wounded. Men died on all sides. Filth accumulated. In the heavy rains, water poured into the cave and the wounded almost drowned. The smell was so bad they could hardly breathe." This scene was repeated in many other caves behind the Shuri Line. Ushijima himself was a compassionate man, but his first consideration was the conduct of the battle, and he decided to retreat. The wounded who could not be taken along would be left with what supplies could be spared and with the means to destroy themselves. Some thousands of healthy troops would stay behind, their mission to fight rear-guard actions. The remainder of the 32nd Army would set up a new cross-island defense line six or seven miles to the south. Ushijima's new headquarters would be established behind the lines in a cave near the southern sea.

The retreat was begun under cover of the rain and a series of aerial operations launched from Japan. In addition to the usual *kamikaze* attacks on the fleet, an airborne raiding force made up of 120 suicide troops was aimed at central Okinawa's Yontan and Kadena airfields, which the Americans had put into busy operation. The Japanese approached in a dozen twin-engine bombers during the night of May 24, when the rain had lulled and there was a full moon. Not parachutists, the raiders intended to ride their planes down for a landing on the runways. As the bombers came in against the moonlit sky, Marine and GI antiaircraft gunners covering the fields let go with a dazzling barrage of 40-millimeter and 90-millimeter shells, thousands of tracers streaking upward, the bursts forming an umbrella of black puffs, the detonations merging into an unbroken roar. This was still another instance when Japanese attackers with lofty hopes were stunned by the enormity of American power. Some of the planes gave up and veered away, while others crashed in flames. Only one completed its mission, making a screeching, spark-throwing belly-landing on the coral of Yontan's main strip. Ten incredibly brave men leaped out and began throwing grenades and demolitions charges in all directions. Before being deluged and slain by American fire, the little band destroyed seven planes, damaged twenty-six others, and turned 70,000 gallons of aviation gasoline into a mass of throbbing flames and billowing smoke. Three Americans died and eighteen were wounded, probably victims of stray bullets from the weapons of their comrades, which also put holes in many aircraft the Japanese missed.

It was several days before the Americans discovered that Ushijima was retreating. The early Japanese columns had only the rain and the mud to contend with. Some of the first to go were the walking wounded, accompanied by young Okinawan nurses. Begging not to be left behind, hundreds of wounded who could not walk tried to join the exodus by crawling or by using such objects as rifles and shovels as crutches. "We couldn't take them," a survivor said later, "and it still bothers me." When a temporary lifting of the overcast enabled American air observers to spot the troops and vehicles clogging the roads southward, interdicting measures were undertaken. All of the routes and the key crossroads were targeted by gunfire support ships, artillery, and aircraft pouring down bullets, bombs and fiery napalm. The work was hampered by the weather, but Ushijima lost a considerable segment of his army.

Disaster came also to thousands of civilians—men, women, and children who, fearing capture by the Americans, retreated in panic with the troops. The dead and dying, both soldiers and civilians, lay thick along the muddy roadbanks. A male schoolteacher who survived the march called it "literally hell." In spite of the military losses, however, Ushijima counted the retreat a success. The general had gone early to his headquarters cave overlooking the southern sea, and the reports that reached him indicated that about 30,000 troops would be able to emplace themselves on the new line.

The old line's days were numbered. Even before the rains brought the American attack to a complete halt, some extra progress had been made on the coastal flanks. In the east the GIs moved past Conical Hill and took the high ground south of the port city of Yonabaru, while in the west the 6th Marine Division left Sugar Loaf behind and crossed the Asato River into the port city of Naha.

There was another break in the weather on May 28. For the fleet, this meant an upsurge in *kamikaze* attacks, but for the Marines and GIs it was a boon, enabling them to start moving again, although the mud was only slightly less than paralyzing. On the morning of May 29 the 1st Marine Division began slogging southeast from Wana Draw toward Shuri Castle. The plum of the long-coveted Japanese line, this bastion was actually in the Army's zone, but the GIs were facing strong opposition from the rear-guard troops in Shuri city's northern environs. The Marines had found a lightly defended route around the flank to the south, where the castle was located.

Pedro del Valle, commanding the 1st Division, sent the 1st Battalion, 5th Marines, pressing in. Captain Julian D. Dusenbury's A Company was in the lead. Brushing aside a small party of the enemy, Dusenbury's men reached the abandoned ruins at 10:15 A.M. An Army historian later grumbled: "The elements of the 1st Marine Division which entered Shuri Castle had crossed over into the 77th Division zone of action and line of fire without giving that unit notice that such a movement was under way." Del Valle took care of this matter just in time to save his Marines from a planned artillery and air strike. Captain Dusenbury had

Flame tank on way to Naha burns out Japanese occupying hillside tombs.

not brought along an American flag; but, a Southerner, he was carrying a small folded Confederate flag in his helmet. The first victory banner to be raised over the castle ruins was not the Stars and Stripes but the Stars and Bars.

By the end of May 31, which had been blessed with sunshine, the 1st Marine Division and the 77th Infantry held the entire core of the Shuri Line—except, of course, for the customary mopping up. From coast to coast the line was now in American hands, and the coastal troops had pushed well below its flanks. Naha's ruins belonged to the 6th Marine Division. The campaign was two months old and had cost Simon Buckner's GIs and Marines 5,655 killed or missing and 23,909 wounded. Many units were heavy with replacements. One of the drafts that reached the Marine lines was made up entirely of sergeants, some with six stripes. An officer told them, "We're sorry, but we're right in the middle of a campaign. We'll treat you like sergeants later. Right now we need riflemen." In effect, the high-ranking NCOs suddenly became privates, but there were few complaints.

Early June saw the Army and the 1st Marine Division pressing south toward Ushijima's last-ditch line while the 6th Marine Division tackled Oroku Peninsula, extending into the western sea just below Naha. Four miles long and two wide, Oroku was held by several thousand naval troops under Rear Admiral Minoru Ota. The 6th employed a pincers movement. With the 22nd Marines stationed at Oroku's base, the 4th and 29th climbed aboard amtracs and, aided by a full-scale sea and air preparation, stormed the peninsula's northern coast. Except for a profusion of land mines that took a toll of the motorized equipment, the invasion was made with little trouble, but the advance against the ridges and hills was strongly opposed. Admiral Ota radioed Tokyo: "Fierce bombings and bombardments may deform the mountains of Okinawa but cannot alter the loyal spirit of our men."

The rains had started again. On June 5 the high winds and sheets of water that swept the island seemed only another part of a wretched sequence, but the storm was more than that to the Navy. A full-blown typhoon, its winds grew as strong as 127 knots and created waves seventy-five feet from trough to crest. Ships caught in the storm's eye pitched violently. The bow of the escort carrier *Windham Bay,* according to her commander, "would alternately plunge deeply with screws clear of the water, racing madly, and then rise to extraordinary heights before plunging again." Ironically, the fleet was extensively damaged at a time when the *kamikaze* attacks were finally easing off. The heavy cruiser *Pittsburgh* lost 100 feet of her bow (which remained afloat and was salvaged); the carriers *Hornet* and *Bennington* had sections of their flight decks crushed; and many other vessels were left in need of major repairs. On the bright side, only a few lives were lost, and two days after the typhoon the long rainy spell gave way to assertive sunshine. On Okinawa, the mud that had slowed the assault, and had also caused grave supply problems and made foxhole life a soupy misery, at last began to dry.

It took the 6th Marine Division ten days to clean out Oroku. Toward the end Admiral Ota radioed Ushijima: "Enemy groups are now attacking our cave headquarters. The Naval Base Force is dying gloriously at this moment." With that, Ota and five members of his staff donned fresh uniforms and committed suicide. An assistant ensured the job by cutting their throats. By the time organized resistance ended on June 14 the peninsula held nearly 5,000 enemy dead, some of them civilians. The Marines counted their losses at 1,608 killed or wounded.

The 1st Marine Division and the Army had now reached Ushijima's last-ditch line, and the 6th moved south to join the attack, taking up its old position on the west coast, with the 1st again sidestepping toward the center of the island to make room. The GIs continued to occupy the rest of the front, their left flank on the east coast. The Japanese fought with all of their usual stubbornness, but Buckner's forces made steady progress. Ushijima had lost most of his artillery, while the heavy support fire of the Americans was now concentrated on this one section of the island, keeping its hills, ridges, ravines, and plateaus almost constantly atremble, and pulverizing many of its defenses. Those that escaped were assaulted by tanks, both regular and flame; by rocket trucks, half-tracks, 37-millimeter guns, and mortars; and by the foot troops with their flamethrowers, bazookas, grenades, and demolitions. The Marines and GIs suffered casualties enough—with the Marines of the 1st Division meeting especially hot opposition at a spot called Kunishi Ridge—but the Japanese died at the rate of 1,000 a day.

As for the civilians mingled with the Japanese military, numbers were induced to come out of their caves and surrender, but many others perished inside. Families sat in circles and exploded grenades in their midst, a procedure that did not always kill everyone outright. A maimed parent might be left holding a dead child, or a maimed child left sobbing against the breast of a dead parent. Civilians were incinerated by American flamethrowers and blasted by American grenades and demolitions. Some were sealed in the caves in total darkness and died slowly of suffocation. Others who might have escaped death by giving themselves up were killed by Japanese soldiers before the soldiers themselves held grenades to their stomachs.

A surrender plea that Buckner addressed to Ushijima and sent by airdrop reached the Japanese general on June 17. "The forces under your command have fought bravely and well, and your infantry tactics have merited the respect of your opponents. . . . Like myself, you are an infantry general long schooled and practiced in infantry warfare. You fully know the pitiful plight of your defense forces. You know that no reinforcements can reach you. I believe, therefore, that you understand as clearly as I that the destruction of all Japanese resistance on the island is merely a matter of days, and that this will entail the necessity of my killing the vast majority of your remaining troops. . . ." Ushijima smiled wryly as he read on to the part about surrendering. His chief of staff, Lieutenant General Isamu Cho, found the suggestion hilarious. As it turned out, the two doomed officers outlived their benevolent adversary. Buckner went to the Marine front on June 18 to take stock of a newly arrived unit. The 8th Regiment of the 2nd Marine Division had been summoned from Saipan, stopping off to capture two isles near Okinawa that Kelly Turner wanted as radar outposts, and then joining Roy Geiger as a reinforcement. While Buckner was watching the 8th begin an attack toward the southern sea he was bracketed by Japanese shellfire. Struck in the chest, the general died ten minutes later. Geiger took Buckner's place as top commander and thus became the first Marine in the nation's history to command a field army.

In this campaign the enemy troops were not united in their will to death. Belief in Japan's invincibility had faded and many thinking men decided there was little glory in dying for a lost cause. "Toward the end of it," relates Marine Colonel John C. McQueen, 6th Division Chief of Staff, "the Japanese started to surrender right and left. They'd had enough. We had a prisoner-of-war enclosure, but it wasn't big enough to hold an additional bunch that came back one evening. I said, 'We'll use an open space next to the enclosure, make imaginary lines, and station a machine gun here and there; and we'll tell the prisoners that if they step outside the lines they'll be liquidated.' (I believe we ended up outlining the lines with lime.) The next morning I went down to see how things were getting on, and all of the prisoners were accounted for. When I went to the regular enclosure, a very snappy little Japanese— a sergeant or a corporal—got up and saluted and said, 'Good morning, Colonel; I just want to let you know we have no trouble here.' I responded, 'You speak perfect English.' He explained, 'My name is Frank, and I went to the University of Chicago. I wish to hell I were back there now! Colonel, you won't have any trouble with these monkeys. They are licked, and they know it.' I asked, 'How did you happen to get thrown into this?' He replied, 'My friends and relatives kept writing me and telling me to come home; and, like a fool, I listened to them; and here I am, a prisoner of war. I am happy to be here. I'm glad it's ending.' "

Roy Geiger declared Okinawa secured on June 21, and on the twenty-second there was a flag-raising ceremony, complete with a band playing the national anthem, at 10th Army headquarters near the Kadena airfield. That same day there was a different kind of ceremony on the south coast. Generals Ushijima and Cho had survived in their cliff cavern, but now they went to a ledge overlooking the sea and committed hara-kiri. Ushijima had radioed his apologies to Tokyo, and Cho had written a final message in which he said: "Our strategy, tactics, and techniques were all used to the utmost. We fought valiantly, but it was as nothing before the material strength of the enemy." Ushijima's last words were: "The Okinawans must be resentful of me." After eighty-three days, the campaign was officially over; only the mopping-up remained.

Okinawa was excessively costly for both sides. The Japanese military lost more than 100,000 dead, while a similar number of civilians perished, most of them needlessly. American casualties came to nearly 50,000: the Navy incurred 4,907 dead and 4,824 wounded, the Army 4,675 and 18,099, and the Marines 2,938 and 13,708. Material casualties were also high. The Japanese lost several thousand aircraft, the Americans 763. With the sinking of the battleship *Yamato*, the Imperial Navy was spent, while the *kamikazes* cost the Americans thirty-six ships sunk and 368 damaged. Both sides were fully aware of the campaign's significance. The Americans had the base they needed for their planned invasion of Japan, and the Japanese knew that the Empire was now mortally threatened.

28 | *The Last Act*

====Few Americans expected Okinawa to be the final battle of the Pacific war. It was known at high levels that the Japanese government was seeking peace, but the overtures were hesitant and conditional. Japan's militarists were prepared to continue fighting, to meet the Americans on the home beaches with 2,350,000 regular troops and some 32 million civilians, women among them, the arms of the civilians to include muzzle-loading rifles, bamboo spears, and bows and arrows saved from feudal times. The hesitation of the peace seekers was dispelled by the atomic bombing of Hiroshima and Nagasaki and Russia's declaration of war against Japan, all of which happened early in August 1945.

News of The Bomb came as a wondrous surprise to the Marines, who were busy preparing for the invasion, coded "Olympic." PFC Henry Berry, with the 22nd Marines on Guam, never forgot the developments of August 6. "We were all thinking about Olympic in November. I was already scared about the invasion. I got the word about Hiroshima from a big sergeant who came running up and yelled, 'Holy Jeez! They just dropped a bomb on Japan so powerful that if it was only the size of a pea it could blow up a whole football field!' Before the day was out we were convinced that all of Japan was in flames and we would not have to invade. No tears were shed for the Nip civilians. Not at that time, anyway." This attitude among the Marines was natural enough. Three years and eight months of war had cost the Corps nearly 92,000 casualties. The dead numbered about 20,000—enough men to fill out a division. The survivors were infinitely glad to see Japan knocked out, whatever the method.

Emperor Hirohito himself made the decision to surrender, telling his ministers of state, "I cannot let my subjects suffer any longer. I wish to save the people at the risk of my own life." Japan's war of conquest, begun with supreme confidence and exceeding success, had ended as a national calamity. On August 15 Admiral Nimitz ordered the cessation of all offensive operations, but felt the need to add, "Beware of treachery." None developed. The Japanese, so intransigent before, accepted their defeat gracefully. The surrender was formalized aboard the battleship *Missouri* in Tokyo Bay on Sunday, September 2. One of the American officers present was Roy Geiger, who had succeeded Holland Smith as the top Marine in the Pacific.

American troops were already on the Japanese mainland. Among the first to go in were the 4th Marines of the 6th Division, the Army's 11th Airborne Division, and several teams of Navy men who began the top-priority job of repatriating the Allied prisoners of war. Accompanying the greater occupation forces that followed were the 2nd and 5th Marine Divisions. The 1st Marine Division and the other regiments of the 6th were sent to China. The 3rd Marine Division was kept at its camp on Guam as a precaution. There were many thousands of Japanese troops on bypassed Pacific islands, and no one could be sure how these men would react to Tokyo's order to lay down their arms. It was feared that some of them might cause trouble. As it turned out, the fears were groundless.

One of the occupied islands was of particular interest to the Marines. Wake had been bypassed but never forgotten. The Navy and the Army Air Forces had remembered it too, making frequent forays into its waters and its air space to clobber its garrison. These visits had accounted for 600 Japanese. Another 1,288 had died of starvation or disease. Before the sea lanes were closed by American submarines, 974

The ruins of Nagasaki.

Fifth Division Marines move into Sasebo, Kyushu, Japan.

were evacuated as hospital cases. Of the 1,262 who remained, 405 were ill, 200 bedridden.

All through the war the atoll's Japanese had been expecting the arrival of a massive American fleet carrying thousands of amphibious troops. When the Americans finally drew up offshore at 7:00 A.M. on September 4, two days after the surrender ceremonies in Tokyo Bay, they numbered a relatively few Marines and sailors on board three lightly armed destroyer escorts. The little force had come up from the Marshall Islands, its Marines commanded by Brigadier General Lawson H. M. Sanderson. Only one of the original Wake Island defenders was present: Walter Bayler, now a colonel, who had flown out just before the Japanese takeover. (Most of the Americans captured and sent to the Orient had survived the ordeal and were being repatriated.) The combat correspondent covering the reoccupation of Wake was Sergeant Ernie Harwell, who would later come to fame in the States as a baseball broadcaster.

At 7:45, with a dawn mist still hanging over the atoll's shoreline, a battered motor launch flying a piece of white cloth at its bow came sputtering out to the flagship *Levy*, and Rear Admiral Shigematsu

Sakaibara and his staff came aboard to consult with General Sanderson and the other American officials. The general waved the visitors into seats by a table on deck and turned to his interpreter, Army Staff Sergeant Larry Watanabe, a Japanese-American. Placing his hand on the sergeant's shoulder, Sanderson said, "This boy was born in U.S. territory. He is an American citizen, not a prisoner." Admiral Sakaibara broke into a smile and responded, "Of course, General. We regret that the Japanese must surrender, but we are glad it is to America." Sanderson seated himself, and there was discussion about the terms and the procedures. When the general expressed concern that the Japanese garrison might be tempted to commit acts of sabotage before the Americans landed, the admiral said, "There need be no worry. None of our men has the strength for such action." Sanderson arranged to provide the garrison with four tons of rice and fish and 550 pounds of medical supplies. The surrender documents were signed in the presence of two movie cameramen and four still photographers. After submitting to a brief conference with reporters, Sakaibara went back ashore to prepare for a flag-raising ceremony set for 1:30 that afternoon.

The Americans started heading in at 10:30 A.M. One of those in the leading boat was Walter Bayler. And now "the last man off Wake Island" became the first to return. As he climbed the short ladder to the boat dock, the colonel was saluted by a Japanese soldier. Moving off the dock, Bayler and his party of Marines and newsmen came to a white frame building serving as a Japanese headquarters. Standing on its veranda were small groups in patched uniforms. Most of these men were glum behind their show of politeness, but one, a major who could speak English, said cheerfully, "We enjoyed American cinemas very much here. The films once belonged to your Marine garrison. Our sound amplifiers would not work, but we did not mind." Pressed to name the movies, the major scribbled on a pad: *"Chicago, Dance in Honolulu, Cowboy A & B, Three People in Heaven, Lost Love, Brave Soldiers, Military Ships,* and *Amusement of Soldiers."*

Eager to make a tour, Bayler and his group commandeered a Japanese truck and took off. Sakaibara's men had fortified the island and made many other changes, but signs of the American occupation remained. Wrecked and rusted industrial machinery was scattered everywhere, and three of the once-formidable Grumman Wildcats stood forlornly in a field, weeds and bushes growing about them. A row of toilet bowls rose from the floor of a leveled officers' barracks. When the Americans reached the old three-legged water tank that had served the Marine garrison as an observation tower, Bayler explained, "It was from

"Last man off Wake Island" becomes first to return.

there that we saw the first wave of attacking Jap planes come over the island on the morning of December 8."

The visitors found the graves of Wake's fallen Marines and civilian workers. But Bayler was left puzzled. He recalled one mass grave holding Americans, but now there were two. Subsequent investigations would disclose that the second mound held the 100 civilians who had been kept on Wake as laborers at the time the rest of the prisoners were sent to Japan. As the American raids on Wake mounted, the civilians were accused of abetting the work by means of radio contact with the U.S. Navy. On the night of October 7, 1943, the unfortunates were lined up on the beach and machine-gunned to death.

The afternoon ceremony at the flagpole was conducted by General Sanderson and was attended by Marines, sailors, newsmen, and a delegation of Japanese led by Admiral Sakaibara. The white-gloved Japanese officers joined the Americans in saluting as the Stars and Stripes went up with a bugler blowing "to the colors." Offshore, the *Levy* boomed a twenty-one-gun tribute. At the fading of the last shot, the general made a brief speech turning the atoll over to the Navy as an air station. Naval Commander William Masek, who would head the new garrison, responded: "I accept this island proudly, because this is Wake Island, not just any island. It was here the Marines showed us how." General Sanderson next approached the Japanese delegation and ad-

Japanese join Americans in saluting reestablished flag.

dressed Sakaibara: "The Japanese fought bravely. Now the war is over, and there will be peace between us." The admiral concluded a gracious response with, "Thank you for your kind treatment of myself and my men." Sakaibara did not know it, but the kindness of the Americans would not last. He and eleven subordinates were to be sentenced to death for the machine-gun massacre of the civilian workmen.

With the return to Wake Island, the Marines completed their task in the Pacific, and the flag that was raised on that afternoon of September 4, 1945, had a special significance. It was a symbol of the greatest story in the history of amphibious warfare.

Bibliography

Adams, Henry H. *1942: The Year That Doomed the Axis.* New York: David McKay Co., 1967.

Aurthur, Robert A., and Kenneth Cohlmia. *The Third Marine Division.* Washington, D.C.: Infantry Journal Press, 1948.

Bartley, Whitman S. USMC Historical Branch. *Iwo Jima: Amphibious Epic.* Washington, D.C.: Government Printing Office, 1954.

Bayler, Walter L. J., and Cecil Carnes. *Last Man Off Wake Island.* Indianapolis and New York: Bobbs-Merrill, 1943.

Belote, James and William. *Typhoon of Steel: The Battle for Okinawa.* New York: Harper & Row, 1970.

Berry, Henry. *Semper Fi, Mac: Living Memories of the U.S. Marines in World War II.* New York: Arbor House, 1982.

Boswell, Rolfe. *Medals for Marines.* New York: Crowell, 1945.

Cass, Bevan G. *History of the Sixth Marine Division.* Washington, D.C.: Infantry Journal Press, 1948.

Chapin, John C. USMC Historical Branch. *The Fifth Marine Division in World War II.* Washington, D.C.: Government Printing Office, 1945.

Coggins, Jack. *The Campaign for Guadalcanal.* Garden City, N.Y.: Doubleday, 1972.

Commager, Henry Steele, ed. *The Pocket History of the Second World War.* New York: Pocket Books, 1945.

Conner, Howard M. *The Spearhead: The World War II History of the Fifth Marine Division.* Washington, D.C.: Infantry Journal Press, 1950.

Cunningham, W. Scott, with Lydel Sims. *Wake Island Command.* Boston: Little, Brown, 1961.

Davis, Burke. *Marine! The Life of Chesty Puller.* Boston: Little, Brown, 1962.

Devereux, James P. S. *The Story of Wake Island.* Philadelphia and New York: Lippincott, 1947.

Fahey, James J. *Pacific War Diary.* New York: Avon Books, 1963.

Fane, Francis Douglas, and Don Moore. *The Naked Warriors.* New York: Appleton-Century-Crofts, 1956.

Frank, Benis M. *Okinawa: The Great Island Battle.* New York: Dutton, 1978.

———. *Okinawa: Touchstone to Victory.* London: Macdonald & Co., 1970.

Frank, Benis M., and Henry I. Shaw, Jr. USMC Historical Branch. *Victory and Occupation: History of U.S. Marine Corps Operations in World War II,* vol. 5. Washington, D.C.: Government Printing Office, 1968.

Garand, George W., and Truman R. Strobridge. USMC Historical Branch. *Western Pacific Operations: History of U.S. Marine Corps Operations in World War II,* vol. 4. Washington, D.C.: Government Printing Office, 1971.

Griffith, Samuel B., II. *The Battle for Guadalcanal.* Philadelphia and New York: Lippincott, 1963.

Hannah, Dick. *Tarawa: The Toughest Battle in Marine Corps History.* U.S. Camera Publishing Corp., 1944.

Hanrahan, Gene Z., ed. *Assault! True Action Stories of the Island War in the Pacific.* New York: Berkley, 1962.

Hashimoto, Mochitsura. *Sunk: The Story of the Japanese Submarine Fleet, 1941–1945.* Trans. E. H. M. Colegrave. New York: Henry Holt, 1954.

Hayashi, Saburo, with Alvin D. Coox. *Kogun: The Japanese Army in the Pacific War.* Quantico, Va.: Marine Corps Association, 1959.

Heinl, Robert D., Jr. USMC Historical Branch. *The Defense of Wake.* Washington, D.C.: Government Printing Office, 1947.

Henri, Raymond. *Iwo Jima: Springboard to Final Victory.* New York: U.S. Camera Publishing Corp., 1945.

Henri, Raymond, Jim G. Lucas, W. Keyes Beech, David K. Dempsey, and Alvin M. Josephy, Jr. *The U.S. Marines on Iwo Jima.* Washington, D.C.: Infantry Journal Press, 1945.

Hoffman, Carl W. USMC Historical Branch. *Saipan: The Beginning of the End.* Washington, D.C.: Government Printing Office, 1950.

————. *The Seizure of Tinian.* Washington, D.C.: Government Printing Office, 1951.

Horan, James D., and Gerold Frank. *Out in the Boondocks.* New York: Putnam, 1943.

Horie, Yoshitaka. *Fighting Spirit: Iwo Jima.* Published in Japan, 1965. Trans. by Horie for private distribution in photocopy to friends in the United States.

Horton, D. C. *New Georgia: Pattern for Victory.* New York: Ballantine Books, 1971.

Hough, Frank O., and John A. Crown. USMC Historical Branch. *The Campaign on New Britain.* Washington, D.C.: Government Printing Office, 1952.

Hough, Frank O., Verle E. Ludwig, and Henry I. Shaw, Jr. USMC Historical Branch. *Pearl Harbor to Guadalcanal: History of U.S. Marine Corps Operations in World War II,* vol. 1. Washington, D.C.: Government Printing Office, 1958.

Howard, Clive, and Joe Whitley. *One Damned Island After Another: The Saga of the Seventh Air Force.* Chapel Hill: University of North Carolina Press, 1946.

Hoyt, Edwin P. *To the Marianas.* New York: Van Nostrand Reinhold, 1980.

Huie, William Bradford. *Can Do! The Story of the Seabees.* New York: Dutton, 1945.

————. *From Omaha to Okinawa: The Story of the Seabees.* New York: Dutton, 1945.

Hunt, George P. *Coral Comes High: A Company on Peleliu.* New York: Harper & Brothers, 1946.

Isely, Jeter A., and Philip A. Crowl. *The U.S. Marines and Amphibious War.* Princeton, N.J.: Princeton University Press, 1951.

Johns, J. Murray, and Bill Compton. *Guadalcanal Twice-Told.* New York: Vantage Press, 1978.

Johnston, Richard W. *Follow Me! The Story of the Second Marine Division in World War II.* New York: Random House, 1948.

Josephy, Alvin M., Jr. *The Long and the Short and the Tall: The Story of a Marine Combat Unit in the Pacific.* New York: Knopf, 1946.

Karig, Walter, and Eric Purdon. *Battle Report, Pacific War: Middle Phase.* New York: Rinehart, 1947.

Kent, Graeme. *Guadalcanal: Island Ordeal.* New York: Ballantine Books, 1971.

Leckie, Robert. *Challenge for the Pacific.* Garden City, N.Y.: Doubleday, 1965.

———. *Strong Men Armed: The United States Marines Against Japan.* New York: Random House, 1962.

Letcher, John Seymour. *One Marine's Story.* Verona, Va.: McClure Press, 1970.

Love, Edmund G. *The 27th Infantry Division in World War II.* Nashville, Tenn.: Battery Press, 1982.

Manchester, William. *Goodbye Darkness: A Memoir of the Pacific War.* New York: Dell, 1982.

McMillan, George. *The Old Breed: A History of the First Marine Division in World War II.* Washington, D.C.: Infantry Journal Press, 1949.

McMillan, George, C. Peter Zurlinden, Jr., Alvin M. Josephy, Jr., David Dempsey, Keyes Beech, and Herman Kogan. *Uncommon Valor: Marine Divisions in Action.* Washington, D.C.: Infantry Journal Press, 1946.

Mercey, Arch A., and Lee Grove, eds. *Sea, Surf and Hell.* Englewood Cliffs, N.J.: Prentice-Hall, 1946.

Metcalf, Clyde H., ed. *The Marine Corps Reader.* New York: Putnam, 1944.

Miller, Thomas G., Jr. *The Cactus Air Force.* New York: Harper & Row, 1969.

Millot, Bernard. *The Life and Death of the Kamikazes.* New York: McCall, 1971.

Monks, John, Jr. *A Ribbon and a Star: The Third Marines on Bougainville.* New York: Henry Holt, 1945.

Morison, Samuel Eliot. *The Rising Sun in the Pacific: History of United States Naval Operations in World War II,* vol. 3. Boston: Little, Brown, 1959.

———. *Coral Sea, Midway and Submarine Action: History of United States Naval Operations in World War II,* vol. 4. Boston: Little, Brown, 1960.

———. *The Struggle for Guadalcanal: History of United States Naval Operations in World War II,* vol. 5. Boston: Little, Brown, 1959.

———. *Breaking the Bismarcks Barrier: History of United States Naval Operations in World War II,* vol. 6. Boston: Little, Brown, 1960.

———. *Aleutians, Gilberts and Marshalls: History of United States Naval Operations in World War II,* vol. 7. Boston: Little, Brown, 1960.

———. *New Guinea and the Marianas: History of United States Naval Operations in World War II,* vol. 8. Boston: Little, Brown, 1960.

———. *Leyte: History of United States Naval Operations in World War II,* vol. 12. Boston: Little Brown, 1958.

———. *Victory in the Pacific: History of United States Naval Operations in World War II,* vol. 14. Boston: Little, Brown, 1960.

Moskin, J. Robert. *The U.S. Marine Corps Story.* New York: McGraw-Hill, 1977.

Nalty, Bernard C. USMC Historical Branch. *The United States Marines on Iwo Jima: The Battle and the Flag Raising.* Washington, D.C.: Government Printing Office, 1970.

Newcomb, Richard F. *Iwo Jima.* New York: Holt, Rinehart & Winston, 1965.

———. *Savo: The Incredible Naval Debacle off Guadalcanal.* New York: Holt, Rinehart & Winston, 1961.

Nichols, Charles S., Jr., and Henry I. Shaw, Jr. USMC Historical Branch. *Okinawa: Victory in the Pacific.* Washington, D.C.: Government Printing Office, 1955.

Okumiya, Masatake, and Jiro Horikoshi, with Martin Caidin. *Zero! The Inside Story of Japan's Air War in the Pacific.* New York: Ballantine Books, 1957.

Pratt, Fletcher. *The Marines' War.* New York: Sloane, 1948.

Proehl, Carl W., ed. Narrative by David Dempsey. *The Fourth Marine Division in World War II.* Washington, D.C.: Infantry Journal Press, 1946.

Rentz, John N. USMC Historical Branch. *Marines in the Central Solomons.* Washington, D.C.: Government Printing Office, 1952.

Roscoe, Theodore. *United States Destroyer Operations in World War II.* Annapolis, Md.: U.S. Naval Institute, 1953.

Rosenthal, Joe, and W. C. Heintz. "The Picture That Will Live Forever." Fifth Marine Division Reunion Journal. Capistrano Beach, Calif.: Gallant/Charger Publications, 1978.

Russ, Martin. *Line of Departure: Tarawa.* Garden City, N.Y.: Doubleday, 1975.

Russell, Michael. *Iwo Jima.* New York: Ballantine Books, 1974.

Sakai, Saburo, with Martin Caidin and Fred Saito. *Samurai! The Personal Story of Japan's Greatest Living Fighter Pilot.* New York: Ballantine Books, 1957.

Schultz, Duane. *Wake Island: The Heroic, Gallant Fight.* New York: St. Martin's, 1978.

Schuon, Karl, ed. *The Leathernecks.* New York: Franklin Watts, 1963.

Shaw, Henry I., Jr. *Tarawa: A Legend Is Born.* New York: Ballantine Books, 1969.

Shaw, Henry I., Jr., and Douglas T. Kane. USMC Historical Branch. *Isolation of Rabaul: History of U.S. Marine Corps Operations in World War II,* vol. 2. Washington, D.C.: Government Printing Office, 1963.

Shaw, Henry I., Jr., Bernard C. Nalty, and Edwin T. Turnbladh. USMC Historical Branch. *Central Pacific Drive: History of U.S. Marine Corps Operations in World War II,* vol. 3. Washington, D.C.: Government Printing Office, 1966.

Sherrod, Robert. *History of Marine Corps Aviation in World War II.* Washington, D.C.: Combat Forces Press, 1952.

———. *On to Westward: War in the Central Pacific.* New York: Duell, Sloan & Pearce, 1945.

———. *Tarawa: The Story of a Battle.* New York: Duell, Sloan & Pearce, 1944.

Silcox, S. G. *A Hillbilly Marine.* Privately printed, 1977.

Simmons, Edwin H. *The United States Marines: The First Two Hundred Years, 1775–1975.* New York: Viking, 1976.

Simmons, Walter. *Joe Foss, Flying Marine.* New York: Dutton, 1943.

Sledge, E. B. *With the Old Breed at Peleliu and Okinawa.* Novato, Calif.: Presidio Press, 1981.

Smith, Holland M., and Percy Finch. *Coral and Brass.* New York: Scribner, 1949.

Smith, S. E., ed. *The United States Marine Corps in World War II.* New York: Random House, 1969.

———, ed. *The United States Navy in World War II.* New York: Morrow, 1966.

Stafford, Edward P. *The Big E.* New York: Dell, 1964.

Toland, John. *But Not in Shame: The Six Months After Pearl Harbor.* New York: Random House, 1961.

————. *The Rising Sun: The Decline and Fall of the Japanese Empire, 1936–1945.* New York: Random House, 1970.

Tregaskis, Richard. *Guadalcanal Diary.* New York: Random House, 1943.

Updegraph, Charles L., Jr. USMC Historical Branch. *U.S. Marine Corps Special Units of World War II.* Washington, D.C.: Government Printing Office, 1972.

Vader, John. *New Guinea: The Tide Is Stemmed.* New York: Ballantine Books, 1971.

Vandegrift, A. A., and Robert B. Asprey. *Once a Marine.* New York: Ballantine Books, 1966.

Wheeler, Richard. *The Bloody Battle for Suribachi.* New York: Crowell, 1965.

————. *Iwo.* New York: Lippincott & Crowell, 1980.

Wilson, Earl J., Jim G. Lucas, Samuel Shaffer, and C. Peter Zurlinden. *Betio Beachhead.* New York: Putnam, 1945.

Wolfert, Ira. *Battle for the Solomons.* Boston: Houghton Mifflin, 1943.

Yukota, Yutaka, and Joseph D. Harrington. *Suicide Submarine!* New York: Ballantine Books, 1962.

Zimmerman, John L. USMC Historical Branch. *The Guadalcanal Campaign.* Washington, D.C.: Government Printing Office, 1949.

Index